FUNDAMENTALS OF FINANCIAL MANAGEMENT

James C. Van Horne
Stanford University

Cecil R. Dipchand
Dalhousie University

J. Robert Hanrahan
Brock University

PRENTICE-HALL CANADA INC.
Scarborough, Ontario

Canadian

5th
Edition

FUNDAMENTALS
OF FINANCIAL
MANAGEMENT

Canadian Cataloguing in Publication Data

Van Horne, James C.
  Fundamentals of financial management

Includes bibliographies and index.
ISBN 0-13-339532-4

1. Corporations—Finance. I. Dipchand, Cecil R.,
1941−   II. Hanrahan, J. Robert, 1934-
III. Title.

HG4011.V343 1985   658.1'5   C84-099304-8

FUNDAMENTALS
OF FINANCIAL MANAGEMENT

Canadian Fifth Edition

©1985 by Prentice-Hall Canada Inc.
Scarborough, Ontario

Original American edition published
by Prentice-Hall Inc., Englewood
Cliffs, New Jersey.

©1983 by Prentice-Hall Inc.

PRENTICE-HALL INC., *Englewood Cliffs, New Jersey*
PRENTICE-HALL INTERNATIONAL, INC., *London*
PRENTICE-HALL OF AUSTRALIA, PTY., LTD., *Sydney*
PRENTICE-HALL OF INDIA PVT., LTD., *New Delhi*
PRENTICE-HALL OF JAPAN INC., *Tokyo*
PRENTICE-HALL OF SOUTHEAST ASIA (PTE.) LTD., *Singapore*
EDITORA PRENTICE-HALL DO BRASIL LTDA., *Rio de Janeiro*
PRENTICE-HALL HISPANOAMERICANA, S.A., *Mexico*

ISBN 0-13-339532-4

Design Supervision: Joe Chin
Production Editor: Clare Rundall
Typesetting: Trigraph Inc.
   2   3   4   5   JD   89   88   87   86   85
Manufactured in Canada by John Deyell Company.

To my father, Ralph Van Horne
— James C. Van Horne

To Betty and daughters Anne,
Christine, Rosemarie, June,
and Elizabeth
— Cecil R. Dipchand

To Mary, Tom, Catherine
Margaret and Robert
— J. Robert Hanrahan

Contents

Contents

11

SPONTANEOUS FINANCING 272

12

SHORT TERM BORROWINGS 283

V. Investing in Capital Assets 309

13

CAPITAL BUDGETING 310

Contents

Preface
to the
American
Edition

Just as financial managers seek a good return on their firms' investments, those who are about to study this introductory course in financial management will want a satisfactory return on the investment of their time. With a good yield as its objective, the book offers a basic understanding of

1. What business finance is
2. Allocation of funds within a business enterprise
3. Raising funds
4. Application of certain theoretical concepts to financial problems.

Most of the concepts are expressed verbally, but elementary algebra is sometimes brought in for clearer understanding.

Structuring financial decisions continues to be the principal subject of the fifth edition. Unless financial managers focus on what is relevant, they will be hopelessly entwined in conflicting considerations, many of them trivial. In the pages that follow, they should find a lucid framework for approaching financial decisions. Theory will be explored not for its own sake, but for the help it can give in sorting out the important from the unimportant and in reaching better decisions.

A number of changes in this edition should enhance the learning experience and the reader's enthusiasm for financial management. Probably the most noticeable change is the comprehensive editing from start to finish. Explanations have been simplified, excess verbiage eliminated, and the writing style has been made more lively.

- The Economic Recovery Tax Act of 1981 is an essential part of the largely rewritten Chapter 2.

- Inflation, as it affects financial market returns, receives increased attention.

- Amortizing a loan is a new section in Chapter 4, which also has a new appendix on the use of a calculator in solving terminal and present values.

- The capital-asset pricing model is presented in a way that is easier to follow and apply.

- Cash and marketable security management incorporates new developments in financial markets, institutions, and practices.

- For judging credit policy decisions, Chapter 10 suggests a method that is different from methods explained in previous editions.

- Accounts receivable management and inventory management are consolidated into one chapter.

- The treatment of short term loans is reshaped in keeping with recent changes in financial markets and institutions.

- Capital budgeting (Chapter 13) conforms to the Tax Act of 1981. A new section analyzes projects with different economic lives.

- Group-specific, or divisional, required returns are introduced in a restructured Chapter 15. Among other improvements, there is a new appendix on adjusting the beta of a proxy company for leverage.

- The theory of dividend payout has been rewritten so that it is easier to follow, and newer arguments are incorporated. The effect of taxes and other imperfections is stressed. A new section reveals the things that managers consider when they decide on a dividend payout.

- Lease financing has been changed to reflect the Economic Recovery Tax Act of 1981.

- Improved examples in the valuation of convertible securities give the treatment more realism.

- Experience and research have made a better Chapter 24 on mergers. A checklist illustrates the multitude of considerations in combining two companies. Tax-free transactions and empirical evidence on valuation vitalize the chapter.

- International financial management, Chapter 25, is substantially revised, particularly the section on currency exposure management. The forward market, the effect of inflation and interest rates, and the interest-rate parity theorem are carefully examined.

- The smaller company and financial management is the subject of the entirely new Chapter 26, which is devoted completely to this significant segment of our economy.

- The Bankruptcy Reform Act of 1978, having modified current procedures and practices, is the basis of the rewritten Chapter 27 on failure and reorganization.

- Of the more than 200 problems at the end of the chapters, 35 percent are either new or revised. Less useful problems from the fourth edition have been eliminated.

- Other chapters have been carefully revised, updated, and improved. In many instances, the interest rates in the examples and problems are higher than in the earlier edition. Rather than use one interest rate throughout, I have used a wide range—6 percent to over 20 percent. Rates vary not only with the maturity and grade of debt instrument, but also with the recent volatility of interest rates overall. In this way the reader is able to apply the principles presented to a variety of interest rate scenarios.

I am grateful to a number of professors who have used the book and have offered helpful comments. In particular, I wish to thank Professors Eric L. Anderson, California State University, Los Angeles; Sheldon D. Balbirer, University of North Carolina, Greensboro; Edward J. Farragher, Eastern Michigan University; Peter G. Goulet, University of Northern Iowa; George A. Hachey, Jr., Merrimack College; Larry C. Nelson, Fisk University; and Raj A. Padmaraj, Bowling Green State University. Finally, I am grateful to Maurine Lewis, formerly of Prentice-Hall, who did a superb job editing the book.

JAMES C. VAN HORNE
Palo Alto, California

Preface to the Canadian Edition

Throughout the Canadian edition of this book, the authors' intentions were to preserve the conceptual framework of the fifth American edition. Since most of the theoretical aspects are well established and since we tended to agree with the point of view presented in controversial areas, the authors had very little difficulty working within this constraint. Although tailored to the Canadian environment, the text is still designed for an introductory course in financial management.

In a revision of this type, it is normal to expect some chapters to go almost untouched, others to require major changes, and the remainder to fall somewhere in between. Chapters requiring major revisions were: Chapter 2, "Organizational Form and Taxes"; Chapter 9, "Cash and Marketable Securities"; Chapter 12, "Short Term Borrowings"; Chapter 13, "Capital Budgeting"; Chapter 19, "Interface with Suppliers of Capital"; Chapter 20, "Term and Lease Financing"; Chapter 26, "The Smaller Company and Financial Management"; and finally Chapter 27 "Failure, Reorganization and Liquidation." Chapters requiring substantial changes but not major revisions were: Chapter 3, "The Role of Financial Markets for Business Firms"; Chapter 6, "Financial Analysis"; Chapter 21, 'Long Term Debt"; and Chapter 24, "Corporate Combinations."

We have once again included approximately seventy-five problems with solutions. Many new problems have been added and many of the older and more controversial ones have been changed or removed.

We wish to thank the many users of the text and reviewers Charles Re, G. Srinivasan and R.A. Kennedy for their constructive criticism and suggested revisions.

CECIL R. DIPCHAND
Halifax, Nova Scotia
J. ROBERT HANRAHAN
St. Catharines, Ontario

INTRODUCTION

The Role
of Financial
Management

At any moment in time, a business firm can be viewed as a pool of funds. These funds come from a variety of sources: investors in the company's preferred and common shares, creditors who lend it money, and past earnings retained in the business. Funds provided from these sources are committed to a number of uses: to purchase fixed assets used in the production of a good or service, inventories used to facilitate production and sales, cash and marketable securities used for transactions and liquidity purposes, and to finance accounts receivable owned by customers. At a given moment, the firm's pool of funds is static. With time, however, the pool changes; and these changes are known as funds flows. In an ongoing business, funds flow continually throughout the enterprise. The term *financial management* means that these flows are directed according to some plan; this book deals with the flow of funds within the firm. The *financial manager* is the person who has primary responsibility for financial management in a firm.

Responsibilities of the Financial Manager

The financial manager has the following responsibilities:[1]

1. Determining the proper amount of funds to employ in the firm (i.e., how large it will be and how fast it will grow) and the efficient allocation of funds for specific assets.

2. Raising funds on as favorable terms as possible, i.e., determining the composition of liabilities.

---

[1] See Ezra Solomon, *The Theory of Financial Management* (New York: Columbia University Press, 1963), Chapter 1.

The financial manager must undertake certain specific duties to carry out these responsibilities satisfactorily. Some of the main duties are summarized below.

1. The financial manager is continuously involved in financial analysis to monitor the financial performance of a firm. Then there is the duty of financial planning which involves the setting of future plans for the firm's operations and the determination of the amount of financing needed to support such plans. Finally, the financial manager ensures that there is adequate financial control such that funds are allocated in an efficient manner.

2. The financial manager must ensure that the firm meets its day-to-day cash requirements. Decisions have to be made regarding the level of investment in current assets (i.e. cash, market securities, accounts receivable and inventories). This duty is usually called working capital management.

3. The financial manager advises on the acquisition of fixed assets (i.e. land, buildings, machinery and equipment, and furniture and fixtures). Fixed asset management seeks to ensure that a firm invests in the types and amounts of fixed assets needed for efficient operation.

4. The current and fixed assets of a firm are usually financed through a combination of current and long-term liabilities, and equity, or shareholders' money. The financial manager must ensure that the "mix" of financing is one that is in the best interest of the firm.

5. The financial manager must pay attention to the welfare of the firm's shareholders. In this regard, there is need to develop and implement a dividend policy which is acceptable to these shareholders.

In years gone by, the financial manager was concerned mainly with the raising of funds. But the role has gradually changed to a point where the financial manager is now involved in general management. The list of duties discussed above attests to this fact. In recent years, the combination of increased competition, persistent inflation, an explosion in technological improvements, increased national concern with environmental and social issues, heightened government regulation of firms, and the growing importance of international operations have had an enormous influence in pushing the financial manager into a general management role.

Moreover, these factors have required the financial manager to have considerable flexibility in order to cope with ever-present change. The "old way of doing things" simply is not good enough in a world in which old ways quickly become obsolete. Competition requires continual adaptation to changing conditions.

How well financial managers adapt to change and how efficient they are in planning the proper amount of funds to employ in the firms, in over-seeing the allocation of these funds, and in raising funds, affect not only the success of the firms in which they are employed but the overall economy as well. To the extent that funds are misallocated, the growth of the economy will be slowed down. In an era of unfilled economic wants and scarcity, this may well work to the detriment of society. Efficient allocation of resources in an economy is vital to optimal growth in that economy; it is also vital in assuring that individuals obtain the highest level of want satisfaction possible. Through effective allocation of funds, financial managers contribute to the fortunes of their firms and to the vitality and growth of the entire economy.

Finance as a Discipline

In order to better understand the nature of financial management, the role of the financial manager and the evolution of the financial manager's functions, it is useful to trace the changing character of finance as an academic discipline.[2] In the early part of this century, corporate finance emerged as a separate field of study, whereas before it was considered primarily as a part of economics. By and large, the field encompassed only the instruments, institutions, and procedural aspects of the capital markets. By the 1900s the framework for our capital market system was fairly well-developed;[3] chartered and savings banks, insurance companies and building societies, and trust and loan companies had all appeared as part of the Canadian business environment.[4] Share ownership by the public was evident and the well-known stock exchanges had emerged about that time. The Montreal Stock Exchange was established in 1874 and the Toronto Stock Exchange in 1878. The Winnipeg Stock Exchange opened in 1903; the Vancouver Stock Exchange in 1907; and the Alberta Stock Exchange (formerly the Calgary Stock Exchange) in 1913. Long-term debt securities were issued primarily by the government and sold mostly in the United Kingdom. With the development of the Canadian securities market came the associated institutional service provided by investment dealers, brokers, and counsellors. Accounting data and financial records, as we know them today, were nonexistent. Only with the advent of regulations did disclosure of financial data become prevalent.[5]

With the era of technological innovation and new industries in the 1920s, firms needed more funds. The result was a greater emphasis on liquidity and financing of the firm. Considerable attention was directed to describing methods of external financing and little to managing a firm internally. One of the important texts of this period was Arthur Stone Dewing's *Financial Policy of Corporations*, which, in a scholarly fashion, drew together existing thought, promulgated certain new ideas, and served to pattern the teaching of finance for many years to come.[6] During this period, there was widespread interest in securities, particularly in common stock. This interest became intense toward the end of the decade, and the role and function of the investment dealer was particularly important in the study of corporate finance at this time.

The depression of the 1930s necessarily focused the study of finance on the defensive aspects of survival. A great deal of attention was directed toward the

---

[2]See J. Fred Weston, *The Scope and Methodology of Finance* (Englewood Cliffs, N.J.: Prentice-Hall, Inc., 1966), Chapter 2.

[3]The development of the capital market system is reviewed in E.P. Neufeld, *The Financial System of Canada: Its Growth and Development* (Toronto: Macmillan of Canada, 1972).

[4]For an interesting review of the business environment in pre- and post-Confederation times, see Merrill Denison, *Canada's First Bank: A History of the Bank of Montreal*, Vols. I & II (Toronto: McClelland and Stewart, 1967).

[5]The history of securities regulation is noted in Peter J. Williamson, *Securities Regulation in Canada* (Toronto: University of Toronto Press, 1960).

[6]Arthur S. Dewing, *The Financial Policy of Corporations* (New York: Ronald Press, 1920).

preservation of liquidity and toward bankruptcy, liquidation, and reorganization. The principal concern in external financing was how a lender could protect himself. Conservatism, naturally, reigned supreme, with considerable emphasis on a company's maintaining a sound financial structure. The large number of abuses with debt—particularly those that occurred in connection with public utility holding companies in the U.S.—were brought into the limelight when many companies collapsed. These failures, together with the fraudulent maltreatment of numerous investors, brought cries for regulation. Regulation and increased controls on business by government were quick to follow. One result of these regulations was an increase in the amount of financial data disclosed by companies. This disclosure made financial analysis more encompassing, because the analyst was able to compare different companies as to their financial condition and performance.

Finance, during the 1940s to the early 1950s, was dominated by a "traditional" approach. This approach, which had evolved during the 1920s and 1930s, was from the point of view of an outsider—such as a lender or investor—analyzing the firm and did not emphasize decision making within the firm. The study of external financing was still largely descriptive. During this period, however, a greater emphasis on analyzing the cash flows of the firm and on the planning and control of these flows from within did develop.

In the mid-1950s, great interest developed in capital budgeting and allied considerations.[7] This topic and the concurrent emphasis on present value served as a catalyst for the sweeping changes that subsequently occurred. With the development of new methods and techniques for selecting capital investment projects came a framework for the efficient allocation of capital within the firm. New fields of responsibility and influence for the financial manager included management of the total funds committed to assets and the allocation of capital to individual assets on the basis of an appropriate and objective acceptance criterion.

As a result of these developments, the financial manager had to come squarely to grips with how investors and creditors valued the firm and how a particular decision affected their respective valuations. Valuation models were developed for use in financial decision making. Interestingly enough, many of the dividend capitalization models developed during the 1950s for the valuation of the firm were offshoots of the classic 1938 work of John Burr Williams.[8] Unfortunately, the impact of this work was not felt in finance for nearly 20 years. With the concern for valuation in the 1950s, however, came a critical evaluation of the capital structure and the dividend policy of the firm in relation to its valuation as a whole.

In 1958 and 1961, Modigliani and Miller presented two studies which argued that in efficient financial markets, the debt and dividend policies of a firm really do not matter from the standpoint of valuation. This hypothesis clashed with the

---

[7]In the early 1950s, Friederich and Vera Lutz expounded a comprehensive theory of the firm in their famous book *The Theory of Investment of the Firm* (Princeton, N.J.: Princeton University Press, 1951). Much of the work on capital budgeting owes its origin to Joel Dean's renowned book *Capital Budgeting* (New York: Columbia University Press, 1951). These works served as building blocks for subsequent theoretical and managerial development in finance.

[8]*The Theory of Investment Value* (Amsterdam: North Holland Publishing, 1964).

opinions of most practitioners and academics.[9] The Modigliani-Miller (MM) propositions were challenged; and since the early 1960s, there have been ongoing studies which have endeavored to identify market imperfections which would affect the valuation of a firm, given a firm's capital structure and dividend policies.

Another major event in the 1960s was the development of portfolio theory and its eventual application to financial management. First expounded by Markowitz in 1952, the theory was later extended and considerably refined by Sharpe, Linter, and others.[10] Within a portfolio context, the valuation of a security is based on that security's marginal contribution to the total risk of a portfolio of securities. As we illustrate later in this book, it is possible to diversify some portion of the risk of individual securities, thus rendering such assets less risky, by including them in a portfolio of assets. Concurrent with this development was considerable theoretical and empirical work on the functioning of financial markets. The simple notion that the firm's debt and equity instruments are traded in markets that may be more or less efficient depending on the circumstances was really never fully understood until much of the work on portfolio theory and efficient markets had been done.

Further refinement of Sharpe's capital-asset pricing model for valuing financial assets brought with it the application of these ideas to financial management in the 1970s. The model suggested that some of the risk of the firm was not relevant to investors in the firm's stock, as this risk could be diversified away in the portfolios of stocks they held. It also brought an increased focus on market imperfections when one judged the firm's selection of assets, financing, and dividends. Recently, the capital-asset pricing model has undergone challenge, particularly from an empirical standpoint. The arbitrage pricing model, an alternative, less restricted approach, has created a good deal of interest.[11] In the ensuing chapters, we will devote considerable attention to the implications of these notions for financial management.

The decade of the 1970s was a period of major developments in the field of finance. Black and Scholes made a landmark contribution by introducing the option[12] pricing model for evaluating financial claims.[13] Corporate financing techniques became more sophisticated; the rights, warrant, conversion, and call options which were in use were supplemented with the extendible and retractable options on new issues of corporate securities. In the same period the secondary market for options trading came into being. The options are written on a firm's common shares which are outstanding and trading in the stock market.

---

[9]Franco Modigliani and M. H. Miller, "The Cost of Capital, Corporation Finance and the Theory of Investment," *American Economic Review*, 48 (June 1958), 261-97; and "Dividend Policy, Growth, and the Valuation of Shares," *Journal of Business*, 34 (Oct. 1961), 411-33.

[10]See Harry M. Markowitz, *Portfolio Selection: Efficient Diversification of Investments* (New York: John Wiley, 1959); William F. Sharpe, "Capital Asset Prices: A Theory of Market Equilibrium under Conditions of Risk," *Journal of Finance*, 19 (Sept. 1964), 425-42; John Lintner, "Security Prices, Risk and Maximal Gains from Diversification," *Journal of Finance*, 20 (Dec. 1965), 587-616; Jan Mossin, *Theory of Financial Markets* (Englewood Cliffs, N.J., Prentice-Hall, 1973); and Eugene F. Fama and Merton H. Miller, *The Theory of Finance* (New York: Holt, Rinehart and Winston, 1972).

[11]See Stephen A. Ross, "The Arbitrage Theory of Capital Asset Pricing," *Journal of Economic Theory*, 13 (December 1976), 341-60.

[12]Options are rights to buy or sell stock at a specified price within a specified time.

[13]Fischer Black and Myron Scholes, "The Pricing of Options and Corporate Liabilities," *Journal of Political Economy*, 81 (May-June 1973), 637-54.

While the Black and Scholes model provides a theoretical framework for the valuation of a "European" option, it has been used in a number of other instances. Several studies have valued convertible securities and warrants and have treated as options such things as the capital structure of the firm, the desire by lenders for restrictions on the borrower, and the call feature on corporate bonds. The application of the option pricing model to corporate finance is expanding and has been a rich source of intellectual inquiry in recent years.

So far in the 1980s, we have witnessed a number of intellectual advances in the valuation of the firm in an uncertain world. Increased attention has been paid to the effect of market imperfections on value. The role of personal taxes in conjunction with corporate taxes has been a particularly fruitful area. Information economics gives us certain insights into the market behavior of financial instruments. Financial signaling, whereby a management action is interpreted by outsiders in terms of its informational content, is receiving a good deal of notice. More and more precision is being added to financial theory, and we can expect this trend to continue.

Recent high and fluctuating inflation has had a profound influence on financial decision making. Although inflation was 2 to 3 percent in the 1950s and 1960s, it was over 10 percent in the early 1980s and fluctuated widely. This change in inflation has caused interest rates to rise dramatically. More and more lenders are avoiding longer-term fixed-rate loans in favor of variable-rate loans where their return is responsive to changes in inflation. Inflation distorts profits reported for accounting purposes. The sale of previously acquired low-cost inventories results in higher reported earnings. Moreover, depreciation charges on existing assets are less than the cost of replacing them. As a result, reported profits and the taxes paid on these profits are higher than the true economic profits of corporations and the taxes that would be paid on such profits. The heightened volatility of inflation in recent years has aggravated the uncertainty that companies face. Forecasts of future demand, prices, and costs become ever so much more difficult. Capital investment and financing decisions are riskier than they would be in an era of stable and low inflation. In turn, these considerations have an adverse effect on the valuation of business firms. We never know what the future will hold; but if high and volatile inflation continues, corporate financial policy will need to be continually modified.

The evolution of finance described above has a great influence on the role and importance of financial management. Finance has changed from primarily a descriptive study to one that encompasses rigorous analysis and normative theory; from a field that was concerned primarily with the procurement of funds to one that includes the management of assets, the allocation of capital, and the valuation of the firm in the overall market; and from a field that emphasized external analysis of the firm to one that stresses decision making within the firm. Finance today is best characterized as ever-changing, with new ideas and techniques. The role of the financial manager is considerably different from what it was 20 years ago and from what it will no doubt be in another 20 years. Academics and financial managers must grow to accept the changing environment and master its challenge. In this regard, they must thoroughly understand the underlying goal or objective of the firm.

The Goal of the Firm

Efficient management of the flow of funds within the firm implies the existence of an objective or goal because judgment as to whether or not a financial decision is efficient must be made according to some standard. Although various objectives are possible and desirable, we have assumed for purposes of clear discussion in this book that the fundamental goal of the firm is to maximize the wealth of its present owners.

Ownership in a company is evidenced by shares of common stock. Each share indicates that its holder owns $1/n$th of the company involved, where n is the total number of shares outstanding. For our purposes, shareholder wealth is represented by the market price per share of the firm's stock. While the market price may not be a perfect measure of wealth for all shareholders, it is the best measure available. When a public market does not exist for the shares, an opportunity price must be used. By analyzing similar companies whose shares are traded publicly, one can approximate the market value of the shares of the company involved.

PROFIT MAXIMIZATION VERSUS WEALTH MAXIMIZATION

Frequently, maximization of profits is regarded as the proper objective of the firm, but it is not as inclusive a goal as that of maximizing shareholder wealth. For one thing, total profits are not as important as earnings per share. A firm could always raise total profits by issuing shares and using the proceeds to invest in Treasury bills. Even maximization of earnings per share, however, is not a fully appropriate objective, partly because it does not specify the timing or duration of expected earnings or returns. Is the investment project that will produce a $100 000 return five years from now more valuable than the project that will produce annual returns of $15 000 in each of the next five years? An answer to this question depends on the time value of money to the firm and to potential investors. Few existing shareholders would think favorably of a project that promised its first return in 100 years, no matter how large this return. In our analysis, we must take into account the time pattern of returns.

Another shortcoming of the objective of maximizing earnings per share is that it does not consider the risk of the prospective earnings stream. Some investment projects are far more risky than others. As a result, the prospective stream of earnings per share would be more risky if these projects were undertaken. In addition, a company will be more or less risky depending on the amount of debt in relation to equity in its capital structure. The risk is known as financial risk; and it, too, contributes to the eventual risk of the prospective stream of earnings per share. Two companies may have the same expected future earnings per share, but if the earnings stream of one is subject to considerably more risk than the earnings stream of the other, the market price per share of its stock may be less.

Finally, this objective does not allow for the effect of dividend policy on the market price of the shares. If the objective were only to maximize earnings per share, the firm would never pay a dividend. At the very least, it would always improve earnings per share by retaining earnings and investing them in marketable securities. To the extent that the payment of dividends can affect the value of the shares, the maximization of earnings per share will not be a satisfactory objective by itself.

For the reasons given above, an objective of maximizing earnings per share may not be the same as maximizing market price per share. The market price of a firm's shares represents the focal judgment of all market participants as to the value of the particular firm. It takes into account present and prospective future earnings per share, the timing and risk of these earnings, the dividend policy of the firm, and any other factors that bear upon the market price of the shares. The market price serves as a performance index or report card of the firm's progress; it indicates how well management is doing on behalf of its shareholders. The management is under continuous review. If a shareholder is dissatisfied with management's performance, he may sell his shares and invest in another company. This action, if taken by other dissatisfied shareholders, will put downward pressure on the market price per share.

MANAGEMENT VERSUS SHAREHOLDERS

In certain situations, the objectives of management may differ from those of the firm's shareholders. In a large company whose shares are widely held, shareholders exert very little control or influence over the operations of the company. When the control of a company is separate from its ownership, management may not always act in the best interests of the shareholders.[14] Managements sometimes are said to be "satisfiers" rather than "maximizers";[15] they may be content to "play it safe" and seek an acceptable level of growth, being more concerned with perpetuating their own existence than with maximizing the value of the firm to its shareholders. To a management of this sort the most important goal may be its own survival. As a result, it may be unwilling to take reasonable risks for fear of making a mistake and thereby becoming conspicuous to outside suppliers of capital. In turn, these suppliers may pose a threat to management's survival. In order to survive over the long run, management may have to behave in a manner that is reasonably consistent with maximizing shareholder wealth, but the goals of the two parties do not necessarily have to be the same.

A NORMATIVE GOAL

As a normative or ideal goal, the principle of maximization of shareholder wealth provides an appropriate guide for the most efficient management of a firm. However, it is not necessarily a guide to the way a firm is actually managed. The purpose of capital markets is to efficiently allocate savings in an economy from ultimate savers to ultimate users of funds who invest in real assets. If savings are to

---

[14]For a discussion of this question, see Gordon Donaldson, "Financial Goals: Management vs. Stockholders," *Harvard Business Review*, 41 (May-June 1963), 116-29; and J. W. Elliott, "Control, Size Growth, and Financial Performance in the Firm," *Journal of Financial and Quantitative Analysis*, 7 (Jan. 1972), 1309-20.

[15]Herbert A. Simon, "Theories of Decision Making Economics and Behavioral Science," *American Economic Review*, 49 (June 1959), 253-83. See also J. Fred Weston, *The Scope and Methodology of Finance* (Englewood Cliffs, N.J.: Prentice-Hall, Inc., 1966), Chapter 2.

be channeled to the most promising investment opportunities, a rational economic criterion must exist that governs their flow. By and large, the allocation of savings in an economy occurs on the basis of expected return and risk. The market value of a firm's common shares reflects both of these factors. It therefore reflects the market's tradeoff between risk and return. If decisions are made in keeping with the likely effect upon the market value of its shares, a firm will attract capital only when its investment opportunities justify the use of that capital in the economy as a whole.

Put another way, the equilibration process by which savings are allocated in an economy occurs on the basis of expected return and risk. Under conditions of equal risk, those economic units (business firms, households, financial institutions, or governments) willing to pay the highest yield are the ones entitled to the use of funds. If rationality prevails, the economic units bidding the highest yields will be the ones with the most promising investment opportunities. As a result, savings will tend to be allocated to the most efficient uses. Maximization of shareholder wealth then embodies the risk-return tradeoff of the market and is the focal point by which funds should be allocated within and among business firms. Any other objective is likely to result in the suboptimal allocation of funds and therefore lead to less-than-optimal capital formation and growth in the economy as well as a less-than-optimal level of economic want satisfaction.

Social responsibility Management should not ignore the question of social responsibility. The social responsibility of business firms is concerned with such things as protecting the consumer, paying fair wages to employees, maintaining fair hiring practices, supporting education, and becoming actively involved in environmental issues such as clean air and water. Many people feel that a firm has no choice but to act in socially responsible ways; they argue that shareholder wealth and, perhaps, the company's very existence depends on its being socially responsible. However, the criteria for social responsibility are not clearly defined, which makes formulation of a consistent social objective difficult.

Moreover, social responsibilty creates certain problems for the firm. One is that it falls unevenly on different companies. Another is that it sometimes conflicts with the objective of wealth maximization. Certain social actions, from the point of view of their long-range effects, are clearly in the best interests of shareholders, and there is little question that they should be undertaken. The need for other actions is less clear, and engaging in them may cause a decline in profits and in shareholder wealth in the long run. From the standpoint of society, this decline may produce a conflict. What is gained in achieving a socially desirable goal may be offset in whole or in part by an accompanying less efficient allocation of resources in society. The latter will result in a less-than-optimal growth of the economy and a lower total level of economic want satisfaction. In an era of unfilled wants and scarcity, the allocation process is extremely important.

Many people feel that management should not be called upon to resolve the conflict posed above. Rather, society, with its broad general perspective, should make the decisions necessary in this area. Only society, acting through Parliament and other representative governmental bodies, can judge the relative tradeoff between the achievement of a social goal and the sacrifice in the efficiency of apportioning resources that may accompany realization of the goal. With these decisions made, companies can engage in wealth maximization and thereby efficiently allocate resources, subject, of course, to certain governmental constraints. Under such a system, companies can be viewed as producing both private and social "goods", and the maximization of shareholder wealth remains a viable corporate objective.

The Development of the Book

The financial manager is concerned with (1) the efficient allocation of funds within the enterprise and (2) the raising of funds on as favorable terms as possible. These two aspects of the job have a combined impact on the investment, financing, and dividend decisions of a firm. The ultimate goal is the maximization of shareholder wealth. By and large, this book is organized according to the two functions mentioned above.

SOME BACKGROUND KNOWLEDGE

Before proceeding to examine the allocation and raising of funds, we take up certain background material and tools of analysis. In the next chapter, we examine the legal setting for financial management as it relates in particular to organizational form and taxes. Also important with respect to background is the function of financial markets and interest rates in our society. These topics are discussed in Chapter 3 and throughout much of the book. In particular, our focus is on how business firms interact with financial markets. Also discussed throughout the book are certain concepts involving valuation and the time value of money. These topics are taken up in Chapters 4 and 5, and an understanding here is essential if one is to make sound financial decisions. Indeed the foundation for maximizing shareholder wealth is valuation. As a result, we take up the basics of valuation and the time value of money early on.

In order to raise funds efficiently and to allocate them, the financial manager must plan carefully. For one thing, the financial manager must project future cash flows and then assess the likely effect of these flows on the financial condition of the firm. On the basis of these projections, the financial manager plans for adequate liquidity to pay bills and other obligations as they come due. These obligations may make it necessary to raise additional funds. In order to control performance, the financial manager needs to establish certain norms. These norms are then used to compare actual performance with planned performance. Because the principles of financial analysis, planning, and control underlie a good deal of the discussion in this book, we examine these topics in Chapters 6 and 7.

ALLOCATION OF FUNDS

The financial manager oversees the allocation of funds among alternative uses. This allocation must be made in accordance with the underlying objective of the firm to maximize shareholder wealth.

Management of working capital   In Part IV, we examine cash, marketable securities, accounts receivable, and inventories. Our concern is with ways of efficiently managing these current assets in order to maximize profitability relative to the amount of funds tied up in the assets. Determining a proper level of liquidity for the firm is very much a part of this management. The optimal level of a current asset depends on the profitability and flexibility associated with that level in relation to the cost involved in maintaining it. In the past, managing the firm's working capital was the major role of the financial manager. Though this traditional function continues to be vital, this role has expanded to include the handling of longer-term assets and liabilities.

Investment in fixed assets   The allocation of funds among fixed assets is considered in Part V, under capital investment. Capital budgeting involves allocating capital to investment proposals whose benefits will be realized in the future. When a proposal has a current-asset component, the latter is treated as part of the capital-budgeting decision and not as a separate working-capital decision. Because the expected future benefits from an investment proposal are uncertain, risk is necessarily involved. Changes in the business-risk complexion of the firm can have a significant influence on its value in the marketplace. Because of this important effect, attention is devoted to the problem of measuring risk for a capital investment project. Capital is apportioned according to an acceptance criterion. It is important that the return required of the project be in accord with the objective of maximization of shareholder wealth.

External growth   In Chapter 24 in Part VIII, we consider mergers and acquisitions from the standpoint of an investment decision. These external investment opportunities can be evaluated in the same general manner as an investment proposal that is generated internally.

International operations   In Chapter 25 in Part VIII, we consider growth through international operations. In recent years, the multinational firm has become increasingly important, so its consideration is particularly germane.

Financial distress and reorganization   Finally, in Chapter 26 in Part VIII, we take up failures and reorganizations, which involve a decision to liquidate a company or to rehabilitate it, often by changing its capital structure. This decision should be based on the same economic considerations that govern the allocation of capital.

In summary, the allocation of funds within the firm determines the total amount of assets of the firm, the composition of these assets, and the business-risk complexion of the firm. All of these factors have an important influence on its value.

THE RAISING OF FUNDS

The second facet of financial management is the acquisition of funds. A wide variety of sources is available. Each has certain characteristics related to cost, maturity, availability, the encumbrance of assets, and other terms imposed by the supplier of capital. On the basis of these factors, the financial manager must determine the best mix of financing for the firm. Its implications on shareholder wealth must be considered when this decision is made.

Short term financing In Chapters 11 and 12 in Part IV, we discuss the various sources of short term financing available to Canadian businesses. Such financing has an important impact on the management of working capital, which is the area of focus in Part IV.

Capital structure and dividend decisions In Part VI, the question of the appropriate capital structure of a firm is considered. The concept of leverage is explored from a number of different angles to obtain a better understanding of financial risk and how this risk is related to operating risk. In addition, retained earnings are analyzed as a source of funds. Because this source represents dividends forgone by shareholders, dividend policy very much impinges on financing policy and vice versa.

Intermediate and long term financing In Part VII, we examine the various sources of intermediate and long term financing. The features, concepts, and problems associated with alternative methods of financing are explored.

Small business financing Special sources of funds for small businesses are discussed in Chapter 26. Most of these sources have some "non-traditional" features and as such are given separate treatment in this book.

Financial management, then, involves the allocation of funds within the firm and the acquisition of funds. The two are interrelated in that a decision to invest in a particular asset necessitates the financing of that asset, whereas the cost of financing affects the decision to invest. The focus of this book is on the allocation and acquisition of funds; together, these activities determine the value of the firm to its shareholders. Mastering the concepts involved is the key to understanding the role of financial management.

Questions

1. The maximization of wealth objective suggests that management should attempt to minimize dollar cost of production at a given level of output. Some costs resulting from production are not paid for by the company (e.g., pollution clean-up). Is the objective of maximizing wealth consistent with the well-being of society as a whole? If the answer is no, what objective would you substitute in its place?
2. Contrast the objective of maximizing earnings and that of maximizing wealth.
3. Maximizing wealth implies maximizing the price of the stock of the firm. Scandals involving stock manipulations suggest that share prices are not an infallible yardstick of performance. Discuss conditions created by management which maximize share prices but which do not necessarily mean efficiency in financial decision making.

4. Is the goal of zero profits for some finite period (three to five years, for example) consistent with the maximization of wealth objective? Explain.

5. Explain why the existence of a goal is necessary for judging the efficiency of any financial decision.

6. What are the two major functions of the financial manager? How are they related?

7. Should the managers of a company own sizable amounts of stock in the company? What are the pros and the cons?

8. In recent years, there have been a number of environmental, hiring and other regulations imposed on businesses. In view of these, is maximization of shareholder wealth still a realistic objective?

9. As an investor, do you think some managers are paid too much? Do their rewards not come at your expense?

10. How does the notion of risk and reward govern the behavior of financial managers?

Selected References

ANTHONY, R. "The Trouble with Profit Maximization." *Harvard Business Review* (November-December, 1960), 126-34.

ASHLEY, C.A. and J.E. SMYTH *Corporation Finance in Canada*, Toronto: Macmillan Company of Canada, 1947.

BERANEK, WILLIAM, "Research Directions in Finance," *Quarterly Review of Economics and Business*, 21 (Spring 1981), 6-24.

BRANCH, BEN, "Corporate Objectives and Market Performance," *Financial Management*, 2 (Summer 1973), 24-29.

BROOKS, JR., L.J., "Social Goals for Canadian Business", *Cost and Management*, March-April, 1984, 2-8.

CISEL, DAVID H., and THOMAS M. CARROLL, "The Determinants of Executive Salaries: An Econometric Survey," *Review of Economics and Statistics*, 62 (February, 1980), 7-13.

COOLEY, PHILLIP L., "Managerial Pay and Financial Performances of Small Business," *Journal of Business*, (September 1979), 267-76.

COWEN, S., and M. SEGAL, "Corporate Responsibility: Part I—Reporting Social Performance," *Financial Executive* (January 1981). 10-16.

DAVIS, K. "Social Responsibility is Inevitable," *California Management Review* (Fall 1976). 14-20.

DE ALESSI, LOUIS, "Private Property and Dispersion of Ownership in Large Corporations," *Journal of Finance*, 28 (Sept. 1973), 839-51.

DENISON, MERRILL, *Canada's First Bank: A History of the Bank of Montreal*, Vols. I&II, Toronto McClelland and Stewart, 1967.

DONALDSON, GORDON, "Financial Goals: Management vs. Stockholders," *Harvard Business Review*, 41 (May-June 1963), 116-29.

ELLIOTT, J.W. "Control, Size, Growth, and Financial Performance in the Firm," *Journal of Financial and Quantitative Analysis*, 7 (Jan. 1972), 1309-20.

FAMA, EUGENE F. "The Effects of a Firm's Investment and Financing Decisions on the Welfare of Its Security Holders," *American Economic Review*, 68 (Sept. 1978), 272-84.

FAMA, E. "Agency Problems and the Theory of the Firm," *Journal of Political Economy* (April 1980), 288-307.

FINDLAY, M. CHAPMAN III and G.A. WHITMORE, "Beyond Shareholder Wealth Maximization," *Financial Management*, 3 (Winter 1974), 25-35.

GERSTNER, LOUIS V. and HELEN M. ANDERSON, "The Chief Financial Officer as Activist," *Harvard Business Review*, 54 (Sept.-Oct. 1976), 100-6.

HILL, LAWRENCE W. "The Growth of the Corporate Finance Function," *Financial Executive*, 44 (July 1976), 33-43.

JENSEN, MICHAEL C. and WILLIAM H. MECKLING, "Theory of the Firm: Managerial Behavior. Agency Costs and Ownership Structure," *Journal of Financial Economics*, 31 (Oct. 1976), 305-60.

KOSHAL, RAJINDAR K., S.B. PRASAD, and R.K. JAIN, "Executives' Remuneration Maximization Behavior: Some Further Evidence," *Atlantic Economic Journal* (Mar. 1977), 65-68.

MASSON, ROBERT TEMPEST, "Executive Motivations, Earnings, and Consequent Equity Performance," *Journal of Political Economy*, 79 (Nov.-Dec. 1971), 1278-92.

NEUFELD, E.P. *The Financial System of Canada*, Toronto: Macmillan of Canada, 1972.

NORR, DAVID, "Management and the Investor," *Financial Analysts Journal* (Mar.-Apr. 1979), 45-48.

SOLOMON, EZRA, *The Theory of Financial Management,* New York: Columbia University Press. 1963, 1 & 2.

SPRAAKMAN, G. "Financial Goal Recognition by Corporations," *Cost and Management* (January-February 1980), 30-34.

WESTON, J. FRED, *The Scope and Methodology of Finance*, Englewood Cliffs, N.J.: Prentice-Hall, Inc., 1966.

WESTON, J. FRED, "Developments in Finance Theory," *Financial Management*, 10 (1981), 5-22.

WILLIAMSON, PETER J. *Securities Regulation in Canada*, Toronto: University of Toronto Press, 1960.

Organizational Form and Taxes

To understand the role of financial managers, we must be familiar with the legal setting in which they operate. When we look at one aspect of the setting, the basic form of business organization, we shall discover advantages and disadvantages of the various forms. Delving into another aspect, the tax environment, we shall not try to become experts, but we do hope to gain a basic understanding of the tax implications of various financial decisions to be considered in this book.

Forms of Organization

In Canada there are three basic forms of business organization: the sole proprietorship, the partnership, and the corporation. The sole proprietorship outnumbers the other two, but the corporation is largest in sales, assets, profits, and contribution to national income. As this section unfolds, we shall see several important advantages to the corporate form.

THE SOLE PROPRIETORSHIP

The sole proprietorship is the oldest form of business organization. As the title suggests, a single person owns the business, holds title to all its assets, and is personally responsible for all of its liabilities. Because of its simplicity, a sole proprietorship can be established with few complications. Simplicity is its greatest virtue; its principal shortcoming is the proprietor's legal responsibility for all obligations the organization incurs. If the organization is sued, the proprietor as an individual is sued and has unlimited liability, which means that his or her personal property as well as the assets of the business may be seized to settle claims. Obviously, this liability places the individual in a risk-prone position.

Another problem with a sole proprietorship is the difficulty in raising capital. In general, this form of organization is not as attractive to investors as are other forms of organization. Moreover, the proprietorship has certain tax disadvantages. Fringe benefits, such as medical coverage and group insurance, are not regarded by Revenue Canada as expenses of the firm and therefore are not deductible for tax purposes. In the case of a company, these and similar benefits are often deductible in whole or in part. Also, the business income from the proprietorship is deemed to be the income of the owner and is taxed at his or her marginal tax rates. This may result in higher taxes which we will discuss later in this chapter.

THE PARTNERSHIP

A partnership is similar to a proprietorship in all aspects except that there is more than one owner. In a *general partnership* all partners have unlimited liability; they are jointly liable for the liabilities of the partnership. Because an individual partner can bind the partnership with obligations, general partners should be selected with care. In most cases there is a formal arrangement, or partnership agreement; this sets forth the powers of an individual partner, the distribution of profits, the amounts of capital to be invested by the partners, procedures for admitting new partners, and procedures for reconstituting the partnership in case of the death or withdrawal of a partner. Legally, the partnership is terminated if one of the partners dies or withdraws. In such cases, settlements invariably are "sticky," and reconstitution of the partnership is a difficult matter. For these reasons, many people view the partnership as an unattractive form of business organization.

The decision-making process of a partnership is often cumbersome. Unless the agreement specifies otherwise, important decisions must be made by majority vote. In most cases, group decisions are difficult, to say the least. On less weighty matters, individual partners may transact business for the firm but must be careful to keep the other partners informed. The powers of an individual partner will vary according to the formal or informal agreement among partners. Some partnerships specify a hierarchy of two or more layers of partners. This hierarchy determines the magnitude of decision an individual partner can make and the degree to which a partner can commit the firm.

Limited partnerships are permitted in all provinces except Prince Edward Island and Nova Scotia. A limited partner contributes capital, and his liability is confined to that amount of capital. There must, however, be at least one general partner in the partnership whose liability is unlimited. Limited partners do not participate in the operation of the business; this is left to the general partner(s). The limited partners are strictly investors, and they share in the profits or losses of the partnership according to the terms of the partnership agreement.

THE COMPANY[1]

Because of the importance of the corporate form in this country, the focus of this book is on companies. A company is an "impersonal" entity, created by law, which can own assets and incur liabilities. The principal feature of this form is that the company exists separately and apart from its owners. An owner's liability is limited to his investment. Limited liability represents an important advantage over the proprietorship and the general partnership. Capital can be raised in the company's name without exposing the owners to unlimited liability. Therefore, personal assets cannot be seized in the settlement of claims. Ownership itself is evidenced by shares of stock, with each shareholder owning that proportion of the enterprise represented by his shares in relation to the total number of shares outstanding.[2] These shares are transferable, representing another important advantage of the corporate form. Moreover, the company can continue even though individual owners may die or wish to sell their shares.

A company is incorporated either federally or provincially. Companies may be incorporated by a special Act of Parliament or of a provincial Legislature or under the provisions of the federal or provincial Companies' Acts. Our concern is primarily with companies incorporated under the latter statutes.[3] Incorporation procedures vary across Canada. The federal government and the provinces of Quebec, Ontario, Manitoba, Prince Edward Island, and New Brunswick follow a *letters patent* system, while the other provinces use the *registration* system. These two systems may differ only in procedural aspects. Upon approval of the letters patent, or the memorandum of association under the registration system, the desired corporate entity is created.

Because of the advantages associated with limited liability, transferability of ownership, and the ability of the company to raise capital apart from its owners, the corporate form of business organization has grown enormously in importance during the last century. With the large demands for capital that accompany an advanced economy, the proprietorship and partnership have proven unsatisfactory, and the company has emerged as the most important organizational form. A possible disadvantage of the company is the tax treatment, which we take up shortly. Even here, the disadvantage exists only under certain circumstances. Minor disadvantages include the length of time required to incorporate and the red tape involved, as well as the incorporation fee that must be paid to the incorporating body. Thus, a company is more difficult to establish than either a proprietorship or a partnership. However, this is not a very serious problem.

---

[1]The word "company" instead of "corporation" usually appears in the company's name. Under the Canada Business Corporations Act and those of some provinces, the word "limited" or "incorporated" must be added. The advantages and disadvantages of incorporation are discussed in Robert H. Morrow, "Reasons for Incorporation," *Certified General Accountant* (May-June 1973), 13-23.

[2]See Chapter 22 for a detailed discussion of common stock.

[3]Companies created by Acts of Parliament or of provincial Legislatures are sometimes established to supervise government-sponsored programs. A few of the companies are discussed in Chapter 26, and the Export Development Corporation is discussed in Chapter 25.

Some Corporate Tax Provisions

Few business decisions are not affected either directly or indirectly by taxes. Through their taxing power, federal, provincial, and municipal governments have a profound influence on the behavior of business organizations and that of their owners. What might be an optimal decision in the absence of taxes may prove to be a very inferior one with taxes. In this section, we trace some of the essentials of taxation. This basic understanding is used in later chapters when we consider specific financial decisions. We begin with corporate tax provisions and then go on to consider non-corporate income taxes.

CORPORATE INCOME TAX

A company's taxable income is found by deducting from income all allowable expenses, including depreciation (capital cost allowance) and interest charges on debt issued by the company. In Canada the amount of tax is determined in part by the category into which the company falls. The general corporate tax rate under the federal Income Tax Act is 46 percent of taxable income. Thus, if a company has revenue of $3 000 000 and allowable expenses total $2 500 000, the taxes payable ($230 000) are computed as follows:

Sales	$3 000 000
Less: expenses	2 500 000
Earnings before tax	500 000
Taxes (46%)	230 000
Earnings after tax	$ 270 000

Companies in all provinces except Ontario and Quebec determine their taxable income according to the provisions of the federal Income Tax Act. The 46 percent tax rate is a general rate which, theoretically, is split 36 percent for the federal government and 10 percent for the provincial government. However, provincial governments have the authority to assess tax at a rate higher than 10 percent; where this is the case, the overall tax rate exceeds 46 percent by the differential between the provincial rate and 10 percent. For example, in Nova Scotia the provincial corporate tax rate is 13 percent, and the overall tax rate is 49 percent instead of the 46 percent in the above illustration. Thus, a Nova Scotia firm would pay taxes of $245 000(49 percent of $500 000) instead of the $230 000 computed above. Most provinces have provincial corporate tax rates higher than 10 percent and hence, the actual tax rate exceeds the stated general rate of 46 percent. For simplicity, we use the general rate of 46 percent which implies 36 percent for the federal government and 10 percent for a provincial government. The reader is advised to adjust this rate for provincial differences, if necessary.

Under tax collection agreements, the federal government collects corporate taxes on behalf of the provinces and then transfers the appropriate amounts to the respective provincial treasuries. In Ontario and Quebec, corporate tax is computed under the Ontario Corporations Tax Act and the Quebec Taxation Act, respectively. The taxation principles embodied in these two statutes are usually consistent with those of the federal statute. Ontario and Quebec collect their own corporate taxes.

Companies are required to make monthly tax payments on what is essentially a current basis. The Act requires that either an estimate of current income is made or that payments are based on the taxable earnings of the previous year. In any case, the remainder of the tax must be paid within two months of the end of the corporation's fiscal year.

Small business tax rate   Some tax relief is offered as an incentive to promote small business development in Canada. A Canadian-controlled private company[4] is taxed at 25 percent on the first $200 000 of taxable income and 46 percent on amounts over $200 000. Thus, if a qualified small business has revenue of $1 000 000 and allowable expenses total $750 000, taxes of $73 000 are computed as follows:

Sales	$1 000 000
Less: expenses	750 000
Earnings before taxes	$ 250 000

Taxes:
  25% of $200 000 = $50 000
  46% of $ 50 000 = 23 000
	73 000

Earnings after taxes	$ 177 000

Where a qualified small business pays dividends, the tax rate on the first $200 000 of taxable income will increase. The firm is required to pay an additional tax of $12\frac{1}{2}$ percent of the dividends paid to shareholders. In the above example, suppose the firm pays $150 000 as dividends. This $150 000 is the earnings after taxes on the first $200 000 of taxable income (or $200 000 less taxes of $50 000). Based on dividends of $150 000, the additional tax is $18 750 ($12\frac{1}{2}$ percent of $150 000) and total tax on the first $200 000 of taxable income is $68 750 ($50 000 plus the additional tax of $18 750). Thus, the effective tax rate on the first $200 000 of taxable income with a dividend payment of $150 000 is 34.4 percent ($68 750 divided by $200 000 times 100). The effective tax rate may be reduced with lower dividends. For example, if the dividends are $50 000 (rather than $150 000), the additional taxes are $6 250 ($12\frac{1}{2}$ percent of $50 000), the total taxes are $56 250

---

[4]A Canadian-controlled private company is one whose shares are not listed on a stock exchange or are not traded over the counter, and is not controlled by non-resident persons or by a company whose shares are listed or traded over the counter, or by a combination of both. For further discussion, see Robert J. Dart, "An Analysis of the Tax Position of Public, Private and Canadian-controlled Private Corporations," *Canadian Tax Journal*, XX (Nov.-Dec. 1972), 521-33.

($50 000 plus $6 250), and the effective tax rate is 28.1 percent ($56 250 divided by $200 000 times 100).

Tax on manufacturing and processing income Some tax relief is also given on Canadian manufacturing and processing income.[5] Since January 1973, such income has been taxed at a general rate of 40 percent instead of the 46 percent mentioned earlier. If a small business qualifies, its manufacturing and processing income is taxed at 20 percent on the first $200 000 and at 40 percent on such income exceeding $200 000. If the firm pays dividends from its small business earnings, it has to pay an additional tax equal to 12½ percent of the dividends as discussed above.

CAPITAL COST ALLOWANCE

The portion of the cost of a depreciable asset that is allowed as a deductible expense for tax purposes in Canada is quite clearly defined in the Income Tax Act. Only the declining balance method of depreciating assets has been generally acceptable since 1949 when the Act was completely revamped.[6] Assets are divided into 35 classes and assigned fixed rates. For example, a brick building is a Class 3 asset and a capital cost allowance of 5 percent is allowed. The method for calculating annual capital cost allowance (CCA) is

Year 1	
Original cost	$100 000
Capital cost allowance ½ ($100 000 × 0.05)	(2 500)
Undepreciated capital cost	97 500
Year 2	
Capital cost allowance ($97 500 × 0.05)	(4 875)
Undepreciated capital cost	92 625
Year 3	
Capital cost allowance ($92 625 × 0.05)	(4 631)
Undepreciated capital cost	87 994
Year n	
Capital cost allowance (undepreciated capital cost in year n − 1 × 0.05)	
Undepreciated capital cost (undepreciated capital cost in year n − 1 less capital cost allowance in year n)	

[5]For discussion, see Ronald C. Knechtel and P. Wayne Penny, "Federal Manufacturing and Processing Incentives," *Canadian Tax Journal*, XXI (Sept.-Oct. 1973), 391-409; and "Federal Manufacturing and Processing Incentives—Rapid Write-Off," *Canadian Tax Journal*, XXI (Nov.-Dec. 1973), 540-45.

[6]The history of depreciation practices since 1900 is outlined in George J. Murphy, "The Influence of Taxation on Canadian Corporate Depreciation Practices," *Canadian Tax Journal*, XX (May-June 1972), 233-39.

Thus, the rate is always applied to the undepreciated capital cost or UCC (cost less accumulated capital cost allowances) of the asset except in the first year, when only one-half of the amount is allowed. It should be noted that a company is not required to charge capital cost allowance, a provision that is useful in years when losses are incurred. However, the maximum of the capital cost allowance claim in any year is limited to a sum equal to the capital cost allowance rate times the UCC of the asset.

Acquisition and disposal of assets All assets of a given class form a pool.[7] Additional assets purchased are added to the pool and when an asset is sold, the lower of the sales proceeds or its original cost is deducted from the pool.[8] After the above adjustments are made, the balance in the asset account is the undepreciated capital cost (UCC) which will be used to compute capital cost allowances (CCA) for the year in which an acquisition or disposal occurs. Continuing with our previous example, suppose that a second brick building was purchased in year 2 for $200 000 and then in year 3 the first brick building was sold for $95 000. Note that the increase in the pool ($200 000) in year 2 is eligible for only one-half the CCA in that year. Annual capital cost allowances for the first three years would then be computed as follows:

Year 1	
Original cost—Building #1	$100 000
CCA ½ ($100 000 × 0.05)	(2 500)
UCC at year end	97 500
Year 2	
Original cost—Building #2	$200 000
UCC for CCA for year 2	297 500
CCA ($97 500 × 0.05) + ($200 000 × 0.05 × ½)	(9 875)
UCC at year end	287 625
Year 3	
Sales proceeds—Building #1	(95 000)
UCC for CCA for year 3	192 625
CCA ($192 625 × 0.05)	(9 631)
UCC at year end	$182 994

Liquidation of a pool of assets Generally, as long as a firm continues to have assets in a given pool, the above calculations will apply. That is, we add the cost of new assets acquired and deduct the lower of the sales proceeds or the original cost of assets which are sold. The adjusted asset balance becomes the base for capital cost

[7]See Schedule B to the Income Tax Regulations.

[8]Where assets are sold at a price higher than their original cost, capital gains equal to the sale price less original cost occur. The treatment of capital gains is discussed later in this chapter.

TABLE 2-1 Disposal of Assets in a Pool

	Case 1	Case 2	Case 3	Case 4
Year 3				
UCC (see earlier calculations)	$182 994	$182 994	$182 994	$182 994
Year 4				
CCA ($182 994 × 0.05)	(9 150)	(9 150)	(9 150)	(9 150)
UCC	173 844	173 844	173 844	173 844
Year 5				
Sale price—Building #2	173 844	150 000	190 000	250 000
Less: UCC	173 844	173 844	173 844	173 844
Balance in account	—	(23 844)	16 156	76 156
Classification of balance				
Terminal loss	—	(23 844)	—	—
Recaptured depreciation	—	—	16 156	26 156
Capital gains	—	—	—	50 000

allowance for the year in which the acquisition or disposal occurs. However, when a firm decides to liquidate all assets in a pool, these calculations do not apply. Let us illustrate by continuing with our previous example.

Suppose that the second brick building is disposed of in year 5 and the asset pool is liquidated. Based on the sale price of that building shown in Table 2-1, we develop four different cases. In Case 1, we assume that the building is sold for its UCC of $173 844 which leaves a zero balance in the pool of assets. Through CCA write-offs over years 2-4 and a sale price of $173 844, the entire cost of the building ($200 000) has been accounted for. Now in Case 2, we assume a sale price of $150 000 which is less than the UCC of $173 844. The differential of $23 844 is a *terminal loss* and is fully chargeable (as an expense) against income in year 5. The asset has actually depreciated much faster than provided for through a CCA rate of 5 percent. In Case 3, where the sale price exceeds the UCC, the opposite situation occurs. Capital cost allowances for tax purposes were higher than necessary, thus we have a case of *recaptured depreciation*. The amount of $16 156 (sale price of $190 000 less UCC of $173 844) is deemed income and is taxed in year 5.

Finally, there is the case where an asset is sold at a price higher than its original cost as in Case 4 in Table 2-1. First, the amount of the recaptured depreciation (original cost less UCC) is determined; this is deemed income and is taxed accordingly. Next, the amount in excess of original cost is deemed *capital gains*; one-half of capital gains is deemed income and is taxed at normal rates. For example, in Case 4 the recaptured depreciation is $26 156 ($200 000-$173 844) and the capital gain is $50 000 ($250 000-$200 000). Additional income arising from the liquidation of the pool of assets will be $51 156 ($26 156 + ½ of $50 000) for year 5.

Accelerated write-offs There are cases where the cost of certain assets may be written off for tax purposes in two or three years. For example, machinery and equipment acquired after May 9, 1972 for the purpose of manufacturing and processing goods in Canada may be written off using the straight-line method over two years.[9] Say a piece of equipment that qualifies for this tax write-off costs $1 000 000; $500 000 may be written off in year 1 and the other $500 000 in year 2. As another example, certain vessels can be written off in three years using the straight line method to calculate CCA. Such accelerated CCA provisions may be viewed as temporary tax measures designed to promote capital investment in selected industrial sectors.

Investment tax credit Companies are allowed an investment tax credit (ITC) on the capital cost of certain fixed assets acquired within certain specified time limits.[10] This ITC ranges from 7 percent to 50 percent of the acquisition cost of a qualified asset depending upon the region of the country, the type of asset purchased and the size of the acquiring company. The amount of the ITC is allowed as a deduction against any federal taxes payable by the acquiring firm. For example, in 1984, Nova Scotia Plastics Ltd. purchased and installed a moulding injection machine at a cost of $250 000. Assuming that this asset qualifies for 20 percent ITC, then $50 000 (or 20 percent of $250 000) may be offset against any federal taxes payable by Nova Scotia Plastics Ltd. If this firm has a 1984 federal tax liability of $80 000, then it will only pay $30 000 (or $80 000 less the ITC of $50 000). Thus, the ITC helps to reduce the acquisition costs of qualified assets and is an incentive to boost capital formation in the economy. Also, the ITC is deducted from the cost of the asset before CCA is calculated. In the above example, the base for CCA calculations will be $200 000 ($250 000 less $50 000) in 1984.

Where a firm has a federal tax liability less than the ITC in the year of acquisition of the qualified asset, there will be some "unused" ITC. For example, if the 1984 federal tax liability for Nova Scotia Plastics Ltd., is $20 000, then $30 000 of the ITC (or $50 000 less taxes of $20 000) cannot be offset in 1984. The firm can offset this $30 000 against federal taxes paid in each of the last three years assuming that it did in fact pay $30 000 or more in federal taxes in those years. Amended tax return(s) will be submitted to Revenue Canada to claim an aggregate refund of $30 000 given the illustration above. If the federal taxes in the last three years are less than the "unused" ITC, then any balance of the ITC not offset against federal taxes paid or payable may be carried forward and be offset against federal taxes payable in each of the next seven years.

---

[9]One study has argued that the reduction in corporate income tax and the allowance of rapid write-off equipment for manufacturing and processing are relatively inefficient and are potentially more beneficial to the U.S. treasury than the Canadian economy. See R. M. Hyndman, "The Efficacy of Recent Corporate Income Tax Reductions for Manufacturing," *Canadian Tax Journal* XXIII (Jan.-Feb. 1974), 84-97. For a rebuttal see R. P. Simon, "The Efficacy of Recent Corporate Income Tax Reductions for Manufacturing—An Unsimulated View," *Canadian Tax Journal*, XXII (Mar.-Apr. 1974), 160-65.

[10]The investment tax credit allowance became effective in 1975 and is available only for prescribed machinery and equipment or buildings acquired within certain time limits and for use in designated activities. See Revenue Canada-Taxation, *Information Circular—Business Investment Tax Credit Rates*, February 11, 1983, for specific locations and for variations for scientific research expenditures and transportation equipment.

The above general provisions for ITC came into effect on April 19, 1983. Transition provisions for ITC on assets acquired prior to 1984 and other specific ITC provisions may be reviewed in the *Information Circular* noted in footnote 10.

INTEREST EXPENSE

Interest charges on debt issued by a company are treated as an expense and are deductible for tax purposes. This treatment contrasts with that for common- and preferred-stock dividends and interest on income bonds, which are not deductible for tax purposes. If a company is profitable and pays taxes, the use of debt in its financing mix results in a significant tax advantage relative to the other forms of raising capital. If the marginal tax rate is 48 percent, the firm would need to earn approximately $1.92 before taxes for every $1 paid out in dividends versus only $1 for the payment of $1 of interest. Thus, we see the tax advantages associated with using debt.

DIVIDEND INCOME

Dividends received by a company from a taxable Canadian company are usually tax-free to the recipient. Under certain specific circumstances, dividends received from nonresident companies carrying on business in Canada and from foreign affiliates are at least partially taxable.

CAPITAL GAINS AND CAPITAL LOSSES

Since January 1, 1972, taxpayers in Canada have had to include in taxable income gains and losses arising from the disposal of capital property. Capital gains arise when the sale price of an asset exceeds the cost of acquisition; one half of such gains is taxed at the marginal tax rate. A capital loss arises when the sale price is less than the cost of acquisition of an asset. (Usually, we talk of capital losses only for assets which are non-depreciable for tax purposes.) Financial assets such as marketable securities and common shares, and real assets such as land, are non-depreciable for tax purposes. If the sale price of such an asset is below acquisition cost, then we have a capital loss. One half of a capital loss is allowed as a deduction against taxable capital gains. In effect, net capital gains are taxed at one half the tax rate charged on other income.

CARRY-BACK AND CARRY-FORWARD

Taxpayers may carry operating or non-capital losses back one year and ahead five years. Table 2-2 provides an example of the treatment of losses under this system. The loss of $140 000 in year 0 is applied to income in years –1, 1, 2, 3, 4, and 5. Remember that taxes were already paid on year –1 income so the firm must submit an amended income tax form for year –1 to claim a tax refund. In future years the firm will not remit monthly tax instalments until the loss is completely written off or until after five years have gone by, whichever comes first. Any losses not written off after five years cannot be offset against income in the sixth and

TABLE 2-2   Carry-back and Carry-forward Calculation

Year	-2	-1	0	1	2	3	4	5
Net income (loss)	$8 000	$12 000	$(140 000)	$25 000	$30 000	$36 000	$30 000	$40 000
Loss carry-over		(12 000)		(25 000)	(30 000)	(36 000)	(30 000)	(7 000)
Taxable income	8 000	—	—	—	—	—	—	33 000

subsequent years. Small businesses are permitted to carry back and forward operating losses three and seven years, respectively.

Operating or non-capital losses may also be offset against taxable capital gains. However, allowable capital losses from the sale of non-depreciable assets can only be written off against taxable capital gains commencing in 1985. Any unabsorbed capital losses may be carried back three years and forward for an indefinite period and applied against taxable capital gains. Where both non-capital (operating) losses and capital losses occur, non-capital losses will be absorbed first against income, and if necessary, against taxable capital gains before deduction is permitted for carried-over capital losses.

Some Non-Corporate Tax Provisions

The subject of non-corporate taxes is extremely comprehensive, but our main concern here is with personal taxes of individuals owning shares in companies. Salaries, wages, and associated benefits constitute the bulk of personal income. Income reported by a sole proprietorship or a partnership becomes income of the owner(s).[11] Finally, individuals receive income in the form of interest, dividends, and capital gains. There are allowable deductions depending on the individual, family size, source of income, and so on. Gross income less all allowable deductions is taxed at prescribed personal tax rates as discussed in the next section.

PERSONAL TAX RATES

Personal income taxes are levied by both federal and provincial governments using a progressive taxation system, i.e., higher levels of taxable income are taxed at higher rates as shown in Table 2-3. The basic federal tax is computed using a schedule of marginal tax rates applied to specified taxable income brackets (see the first two columns of Table 2-3).

---

[11]The tax status of the partnership is reviewed in Glen A. Russell, "Tax Problems Facing Partnerships," *Canadian Chartered Accountant* (Dec. 1972), 32-40; and Howard J. Kellough, "The Business of Defining a Partnership under the Income Tax Act," *Canadian Tax Journal*, XXII (Mar.-Apr. 1974), 190-212.

TABLE 2-3 Rate of Federal Income Tax and Total Marginal Tax Rate for Ontario 1982

Brackets of Taxable Income	Federal Income Tax*	Total Average Tax Rate**	Total Marginal Tax Rate
$ 1 112 or less	6% = $67	8.9%	8.9%
1 112– 2 224	67 + 16% on next 1 112	16.3	23.7
2 224– 4 448	245 + 17% on next 2 224	20.7	25.2
4 448– 6 672	623 + 18% on next 2 224	22.7	26.7
6 672–11 120	1 023 + 19% on next 4 448	24.9	28.1
11 120–15 568	1 868 + 20% on next 4 448	26.2	29.6
15 568–20 016	2 758 + 23% on next 4 448	28.0	34.0
20 016–31 136	3 781 + 25% on next 11 120	31.2	37.0
31 136–53 376	6 561 + 30% on next 22 240	36.7	44.4
53 376 & over	13 233 + 34% on remainder	—	50.3

*There is a federal tax reduction to a maximum of $200 which is not taken into account in these calculations.
**These rates are calculated based on the upper level in each taxable income group and using the Ontario tax of 48 percent of the basic federal tax.

All provinces (except Quebec) levy personal income taxes using a percentage of the basic federal tax payable. For example, assume that a resident of Ontario has a taxable income of $11 120. Then the federal tax payable is $1 868 ($1 023 tax on the first $6 672 of taxable income plus 19 percent on the next $4 448 of taxable income as shown in Row 5, Table 2-3). The provincial tax will be $897 (48 percent of the federal tax of $1 868). Thus, the total tax payable is $2 765 ($1 868 + $897) based on a taxable income of $11 120—this works out to an average tax rate of 24.9 percent ($2 765 divided by $11 120 times 100). Note that the average tax rate is higher as taxable income increases (Column 3, Table 2-3)—this is a feature of a progressive taxation system.

Another feature shown in Table 2-3 is the fact that the marginal tax rate is higher than the average tax rate for each bracket of taxable income (except that for a taxable income of $1 112 or less). The marginal tax rate for a bracket of taxable income is computed as the sum of the marginal federal and provincial tax rates for that bracket. Let us take the bracket of taxable income starting at $6 672 in Table 2-3. The marginal federal tax rate for taxable income in excess of $6 672 is 19 percent. Then the marginal provincial tax rate is 9.1 percent (or 48 percent of the marginal federal tax rate of 19 percent). Thus, the total marginal tax rate for the bracket of taxable income in excess of $6 672 is 28.1 percent (19 percent plus 9.1 percent)—this is higher than the average tax rate of 24.9 percent which was computed earlier.

The federal government collects the taxes for the provinces then effects transfers to provincial treasuries. Quebec levies personal income taxes under the Quebec Taxation Act. The Quebec tax rate varies from 13 percent to 33 percent for stated taxable income classes. The province collects its own taxes, and federal taxes are paid directly to Ottawa by the taxpayer.

DIVIDENDS

Dividends paid by taxable Canadian companies are subject to tax in the hands of individual shareholders. However, to alleviate in some measure the effects of double taxation, each shareholder is allowed the first $1000 of dividends tax-free and a dividend tax credit is applied to reduce personal taxes on dividends over $1000.

Let us illustrate how this system works. Suppose an individual received $6000 in dividends. Assuming federal marginal tax rates of 25 percent, 30 percent and 34 percent, taxes payable are computed as follows:

Taxpayers' federal marginal tax rate	25%	30%	34%
Dividend	$6 000	$6 000	$6 000
Add: Gross up (50%)	3 000	3 000	3 000
Taxable dividend	9 000	9 000	9 000
Less: Dividend and interest deduction	1 000	1 000	1 000
Taxable income	8 000	8 000	8 000
Federal tax	$2 000	$2 400	$2 720
Less: Dividend tax credit (22 2/3% of taxable dividend)	2 040	2 040	2 040
Basic federal tax	(40)*	360	680
Add: Ontario tax (0.48 × basic federal tax)	(19)	173	326
Total tax	(59)	533	1006
Dividend after tax	6 059	5 467	4 994
Effective tax rate on dividends	(1%)	8.9%	16.8%
Marginal tax rate on ordinary income to Ontario resident	37%	44.4%	50.3%

*We assume that the taxpayer has other taxable income.

Thus we see that dividends received are grossed up by 50 percent before the $1000 allowance is deducted. Taxes payable are then reduced by a dividend tax credit of 22 2/3 percent of taxable dividends to a maximum of the *total* federal taxes payable. It is important to note that the tax payable is in part a function of the marginal tax rate of the taxpayer. This feature is discussed further in Chapter 18, which deals with the dividend policy of a firm.

CAPITAL GAINS AND LOSSES

The capital gains and losses of individual taxpayers are treated in the same way as those of a company. That is, one half of capital gains is taxable and one half of capital losses is allowable as a deduction from taxable capital gains. In addition, individuals are allowed to deduct up to $2 000 of unused allowable capital losses from income from other sources. Moreover, this amount may be deducted in the year in which it occurs, the previous year, or in any subsequent year. Also, the first $1 000 of capital gains from the sale of Canadian securities is tax-free except when this allowance is claimed for dividends and interest.

INTEREST INCOME

Interest received on fixed-income securities is deemed income and is taxed in a manner similar to salaries and wages. However, since 1975 interest on the first $1 000 has been tax-free except when this allowance is claimed for dividends and capital gains. That is, where a person receives capital gains, dividends, and interest, the aggregate tax-free limit is $1 000 in a given taxation year.

Summary

In this chapter, the three basic forms of business organization were considered—the sole proprietorship, the partnership, and the company. The advantages and disadvantages of each were discussed, and it was concluded that, in a modern economy, the corporate form offers a number of advantages. As a result, we have seen a significant growth in the importance of the company in the last century.

The tax environment has a profound influence on business decisions. We briefly examined certain basic features of the tax law as they apply to companies and individuals. This chapter serves only as an introduction to the issue; relevant taxes and their implications will be discussed throughout the book when we consider specific financial decisions.

Questions

1. What are the advantages of the corporate form of business organization? Discuss their importance (a) to the owner of a small family restaurant and (b) to a wealthy entrepreneur who owns several businesses.
2. Explain the impact on earnings of the double declining balance method of depreciation.
3. The method of calculating capital cost allowance does not alter the total amount of deductions from income during the life of an asset. What does it alter and why is that important?
4. Is there any theoretical justification for allowing the deduction of debt service charge from income for tax purposes, yet disallowing the deduction of dividends on preferred and common stock? Discuss.
5. Tax laws have become extremely complex. In addition, there is little theoretical or moral justification for a substantial number of tax incentives (loopholes). Why and how are these incentives created? In your opinion, is there any indication that these incentives will be eliminated?
6. What is the purpose of the carry-back and the carry-forward provisions in the tax laws?
7. If the investment tax credit were raised, what is the likely effect on business investment?

Problems with Solutions

1. A company purchases an asset during 198A for $40 000. The asset falls into class 10 for income tax purposes and thus the company is allowed to use a 30 percent rate to calculate capital cost allowance. During 198C the asset is sold for $16 000 and a new asset in the same class is purchased for $50 000. Calculate the capital cost allowance.

Capital cost allowance	
198A ($40 000 × 0.3 × 1/2)	$ 6 000
198B ($40 000 − $6 000) 0.3	10 200
198C ($40 000 − $6 000 − $10 200) 0.3 + ($50 000 − $16 000) (0.3) (1/2)	12 240
198D ($40 000 − $6 000 − $10 200 − $16 000 + $50 000 − $12 240) 0.3	13 668
Balance in the pool at end of 198D ($40 000 − $6 000 − $10 200 − $16 000 + $50 000 − $12 240 − $13 668)	31 892

work thru this

2. A company purchases an asset during 198A for $50 000. The asset falls into Class 8 and thus a 20 percent capital cost allowance is chargeable. A new asset in the same class is purchased during 198C for $100 000 and the old asset sold at the same time. Calculate the tax the company would pay in 198C on income of $200 000 before capital cost allowance assuming the old asset is sold for a) $26 000 b) $36 000 c) $44 000 d) $56 000 using tax rate of 46 percent. Also calculate the net income after tax.

	(a)	(b)	(c)	(d)
Original cost (old)	$ 50 000	$ 50 000	$ 50 000	$ 50 000
CCA ($5 000 + $9 000)	14 000	14 000	14 000	14 000
UCC at time of sale	36 000	36 000	36 000	36 000
Sale of old asset	(26 000)	(36 000)	(44 000)	(56 000)
Capital gain				6 000
Purchase of new asset	100 000	100 000	100 000	100 000
UCC after purchase of new asset	110 000	100 000	92 000	86 000
Taxable income before CCA	$200 000	$200 000	$200 000	$200 000
Capital gain × 0.5				3 000
CCA*	(14 600)	(13 600)	(12 800)	(12 200)
Taxable income	185 400	186 400	187 200	190 800
Tax (taxable income) (0.46)	85 284	85 744	86 112	87 768
Net income after tax	$100 116	$100 656	$101 088	$103 032

*($36 000 × 0.2) + (UCC after purchase − $36 000) × 0.2 × 1/2.

3. Recalculate problem 2 assuming that when the old asset is sold it is the only asset in the class and no new asset is purchased.

	(a)	(b)	(c)	(d)
UCC at time of sale (see problem 2)	$ 36 000	$ 36 000	$ 36 000	$ 36 000
Sale of asset	(26 000)	(36 000)	(44 000)	(56 000)
Terminal loss	$ 10 000	—	—	—
Recaptured depreciation	—	—	$ 8 000	$ 14 000
Capital gain	—	—	—	6 000
Taxable income before adjustments for terminal loss, recaptured depreciation and capital gain	$200 000	$200 000	$200 000	$200 000
Terminal loss	(10 000)	—	—	—
Recaptured depreciation	—	—	8 000	14 000
Capital gain × 0.5	—	—	—	3 000
Taxable income	$190 000	$200 000	$208 000	$217 000
Tax (taxable income) (0.46)	87 400	92 000	95 680	99 820
Net income after tax	$102 600	$108 000	$112 320	$117 180

4. A company purchases an asset for $500 000 that qualifies for a 10 percent investment tax credit. The CCA rate is 20 percent. Calculate the tax paid and the after tax net income if the company earns the following amounts before tax and CCA: 198A $150 000; 198B $250 000; 198C $250 000. The tax rate is 46 percent.

	198A	198B	198C
Earnings before Tax and CCA	$150 000	$250 000	$250 000
CCA*	45 000	81 000	64 800
Earnings before tax	105 000	169 000	185 200
Tax at 46 percent	43 700	77 740	85 192
Less: ITC	(43 700)	(6 300)**	—
Tax paid	0	71 440	85 192
Earnings after tax	105 000	97 560	100 008

*Calculation of CCA

Cost	500 000	
Less: ITC	50 000	
	450 000	
198A	45 000	(½ × 0.2 × $450 000)
UCC	405 000	
198B	81 000	(0.2 × $405 000)
UCC	324 000	
198C	64 800	(0.2 × $324 000)
UCC	$259 200	

**This is the balance of ITC not deducted in 198A.

5. A company shows the following results for the seven year period ended Dec. 31, 198G:

Year	Net income (loss) excluding capital gains and losses	Net taxable capital gains (losses)*
198A	$ 8 000	$ —
8B	12 000	3 000
8C	(55 000)	4 000
8D	25 000	(6 000)
8E	30 000	2 000
8F	36 000	9 000
8G	42 000	—

*All capital gains and capital losses from the sale of non-depreciable assets have been multiplied by 0.5 to derive taxable amounts.

Show how carry-back and carry-forward provisions would be used in the above circumstances.

Year	Net income (loss) excluding capital gains and losses	Net taxable capital gains (losses)	Non-capital loss carry back/ forward	Capital loss carry forward	Taxable income
198A	$ 8 000	$ —	$ —	$ —	$ 8 000
8B	12 000	3 000	(15 000)	—	—
8C	(55 000)	4 000	—	—	—
8D	25 000	(6 000)	(25 000)	—	—
8E	30 000	2 000	(11 000)	(2 000)	19 000
8F	36 000	9 000	—	(4 000)	41 000
8G	42 000	—	—	—	42 000

6. An Ontario taxpayer whose federal marginal tax rate is 34 percent receives interest income of $3 000 and dividends from taxable Canadian companies of $6 000. Calculate tax payable and after tax income. The Ontario tax rate is 48 percent.

Interest income		$ 3 000
Dividend income	$6 000	
Gross up 50%	3 000	9 000
		12 000
$1 000 allowable deduction		1 000
Taxable income		$11 000
Federal tax 0.34 ($11 000)		$ 3 740
Dividend tax credit (22 2/3% of $9 000)		2 040
Basic federal tax		1 700
Ontario tax (0.48) ($1 700)		816
Additional tax		$ 2 516

After tax income = $9 000 – $2 516 = $6 484

Problems

1. In 1983 the Laiken Company Ltd. purchased a special purpose machine for $30 000. The machine is a Class 10 asset with a capital cost allowance rate of 30 percent. Assume that this is the only asset in the pool of Class 10 assets and no replacement is contemplated. Two years later the machine is sold.
   (a) If the sale price were $35 000 and the tax rate 46 percent, how much tax would the company pay on the sale of the machine?
   (b) If the sale price were $5000, how much tax would be saved?

2. The Cawsey Company Ltd., a Canadian-controlled private company, was established in 1984 and was expected to have the following taxable income:

1984	$ 30 000
1985	50 000
1986	190 000
1987	250 000
1988	220 000
1989	210 000
1990	40 000
1991	80 000
1992	150 000

   (a) The company pays no dividends. Calculate the taxes payable each year from 1984 to 1992.
   (b) The company pays 20 percent of after tax income as calculated in (a) in dividends each year. Calculate the taxes payable each year.
   (c) Discuss the reasons for the differences in the answers obtained in (a) and (b).

3. Prout Manufacturing Company Ltd. projects income to be:

	Net income (loss)	Dividends	Capital gains (losses)
Year 1	$ 25 000	$3 000	—
Year 2	(150 000)	3 500	5 000
Year 3	45 000	4 000	(15 000)
Year 4	70 000	4 500	3 000
Year 5	75 000	5 000	5 000
Year 6	80 000	5 500	17 000

   Net income (loss) excludes dividends and capital gains (losses). Assume that (a) the dividends are received from a taxable Canadian company, and (b) the corporate tax is 46 percent. Calculate the annual taxes payable after taking into account carry-back and carry-forward adjustments.

4. In January, 19X1 a resident of Ontario is given the opportunity to invest in either of three proposals for incremental income. Proposal 1 offers interest income of $16 000 (16 percent on $100 000); Proposal 2 offers $10 000 dividends on an investment of $100 000 in a 10 percent preferred stock issue; and Proposal 3 offers expected capital gains of $10 000 for an

investment of $100 000. Income from any of the investments will be received by December, 19X1. Assume that the federal tax rate shown in Table 2-3 applies, that the Ontario personal tax rate is 48 percent of the basic federal tax payable, and that the investor expects to have a taxable income of $53 376 for 19X1 from sources other than the investments noted above. Which proposal should the investor accept? Why?

5. Rework problem 4 under the assumption that the investor expects his taxable income to be $1 112 instead of $53 376. Which proposal should the investor accept? Why? Is your answer different from that in problem 4? Why?

Selected References

BOSSON, JOHN. "Implementing Capital Gains Tax Reform," *Canadian Tax Journal* (Mar.-Apr. 1979), 145-56.

BUCOVETSKY, MEYER W. "Inflation and the Personal Tax Base: The Capital Gains Issue," *Canadian Tax Journal* (Jan.-Feb. 1977), 77-107.

HYNDMAN, R. M. "The Efficacy of Recent Corporate Tax Reductions for Manufacturing," *Canadian Tax Journal*, XXII (Jan.-Feb. 1974), 84-97.

IZARD, RICHARD. "Corporate Taxes: Death to Capital Investments?", *CA Magazine* (Nov. 1979), 42-48.

KELLOUGH, HOWARD J. "The Business of Defining a Partnership under the Income Tax Act," *Canadian Tax Journal*, XXII (Mar.-Apr. 1974), 190-212.

KNECHTEL, RONALD C. and P. WAYNE PENNY. "Federal Manufacturing and Processing Incentives," *Canadian Tax Journal*, XXI (Sept.-Oct. 1973), 391-409.

———. "Federal Manufacturing and Processing Incentives—Rapid Write-Off," *Canadian Tax Journal*, XXI (Nov.-Dec. 1973), 540-45.

LACHANCE, R.A. and G.D. ERIKS, *Preparing Your Income Tax Returns*, 1974 ed. Don Mills, Ont.: CCH Canadian Ltd., 1974.

McCALLUM, JOHN S. "The Impact of the Capital Gains Tax on Bond Yields," *National Tax Journal*, XXVI (Dec. 1973), 575-83.

MORROW, ROBERT H. "Reasons for Incorporation," *Certified General Accountant* (May-June 1973), 13-23.

MURPHY, GEORGE J. "The Influence of Taxation on Canadian Corporate Depreciation Practices," *Canadian Tax Journal*, XX (May-June 1972), 233-39.

RUSSELL, GLENN A. "Tax Problems Facing Partnerships," *Canadian Chartered Accountant* (Dec. 1972), 32-40.

SHINDER, BERNARD, "The Taxation of Small Business: An Historical and Technical Review", *Canadian Tax Journal*, January-February, 1984, 1-53.

SIMON, R.P. "The Efficacy of Recent Corporate Income Tax Reductions for Manufacturing—An Unsimulated View," *Canadian Tax Journal*, XXII (Mar.-Apr. 1974), 160-65.

SMITH, ERNEST H. "Allocating to Provinces the Taxable Income of Corporations: How the Federal-Provincial Allocation Rules Evolved," *Canadian Tax Journal* (Sept.-Oct. 1976), 543-71.

WOODSIDE, KEN. "Tax Incentives vs. Subsidies: Political Considerations in Government Choice," *Candian Public Policy* (Spring 1979), 248-56.

II

PRINCIPLES OF FINANCIAL RETURNS

The Role
of Financial
Markets for
Business Firms

3

In varying degrees, all business firms operate within the financial system. When a product or service is sold, the seller receives either cash or a financial asset in the form of an account receivable. In addition, the firm invests idle funds in marketable securities, and here it has direct contact with the financial markets. More importantly, most firms use financial markets to finance their investment in assets. In final analysis, the market prices of a company's securities are the test of whether it is a success or a failure. While business firms compete with each other in the product markets, they must continually interface with the financial markets. The financial system consists of a number of institutions and markets serving business firms, individuals, and governments. Because of the importance of this environment to the financial manager as well as to the individual as a consumer of financial services, this chapter is devoted to exploring the financial system.

The Purpose of Financial Markets

Financial assets exist in an economy because the savings of various individuals, corporations, and governments during a period of time differ from their investment in real assets. By real assets, we mean such things as houses, buildings, equipment, inventories, and durable goods. If savings equalled investment in real assets for all economic units in an economy over all periods of time, there would be no external financing, no financial assets, and no money and capital markets. Each economic unit would be self-sufficient; current expenditures and investment in real assets would be paid for out of current income. A financial asset is created only when the investment by an economic unit in real assets exceeds its savings, and it finances this excess by borrowing or issuing equity securities. For an economic unit to finance, of course, another economic unit must be willing to lend. This interaction of borrowers with lenders determines interest rates. In the economy as a whole, funds are provided by savings-surplus economic units whose savings exceed their investment in real assets to savings-deficit units whose investment in real assets exceeds their savings. This exchange of funds is evidenced by pieces of paper representing a financial asset to the holder and a financial liability to the issuer.

PRIMARY AND SECONDARY DISTRIBUTION

A financial asset is created only once. The first issue of the asset is termed a *primary* distribution. For example, a new common stock issue of a company will be a primary distribution. Investors use current savings to purchase these securities. However, these investors are not obligated to hold the shares forever. For a number of reasons, an investor may desire to liquidate his investment and he is able to sell his securities because there are other investors who are willing to buy them. Trading activities after the primary distribution are termed *secondary* distribution of the securities. Under the secondary distribution process, the ownership of financial assets may change many times.

EFFICIENCY OF FINANCIAL MARKETS

The purpose of financial markets is to allocate savings efficiently in an economy to ultimate users. If those economic units that saved were the same as those that engaged in capital formation, an economy could prosper without financial markets. In modern economies, however, the economic units most responsible for capital formation—non-financial corporations—invest in real assets in an amount in excess of their total savings. Households, on the other hand, have total savings in excess of total investment in real assets. The more diverse the patterns of desired savings and investment among economic units, the greater the need for efficient financial markets to channel savings to ultimate users. The ultimate investor in real assets and the ultimate saver should be brought together at the least possible cost and/or inconvenience to both.

Efficient financial markets are absolutely essential to assure adequate capital formation and economic growth in an economy. If there were no financial assets other than paper money, each economic unit could invest only to the extent that it saved. Without financial assets, then, an economic unit would be greatly constrained in its investment behavior. If the amounts required for investment in a real asset were large in relation to current savings, an economic unit would simply have to postpone investment until it had accumulated sufficient savings in the form of paper money. In the absence of financing, many worthwhile investment opportunities would have to be postponed or abandoned by economic units lacking sufficient savings.

In such a system, savings in the economy would not be channeled to the most promising investment opportunities; and capital would be less than optimally allocated. Those economic units which lacked promising investment opportunities would have no alternative but to accumulate money. Likewise, economic units with very promising opportunities might not be able to accumulate sufficient savings rapidly enough to undertake the projects. Consequently, inferior investments might be undertaken by some economic units while very promising opportunities would be postponed or abandoned by others. It is not difficult to see the importance of one unit being able to issue financial assets to another. However, even with this ability, the efficiency with which savings are channeled to investment opportunities is not always the highest.

THE GENERAL STRUCTURE OF FINANCIAL MARKETS

In advanced economies, a system of efficient capital markets has evolved; the general structure of such a system is shown in Fig. 3-1. We should note, however, that not all components of the capital market system are equally efficient. The term *efficient market* usually refers to markets for publicly traded securities of large firms. This stock market (of which the Toronto Stock Exchange is a part) is an example of a relatively efficient Canadian capital market. Other markets such as the over-the-counter and mortgage markets are less efficient.

Savings which move directly from savings-surplus economic units to savings-deficit economic units constitute a direct flow of funds. An indirect flow of funds, shown in Fig. 3-1, moves from the savings-surplus economic units to the users by way of the financial institutions. A number of institutions have developed to enhance the efficiency of the flow of funds. One institution is the investment dealer/broker/counselor whose primary purpose is to find savers and put them in touch with economic units needing funds. Because the investment dealer or broker is a specialist in the business of matching the demand for funds with the supply, the dealer can usually do it more efficiently and at a lower cost than would the individual economic units themselves. Other institutions that enhance the efficiency of the flow of savings are the securities markets, where existing securities can be bought or sold. With a viable secondary market, a financial instrument is marketable. If the purchaser wishes to sell the security sometime in the future, he or she will be able to do so. Thus, the existence of a strong secondary market enhances the primary market in which funds flow from ultimate savers to ultimate users.

Financial intermediaries (Fig. 3-1) as a group have become a dominant factor in the indirect flow of funds process. Financial institutions can accumulate small amounts of individual savings and direct them in larger blocks to the savings-deficit units at relatively lower costs. The operations of the above-mentioned institutions are discussed in greater detail later in this chapter.

SECURITIES REGULATION

The efficiency of the financial markets is enhanced by the various regulations enacted to protect investors. The creation, distribution, and trading of securities are of national interest and over the years governments have intervened in the operations of financial markets to set minimum acceptable standards for all participants. The threat of prosecution is undoubtedly a positive force in promoting market efficiency. Relevant statutory provisions are discussed later in this chapter.

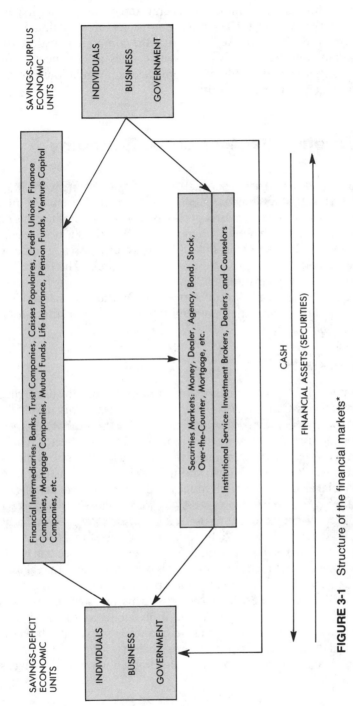

FIGURE 3-1 Structure of the financial markets*

* This figure is a modified version of the diagram in David C. Shaw and T. Ross Archibald, *Canada's Capital Markets* (Toronto: The Toronto Stock Exchange and London: The School of Business Administration, U.W.O., 1972), 3.

We now move to a review of a model which is used to identify and evaluate the flow of funds through the economy in general, and business firms in particular. Then we focus on the role of interest rates as a means for allocating funds in the economy. With this background, we then review the component institutions in the financial markets and evaluate their respective roles as suppliers of funds to businesses. Finally, we identify and review some relevant regulations governing the issuing and trading of corporate securities.

Flow of Funds Through Sectors of the Economy

There are four main sectors in the economy: households, non-financial business firms, governments and financial institutions (which include financial intermediaries). These four sectors form a matrix of claims against one another; this matrix is illustrated in Fig. 3-2, which shows a hypothetical balance sheet for each sector. Households are the ultimate owners of all business enterprises, whether they be non-financial corporations or private financial institutions. The figure illustrates the distinct role of financial institutions. Their assets are primarily financial assets; they hold a relatively small amount of real assets. On the right-hand side of their balance sheet, financial liabilities predominate. Financial institutions link all sectors of the economy.

FLOW OF FUNDS MATRIX

We can study the flow of savings between sectors through the use of funds data published in Statistics Canada's *Financial Flow Accounts*. This system of social accounting provides a picture of interlocking funds flows in the economy.[1] Essentially, a source and use of funds statement is prepared for each sector. The starting point is a balance sheet at the beginning of the period as well as one at the end. The balance sheet is similar to that shown in Fig. 3-2. However, it is useful to break down the financial asset category into money and other financial assets, i.e., paper claims. The flows are simply the changes in balance sheet figures between two moments in time. When source and use statements are combined, we obtain a matrix for the entire economy. A hypothetical matrix for a closed economy consisting of four sectors is shown in Table 3-1. In the table, we see that total uses of funds equal total sources for each sector; that is, the investment in real assets plus changes in financial assets must equal savings plus changes in financial liabilities.

We also see that, on the whole, business firms invested in real assets to a greater extent than they were saving. The difference was financed by issuing financial liabilities in excess of the increase in financial assets held. The existence of this large savings-deficit sector implies the existence of one or more savings-surplus sectors. When we analyze the matrix, we see that households were a savings-surplus

---

[1]See James C. Van Horne, *Financial Market Rates and Flows* (Englewood Cliffs, N.J.: Prentice-Hall, Inc., 1978), Chapter 2, for a further analysis of this system.

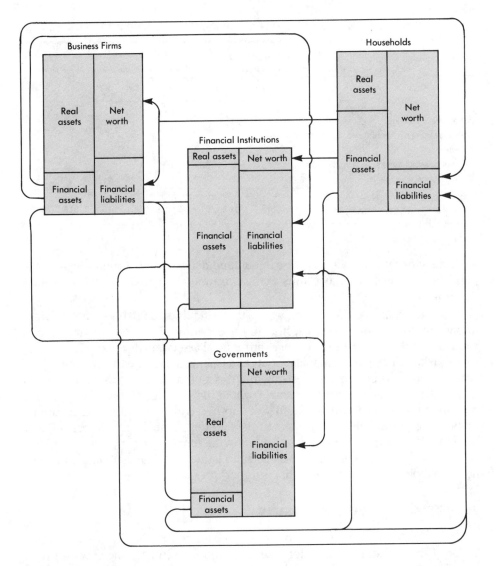

FIGURE 3-2 Relationship of claims

sector and that they were primarily responsible for financing the business firms sector on a net basis. In addition, financial institutions were a savings-surplus sector, although the excess of savings over investment for this sector was small. This sector acts almost entirely as an intermediary, increasing its holdings of financial assets by issuing financial liabilities. Finally, governments, the fourth category, were a savings-deficit sector.

The budget deficit for governments is financed by an increase in financial liabilities in excess of the increase in financial assets. Because the financial institutions sector contains commercial banks and the monetary authorities, it "provides" money for other sectors in the economy. The $5 billion source of money

TABLE 3-1   Matrix of Funds Flow in the Entire Economy 19XX

	Households		Business Firms		Financial Institutions		Governments		All Sectors	
	U	S	U	S	U	S	U	S	U	S
Net worth (savings)		101		77		4		−3		179
Real assets (investment)	82		96		1				179	
Money	2		2			5	1		5	5
Other financial assets	37		18		60		17		132	
Financial liabilities		20		39		52		21		132
	121	121	116	116	61	61	18	18	316	316

for this sector represents an increase in demand deposits and currency held by the public and governments as claims against commercial banks and the monetary authorities.

In the "All Sectors" column, we see that total uses equal total sources. More important, total savings for all sectors in the economy equal the total increase in real assets. Likewise, the total change in financial assets equals the total change in financial liabilities. Thus, financial assets and financial liabilities balance out in the economy as a whole. In other words, there is no such thing as saving through financial assets for the economy as a whole. The financial asset held by one economic unit is the financial liability of another. However, individual economic units can save through financial assets; the fact that financial assets "cancel out" when they are totaled for all economic units in the economy is simply a mathematical truism. It is the interaction between the issuers of financial claims and the potential holders of those claims that is important.

FUNDS FLOW FOR BUSINESS FIRMS

Our previous discussion showed that business firms are a savings-deficit sector of the economy. The major sources of funds to finance the excess of their investment in real assets over savings are individuals and financial institutions. The former represent a direct flow, while the latter represent an indirect one. Of course, business firms finance each other through accounts receivable and other arrangements, but these funds flows cancel out when we consider all business firms. A general breakdown of the sources and uses of funds by incorporated business firms during the 1976–82 period is shown in Table 3-2.

We see that the principal use of funds by business firms was for plant and equipment. Of the total sources of funds internal sources—comprised of retained earnings and depreciation allowances—accounted for about two thirds of total funds. Of the external sources, new bond and stock issues and bank loans were the most important sources, followed by other loans and commercial paper and mortgage debt.

TABLE 3-2   Sources and Uses of Corporate Funds ($ billions)

	Annual Net Increases in Amounts Outstanding						
	1976	*1977*	*1978*	*1979*	*1980*	*1981*	*1982*
Uses of funds:							
Plant, other real estate & equipment	20.07	21.80	23.40	29.51	37.11	44.16	37.61
Inventories adjusted for valuation	0.48	−0.44	0.90	3.42	−1.35	0.02	−10.01
Nonfinancial asset investment	20.55	21.36	24.30	32.93	35.76	44.18	27.60
Net trade & consumer credit	1.06	1.76	2.54	0.63	−0.06	1.01	2.37
Currency & bank deposits	0.86	0.58	1.32	−0.44	1.36	0.79	−2.63
Deposits in other institutions	0.06	0.00	0.26	0.23	−0.18	−0.43	0.35
Foreign currency & deposits	0.58	−0.14	0.92	0.29	0.08	−0.73	1.78
Government securities	0.00	0.00	0.00	0.05	0.06	0.26	1.38
Finance co. & other short-term paper	−0.24	0.34	0.36	1.15	1.11	−0.84	0.40
Direct investment in other companies (net)	0.35	1.26	2.38	4.91	3.72	11.77	1.90
Other financial assets (net)	0.38	0.89	2.42	3.50	4.23	3.50	2.28
Financial asset investment	3.05	4.69	10.20	10.32	10.42	15.29	7.83
Total uses	23.60	26.05	34.50	43.25	45.58	59.51	35.43
Sources of funds:							
Retained earnings	5.70	6.39	7.45	10.90	8.84	3.86	1.53
Depreciation & misc. valuation adjustments	10.38	11.52	12.50	14.74	17.82	20.73	22.72
Total internal sources	16.08	17.91	19.95	25.64	26.66	24.59	24.25
Bank loans	2.97	1.56	3.90	5.30	6.47	17.57	0.02
Other loans & commercial paper	1.07	0.94	1.20	3.03	1.62	4.11	2.74
Mortgage debt	0.76	1.68	0.32	0.87	1.79	0.96	1.34
New bond issues	2.13	1.96	1.23	0.47	2.14	5.38	2.84
New stock issues	0.93	2.83	4.87	5.26	5.56	6.64	3.80
Miscellaneous liabilities	0.68	1.01	3.73	4.68	3.19	3.79	0.19
Total financial liabilities	8.54	9.98	15.25	19.61	20.77	38.45	10.93
Error term	(1.02)	(1.84)	(0.70)	(2.00)	(1.25)	(3.53)	0.25
Total sources	23.60	26.05	34.50	43.25	45.58	59.51	35.43

Source: Statistics Canada, *Financial Flow Accounts*. The data apply to nonfinancial private companies; government nonfinancial businesses are not included.

Funds flows to business firms may come directly from savings-surplus economic units or indirectly through the financial intermediaries (Fig. 3-1). The institutions and procedures involved in these flow-of funds processes are important to the financial manager. However, before we review this topic we should consider another equally important factor—the role of interest rates in the allocation of savings.

Allocation of Funds Through Yields

The allocation of savings in an economy is made primarily on the basis of price, expressed in terms of expected yield. Economic units in need of funds must outbid others for their use. Although the allocation process is somewhat affected by capital rationing, government restrictions, and institutional constraints, yields are the primary mechanism whereby supply and demand are brought into balance for a particular financial instrument across financial markets. If all investment projects carried the same degree of risk, those economic units willing to pay the highest yield would be the ones entitled to the use of funds. If rationality prevails, the economic units bidding the highest prices will be the ones with the most promising investment opportunities. As a result, savings will tend to be allocated to the most efficient users.

However, it is important to recognize that the equilibration process by which savings are allocated in an economy occurs not only on the basis of expected return but on the basis of risk as well. Different financial instruments have different degrees of risk. In order for them to compete for funds, these instruments must provide different expected returns or yields. If all financial instruments had exactly the same risk characteristics, they would provide the same yield. Because of differences in maturity, default risk, marketability, and taxability, however different instruments carry different degrees of risk and provide varying expected returns to the investor. Some other factors (callable, extendible, and refundable options) which also affect yields are discussed later in Chapter 21.

MATURITY

The relationship between yield and maturity can be studied graphically by plotting yield to maturity for securities differing only in the length of time to maturity. In practice, this means holding the degree of default risk constant. For example, we could study the yield-maturity relationship for default-free Government of Canada securities. An example of the yield-maturity relationship for Canada bonds is shown in Fig. 3-3. Maturity is plotted on the horizontal axis and yield on the vertical; their relationship is described by a yield curve fitted to the observations. Note that a yield curve depicts yield-maturity relationship at a point in time; this relationship usually changes with the passage of time.

Generally, when interest rates are expected to rise, the yield curve is upward-sloping, whereas it is downward-sloping at the long end of the yield curve when they are expected to fall. However, the yield differential between short and long term securities is greater for the steepest upward-sloping yield curve. In other words, there is a tendency towards positive-sloped yield curves. Most economists attribute this tendency to the presence of risk for those who invest in long term securities vis-à-vis short term securities. In general, the longer the maturity, the greater the risk of fluctuation in the market value of the security. Consequently, investors need to be offered a risk premium to induce them to invest in a long term securities. Only when interest rates are expected to fall significantly are they willing

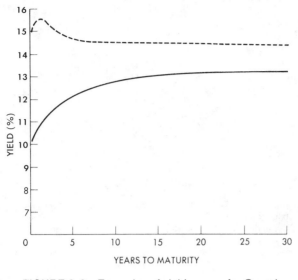

FIGURE 3-3 Examples of yield curves for Canada
Bonds

to invest in long term securities yielding less than short and intermediate term securities.[2]

DEFAULT RISK

When we speak of default risk, we mean the risk of default on the part of the borrower in the payment of principal or interest. Investors demand a risk premium before they invest in other than default-free securities. The greater the possibility that the borrower will default in his or her obligation, the greater the default risk and the premium demanded by the marketplace. Government of Canada securities are usually regarded as default-free, and other securities are judged in relation to them. The greater the default risk of a security issuer, then, the greater the expected return or yield of the security, all other things being the same.[3] This relationship is shown in Fig. 3-4. Holding maturity constant, a higher risk premium is required to encourage investors to buy securities from issuers with higher probabilities of default.

Quality differentials across Canadian corporate bond issues are determined by underwriters pricing the issue or by rating agencies.[4] In 1972 the Canadian Bond Rating Service Ltd. (CBRS) was established. This firm, located in Montreal, gives a credit rating similar to that used by Moody's or Standard & Poor's (Table 3-3), to all major Canadian bond issues. The top credit is A++, followed by A+, A, B++, B+, C,

---

[2]For a much deeper discussion of this concept, see Van Horne, *Financial Market Rates and Flows*, Chapter 4.

[3]For an extended discussion of the influence of default risk on yields as well as a review of the various empirical studies, see Van Horne, *Financial Market Rates and Flows*, Chapter 6.

[4]For an analysis of bond rating methods, see James S. Ang and Kiritkumar A. Patel, "Bond Rating Methods: Comparison and Validation," *Journal of Finance*, 30 (May 1975), 631–40.

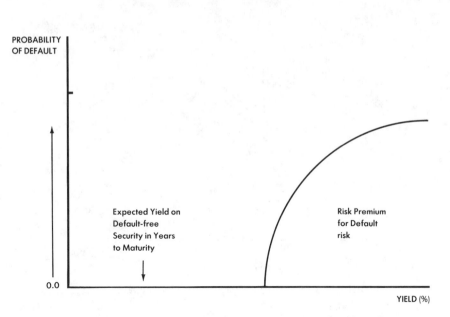

FIGURE 3-4 Illustration of risk premium/default risk relationship

and D. Companies issuing bonds or investors desiring to buy bonds may, upon payment of a fee, request a rating. There is also the Dominion Bond Rating Service Ltd. which rates commercial paper. This Toronto firm was established early in the 1970s and rates these securities on a request basis. Generally, the rating agencies assign letter grades which are available for the use of investors. In their ratings, the agencies attempt to rank issues according to the probability of default. A number of factors go into the analysis of an issue by an agency, including the cash-flow ability of the issuer to service debt, the amount and composition of existing debt, and the stability of cash flows. The highest grade securities, whose default risk is felt to be negligible, are rated triple-A. The ratings used by the two U.S. agencies are shown in Table 3-3.

MARKETABILITY

The marketability of a security relates to the possibility of converting it into cash. There are two dimensions: the price which can be realized and the amount of time required to sell the asset. The two are interrelated in that it is often possible to sell an asset in a short period of time if enough price concession is given. For financial instruments, marketability is judged in relation to the ability to sell a significant volume of securities in a short period of time without significant price concession. The more marketable the security, the greater the ability to execute a large transaction near the quoted price. In general, the lower the marketability of a security, the greater the yield necessary to attract investors. Thus, the demand differential between different securities of the same maturity is caused not only by differences in default risk but also by differences in marketability.

TABLE 3-3 Ratings by Investment Agencies

Moody's	
Aaa	Best quality
Aa	High quality
A	Higher medium grade
Baa	Lower medium grade
Ba	Possess speculative elements
B	Generally lack characteristics of desirable investment
Caa	Poor standing; may be in default
Ca	Speculative in a high degree; often in default
C	Lowest grade

Standard & Poor's	
AAA	Highest grade
AA	High grade
A	Upper medium grade
BBB	Medium grade
BB	Lower medium grade
B	Speculative
CCC-CC	Outright speculation
C	Reserved for income bonds
DDD-D	In default, with rating indicating relative salvage value

TAXABILITY

Another factor affecting observed differences in market yields is the differential impact of taxes. The return on a bond investment comes from interest income and capital gains if selling or redemption price exceeds purchase price. Capital losses arise if selling or redemption price is below purchase price. There is a differential impact on yields because interest income is taxed at the marginal income tax rate while only half of capital gains is so taxed.[5] As a result, fixed-income securities that sell at a discount because of a low coupon rate in relation to prevailing yields are attractive to investors. The reason is that part of the return is a capital gain. For example, if the face value of a bond is $1 000 and the current market price is $900, the bond must rise in price to $1 000 at maturity. The $100 rise represents a capital gain which is taxed at a more favorable rate than the interest income on the bond. Because of the desirability of discount bonds, their yield to maturity tends to be lower than the yield on comparable bonds with higher coupon rates.[6] The greater the discount, the greater the capital-gains attraction and the

---

[5]Remember that the first $1 000 of interest and taxable capital gains are usually not taxable. See Chapter 2 for further discussion.

[6]For further discussion, see Cecil R. Dipchand, "The Influence of Coupon on Canadian Corporate Bond Yields," *Journal of Business Administration*, 6(Fall 1974), 16–32; and William H. Gross, "Coupon Valuation and Interest Rate Cycles," *Financial Analysts Journal* (Jul.–Aug. 1979), 68–71.

lower its yield relative to what it would be if the coupon rate were such that the security sold at par.

INFLATION

In addition to these factors, which affect the yield of one security relative to that of another, inflation expectations have a substantial influence on interest rates overall. It generally is agreed that the nominal rate of interest on a security embodies a premium for inflation. The higher the expected inflation, the higher the nominal yield on the security; and the lower the expected inflation, the lower the nominal yield. Many years ago Irving Fisher expressed the nominal rate of interest on a bond as the sum of the real rate of interest and the rate of price change expected to occur over the life of the instrument.[7] If the annual real rate of interest in the economy were 4 percent for prime risks, and inflation of 8 percent per annum were expected over the next ten years, this would imply a yield of 12 percent for ten-year, high-grade bonds. This states merely that lenders require a nominal rate of interest high enough to earn the real rate of interest.

Fig. 3-5 indicates that interest rates tend to move in the same direction as the inflation rate as measured by the Consumer Price Index. This relationship suggests that as inflation increases or decreases, nominal interest rates follow a similar pattern.

It is important to differentiate between expected inflation and unexpected inflation. If inflation over the life of a security is exactly that which was anticipated when the terms of the loan were set, neither the borrower nor the lender gains (or loses) with respect to inflation. In other words, the terms of the loan reflect expected inflation, and the debt obligation is paid in keeping with the inflation that actually occurs. If part of the inflation which occurs is unanticipated, there is a redistributional effect from lender to borrower, or vice versa. With an unanticipated increase in inflation, the lender suffers by receiving a real rate of return lower than that anticipated at the time the terms of the loan were set.

To illustrate: the nominal rate of interest on a ten-year loan is 12 percent, of which 4 percent is the expected real rate and 8 percent is a premium for expected inflation. Over the ten years, inflation of 10 percent per annum actually occurs. As a result, the borrower's real interest cost is 2 percent instead of 4 percent. The lender loses, of course, because its real return is less than it anticipated at the time the loan contract was made. With an unanticipated decrease in inflation, the borrower loses in having to repay the loan in more "expensive" dollars than originally anticipated, whereas the lender gains.

Unanticipated increases in inflation result in a transfer of real wealth from net creditors to net debtors, whereas the opposite occurs with unanticipated decreases. A *net creditor* is defined as one whose financial assets exceed its financial liabilities; for the *net debtor*, the opposite holds. Whether a given company gains or loses with respect to inflation depends upon whether there is an unanticipated increase or

---

[7] *Appreciation and Interest* (New York: MacMillan, 1896). Actually, Fisher expressed the nominal rate as $R + \alpha + R\alpha$, where R is the real rate, α is the expected rate of inflation, and $R\alpha$ is the product of the two. Like others, we ignore the product term, as it has not been found to be important.

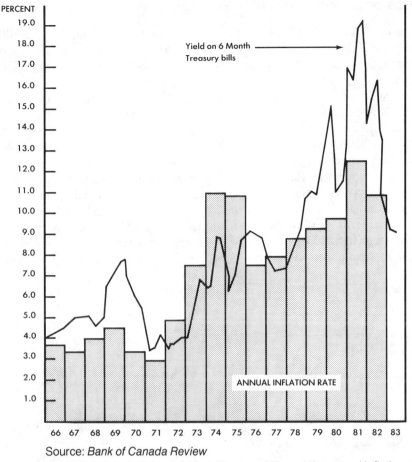

PERCENT

Yield on 6 Month
Treasury bills ————————→

ANNUAL INFLATION RATE

66 67 68 69 70 71 72 73 74 75 76 77 78 79 80 81 82 83

Source: *Bank of Canada Review*

FIGURE 3-5   Yield on six month Treasury bills and the annual inflation rate

decrease in inflation and whether the firm is a net debtor or a net creditor. In the aggregate, nonfinancial corporations have been consistent net debtors. Individually, companies can be net debtors or net creditors, and this can vary over time.

In the post-World War II period, a sizable portion of the inflation was unanticipated. Twenty years ago, no one would have thought present levels of inflation were possible. How much was unanticipated is difficult to say because we do not know what was expected, but it is not uncommon to see estimates that one-third of the inflation was unanticipated several years in advance. These estimates means that nonfinancial corporations as net debtors, in the aggregate, have gained in the post-World War II period. Put another way, there has been a drop in the value of existing debt instruments, accruing to the benefit of the firm and its stockholders.

The important point here is that while nominal yields embody a premium for expected inflation, those expectations are not necessarily realized. In an uncertain world, unanticipated changes in inflation cause a relative redistribution of real return from lender to borrower, or vice versa.

BEHAVIOR OF YIELDS ON CORPORATE SECURITIES

As a result of differences in maturity, default risk, marketability, taxability and changes in inflation expectations over time, the costs of funds to business vary over time. Generally, long-term funds cost more than short-term funds. This means that lenders want a higher expected yield or return on long-term securities relative to short-term securities. The maturity of a short-term instrument, by definition, is near. At maturity, the investor receives the face value of the instrument, assuming there is no default. Accordingly, there is far less investor uncertainty with respect to fluctuations in the market value of the instrument than there is with a long-term security.

Fig. 3-6 shows the yields for ten industrial bonds (which are long-term securities) and 90 day finance company paper (or 90 day commercial paper). Throughout most of the 1970s the bonds were sold to yield more than the commercial paper. This is the yield relationship we expect between long-term and short-term securities. However, we may find exceptions to this rule. Note in Fig. 3-6 that commercial paper had a yield higher than bonds over the 1979–81 period.

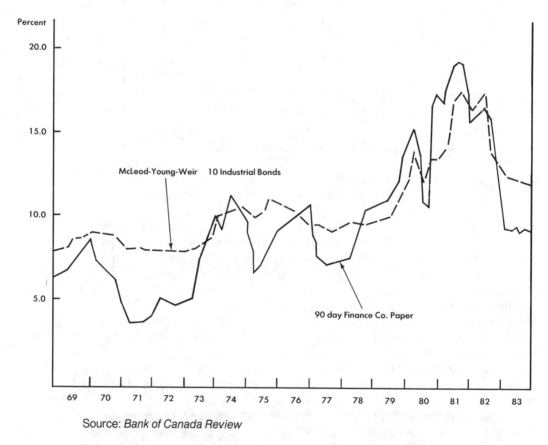

Source: *Bank of Canada Review*

Figure 3–6　Yields on McLeod-Young-Weir 10 Industrial Bonds and 90 day Finance Company Paper—Quarterly Series

This phenomenon is due largely to investors' expectations of the future level of interest rates.

The relevant expectations for commercial paper involve only the near future. The relevant expectations for bonds involve a much longer period of time. To illustrate the difference, suppose the economy was in a period of excessive inflation and the monetary authorities had begun to tighten money. The accompanying reduction in the growth of the money supply would put upward pressure on short-term rates. However, by virtue of the monetary authorities tightening money, investors might believe that inflation would ultimately come under control and that interest rates would decline after a year or so. As a result, long-term bond yields might not rise and could actually decline somewhat in anticipation of interest rates eventually moving down. Thus, the two rates might temporarily move in opposite directions as shown in Fig. 3-3. Over the long run, however, short and long rates tend to move in the same direction, as shown in the figure. The important point in all of this discussion, however, is that short-term rates reflect immediate supply-and-demand pressures in financial markets, while long-term rates are more influenced by long-run expectations.

Fig. 3-7 shows the yields on corporate bonds and bonds issued by the government of Canada. Both securities have about the same term to maturity and yield differences are due mainly to default risk. Government bonds are considered default-free and are sold to yield less than corporate bonds, other factors held constant.

Throughout the time span shown in Fig. 3-6 and Fig. 3-7, the secular trend in interest rates was steadily upward. Each cyclical peak in interest rates exceeded the previous interest rate peak. This trend is primarily attributable to changing inflation and inflation expectations. In the mid-1960s, the rate of inflation was around 4 percent and reasonably stable; by the 1980s, it was above 10 percent and was quite volatile. This changing level and volatility of inflation, as well as the efforts of the monetary authorities to quell it, largely explains movements in the overall levels of interest rates in the 1964–1983 period reflected in figures.

FACTORS AFFECTING EXPECTATIONS

The most important factors affecting interest-rate expectations are general economic conditions, monetary policy, and fiscal policy. Economic conditions are the underlying determinant of the real rate of interest as well as of inflation. When the economy is booming, there is usually a high demand for funds to finance investment in real assets relative to savings. Moreover, inflation often increases in the latter part of a boom. As a result interest rates tend to rise. In a recession, on the other hand, demand for funds tends to be lower in relation to the supply, and inflation tends to decline in the face of excess capacity in productive resources and labor. As a result, interest rates tend to decline.[8] Thus, expectations of the future state of the economy have an extremely important effect on interest rates in general and on long-term rates in particular.

---

[8]There are exceptions; for example, in 1974 inflation and interest rates rose despite a recession. The topic of inflation is complicated and a detailed discussion is beyond the scope of this book.

Monetary policy is an attempt to influence the rate of growth in economic activity and the rate of inflation by control over the supply of money. Consequently, it affects interest-rate expectations. Fiscal policy also influences economic activity and inflation because of the significant role the government plays in the economy. Policies on expenditures, taxation, and borrowing have a substantial impact on

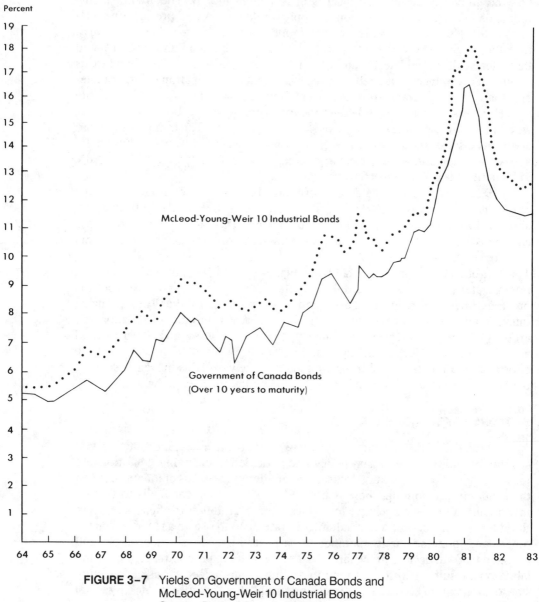

Percent

McLeod-Young-Weir 10 Industrial Bonds

Government of Canada Bonds
(Over 10 years to maturity)

FIGURE 3–7 Yields on Government of Canada Bonds and McLeod-Young-Weir 10 Industrial Bonds
Source: *Bank of Canada Review*

economic activity and inflationary expectations and, as a result, they affect interest-rate expectations. Moreover, the federal government is the largest single borrower in the money and capital markets. Therefore, it has a direct effect on the supply of securities in these markets and on interest rates. In summary, all of these factors—economic activity, monetary policy, and fiscal policy—have an important influence on interest-rate expectations.

BONDS VERSUS STOCK YIELDS

It is not appropriate to compare dividend yields on common shares—that is, the dividend per share divided by the market price per share—with yields on bonds. The expected return on a common share is comprised of dividends plus (or minus) the capital gain (or loss) that arises from the sale of the share at the end of a holding period. Dividends are paid from earnings available after the firm has met interest and preferred dividend payments. Capital gains have to come from price appreciation of the shares. These components of the return on a share are not as certain as those determining the yield to maturity on a bond. Given these considerations, the expected return for common shares is not as easily measured as the expected return for bonds. The capital gains component and future trend in dividends must be estimated. The current dividend yield alone simply omits the prospect for capital gains.

To illustrate this point, consider Fig. 3-8, where the average dividend yields for common shares listed on the Toronto Stock Exchange are compared with yields on the McLeod, Young & Weir ten industrial bonds over the 1956-83 period. The 1956-83 period yields on bonds were higher than the dividend yield on common shares. Such results are not consistent with the notion that securities subject to greater degrees of risk should offer returns higher than securities exposed to lesser degrees of risk. The dividend yield measure excludes capital gains considerations. As a result, the *direct* comparison of corporate bond and dividend yields is *not* an accurate guide to differences in expected return and risk.

Financial Intermediaries

Financial intermediaries include such institutions as commercial banks, trust companies, credit unions, life insurance companies, and pension funds. These intermediaries come between ultimate borrowers and lenders by transforming direct claims into indirect ones. They purchase primary securities and, in turn, issue their own securities. For example, the primary security that a trust company purchases is a mortgage; the indirect claim issued is a savings account or a certificate of deposit. A life insurance company, on the other hand, purchases corporate bonds, among other things, and issues life insurance policies.

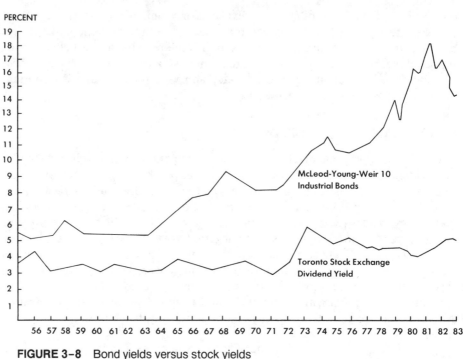

PERCENT

FIGURE 3-8   Bond yields versus stock yields
Source: *Bank of Canada Review*

Financial intermediaries transform funds in such a way as to make them more attractive. They provide a variety of services and are often able to cut costs as well. For one, economies of scale are possible which result in lower operational costs; these savings may be passed on to the borrower and lender. A financial intermediary is also able to pool savings to purchase primary securities of varying sizes. Most individual savers would have difficulty investing in a $20 000 mortgage. By putting funds in a trust company, however, they are able to invest indirectly in a mortgage. Another service provided is diversification of risk, something the individual saver acting alone would find difficult to accomplish. Also, financial intermediaries are able to transform the maturity of a primary security into indirect securities of different maturities. The new maturities may be more attractive to the ultimate lender than the maturity of the original direct loan. Finally, the financial intermediary has expertise in investing in primary securities which is something many individuals do not have.

Thus, financial intermediaries tailor the denomination and type of indirect securities they issue to the needs of savers. Their purpose, of course, is to make a profit by purchasing primary securities yielding more than the return they must pay on the indirect securities issued and the cost of their overhead. In so doing, they channel funds from the ultimate lender to the ultimate borrower at a lower cost or with less inconvenience (or both) than is possible through a direct purchase of primary securities by the ultimate lender. Otherwise, financial intermediaries have no reason to exist.

As indicated in Fig. 3-1, a number of financial institutions are involved in the financial market system. However, only a handful invest heavily in the securities of business firms. In the section that follows, we study those institutions involved in the buying and selling of corporate securities.[9]

DEPOSIT INSTITUTIONS

Deposit institutions include commercial banks and near-banks (trust companies, savings banks, credit unions and caisses populaires, and mortgage loan companies). These institutions acquire demand, savings, and time deposits from individuals, companies, and governments and in turn make loans and investments. Commercial banks as a group dominate this sector. In 1983, banks in Canada reported total domestic assets of $211.8 billion; this represented about 65 percent of the total assets of deposit institutions. With this financial strength, commercial banks are an important source of funds for business firms. Banks are primarily involved in lending on a short- and intermediate-term basis. In recent years, general loans to business firms averaged about 20 percent of the total assets of banks. Banks also invest in some corporate mortgage and other long-term bonds. The larger banks (the Royal Bank, the Bank of Montreal, the Canadian Imperial Bank of Commerce, the Bank of Nova Scotia, and the Toronto-Dominion Bank) have branches across the country and can thus provide for the regional banking needs of business firms.

Bank credit, which will be discussed later in Chapters 12 and 20, is a rather important source of funds for business firms. Here we should note that this market for bank credit is a rather "personal" market as compared to the bond or stock market. Usually, bank loans are negotiated between the lender (the bank) and the borrower (the business firm). The interest cost of the loan and other terms should be mutually agreed upon by both lender and borrower. For several reasons, however, a borrower may be able to negotiate a loan with an interest cost and other terms which may vary from bank to bank. That is, the terms of a loan from Bank A may vary (and sometimes significantly) from those of Bank B. Competition among banks is a primary reason for such inconsistencies, and firms sometimes shop around for better deals.

On the other hand, banks have been criticized for being too conservative in their lending policies. Critics claim that the degree of competition among banks is inadequate, that the market for bank credit is somewhat oligopolistic, and that smaller and well-deserving firms are denied full access to bank credit. These criticisms may have some validity—in recent years our legislators have encouraged the expansion of the banking system beyond the "big five". Also, foreign banks are allowed freer access to the Canadian market.[10]

---

[9]Our discussion here is rather limited. For details, see E. P. Neufeld, *The Financial System of Canada* (Toronto: Macmillan Co. of Canada Ltd., 1972) and R. A. Shearer, John F. Chant and David E. Bond, *The Economics of the Canadian Financial System* (Scarborough, Ont.: Prentice-Hall of Canada, Inc., 1984).

[10]Recent revisions to the Bank Act permitted foreign banks to set up subsidiaries in Canada. As of October 1983, about 58 foreign banks took advantage of these privileges and they are permitted to hold in aggregate, about 16 percent of total assets in the banking industry.

The near-banks are primarily involved with individuals. They take individual savings deposits and make mortgage and consumer loans. They are not an important source of financing for business firms. Trust companies and some credit unions invest some of their assets in loans to businesses. However, the amounts involved are relatively small compared to business loans from the banks.

INSURANCE COMPANIES

Insurance companies collect periodic premiums from those they insure in return for providing a payout should some adverse event happen. With funds received in advance premium payments, companies build reserves, which, together with a portion of their capital, are invested in financial assets. Insurance companies are broken down into two types: life insurance companies and fire and casualty insurance companies. The latter group is usually referred to as general insurance companies.

Life insurance companies insure against loss of life. Because the mortality of a large group of individuals is highly predictable, these companies are able to invest in long-term securities. In 1982, the Canadian assets of life insurance companies were about $30 billion. About one third of these assets were invested in long-term corporate debt and equity securities. Generally, life insurance companies invest heavily in fixed-income securities such as corporate and government bonds and mortgages. Investments in corporate stocks have accounted for less than 10 percent of the investment portfolios of these companies.

General insurance companies insure against fire, theft, car accidents, and other unexpected occurrences. These companies invest largely in government bonds, and to a lesser extent, in corporate bonds and equities. Their Canadian assets are less than one quarter those for life insurance companies and as such, they play a relatively smaller role in corporate financing.

PENSION FUNDS

Pension funds and other retirement funds, such as the Registered Retirement Savings Plan (RRSP), were established to provide income to individuals upon retirement. Individuals usually contribute to the fund during their working lives. Employers also contribute on behalf of their employees. The fund invests these contributions, and upon retirement of the employee, the fund either pays out the cumulative amount over a period of time or arranges an annuity. Trust and insurance companies administer most of the private pension funds in the country. They develop and sell their own funds (e.g., the RRSP) or they administer corporate pension funds for a fee. The federal, provincial, and municipal governments also have pension funds, the more well-known ones being the Canada Pension Plan and the Quebec Pension Plan. In 1983, the total assets of Canadian trusteed pension funds were about $81 billion.

Because of the long-term nature of their liabilities, pension funds invest in longer-term securities. In recent years, about one third of the assets of these funds has been invested in corporate bonds and stocks. Pension funds rank as the second largest investor (after insurance companies) in corporate bonds and as the largest single institutional investor in corporate stocks. While individuals and some other investors have been reducing their investment in common shares, pension funds have been a significant net buyer in recent years.

OTHER FINANCIAL INTERMEDIARIES

Mutual funds are another important investor in corporate shares. These funds accept monies contributed by a number of individuals and invest them in specific types of financial assets. Professional investment management of the fund is usually provided by a management company which charges a fee for such services. Each individual owns a specified percentage of the mutual fund depending on his investment in the fund. The individual can sell his shares at any time as the mutual fund is required to redeem them. While most mutual funds invest in common shares, there are also "balanced funds" which invest in both shares and bonds. The various funds have different investment goals ranging from income and safety to highly aggressive growth. In all cases, the individual obtains a diversified portfolio managed by professionals. However, there is little evidence that such management results in consistently superior performances.

The assets of Canadian mutual funds were about $9 billion in 1983. Mortgages accounted for about 40 percent of total investment; corporate shares, 30 percent; other securities, 30 percent. When stock market conditions are favorable, mutual funds increase their holdings of equities; the reverse is true under adverse market conditions.

Financial corporations (sales and consumer loan companies) are private corporations established to make instalment loans, personal loans, and secured business loans. These companies raise capital through stock issues and through borrowings. In turn, the finance company invests primarily in loans. Their role in business financing is relatively small and is generally restricted to term loans, equipment financing, and leasing.

In summary, we may note that of the financial institutions considered, the commercial banks are the most important sources of financing for business firms. However, their investments are primarily short- and intermediate-term loans. Corporate bonds and stocks are popular investments for insurance companies, pension funds, and mutual funds. However, commercial banks do invest a relatively small percentage of their assets in corporate bonds. On the whole, the role of financial institutions in providing external financing for business firms will continue to grow in importance.

The Securities Markets

In addition to the financial institutions already discussed, various securities markets, with their associated exchanges, facilitate the smooth functioning of the financial system. In general, these securities markets and exchanges are involved in the secondary trading of existing and outstanding financial assets. These secondary trading transactions do not increase the total stock of financial assets outstanding.

However, the presence of viable secondary markets increases the liquidity of financial assets and therefore enhances the primary or direct markets for securities. A firm whose common shares are actively traded on the Toronto Stock Exchange (the secondary market) will find it relatively easier to float a new issue of similar securities to interested investors (the primary market) than would otherwise be the case. The marketability of the shares in the secondary market is one of several factors which potential investors consider when evaluating the new issue.

THE MEETING PLACE

There are essentially two types of meeting places where buyers and sellers of securities interact for business purposes. The *organized security exchange* is a statutory body established under provincial securities regulation. Usually, the exchange has its own physical facilities (a building, communication systems, and so on) where members can meet to trade in designated financial assets. Qualified individuals associated with investment dealer firms hold "seats" on the exchange and thus have the right to trade there. The exchange is basically an auction market where the sellers of a security "ask" a price for the asset and potential buyers return with "bid" prices. Negotiations continue until a sale is made.

Firms that want a viable secondary market for their securities "list" such securities on the exchange. Permission to list is possible only if the firm meets the listing requirements specified by the governing body of the exchange. These listing requirements, which relate to minimum size, earnings capacity and corporate standing in general, are rather restrictive from the point of view of smalller firms because in essence, only the larger firms can meet the conditions necessary for listing. Once listed, firms have prescribed reporting functions and the conduct of management is subject to specific regulations. It is a general rule that members of the exchange should trade listed securities on the "floor" of the exchange. Exchange permission is necessary to sell listed securities outside the exchange.

In Canada there are five organized stock exchanges—the Toronto Stock Exchange, the Montreal Stock Exchange, the Vancouver Stock Exchange, the Calgary Stock Exchange, and the Winnipeg Stock Exchange. The Toronto Stock Exchange is the largest and most prestigious, has the most stringent regulations on its membership and listing firms, and has the largest number of listed firms. Investment dealers can have seats on more than one exchange and firms can interlist securities across exchanges. In practice, the larger firms (about 60 of them) interlist on the Toronto and Montreal Stock Exchange.

Canada has organized exchanges only for the trading of listed corporate stocks (preferred and common shares). Other securities such as unlisted corporate stocks and bonds trade in the *over-the-counter market*. This types of market lacks precise definition. In practice, the over-the-counter market consists of investment dealers (or brokers) who hold inventories of unlisted securities and stand ready to trade in these securities. Investors can buy the securities over the counter from the dealer, and vice versa. The market is an auction market with the dealer quoting "ask" prices for the sale of securities and "bid" prices for purchases. Usually, buyers and sellers "meet" by telephone to transact business deals in the over-the-counter market.

MONEY AND CAPITAL MARKETS

Different securities markets may be classified according to the final maturity of the financial instrument they deal in. *Money* markets deal in financial assets that are short-term, that are highly marketable, and that have a low degree of risk. These instruments are traded in highly impersonal markets, where funds move on the basis of price and risk alone. Thus, a short-term loan negotiated between a company and a bank is not considered a money-market instrument. *Capital* markets include instruments with longer terms to maturity and often with less liquidity. The maturity boundary that divides the money and capital markets is rather arbitrary, about one to five years, depending on who is doing the classifying.

The *securities* markets may also be classified according to the type of financial assets trading in such markets. Very often we hear of such terms as the Treasury bill market, the bond market, the stock market, and so on.

The money market The money market is highly sophisticated and is comprised of a number of security dealers and various financial institutions. It is a national market, though the center of activity is Toronto. Interest rates on money market instruments are extremely sensitive to constantly changing supply and demand conditions. New information is quickly acted upon and can affect price almost immediately. Fund transfers between buyers and sellers are done by computer, which allows prompt settlement of transactions.

An efficient money market serves the liquidity needs of the nation. Large numbers of securities can be sold or bought quickly with little change from the previous traded price. Given this liquidity, financial institutions, corporations, and individuals can manage and plan their overall investment portfolios better. Examples of money market instruments are *Treasury bills, commercial paper,* and *bankers' acceptances*. These instruments are examined in some detail in Chapter 9, when we consider the investment of idle cash by the business firm. The use by the business firm of the money market for short-term borrowing is discussed in Chapter 12.

The capital markets The capital markets tend to be more varied than the money market, being comprised of a handful of distinctly different instruments. The *bond market* comprises the outstanding long-term debt of government (federal, provincial, and municipal) and corporations. In 1982, the total amount of bonds outstanding was about $273 billion. Corporate issues accounted for about 22 percent of this amount and government issues, 78 percent (provincial 41 percent, federal 31 percent and municipal 6 percent. The market for federal government bonds is highly organized and dealers are strong. Because these bonds are free of default risk and are highly marketable, they command the lowest yield.

In contrast, the market for provincial and municipal bonds is largely an aggregation of regional and local markets. Interest rates, fees, and terms vary geographically depending on the perceived quality of the issuers. Finally, in the corporate bond market, the issues of larger firms are usually marketed nationally through investment dealers. Issues of lesser known firms are less marketable and are thinly placed among investors (primarily financial institutions) in the larger metropolitan centers. In general, corporate bonds are not as marketable as Canada bonds and bonds of the larger provinces. (The procedures involved in issuing corporate bonds are discussed in Chapter 19.)

Another market is the *stock market* which trades in corporate stocks. Stocks are evidences of ownership in companies; the rights, privileges, and risks attached to such ownership are different from those of debt holders. Corporate stocks may be traded on the organized exchanges if they are listed; otherwise they trade over the counter. The stock market also trades in preferred shares, and rights and warrants, which are options entitling holders to buy common shares.

Domestic versus foreign securities markets   Canadian business firms raise funds in both the domestic and foreign money and capital markets. In recent years, non-financial companies have used such U.S. financial centers as New York, Boston, and Chicago to issue a relatively small amount of commercial paper. In the case of bonds, about 20 percent of the net new issues of these companies are floated in foreign markets. The U.S. bond market accounts for about 50 percent of new foreign issues followed by some European countries (U.K., Germany, France, and so on), and others. Finally, some rather small amounts of preferred and common stocks are sold primarily in the U.S.

SECURITIES FIRMS

Institutional services for the financial markets are provided by a group of securities firms with specialists performing dealer, broker, and counselling functions. Securities firms, or investment dealers as they are called, are probably best known as underwriters of new or primary issues and for the support they provide for the secondary trading of outstanding issues. When a company decides to raise funds, an investment dealer often buys the issue and then turns around and sells it to investors. Because the investment dealer is continually in the business of matching users of funds with suppliers, he or she can sell the issue more efficiently than can the issuing company. For this service, the investment dealer receives a fee in the form of the difference between the amount received from the sale of the securities to the public and the amount paid to the company. (The role of investment dealers will be discussed further in Chapter 19.)

Securities firms also have the organizational structure (administration, research, management, marketing and so on) to provide a continuous brokerage and counselling service to investors as well as their corporate clientele. They maintain inventories of corporate securities, act as buy and sell agents for investors, provide investment advice, act as fiscal agents to companies, and provide associated services on a year-round basis.

The employees and activities of securities firms are closely regulated by the various provincial securities laws. The Investment Dealers Association (IDA), an unincorporated non-profit national body, is the professional association of securities firms. On behalf of its membership, the IDA sets and maintains desirable ethical standards, provides educational programs for employees, maintains a constant liaison with securities authorities and other relevant institutions, and in general, provides services for the goodwill of the industry. The association's principal objective is to protect investors by ensuring that its members are ethically responsible, educated, and responsive to the needs of the varied clientele.

Government Regulation of Securities Offerings

The corporate entity is created by incorporation procedures embodied in the Canada Business Corporations Act and the various provincial Companies Acts as discussed in Chapter 2. The corporate authority to issue new securities is contained in the corporate charter. The underwriting, distribution, and trading of corporate securities are governed by the "Securities Acts" which are administered by a Securities Commission or similar agency of the provincial governments. In Ontario, for example, the Ontario Securities Act is administered by the Ontario Securities Commission which reports to the Ministry of Consumer and Commercial Relations. Some of the smaller provinces do not have a separate commission and the administration of the Securities Acts comes under another body.

The underlying philosophy behind government regulation is to ensure that there is "full, true and plain disclosure" of facts on an issue and the issuer of the security so that investors can make informed decisions. Although a discussion of all facets of securities regulation is beyond the scope of this book, we will review briefly the standards used by securities authorities—licencing, full disclosure, and investigation and prosecution—to regulate the sale and distribution of corporate securities using the provisions of the Ontario Securities Act as an example. Throughout the book and where desirable, we identify securities regulations relating to specific topics.

LICENSING

Securities firms and employees involved in the underwriting, distribution, and trading of securities must be licensed by the Ontario Securities Commission (OSC). Usually, the employees have to show a basic knowledge of the securities markets and their operations before being licensed. The OSC has the right to withdraw or suspend a license if it is deemed to be in the public interest. There are rules prohibiting the sale of securities by telephone, across provinces, and by illegal representations. Also, the sale to the public of securities not approved by the securities authorities is prohibited.

FULL DISCLOSURE

The term *full disclosure*, as it applies to the issuing company, embraces a number of topics related to the sale and distribution of corporate securities. We look at some of the more important ones.

Prospectus requirements   All Ontario companies selling securities to the public must register the issue with the Ontario Securities Commission. A *preliminary* or *"red herring" prospectus* is filed with the Commission. This prospectus contains such information as the nature and history of the company, the use of the proceeds of the issue, financial statements, the identities of those in management and the directors plus their security holdings, legal opinions, and a description of the security issued. This "red herring" proposal is also available to prospective investors and others who request it. The front cover of this prospectus has a statutory statement informing the readers that the issue is not yet approved by the Commission. Meanwhile, the Commission reviews the prospectus to see that all the required information is presented and that it is not misleading. If the Commission is satisfied with the information, it approves the registration, and the company is given permission to sell the securities. If not, the Commission can issue an *order to cease* distribution of the securities. In this case, the company has to revise the prospectus to the satisfaction of the Commission.

The approval by the Commission is not to be construed as a recommendation to buy the securities. The Commission is not concerned with the investment value of the securities being issued, only with the presentation of complete and accurate information. The investor must make his own decision based on this information. The security being issued may well be a highly speculative one subject to considerable risk. As long as the information is correct, the Commission will not prevent its sale.

The registration period is usually at least ten days and is viewed as a "cooling-off" period. During this time, investors can evaluate the information in the prospectus and reach a decision. On receiving approval, the company prepares a *final prospectus* incorporating the approved preliminary prospectus plus the offering price to the public, the proceeds to the company (and/or the selling shareholders), the underwriting discount, and any other required information which is not in the preliminary prospectus. This final prospectus is made available to the prospective investors. The company may list a stock issue for trading on the Toronto Stock Exchange which is subject to control by the Ontario Securities Commission, or alternatively, the issue may be traded on the over-the-counter market. Though this latter market is not an organized exchange requiring formal listing, the Commission still has authority to enquire into trading activities.

Purchaser's rights of withdrawal and rescission Under certain circumstances, a purchaser of a new issue may withdraw or rescind his order of purchase, usually within 90 days. Generally, this right can be exercised if the prospectus contains untrue or misleading statements or if material facts have been omitted.

Financial statement disclosure All companies listed on the TSE are required to submit annual and interim financial statements to the OSC. These statements are available for public inspection.

Takeover bids A takeover bid is an offer by an investor to buy shares which, together with existing holdings, will account for at least 20 percent of the outstanding common shares of a particular firm. We discuss some of the specific statutory requirements for takeover bids in Chapter 24.

Insider trading "Insiders" include all directors and senior officers of the company and shareholders owning at least 10 percent of the common shares. Insiders are required to report all trading transactions within ten days of the end of the month in which they take place. The principle here is that the investors should be informed regularly of the market activity of insiders of a company. Because directors and senior officers of a company usually have access to information before such information is made public, it would be unethical for such individuals to use their privileged position for personal gain.

Proxies and Proxy Solicitation   The existing management team may solicit proxies from shareholders to vote for its continued existence in the company. The tendency for abuse exists and securities regulation contains provisions relating to solicitation of proxies, the form and documents involved, and the information that should be provided to shareholders. These topics are reviewed in Chapter 22.

INVESTIGATION AND PROSECUTION

Securities regulations provide for investigation and prosecution for violations of the Securities Act. The authority to prosecute usually comes from the Attorney General. Fines can be imposed or licenses suspended where employees of securities firms are convicted of fraud, misrepresentation, or intentional omission of important facts in the underwriting, distribution, or trading of securities. Companies and associated executives may also be subject to criminal proceedings for fraudulent acts connected with the preparation and filing of prospectuses.

Summary

Financial assets exist in an economy because the investment in real assets by various economic units frequently differs from those units' savings. An excess of investment over savings is financed by issuing a financial liability instrument, while a surplus of savings over investment in real assets is held in the form of financial assets. The purpose of financial markets is to efficiently allocate savings in an economy to ultimate users of funds. A number of factors make financial markets efficient. Among the most important is the presence of financial intermediaries. A financial intermediary transforms the direct claim of an ultimate borrower into an indirect claim, which is sold to ultimate lenders. Intermediaries channel savings from ultimate savers to ultimate borrowers at a lower cost and with less inconvenience than is possible on a direct basis.

We can study the flow of savings from ultimate savers to ultimate borrowers through flow-of-funds data. We saw that for the economy as a whole, investment in real assets must equal savings. However, this is not true for individual economic units; there can be considerable divergence between savings and investment for a particular period. For business firms, the principal means for supporting investment in real assets is internal financing, or savings. However, business firms are a savings-deficit sector and make extensive use of external financing. The predominant sources of external financing are bond issues, stock issues, mortgage debt, and bank loans. The greatest portion of funds received do not come directly from individuals but indirectly from financial intermediaries. The most important institutions for business firms are chartered banks, life insurance companies, finance companies, pension funds, and mutual funds. Each was discussed along with other less important financial intermediaries. Finally, the secondary market is enhanced by the presence of strong security exchanges, over-the-counter markets, and securities regulations governing the operations of these markets.

The allocation of savings in an economy is done primarily on the basis of expected return and risk. In turn, the overall risk of a security depends on the likelihood of default, its marketability, its maturity, and certain tax considerations. In addition, expected and unanticipated inflation have a major effect on all yields. Different financial instruments provide different yields over time because of differences in these factors. The differences in yields of Government of Canada bonds, industrial bonds, commercial paper, and Treasury bills were studied in light of these factors. With respect to maturity, interest-rate expectations play an important role in distinguishing short term instruments from long term ones. The primary factors affecting such expectations are economic conditions, monetary policy, and fiscal policy. The expected return on investment in a common share must include expected capital appreciation as well as the current dividend. The true expected return on a share is greater than its dividend yield, if future growth in earnings and dividends is expected. For this reason, it is inappropriate to compare the dividend yield on common shares with the yield on bonds.

Financial markets are described as money or capital markets depending on the term to maturity of the instruments they deal in. Money markets deal in short-term, highly marketable financial assets with little risk. Capital markets deal in instruments with longer terms to maturity where there is much more variation among instruments with respect to marketability and default risk.

Questions

1. What is the purpose of financial markets? How is this purpose accomplished efficiently?

2. Discuss the functions of financial intermediaries.

3. Business firms finance about two thirds of their needs internally. As a result, many argue that professional management teams are isolated from investors and that they run an enterprise for management, not for shareholders.

(a) What forces in the economy might break down management's isolation from investors?

(b) If management teams do in fact become isolated, what will be the impact of this isolation on the efficiency of the economy?

4. The Braniff Airlines bankruptcy, the Equity Funding scandal, Penn Central's bankruptcy, the near collapse of Chrysler Corporation, Massey Ferguson, and International Harvester, and other incidents that have made headlines cause investors to revise their expectation of risk and return associated with financial instruments. What is the impact of such incidents on capital formation and on the economic development of our society?

5. What is the function of stock exchanges such as the TSE or VSE?

6. What would be the effect of the following occurrences on the money and capital of markets?

(a) The savings rate of individuals in the country declines.

(b) Individuals increase their savings in mortgage loan companies and decrease their savings in banks.

(c) The government taxes all capital gains at the ordinary income tax rate.

(d) Unanticipated inflation of substantial magnitude occurs and price levels rise rapidly.

(e) Savings institutions and lenders increase the transaction charge for investing savings and for making loans.

7. Suppose non-financial corporations had great liquidity. Nonetheless, a great demand for funds by municipalities and the federal government developed. How would this affect interest rates of corporate bonds? What would be the effect if corporations developed a need for large amounts of funds but first financed themselves by reducing their liquidity?

8. Can you name an innovation in a financial instrument, an institution, or a practice? What is the principal characteristic of a financial innovation? Who do financial innovations benefit?

9. Pick a financial intermediary with which you are familiar and explain its economic role. Does it make the financial markets more efficient?

10. What is the difference between the money markets and the capital markets? Is the difference real or artificial?

11. How do transaction costs affect the flow of funds and the efficiency of financial markets? Are transaction costs justified?

12. What are the major sources of external financing for business firms?

13. In addition to financial intermediaries, what other institutions and arrangements facilitate the flow of funds to and from business firms?

Problems with Solutions

1. The yields to maturity for Government of Canada securities at selected dates are presented below.

	Treasury bills		Average bond yields			
			1–3	3–5	5–10	>10
Date	90 days	180 days	years	years	years	years
Dec., 1980	17.01%	15.30%	12.95%	12.47%	12.63%	12.67%
Dec., 1981	14.41%	14.51%	15.19%	14.80%	15.29%	15.27%
Dec., 1982	9.80%	9.39%	9.85%	10.10%	11.03%	11.69%
Dec., 1983	9.71%	9.86%	9.15%	10.51%	11.41%	12.02%

Source: *Bank of Canada Review*

(a) Make a rough sketch of the yield of the yield-maturity relationships (or the term structure of interest rates) as at Dec., 1980. What observations can you make?

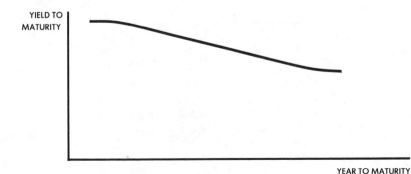

YIELD TO MATURITY

YEAR TO MATURITY

Short term rates were higher than long term rates. Apparently, investors were expecting inflation and the general level of interest rates to fall in the future. However, this did not occur in the next two years as shown in Fig. 3-5. Investors might have suffered from unanticipated inflation.

(b) Make a rough sketch of the yield-maturity relationships as at December, 1983. What observations can you make?

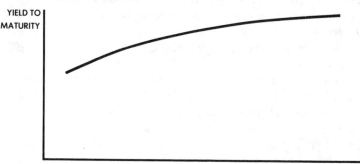

The yield curve is upward sloping and long-term securities are offering a yield higher than short term securities. Investors wanted (and received) a premium to buy longer term securities to protect the purchasing power of their money.

2. The yields to maturity for some corporate securities at selected dates are presented below.

Date	Commercial Paper 90 days	McLeod Young Weir Corporate Bonds 10 years
Dec., 1980	17.75%	13.63%
Dec., 1981	15.65%	16.54%
Dec., 1982	10.25%	12.93%
Dec., 1983	9.85%	12.95%

(a) Calculate the risk premium required for default risk for commercial paper. What observations can you make?

The risk premium is computed as the yield on commercial paper less the yield on Treasury bills 90 days to maturity. See problem 1 above for Treasury bill yields. Both instruments must have the same maturity structure when default risk is considered.

Date	Commercial Paper 90 days	Treasury bills 90 days	Risk premium
Dec., 1980	17.75%	17.01%	0.74%
Dec., 1981	15.65%	14.41%	1.24%
Dec., 1982	10.25%	9.80%	0.45%
Dec., 1983	9.85%	9.71%	0.14%

The risk premium is not constant over time. Generally, risk premiums are larger in recessionary periods when the fear of default is high. They tend to be smaller in times of economic prosperity since expectations of default are generally lower.

(b) Calculate the average risk premium required for default risk for corporate bonds with maturity over 10 years. What observations can you make?

The average risk premium is computed as the yield on corporate bonds less the yield on Government of Canada bonds with maturity greater than 10 years. See problem 1 above for yields on Government of Canada bonds.

Date	Corporate bonds > 10 years	Government of Canada bonds > 10 years	Risk premium
Dec., 1980	13.63%	12.67%	0.96%
Dec., 1981	16.54%	15.27%	1.27%
Dec., 1982	12.93	11.69%	1.24%
Dec., 1983	12.95	12.02%	0.93%

Corporate bonds offer a risk premium for possible default risk. The risk premium is greater than that on commercial paper and this is likely due to the longer term nature of the bonds. Business cycles play some role in the variations of risk premiums across time as discussed for commercial paper above.

Problems

1. Loquat Foods Company Ltd. is able to borrow at an interest rate of 14 percent for one year. For the year, market participants expect 10 percent inflation.
   (a) What approximate real rate of return does the lender expect? What is the inflation premium embodied in the nominal interest rate?
   (b) If inflation proves to be 7 percent for the year, does the lender suffer? Does the borrower suffer? Why?
   (c) If inflation proves to be 13 percent, who gains and who loses?

2. Suppose that 90-day Treasury bills currently yield 9 percent to maturity and that 25-year Government of Canada bonds yield $10\frac{1}{4}$ percent. Lopez Pharmaceutical Company Ltd. has recently issued long-term, 25-year bonds that yield 12 percent to maturity.
   (a) What premium in yield is required for the default risk and lower marketability associated with the Lopez bonds?
   (b) What premium in yield above the short-term risk-free rate is attributable to maturity?

3. For 19XX, suppose that the following changes in the balance sheets of business firms, households, and governments in the aggregate occur (in billions):

	Business firms	Households	Governments
Net worth (savings)	$220	$380	−$50
Real assets	275	280	
Money	5	10	2
Other financial assets	75	215	70
Financial liabilities	135	125	122

(a) Which sectors are savings-deficit sectors? Savings-surplus sectors? Why?

(b) From which sector do the savings-deficit sectors finance their deficits? How is it done?

4. In problem 3, suppose the economy is comprised of the three sectors described, along with a financial-institutions sector. For the year, the change in balance sheet for *all sectors* is as follows (in billions):

	Change	
Net worth (savings)	$565	
Real assets	565	
Money	0	net ($17 use, $17 source)
Other financial assets	560	
Financial liabilities	560	

(a) Using a flow-of-funds matrix, derive the sources and uses of funds for the financial-institutions sector on the basis of the information presented in these two problems.

(b) What are the characteristics of the financial-institutions sector?

5. Companies X and Y have the following balance sheets at the latest year end (in thousands):

	Company X	Company Y
Cash	$1 000	$ 500
Receivables	7 000	2 000
Inventories	2 000	4 000
Net fixed assets	2 000	5 500
Total	$12 000	$12 000
Current liabilities	2 000	3 000
Long term debt	1 000	5 000
Net worth	9 000	4 000
Total	$12 000	$12 000

(a) Are the companies net monetary creditors or debtors?

(b) If the rate of inflation should increase unexpectedly from 8 percent presently to 10 percent, who gains and who loses?

(c) If inflation unexpectedly drops from 8 percent to 6 percent, what happens?

6. From a recent Monday Globe and Mail, collect information on yields for a long term Government of Canada bond, a public utility bond, provincial bonds, Treasury bills, and commercial paper. (This information appears at the back of the paper under the Bond Market section, the Money Market Rates section, and the Treasury Issues section.) What reasons can you give for the differences in yield on these various instruments?

Selected References

ANG, JAMES S. and KIRITKUMAR A. PATEL. "Bond Rating Methods: Comparison and Validation," *Journal of Finance*, 30 (May 1975), 631-40.

CARGILL, THOMAS F., *Money, The Financial System, and Monetary Policy*, Englewood Cliffs, N.J.: Prentice-Hall, 1979.

COOPER, S. KERRY, and DONALD R. FRASER, *The Financial Marketplace*, Reading, Mass.: Addison-Wesley, 1982.

DIPCHAND, CECIL R. "The Influence of Coupon on Canadian Corporate Bonds Yields," *The Journal of Business Administration*, 6 (Fall 1974), 16-32.

DOUGALL, HERBERT E. *Capital Markets and Institutions*. 4th ed. Englewood Cliffs, N.J.: Prentice-Hall, Inc., 1980.

HOMER, SIDNEY, and MARTIN L. LEIBOWITZ, *Inside the Yield Book*. Englewood Cliffs, N.J.: Prentice-Hall, 1972.

HORVITZ, PAUL M., *Monetary Policy and the Financial System*, 4th ed., Englewood Cliffs, N.J.: Prentice-Hall, 1979.

IBBOTSON, ROGER G., and REX A. SINQUEFIELD, *Stocks, Bonds, Bills, and Inflation*. Charlottesville, Va.: Financial Analysts Research Foundation, 1979.

JONES, FRANK J., *Macrofinance*. Cambridge, Mass.: Winthrop Publishers, 1978.

KAUFMAN, GEORGE G., *The U.S. Financial System: Money, Markets, and Institutions*. Englewood Cliffs, N.J.: Prentice-Hall, 1980.

KIDWELL, DAVID S., and RICHARD L. PETERSON, *Financial Institutions, Markets, and Money*. Hinsdale, Ill.: Dryden Press, 1981.

LIGHT, J. O., and WILLIAM L. WHITE, *The Financial System*. Homewood, Ill.: Irwin, 1979.

NEUFELD, E.P. *The Financial System of Canada*. Toronto: Macmillan Company of Canada Ltd., 1972.

PEEK, JOE and JAMES A. WILCOX, "The Postwar Stability of the Fisher Effect," *Journal of Finance*, September 1983, 1111-1123.

RITTER, LAWRENCE S. and WILLIAM L. SILBER. *Principles of Money, Banking, and Financial Markets*. New York: Basic Books, Inc., 1974.

ROBERTS, GORDON S. "Term Premiums in the Term Structure of Interest Rates," *Journal of Money, Credit and Banking*, forthcoming.

ROBINSON, ROLAND I. and DWAYNE WRIGHTSMAN. *Financial Markets: The Accumulation and Allocation of Wealth*. New York: McGraw-Hill Book Co., 1974.

SHAW, DAVID C. and T. ROSS ARCHIBALD. *A Survey of Research Operations of Brokerage Firms in Canada*. Toronto: The Toronto Stock Exchange, and London: The School of Business Administration, U.W.O., 1972.

_____. *The Securities Firm in the Canadian Capital Market*. Toronto: The Toronto Stock Exchange, and London: The School of Business Administration, U.W.O., 1975.

_____. *Canada's Capital Markets*, Toronto: The Toronto Stock Exchange, 1972.

SHEARER, R. A., J. F. CHANT and D. E. BOND, *The Economics of the Canadian Financial System*. Scarborough, Ont.: Prentice-Hall of Canada, Inc., 1984.

SMITH, PAUL F. *Money and Financial Intermediation*. Englewood Cliffs, N.J.: Prentice-Hall, Inc., 1978.

VAN HORNE, JAMES C. *Financial Market Rates and Flows*. Englewood Cliffs, N.J.: Prentice-Hall, Inc., 1978.

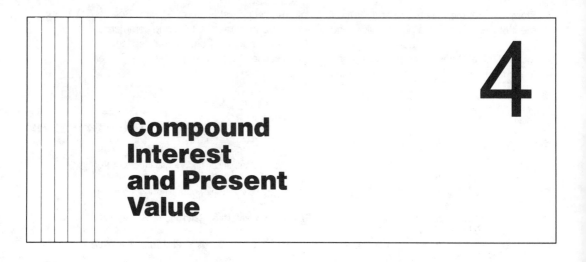

Compound
Interest
and Present
Value

Because finance is concerned with decisions involving monetary variables, and because the price of money is the interest rate, most financial decisions involve interest-rate considerations. This chapter deals with the mathematics of compound interest and present value. We have placed the material here because of the important role it plays in the development of the book. Although the discussion obviously is mathematical in orientation, we focus on only a handful of formulas, so that we may easily grasp the essentials. The examples frequently involve numbers that must be raised to the nth power, an operation that is difficult to work by hand, but most readers have access to a calculator, with which these examples can be easily verified.

Compound Interest and Terminal Values

The notion of compound interest is central to understanding the mathematics of finance. The term itself merely implies that interest paid on a loan or an investment is added to the principal. As a result, interest is earned on interest. This concept can be used to solve a class of problems illustrated in the following examples.

To begin with, consider a person who has $100 in a savings account. If the interest rate is 8 percent compounded annually, how much will the $100 be worth at the end of a year? Setting up the problem, we solve for the terminal value of the account at the end of the year (TV_1)

$$TV_1 = \$100(1 + 0.08) = \$108$$

For a deposit of 2 years, the $100 initial deposit will become $108 at the end of the first year at 8 percent interest. Going to the end of the second year, $108 becomes $116.64, as $8 in interest is earned on the initial $100 and $0.64 is earned on the $8 in interest paid at the end of the first year. In other words, interest is earned on previously earned interest, hence the name compound interest. Therefore, the terminal value at the end of the second year is $100 times 1.08 squared, or times 1.1664. Thus

$$TV_2 = \$100(1.08)^2 = \$116.64$$

At the end of three years the depositor would have

$$TV_3 = \$100(1.08)^3 = \$125.97$$

Looked at in a different way, $100 grows to $108 at the end of the first year if the interest rate is 8 percent, and when we multiply this amount by 1.08 we obtain $116.64 at the end of the second year. Multiplying $116.64 by 1.08, we obtain $125.97 at the end of the third year.

Similarly, at the end of n years the terminal value of a deposit is

$$TV_n = X_0(1 + r)^n \tag{4-1}$$

where X_0 = amount of savings at the beginning
r = interest rate.

A calculator makes the equation very simple to use. Table 4-1, showing the terminal values for our example problem at the end of years 1 through 10, illustrates the concept of interest being earned on interest.

TABLE 4-1   Illustration of Compound Interest with $100 Initial Deposit and 8 Percent Interest

Period	Beginning Value	Interest Earned During Period (8 Percent of Beginning Value)	Terminal Value
1	$100.00	$ 8.00	$108.00
2	108.00	8.64	116.64
3	116.64	9.33	125.97
4	125.97	10.08	136.05
5	136.05	10.88	146.93
6	146.93	11.76	158.69
7	158.69	12.69	171.38
8	171.38	13.71	185.09
9	185.09	14.81	199.90
10	199.90	15.99	215.89

Eq. (4-1) is our fundamental formula for calculating terminal values. Obviously, the greater the interest rate r, and the greater the number of periods n, the greater the terminal value. In Fig. 4-1 we graph the growth in terminal value for a $100 initial deposit with interest rates of 5, 10, and 15 percent. As can be seen, the greater the interest rate, the steeper the growth curve by which terminal value increases. Also, the greater the number of years during which compound interest can be earned, obviously the greater the terminal value.

Although our concern has been with interest rates, the concept involved applies to compound growth of any sort. Suppose that the earnings of a firm are

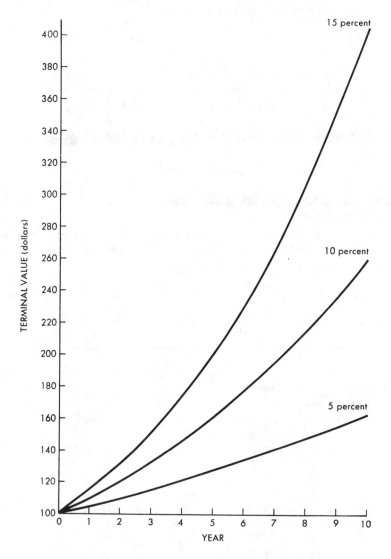

FIGURE 4-1 Compound values with $100 initial deposit and 5, 10 and 15 percent interest rates

$100 000, but we expect them to grow at a 10 percent compound rate. At the end of years 1 through 5 they will be as follows:

Year	Growth factor	Expected earnings
1	(1.10)	$110 000
2	$(1.10)^2$	121 000
3	$(1.10)^3$	133 100
4	$(1.10)^4$	146 410
5	$(1.10)^5$	161 051

Similarly, we can determine the level at the end of so many years for other problems involving compound growth. The principle is particularly important when we consider certain valuation models for common stock, as we shall do in the next chapter.

TABLES OF TERMINAL VALUES

Using Eq. (4-1), we can derive tables of terminal values (also known as future values). Table 4-2 is an example showing interest rates of 1 to 10 percent. In the 8 percent column, we note that the terminal value shown for $1 invested at this compound rate corresponds to our calculations for $100 in Table 4-1. Notice, too, that in rows tabulating two or more years, the proportional increase in terminal value becomes greater as the interest rate rises. This heightened growth is impressive when we look a century ahead. A dollar deposited today will be worth only $2.70 if the interest rate is 1 percent, but it will fatten to $13 780.59 if the interest rate is 10 percent. Behold (or let your heirs behold) the wonders of compound interest.

In 1790 John Jacob Astor bought approximately an acre of land on the east side of Manhattan Island for $58. Astor, who was considered a shrewd investor, made many such purchases. How much would his descendants have in 1990 if, instead of buying the land, Astor had invested the $58 at 6 percent compound interest? In Table 4-2 we see that $1 compounded at an interest rate of 6 percent is worth $339.30 in 100 years. Therefore, the value of $1 in 200 years is simply

$$\$1 \times 339.30 \times 339.30 = \$115\ 124.49$$

For an investment of $58, we have a value of

$$\$58 \times 115\ 124.49 = \$6\ 677\ 220.42$$

in 1990 at a compound interest rate of 6 percent. This translates into a value of about $153 a square foot. Perhaps John Jacob would have been better off if he had forgone that particular purchase because the current market value of the land is less than $153 a square foot.

TABLE 4-2   Terminal Value of $1 at the End of n Years

Year	1%	2%	3%	4%	5%	6%	7%	8%	9%	10%
1	1.0100	1.0200	1.0300	1.0400	1.0500	1.0600	1.0700	1.0800	1.0900	1.1000
2	1.0201	1.0404	1.0609	1.0816	1.1025	1.1236	1.1449	1.1664	1.1881	1.2100
3	1.0303	1.0612	1.0927	1.1249	1.1576	1.1910	1.2250	1.2597	1.2950	1.3310
4	1.0406	1.0824	1.1255	1.1699	1.2155	1.2625	1.3108	1.3605	1.4116	1.4641
5	1.0510	1.1041	1.1593	1.2167	1.2763	1.3382	1.4026	1.4693	1.5386	1.6105
6	1.0615	1.1262	1.1941	1.2653	1.3401	1.4185	1.5077	1.5869	1.6771	1.7716
7	1.0721	1.1487	1.2299	1.3159	1.4071	1.5036	1.6058	1.7138	1.8280	1.9487
8	1.0829	1.1717	1.2668	1.3688	1.4775	1.5938	1.7182	1.8509	1.9926	2.1436
9	1.0937	1.1951	1.3048	1.4233	1.5513	1.6895	1.8385	1.9990	2.1719	2.3579
10	1.1046	1.2190	1.3439	1.4802	1.6289	1.7908	1.9672	2.1589	2.3674	2.5937
11	1.1157	1.2434	1.3842	1.5395	1.7103	1.8983	2.1049	2.3316	2.5804	2.8531
12	1.1268	1.2682	1.4258	1.6010	1.7959	2.0122	2.2522	2.5182	2.8127	3.1384
13	1.1381	1.2936	1.4685	1.6651	1.8856	2.1329	2.4098	2.7196	3.0658	3.4523
14	1.1495	1.3195	1.5126	1.7317	1.9799	2.2609	2.5785	2.9372	3.3417	3.7975
15	1.1610	1.3459	1.5580	1.8009	2.0789	2.3966	2.7590	3.1772	3.6425	4.1772
20	1.2202	1.4859	1.8061	2.1911	2.6533	3.2071	3.8697	4.6610	5.6044	6.7275
25	1.2824	1.6406	2.0938	2.6658	3.3864	4.2919	5.4274	6.8485	8.6231	10.8347
50	1.6466	2.6916	4.3839	7.1067	11.4674	18.4201	29.4570	46.9016	74.3575	117.3907
100	2.7048	7.2446	19.2186	50.5049	131.5010	339.3014	867.7149	2 199.7569	5 529.0304	13 780.5890

COMPOUND VALUE WITH UNIFORM PAYMENTS OR RECEIPTS

Consider now a situation in which an individual makes an initial deposit but adds to it a given amount at the end of each period. Continuing with our earlier example, suppose the initial deposit is $100 and the compound annual interest rate 8 percent, but the individual adds to it $50 per year. At the end of one year the terminal value would be

$$TV_1 = \$100(1.08) + \$50 = \$158$$

At the end of two years it would be

$$TV_2 = \$158(1.08) + \$50 = \$220.64$$

Although we could calculate the terminal value at the end of any period in this step-by-step manner, a more general formula is available for solution of the problem. It is

$$TV_n = \left(X_0 + \frac{x}{r}\right)(1 + r)^n - \frac{x}{r} \qquad (4\text{-}2)$$

where x is the increment which is added each period. For the example above, the terminal value at the end of two years would be

$$TV_2 = \left(\$100 + \frac{\$50}{0.08}\right)(1.08)^2 - \frac{\$50}{0.08}$$

$$= (\$100 + \$625)(1.1664) - \$625$$

$$= \$220.64$$

which, of course, is the same as calculated before. The terminal value at the end of five years would be

$$TV_5 = (\$100 + \$625)(1.08)^5 - \$625$$

$$= \$440.26$$

The formula in Eq. (4-2) is complicated, but it has widespread applicability. With the use of a calculator and with care to detail, one should have no difficulty. Remember that there is such a formula, but do not memorize it.

Annuities An *annuity* can be defined as a series of uniform receipts occurring over a specified number of years, which result from an initial deposit. Figure 4-2 shows the cash-flow sequence for an annuity. An initial deposit is followed by a series of equal withdrawals over a given period of time. In our illustration we have assumed five years. Total withdrawals over the five years exceed the initial deposit because of the presence of compound interest.

Let us imagine that you inherit $10 000 and wish to have a steady income over the next ten years. A life insurance company sells annuities that will pay you, or your beneficiary if you should die, a fixed dollar amount annually for ten years. The insurance company calculates the amount of distribution on the basis of a 5 percent return. What is the annual amount it will pay? Referring to Eq. (4-2), the terminal value at the end of ten years would be zero, as everything would be paid out. We know also that X_0 is $10 000, r is 0.05, and n is 10. Therefore, we must solve for x, which we know will be negative, as it is a withdrawal. Setting the problem up in this manner, we have

$$0 = \left(\$10\ 000 - \frac{x}{0.05}\right)(1.05)^{10} + \frac{x}{0.05}$$

$$= (\$10\ 000 - 20x)(1.628894) + 20x$$

$$32.57788x - 20x = 16\ 288.94$$

$$12.57788x = 16\ 288.94$$

$$x = \$1\ 295.05$$

Thus, you are able to obtain $1 295.05 per year for ten years with an annuity.

Reversing our earlier problem, we also are able to determine the amount of initial deposit or balance that is necessary to afford a person a withdrawal of a certain amount over so many years. You may want to be able to withdraw $5 000 per year over the next ten years. If a savings institution pays 8 percent per annum,

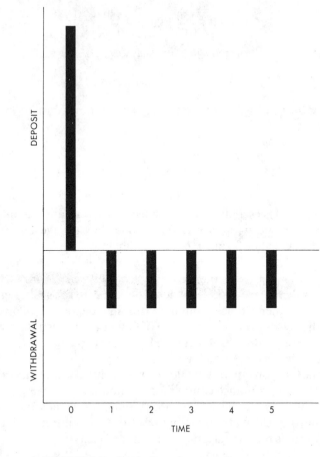

FIGURE 4-2 Illustration of an annuity

how much will you need to deposit for this to happen? In this case, x in Eq. (4-2) is − $5 000. At the end of ten years there will be no terminal value, so $TV_n = 0$. With an interest rate of 8 percent, we have

$$0 = \left(X_0 - \frac{\$5\ 000}{0.08}\right)(1.08)^{10} + \frac{\$5\ 000}{0.08}$$

where we wish to solve for X_0. We have

$$0 = (X_0 - \$62\ 500)(2.1589) + \$62\ 500$$

$$2.1589X_0 = \$72\ 431$$

$$X_0 = \$33\ 550$$

Therefore, $33 550 must be deposited initially in order for the annuity to pay $5 000 at the end of each of the next ten years.

COMPOUNDING MORE THAN ONCE A YEAR

Up to now, we have assumed that interest was paid annually. It is easiest to work with this assumption. Now we consider the relationship between terminal value and interest rates for different periods of compounding. To begin, suppose that interest were paid semiannually. If one then deposited $100 in a savings account at 8 percent, the terminal value at the end of six months would be

$$TV_{1/2} = \$100\left(1 + \frac{0.08}{2}\right) = \$104.00$$

In other words, at the end of one-half year one would receive 4 percent in interest, not 8 percent. At the end of a year the terminal value of the deposit would be

$$TV_1 = \$100\left(1 + \frac{0.08}{2}\right)^2 = \$108.16$$

This amount compares with $108.00 if interest were paid only once a year. The $0.16 difference is attributable to the fact that during the second six months, interest is earned on the $4.00 in interest paid at the end of the first six months. The more times during a year that interest is paid, the greater the terminal value at the end of a given year.

The general formula for solving for the terminal value at the end of year n where interest is paid m times a year is

$$TV_n = X_0\left(1 + \frac{r}{m}\right)^{mn} \tag{4-3}$$

To illustrate, suppose that in our previous example interest were paid quarterly and that we wished again to know the terminal value at the end of one year. It would be

$$TV_1 = \$100\left(1 + \frac{0.08}{4}\right)^4 = \$108.24$$

which, of course, is higher than it would have been with semiannual or annual compounding.

The terminal value at the end of 3 years for the example above with quarterly interest payments is

$$TV_3 = \$100\left(1 + \frac{0.08}{4}\right)^{12} = \$126.82$$

Compared to a terminal value with semiannual compounding of

$$TV_3 = \$100\left(1 + \frac{0.08}{2}\right)^6 = \$126.53$$

and with annual compounding of

$$TV_3 = \$100\left(1 + \frac{0.08}{1}\right)^3 = \$125.97$$

Thus, the more frequently each year interest is paid, the greater the terminal value. In Appendix A to this chapter we show how to determine terminal value when interest is compounded continuously. As m in Eq. (4-3) increases, terminal value increases at a decreasing rate until ultimately it approaches that achieved with continuous compounding. With continuous compounding, for example, the terminal value for our example problem is $127.12.

In summary, then, the terminal value of $100 at the end of three years with a 8 percent interest rate under various compounding intervals is as follows:[1]

Compounding	Terminal value
Annual	$125.97
Semiannual	126.53
Quarterly	126.82
Monthly	127.02
Continuous	127.12

We see that as the compounding interval shortens, terminal value increases but at a decreasing rate. The limit is continuous compounding. In order to attract deposits by paying a higher effective interest rate, many financial institutions have shortened their compounding period.

TO DOUBLE YOUR MONEY!

Several rules of thumb apply to compound interest and doubling your money over a particular period of time. One is the rule of 72: divide 72 by the interest rate to find the number of years it will take you to double your money. If the interest rate on time deposits is 4 percent and you deposit $1 now, it will take roughly 18 years to double your money. If the interest rate is 6 percent, the number of years becomes 12; if 8 percent, 9 years. Referring to Table 4-2, we see that for annual compounding, $1 at 6 percent rate is worth $2.01 in 12 years, and at an 8 percent rate it is worth $2.00 in 9 years. Therefore, the rule of 72 seems to give reasonable answers.

Indeed, for most interest rates one encounters, the rule of 72 gives a good approximation of the number of years required to double your money, but the answer is not exact. At 2 percent interest, the rule tells us our money will double in 36 years. In fact, our money will double in 35 years. At 24 percent interest, the rule tells us that we will double our money in 3 years. In fact, it will take a bit longer— 3.2 years with annual compounding. Also, when interest is paid more than once a year, it will take somewhat less time to double our money than with annual compounding. With quarterly compounding it will take 11.6 years to double our

---

[1]With monthly compounding, m in Eq. (4-3) is 12, and mn is 36.

money if the interest rate is 6 percent as opposed to 11.9 years with annual compounding. (The rule of 72 tells us 12 years.)

Another rule of thumb is the 7-10 rule. This rule tells us that our money will double in 10 years at 7 percent interest and in 7 years at 10 percent interest. Turning to Table 4-2, we see that with annual compounding, $1 is worth $1.97 at the end of ten years at an interest rate of 7 percent, whereas it is worth $1.95 at the end of seven years at an interest rate of 10 percent. However, with quarterly compounding, $1 at the end of ten years at 7 percent interest is worth

$$TV_{10} = \$1\left(1 + \frac{0.07}{4}\right)^{40} = \$2.002$$

and $1 at the end of seven years at 10 percent interest is worth

$$TV_{10} = \$1\left(1 + \frac{0.10}{4}\right)^{28} = \$1.996$$

Therefore, the rule of 7-10 gives accurate results if the compounding interval is quarterly, but only approximate results if it is annual.

Both of these rules of thumb are useful to remember. They allow you to make certain compound-interest approximations in your head. Not only can you estimate the number of years it will require to double your money at a given interest rate, but also the interest rate required in order to double your money in a given number of years. For example, if you wish to know the interest rate necessary to double your money in eight years, the rule of 72 tells you it is 9 percent.

Present Values

Having considered compound interest, we now are ready to take up present values. In any economy in which capital has value, a dollar today is worth more than a dollar to be received one year, two years, or three years from now. Therefore, we need a means for standardizing differences in timing of cash flows so that the time value of money is properly recognized. Calculating the present value of future cash flows allows us to isolate differences in the timing of these cash flows.

Perhaps you will be given an opportunity to receive, with complete certainty, $1 000 at the end of each of the next two years. If your opportunity cost of funds is 8 percent per annum, what is this proposal worth to you today? We might begin by asking, What amount today would grow to be $1 000 at the end of one year at 8 percent interest? In calculating the terminal value in the preceding section, we multiplied the initial deposit by $(1 + r)$, where r is the rate of interest, to obtain the terminal value. In this case, we are given the terminal value as well as the required interest rate and must solve the appropriate beginning value. Consequently, we divide the terminal value by the required rate of interest, and this operation is known as *discounting*. For our example, the present value of $1 000 to be received at the end of one year is

$$PV = \frac{\$1\ 000}{(1.08)} = \$925.93$$

Similarly, the present value of $1 000 to be received at the end of two years is

$$PV = \frac{\$1\ 000}{(1.08)^2} = \$857.34$$

Thus, $1 000 received two years from now has a lower present value than $1 000 received one year from now. That is the whole idea of the time value of money. Overall then, the opportunity is worth $925.93 + $857.34 = $1 783.27 to us today.

In solving present-value problems, it is useful to express the interest factor separate from the amount to be received in the future. For example, our problem above involving $1 000 to be received at the end of two years can be expressed as

$$PV = \$1\ 000\left[\frac{1}{(1.08)^2}\right] = \$857.34$$

In this way we are able to isolate the interest factor, and this isolation facilitates present-value calculations. In such calculations, the interest rate is known as the *discount rate*. The general formula for finding the present value of X_n to be received at the end of year n where k is the discount rate is

$$PV = X_n\left[\frac{1}{(1+k)^n}\right] \tag{4-4}$$

Note that Eq. (4-4) for discounting is simply the reciprocal of the formula for finding the terminal value, Eq. (4-1), of x dollars so many years hence.

Fig. 4-3 illustrates the present value of $100 received from one through ten years in the future with discount rates of 5, 10, and 15 percent. This graph shows that the present value of $100 decreases by a decreasing rate the further in the future it is to be received. The greater the interest rate, of course, the lower the present value but also the more pronounced the curve. At a 15 percent discount rate, $100 to be received ten years hence is worth only $24.72 today.

For an annuity involving a series of uniform receipts for a specified number of periods, the present value of the stream is

$$PV = \sum_{t=1}^{m} \frac{X}{(1+k)^t} \tag{4-5}$$

where m is the number of periods over which receipts of X occur at the end of each period, and the capital Greek sigma denotes the sum of discounted receipts at the end of period 1 through period m. If $1 000 were expected at the end of each of the next two years and the discount rate were 8 percent, we would have

$$PV = \frac{\$1\ 000}{(1.08)} + \frac{\$1\ 000}{(1.08)^2} = \$925.93 + \$857.34 = \$1\ 783.27$$

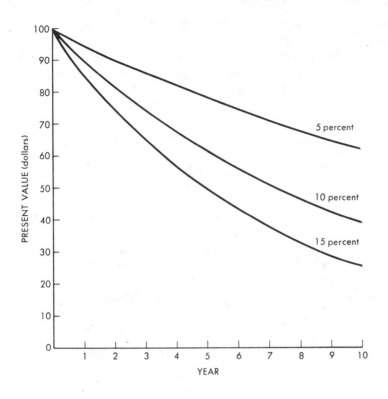

FIGURE 4-3 Present values with $100 cash flow and 5, 10, and 15 percent interest rates

CONSTRUCTION OF PRESENT-VALUE TABLES

Fortunately, one does not have to calculate present values by hand using Eq. (4-4). Present-value tables allow us easily to determine the present value of $1 received so many years from now at such and such a rate. To illustrate the construction of such a table, we make a few calculations using a discount rate of 10 percent. Suppose we wish to know the present value of $1 to be received one year from today. The formula is

$$PV = \frac{1}{(1 + 0.10)} = 0.90909$$

Similarly, if we wish to know the present value of $1 received two years from today, the formula is

$$PV = \frac{1}{(1 + 0.10)^2} = \frac{1}{1.21} = 0.82645$$

A present-value table relieves us of making these calculations every time we have a problem to solve; it is shown in Table A in the Appendix at the end of the book. We see in the table that for a 10 percent discount rate, the discount factors for one and two years in the future are 0.90909 and 0.82645, respectively—just as we calculated by hand.

If we had an uneven series of cash flows—$1 one year hence, $3 two years hence, and $2 three years from now—the present value of this series, using a 10 percent discount rate, would be

PV of $1 to be received at the end of 1 year $1(0.90909)   = $0.90909

PV of $3 to be received at the end of 2 years $3(0.82645)   =   2.47935

PV of $2 to be received at the end of 3 years $2(0.75131)   =   1.50262
Present value of series $4.89106

With a present-value table, we are able to calculate the present value for any series of future cash flows in the above manner.

The procedure can be simplified for a series if the cash flows in each future period are the same; that is, for an annuity. Suppose that in a series of future cash flows, $1 is to be received at the end of each of the next 3 years. The calculation of the present value of this stream, using the procedure above, is

PV of $1 to be received in 1 year   = $0.90909

PV of $1 to be received in 2 years   =   0.82645

PV of $1 to be received in 3 years   =   0.75131
Present value of series $2.48685

With an even series of future cash flows, it is unnecessary to go through these calculations. The discount factor, 2.48685, can be applied directly. Simply multiply $1 by 2.48685 to obtain $2.48685.

Present-value tables for even series of cash flows allow us to look up the appropriate compound discount factor (see Table B at the end of the book). We note that the discount factor for an even series of cash flows for 3 years, using a 10 percent discount rate, is 2.4868, as we calculated. Thus, for an even series of cash flows, we simply multiply the appropriate discount factor times the cash flow.

USE OF TABLES

Using the present-value tables A and B at the end of the book, we are able to calculate the present value of various future streams of cash flows. If we trace across any of the rows in Tables A and B, we see that the higher the discount rate the lower the discount factor. It is not a linear relationship, because the discount factor decreases less and less as the discount rate increases. Therefore, the present value of an amount of money to be received in the future decreases at a decreasing rate as the discount rate increases. The relationship is illustrated in Fig. 4-3. At a zero rate of discount, the present value of $1 to be received in the future is $1. In other words, there is no time value of money. As the discount rate increases, however, the present value declines but at a decreasing rate. As the discount rate approaches infinity, the present value of the future $1 approaches zero.

As an additional illustration of the use of these tables, suppose that we wished to determine the present value of $500 to be received at the end of one year, $400 to be received at the end of 2 years, $300 to be received at the end of 3 years, and $200 to be received at the end of years 4 through 10, all at a discount rate of 12 percent. Here we have an uneven series for the first 3 years and an even series, or annuity, for years 4 through 10. Consequently, we use Table A for the first series and Table B for the second. For the first series, the present value is

$$PV \text{ of } \$500 \text{ at the end of 1 year} - \$500(0.89286) = \$446.43$$

$$PV \text{ of } \$400 \text{ at the end of 2 years} - \$400(0.79719) = 313.88$$

$$PV \text{ of } \$300 \text{ at the end of 3 years} - \$300(0.71178) = \underline{213.53}$$
$$\$978.84$$

For the second series, the annuity, begins not at time 0, but at the beginning of the fourth year. Referring to Table B, we calculate the present value of an annuity of 10 years and subtract from it the present value of an annuity of 3 years to obtain the present value of an annuity from years 4 through 10.

$$PV \text{ of } \$200 \text{ for } 10 \text{ years} - \$200(5.6502) = \$1\,130.04$$

$$PV \text{ of } \$200 \text{ for } 3 \text{ years} - \$200(2.4018) = \underline{\quad 480.36}$$
$$\$649.68$$

Thus, the present value of the whole series is

$$PV \text{ of uneven series} \qquad \$\quad 978.84$$

$$PV \text{ of annuity} \qquad \underline{\quad 649.68}$$
$$\$1\,628.53$$

A wide variety of present-value problems could be illustrated. Be sure to do the problems at the end of this chapter.

In Appendix B to this chapter, we learn how to use an electronic calculator instead of present-value tables to determine present values and terminal values. There still are occasions when it is easier to use the tables, however, and that is the reason for our attention to them here.

PRESENT VALUE WHEN INTEREST IS COMPOUNDED MORE THAN ONCE A YEAR

When interest is compounded more than once a year, the formula for calculating present values must be revised along the same lines as for the calculation of terminal value. Instead of dividing the future cash flow by $(1 + k)^n$ as we do when annual compounding is involved, we determine the present value by

$$PV = \frac{x_n}{\left(1 + \dfrac{k}{m}\right)^{mn}} \qquad (4\text{-}6)$$

where, as before, x_n is the cash flow at the end of year n, m is the number of times a year interest is compounded, and k is the discount rate. The present value of $100 to be received at the end of year 3, the discount rate being 10 percent compounded quarterly, is

$$PV + \frac{\$100}{\left(1 + \frac{0.10}{4}\right)^{(4)(3)}} = \$74.36$$

On the other hand, if the discount rate is compounded only annually, we have

$$PV = \frac{\$100}{(1.10)^3} = \$75.13$$

Thus, the fewer times a year the discount rate is compounded, the greater the present value. This relationship is just the opposite of that for terminal values. In Appendix A to this chapter, we show how to calculate present values when interest is compounded continuously. To illustrate the relationship between present value and the number of times a year the discount rate is compounded, consider again our example involving $100 to be received at the end of 3 years with a discount rate of 10 percent. The following present values result from various compounding intervals.[2]

Compounding	Present value
Annual	$75.13
Semiannual	74.62
Quarterly	74.36
Monthly	74.17
Continuous	74.08

We see that present value decreases but at a decreasing rate as the compounding interval shortens, the limit being continuous compounding.

While it is important to understand discounting where interest is compounded more than once a year, all of the present-value calculations in this book will involve annual compounding. However, the reader should be able to adjust any of the discount calculations undertaken for compounding more than once a year.

SOLVING FOR THE NUMBER OF PERIODS

In the preceding section we solved for the present value, given the interest rate, number of periods, and cash flows. In this section we wish to solve for the number of periods given the other three variables. To illustrate such a problem,

[2]For semiannual compounding, m is 2 in Eq. (4-6) and mn is 6. With monthly compounding, m is 12 and mn is 36.

suppose that for $10 000 you can acquire an asset that will generate cash inflows of $2 000 at the end of each year until it becomes obsolete, after which no more cash flows are generated and the asset has no salvage value. If the opportunity cost of funds is 18 percent, how long must the asset last to be a worthwhile investment? In this case, we have an annuity producing $2 000 a year. Setting up the problem, we have

$$\$10\,000 = \frac{\$2\,000}{(1.18)} + \frac{\$2\,000}{(1.18)^2} + \ldots + \frac{\$2\,000}{(1.18)^n}$$

We must determine that value of n where the cumulative sum on the righthand side of the equation equals $10 000. To do so, we first divide the amount of the investment, $10 000, by the annual cash flow, $2 000, and obtain 5.0. When we go to Table B at the back of the book, we find that for 18 percent the discount factor is 5.0081 for 14 years, whereas it is 4.9095 for 13 years. Therefore, the asset must last nearly 14 years if it is to be a worthwhile investment.

Amortizing a Loan

Certain loans require the repayment of both interest and principal in a series of equal installments. Examples include mortgage loans, automobile loans, and some business loans. A bank may make you an $80 000 loan at 15 percent interest to be repaid in 10 equal annual installments. From the bank's standpoint, the cash flow stream represents an annuity with a cash outflow at time 0, followed by a series of even annual cash inflows. The amount of annual payment may be calculated by solving the following equation for x:

$$\$80\,000 = \sum_{t=1}^{10} \frac{x}{(1.15)^t} \tag{4-6}$$

Looking under the 15 percent column in Table B at the back of the book, we see that the discount factor for an even stream of cash flows for 10 years is 5.0188. Therefore, we have

$$\$80\,000 = 5.0188x$$

$$x = \$15\,940$$

Thus, $15 940 is the annual payment necessary to pay off the loan in 10 years and return the lender 15 percent. In Table 4-3, the loan amortization schedule is shown. The interest payment is based on the amount owed at the beginning of the year. In the first year, it is 15 percent of $80 000, or $12 000. The principal payment in the first year is $15 940 minus $12 000, or $3 940. Therefore, the balance owing at the end of the year is $80 000 − $3 940 = $76 060, and this becomes the base on which the interest payment in the second year is calculated:

$76\ 060 \times 0.15 = \$11\ 409$. And so the process goes through successive iterations through year 10. Note that in the early years, the payment is comprised largely of interest, whereas at the end it is mainly principal. This relationship reflects the decline in interest as the principal amount is paid down. Similar to present-value tables, mortgage payment tables allow one to look up the amount of payment required.

Summary

Mastering the concept of compound interest and growth is fundamental to understanding much of what goes on in financial management. In an economy where capital has value, interest rates are positive; and these rates must be embodied in any analysis involving future payments or receipts. In this chapter we considered the determination of terminal, or compound, values, as well as the determination of present values.

The terminal value at the end of year n for an initial deposit of X_0 that grows at a compound annual rate or r is

$$TV = X_0(1 + r)^n$$

This basic formula may be modified to take account of payment of interest more than once a year by

$$TV = X_0\left(1 + \frac{r}{m}\right)^{mn}$$

The greater the number of times a year interest is paid, the greater the terminal value.

TABLE 4-3   Loan Amortization Schedule (Rounded to Nearest Dollar)

End of Year	Payment	Interest	Principal Repayment	Remaining Principal Amount Owing
1	$15 940	$12 000	$ 3 940	$76 060
2	15 940	11 409	4 531	71 529
3	15 940	10 729	5 211	66 318
4	15 940	9 948	5 992	60 326
5	15 940	9 049	6 891	53 435
6	15 940	8 015	7 925	45 510
7	15 940	6 826	9 114	36 396
8	15 940	5 459	10 481	25 915
9	15 940	3 887	12 053	13 862
10	15 941	2 079	13 862	0

We may also determine the terminal value when there are uniform payments or receipts over n years. Where receipts are involved, the situation is known as an *annuity*. Rules of thumb can be used to approximate the time required for one to double one's money, given a particular compound rate of interest.

The second major concept we considered was the determination of the present value of a future cash flow. It can be expressed as

$$PV = \frac{x_n}{(1 + k)^n}$$

where x_n is a cash flow at the end of year n, and k is the discount rate or interest rate required. As in the previous case, this formula may be modified for compounding more than once a year. We proceeded to show how present-value tables are constructed and used. Also, we considered how to solve for n, given the other three variables in the present-value equation. Finally, we showed how a loan may be amortized with equal installment payments and how to solve for the correct annual payment.

Appendix A: Continuous Compounding

In practice, interest sometimes is compounded continuously. Certain valuation models in finance also employ continuous compounding. Therefore, it is useful to consider how it works. Recall from the chapter that the general formula for solving for the terminal value at the end of year n is

$$TV_n = X_0\left(1 + \frac{r}{m}\right)^{mn} \tag{4A-1}$$

where X_0 = the initial deposit
r = the interest rate
m = number of times a year interest is paid.

If interest were compounded daily on the basis of a 365-day year, the terminal value of an X_0 initial deposit at the end of n years would be

$$TV_n = X_0\left(1 + \frac{r}{365}\right)^{365n}$$

As m approaches infinity, the term $(1 + r/m)^{mn}$ approaches e^{rn}, where e is approximately 2.71828 and is defined as

$$e = \lim_{m \to \infty}\left(1 + \frac{1}{m}\right)^{m} \tag{4A-2}$$

where ∞ is the sign for infinity. To see that e approaches 2.71828 as m increases, simply increase m in the above expression from, say, 5 to 10 to 20 and solve for e.

The terminal value at the end of n years of an initial deposit of X_0 where interest is compounded continuously at a rate of r is

$$TV_n = X_0 e^{rn} \tag{4A-3}$$

For our earlier example problem, the terminal value at the end of 3 years would be

$$TV_3 = \$100(2.71828)^{(0.08)(3)} = \$127.12$$

This compares with a terminal value with annual compounding of

$$TV_3 = \$100(1.08)^3 = \$125.97$$

Continuous compounding results in the maximum possible terminal value at the end of n periods for a given rate of interest.

When interest is compounded continuously, the present value of a cash flow at the end of year n is

$$PV = \frac{X_n}{e^{rn}} \tag{4A-4}$$

The present value of $1 000 to be received at the end of ten years with a discount rate of 20 percent compounded continuously is

$$PV = \frac{\$1\ 000}{2.71828^{(0.20)(10)}} = \$135.34$$

We see then that present-value calculations involving continuous compounding are merely the reciprocal of terminal-value calculations. While continuous compounding results in the maximum possible terminal value, it results in the minimum possible present value.

Appendix B: Use of Electronic Calculators

With an electronic calculator, especially one equipped with a memory, we can easily and quickly compute the compound value and the present value of a series of cash flows.

CALCULATING TERMINAL VALUE

An investor deposits $3 000 in a bank account at the start of year 1, withdraws $1 000 at the start of year 2, and deposits $2 500 at the start of year 3. If the bank account earns interest at the rate of 5.875 percent compounded yearly, what is the compound value of the investment at the end of year 3?

With an electronic calculator, follow the accumulation process step by step.

Calculation step	Display shows
Enter the factor 1.05875	1.05875
Transfer it into the memory	1.05875 or 0.*
Enter the cash flow at start of year 1: + $3 000	3 000.
Multiply by the factor in the memory	3 176.25
Add the cash flow at start of year 2: − $1 000	2 176.25
Multiply by the factor in the memory	2 304.1046
Add the cash flow at start of year 3: + $2 500	4 804.1046
Multiply by the factor in the memory	5 086.3457

*Depending on type of calculator used.

In the above calculations, each multiplication by the factor 1.05875 carries the calculation forward by one year. The first multiplication finds and adds the interest earned during year 1. The negative cash flow, which occurs at the start of year 2, is then added, and the next multiplication finds and adds the interest earned during year 2. The positive cash flow at the start of year 3 is now added, and the last multiplication finds and adds the interest earned during year 3. Thus the compound value of the investment at the end of year 3 is $5 086.35.

CALCULATING A PRESENT VALUE

We have seen that the easiest way of calculating the terminal value of a series of cash flows is to proceed step by step, moving forward one period at a time. Similarly, the easiest way of calculating the present value of a series of cash flows is to proceed step by step, moving *backward* one period at a time. This involves starting with the *last* cash flow of the series, *dividing* by the factor $(1 + k)$, adding the next-to-last cash flow, dividing by the factor again, and so on, ending with the cash flow (if any) at time 0.

An investment opportunity is expected to provide cash inflows of $6 000, $9 000 and $7 000, respectively at the end of each of the next 3 years. What is the present value of this series discounted at 10.5 percent per annum? The steps and results of this calculation are shown below.

Calculation step	Display shows
Enter the factor 1.105	1.105
Transfer it into the memory	1.105 or 0
Enter the cash flow at end of year 3: + $7 000	7 000.
Divide by the factor in the memory	6 334.8416
Add the cash flow at end of year 2: + $9 000	15 334.842
Divide by the factor in the memory	13 877.685
Add the cash flow at the end of year 1: + $6 000	19 877.685
Divide by the factor in the memory	17 988.855

In this table, each division by the factor 1.105 carries the calculation backward by one year. The third division carries it back to the start of the first year. As no cash flow at that time has been specified, this last division completes the calculation: the present value of the series is $17 988.85.

The use of an electronic calculator allows us to solve for problems without having to interpolate, as we must when we use present value tables. Therefore, the answers we obtain will often be more accurate.

Questions

1. What is compound interest? Why is it important?
2. What kinds of personal financial decisions have you made that involve compound interest?
3. In calculating the terminal value, we compute the terminal value factor as one plus the interest rate to the nth power then multiply by the dollar value of the initial deposit. In calculating the present value, we compute the present value factor as one divided by one plus the interest rate to the nth factor, then multiply by the dollar value expected to be received in a future period. Is the present value factor the reciprocal of the terminal value factor?
4. What is an annuity? Suppose you are offered $100 a year for 5 years or $500 as a lump sum payment today, which offer will you accept? Why?
5. What type of compounding would you prefer in your savings account? Why?
6. Contrast the calculation of terminal value with the calculation of present value. What is the difference?
7. What is the advantage of present-value tables over hand calculations?
8. If you were to receive a sum of money 5 years hence but wished to sell your contract for its present value, which type of compounding would you prefer? Why?
9. In order to solve for the number of periods in a present-value situation, what do you need to know?
10. The 7-10 rule of thumb suggests that an amount will double in seven years at a 10 percent compound annual rate or double in ten years at a 7 percent annual rate. Is this a useful rule and is it an accurate one?
11. Does present value decrease at a linear rate, at an increasing rate, or at a decreasing rate with the discount rate? Why?
12. Does present value decrease at a linear rate, at an increasing rate, or at a decreasing rate with the length of time in the future the payment is to be received? Why?

Problems with Solutions

1. Calculate earnings at the end of year 7 if present earnings of $100 000 are expected to grow at (a) 12 percent compound rate; (b) 14 percent compound rate; (c) 20 percent compound rate; (d) 12 percent rate compounded semi annually; and (e) 12 percent rate compounded quarterly.

   (a) $100 000 (1 + 0.12)^7 = $221 068
   (b) $100 000 (1 + 0.14)^7 = $250 227
   (c) $100 000 (1 + 0.20)^7 = $358 318
   (d) $100 000 \left(1 + \dfrac{0.12}{2}\right)^{7\times2} = $226 090

(e) $\$100\ 000 \left(1 + \dfrac{0.12}{4}\right)^{7 \times 1} = \$228\ 793$

Note that if compounding takes place more than once a year, the annual rate is divided by and number of years is multiplied by the number of times compounding takes place each year.

2. Calculate the value at the end of year 5 of an initial $1000 deposit and additional deposits of $400 at the end of each year at an annual rate of 10 percent. Use Eq. (4-2).

$$\text{Terminal value} = \left(1\ 000 + \dfrac{400}{0.1}\right)(1 + 0.10)^5 - \dfrac{400}{0.1}$$

$$= (5\ 000)(1 + 0.10)^5 - 4\ 000 = \$4\ 053$$

3. John Holland, age 65, has decided to purchase an annuity with the proceeds of a retirement savings plan. The total amount available in the plan is $100 000. An insurance company representative has told Mr. Holland that his money would be invested to net 8 percent and that he would receive annuity payments for 10 years. How much would he receive?

Since the terminal value is zero and annual amount x are being withdrawn, Eq. (4-2) becomes

$$0 = \left(\$100\ 000 - \dfrac{x}{0.08}\right)(1 + 0.08)^{10} + \dfrac{x}{0.08}$$

$$0 = (\$100\ 000 - 12.5x)(1 + 0.08)^{10} + 12.5x$$

$$0 = (100\ 000 - 12.5x)\,2.15894 + 12.5x$$

$$= 215\ 894 - 26.98675x - 12.5x$$

$$26.98675x = 12.5x = 215\ 894$$

$$14.48675x = 215\ 894$$

$$x = \$14\ 903$$

We can solve the problem in another way using present value analysis. The $100 000 can be viewed as the present value of annual receipts of $x received over 10 years discounted at 8 percent.

$\$100\ 000 = \$\,x$ times present value factor of an annuity over 10 years

$$= \$\,x\ (6.7101 \text{ from Table B at the back of the book})$$

$$\dfrac{\$100\ 000}{6.7101} = \$\,x = \$14\ 903$$

4. How much would John Holland (Problem 3) pay for $16 000 annuity if his life expectancy were 12 years and the insurance company could invest to net 10 percent after company profits?

With terminal value analysis and using Eq. (4-2), the calculations are as follows:

$$0 = \left(y - \dfrac{\$16\ 000}{0.10}\right)(1 + 0.10)^{12} + \dfrac{16\ 000}{0.10}$$

$$0 = (y - \$160\ 000)\,3.1384 + \$160\ 000$$

$$= 3.1384\,y - \$502\ 144 + \$160\ 000$$

$$= 3.1384\,y = \$502\ 144 - \$160\ 000$$

$$y = \$109\ 019$$

Using present value analysis, the present value ($ y$) of the series of receipts ($16 000 in each of 12 years) is calculated as follows:

y = $16 000 times present value factor of an annuity over 12 years at 10 percent

= $16 000 (6.8137 from Table B at the back of the book)

= $109 019

5. Find the present value of the following cash flows using a discount rate of 10 percent.

			Situation	
	A	B	C	D
Cash flows end of:				
Year 1	$ 0	$3 000	$4 000	$2 000
Year 2	0	3 000	3 000	3 000
Year 3	9 000	3 000	2 000	4 000

Situation A: Use table for the present value of $1 due at end of N years. Factor for 3 years at 10% = 0.75131 (Table A at the back of the book).
Present Value = $9 000 × 0.75131 = $6 762
This means that if an investment of $6 762 were made at a rate of 10 percent it would grow to $9 000 at the end of year 3.

Situation B: Use table for present value of $1 per year. Three years at 10 percent gives a factor of 2.4868 (Table B at the back of the book).
Present value = $3 000 × 2.4868 = $7 460
This means that an investment of $7 460 at 10 percent would return $3 000 a year for a 3-year period to the investor.

Situations C & D: Use table for the present value of $1 due at the end of year N three times

	C		D
4 000 × 0.90909 =	$3 636	$2 000 × 0.90909 =	$1 818
3 000 × 0.82645 =	2 479	3 000 × 0.82645 =	2 479
2 000 × 0.75131 =	1 503	4 000 × 0.75131 =	3 005
Present value	$7 618		$7 302

Summary Present value:
Situation
A $6 762
B 7 460
C 7 618
D 7 302

Situation C has the highest present value since the largest amounts are received in the early years.

Problems

1. The following are exercises in terminal values:
(a) At the end of 3 years, how much is an initial deposit of $100 worth, assuming an annual interest rate of (1) 10 percent? (2) 100 percent? (3) 0 percent?

(b) At the end of 5 years, how much is an initial $500 deposit plus annual $100 payments worth, assuming an annual interest rate of (1) 10 percent? (2) 5 percent? (3) 0 percent?

(c) At the end of 3 years, how much is an initial $100 deposit worth, assuming a quarterly compounded interest rate of (1) 10 percent? (2) 100 percent?

(d) Why does your answer to part c differ from that to part a?

(e) At the end of 10 years, how much is a $100 initial deposit worth, assuming an interest rate of 10 percent compounded (1) annually? (2) semiannually? (3) quarterly? (4) continuously?

2. The following are exercises in present values:

(a) $100 at the end of 3 years is worth how much today, assuming a discount rate of (1) 10 percent (2) 100 percent? (3) 0 percent?

(b) What is the aggregate present value of $500 received at the end of each of the next 3 years, assuming a discount rate of (1) 4 percent? (2) 25 percent?

(c) $100 is received at the end of one year, $500 at the end of 2 years, and $1 000 at the end of 3 years. What is the aggregate present value of these receipts, assuming a discount rate of (1) 4 percent? (2) 25 percent?

(d) $1 000 is to be received at the end of one year, $500 at the end of 2 years, and $100 at the end of 3 years. What is the aggregate present value of these receipts assuming a discount rate of (1) 4 percent? (2) 25 percent?

(e) Compare your solutions in 2(c) with those in 2(d) and explain the reason for the differences.

3. Sally Ronk is considering two different savings plans. The first plan would have her deposit $500 every 6 months, and she would receive interest at a 7 percent annual rate, compounded semi-annually. Under the second plan she would deposit $1 000 every year with a rate of interest of 7½ percent, compounded annually. The initial deposit with plan 1 would be made 6 months hence and with plan 2 one year hence.

(a) What is the terminal value of the first plan at the end of 10 years?

(b) What is the terminal value of the second plan at the end of 10 years?

(c) Which plan should Ronk use, assuming her only concern is with the value of her savings at the end of 10 years?

(d) Would your answer change if the rate of interest on the second plan were 7 percent?

4. Joe Hing has inherited $25 000 and wishes to purchase an annuity that will provide him with a steady income over the next twelve years. He has heard that the local savings and loan association is currently paying 6 percent on an annual basis. If he were to deposit his funds here, how much would he be able to withdraw annually (to the nearest dollar)?

5. You need to have $50 000 at the end of ten years. To accumulate this sum, you have decided to save a certain amount at the end of each of the next ten years and deposit it in the bank. The bank pays 8 percent interest compounded annually for long-term deposits. How much will you have to save each year (to the nearest dollar)?

6. Mr. Joel Dunway wishes to borrow $10 000 for 3 years. A group of individuals agrees to lend him this amount if he contracts to pay them $18 000 at the end of the three years. What is the implicit annual interest rate to the nearest percentage?

7. You have been offered a note with 4 years to maturity, which will pay $3 000 at the end of each of the four years. The price of the note to you is $10 200. What is the implicit interest rate you will receive to the nearest percentage?

8. Sales of the H. L. Cramer Company Ltd. were $500 000, and they are expected to grow at a compound rate of 20 percent for the next 6 years. What will the sales be at the end of each of the next 6 years?

9. The H & L Bark Company Ltd. is considering the purchase of a scraping machine that is expected to provide cash flows as follows:

Year	1	2	3	4	5	6	7	8	9	10
Cash flow	$1 200	$2 000	$2 400	$1 900	$1 600	$1 400	$1 400	$1 400	$1 400	$1 400

If the appropriate discount rate is 14 percent, what is the present value of this cash-flow stream?

10. Suppose you were to receive $1 000 at the end of 10 years. If your opportunity rate is 10 percent, what is the present value of this amount if interest is compounded annually? If compounded quarterly? if compounded continuously?

11. As treasurer of Roberts Ltd., you are involved in negotiating a loan of $50 000 from your bank. The lender (i.e. the bank) requires that the loan be amortized over 3 years, that payments be made semiannually and that the annual interest rate be 14 percent. Determine the amount of each payment and prepare a schedule to show the periodic principal repayment and interest charges.

12. Patricia Van Auken is a prospective buyer of an apartment building on leased land. At the end of 20 years the land and the building revert to the lessor with no terminal value to the buyer. Annual rentals on the building are expected to be $126 000, while maintenance and other cash expenses and taxes are expected to average $60 000 per year. If Van Auken's opportunity cost of funds is 13 percent, what is the maximum price she should pay for the building?

13. Toby Markovich wishes to purchase an annuity contract that will pay him $7 000 a year for the rest of his life. St. Lambert Life Insurance Company figures that his life expectancy is 21 years based on its actuary tables. The company assigns an interest rate of 6 percent in its annuity contracts.
    (a) How much will Mr. Markovich have to pay for the annuity?
    (b) How much would he have to pay if the interest rate were 8 percent?

14. Belleville Mines, Inc., Ltd. is considering investing in Peru. It makes a bid to the government to participate in the development of a mine, the profits of which will be realized at the end of 5 years. The mine is expected to produce $5 million in cash to Belleville at that time. Other than the bid at the outset, no other cash flows will occur, as the government will reimburse the company for all costs. If Belleville requires a return of 20 percent, what is the maximum bid it should make for the participation right if interest is compounded (a) annually? (b) semi-annually? (c) quarterly? (d) continuously?

Selected References

CISSELL, ROBERT, HELEN CISSELL, and DAVID C. FLASPOHLER, *Mathematics of Finance*, 5th ed. Boston: Houghton, Mifflin, 1978.

DRAPER, JEAN E., and JANE S. KLINGMAN, *Mathematical Analysis*, 2nd ed. New York: Harper, 1972.

HAEUSSLER, ERNEST F., and RICHARD S. PAUL, *Introductory Mathematical Analysis for Students of Business and Economics*, 2nd ed. Reston, Va.: Reston Publishing Company, 1976.

HOWELL, JAMES E., and DANIEL TEICHROEW, *Mathematical Analysis for Business Decisions*, 2nd ed. Homewood, Ill.: Irwin, 1971.

KEMENY, JOHN G., ARTHUR SCHLEIFER, JR., J. LAURIE SNELL, and GERALD L. THOMPSON, *Finite Mathematics with Business Applications*, 2nd ed. Englewood Cliffs, N.J.: Prentice-Hall, 1972, Chapter 7.

SHAO, STEPHEN P., *Mathematics for Management and Finance*, 3rd ed. Cincinnati: South-Western, 1974.

SNYDER, LLEWELLYN R., and WILLIAM F. JACKSON, *Essential Business Mathematics*, 7th ed. New York: McGraw-Hill, 1979.

VICHAS, ROBERT P., *Handbook of Financial Mathematics, Formulas, and Tables*. Englewood Cliffs, N.J.: Prentice-Hall, 1979.

5

Foundations
for Valuation

In the last chapter we investigated the wonders of compound interest as well as the time value of money. We now are able to apply these concepts to the valuation of different securities. By *valuation* we mean the process by which the market price of a security is determined. In particular, we are concerned with the valuation of bonds, preferred stocks, and common stocks, though the principles discussed apply to other financial instruments as well. These principles will underlie much of the later development of the book. Because the major decisions of a company are all related in their effect on valuation, we must understand how investors value the financial instruments of a company.

Valuation in General

A key factor in the valuation of any financial instrument is an implied positive relationship between risk and expected return. It has been shown that investors overall dislike risk. As a result, they must be offered additional expected return for taking greater risk. Assume for purposes of illustration that you are among investors who concentrate upon some common holding period—say one year. The return from holding a security is simply the change in market price, plus any cash payments received from the company, divided by the beginning price. You might buy a security for $100 that paid $7 in cash to you and was worth $106 one year hence. The return would be ($7 + $6)/$100 = 13 percent. Assume further that you are concerned with what we shall call *unavoidable risk*, the risk that cannot be avoided by diversification of the securities you hold. In other words, if you invest in a number of securities, some of the individual security risks cancel out. What is left over we call the unavoidable risk. Much more will be said about this later in the chapter; for now, our purpose is to illustrate a simple but fundamental concept.

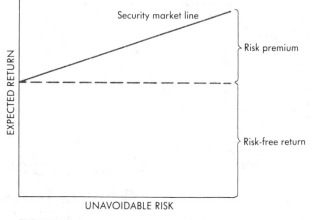

FIGURE 5-1 The security market line

If investors overall are averse to risk, there exists a relationship between the return they expect from holding a security and its unavoidable risk. This relationship, known as the *security market line*, is illustrated in Fig. 5-1. The expected one-year return is shown on the vertical axis, and unavoidable risk is on the horizontal. At zero risk, the security market line has an intercept on the vertical axis at a positive expected rate of return. As no risk is involved, this rate is known as the *risk-free rate*. As risk increases, the required rate of return increases in the manner depicted. Thus, there is a positive relationship between risk and expected return, which, as we shall see, governs the valuation of marketable securities.[1]

The slope of the security market line tells us the degree to which investors are risk-averse. The steeper the slope, the more averse they are to risk. If investors were not at all averse to risk, the security market line would be horizontal. In other words, they would require the same expected return on Treasury bills as they would on the securities of the most speculative of companies. As this equality of expected returns is not the case, we shall assume that the line has a positive slope.

CHANGES IN SECURITY MARKET LINE

We must be alert to the fact that the security market line depicts the tradeoff between expected return and unavoidable risk at a particular moment. This line can change over time with changes in interest rates and investor psychology. For one thing, the risk-free rate is expressed in nominal terms; that is, it is not adjusted for inflation. As we discussed in Chapter 3, the nominal rate of interest can be thought of as comprised of the real rate of interest plus a premium for inflation. Suppose for purposes of illustration that the real rate of interest on short-term securities is 1 percent and the inflation premium 9 percent, making the nominal risk-free rate 10 percent. Now if there were an unanticipated burst in inflation of 3

---

[1]The concepts underlying the security market line will be explored in more depth in the latter part of this chapter when we take up the valuation of common stocks.

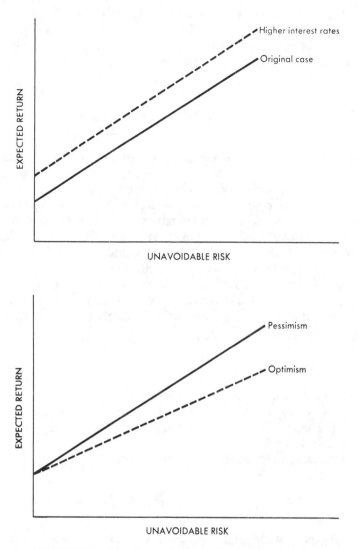

FIGURE 5-2 Security market line with changes in interest
rates and investor psychology

percent, the inflation premium would go to 12 percent and the nominal rate to 13
percent. As a result, the security market line would shift upward. This shift might
be depicted by the graph in the upper panel of Fig. 5-2. Note that the line shifts
upward by a given amount throughout.

In the lower panel of the figure we show a hypothetical change in investor
psychology from pessimism regarding the economy to optimism. Note here that
the slope of the security market line decreases, as opposed to a shift throughout.
The same expected return as before is required for a risk-free security. However,
lower returns are required for all risky securities; the greater the unavoidable risk,
the lower the return required relative to the pessimistic period. Thus, we must allow

for the fact that the relationship between risk and expected return is not necessarily stable. The degree of risk aversion of the market can and does change over time. With these general valuation concepts in mind, we are able to explore in more detail the valuation of specific types of securities.

Valuation of Fixed-Income Securities

A fixed-income security is one that pays a stated amount of money to the investor each period until it is retired by the issuing company. Before we can understand the valuation of such securities, certain terms must be discussed. For one thing, the instrument has a stated *face value*. This value is almost always $1 000 per bond and usually $50 or $100 per share of preferred stock. The bond also has a stated *maturity*, which is the time when the company must pay the holder the face value of the instrument. Preferred stock, on the other hand, has no stated maturity; like common stock, it is perpetual. Finally, the *coupon rate of interest* is stated, and it is paid each year. If the coupon rate is 12 percent on a $1 000 face value bond, the company pays the holder $120 each year until the bond matures. Remember that the terms of a fixed-income security are established at the time it is originally issued and cannot be changed.

BOND VALUATION

The terms of a bond call for the payment of a stated amount of interest over a given number of years, at the conclusion of which the face value of the instrument must be paid. The value of the instrument can be viewed as simply the present value of this cash-flow stream. The valuation equation for a bond that pays interest at the end of the year and has a face value of $1 000 is

$$P = \frac{C}{(1 + K)} + \frac{C}{(1 + K)^2} + \ldots + \frac{C}{(1 + K)^n} + \frac{\$1\ 000}{(1 + K)^n} \tag{5-1}$$

where P is the present value of the payment stream, C is the annual interest payment as given by the coupon rate, n is the number of years to final maturity, and k is the required rate of return, given its risk. The latter also is known as the *yield to maturity*.

We may wish to determine the market price necessary for a bond with a 12 percent coupon and ten years to maturity to provide a return of 14 percent. This shift upward in market rates might occur if there were an unanticipated increase in inflation. The coupon rate corresponds to interest payments of $120 a year. Therefore,

$$P = \frac{\$120}{(1.14)} + \frac{120}{(1.14)^2} + \ldots + \frac{\$120}{(1.14)^{10}} + \frac{\$1\ 000}{(1.14)^{10}}$$

Referring to Table B at the back of the book, we find that the present-value discount factor for 10 years of annual payments at a 14 percent discount rate is 5.2161. From

Table A, again at the back of the book, we find under the 14 percent column that the discount factor for a single payment 10 years in the future is 0.26974. Therefore, the value, P, of the bond is

Period	Payment	Discount factor	Present value
1-10	$ 120	5.2161	$625.93
10	1 000	0.26974	269.74
		Value of bond	$895.67

Expressed differently, the value of the bond is simply the sum of the present value of the stream of future interest payments plus the present value of the final payment at maturity.

If, instead of 14 percent, the bond provided only a 10 percent return, the valuation equation would become

$$P = \frac{\$120}{(1.10)} + \frac{120}{(1.10)^2} + \ldots + \frac{\$120}{(1.10)^{10}} + \frac{\$1\,000}{(1.10)^{10}}$$

Looking up the appropriate discount factors in Tables A and B at the back of the book, we find the following:

Period	Payment	Discount factor	Present value
1-10	$ 120	6.1446	$ 737.35
10	1 000	0.38554	385.54
		Value of bond	$1 122.89

In this case, the value of the bond is in excess of its $1 000 face value, whereas before it was less than its face value.

Behavior of bond values   On the basis of these examples, a number of observations can be made concerning the valuation of bonds.

1. When the required rate of return is more than the stated coupon rate, the value of the bond will be *less* than its face value. Such a bond is said to be selling at a *discount*.
2. When the required rate of return is less than the stated coupon rate, the value of the bond will be *greater* than its face value. Such a bond is said to be selling at a *premium*.
3. When the required rate of return equals the stated coupon rate, the value of the bond will equal to its face value.
4. If interest rates rise so that the required rate of return increases, the bond will decline in value. If interest rates fall, it will increase in value.

A further relationship, not apparent from the previous examples, needs to be illustrated separately.

5. For a given change in required return, the value of a bond will change by a greater amount, the longer its maturity.[2]

To illustrate, consider a five-year bond with annual interest payments of $120 a year and a required rate of return of 14 percent. Its valuation is

$$P = \frac{\$120}{(1.14)} + \frac{\$120}{(1.14)^2} + \ldots + \frac{\$120}{(1.14)^5} + \frac{\$1\ 000}{(1.14)^5} = \$931.34$$

which is determined in the same manner as illustrated before. Suppose now that interest rates fall so that the required rate of return is 10 percent. The value of the bond now is

$$P = \frac{\$120}{(1.10)} + \frac{\$120}{(1.10)^2} + \ldots + \frac{\$120}{(1.10)^5} + \frac{\$1\ 000}{(1.10)^5} = \$1\ 075.82$$

The increase in value for the bond is $1 075.82 − $931.34 = $144.48. Yet this illustration is exactly the same as our earlier one except for a maturity of 10 years instead of 5. In the former example the bond increased in value from $895.67 to $1 122.89. The absolute increase was $227.22. Thus, the change in value accompanying a decline in the required rate of return is greater for a 10-year bond than for a 5-year bond.

Similarly, one is able to take other maturities and demonstrate that, in general, the longer the maturity, the greater the price fluctuation associated with a given change in yield. Once can think of the face value of $1 000 serving as an anchor. The closer it is to being realized, the less important are interest payments in determining the market price, and the less important is a change in required return on the market price of the security. In general, then, the longer the maturity of a bond, the greater the risk of price change to the investor when changes occur in the overall level of interest rates.

Paying interest more than once a year If interest is paid more than once a year, Eq. (5-1) needs to be modified along the lines of our discussion in Chapter 4. If interest is paid twice a year, or semiannually, we have

$$P = \frac{C/2}{[1 + (k/2)]} + \frac{C/2}{[1 + (k/2)]^2} + \frac{C/2}{[1 + (k/2)]^3} \qquad (5\text{-}2)$$

$$+ \ldots + \frac{C/2}{[1 + (k/2)]^{2n}} + \frac{\$1\ 000}{[1 + (k/2)]^{2n}}$$

---

[2]For bonds selling at a discount with very long maturities, it is possible for prices to change by a lesser amount, the longer the maturity. This occurrence is unusual, so we shall not discuss it further. The interested reader may look into Michael H. Hopewell and George G. Kaufman, "Bond Price Volatility and Term to Maturity," *American Economic Review*, 63 (September 1973), 749-53.

For our first example above, we have

$$P = \frac{\$60}{(1.07)} + \frac{60}{(1.07)^2} + \frac{\$60}{(1.07)^3} + \ldots + \frac{\$60}{(1.07)^{20}} + \frac{\$1\,000}{(1.07)^{20}}$$

We see that the discount rate is one-half of 14 percent, or 7 percent. Looking up the appropriate discount factors for 7 percent at the back of the book, we find the value of the bond to be

Period	Payment	Discount factor	Present value
1-20	$ 60	10.5940	$635.64
20	1 000	0.25842	258.42
			$894.06

where each period represents one-half year.

We see that the value of the bond with semiannual interest payments is slightly less than that with annual payments.[3] While the present value of the interest stream is greater, owing to earlier payment on average, the present value of the final $1 000 payment is less. The net result is a slight decrease in overall present value.

If interest on a bond is paid more than once a year, Eq. (5-2) can be modified in keeping with our discussion in the previous chapter; however, most bonds issued today have semiannual interest payments. Rather than having to solve for value by hand, we can turn to bond value tables. Given the maturity, coupon rate, and yield, we can look up the market price. Similarly, given any three of these four factors, we can look up the fourth.

PERPETUAL BONDS AND PREFERRED STOCK

It is possible to have a bond that is a perpetuity. The British Consol, a bond issued in the early nineteenth century with no maturity date, carries to obligation of the British government to pay a fixed coupon perpetually. If an investment promises fixed annual payment of C forever, its present value is

$$P = \frac{C}{k} \qquad (5\text{-}3)$$

Here k is the yield required on a perpetual investment. Suppose we could buy a security that paid $50 a year forever. If the appropriate yield, k, were 12 percent, the market value of the security would be

$$P = \frac{\$50}{0.12} = \$416.67$$

_____

[3]If the required rate of return were less than the coupon rate, semiannual payments would result in a slightly higher present value.

Preferred stock is a fixed-income security in the sense that it specifies a fixed dividend to be paid at regular intervals. The features of this financial instrument are discussed in Chapter 22. While virtually all preferred stock issues have a call feature and many are eventually retired, they have no maturity as such. Therefore, they can be treated as perpetuities when it comes to valuation. Thus, we have

$$P = \frac{D}{k} \qquad (5\text{-}4)$$

where P as before is the market price, D is the stated dividend per share, and k is the appropriate discount rate. If Hi-LoCompany Ltd. had a 9 percent, $100 par value preferred-stock issue outstanding where the appropriate yield was 14 percent, its value per share would be

$$P = \frac{\$9}{0.14} = \$64.29$$

APPROPRIATE RETURN FOR A FIXED-INCOME SECURITY

As illustrated in several instances above, the valuation of a fixed-income security simply involves capitalizing interest payments or preferred stock dividends, using an appropriate discount rate. This rate can be thought to be comprised of the risk-free rate plus a premium for risk. Thus,

$$k = i + \theta \qquad (5\text{-}5)$$

where i = risk-free rate

θ = risk premium

If the security involved were a Treasury bill, there would be no risk of default, and we would expect θ to approximate zero.[4] Fixed-income securities of corporations obviously possess greater default risk than do Treasury bills. Therefore, there must exist a risk premium. The risk involved varies according to the company. Moreover, the financial instruments of an individual company possess more or less risk, depending upon their maturity, whether they are secured, and so forth. All of this is in keeping with our discussion in Chapter 3 of the reasons that different interest rates prevail in the financial markets.

If we assume that investors overall are concerned with unavoidable risk, as described in the opening section of this chapter, the appropriate discount rate can be approximated by use of the security market line. Given the degree of risk, one traces up to the security market line in Fig. 5-1, then over to the vertical axis to

---

[4]Even with Treasury bills, there are fluctuations in market price caused by changes in interest rates. Moreover, there is uncertainty about the return available upon reinvestment at maturity if one's holding period is longer than the maturity of the instrument. Nonetheless, Treasury bills are thought to represent a good proxy for the risk-free rate.

obtain the appropriate required rate of return. Similar securities, such as 30-year bonds issued by public utilities and rated Aa, will cluster at approximately the same degree of risk and, accordingly, require about the same rate of return. The risk associated with 5-year bonds of Bell Canada however, will be considerably less than that associated with the preferred stock of a new company in the electronics industry.

Our discussion of risk has been general, but it is possible to measure unavoidable risk and, as a result, approximate the required rate of return. As the work in this regard has been concerned primarily with the valuation of common stocks, we have deferred its illustration to the subsequent section. In closing, it is appropriate to stress that the same concepts that apply to the evaluation of fixed-income securities apply also to the valuation of common stocks.

Valuation of Common Stocks

The theory surrounding the valuation of common shares has undergone profound change during the last two decades. It is a subject of considerable controversy, and no one method for valuation is universally accepted. Still, in recent years there has emerged growing acceptance of the idea that individual common stocks should be analyzed as a part of a total portfolio of common shares the investor might hold. In other words, investors are not concerned with whether a particular stock goes up or down but with what happens to the overall value of their portfolios. We shall explore the valuation of common stocks in a portfolio context later in this section. First, however, we need to take up what is meant by the return to the common stock investor.

DIVIDENDS AND CAPITAL GAINS

If an investor's holding period were one year, most of us would agree that the return on investment in a common stock would be the sum of cash dividends received plus the selling price, all over the purchase price, minus one. More formally, the one-period return is

$$r = \frac{\text{Dividends} + \text{Ending price}}{\text{Beginning price}} - 1 \qquad (5\text{-}6)$$

On your next birthday, someone may give you a share of DSS Company Ltd. worth $50 a share. The company is expected to pay a $2 dividend at the end of the year, and its market price after the payment of the dividend is expected to be $53½ a share. Your expected return will be

$$k = \frac{\$2 + \$53.50}{\$50} - 1 = 11 \text{ percent}$$

Solving for the return Another way to solve the expected return is to set the problem up as follows

$$\$50 = \frac{\$2}{(1+k)} + \frac{\$53.50}{(1+k)}$$

In this formulation, we are interested in solving for the rate of return, k, which will equate the present value of the dividend and the terminal value at the end of year 1 with the beginning value. We want to determine the discount factor which, when multiplied by $2 plus $53.50, will equal the beginning value of $50. If we start with a discount rate of 11 percent, we find in Table A at the back of the book that the discount factor for one year is 0.90090. Therefore, the present value of the amounts to be received at the end of the year is 0.90090 x $55.50 = $50, or the exact value of the stock at the beginning of the year. Therefore, the expected return is 11 percent.

Now suppose that, instead of holding the security one year, you intend to hold it two years and sell it at the end of that time. Moreover, you expect the company to pay a $3 dividend at the end of year 2 and the market price of the stock to be $57 after this dividend is paid. Your expected return can be found by solving the following equation for k:

$$\$50 = \frac{\$2}{(1+k)} + \frac{\$3}{(1+k)^2} + \frac{57}{(1+k)^2}$$

Here solving for k is more difficult. Suppose we start with two discount rates, 11 and 12 percent, because we have a "feel" from the numbers that the return will be somewhat higher than the 11 percent calculated before. Using this discount rates and Table A at the back of the book, we find:

Year	Discount rate	Discount factor	Cash flow	Present value
1	11%	0.90090	$2	$ 1.8018
2	11	0.81162	60	48.6972
			Total	$50.4990
1	12%	0.89286	$2	$ 1.7857
2	12	0.79719	60	47.8314
			Total	$49.6171

As the beginning value of $50 lies between these two total present-value figures, we know that the expected return falls between 11 and 12 percent. To approximate the actual rate, we interpolate as follows:

	Discount rate	Present value
	11%	$50.4990
	12	49.6171
Difference	1%	0.8819

$$\frac{0.4990}{0.8819} = 0.57 \quad 11\% + 0.57\% = 11.57\%$$

Thus, the rate of return necessary to equate the present value of the expected dividends and terminal value with the beginning value is approximately 11.57 percent. With trial and error then, we can solve for the expected return on a particular investment. With practice, a person can come surprisingly close in selecting the discount rates from which to begin. Fortunately, computer programs and now even special calculators exist for solving for the rate of return, and these eliminate the need for the calculations illustrated above.

Multiple year holding period returns　For general purposes, the return formula for a two-year holding period can be expressed as

$$P_0 = \sum_{t=1}^{2} \frac{D_t}{(1+k)^t} + \frac{P_2}{(1+k)^2} \tag{5-7}$$

where P_o is the market price at time 0; D_t is the expected dividend at the end of period t; the capital Greek sigma denotes the sum of discounted dividends at the end of periods 1 and 2; and P_2 is the expected terminal value at the end of period 2.

If an investor's holding period were 10 years, the expected rate of return would be determined by solving the following equation for k:

$$P_0 = \sum_{t=1}^{10} \frac{D_t}{(1+k)^t} + \frac{P_{10}}{(1+k)^{10}} \tag{5-8}$$

The investor might be a perpetual trust fund, and the trustee expects to hold the stock forever. In this case, the expected return would consist entirely of cash dividends and perhaps a liquidating dividend. Thus, the expected rate of return would be determined by solving the following equation for k:

$$P_0 = \sum_{t=1}^{\infty} \frac{D_t}{(1+k)^t} \tag{5-9}$$

where ∞ is the sign for infinity.

It is clear that the intended holding period of different investors will vary greatly. Some will hold a share only a few days; others might expect to hold it forever. Investors with holding periods shorter than infinity expect to be able to sell the share in the future at a price higher than they paid for it. This assumes, of course, that at that time there will be investors willing to buy it. In turn, these investors will base their judgments of what the share is worth on expectations of future dividends and future terminal value beyond that point. That terminal value will depend upon the willingness of other investors at that time to buy the share. The price they are willing to pay will depend upon their expectations of dividends and terminal value. And so the process goes through successive investors. Note that the total cash return to all successive investors in a stock is the sum of the dividends paid, including any liquidating dividend. Thus, cash dividends are all that stockholders as a whole receive from their investment; they are all the company pays out.

Consequently, the foundation for the valuation of common shares must be dividends.

The logical question to be raised at this time is, Why do the shares of companies that pay no dividends have positive, often quite high values? The answer is that investors expect to sell the shares in the future at a price higher than they paid for it. Instead of a dividend income plus terminal value, they rely only upon the terminal value. In turn, terminal value will depend upon the expectations of the marketplace at the end of the horizon period. The ultimate expectation is that the firm eventually will pay dividends, either regular or liquidating ones, and that future investors will receive a cash return on their investment. In the interim investors are content with the expectation that they will be able to sell the shares at a subsequent time, because there will be a market for it. In the meantime, the company is reinvesting earnings and, everyone hopes, enhancing its future earning power and ultimate dividends.

GROWTH MODELS

We saw that the return on investment is the rate of discount that equates the present value of the stream of expected future dividends with the current market price of the share. If dividends of a company are expected to grow at a constant rate, g, in keeping, say, with a growth in earnings, Eq. (5-9) becomes

$$P_0 = \frac{D_0(1 + g)}{(1 + k)} + \frac{D_0(1 + g)^2}{(1 + k)^2} + \ldots + \frac{D_0(1 + g)^\infty}{(1 + k)^\infty} \qquad \text{(5-10)}$$

where D_0 is the present dividend per share. Thus, the dividend expected in period n is equal to the most recent dividend times the compound growth factor, $(1 + g)^n$.

Assuming k is greater than g, Eq. (5-10) can be expressed as[5]

$$P_0 = \frac{D_1}{k - g} \qquad \text{(5-11)}$$

_____

[5]If we multiply both sides of Eq. (5-10) by $(1 + k)/(1 + g)$ and subtract Eq. (5-10) from the product, we obtain

$$\frac{P_o(1 + k)}{(1 + g)} - P_o = D_o - \frac{D_o(1 + g)^\infty}{(1 + k)^\infty}$$

Because k is greater than g, the second term on the right side will be zero. Consequently,

$$P_o \left[\frac{1 + k}{1 + g} \right] = D_o$$

$$P_o \left[\frac{(1 + k) - (1 + g)}{1 + g} \right] = D_o$$

$$P_o[k - g] = D_o(1 + g)$$

$$P_o = \frac{D_1}{k - g}$$

Rearranging, the expected return becomes

$$k = \frac{D_1}{P_0} + g \qquad (5\text{-}12)$$

The critical assumption in this valuation model is that dividends per share are expected to grow perpetually at a compound rate of g. For many companies, this assumption may be a fair approximation of reality. To illustrate the use of Eq. (5-12), suppose that A & G Company's dividend per share at $t = 1$ was expected to be $3, that it was expected to grow at a 6 percent rate forever, and that the appropriate discount rate was 12 percent. The market price would be

$$P_0 = \frac{\$3}{0.12 - 0.06} = \$50$$

When the pattern of expected growth is such that a perpetual growth model is not appropriate, modifications of Eq. (5-10) can be used. A number of valuation models are based upon the premise that the growth rate will taper off eventually. The transition might be from a present above-normal growth rate to one that is considered normal. If dividends per share were expected to grow at a 10 percent compound rate for 5 years and thereafter at a 6 percent rate, Eq. (5-10) would become

$$P_0 = \sum_{t=1}^{5} \frac{D_0(1.10)^t}{(1 + k)^t} + \sum_{t=6}^{\infty} \frac{D_5(1.06)^{t-5}}{(1 + k)^t} \qquad (5\text{-}13)$$

If the current dividend, D_0, were $2 per share and the required rate of return, k, were 12 percent, we would solve for P_0 in the following manner:

End of Year	Dividend		Present value of dividend at 12 percent
1	$2(1.10) = \$2.20$	x	$0.89286 = \$1.96$
2	$2(1.10)^2 = 2.42$	x	$0.79719 = 1.93$
3	$2(1.10)^3 = 2.66$	x	$0.71178 = 1.89$
4	$2(1.10)^4 = 2.93$	x	$0.63552 = 1.86$
5	$2(1.10)^5 = 3.22$	x	$0.56743 = 1.83$

Present value of dividends: first five years = $9.47

Dividend at the end of year 6 = $3.22 (1.06) = $3.41

Market value at the end of year 5 = $\dfrac{D_6}{k - g} = \dfrac{\$3.41}{0.12 - 0.06} = \$56.83$

Present value of $56.83 at the end of year 5 = $56.83 × 0.56743 = $32.25

$P_0 = \$9.47 + \$32.25 = \$41.72$

The transition from an above-normal to a normal rate of growth could be specified as more gradual than the rate above. We might expect dividends to grow at a 10 percent rate for 4 years, followed by an 8 percent rate for the next 4 years and a

6 percent growth rate thereafter. The more growth segments that are added, the more closely the growth in dividends will approach a curvilinear function. But even IBM cannot grow at an above-normal rate forever. Typically, companies tend to grow at a very high rate initially, after which their growth opportunities slow down to a rate that is normal for companies in general. If maturity is reached, the growth rate may stop altogether. For any growth model, Eq. (5-10) can be modified so that it portrays the expected stream of future dividends.

Required Rate of Return on a Share

We have seen that the expected return on a share is the rate of discount that equates the present value of the stream of expected future dividends with the market price of the share. Conversely, the market price of a share might be thought to be the stream of expected future dividends discounted to their present value using the required rate of return. Frequently, the terms *required* and *expected* are used interchangeably. The two rates of return are the same in market equilibrium, but they are not the same when disequilibrium prevails. To appreciate the distinction and to understand the equilibrating process, we explore in detail the required rate of return for a share

RISK AND RETURN IN A PORTFOLIO CONTEXT

Picking up on our previous discussion of the security market line, we now want to consider how this line is derived and how the required rate of return is determined for a common share. We do this in the context of Sharpe's capital-asset pricing model, which was developed in the 1960s. Like any model, this one is a simplification of reality. Nevertheless, it allows us to draw certain implications about the required rate of return for a share assuming the market for shares overall is in equilibrium. As we shall see, the value of an individual security depends upon its risk in relation to the risk of other securities available for investment. Because a complete and mathematically rigorous presentation of the model is beyond the scope of an introductory book, we shall concentrate on the general aspects of the model and its important implications.[6] Certain corners have been cut in the interest of simplicity.

As with any model, there are assumptions to be made. First, we assume that capital markets are efficient in that investors are well informed, transaction costs are low, there are negligible restrictions on investment, and no investor is large enough to affect the market price of a stock. We assume also that investors are in general agreement about the likely performance of individual securities and that their expectations are based on a common holding period, say one year. There are two types of investment opportunities with which we will be concerned.[7] The first is

---

[6]See William F. Sharpe, *Investments* 2d ed. (Englewood Cliffs, N.J.: Prentice-Hall, 1981), for a more complete discussion of the model.

[7]The immediate subsequent development draws upon William F. Sharpe, "Efficient Capital Markets with Risk," Research Paper (Stanford Graduate School of Business).

a risk-free security whose return over the holding period is known with certainty. Frequently, the rate of Treasury bills is used as surrogate for the risk-free rate. The second is the market portfolio of common shares. It is represented by all available shares weighted according to their market values outstanding. As the market portfolio is a somewhat unwieldy thing with which to work, most people use a surrogate such as the TSE 300-Stock Index.

Earlier we discussed the idea of *unavoidable risk*; it was defined as risk that cannot be avoided by efficient diversification. Because one cannot hold a more diversified portfolio than the market portfolio, it represents the limit to attainable diversification. Thus, the risk associated with the market portfolio is unavoidable, or "systematic." Put another way, the only risk remaining after efficient diversification is systematic in the sense that it affects all securities. In essence, this is the risk of market swings caused by things such as changes in the economy or the political situation. It affects all shares no matter how efficiently one is diversified.

THE CHARACTERISTIC LINE

Now we are in a position to compare the expected return for an individual stock with the expected return for the market portfolio. In our comparison, it is useful to deal with returns in excess of the risk-free rate. The *excess return* is simply the expected return less the risk-free return. Fig. 5-3 shows an example of a comparison of expected excess returns for a specific stock with those for the market portfolio. The dark line is known as the characteristic line; it depicts the expected relationship between excess returns for the stock and excess returns for the market portfolio. This expected relationship may be based upon past experience, in which case actual excess returns for the share and for the market portfolio would be plotted on the graph, and a line would be drawn, best characterizing the historical relationship. Such a situation is illustrated by the scatter diagram shown in the figure. Each point represents the excess return of the share and that of the TSE 300-Stocks Index for a given month in the past, sixty in total. We see that when returns on the market portfolio are high, returns on the share tend to be high as well. Instead of using historical return relationships, one might obtain future return estimates from security analysts who follow the stock. As this approach usually is restricted to investment organizations with a number of security analysts, we illustrate the relationship assuming the use of historical data.

In the figure, three measures are important. The first, known as the *alpha*, is simply the intercept of the characteristic line on the vertical axis. If the excess return for the market portfolio were expected to be zero, the alpha would be the expected excess return for the stocks. In theory, the alpha for an individual share should be zero.[8] Using past data to approximate the characteristic line, however, we

---

[8]If the alpha of a share were above zero, market participants would recognize the opportunity for an expected return greater than that required for the systematic risk involved. They would buy the share and this buying pressure would raise the price of the share and lower its expected return. As a result, the characteristic line would decline throughout. Such buying would continue until the share provided the same expected return as other shares with that systematic risk. At this point, the vertical intercept of the characteristic line would be zero. If the alpha of a stock is negative, market participants will sell it, and these sales will cause the market price to decline. With this decline, the share's expected return will rise, as will the characteristic line until it passes through zero.

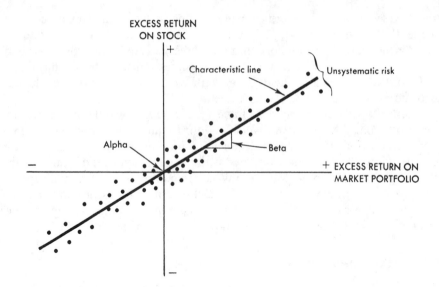

FIGURE 5-3 Relationship between excess returns for stock and excess returns for market portfolio

might observe alphas that differ from zero if the market were in disequilibrium, if there were market imperfections, or if there were statistical problems in measurement. We assume for now, however, that the alpha for a particular share is zero.

The second measure with which we are concerned, and the most important, is the *beta*. The beta is simply the slope of the characteristic line. If the slope is one, it means that excess returns for the share vary proportionally with excess returns for the market portfolio. In other words, the share has the same unavoidable risk as the market as a whole. If the market goes up and provides an excess return of 5 percent for a month, we would expect on average for the share's excess return to be 5 percent as well. A slope steeper than one means that the share's excess return varies more than proportionally with the excess return of the market portfolio. Put another way, it has more unavoidable risk than the market as a whole. This type of share is often called an "aggressive" investment. A slope of less than one means that the share has less unavoidable or systematic risk than the market as a whole. This type of share is often called a "defensive" investment. Examples of the three types of relationships are shown in Fig. 5-4.

The greater the slope of the characteristic line for a share, as depicted by its beta, the greater its systematic risk. This means that for both upward and downward movements in market excess returns, movements in excess returns for the individual share are greater or less depending on its beta. Thus, the beta is a measure of a share's systematic or unavoidable risk. This risk cannot be diversified away by investing in more stocks, as it depends upon such things as changes in the economy and in the political atmosphere, which affect all stocks. In summary, the beta of a share represents its contribution to the risk of a highly diversified portfolio of shares.

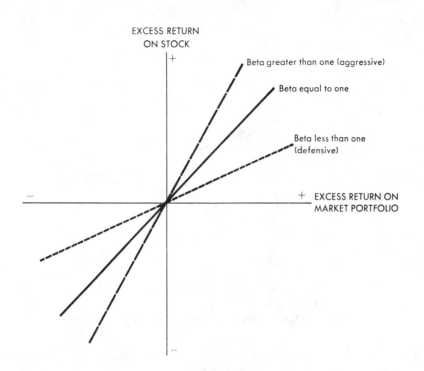

EXCESS RETURN
ON STOCK

Beta greater than one (aggressive)

Beta equal to one

Beta less than one
(defensive)

EXCESS RETURN ON
MARKET PORTFOLIO

FIGURE 5-4   Examples of characteristic lines with different betas

UNSYSTEMATIC RISK

The last of the three measures with which we are concerned is the unsystematic risk of a share. This risk is described by the dispersion of the estimates involved in predicting a share's characteristic line. In Fig. 5-3 it is represented by the relative vertical distance of the dots from the solid line. If all of the points in the scatter diagram were plotted along the characteristic line, there would be no unsystematic risk. All risk would be market related. If the points are widely scattered around the characteristic line, this occurrence implies that a good deal of the total risk of the share is company related. The greater the dispersion of the points in the figure, the greater the unsystematic risk of the share. By diversification of shares in one's portfolio, however, we can reduce unsystematic risk. It has been shown that unsystematic risk is reduced at a decreasing rate toward zero as more stocks are added to the portfolio. Thus, a substantial proportion of the unsystematic risk of a share can be eliminated with a relatively moderate amount of diversification—say 10 or 15 stocks. For the well-diversified portfolio, unsystematic risk approaches zero. Conceptually, this can be illustrated as in Fig. 5-5. As the number of randomly selected securities held in the portfolio increases, the total risk of the portfolio is reduced in keeping with the reduction in unsystematic risk. However, this reduction is at a decreasing rate, as seen in the figure.

Thus, the total risk involved in holding a share is comprised of two parts:

$$\text{Total risk} = \begin{matrix}\text{Systematic risk} \\ \text{(Nondiversifiable)}\end{matrix} + \begin{matrix}\text{Unsystematic risk} \\ \text{(Diversifiable)}\end{matrix} \qquad \textbf{(5-14)}$$

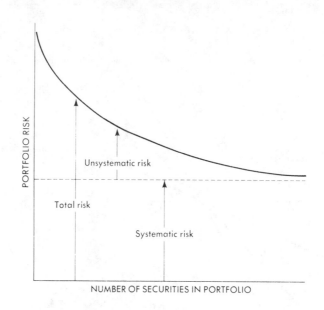

FIGURE 5-5 Total, unsystematic, and systematic risk

The first part is due to the overall market risk—changes in the economy, tax reform by Parliament, a change in the world energy situation—risks that affect securities overall and, consequently, cannot be diversified away. In other words, even the investor who hold a well-diversified portfolio will be exposed to this type of risk. The second risk component, however, is unique to a particular company, being independent of economic, political, and other factors that affect securities in a systematic manner. A wildcat strike may affect only one company; a new competitor may produce essentially the same product; a technological breakthrough can make obsolete an existing product. For the typical share unsystematic risk accounts for somewhere around two-thirds of its total risk. By diversification, this kind of risk can be reduced or even eliminated if diversification is efficient. Therefore, not all of the risk involved in holding a share is relevant; part of it can be diversified away.

MEASURING THE REQUIRED RATE OF RETURN

If we assume that financial markets are efficient and that investors as a whole are efficiently diversified, unsystematic risk is a minor matter. The major risk associated with a share becomes its unavoidable or systematic risk. The greater the beta of a share the greater the risk of that share, and the greater the return required. If we assume that unsystematic risk is diversified away, the required rate of return for stock j is

$$\overline{R}_j = i + (\overline{R}_m - i)\beta_j \tag{5-15}$$

where i is the risk-free rate, $\overline{R}_m$ is the expected return for the market portfolio, and β_j is the beta coefficient for stock j as defined earlier.

Put another way, the required rate of return for a share is equal to the return required by the market for a riskless investment plus a risk premium. In turn, the risk premium is a function of: (1) the expected market return less the risk-free rate, which represents the risk premium required for the typical share in the market; and (2) the beta coefficient. Suppose that the expected return on short-term Treasury bills is 10 percent, the expected return on the market portfolio is 15 percent, and the beta of Pro-Fli Company Ltd. is 1.3. The beta indicates that Pro-Fli has more systematic risk than the typical share. Given this information and using Eq. (5-15), we find that the required return on Pro-Fli's shares would be

$$\overline{R}_j = 0.10 + (0.15 - 0.10)1.3 = 16.5 \text{ percent}$$

What this tell us is that on average the market expects Pro-Fli to show a 16.5 percent annual return. Because Pro-Fli has more systematic risk, this return is higher than that expected of the typical share in the marketplace. For the typical share the expected return would be

$$\overline{R}_j = 0.10 + (0.15 - 0.10)1.0 = 15.0 \text{ percent}$$

Suppose now that we are interested in a defensive share whose beta coefficient is only 0.7. Its expected return is

$$\overline{R}_j = 0.10 + (0.15 - 0.10)0.7 = 13.5 \text{ percent}$$

OBTAINING INFORMATION FOR THE MODEL

If past performance is a good gauge of the future, one can use past data on excess returns for the stock and for the market to calculate the beta. In Canada, betas for selected stocks are prepared by some securities firms for internal use. There is no published information on betas available to the investing public. Access to beta information is possible if a firm is a client of a securities firm which prepares such information. Table 5-1 shows the beta statistics supplied by Burns Fry Ltd. of Toronto, a firm that computes betas for about 350 Canadian stocks on a quarterly basis, using data of the previous 54 months.

In addition to the beta, it is important to use the best possible estimates of the future for the market return and for the risk-free rate. Past data may or may not provide good bases. For example, if in the past there was relative economic stability but a high inflation rate is forecast for the future, averages of past market returns and past risk-free rates would be biased and low estimates of the future would result. In this case, it would be a mistake to use historical average returns in the calculation of the required return for a project. In another situation, market returns realized in the not-so-distant past might be very high and not expected to continue. As a result, the use of past data might result in too high an estimate of the future market return.

In situations of this sort, direct estimates of the market return and of the risk-free rate must be made. These estimates might be consensus estimates of security analysts, economists, and others who regularly predict such returns. In recent

TABLE 5-1   Betas for Selected Stocks

Industry Group and Selected Companies	Beta	Industry Group and Selected Companies	Beta
Integrated Mines		Paper & Forest Products	
Alcan	1.0	Brinco	0.2
Falconbridge	2.0	Abitibi	0.7
Inco	1.3	DomTar	0.3
Metal Mines		Distilleries	
Vestgron Mines	0.7	Corby	0.7
Un Keno Hill	2.1	Seagram	0.3
Northgate Ex	1.4	Walker	0.4
Golds		Telephone	
Camp Red Lake	1.1	B.C. Tel	0.2
Pegasus Gold	3.7	Bell	0.3
Lake Shore	1.6	Maritime Tel & Tel	0.3
Integrated Oils		Banks	
Shell Canada	1.0	Can. Imperial	0.2
Husky	1.5	Northland	0.9
Gulf Canada	1.5	Royal	0.3
Oil & Gas Producers		Trust, Savings & Loan	
Ram Pete	0.3	Central Trust	0.2
Q.M.G. Holding	2.8	National	0.3
Rupertsland	1.1	Royal	0.3
		Broadcasting	
		Baton A	0.9
		Chum B	0.2
		Standard	0.3

Source: *Burns Fry Ltd.*, Toronto. The sample of betas was computed as of June 30, 1983. In the above table, we report the minimum and maximum beta available within an industry sector and a third selected beta.

years, consensus estimates over time of the expected market return have ranged between 10 percent and 16 percent and estimates of the short-term risk-free rate between 8 percent and 11 percent. In periods of anticipated high inflation, such estimates tend to be in the upper part of these ranges. It is important that the market return and the risk-free rate used in Eq. (5-15) be the current, market consensus of the expected return on common shares and the expected return on short term treasury securities.

Equilibrium Returns and Stock Prices

The capital-asset pricing model provides us a means by which to estimate the required rate of return on a security. This return then can be used as the discount rate in a dividend-capitalization model. You will recall that the market price per share of a stock can be expressed as the present value of the stream of expected future dividends.

$$P_0 = \sum_{t=1}^{\infty} \frac{D_t}{(1 + k)^t}$$ (5-16)

where D_t is the expected dividend in period t; k is the required rate of return for the stock, and Σ is the sum of the present value of future dividends going from period 1 to infinity.

Suppose that we wished to determine the value of the share of Pro-Fli Company Ltd. and that the perpetual dividend growth model was appropriate. This model is

$$P_0 = \frac{D_1}{k - g}$$ (5-17)

where g is the expected future growth rate in dividends per share. Suppose that Pro-Fli's expected dividend in period 1 is $2 per share, and that the expected annual growth rate in dividends per share is 10 percent. In previous computations we determined that the required rate of return for Pro-Fli was 16.5 percent. On the basis of these expectations, the value of the stock is

$$P_0 = \frac{\$2.00}{0.165 - 0.100} = \$30.77$$

This represents the *equilibrium price* of the share based on investor expectations about the company, about the market as a whole, and about the return available on a riskless asset.

These expectations can change; and when they do, the value of the share changes. Suppose that inflationary pressures in the economy abate, and we enter a period of relatively stable growth. As a result, interest rates decline, and investor risk aversion lessens. Moreover, suppose that Pro-Fli develops a new product line that has much less systematic risk than its existing product lines. However, the growth rate of the company also declines somewhat. The variables before and after these changes are

	Original	New
Risk-free rate	0.10	0.08
Market return	0.15	0.12
Pro-Fli Beta	1.30	1.10
Pro-Fli growth rate	0.10	0.09

The required rate of return for Pro-Fli's stock becomes

$$\overline{R}_j = 0.08 + (0.12 - 0.08)1.10 = 12.4 \text{ percent}$$

Using this rate as k, the new value of the share is

$$P_0 = \frac{\$2.00}{0.124 - 0.09} = \$58.82$$

Thus, the combination of these events causes the value of the share to go from $30.77 to $58.82, per share, almost doubling. Thus, the equilibrium price of a share can change very quickly as expectations in the market place change.

MARKET-DETERMINED RELATIONSHIP

From these examples, we see that the greater the systematic or unavoidable risk of a share, as denoted by its beta, the higher the return that is expected. Given the assumptions of the model, there exists a linear and positive relationship between the beta of a particular share and its required rate of return. This relationship is known as the security market line, and it was illustrated for securities in general in Fig. 5-1. The work to date on devising return measures for combinations of fixed-income securities and common shares leaves something to be desired. As a result, it is difficult in practice to derive satisfactory beta information for fixed-income securities and common shares. In contrast, when the market portfolio is restricted to common shares, beta information is well developed and readily available. For this reason, most of the work on the capital-asset pricing model has involved common shares. The concept of the relationship between unavoidable risk and the required return is important, however, for both fixed-income securities and common shares.

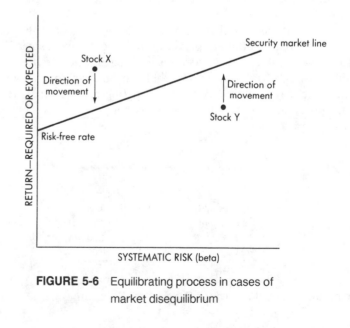

FIGURE 5-6 Equilibrating process in cases of market disequilibrium

Returns in disequilibrium situations   We said earlier that in market equilibrium the required rate of return on a share equals its expected return. What happens when this is not so? Suppose that in Fig. 5-6 the security market line is drawn on the basis of what investors as a whole know to be the appropriate relationship between the required rate of return and systematic or unavoidable risk. For some reason, two shares—call them X and Y—are improperly priced. Share X is underpriced relative to the security market line, while share Y is overpriced.

As a result, share X provides a higher expected return than the security market line for the systematic risk involved, while share Y provides a lower expected return. Investors seeing the opportunity for superior returns by investing in share X should rush to buy it. This action would drive the price up and the expected return down. How long would this continue? It would continue until the market price was driven up and the expected return down to the point at which the expected return was on the security market line. In the case of share Y, investors holding this share would sell it, recognizing that they could obtain a higher return for the same amount of systematic risk with other shares. This selling pressure would drive Y's market price down and its expected return up until the expected return was on the security market line.

When the expected returns for these two shares were both on the security market line, market equilibrium would again prevail. As a result, the expected returns for the two share would equal their required returns. Available evidence suggests that disequilibrium situations in share prices do not long persist and that share prices adjust rapidly to new information. With the vast amount of evidence indicating market efficiency, the security market concept becomes a useful means for determining the expected and required rate of return for a share. This rate then can be used as the discount rate in the valuation procedures described earlier.

This brings to a close our examination of valuation. Given the expected cash payments together with the appropriate required rate of return for a financial instrument, we are able to determine its present value and, accordingly, attach a proper valuation to the investment.

Summary

The valuation of any financial instrument involves a capitalization of its expected income stream by a discount rate appropriate for the risk involved. The important risk to the investor is that which cannot be avoided by diversification. This risk, known as *unavoidable risk*, is systematic in the sense that it affects all securities, although in different degrees. Unsystematic risk is company specific in that it does not depend upon general market movements. This risk is avoidable through proper diversification of one's portfolio. If we assume that investors as a whole are efficiently diversified in the securities they hold, the important risk to the investor is the security's systematic risk.

The degree of systematic risk a security possesses can be determined by drawing a *characteristic line*. This line depicts the relationship between expected returns in excess of the risk-free rate for the specific security involved and for the market portfolio. The slope of this line, know as *beta*, is a measure of systematic risk. The greater the beta, the greater the unavoidable risk of the security involved. The relationship between the required rate of return for a security and its beta is known as the *security market line*. It is linear and reflects a positive relationship between the return investors require and systematic risk. Thus, the required return is the risk-free rate plus some premium for systematic risk.

With the security-market-line concept, one is able to approximate the appropriate discount rate for both fixed-income securities and common shares. Bonds and preferred stocks represent fixed-income securities in the sense that the cash payment, whether interest or preferred dividend, is established at issuance and is invariant. We illustrated the calculation of the present value of a bond under various assumptions as to the number of times a year interest is paid as well as the valuation of a perpetuity. In addition, the price behavior accompanying a change in interest rates was explored.

Expected future dividends are the foundation for the valuation of common shares. The dividend-capitalization model embodies the notion of capital gains. We went on to consider various growth models in which dividends are expected to grow over time either at a constant rate or at different rates. In all cases, determination of value involves calculating the present value of the expected future stream of dividends. The key to valuation is determining the appropriate discount rate that properly takes account of risk. Several examples demonstrated how to calculate the required rate of return for a stock and how to obtain the necessary information. Once the discount rate is determined, it can be used in a dividend-capitalization model to determine the value of a share.

Questions

1. Define the determination of the present value of an income stream approach to valuation.
2. Why do we treat bonds and preferred stock in the same way when it comes to valuation?
3. Why do bonds with long maturities fluctuate more in value than bonds with short maturities, given the same change in yield to maturity?
4. Why are dividends the basis for the valuation of common shares?
5. Suppose controlling stock of IBM Corporation were placed in a perpetual trust with an irrevocable clause that cash or liquidating dividends would never be paid. Earnings per share continued to grow. What would be the value of the company?
6. Why is the growth rate in earnings and dividends of a company likely to taper off in the future? Could not the growth rate increase as well? If it did, what would be the effect?
7. Explain the importance of the assumption of efficient capital markets when it comes to deriving the security market line.
8. Define the *characteristic line* and its *alpha* and *beta*.
9. Why is beta a measure of systematic risk? What is its meaning?
10. What is the required rate of return of a share? How can it be measured?
11. Is the security market line constant over time?
12. What would be the effect of the following changes on the market price of a company's shares all other things the same?
    (a) Investors demand a higher required rate of return for shares in general.

(b) The covariance between the company's rate of return and that for the market decreases.

(c) The standard deviation of the probability distribution of rates of return for the company's shares increases.

(d) Market expectations of the growth of future earnings of the company are revised downward.

13. Why should the required rate of return for preferred shares of a company be lower than that for its common shares?

14. In a world of complete certainty, would there be any difference between the debt and equity instruments of a company?

Problems with Solutions

1. An investor measures unavoidable risk on a scale from 0 to 10. Plot a security market line if the risk free rate is 8 percent and at 6 on the unavoidable risk scale the investor expects a return of 14 percent.

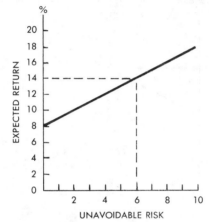

2. Suppose in question 1 (a) the investor was not at all risk averse, (b) he was more pessimistic and (c) the risk free rate rose to 10 percent. Plot the security market line under each condition.

(a)

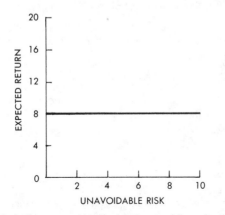

The investor is not at all concerned with risk; he would require the same return (the risk-free rate) from all securities.

(b)

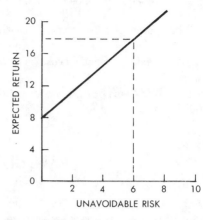

The slope of the security market line is steeper than in question 1. For example, the investor requires a return of 18 percent instead of 14 percent at 6 on the unavoidable risk scale. He thinks there is more risk and thus requires a higher return.

(c)

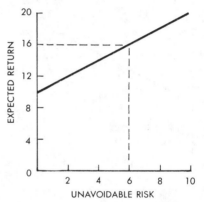

The slope of the line is the same as in question 1 but the origin is 10 percent not 8 percent. Thus the required return is higher at all levels of risk. At 6 the required return is 16 percent.

3. What is the market value of 10 percent, 10 year, $1 000 bond with (a) interest payable annually or (b) interest payable semiannually, if the required market yield is 12 percent?

Let P = Market value of the bond

(a) $P = \dfrac{100}{(1 + 0.12)} + \dfrac{100}{(1 + 0.12)^2} + \dfrac{100}{(1 + 0.12)^3} + \ldots + \dfrac{100}{(1 + 0.12)^{10}} + \dfrac{1\,000}{(1 + 0.12)^{10}}$

$100 received annually for 10 years discounted at 12 percent = $100 × 5.6502 = $565.02
$1 000 received at the end of year 10 discounted at 12 percent = $1 000 × 0.32197 = $321.97
$P = $565.02 + $321.97 = $886.99

(b) Divide the market yield by 2 and multiply years by 2 since interest is paid semiannually.

$P = \dfrac{50}{(1 + 0.06)} + \dfrac{50}{(1 + 0.06)^2} + \dfrac{50}{(1 + 0.06)^3} + \ldots + \dfrac{50}{(1 + 0.06)^{20}} + \dfrac{1\,000}{(1 + 0.06)^{20}}$

$50 received semiannually for 10 years discounted at 6 percent = $50 × 11.4699 = $573.50
$1 000 received at the end of year 10 discounted at 12 percent compounded semi-

annually = $1 000 × 0.31180 = $311.80
P = $573.50 + $311.80 = $885.30

4. On January 1, 19X1, a 14 percent Government of Canada bond with 20 years to maturity sold at its par value of $1 000. At that time, investors as a whole expected inflation to average 10 percent annually. However, by January 1, 19X2, the average annual inflation rate had fallen to 6 percent. Assume that expectations about the real rate of return are constant. What was the likely maximum price of the bond on January 1, 19X2?

(a) The real rate of return on January 1, 19X1, was 4 percent (14 percent yield to maturity less 10 percent inflation. See Chapter 3 for further discussion on this calculation.)

(b) The likely minimum yield to maturity for the bond on January 1, 19X2, was 10 percent (4 percent real rate plus 6 percent inflation). If investors are skeptical about the low inflation rate, they may want a yield to maturity higher than 10 percent.

(c) The likely maximum price for the bond on January 1, 19X2, should be:

$$P + \frac{\$140}{(1+0.10)} + \frac{\$140}{(1+0.10)^2} + \ldots + \frac{\$140}{1+0.10)^{19}} + \frac{\$1\ 000}{(1+0.10)^{19}}$$

We assume that interest is paid annually. Also, note that only 19 years remain to maturity.
$140 discounted for 19 years at 10 percent = $140 × 8.3649 = $1171.08
$1 000 received at the end of 19 years at 10 percent = $1 000 × 0.16351 = 163.51
P = $1 171.08 + $163.51 = $1 334.59

5. A company expects earnings to grow at a rate of 10 percent for three years, then at 5 percent for three additional years after which earnings should be constant. The present dividend of $2.00 is expected to increase at the same rate. The cost of equity capital is 10 percent. Calculate the price of the share.

Note that P_o (i.e. the share price today) is based on dividends expected in the future. Current dividends are $2.00 per share and this has to be increased for future periods. Thus, we start the calculation with dividends expected one period from now.

End of year	Expected dividend	P.V. factor 10%	Present value (rounded)
1	$2.20	0.90909	$2.00
2	2.42	0.82645	2.00
3	2.66	0.75131	2.00
4	2.80	0.68301	1.91
5	2.93	0.62092	1.82
Present value of dividends for first five years			9.73

The dividend is expected to be $3.08 at the end of year 6 and remain at that level forever. So using Eq. (5-11), the price at the end of year 5 (for dividends in year 6 and beyond) is:

$$P_5 = \frac{3.08}{0.10-0.0} = \$30.80$$

The present value of $30.80 is: = $19.12
Price of share (P_o) = $19.12 + 9.73 = $28.85

6. An investor in a share expects to receive a dividend of $1 at the end of year 1. He also expects that the dividend will grow at a 3 percent rate indefinitely. On investments of this type he requires a return of 11 percent. Using Eq. (5-10) calculate the price of a share. Also use Eq. (5-11) to make the same calculation.

Let P_o = price of a share now, D_o = the dividend now, g = the growth rate of dividends and k the required rate of return

$$P_o = \frac{D_o(1 + g)}{(1 + k)} + \frac{D_o(1 + g)^2}{(1 + k)^2} + \ldots + \frac{D_o(1 + g)^\infty}{(1 + k)^\infty}$$ **Eq. (5-10)**

$$P_o = \frac{D_o(1 + 0.03)}{1 + 0.11} + \frac{D_o(1 + 0.03)^2}{(1 + 0.11)^2} + \ldots + \frac{D_o(1 + 0.03)^\infty}{(1 + 0.11)^\infty}$$ (1)

Multiplying both sides of equation (1) by $(1 + 0.11)/(1 + 0.03)$ we get:

$$P_o \frac{(1 + 0.11)}{(1 + 0.03)} = \frac{D_o(1 + 0.03)^\infty(1 + 0.11)}{(1 + 0.11)^\infty(1 + 0.03)} + \frac{D_o(1 + 0.03)^2(1 + 0.11)}{1 + 0.11)^2(1 + 0.03)}$$

$$+ \ldots + \frac{D_o(1 + 0.03)^\infty(1 + 0.11)}{(1 + 0.11)^\infty(1 + 0.03)}$$ (2)

Subtract equation (1) from equation (2)

$$P_o \frac{(1 + 0.11)}{(1 + 0.03)} - P_o = D_o - D_o \frac{(1 + 0.03)^\infty}{(1 + 0.11)^\infty}$$

The term $D_o \dfrac{(1 + 0.03)^\infty}{(1 + 0.11)^\infty}$ approaches 0, therefore:

$$P_o \left[\frac{(1 + 0.11)}{(1 + 0.03)} - 1 \right] = D_o \quad P_o \frac{(1 + 0.11) - (1 + 0.03)}{(1 + 0.03)} = D_o$$

$$P_o (0.11 - 0.03) = D_o (1 + 0.03) \text{ but } D_o (1 + 0.03) = D_1 = \$1$$

$$P_o(0.11 - 0.03) = \$1, \ P_o = \frac{\$1}{0.08} = \$12.50$$

$$P_o = \frac{D_1}{k - g} = \frac{\$1}{0.11 - 0.03} = \frac{\$1}{0.08} = \$12.50$$ **Eq. (5-11)**

7. An investor is considering an investment in three shares; the first has a beta of 8, the second has a beta of 1.2 and the third a beta of 1. The risk free rate is 11 percent and the expected return on the Toronto Stock Exchange index is 14 percent. Calculate the required rate of return on the three shares. What conclusions can be drawn about the risk associated with investment in the three shares.

Use Eq. (5-15)
Share 1: $\overline{R_j} = 0.11 + (0.14 - 0.11)\,0.8 = 13.4\%$
Share 2: $\overline{R_j} = 0.11 + (0.14 - 0.11)\,1.2 = 14.6\%$
Share 3: $\overline{R_j} = 0.11 + (14 - 0.11)1 = 14\%$
Share 1 has less unavoidable risk than the market as a whole; it is a defensive share. Share 2 is aggressive; it has more risk than the entire market. Share 3 has the same risk as the market as a whole and the same expected return.

8. What would be the price of the three shares in the previous problem if each paid a dividend of $2 and was expected to grow at a rate of 10 percent?

$$\text{Share 1: Price of share 1} = \frac{\$2}{0.134 - 10} = \frac{\$2}{0.034} = \$58.82$$

$$\text{Price of share 2} = \frac{\$2}{0.146 - 10} = \frac{\$2}{0.046} = \$43.48$$

$$\text{Price of share 3} = \frac{\$2}{0.14 - 10} = \frac{\$2}{0.04} = \$50.00$$

Problems

1. La Fleur Electric Company Ltd. has outstanding a 3-year, 10 percent bond issue with a face value of $1 000 per bond. Interest is payable annually. The bonds are privately held by Suresafe Fire Insurance Company Ltd. Suresafe wishes to sell the bonds and is negotiating with another party. It estimates that in current market conditions, the bonds should provide a return of 14 percent (yield to maturity). What price per bond should Suresafe be able to realize on their sale?

2. What would be the price per bond in problem 1 if interest payments were semiannual?

3. Superior Cement Company Ltd. has an 8 percent preferred-stock issue outstanding, with each share having a $100 face value. Currently, the yield is 10 percent. What is the market price per share? If interest rates in general should rise so that the required return becomes 12 percent, what will happen to the market price per share?

4. The stock of the Health Company Ltd. is currently selling for $20 a share and is expected to pay a $1 dividend at the end of the year. If you bought the stock now and sold it for $23 after receiving the dividend, what rate of return would you earn?

5. Delphi Products Company Ltd. currently pays a dividend of $2 per share, and this dividend is expected to grow at a 15 percent annual rate for 3 years, then at a 10 percent rate for the next 3 years, after which it is expected to grow at a 5 percent rate forever. What value would you place on the share if an 18 percent rate of return were required?

6. Suppose that you were given the following data for past excess quarterly returns for Karochi Company Ltd. and for the market portfolio:

Quarter	Excess returns Karochi	Excess returns market portfolio
1	0.04	0.05
2	0.05	0.10
3	-0.04	-0.06
4	-0.05	-0.10
5	0.02	0.02
6	0.00	-0.03
7	0.02	0.07
8	-0.01	-0.01
9	-0.02	-0.08
10	0.04	0.00
11	0.07	0.13
12	-0.01	0.04
13	0.01	-0.01
14	-0.06	-0.09
15	-0.06	-0.14
16	-0.02	-0.04
17	0.07	0.15
18	0.02	0.06
19	0.04	0.11
20	0.03	0.05
21	0.01	0.03
22	-0.01	0.01
23	-0.01	-0.03
24	0.02	0.04

On the basis of this information, graph the relationship between the two sets of excess returns and draw a characteristic line. What is the approximate alpha? The approximate beta? What can you say about the systematic risk of the stock, based upon past experience?

7. Assuming the capital-asset-pricing-model approach is appropriate, compute the required rate of return for each of the following stocks, given a risk-free rate of 0.07 and an expected return for the market portfolio of 0.13:

Share	A	B	C	D	E
Beta	1.5	1.0	0.6	2.0	1.3

What implications can you draw?

8. North Great Timber Company Ltd. will pay a dividend of $1.50 a share next year. After this, earnings and dividends are expected to grow at a 9 percent annual rate indefinitely. Investors presently require a rate of return of 13 percent. The company is considering several business strategies and wishes to determine the effect of these strategies on the market price per share of its stock.

(a) Continuing the present strategy will result in the expected growth rate and required rate of return shown above.

(b) Expanding timber holdings and sales will increase the expected dividend growth rate to 11 percent, but will increase the risk of the company. As a result, the rate of return required by investors will increase to 16 percent.

(c) Integrating into retail stores will increase the dividend growth rate to 10 percent and increase the required rate of return to 14 percent.

From the standpoint of market price per share, which strategy is best?

9. On the basis of an analysis of past returns and of inflationary expectations, Maria Goncalves feels that the expected return on stocks in general is 15 percent. The risk-free rate on short-term Treasury securities is now 10 percent. Ms. Goncalves is particularly interested in the return prospects for Kessler Electronics Company Ltd. Based upon monthly data for the past 5 years, she has fitted a characteristic line to the responsiveness of excess returns of the stock to excess returns of the Toronto Stock Exchange Index and has found the slope of the line to be 1.67. If financial markets are believed to be efficient, what return can she expect from investing in Kessler?

10. Currently, the risk-free rate is 10 percent and the expected return on the market portfolio is 15 percent. The expected returns for four stocks are listed below, together with their expected betas.

Stock	Expected return	Expected beta
1. Stillman Zinc Company Ltd.	17.0%	1.3
2. Union Paint Company Ltd.	14.5	0.8
3. National Automobile Company Ltd.	15.5	1.1
4. Parker Electronics Company Ltd.	18.0	1.7

(a) On the basis of these expectations, which stocks are overvalued? Which are undervalued?

(b) If the risk-free rate were to rise to 12 percent and the expected return on the market portfolio to 16 percent, which shares would be overvalued? Which would be under-valued? (Assume the betas stay the same.)

11. On the morning of January 2, 19X1, Mr. Prout purchased, at par, two Government of Canada bonds—10 percent due in 5 years and 12 percent due in 20 years.

(a) At the end of that day, the bank rate was increased rather significantly and on January 3, 19X1, the 5-year bond was priced to sell at $963.00 (for a yield to maturity of 11 percent) and the 20-year bond at $926.70 (for a yield to maturity of 13 percent). If Mr. Prout sold both bonds on January 3, compute his capital loss in percentage terms.

(b) Now disregard part (a) above. At the end of the day (January 2), the bank rate was significantly reduced and on January 3, 19X1, the 5-year bond was priced at $1 038.90 (for a yield to maturity of 9 percent) and the 20-year bond at $1 084.20 (for a yield to maturity of 11 percent). If Mr. Prout sold both bonds on January 3, compute his capital gains in percentage terms.

(c) Now consider your results in parts (a) and (b) above. Can you identify some relationships between bond prices and changes in yields for a given maturity and across different maturities? Try to graph observed relationships.

Selected References

BAUMAN, W. SCOTT, "Investment Returns and Present Values," *Financial Analysts Journal*, 25 (November-December 1969), 107-18.

BLUME, MARSHALL E., "On the Assessment of Risk," *Journal of Finance*, 26 (March 1971), 1-10.

ELTON, EDWIN J., and MARTIN J. GRUBER, "Earnings Estimates and the Accuracy of Expectational Data," *Management Science*, 18 (April 1972), 409-24.

EVANS, JACK, and STEPHEN H. ARCHER, "Diversification and the Reduction of Dispersion: An Empirical Analysis," *Journal of Finance*, 23 (December 1968), 761-67.

FAMA, EUGENE F., "Components of Investment Performance," *Journal of Finance*, 27 (June 1972), 551-67.

_____, *Foundations of Finance*, New York: Basic Books, 1976.

_____, and MERTON H. MILLER, *The Theory of Finance*, New York: Holt, 1972.

IBBOTSON, ROGER G., and REX A. SINQUEFIELD, *Stocks, Bonds, Bills, and Inflation: Historical Returns*. Charlottesville, Va.: Financial Analysts Foundation, 1977.

LORIE, JAMES H., and MARY T. HAMILTON, *The Stock Market*, Homewood. Ill.: Irwin, 1973.

MAO, JAMES C. T., "The Valuation of Growth Stocks: The Investment Opportunities Approach," *Journal of Finance*, 21 (March 1966), 95-102.

MODIGLIANI, FRANCO, and GERALD A. POGUE, "An Introduction to Risk and Return," *Financial Analysts Journal*, 30 (March-April 1974), 68-80, and (May-June 1974), 69-86.

POGUE, GERALD A., and KISHORE LALL, "Corporate Finance: an Overview," *Sloan Management Review*, 15 (Spring 1974), 19-38.

ROGALSKI, RICHARD J. and SEHA M. TINIC, "Risk-Premium Curve vs. Capital Market Line: A Re-examination," *Financial Management*, 7 (Spring 1978), 73-84.

ROLL, RICHARD, "Performance Evaluation and Benchmark Errors," *Journal of Portfolio Management*, 6 (Summer 1980), 5-12.

ROSENBERG, BARR, "The Capital Asset Pricing Model and the Market Model," *Journal of Portfolio Management*, 7 (Winter 1981), 5-16.

ROSENBERG, BARR, and JAMES GUY, "Beta and Investment Fundamentals," *Financial Analysts Journal*, 32 (May-June 1976), 60-72.

SCHALLHEIM, JAMES, and ROBIN DeMAGISTRIS, "New Estimates of the Market Parameters," *Financial Management*, 9 (Autumn 1980), 60-68.

SHARPE, WILLIAM F., "Capital Asset Prices: A Theory of Market Equilibrium under Conditions of Risk," *Journal of Finance*, 19 (September 1964), 425-42.

_____, "A Simplified Model for Portfolio Analysis," *Management Science*, 10 (January 1963), 277-93.

_____, *Investments*, 2d. ed. Englewood Cliffs, N.J.: Prentice-Hall, 1981.

VAN HORNE, JAMES C., *Financial Market Rates and Flows*. Englewood Cliffs. N.J.: Prentice-Hall, 1978.

TOOLS
OF FINANCIAL
ANALYSIS
AND
PLANNING

6

Financial Analysis

Financial analysis means different things to different people. A trade creditor, for example, is primarily interested in the liquidity of the firm being analyzed. His or her claim is short term in nature, and the ability of the firm to pay this claim can best be judged by an analysis of its liquidity. The claim of a bondholder, on the other hand, is long term. Accordingly, he or she is interested in the cash-flow ability of the firm to service debt over a long period of time. The bondholder may evaluate this ability by analyzing the capital structure of the firm, the major sources and uses of funds, the firm's profitability over time, and projections of future profitability. Finally, an investor in a company's common stock is concerned principally with present and expected future earnings as well as with the stability of these earnings about a trend. As a result, the investor usually concentrates his or her analysis on the profitability of the firm.

The point of view of the analyst may be either external or internal. In the cases described, it was external, involving suppliers of capital. From an internal standpoint, the firm needs to undertake financial analysis in order to effectively plan and control. To plan for the future, the financial manager must realistically assess the firm's current financial position and evaluate opportunities in relation to their effect on this position. With respect to internal control, the financial manager is particularly concerned with return on investment of the various assets of the company and in the efficiency of asset management. Finally, in order to bargain effectively for outside funds, the financial manager needs to be attuned to all aspects of financial analysis that outside suppliers of capital use in evaluating the firm. We see, then, that the type of financial analysis varies according to the particular interests of the analyst.

Financial Statements

Financial analysis involves the use of financial statements, which come in different forms. The *balance sheet* shows the assets and liabilities of a business firm at a moment in time, usually at the end of a year or a quarter. An *income statement* shows the revenues, expenses, taxes, and profits of a firm for a particular period of time, again usually a year or a quarter. While the balance sheet shows a snap shot of the firm's financial position at a moment in time, the income statement depicts its profitability over time. From these statements, certain information can be derived, such as a statement of retained earnings and a source and use of funds statement. (We consider the latter in the next chapter.)

BALANCE SHEET INFORMATION

In Table 6-1, the balance sheet of King Manufacturing Company Ltd. is shown for the fiscal years ending March 31, 1984 and March 31, 1983. The assets are shown in the upper panel and are listed according to their relative degree of liquidity. For example, cash and marketable securities are the most liquid of assets and they appear first; fixed assets, long-term investment, and goodwill are the least liquid and they appear last. Accounts receivable are IOUs from customers that should convert into cash within a given billing period, usually 30 to 60 days. Inventories, on the other hand, are used in the manufacture of a product. The product must first be sold and a receivable generated before it can go the next step and be converted into cash. One should recognize that goodwill is not a tangible asset. Rather, it represents the imputed value associated with a brand label, a product line, or the like. Its value, if realized at all, will come from future earnings of the firm.

The bottom panel of the table shows the liabilities and net worth of the company. These are ordered according to which are likely to be paid first. For example, all of the current liabilities are payable within one year, whereas the long-term debt is payable beyond one year. Shareholders' equity will be paid only through regular dividends and, perhaps, a final liquidation dividend. Shareholders' equity; or *net worth* as it is called, consists of several sub-categories. The first, common stock, represents stock purchased by investors and paid into the company in years gone by. As will be discussed in Chapter 22, a par value can be assigned to the stock. In this case, the par value is $10 per share, which means that on March 31, 1984, there were 44 000 shares of common stock outstanding. The contributed capital section is the excess of monies paid for the stock above its par value. For example, if the company were to sell an additional share of stock for $16, there would be a $10 increase in the common stock section and a $5 increase in the contributed capital section.[1] Retained earnings are the cumulative profits of a company after dividends are paid. In this sense, it is a residual.

---

[1] Only no-par issue shares can be issued under the Canada Business Corporations Act, in this situation the entire sale price of the shares is credited to the common stock account.

TABLE 6-1 Balance Sheet of King Manufacturing Ltd.

Assets	March 31, 1984	March 31, 1983
Cash and marketable securities	$ 488 000	$ 484 000
Accounts receivable (net)	531 000	502 000
Inventories, at the lower of cost or market	788 000	750 000
Prepaid expenses	67 000	34 000
Current assets	$1 874 000	$1 770 000
Fixed assets at cost	1 807 000	1 730 000
Less accumulated depreciation	863 000	773 000
Net fixed assets	$ 944 000	$ 957 000
Investment—Long-term	55 000	—
Goodwill	298 000	298 000
	$3 171 000	$3 025 000

Liabilities and Shareholders' Equity	March 31, 1984	March 31, 1983
Bank loans and notes payable	$ 666 000	$ 615 000
Accounts payable	176 000	188 000
Accrued liabilities	192 000	153 000
Current liabilities	$1 034 000	$ 956 000
Long-term debt	302 000	285 000
Shareholders' equity		
Common stock, $10 par value	440 000	440 000
Contributed capital—premium on common shares	382 000	382 000
Retained earnings	1 013 000	962 000
Total shareholders' equity	$1 835 000	$1 784 000
	$3 171 000	$3 025 000

We see in the table that total assets equal total liabilities plus net worth. Indeed, that is an accounting identity. Also, it follows that assets less liabilities equals net worth. For the most part, the liabilities of a firm are known with certainty. Most accounting questions concerning the balance sheet are about numbers attached to the assets. We must remember that the figures are accounting numbers and not estimates of the economic value of assets. The value of fixed assets is based on actual costs, not what they would cost today. (The latter is known as the *replacement cost*.) Inventories are valued at cost or market value, whichever is lower, while receivables may include some accounts which may prove to be bad debts. Thus, on many occasions, it is necessary to go beyond the reported figures in order to properly analyze the financial condition of the firm. Depending on the analysis, the net worth figure shown on the financial statement, which is a residual, may or may not be a reasonable approximation of the true net worth of the firm.

INCOME STATEMENT

The income statement in Table 6-2 shows the revenues and net income of King Manufacturing Ltd. for the two fiscal years. The cost of goods sold is the actual cost of producing the goods. Included here are purchases of raw materials and other items, labor costs associated with production, and other manufacturing expenses. Selling, general, and administrative expenses are shown separately from the costs of goods sold so that we can analyze them directly. Depreciation was discussed in Chapter 2. It is important to point out, however, that depreciation is based on historical costs, which in a period of inflation do not conform to economic costs. Therefore, the profit figure may be distorted. The subject of inflation and financial analysis is explored in the appendix to this chapter.

The last three rows of the income statement shown in Table 6-2 represent a simplified statement of retained earnings. Dividends are deducted from earnings after taxes to give the increase in retained earnings. The increase of $51 000 in fiscal year 1984 should agree with the balance sheet figures shown in Table 6-1. On the two dates, retained earnings were $1 013 000 and $962 000, their difference being $51 000. Therefore, there is agreement. It is important to recognize that retained earnings are a residual claim on assets after all liabilities have been paid. They are not to be considered as funds available to the shareholders since such availability depends on the firm's liquidity.

A Possible Framework for Analysis

There are a number of conceptual frameworks that might be used in analyzing a firm. Many analysts have a favorite procedure for making some generalizations

TABLE 6-2 Income Statement of King Manufacturing Ltd.

	Year Ended March 31, 1984	Year Ended March 31, 1983
Net sales	$2 501 000	$2 493 000
Cost of goods sold	1 900 000	1 914 000
Gross margin	$ 601 000	$ 579 000
Selling, general and administration expenses	261 000	283 000
Depreciation	90 000	97 000
Interest expenses	64 000	58 000
Earnings before taxes	186 000	141 000
Income taxes	91 000	70 000
Earnings after taxes	$ 95 000	$ 71 000
Cash dividends	44 000	44 000
Increase in retained earnings	$ 51 000	$ 27 000

about the firm being analyzed. At the risk of treading on some rather sacred ground, we present a conceptual framework lending itself to situations in which external financing is contemplated. The factors to be considered are shown in Fig. 6-1.

Taking them in order, our concern in the first case is with the trend and seasonal component of a firm's funds requirements. How much will be required in the future and what is the nature of these needs? Is there a seasonal component to the needs? Analytical tools used to answer these questions include source and use of funds statements and the cash budget, both of which are considered in Chapter 7. The tools used to assess the financial condition and performance of the firm are financial ratios, a topic taken up in this chapter. With these ratios, the skilled analyst examines the company being analyzed from a number of different angles, in the hope of obtaining valuable insight into its financial condition and profitability. The last factor in the first row of Fig. 6-1, business risk, relates to the risk inherent in the operations of the enterprise. Some companies are in highly volatile lines of endeavor, while others are in very stable lines. A machine tool company would fall in the former category, while an electric utility would be in the latter. The analyst needs to estimate the degree of business risk of the firm being analyzed.

All three factors should be used in determining the financing needs of the firm. Moreover, they should be considered jointly. The greater the funds requirements, of course, the greater the total financing that will be necessary. The nature of the funds needs influences the type of financing that should be used. If there is a seasonal aspect to the business, it will influence short term financing, and bank loans in particular. The basic business risk of the firm also has an important effect on the type of financing that should be used. The greater the business risk, the less desirable debt financing becomes relative to common-stock financing. In other words, equity financing is safer in that there is no contractual obligation to pay interest and principal as there is with debt. A firm with a high degree of business

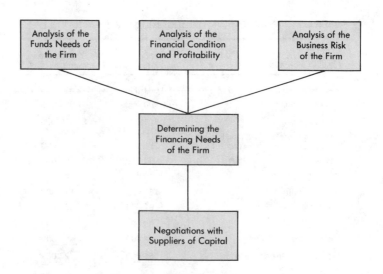

FIGURE 6-1 Framework for financial analysis

risk is generally ill-advised to take on considerable financial risk as well. The financial condition and performance of the firm also influence the type of financing that should be used. The greater the liquidity, the stronger the overall financial condition, and the greater the profitability of the firm, the more risk that can be incurred with respect to the type of financing. That is, debt financing becomes more attractive with improvements in liquidity, financial condition, and profitability.

The last box in Fig. 6-1 gives recognition to the fact that it is not sufficient simply to determine the best financing plan from the standpoint of the firm and assume that it can be consummated. The plan needs to be sold to outside suppliers of capital. The firm may determine that it needs $1 million in short term financing but lenders may not go along with either the amount or the type of financing. In the end, the firm may have to compromise on its plan to meet the realities of the marketplace. The interaction of the firm and these suppliers of capital determine the amount, terms, and price of financing. The fact that the firm must negotiate with outside suppliers of capital serves as a feedback mechanism for the other four factors in Fig. 6-1. Analysis cannot be undertaken disregarding the fact that ultimately an appeal will need to be made to suppliers of capital. Similarly, suppliers of capital must recognize that a company may approach the question of financing from a different point of view than their own and learn to appreciate the difference.

Thus, there are a number of facets to financial analysis. Presumably, analysis will be in relation to some structural framework similar to that presented above. Otherwise, it is likely to be loose and not really answer the questions for which it was intended. As we have seen, an integral part of financial analysis is the analysis of financial ratios; and that will occupy our attention in the remainder of this chapter.

USE OF FINANCIAL RATIOS

To evaluate the financial condition and performance of a firm, the financial analyst needs certain yardsticks. The yardstick frequently used is a ratio, or index, relating two pieces of financial data to each other. Analysis and interpretation of various ratios should give an experienced and skilled analyst a better understanding of the financial condition and performance of the firm than he or she would obtain from analysis of the financial data alone. The analysis of financial ratios involves two types of comparison.

Internal comparisons First, the analyst can compare a present ratio with past and expected future ratios for the same company. For example, the current ratio (the ratio of current assets to current liabilities) for the current year end could be compared with the current ratio for the previous year end. When financial ratios are arrayed on a spread sheet over a period of years, the analyst can study the composition of change and determine whether there has been an improvement or deterioration in the financial condition and performance of the firm over time. Financial ratios can also be computed for projected or *pro forma* statements and compared with present and past ratios.

External comparisons The second method of comparison involves comparing the ratios of one firm with those of similar firms or with industry averages at the same point in time. Such a comparison gives insight into the relative financial condition and performance of the firm. Financial ratios for various industries are published by Dun & Bradstreet and various other credit agencies and trade associations.[2] The analyst should avoid using "rules of thumb" indiscriminately for all industries. For example, the criterion that all companies should have at least 2 to 1 current ratio is inappropriate. The analysis must be in relation to the type of business in which the firm is engaged and to the firm itself. Many sound companies have current ratios of less than 2 to 1. Only by comparing the financial ratios of one firm with those of similar firms can one make a realistic judgment.

TYPES OF RATIOS

For our purposes, financial ratios can be divided into four types: liquidity, debt, profitability, and coverage ratios. The first two types are ratios computed from the balance sheet; the last two are ratios computed from the income statement and, sometimes, from both the income statement and the balance sheet. It is important to recognize from the outset that no one ratio gives us sufficient information to judge the financial condition and performance of the firm. Only when we analyze a group of ratios are we able to make reasonable judgments. In addition, it is very important to take into account any seasonal character in a business. Underlying trends may be assessed only through a comparison of raw figures and ratios at the same time of year. For example, we would not compare a December 31 balance sheet with a May 31 balance sheet but would compare December 31 with December 31.

Although the number of financial ratios that might be computed increases geometrically with the amount of financial data, only the more important ratios are considered in this chapter. Actually, the ratios needed to assess the financial condition and performance of a company are relatively few in number. To compute unneeded ratios complicates the analysis and creates confusion. Also, accounting data from different companies should be standardized as much as possible. It is important to compare apples with apples and oranges with oranges. Even with standardized figures, however, the analyst should use caution in interpreting the comparisons.

In order to illustrate the ratios taken up in this chapter, we use the balance sheet and income statements of King Manufacturing Ltd. shown in Tables 6-1 and 6-2. We will compute the ratios for 1984 and show how they are used to assess the financial position of the firm for that year. Where possible, we will compare the firm's ratios with those for its industry as reported by Dun & Bradstreet. Later in this chapter, we will present the financial ratios for King Manufacturing Ltd. for the period 1975–84.

---

[2]Dun & Bradstreet calculates annually 11 important ratios for 166 lines of business. Statistics Canada publishes some financial ratios by industries. These ratios are published in several sources: *Industrial Corporations, Manufacturing Industries of Canada*, and *Corporation Financial Statistics*. The Financial Post publishes a variety of ratios for individual companies. See *Financial Post Yellow Cards* and *Financial Post Computer Services*.

Liquidity ratios are used to judge a firm's ability to meet short-term obligations.[3] From them, much insight can be gained into the cash solvency position of the firm and its ability to remain solvent.

CURRENT RATIO

One of the most general and frequently used liquidity ratios is the *current ratio* measured as

$$\frac{\text{Current assets}}{\text{Current liabilities}}$$

As you can see, this ratio indicates the number of times that cash and proceeds from the liquidation of other current assets (accounts receivable and inventories in particular) can cover (or pay off) total current liabilities. We assume that all current assets may be liquidated at 100 percent of book values shown in the balance sheet. From Table 6-1, the 1984 current ratio for King is

$$\frac{1\ 874\ 000}{1\ 034\ 000} = 1.81 \text{ (times)}$$

King is engaged in making general electrical equipment. Its current ratio is somewhat above the median ratio for the industry of 1.52. (The median for the industry is found in Dun & Bradstreet, *Key Business Ratios in Canada*.) Though comparisons with industry averages do not always reveal financial strength or weakness, they are meaningful in identifying companies that are out of line. Where a significant deviation occurs, the analyst will want to determine the reasons for this occurrence. Perhaps the industry is overly liquid and the company being examined is basically sound despite a lower current ratio. In another situation, the company being analyzed may be too liquid, relative to the industry, with the result that it forgoes profitability. Whenever a "red flag" is raised, it is important for the analyst to search out the reasons behind it.

In computing the current ratio, we assume that the current assets can be liquidated at 100 percent of book values. This may not always be the case—there may be bad debts and inventories may be sold at less than cost. As a financial analyst, you can assess the extent to which the value of current assets can fall without impairing the firm's ability to pay its current liabilities. For example, in 1984, King would have to realize $0.55 (1/1.81) on every dollar of current assets to meet its current liabilities.

---

[3]We have defined liquidity as the ability to realize value in money, the most liquid of assets. Liquidity has two dimensions: (1) the time required to convert the asset into money and (2) the certainty of the realized price. To the extent that the price realized on receivables is as predictable as that realized on inventories, receivables would be a more liquid asset than inventories, owing to the shorter time required to convert the asset into money. If the price realized on receivables is more certain than that on inventories, receivables would be regarded as being even more liquid.

Supposedly, the higher the current ratio, the greater the ability of the firm to pay its bills. However, the ratio must be regarded as crude because it does not take into account the liquidity of the individual components of the current assets. A firm having current assets composed principally of cash and current receivables is generally regarded as more liquid than a firm whose current assets consist primarily of inventories. Consequently, we must turn to "finer" tools of analysis if we are to evaluate critically the liquidity of the firm.

ACID-TEST RATIO

A somewhat more accurate guide to liquidity is the *quick*, or *acid-test, ratio*.

$$\frac{\text{Cash and marketable securities} + \text{Receivables}}{\text{Current liabilities}}$$

From Table 6-1, the 1984 quick or acid test ratio for King is:

$$\frac{\$488\ 000 + \$531\ 000}{1\ 034\ 000} = 0.99\ (times)$$

The ratio concentrates on cash, marketable securities, and receivables, the most liquid of the current assets, in relation to current obligations and, thus, provides a more penetrating measure of liquidity than does the current ratio. Dun & Bradstreet does not publish an industry acid-test ratio so we cannot compare King's acid test ratios with other firms in the same industry. However, the ratio indicates that the firm can just about pay its current debts with cash and proceeds from the liquidation of marketable securities and receivables (assuming that these assets can be liquidated at 100 percent of book values shown in the balance sheet).

LIQUIDITY OF RECEIVABLES

The current and acid test ratios assume that receivables are liquid (i.e. they are collected on time). However, this may not always be the case. A firm may have a large investment in receivables and this may enhance the current and acid test ratios, but a large percentage of those receivables may be months overdue. Thus the current and acid test ratios could give a misleading favorable impression of the liquidity of the firm. The financial analyst should assess the liquidity of receivables. To do this, we have two basic ratios, the first of which is the *average collection period* ratio.

$$\frac{\text{Receivables} \times \text{Days in year}}{\text{Annual credit sales}}$$

From Table 6-1, the 1984 average collection period ratios for King is

$$\frac{\$531\ 000 \times 365}{\$2\ 501\ 000} = 78\ \text{days}$$

The average collection period tells us the average number of days receivables are outstanding.

The second ratio is the *receivable turnover ratio*.

$$\frac{\text{Annual credit sales}}{\text{Receivables}}$$

From Table 6-1, 1984 receivable turnover ratio for King is

$$\frac{\$2\ 501\ 000}{\$531\ 000} = 4.71 \text{ (times)}$$

Actually, these two ratios are inverses of each other. For example, for 1984, the number of days in the year, 365, divided by the average collection period, 78 days, gives the receivable turnover ratio, 4.71. The number of days in the year divided by the turnover ratio gives the average collection period. Thus either of these two ratios can be employed.

When credit sales figures for a period are not available, we must resort to total sales figures. The receivable figure used in the calculation ordinarily represents year-end receivables. However, when sales are seasonal or have grown considerably over the year, using the year-end receivable balance may not be appropriate. With seasonality, an average of the monthly closing balances may be the most appropriate figure to use. With growth, the receivable balance at the end of the year will be deceptively high in relation to sales. In this case, an average of receivables at the beginning and at the end of the year might be appropriate in the former calculation if the growth in sales was steady throughout the year.

The average industry receivable turnover ratio is 6.4, which tells us that King's receivables are considerably slower in turning over than is typical for the industry (78 days versus 57 days). The finding should cause the analyst concern. One thing he or she should check is the billing terms given on sales. For example, if the average collection period is 78 days and the terms given are 2/10, net 30,[4] he or she would know that a sizable proportion of the receivables are past due beyond the final due date of 30 days. On the other hand, if the terms are net 60, the typical receivable is being collected 18 days after the final due date. Suppose that on further investigation the analyst finds King's credit policy to be too liberal. As a result, many receivables are past due, with some uncollectible. Profits are less than those possible owing to bad debt losses and the need to finance a large investment in receivables. In short, the investigation reveals that King is considerably less liquid with respect to receivables than is suggested by a cursory glance at its current asset position.

Although too high an average collection period is usually bad, a very low average collection period may not necessarily be good. It may be that credit policy is excessively restrictive. The receivables on the book may be of prime quality and yet sales may be curtailed unduly—and profits less than they might be—because of this policy. In this situation, credit standards for an acceptable account might be relaxed somewhat.

Another means by which we can obtain insight into the liquidity of receivables is through an *aging of accounts*. With this method, we categorize the

---

[4]The notation means that the supplier gives a 2 percent discount if the receivable invoice is paid within 10 days, and payment is due within 30 days if the discount is not taken.

receivables at a moment in time according to the month when the credit sales were made. We might have the following hypothetical aging of accounts receivable at December 31:

Proportion of Receivables Billed in

December	November	October	September	August and before	Total
67%	19%	7%	2%	5%	100%

If the billing terms are 2/10, net 30, this aging tells us that 67 percent of the receivables at December 31 are current, 19 percent are up to one month past due, 7 percent are one to two months past due, and so on. Depending upon the conclusions drawn from our analysis of the aging, we may want to examine more closely the credit and collection policies of the company. In the example above, we might be prompted to investigate the individual receivables that were billed in August and before, in order to determine if any should be charged off. The receivables shown on the books are only as good as the likelihood that they will be collected. An aging of accounts receivable gives us considerably more information than the calculation of the average collection period, because it pinpoints the trouble spots more specifically.

Both the average collection period and the aging of accounts receivable are affected by the pattern of sales. With rising sales, the average collection period and the aging will be more current than if sales are level, all other things the same. The reason is that a greater portion of sales is billed currently. On the other hand, when sales are declining over time, the average collection period and the aging will be less current than if sales are level. Here the reason is that a lower portion of sales is billed currently. Although the average collection period and the aging measures will not be significantly affected if there is only a modest and steady trend in sales, they will be affected if there is a rapid change in the pattern of sales or if there is a fluctuating pattern of sales behavior over time. For these situations, the average collection period and the aging schedule are not realistic portrayals of the liquidity of receivables. Adjustments in analysis should be made. For seasonal sales patterns, it is useful to compare the average collection period and aging at one point with the average collection period and aging at the same point in another year. We might compare the average collection period and an aging at the end of May with those at the end of May in another year.

The meaningful thing is to try to separate changes in the payment behavior of customers from changes in the pattern of sales. One way to do so is with a conversion matrix of receivables into cash.[5] Such a matrix is illustrated in Table 6-3. As we see, the matrix tells us the amount of credit sales in a given month and the

---

[5]Similar approaches have been proposed by W. G. Lewellen and R. W. Johnson, "Better Way to Monitor Accounts Receivable," *Harvard Business Review*, 50 (May-June 1972), 101–9; W. G. Lewellen and R. O. Edmister, "A General Model for Accounts Receivable Analysis and Control," *Journal of Financial and Quantitative Analysis*, 8 (March 1973), 195–206; and Bernell K. Stone, "The Payments-Pattern Approach to the Forecasting and Control of Accounts Receivable," *Financial Management*, 5 (Autumn 1976), 65–82. All three article give a detailed analysis of the problem as it relates in particular to the average collection period and the aging of accounts receivable.

TABLE 6-3 Conversion Matrix of Credit Sales to Cash

Month	Credit Sales	Month When Cash is Received					
		Jan., 19X2	Feb.	Mar.	Apr.	May	June
Oct., 19X1	$6 000	$ 600 (10%)[a]					
Nov.	4 000	900 (23%)	$ 300 (8%)	$ 125 (3%)			
Dec.	3 000	1 400 (47%)	700 (23%)	400 (13%)			
Jan., 19X2	5 000	700 (14%)	2 500 (50%)	1 200 (24%)	$ 600 (12%)		
Feb.	6 000		900 (15%)	3 200 (53%)	1 500 (25%)	$ 400 (7%)	
Mar.	7 000			1 200 (17%)	3 300 (47%)	1 900 (27%)	$ 600 (9%)
Apr.	8 000				1 110 (14%)	4 100 (51%)	1 900 (24%)
May	7 000					1 300 (19%)	3 300 (47%)
Jun.	5 000						700 (14%)
Total collections		$3 600	$4 400	$6 125	$6 500	$7 700	$6 500

[a] The percentages are in relation to credit sales shown in the second column.

months when the receivables so generated are collected. At the right of each collection amount, the percentage that amount represents in relation to total credit sales is shown. At the bottom, total collections are shown for each month. The advantage of this type of calculation is that it permits the financial analyst to concentrate on the payment pattern of customers month-by-month as opposed to the combined payment and sales patterns. By tracing the collections in a month to the date of sales, we can determine if the firm's collection experience is improving or deteriorating. If sales change significantly over time, this isolation of payments behavior from sales behavior is critical. The principal limitation to the use of a conversion matrix is that such information is available only from the company and cannot be derived from financial statements. The same limitation applies to an aging of accounts receivable. In fact, the same information necessary to prepare an aging schedule can be used to derive a conversion matrix.

DURATION OF PAYABLES

From a creditor's point of view, it is desirable to obtain an *aging of accounts payable* or a *conversion matrix for payables*. These measures, combined with the less exact *turnover of payables* (annual purchases divided by payables), enable the firm to analyze payables in much the same manner as receivables. Also, the firm can compute the average age of its accounts payable. The *average age of payables* is

$$\frac{\text{Accounts payable} \times 365}{\text{Purchase of raw materials}}$$

where accounts payable is the average balance outstanding for the year; and the denominator is the purchase of raw material during the year. This information is valuable in evaluating the probability that a credit applicant will pay on time. If the average age of payables is 48 days, and the terms in the industry are net 30, we know that a portion of the applicant's payables are not being paid on time. A credit check of other suppliers will give insight into the severity of the problem.

LIQUIDITY OF INVENTORIES

When we assess the liquidity of a firm, we should review the liquidity of inventories to determine if the levels of stocks held by the firm are appropriate given its operations. We may compute the *inventory turnover ratio* and regard it as an indicator of the liquidity of inventory. It is calculated for a specific period and this period should be stated when the ratio is given.

$$\text{Inventory turnover} = \frac{\text{Cost of goods sold}}{\text{Average inventory}}$$

From Table 6-1 and 6-2, the 1984 inventory turnover ratio for King is

$$\frac{\$1\ 900\ 000}{(\$788\ 000 + \$750\ 000)/2} = \frac{\$1\ 900\ 000}{\$769\ 000} = 2.47(\text{times})$$

The figure for cost of goods sold used in the numerator is for the period being studied—usually one year; the average inventory figure used in the denominator typically is an average of beginning and ending inventories for the period. As with receivables, however, it may be necessary to compute a more sophisticated average when there is a strong seasonal element. The inventory turnover ratio tells us the rapidity with which the inventory is turned over into receivables through sales. This ratio, like other ratios, must be judged in relation to past and expected future ratios of the firm and in relation to ratios of similar firms, the industry average, or both.

Generally, the higher the inventory turnover, the more efficient the inventory management of a firm. However, a relatively high inventory turnover ratio may be the result of too low a level of inventory and frequent stockouts. It might also be the result of too many small orders for inventory replacement. Either of these situations may be more costly to the firm than carrying a larger investment in inventory and having a lower turnover ratio. Again, caution is necessary in interpreting the ratio. When the inventory turnover ratio is relatively low, it indicates slow-moving inventory or obsolescence of some of the stock. Obsolescence may necessitate substantial write-downs, which, in turn, would negate the treatment of inventory as a liquid asset. Because the turnover ratio is a somewhat crude measure, we would want to investigate any perceived inefficiency in inventory management. In this regard, it is helpful to compute the turnover of the major categories of inventory to see if there are imbalances, which may indicate excessive investment in specific components of the inventory. Once we have a hint of a problem, we must investigate it more specifically to determine its cause.

King's inventory turnover ratio of 2.47 compares with an average turnover for the industry of 4.2. This unfavorable comparison suggests that the company is less efficient in inventory management than is the industry and that it holds excessive stock. A question also arises as to whether the inventory on the books is worth its stated value. If not, the liquidity of the firm is less than the current or quick ratio alone suggests. The whole problem should be investigated along the lines of our previous discussion to determine its cause.

SUMMARY OF KING'S LIQUIDITY

Although a comparison of King's current ratio with the average for the industry is favorable, a more detailed examination of receivables and inventory reveals some problems. The turnover ratios for both of these assets are significantly less than the average ratios for the industry. These findings suggest that the two assets are not entirely current, and this factor detracts from the favorable current ratio. A sizable portion of receivables are slow and there appear to be inefficiencies in inventory management. On the basis of our analysis, we conclude that the assets are not particularly liquid in the sense of turning over into cash in a reasonable period of time.

Debt Ratios

Extending our analysis to the long-term liquidity of the firm (i.e., its ability to meet long-term obligations), we may use several debt ratios. The *debt-to-net-worth ratio* is computed by simply dividing the total debt of the firm (including current liabilities) by its net worth.

$$\frac{\text{Total debt}}{\text{Net worth}}$$

From Table 6-1, the 1984 *debt-to-net worth ratio* for King is

$$\frac{\$1\ 336\ 000}{\$1\ 835\ 000} = 0.73$$

Total debt financing is 0.73 times (or 73%) of net worth or shareholders' equity. The median debt-to-net worth ratio for the industry is 2.08 so King is more conservatively financial than other companies in the industry. Presumably it would not experience difficulty with creditors because of an excessive debt ratio.

Sometimes we may want to check to see if there are imbalances between current liabilities and long-term debt. Too many current liabilities may put strain on a firm's short-term liquidity position since these debts mature in the near future. We can use the *current liabilities-to-net worth ratio* to help in such an assessment. This ratio is measured as

$$\frac{\text{Current liabilities}}{\text{Net worth}}$$

From Table 6-1, the 1984 current liabilities-to-net worth ratio for King is

$$\frac{\$1\ 034\ 000}{\$1\ 835\ 000} = 0.56$$

The median current *liabilities-to-net worth ratio* for the industry is 1.43 so King is using proportionately less current liabilities relative to other companies in the industry.

When intangible assets are significant, they frequently are deducted from net worth to obtain the tangible net worth of the firm. Depending upon the purpose for which the ratio is used, preferred stock sometimes is included as debt rather than as net worth. Preferred stock represents a prior claim from the standpoint of the investors in common stock; consequently, we might include preferred stock as debt when analyzing a firm. The ratio of debt to equity will vary according to the nature of the business and volatility of cash flows. An electric utility, with very stable cash flows, usually will have a higher debt ratio than will a machine tool company, whose cash flows are far less stable. A comparison of the debt ratio for a given company with those of similar firms gives us a general indication of the credit-worthiness and financial risk of the firm.

In addition to the ratio of total debt to equity, we may wish to compute the following ratio, which deals with only the long term capitalization of the firm:

$$\frac{\text{Long term debt}}{\text{Total capitalization}}$$

where total capitalization represents all long-term debt and net worth. From Table 6-1, the 1984 *long-term debt-to-total capitalization ratio* for King is

$$\frac{\$302\ 000}{\$2\ 137\ 000} = 0.14$$

This measure tells us the relative importance of long-term debt in the capital structure. Again this ratio is well below the median ratio of 0.65 for the industry.

The debt ratios computed above have been based upon book-value figures; it is sometimes useful to calculate these ratios using market values. In summary, debt ratios tell us the relative proportions of capital contribution by creditors and by owners.

CASH FLOW TO DEBT

A measure of the ability of a company to service its debt is the relationship of annual cash flow to the amount of debt outstanding. The cash flow of a company usually is defined as the cash generated from the operations of the company. In the case of a profitable company, it is comprised of net income and depreciation. The *cash-to-flow total liabilities* ratio is simply

$$\frac{\text{Cash flow}}{\text{Total liabilities}}$$

From Tables 6-1 and 6-2, the 1984 *cash flow-to-total liabilities ratio* is

$$\frac{\$185\ 000}{\$1\ 336\ 000} = 0.14$$

The cash flow is computed as earnings after taxes of $95 000 plus depreciation of $90 000. We see that in 1984, cash flow could pay off about 14 percent of total liabilities. This ratio is useful in assessing the credit worthiness of a company seeking short- or intermediate-term debt, such as a bank loan. Another ratio is the *cash flow-to-long-term debt ratio*

$$\frac{\text{Cash flow}}{\text{Long term debt}}$$

From Tables 6-1 and 6-2, the 1984 *cash flow-to-long-term debt ratio* is

$$\frac{\$185\ 000}{\$302\ 000} = 0.61$$

This ratio tends to be used in the evaluation of the bonds of a company. The two cash flow ratios described above have proven useful in predicting the deteriorating financial health of a company. Unfortunately, median ratios for the industry are not available for comparison.

Profitability Ratios

Profitability ratios are of two types: those showing profitability in relation to sales and those showing profitability in relation to investment. Together, these ratios give us an indication of the firm's efficiency of operation.

PROFITABILITY IN RELATION TO SALES

The first ratio we consider is the *gross profit margin*.

$$\frac{\text{Sales less cost of goods sold}}{\text{Sales}}$$

From Table 6-2, the 1984 gross profit margin for King is

$$\frac{\$601\ 000}{\$2\ 501\ 000} = 24\%$$

This ratio tells us the profit of the firm relative to sales after we deduct the cost of producing the goods sold. It indicates the efficiency of production as well as how products are priced. King's gross profit margin is about the same as the industry average of 23.5 percent.

A more specific ratio of profitability is the *net profit margin*

$$\frac{\text{Net profits after taxes}}{\text{Sales}}$$

For King, this ratio is

$$\frac{\$95\ 000}{\$2\ 501\ 000} = 3.8\%$$

The net profit margin tells us the relative efficiency of the firm after taking into account all expenses and income taxes. King's net profit margin is again about the same as the average margin for the industry: 3.97%.

By considering both ratios jointly, we are able to gain considerable insight into the operations of the firm. For example, if the gross profit margin is essentially unchanged over a period of several years, but the net profit margin has declined over the same period, we know that the cause is either higher expenses relative to sales or a higher tax rate. Therefore, we would analyze these factors more specifically to determine the cause of the problem. On the other hand, if the gross profit margin falls, we know that the cost of producing the goods relative to sales has increased. This occurrence, in turn, may be due to lower prices or to lower operating efficiency in relation to volume. If expenses are constant in relation to sales, we would know that the lower net profit margin is due entirely to the higher cost of producing the goods relative to sales.

There are any number of combinations of changes possible in the gross and net profit margins. Indications of the sort illustrated above tell us where we should investigate further. In our analysis, it is useful to examine over time each of the individual expense items as a percentage of sales. By so doing, we can pick out specific areas of deterioration or improvement.

PROFITABILITY IN RELATION TO INVESTMENT

The second group of profitability ratios relates profits to investments. One of these measures is the *rate of return on common stock equity*.

$$\frac{\text{Net profits after taxes less preferred stock dividend}}{\text{Net worth less par value of preferred stock}}$$

From Tables 6-1 and 6-2, the 1984 *rate of return on common equity* is

$$\frac{\$95\ 000}{\$1\ 835\ 000} = 5.18\%$$

This ratio tells us the earning power on shareholders' book investment and is frequently used in comparing two or more firms in an industry. King's rate of return is well below the average return for the industry of 19.5 percent. Thus, while King has the same profit margin on its sales as the industry, it has a lower return on its net worth. This phenomenon suggests that King uses relatively greater investment by shareholders than do most other firms in the industry.

To investigate the problem directly, we turn to the *return-on-assets ratio*.

$$\frac{\text{Net profit after taxes}}{\text{Total tangible assets}}$$

From Tables 6-1 and 6-2, the 1984 *return-on-assets ratio* for King is

$$\frac{\$95\ 000}{\$2\ 873\ 000} = 3.31\%$$

where goodwill is deducted from total assets to obtain total tangible assets. This ratio compares with an average for the industry of 9.34 percent. With the same profitability per dollar of sales but a lower return on assets, we know that King must employ more assets to generate a dollar of sales than does the industry on the average.

TURNOVER AND EARNING POWER

The relationship of sales to total assets is the asset turnover, known as the *turnover ratio*.

$$\frac{\text{Sales}}{\text{Total tangible assets}}$$

King's turnover for the 1984 fiscal year was

$$\frac{\$2\ 501\ 000}{\$2\ 873\ 000} = 0.87\text{(times)}$$

The median turnover for the industry is 2.36, so it is clear that King employs more assets per dollar of sales than does the industry on the average. The turnover ratio tells us the relative efficiency with which a firm utilizes its resources to generate output. King is less efficient than the industry in this regard. Our previous analysis of King's liquidity indicates that this occurrence could well be the result of excessive investments in receivables and inventories.

When we multiply the asset turnover of the firm by the net profit margin, we obtain the return-on-assets ratio, or *earning power* on total tangible assets

$$\begin{aligned}
\text{Earning power} &= \frac{\text{Sales}}{\text{Total tangible assets}} \times \frac{\text{Net profit after taxes}}{\text{Sales}} \\
&= \frac{\text{Net profit after taxes}}{\text{Total tangible assets}} \\
&= \text{Return on assets ratio}
\end{aligned}$$

For King,

$$\text{Earning power} = 0.87 \times 3.8 = 3.31\%$$

Earning power for the industry is 9.37 percent (2.36 × 3.97). Neither the net profit margin nor the turnover ratio by itself provides an adequate measure of operating efficiency. The net profit margin ignores the utilization of assets, whereas the turnover ratio ignores profitability on sales. The return on assets ratio, or earning power, resolves these shortcomings. An improvement in the earning power of the firm will result if there is an increase in turnover on existing assets, an increase in the net profit margin, or both. The interrelation of these ratios is shown in Fig. 6-2. Two firms with different asset turnovers and net profit margins may have the same earning power. For example, Firm A, with an asset turnover of 4 to 1 and net profit of 3 percent has the same earning power—12 percent—as Firm B, with an asset turnover of 1.5 to 1 and a net profit margin of 8 percent.

With all of the profitability ratios, comparisons of a company with similar companies are extremely valuable. Only by comparison are we able to judge whether the profitability of a particular company is good or bad, and why. Absolute figures provide some insight, but it is relative performance that is most important.

Coverage Ratios

Coverage ratios are designed to relate the financial charges of a firm to its ability to service them. Such bond rating services as Moody's Investors Service and Standard

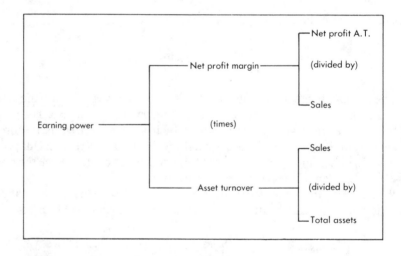

FIGURE 6-2 Determination of earning power

& Poor's make extensive use of these ratios. One of the most traditional of the coverage ratios is the *interest coverage ratio*, simply the ratio of earnings before interest and taxes for a particular reporting period to the amount of interest charges for the period. It is important to differentiate which interest charges should be used in the denominator. The *overall coverage method* stresses the importance of a company's meeting all fixed interest, regardless of the seniority of the claim. Suppose that we have the following financial data for a hypothetical company:

Average earnings	$2 000 000
Interest on senior 10% bonds	– 400 000
	$1 600 000
Interest on junior 12% bonds	160 000

The overall interest coverage would be 2 000 000/560 000, or 3.57. This method implies that the credit-worthiness of the senior bonds is only as good as the firm's ability to cover all interest charges.

Of the various coverage ratios, the most objectionable is the *prior deductions method*. Using this method, we deduct interest on the senior bonds from average earnings and then divide the residual by the interest on the junior bonds. We find that the coverage on the junior bonds in our example is ten times ($1 600 000/160 000). Thus, the junior bonds give the illusion of being more secure than the senior obligations. Clearly, this method is inappropriate.

The *cumulative deduction method* is superior to the overall coverage and prior deductions methods and is perhaps the most widely used method of computing interest coverage. With this method, coverage for interest on the senior bonds is calculated first. Interest on the senior bonds is then added to that for the junior bonds and another coverage ratio is computed for the junior bonds. For example, in the above illustration, coverage for the senior bonds is five times ($2 000 000/$400 000) and that for the junior bonds is 3.57 times ($2 000 000/$560 000). Thus we see that the coverage ratio for the junior bonds also takes into account the interest on the senior debt obligations. This aspect is not taken into account under the prior deductions method as we discussed in the previous paragraph. Finally, the overall coverage method only shows the coverage for all debt whereas the cumulative deductions method shows the coverage for debt obligations ranked by their seniority of claims.

One of the principal shortcomings of an interest coverage ratio is that a firm's ability to service debt is related to both interest and principal payments. Moreover, these payments are not met out of earnings per se, but out of cash. Hence, a more appropriate coverage ratio relates the cash flow of the firm (approximated by earnings before interest and taxes plus depreciation) with the sum of interest and principal payments. The *cash flow coverage ratio* may be expressed as

$$\frac{\text{Annual cash flow before interest and taxes}}{\text{Interest} + \text{principal payments}\ [1/(1 - t)]}$$

where t is the federal income tax rate. As principal payments are made after taxes, it is necessary to adjust this figure by $1/(1 - t)$ so that it corresponds to interest payments, which are made before taxes.[6]

A broader type of analysis would evaluate the ability of the firm to cover all charges of a fixed nature in relation to its cash flow. In addition to interest and principal payments on debt obligations, we would include preferred stock dividends, lease payments, and possibly even certain essential capital expenditures. As explained in Chapter 16, an analysis of this type is a far more realistic gauge than is a simple interest coverage ratio in determining whether a firm has the ability to meet its long-term obligations.

Trend Over Time

Up to now, we have concentrated on presenting the various financial ratios, explaining their use in analysis, and comparing the ratios computed for our hypothetical company with industry averages. As we pointed out earlier, it also is valuable to compare the financial ratios for a given company over time. In this way, the analyst is able to detect any improvement or deterioration in its financial condition and performance.

To illustrate trend over time, we present in Table 6-4 some of the financial ratios we have studied for King Manufacturing Ltd. over the 1975–84 period. The table shows that the current and acid-test ratios tended to remain relatively constant to 1979 and then increased thereafter. Paralleling this behavior were

TABLE 6-4   Financial Ratios of King Manufacturing Ltd. for Fiscal Years 1975-84

	1975	1976	1977	1978	1979	1980	1981	1982	1983	1984
Current ratio	1.59	1.55	1.56	1.54	1.51	1.62	1.80	1.79	1.85	1.81
Acid-test ratio	0.92	0.88	0.93	0.91	0.89	0.97	1.00	1.02	1.03	0.99
Average receivable collection period (days)	41	45	50	54	58	60	63	68	73	78
Inventory turnover	3.21	3.13	3.09	2.91	2.86	2.74	2.78	2.71	2.59	2.47
Total debt/ net worth	0.91	0.93	0.90	0.89	0.89	0.88	0.83	0.85	0.70	0.73
Gross profit margin	25.2%	25.0%	24.8%	24.6%	23.9%	24.3%	23.0%	23.7%	23.2%	24.0%
Net profit margin	4.61%	4.01%	2.72%	3.08%	3.41%	3.51%	2.67%	2.71%	2.85%	3.80%
Return on assets	4.66%	4.17%	2.69%	3.08%	3.31%	3.26%	2.54%	2.44%	2.60%	3.31%
Turnover ratio	1.01	1.04	0.99	1.00	0.97	0.93	0.95	0.90	0.91	0.87

---

[6]For an analysis of various approaches to coverage ratios when principal payments are involved, see M. Chapman Findlay III and Edward E. Williams, "Toward More Adequate Debt Service Coverage Ratios," *Financial Analysts Journal*, 31 (Nov.–Dec. 1975), 58–61.

movements in the average receivable collection period and the inventory turnover ratio. The former increased steadily from 1975 through 1984, while the latter decreased steadily throughout. The trends here tell us that there has been a relative buildup in receivables and inventory. The turnover of both has slowed down, which raises questions as to the quality of these assets. When a trend analysis of receivables and inventory is coupled with a comparison with the average ratios for the industry, the only conclusion possible is that a problem exists. The analyst would want to investigate the credit policies of King, the company's collection experience, and its bad debt losses. Moreover, he should investigate inventory management, obsolescence of inventory, and any imbalances that might exist. Thus, despite the overall improvement in current and acid-test ratios, the apparent deterioration in receivables and inventory is a matter of concern and needs to be investigated in depth.

The debt-to-net-worth ratio has declined somewhat since 1976, indicating some improvement in overall condition from the standpoint of creditors, all other things remaining the same. The gross profit margin and net profit margin have fluctuated over time in keeping with economic cycles. Since 1981, however, both ratios have shown slight improvement, which is perhaps encouraging. There is no particular disparity between the two series which would indicate less efficiency in controlling expenses vis-à-vis the cost of producing electrical equipment or vice-versa. The return on assets has fluctuated over the 1975–84 period in keeping with economic cycles. Abstracting from these fluctuations, however, it is disturbing that the return on assets did not increase as much over the 1982–84 period as did the net profit. With greater profitability in absolute terms, there must have been offsetting increases in total assets that caused the return on assets to lag during the period. This reasoning is confirmed when we analyze the turnover ratio (Sales/Total assets). During the last four years there was an overall decline indicating that more assets were needed to generate a dollar of sales. From our analysis of liquidity, we know that the primary cause was the large relative increase in receivables and inventory.

We see then that the analysis of the trend of financial ratios over time can give the analyst valuable insight into the changes that have occurred in a firm's financial condition and performance. When a trend analysis and comparisons with like companies and the industry average are combined, the depth of analysis possible is considerably increased.

Finally, we should remember that the balance sheet and, to some extent, the income statement for King are historical. Financial ratios which are computed using such historical data will permit an evaluation of management performance in the past. While ex-post analyses and evaluation are worthwhile, we should never lose sight of the fact that future performance is important. The evaluation of management performance in the past helps us to identify strengths and weaknesses and their effects on the firm's financial position. Other factors being constant, the financial analyst may safely assume that acceptable performance by management in the past will continue in the future. However, where weaknesses are observed, their causes should be identified and any repetition in the future should be avoided. The financial analyst must advise management on how to improve on unacceptable past performance.

Common-Size and Index Analysis

In addition to financial ratio analysis over time, it is often useful to express balance sheet and income statement items as percentages. The percentages can be related to totals, such as total assets or total sales, or to some base year. Called common size and index analyses respectively, the evaluation of trends in financial statement percentages over time affords the analyst insight into the movement of funds. While a good portion of this insight is revealed in source and use of funds statements, a deeper and broader understanding of a firm's funds flows is possible when the analysis is extended to include the above considerations. To illustrate these two types of analyses, we shall use the balance sheet and income statements of Howard Chemical Company Ltd. for the 1981–84 fiscal years. These statements are shown in Tables 6-5 and 6-6.

STATEMENT ITEMS AS PERCENTAGES OF TOTALS

In common-size analysis, the various components of a balance sheet are expressed as percentages of the total assets of the company. This can also be done

TABLE 6-5 Howard Chemical Company Ltd. Balance Sheet (in thousands)

	1981	1982	1983	1984
ASSETS:				
Cash	$ 2 507	$ 4 749	$ 11 310	$ 19 648
Accounts receivable	70 360	72 934	85 147	118 415
Inventory	77 380	86 100	91 378	118 563
Other current assets	6 316	5 637	6 082	5 891
Current assets	156 563	169 420	193 917	262 517
Fixed assets—net	79 187	91 868	94 652	115 461
Other long term assets	4 695	5 017	5 899	5 491
Total assets	$240 445	$266 305	$294 468	$383 469
LIABILITIES AND EQUITY:				
Accounts payable	35 661	31 857	37 460	62 725
Notes payable	20 501	25 623	14 680	17 298
Other current liabilities	11 054	7 330	8 132	15 741
Current liabilities	67 216	64 810	60 272	95 764
Long term debt	888	979	1 276	1 917
Total liabilities	68 104	65 789	61 548	97 681
Preferred stock	0	0	0	2 088
Common stock	12 650	25 649	26 038	26 450
Contributed capital	36 134	33 297	45 883	63 049
Retained earnings	123 557	141 570	160 999	194 201
Total equity	172 341	200 516	232 920	283 700
Total liabilities and equity	$240 445	$266 305	$294 468	$383 469

TABLE 6-6 Howard Chemical Company Ltd. Income Statement (in thousands)

	1981	1982	1983	1984
Sales	$323 780	$347 322	$375 088	$479 077
Cost of goods sold	148 127	161 478	184 507	223 690
Gross profit	175 653	185 844	190 581	255 387
Selling expenses	79 399	98 628	103 975	125 645
General and administrative expenses	43 573	45 667	45 275	61 719
Total expenses	122 972	144 295	149 250	187 364
Earnings before interest and taxes	52 681	41 549	41 331	68 023
Interest	1 757	4 204	2 963	3 017
Earnings before taxes	54 438	45 753	44 294	71 040
Taxes	28 853	22 650	20 413	32 579
Earnings after taxes	$ 25 585	$ 23 103	$ 23 881	$ 38 461

TABLE 6-7 Howard Chemical Company Ltd. Common Size Balance Sheet

	1981	1982	1983	1984
ASSETS:				
Cash	1.0	1.8	3.8	5.1
Accounts receivable	29.3	27.4	28.9	30.9
Inventory	32.2	32.3	31.0	30.9
Other current assets	2.6	2.1	2.1	1.5
Current assets	65.1	63.6	65.9	68.5
Fixed assets—net	32.9	34.5	32.1	30.1
Other long term assets	2.0	1.9	2.0	1.4
Total assets	100.0	100.0	100.0	100.0
LIABILITIES AND EQUITY:				
Accounts payable	14.8	12.0	12.7	16.4
Notes payable	8.5	9.6	5.0	4.5
Other current liabilities	4.6	2.8	2.8	4.1
Current liabilities	28.0	24.3	20.5	25.0
Long term debt	0.4	0.4	0.4	0.5
Total liabilities	28.3	24.7	20.9	25.5
Preferred stock	0.0	0.0	0.0	0.5
Common stock	5.3	9.6	8.8	6.9
Contributed capital	15.0	12.5	15.6	16.4
Retained earnings	51.4	53.2	54.7	50.6
Total equity	71.7	75.3	79.1	74.0
Total liabilities and equity	100.0	100.0	100.0	100.0

TABLE 6-8   Howard Chemical Company Ltd.
Common Size Income Statement

	1981	1982	1983	1984
Sales	100.0	100.0	100.0	100.0
Cost of goods sold	45.7	46.5	49.2	46.7
Gross profit	54.3	53.5	50.8	53.3
Selling expenses	24.5	28.4	27.7	26.2
General and administrative expenses	13.5	13.1	12.1	12.9
Total expenses	38.0	41.5	39.8	39.1
Earnings before interest and taxes	16.3	12.0	11.0	14.2
Interest	0.5	1.2	0.8	0.6
Earnings before taxes	16.8	13.2	11.8	14.8
Taxes	8.9	6.5	5.4	6.8
Earnings after taxes	7.9	6.7	6.4	8.0

for the income statement but here items are related to sales. The gross and net profit margins, which we took up earlier, are examples of common-size analysis; it can be extended to all of the items on the income statement. The expression of individual financial statement items as percentages of totals usually permits insights not possible from a review of the raw figures themselves.

To illustrate, we will study the common-size balance sheet and income statements of Howard Chemical for fiscal years 1981–84 in Tables 6-7 and 6-8. In Table 6-7 we see that in the four-year period, the percentage of current assets increased and that this was particularly true for cash. We also see that there is an accounts receivable increase from 1983 to 1984. On the liability and net worth side of the balance sheet, the debt of the company declined on a relative basis from 1981 to 1984. However, with the large absolute increase in assets which occurred in 1984 the debt ratio increased from 1983 to 1984. This is particularly apparent in accounts payable, which increased substantially in both absolute and relative terms.

The common-size income statement shown in Table 6-8 shows the gross profit margin fluctuating from year to year. When this is combined with selling, general, and administrative expenses, which also fluctuate periodically, the result is a profit picture that varies from year to year. While 1984 shows a sharp improvement (over 1983 and 1982) it still is not as good as 1981 on a pre-tax basis.

STATEMENT ITEMS AS INDEXES RELATIVE TO A BASE YEAR

The common-size balance sheet and income statement can be supplemented by expressing the items as trends from a base year. For Howard Chemical Company Ltd., the base year is 1981 and all financial statement items are 100.0 for that year. Items for the three subsequent years are expressed as an index relative to that year. For example, if a $22 500 item were compared with $15 000 in the base year, the

TABLE 6-9   Howard Chemical Company Ltd.
Indexed Balance Sheet

	1981	1982	1983	1984
ASSETS:				
Cash	100.0	189.4	451.1	783.7
Accounts receivable	100.0	103.7	121.0	168.3
Inventory	100.0	111.3	118.1	153.2
Other current assets	100.0	89.2	96.3	93.3
Current assets	100.0	108.2	123.9	167.7
Fixed assets—net	100.0	116.0	119.5	145.8
Other long term assets	100.0	106.9	125.6	117.0
Total assets	100.0	110.8	122.5	159.5
LIABILITIES AND EQUITY:				
Accounts payable	100.0	89.3	105.0	175.9
Notes payable	100.0	125.0	71.6	84.4
Other current liabilities	100.0	66.3	73.6	142.4
Current liabilities	100.0	96.4	89.7	142.5
Long term debt	100.0	110.2	143.7	215.9
Total liabilities	100.0	96.6	90.4	143.4
Preferred stock	0.0	0.0	0.0	0.0
Common stock	100.0	202.8	205.8	209.1
Contributed capital	100.0	92.1	127.0	174.5
Retained earnings	100.0	114.6	130.3	157.2
Total common equity	100.0	116.3	135.2	165.8
Total liabilities and equity	100.0	110.8	122.5	159.5

TABLE 6-10   Howard Chemical Company Ltd.
Indexed Income Statement

	1981	1982	1983	1984
Sales	100.0	107.3	115.8	148.0
Cost of goods sold	100.0	109.0	124.6	151.0
Gross profit	100.0	105.8	108.5	145.4
Selling expenses	100.0	124.2	131.0	158.2
General and administrative expenses	100.0	104.8	103.9	141.6
Total expenses	100.0	117.3	121.4	152.4
Earnings before interest and taxes	100.0	78.9	78.5	129.1
Interest	100.0	239.3	168.6	171.7
Earnings before taxes	100.0	84.0	81.4	130.5
Taxes	100.0	78.5	70.7	112.9
Earnings after taxes	100.0	90.3	93.3	150.3

index would be 150. Tables 6-9 and 6-10 show indexed balance sheet and income statements. In Table 6-9 the buildup in cash from the base year is obvious and agrees with our previous assessment. There is also a large increase in accounts receivable and inventories from 1983–84. The latter was not apparent in the common-size analysis. To a lesser extent, there was an increase in fixed assets. On the liability side of the balance sheet, we note the large increase in accounts payable and in other current liabilities from 1983–84. This, coupled with retained earnings and the sale of common shares, financed the large increase in assets for the same period.

The indexed income statement in Table 6-10 and the common-size income statement both give the same picture, namely fluctuating behavior. However, the sharp improvement in 1984 profitability is more easily seen in the indexed statement than in the common-size statement. The indexed statement also gives us information on the magnitude of absolute change in profits and expenses; in the common-size statement, there is no more information about how total assets or total sales change over time.

In summary, the standardization of balance sheet and income statement items as percentages of totals and as indexes to a base year often gives us insights additional to those obtained from analyses of financial ratios. This supplemental information can be valuable in providing a better understanding of a company's underlying uses of funds and how those uses are financed over time.

Summary

Financial analysis necessarily involves the study of financial statements. In this chapter, important items on the balance sheet and the income statement were presented, and their relationship discussed. In financial analysis, one is concerned with the funds needs of the firm, its financial condition and performance, and its business risk. These factors enable one to determine the financing needs of the firm and how it negotiates with outside suppliers of capital. The framework proposed provides an interlocking means for structuring analysis.

The tools used to analyze financial condition and performance are the financial ratios. These ratios can be divided into four types: liquidity, debt, profitability, and coverage. No one ratio is sufficient by itself to realistically assess the financial condition and performance of a firm, but by using a group of ratios, reasonable judgments can be made. The number of ratios needed for this purpose is not particularly large—about a dozen.

The ratios taken up in this chapter are used extensively by outside creditors and investors. These ratios are also helpful for managerial control and for providing a better understanding of what outside suppliers of capital expect in the way of financial condition and performance. The usefulness of the ratios depends on the ingenuity and experience of the financial analyst who employs them. By themselves, financial ratios are fairly meaningless; they must be analyzed on a comparative basis. A comparison of ratios of the same firm over time is important in evaluating changes and trends in the firm's financial condition and profitability.

Insights into company performance can also be made through common size and index analyses. In common size analysis the various balance sheet items are expressed as percentages of total assets and the income statement items, as percentages of total sales. In index analysis, balance sheet and income statement items are expressed as an index relative to an initial base year. In addition to historical comparisons for the same company, financial ratios may be judged by comparing them with those of similar firms in the same line of business and, when appropriate, with an industry average. Much can be gleaned from a thorough analysis of financial ratios about the financial condition and performance of the firm.

Appendix: Inflation and Financial Analysis

In financial ratio analysis, it is important to recognize that inflationary forces may mask the results. Part of the financial performance of a company for a period of time may be due to management decisions and part to external factors over which management has little control. In particular, inflation may result in holding period gains which are not attributable to management decisions involved in running the enterprise. The problem with holding period gains is that they vary with inflation and thus cloud the analysis of the overall results. If the financial analyst wishes to differentiate performance based on conventional accounting data from that based on economic profitability, he or she will need to adjust the accounting numbers.

THE PROBLEM ILLUSTRATED

To illustrate the problem with a simple example, suppose that Foster Tool Company Ltd., a wholesaler of tools, began business on December 31, 19X1, and had the following balance sheet at that time:

Assets		Liabilities and net worth	
Cash	$ 40 000		
Inventory	100 000	Common stock	$240 000
Net fixed assets	100 000		
	$240 000		$240 000

It is assumed that the fixed assets have a depreciable life of ten years and that inventory is reported on a first in first out (FIFO) basis.[7] It is also assumed that sales

---

[7]This example is based on Lawrence Revsine, *Accounting in an Inflationary Environment*, Laventhol & Horwath, 1977.

occur entirely at the end of the first year of operation and that inflation for that year is 20 percent. It is further assumed that inflation occurred at the beginning of 19X2 and that there are no taxes.

Operations for 19X2 are reported on a historical cost basis and are as follows:

Income statement		
Sales		$170 000
Cost of goods sold		
Beginning inventory	$ 100 000	
Purchases	120 000	
Ending inventory	(120 000)	100 000
Depreciation ($100 000/10)		10 000
Selling and administrative expenses		30 000
Net profit		$ 30 000

Note that the company's ending inventory is higher than its beginning inventory by the percentage increase in prices, namely 20 percent. The balance sheet of the company at December 31, 19X2 would be

Assets		Liabilities and net worth	
Cash	$ 60 000		
Inventory	120 000	Common stock	$240 000
Net fixed assets	90 000	Retained earnings	30 000
	$270 000		$270 000

If we compute two of the more widely used profitability ratios, we find them to be

Net profit margin ($30 000/$170 000) = 17.65%

Return on assets ($30 000/$240 000 = 12.50%

In both cases, the underlying economic profitability of the company is overstated. For one thing, with the FIFO method, inventories which are sold are assumed to have been purchased at the prices prevailing when the oldest items in the inventory were purchased. With inflation, these prices are considerably below their replacement costs. In the case of Foster Tool Company Ltd., for accounting purposes the inventories sold are valued at $100 000, whereas their replacement cost at the time they were sold was $120 000. The costing of inventories in this manner tends to understate economic costs and to overstate economic profits. Like inventory valuation, depreciation charges are based on the original cost of the fixed assets, less accumulated depreciation. Again with inflation, the original cost is less than the current replacement cost of these assets. If these assets increase in value by 20 percent, their replacement value is $120 000 and economic depreciation is $12 000 instead of the $10 000 used for accounting depreciation purposes.

On a replacement-cost basis, the income statement of Foster Tool Company Ltd. for 19X2 is

Income statement	
Sales	$170 000
Cost of goods sold (replacement cost)	120 000
Depreciation ($120 000/10)	12 000
Selling and administrative expenses	30 000
Net profit	$ 8 000

When economic profits instead of profits on a historical cost basis are used, the profitability ratios are

$$\text{Net profit margin } (\$8\ 000/\$170\ 000) = 4.70\%$$

$$\text{Return on assets } (\$8\ 000/\$240\ 000 = 3.33\%$$

We see then that the economic performance results are substantially lower than accounting data results.

Suppose that a year later in 19X3 there is no inflation and that the income statement of the company on a historical cost basis is as follows:

Income statement		
Sales		$170 000
Cost of goods sold		
Beginning inventory	$ 120 000	
Purchases	120 000	
Ending inventory	(120 000)	120 000
Depreciation ($100 000/10)		10 000
Selling and administrative expenses		30 000
Net profit		$ 10 000

Thus, we see that the profits of the company drop substantially from the $30 000 reported the previous year, again using historical costs to compute the profit figure.

However, this "worsening" of the profit performance is primarily attributable to inflation, not to management. If we look at the income statement on a replacement cost basis for 19X3, we find

Income statement	
Sales	$170 000
Cost of goods sold	120 000
Depreciation ($120 000/10)	12 000
Selling and administrative expenses	30 000
Net profit	$ 8 000

To compute the return-on-assets ratio on this basis, we need to recast the 19X2 balance sheet to reflect replacement costs. This balance sheet becomes

Assets		Liabilities and net worth	
Cash	$ 60 000	Common stock	$240 000
Inventories	120 000	Retained earnings	8 000
Net fixed assets	108 000	Holding-period gain	40 000
	$288 000		$288 000

The gross fixed assets are adjusted upward for inflation by 20 percent to $120 000. When the 19X2 economic depreciation of $12 000 is subtracted from this amount, we get net fixed assets of $108 000. The holding period gain of $40 000 is comprised of the inventory profit of $20 000, which arises from the FIFO method, and of the increase in value of the fixed assets of $20 000. Both these gains are attributed to inflation during 19X2. With $288 000 as the asset value, the profitability ratios for 19X3, using replacement cost data are

$$\text{Net profit margin } (\$8\ 000/\$170\ 000) = 4.70\%$$

$$\text{Return on assets } (\$8\ 000/\$288\ 000 = 2.78\%$$

While the net profit margin in 19X3 is the same as in 19X2, the return on assets is lower. This is because the denominator, beginning total assets, is higher than the previous year's.

IMPLICATIONS

The above example shows the problems the analyst faces when comparing the financial ratios of a company over time in the face of differing rates of inflation. We see that historical cost accounting data are distorted from year to year because of inflation. Financial ratios, especially those dealing with profitability, are also distorted. The operating results are partly due to inflation, which is beyond management's control. What may appear to be a significant change in profitability may prove, on closer scrutiny, simply to be due to the vagaries of inflation. In most cases it is important that the financial analyst not only recognize the underlying cause of the distortion but that he or she make appropriate modifications in assessing of the financial performance of the company over time.

Like a company's financial ratios, inter-company comparisons may also be distorted over time. When historical costs are used, the company with older fixed assets will often show a higher return on investment in an inflationary environment than will a company whose fixed assets are more recently acquired. The depreciation charges for the former company will be lower, resulting in greater reported profits; total assets will also be lower. This combination of higher profits and lower investment will mean a higher return-on-investment ratio, all other things remaining constant. However, the difference in returns may be due entirely to assets being purchased at different times, and not to management efficiency. The danger is that the company with older fixed assets may appear to be less efficient in an economic sense, but its return on investment, based on conventional accounting data, may in fact be as good as, if not better than, that of a more efficient producer. Therefore, comparisons of return-on-investment ratios based on historical costs may lead to incorrect conclusions.

In making financial-ratio and intercompany comparisons, the financial analyst must be aware that inflation can result in inaccurate economic assessments. In periods of runaway inflation, it is often desirable to recompute financial ratios using replacement-cost accounting data. In this way, the financial analyst can differentiate that portion of overall performance which is influenced by inflation from that which is more directly related to management efficiency. Thus, the analyst can get a better picture of the economic return instead of the accounting return of a company.

Questions

1. What is the purpose of financial statements? What are the major components of a financial statement?
2. Why is the analysis of trends in financial ratios important?
3. Zokar Manufacturing Company Ltd. has a current ratio of 4 to 1 but is unable to pay its bills. Why?
4. Can a firm generate a 25 percent return on assets and still be technically insolvent? Explain.
5. The traditional definitions of *collection period* and *inventory turnover* are criticized because in both cases balance sheet figures that are a result of the last month of sales are related to annual sales. Why do these definitions present problems? Suggest a solution.
6. Explain why a long-term creditor should be interested in liquidity ratios.
7. Which financial ratios would you be most likely to consult if you were the following? Why?
   (a) A banker considering the financing of seasonal inventory
   (b) A wealthy equity investor
   (c) The manager of a pension fund considering the purchase of bonds
   (d) The president of a consumer products firm

8. Ratio analysis is valuable in assessing the financial position of a firm only when the ratios are compared with industry norms. In the current business environment, many corporations are conglomerates whose holdings cut across all industries. Suggest methods for analyzing conglomerates.

9. Why might it be possible for a company to make large operating profits, yet still be unable to meet debt payments when due? What financial ratios might be employed to detect such a condition?

10. Does increasing a firm's inventory turnover ratio increase its profitability? Why is this ratio computed using cost of goods sold (rather than sales, as is done by some compilers of financial statistics)?

11. Which financial ratios are likely to be affected if the firm's accounting statements are reported on a cost basis rather than on a market basis?

12. Which firm is more profitable? Firm A with a turnover of 10.0 and a net profit margin of 2 percent, or Firm B with a turnover of 2.0 and a net profit margin of 10 percent? Provide examples of both types of firms.

13. Why do short-term creditors, such as banks, emphasize balance sheet analysis when considering loan requests? Should they also analyze projected income statements? Why?

14. How can index analysis be used to reinforce the insight gained from a trend analysis of financial ratios?

Problems with Solutions

1. Rocky Mountain Romano Company Ltd. has the following balance sheet and income statement for 19X2 (in thousands)

Balance sheet	19X2	Income statement	
Cash	$ 400	Net sales (all credit)	$12 680
Accounts receivable	1 300	Cost of goods sold*	8 930
Inventories ($1 800 for 19X1)	2 100	Gross profit	3 750
Current assets	3 800	Selling, general and admin. expenses	2 230
Net fixed assets	3 320	Interest expense	460
Total assets	$7 120	Profit before taxes	1 060
Accounts payable	$ 320	Taxes	490
Accruals	260	Profit after taxes	$ 570
Short-term loans	1 100	*Includes depreciation of $480	
Current liabilities	1 680		
Long-term debt	2 000		
Net worth	3 440		
Total liabilities and net worth	$7 120		

With the above information, compute the main financial ratios discussed in this chapter.

Financial ratios	Method of calculation	Answers
A. Liquidity ratios		
Current ratio	Current assets/current debts = $3 800/$1 680	2.26
Acid-test ratio	Current assets less inventories/current debts = ($3 800 − $2 100)/$1 680	1.01
Average collection period	Receivables times 365/credit sales = ($1 300 × 365)/$12 680	37 days
Inventory turnover	Cost of goods sold/average inventory = $8 930/($1 800 + $2 100) ÷ 2	4.58
B. Debt ratios		
Total debt to net worth	Total debt/net worth = $3 680/$3 440	1.07
Current debt to net worth	Current debt/net worth = $1 680/$3 440	0.49
Long term debt to net worth	Long term debt/net worth = $2 000/$3 440	0.58
Long term debt to total capitalization	Long term debt/long term debt plus net worth = $2 000/($2 000 + $3 440)	0.37
C. Profitability ratios		
Gross profit margin	Gross profit as a percent of sales = ($3 750/$12 680) × 100	29.57%
Net profit margin	Net profit as a percent of sales = ($570/$12 680) × 100	4.50%
Total asset turnover	Sales/total assets = $12 680/$7 120	1.78
Earning power or return on investment or total assets	Net profit margin times total asset turnover = 4.50% × 1.78 or, earnings after taxes as percent of total assets = ($570/$7 120) × 100	8.01% 8.01%
Return on equity	Earnings after taxes/net worth = ($570/$3 440) × 100	16.57%
D. Coverage ratios		
Interest coverage	Earnings before interest and taxes/interest = ($1 060 + $460)/$460	3.30

You may use the above format as a reference in financial ratio analysis. You will encounter other ratios but once you understand how they are computed, you can derive them and add to the above listing.

2. Complete the following Income Statement and Balance Sheet (Assume a 360 day year)

Revenue	$480 000	
Cost of goods sold	‾‾‾‾‾‾	
Gross profit	$	
Expenses	70 000	
Net operating income	$	
Interest expense		
Net income before tax	$	
Tax 40%	‾‾‾‾‾‾	
NET INCOME	$	

Cash	$	Current liabilities	$	
Accounts receivable		Long term debt 10%	‾‾‾‾‾	
Inventory	‾‾‾‾‾	Total liabilities	$	
Current assets	$			
Plant and equipment	‾‾‾‾‾	Shareholders' equity	800 000	
		TOTAL LIABILITIES AND		
TOTAL ASSETS	$	SHAREHOLDERS' EQUITY	$	

Inventory turnover (beginning inventory $200 000)	1.5 times
Collection period accounts receivable	30 days
Gross profit percentage	25%
Total debt to net worth	0.25
Current ratio	5.5 : 1
Acid test ratio	2.7 : 1

Gross profit = 25 percent of sales = 25 percent of $480 000 = $120 000.
Net operating income = gross profit less expenses
$$= \$120\ 000 - \$70\ 000 = \$50\ 000$$
Total debt to net worth = 0.25
Where total debt equals current liabilities plus long-term debt

$$\frac{\text{Total debt}}{\$800\ 000} = 0.25$$

$800\ 000(0.25) = $ Total debt
∴ Total debt = $200 000

Inventory turnover (Beginning inventory $200 000) = 1.5 times

$$\text{Inventory turnover} = \frac{\text{Cost of goods sold}}{\text{Average inventory}}$$

$$1.5 = \frac{\$360\ 000}{\text{Average inventory}}$$

1.5 Average inventory = $360 000

$$\text{Average inventory} = \frac{\$360\ 000}{1.5}$$

Beginning inventory is $200 000, and the Average inventory is $240 000
∴ the Ending inventory is $280 000

Collection period accounts receivable = 30 days

$$\frac{\text{Receivables} \times \text{days in year}}{\text{Annual sales}} = 30 \text{ days}$$

$$\frac{\text{Receivables} \times 360}{\$480\,000} = 30 \text{ days}$$

$$\$480\,000 \times 30 \text{ days} = \text{Receivables} \times 360 \text{ days}$$

$$\frac{\$480\,000 \times 30}{360} = \text{Receivables}$$

$$\therefore \text{Accounts receivable} = \$40\,000$$

Current ratio = 5.5 : 1

$$= \frac{\text{Cash} + \text{Accounts receivable} + \text{Inventory}}{\text{Current liabilities (CL)}}$$

$$\therefore 5.5 = \frac{\text{Cash} + \$40\,000 + \$280\,000}{\text{Current liabilities}}$$

$$5.5 \text{ CL} = \text{Cash} + \$320\,000$$

Acid Test Ratio $\quad$ = 2.7 : 1

$$= \frac{\text{Cash} + \text{Accounts receivable}}{\text{Current liabilities (CL)}}$$

$$\therefore 2.7 = \frac{\text{Cash} + \$40\,000}{\text{Current liabilities (CL)}}$$

$$2.7 \text{ CL} = \text{Cash} + \$40\,000 \text{ (b)}$$

$$(a) - (b) \quad 5.5 \text{ CL} = \text{Cash} + \$320\,000$$

$$-2.7 \text{ CL} = -\text{Cash} - \$40\,000$$

$$2.8 \text{ CL} = 0 + \$280\,000$$

$$\text{CL} = \frac{\$280\,000}{2.8}$$

$$\therefore \text{Current liabilities} = \$100\,000$$

$$5.5 = \frac{\text{Cash} + \$40\,000 + \$280\,000}{\$100\,000}$$

$$5.5(\$100\,000) = \text{Cash} + \$40\,000 + \$280\,000$$

$$\$550\,000 - \$40\,000 - \$280\,000 = \text{Cash}$$

$$\therefore \text{Cash} = \$230\,000$$

Total liabilities less Current liabilities = Long term debt

$$\$200\,000 - \$100\,000 = \$100\,000$$

$$\therefore \text{Long-term debt} = \$100\,000$$

Current liabilities + Long term debt + Shareholders' equity = Total liabilities and Shareholders' equity

$$\$100\,000 + \$100\,000 + \$800\,000 = \$1\,000\,000$$

$$\therefore \text{Total liabilities and Shareholders' equity} = \$1\,000\,000$$

also total assets equal $1 000 000

Cash + Accounts receivable + Inventory + Plant and Equipment = Total assets

$$\$230\,000 + 40\,000 + 280\,000 + \text{Plant and equipment} = \$1\,000\,000$$

$$\therefore \text{Plant and equipment} = \$450\,000$$

Interest expense = Long term debt × 10%

$$= \$100\,000 \times 0.10$$

$$= \$10\,000$$

Income statement		
Revenue	$480 000	
Cost of goods sold	360 000	
Gross profit	$120 000	
Expenses	70 000	
Net operating income	$ 50 000	
Interest expense	10 000	
Net income before tax	$ 40 000	
Tax 40%	16 000	
Net income	$ 24 000	

Balance sheet				
Cash	$230 000	Current liabilities	$100 000
Accounts receivable	40 000	Long term debt (10%)	100 000
Inventory	280 000	Total liabilities	$200 000
Current assets	$550 000		
Plant and equipment	450 000	Shareholders' equity	800 000
		Total liabilities and	
Total assets	$1 000 000	Shareholders' equity	$1 000 000

This problem illustrates the use of financial ratios in preparing *pro forma* income statements and balance sheets—a topic discussed in the next chapter.

Problems

1. The data for various companies in the same industry are as follows:

Company	A	B	C	D	E	F
Sales (in millions)	$10	$20	$ 8	$ 5	$12	$17
Total assets (in millions)	8	10	6	2.5	4	8
Net income (in millions)	0.7	2	0.8	0.5	1.5	1

(a) Determine the asset turnover, net profit margin, and earning power for each of the companies.

(b) Compute the average earning power for the industry. Identify those firms which fail to achieve this average and provide reasons for this occurrence given your information in (a) above.

2. Using the following information, complete the balance sheet below:

Long term debt to net worth	0.5 to 1
Total asset turnover	2.5 times
Average collection period*	18 days
Inventory turnover	9 times
Gross profit margin	10%
Acid-test ratio	1 to 1

*Assume a 360-day year, and all sales on credit.

Cash	$_____	Notes and payables	$100 000
Accounts		Long term debt	
receivable	_____	Common stock	$100 000
Inventory	_____	Retained earnings	100 000
Plant and		Total liabilities	
equipment	_____	and worth	$_____
Total assets	$_____		

3. Selected financial ratios for PET Company Ltd. are as follows:

	1981	1982	1983
Current ratio	4.2	2.6	1.8
Quick ratio	2.1	1.0	0.6
Debt to total assets	23	33	47
Inventory turnover	8.7X	5.4X	3.5X
Average collection period	33	36	49
Fixed-assets turnover	11.6X	10.6X	12.3X
Total-assets turnover	3.2X	2.6X	1.9X
Profit margin on sales	3.8	2.5	1.4
Return on total assets	12.1	6.5	2.8
Return on net worth	15.7	9.7	5.4

(a) Why did return on assets decline?
(b) Was the increase in debt a result of greater current liabilities or of greater long-term debt? Explain.

4. The following information is available on the Vanier Corporation Ltd.:

Balance sheet December 31, 19X6 (in thousands of dollars)			
Cash and marketable securities	$500	Accounts payable	$ 400
Accounts receivable	____	Bank loan	
Inventories	____	Accruals	200
Current assets	____	Current liabilities	____
Net fixed assets	____	Common stock and retained earnings	3 750
Total assets	====	Total liabilities and net worth	====

Income statement for 19X6 (in thousands of dollars)	
Credit sales	$8 000
Cost of goods sold	_____
Gross profit	_____
Selling and admin. expenses	_____
Interest expense	400
Profit before taxes	_____
Taxes (44 percent rate)	_____
Profit after taxes	$ ____

Other information	
Current ratio	3 to 1
Depreciation	$500
Cash flow/long-term debt	0.40
Net profit margin	7%
Total liabilities/net worth	1 to 1
Average collection period	45 days
Inventory turnover ratio	3 to 1

Assuming sales and production are steady throughout the year and a 360-day year, complete the balance sheet and income statement for Vanier Corporation.

5. A company has total annual sales (all credit) of $400 000 and a gross profit margin of 20 percent. Its current assets are $80 000; current liabilities, $60 000; inventories, $30 000; and cash, $10 000.

(a) How much average inventory should be carried if management wants the inventory turnover to be 4?

(b) How rapidly (in how many days) must accounts receivable be collected if management wants to have an average of $50 000 invested in receivables? (Assume a 360-day year.)

6. Stella Stores Co. Ltd., has sales of $6 million, an asset-turnover ratio of 6 for the year, and net profits of $120 000.
   (a) What is the company's return on assets or earning power?
   (b) The company is considering the installation of new point-of-sales cash registers throughout its stores. This equipment is expected to increase efficiency in inventory control, reduce clerical errors, and improve record keeping throughout the system. The new equipment will increase the investment in assets by 20 percent and is expected to increase the net profit margin from 2 to 3 percent. No change in sales is expected. What is the effect of the new equipment on the return-on-assets ratio or earning power?

7. The long term debt section of the balance sheet of the Diters Corporation Ltd. appears as follows:

9¼% mortgage bonds of 2005	$2 500 000
12⅜% second mortgage bonds of 1998	1 500 000
10¼% debentures of 2001	1 000 000
14½% subordinated debentures of 2008	1 000 000
	$6 000 000

   (a) If the average earnings before interest and taxes of the Diters Corporation are $1.5 million, what is the overall interest coverage?
   (b) Using the cumulative deduction method, determine the coverage for each issue.

8. Tic Tac Homes Ltd. had the following balance-sheet statements (in thousands) in the past four years:

	19X1	19X2	19X3	19X4
Cash	$ 214	$ 93	$ 42	$ 38
Receivables	1 213	1 569	1 846	2 562
Inventories	2 102	2 893	3 678	4 261
Net fixed assets	2 219	2 346	2 388	2 692
Total assets	5 748	6 901	7 954	9 553
Accounts payable	1 131	1 578	1 848	2 968
Notes payable	500	650	750	750
Accruals	656	861	1 289	1 743
Long term debt	500	800	800	800
Common stock	200	200	200	200
Retained earnings	2 761	2 812	3 067	3 092
Total liabilities and net worth	$5 748	$6 901	$7 954	$9 553

Using index analysis, what are the major problems in the company's financial condition?

9.

Canada Corporation Ltd. Balance Sheet, December 31, 19X3

Assets		Liabilities and stockholders' equity	
Cash	$ 1 000 000	Notes payable—Bank	$ 4 000 000
Accounts receivable	5 000 000	Accounts payable	2 000 000
Inventory	7 000 000	Accrued wages and taxes	2 000 000
Fixed assets, net	15 000 000		
Excess over book value of assets acquired	2 000 000	Long term debt	12 000 000
		Preferred stock	4 000 000
		Common stock	2 000 000
		Retained earnings	4 000 000
Total assets	$30 000 000	Total liabilities and equity	$30 000 000

Canada Corporation Ltd. Statement of Income and Retained Earnings, Year Ended December 31, 19X3

Net sales:		
Credit		$16 000 000
Cash		4 000 000
Total		$20 000 000
Costs and expenses		
Cost of goods sold	$12 000 000	
Selling, general, and administrative expenses	2 000 000	
Depreciation	1 400 000	
Interest on long-term debt	600 000	16 000 000
Net income before taxes		$ 4 000 000
Taxes on income		2 000 000
Net income after taxes		$ 2 000 000
Less: Dividends on preferred stock		240 000
Net income available to common		$ 1 760 000
Add: Retained earnings at 1/1/19X3		2 600 000
Subtotal		$ 4 360 000
Less: Dividends paid on common		360 000
Retained earnings at 12/31/19X3		$ 4 000 000

(a) Fill in the 19X3 column.

Canada Corporation Ltd.

Ratio	19X1	19X2	19X3	Industry norms
1. Current ratio	250%	200%		225%
2. Acid-test ratio	100%	90%		110%
3. Receivables turnover	5.0X	4.5X		6.0X
4. Inventory turnover	4.0X	3.0X		4.0X
5. Long term debt/Total capitalization	35%	40%		33%
6. Gross profit margin	39%	41%		40%
7. Net profit margin	17%	15%		15%
8. Rate of return on equity	15%	20%		20%
9. Return on assets	15%	12%		10%
10. Tangible asset turnover	0.9X	0.8X		1.0X
11. Overall interest coverage	11X	9X		10X
12. Cash flow/long-term debt	0.46	0.39		0.40

(b) Evaluate the position of the company from the above table. Cite specific ratio levels and trends as evidence.

(c) Indicate which ratios would be of most interest to you and what your decision would be in each of the following situations:

  (1) Canada Corp. wants to buy $500 000 worth of raw materials from you, with payment to be due in 90 days.

  (2) Canada Corp. wants you, a large insurance company, to pay off its note at the bank and assume it on a ten-year maturity basis at the current coupon of 14 percent.

  (3) There are 100 000 shares outstanding and the stock is selling for $80 a share. The company offers you an opportunity to buy $50 000 additional shares at this price.

Appendix Problem

10. Using historical costs, Patel Patterns Ltd., had the following income statement (in thousands of dollars) for the year, during which 15 percent inflation occurred:

Sales		$5 000
Cost of goods sold		
Beginning inventory	$ 800	
Purchases	3 200	
Ending inventory	(920)	3 080
Depreciation		500
Selling and admin. expenses		800
Profit before taxes		620
Taxes (40 percent)		248
Profit after taxes		$ 372

At the beginning of the year, the fixed assets of the company amounted to $6 million on a historical cost basis, and they were depreciated on a straight-line basis with an average depreciable life of 12 years. The FIFO method is used for inventories.

(a) Determine the income statement on a replacement cost basis.

(b) What is the difference between the two methods?

Selected References

Almanac of Business and Industrial Ratios, Englewood Cliffs, N.J.: Prentice-Hall, 1983.

ALTMAN, EDWARD I., "Financial Ratios, Discriminant Analysis and the Prediction of Corporate Bankruptcy," *Journal of Finance*, 23 (September 1968), 589-609.

———, ROBERT G. HALDEMAN, and P. NARAYNAN, "Zeta Analysis: A New Model to Identify Bankruptcy Risk of Corporations," *Journal of Banking and Finance*, 1 (June 1977).

ALTMAN, EDWARD I., and ARNOLD W. SAMETZ, eds., *Financial Crises*, New York: Wiley, 1977.

BACKER, MORTON, and MARTIN L. GOSMAN, "The Use of Financial Ratios in Credit Downgrade Decisions," *Financial Management*, 9 (Spring 1980), 53-56.

BEAVER, WILLIAM, H., *Financial Reporting: An Accounting Revolution.* Englewood Cliffs, N.J.: Prentice-Hall, 1981.

CHEN, KUNG H., and THOMAS A. SHIMERDA, "An Empirical Analysis of Useful Financial Ratios," *Financial Management*, 10 (Spring 1981), 51-60.

DAMBOLENA, ISMAEL G., and SARKIS J. KHOURY, "Ratio Stability and Corporate Failure," *Journal of Finance*, 35 (September 1980), 1017-26.

EDMISTER, ROBERT O., "An Empirical Test of Financial Ratio Analysis for Small Business Failure Prediction," *Journal of Financial and Quantitative Analysis*, 7 (March 1972), 1477-93.

EMERY, GARY W. and KENNETH O. COGGER, "The Measurement of Liquidity," Working Paper, Washington University in St. Louis, 1980.

FINDLAY, M. CHAPMAN III, and EDWARD E. WILLIAMS, "Toward More Adequate Debt Service Coverage Ratios," *Financial Analysts Journal*, 31 (November-December 1975), 58-61.

FORD, JOHN KINGSTON, *A Framework for Financial Analysis*. Englewood Cliffs, N.J.: Prentice-Hall 1981, Chapters 2 and 3.

FOSTER, GEORGE, *Financial Statement Analysis*, Englewood Cliffs, N.J.: Prentice-Hall, 1978.

GOMBOLA, MICHAEL J., and J. EDWARD KETZ, "Financial Ratio Patterns in Retail and Manufacturing Organizations," *Financial Management*, Summer 1983, 45-56.

HELFERT, ERICH A., *Techniques of Financial Analysis*, 5th ed. Homewood, Ill.: Irwin, 1981, Chapter 2.

HORRIGAN, JAMES C., "A Short History of Financial Ratio Analysis," *Accounting Review*, 43 (April 1968), 284-94.

JAEDICKE, ROBERT K., and ROBERT T. SPROUSE, *Accounting Flows: Income, Funds, and Cash.* Englewood Cliffs, N.J.: Prentice-Hall, 1965, Chapter 7.

JOHNSON, W. BRUCE, "The Cross-Sectional Stability of Financial Ratio Patterns," *Journal of Financial and Quantitative Analysis*, 14 (December 1979), 1035-48.

LEV, BARUCH, *Financial Statement Analysis: A New Approach*, Englewood Cliffs, N.J.: Prentice-Hall, 1974.

LEWELLEN, W. G., and R. O. EDMISTER, "A General Model for Accounts Receivable Analysis and Control," *Journal of Financial and Quantitative Analysis*, 8 (March 1973), 195-206.

LEWELLEN, W. G., and R. W. JOHNSON, "Better Way to Monitor Accounts Receivables," *Harvard Business Review*, 50 (May-June 1972), 101-109.

PINCHES, GEORGE E., J. CLAY SINGLETON, and ALI JAHANKHANI, "Fixed Coverage as a Determinant of Electric Utility Bond Ratings," *Financial Management*, 7 (Summer 1978), 45-55.

REVSINE, LAWRENCE, *Accounting in an Inflationary Environment*. Laventhol & Horwath, 1977.

RICHARDS, VERLYN D., and EUGENE J. LAUGHLIN, "A Cash Conversion Cycle Approach to Liquidity Analysis," *Financial Management*, 9 (Spring 1980), 32-38.

STONE, BERNELL K., "The Payments-Pattern Approach to the Forecasting of Accounts Receivable," *Financial Management*, 5 (Autumn 1976), 65-82.

Funds Analysis and Financial Planning

The second portion of our examination of the tools of financial analysis and planning deals with the analysis of funds flows and financial forecasting. A funds-flow statement is a valuable aid to a financial manager or a creditor in evaluating the uses of funds by a firm and in determining how those uses are financed. In addition to studying past flows, the analyst can evaluate future flows by means of a funds statement based on forecasts. Such a statement provides an efficient method for the financial manager to assess to growth of the firm and its resulting financial needs, and to determine the best way to finance those needs. In particular, funds statements are very useful in planning intermediate- and long-term financing.

Closely related to a projected funds-flow statement are the cash budget and *pro forma* statements. The cash budget is indispensable to the financial manager in determining the short-term cash needs of the firm and, accordingly, in planning its short-term financing. When cash budgeting is extended to include a range of possible outcomes, the financial manager can evaluate the business risk and liquidity of the firm and plan a more realistic margin of safety. This margin of safety might come from adjusting the firm's liquidity cushion, rearranging the maturity structure of its debt, arranging a line of credit with a bank, or a combination of the three. Cash budgets prepared for a range of possible outcomes are valuable also in appraising the ability of the firm to adjust to unexpected changes in cash flows. The preparation of *pro forma* balance sheets and income statements enables the financial manager to analyze the effect of various policy decisions on the future financial condition and performance of the firm. We examine each of these three tools in turn.

Flow of Funds in a Business Firm

The flow of funds in a firm may be visualized as a continuous process. For every use of funds, there must be an offsetting source. In a broad sense, the assets of a firm represent the net uses of funds; its liability and net worth represent net sources. A funds-flow cycle for a typical manufacturing company is shown in Fig. 7-1. For the going concern, there is really no starting or stopping point. A finished product is produced with a variety of inputs—namely, raw material, net fixed assets, and labor. These inputs ultimately are paid for in cash. The product then is sold either for cash or on credit. A credit sale involves a receivable, which, when collected, becomes cash. If the selling price of the product exceeds all costs (including depreciation on assets) for a period of time, there is a profit for the period; if not, there is a loss. The reservoir of cash, the focal point in the figure, fluctuates over time with the production schedule, sales, collection of receivables, capital expenditures, and financing. On the other hand, reservoirs of raw materials, work in process, finished goods inventory, accounts receivable, and trade payables fluctuate with sales, the production schedule, and policies with respect to managing receivables, inventories, and trade payables.

The funds statement is a method by which we study the net funds flow between two points in time. These points conform to beginning and ending financial statement dates for whatever period of examination is relevant—a quarter, a year, or five years. It is important to emphasize that the funds statement portrays net rather than gross changes between two comparable financial statements at different dates. Gross changes include all the individual changes that occur between the two statement dates rather than the sum of these changes—the net change as defined.

Although an analysis of the gross funds flow of a firm over time would be much more revealing than an analysis of the net funds flow, we are usually constrained by the financial information available—namely, balance sheets and income statements that span particular periods of time. Funds may be defined in several different ways, depending on the purpose of the analysis. While they are often defined as cash, many analysts treat funds as working capital (current assets less current liabilities)—a somewhat broader definition. Other definitions are possible, although the two described are by far the most common. Depending on the analyst's objective, the definition can be broadened or narrowed. Because a funds-flow analysis on a cash basis serves as a building block for analyses using broader definitions of funds, we begin by defining funds as cash.

SOURCE AND USE STATEMENTS

Basically, one prepares a funds statement on a cash basis by: (1) classifying net balance sheet changes that occur between two points in time into changes that increase cash and changes that decrease cash; (2) classifying, from the income statement and the statement of retained earnings, the factors that increase cash and the factors that decrease cash; and (3) consolidating this information in a source and use of funds statement form.

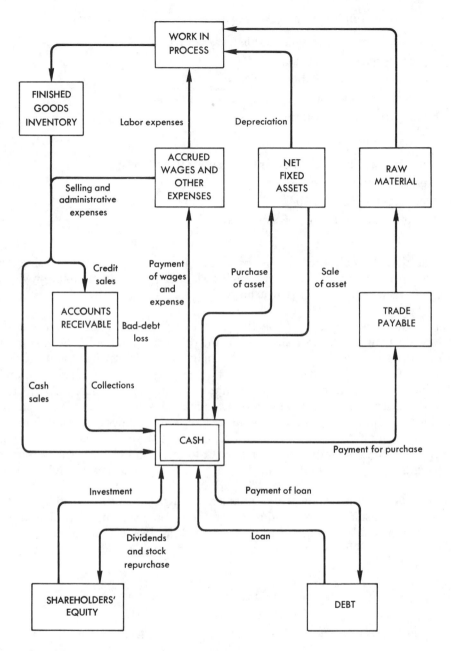

FIGURE 7-1 Funds flow within the firm

Sources of funds that increase cash are

1. A net decrease in any asset other than cash of fixed assets;
2. A gross decrease in fixed assets;
3. A net increase in any liability;
4. Proceeds from the sale of preferred or common shares;
5. Funds provided by operations.

Uses of funds include:

1. A net increase in any asset other than cash or fixed assets;
2. A gross increase in fixed assets;
3. A net decrease in any liability;
4. A retirement or purchase of shares;
5. Cash dividends.

We can show how a source and use of funds statement is computed by using the balance sheet and income statement of King Manufacturing Ltd. from the previous chapter (Tables 6-1 and 6-2) as an example.

Net balance sheet changes   The first of the three steps noted above simply involves placing one balance sheet beside the other and computing the change in the various accounts. This approach is shown in Table 7-1 for King Manufacturing Ltd. for 1983-84. Note that the changes for the Accumulated Depreciation and Retained Earnings accounts are not computed in that table. These accounts are considered separately when we focus on the income statement and statement of retained earnings. Furthermore, a positive change in liabilities and equity (preferred and common stock and contributed capital accounts) and a negative change in assets are sources of funds. The reverse is true for uses of funds—a negative change in liabilities and equity and a positive change in assets reflect uses of funds.

Income statement and statement of retained earnings   Funds provided by operations are not usually expressed directly on the income statement. To determine them; we must add back non-cash charges (such as depreciation) to net income after taxes. For King Manufacturing Ltd., our example in the previous chapter (Table 6-1), we have

Net income after taxes	$ 95 000
Add noncash expenses: depreciation	90 000
Funds provided by operations	$185 000

Thus, the net income of King understates funds provided by operations by $90 000. Depreciation is not a source of funds, for funds are generated only from operations.[1] If operating losses before depreciation are sustained, funds are not

---

[1]For an extensive discussion of this concept, see Robert K. Jaedicke and Robert T. Sprouse, *Accounting Flows: Income, Funds and Cash* (Englewood Cliffs, N.J.: Prentice Hall, Inc., 1965), 80-86.

TABLE 7-1 Balance Sheet of King Manufacturing Ltd. and Changes in Selected Items

Assets	March 31, 1984	March 31, 1983	Changes 1983-84
Cash and marketable securities	$ 488 000	$ 484 000	+ 4 000
Accounts receivable (Net)	531 000	502 000	+ 29 000
Inventories, at the lower of cost or market	788 000	750 000	+ 38 000
Prepaid expenses	67 000	34 000	+ 33 000
Current assets	$1 874 000	$1 770 000	+ 104 000
Fixed assets at cost	1 807 000	1 730 000	+ 77 000
Less accumulated depreciation	863 000	773 000	*
Net fixed assets	944 000	957 000	**
Investment—Long-term	55 000		+ 55 000
Goodwill	298 000	298 000	0
	$3 171 000	$3 025 000	

Liabilities and Shareholders' Equity	March 31, 1984	March 31, 1983	Changes 1983-84
Bank loans and notes payable	$ 666 000	$ 615 000	+ 51 000
Accounts payable	176 000	188 000	− 12 000
Accrued liabilities	192 000	153 000	+ 39 000
Current liabilities	$1 034 000	$ 956 000	+ 78 000
Long-term debt	302 000	285 000	+ 17 000
Shareholders' Equity			
Common stock $10 par value	440 000	440 000	0
Contributed capital—premium on common shares	382 000	382 000	0
Retained earnings	1 013 000	962 000	*
Total shareholders' equity	1 835 000	1 784 000	
	$3 171 000	$3 025 000	

*These accounts are taken into consideration when we analyze the income statement and the statement of retained earnings.

**In cases where only the net fixed assets are reported, we have to recast the account to ascertain gross change in fixed assets. For example, the net fixed assets are $957 000 in 1983 and $944 000 in 1984, and depreciation in 1984 is $90 000 (Table 6-2). The gross change in fixed assets is $944 000 ($957 000 − $90 000) = $77 000.

provided regardless of the magnitude of depreciation charges.

The statement of retained earnings is usually analyzed to see if any dividends were paid. In King's case, the income statement (Table 6-2) reported that $44 000 were paid as dividends in 1984. In a number of cases, the dividend payments may not be given in the income statement and there may not be a statement of retained earnings. Here the approach will be to prepare a simple version of the statement of retained earnings to identify payments. For King the statement of retained earnings would read as follows:

Retained earnings—March 31, 1983	$	962 000
Add net income		95 000
		$1 057 000
Less dividends		44 000
Retained earnings—March 31, 1984		$1 013 000

The source and use of funds statement Once all sources and uses figures are computed, they may be arranged in statement form so that we can analyze them better. Table 7-2 shows a source and use of funds statement for King Manufacturing Ltd. for the fiscal year ended March 31, 1984. The balance sheet and income statement for this company, on which the funds statement is based, are shown in Tables 6-1 and 6-2 of Chapter 6 and in Table 7-1. When we subtract the total uses of funds in Table 7-2 from the total sources, the difference should equal the actual change in cash position between the two statement dates. If it does not, then the analyst must search for the cause of the discrepancy. Frequently, discrepancies will be due to surplus adjustments; the analyst should be alert to this possibility.[2]

In Table 7-2, we see that the principal uses of funds for the 1984 fiscal year were additions to fixed assets and increases in investments, inventories, prepaid expenses, and accounts receivable. These uses were financed primarily from funds provided by operations in excess of dividends, and from increases in bank loans and accruals. As sources slightly exceeded the uses of funds, the cash balance rose by $4 000.

FUNDS AS WORKING CAPITAL

Financial analysts frequently also prepare a source and use of working capital statement. This statement is very similar to the source and use of funds statement, but takes into account working capital instead of cash. A source and use of working capital statement for King Manufacturing Ltd. for the year ended March 31, 1984 is shown in Table 7-3. We see that the only difference between this statement and a funds statement on a cash basis is the omission of changes in the various components of current assets and current liabilities.

The increase in working capital of $26 000 in Table 7-3 may be verified as follows:

Net working capital—March 31, 1984	$840 000
(Current assets of $1 874 000 less current liabilities of $1 034 000, Table 7-1)	
Less: net working capital—March 31, 1983	$814 000
(Current assets of $1 770 000 less current liabilities of $956 000, Table 7-1)	
Equals: net increase in working capital	$ 26 000

---

[2]For a more detailed description of the preparation of a funds-flow statement, see Myron J. Gordon and Gordon Shillinglaw, *Accounting: A Management Approach*, 4th ed. (Homewood, Ill.: Richard D. Irwin, Inc., 1969), 497-512.

TABLE 7-2 King Manufacturing Ltd.,—
Sources and Uses of Funds for the Period
March 31, 1983–March 31, 1984
(in thousands)

Sources of Funds			Percent*
Funds from operation			
Net profit	$95		
Depreciation	90	$185	63%
Sale of fixed assets		0	0
Liquidation of current assets (except cash)		0	0
Increase in current liabilities			
Bank loans	$51		
Accruals	39	90	31
Increase in long term debts		17	6
Increase in shareholders' investment			
Common shares	$ 0		0
Contributed capital	0	0	
Total Sources		$292	100%

Uses of Funds			
Increase in current assets (except cash)			
Accounts receivable	$29		
Inventories	38		
Pre-paid expenses	33	$100	35%
Increase in fixed assets		77	26%
Increase in other assets			
Investments		55	19%
Decrease in current liabilities			
Accounts payable		12	4%
Decrease in long term debts		0	0%
Payments to shareholders			
Dividends		44	15%
Sub-total		$288	99%
Increase in cash		4	1%
Total uses		$292	100%

*Percentages are rounded to the nearest whole number.

This statement is analyzed much as the source and use of funds statement is. A source and use of working capital statement is used frequently by bankers, for they often require a borrower to maintain some sort of minimum working capital. It is used also by other lenders and by management for the purpose of internal control.

TABLE 7-3 King Manufacturing Ltd.—Sources and Uses of Working Capital for the period March 31, 1983–March 31, 1984* (in thousands)

Sources of Working Capital			Percent
Funds from operation			
Net profit	$95		
Depreciation	90	$185	92%
Sale of fixed assets		0	0
Increase in long term debts		17	8
Increase in shareholders' investment		0	0
Total sources		$202	100%

Uses of Working Capital		Percent
Increase in fixed assets	$ 77	38%
Increase in other assets		
Investments	55	27%
Decrease in Long term debts	0	0
Payments to shareholders		
Dividends	44	22%
	$176	87%
Increase in working capital	26	13%
Total uses	$202	100%

*The items listed here are taken from Table 7-2.

IMPLICATIONS

The analysis of cash and working capital funds statements give us a valuable insight into the financial operations of a firm—an insight which is especially useful to the financial manager in analyzing past and future expansion plans of the firm and the impact of these plans on liquidity. He or she can detect imbalances in the uses of funds and undertake appropriate corrective actions. For example, an analysis spanning the past several years might reveal a growth in inventories out of proportion to the growth of other assets and with sales. On analysis, he or she might find that the problem was the result of inefficiencies in inventory management. Thus, a funds statement alerts the financial manager to problems that can be analyzed in detail and proper actions taken to correct. When a company has a number of divisions, individual funds statements may prove useful. These statements enable top management to appraise the performance of divisions in relations to the funds committed to them.

Another use of funds statements is in the evaluation of the firm's financing. An analysis of the major sources of funds in the past reveals what portion of the firm's growth was financed internally and what portion externally. In evaluating the firm's financing, the analyst will wish to evaluate the ratio of dividends to earnings relative to the firm's total need for funds. Funds statements are useful also in judging whether the firm has expanded at too fast a rate and whether financing is strained. For example, we can determine if trade credit has increased out of proportion to increases in current assets and to sales. If trade credit has increased at a significantly faster rate, we would wish to evaluate the consequences of increased slowness in trade payments on the credit standing of the firm and its ability to finance future operations. It is also revealing of the firm and its ability to finance future operations. It is also revealing to analyze the mix of short- and long-term financing in relation to the funds needs of the firm. If these needs are primarily for fixed assets and permanent increases in working capital, we might be disturbed if a significant portion of total financing came from short-term sources.

An analysis of a funds statement with an eye to the future is extremely valuable to the financial manager in planning the immediate and long-term financing of the firm. It tells him or her the firm's total prospective need for funds, the expected timing of these needs, and their nature—that is, whether the increased investment is primarily for inventories, fixed assets, and so forth. Given this information, along with the expected changes in trade payables and the various accruals, the financial manager can arrange the firm's financing more effectively. In addition, the expected closing cash position of the firm can be determined simply by adjusting the beginning cash balance for the change in cash reflected in the projected source and use statement. In essence, the projected change in cash is a residual. Alternatively, the financial manager can forecast future cash positions of the firm through a cash budget, where direct estimates of future cash flows are made.

Cash Flow Forecasting

A cash budget involves a projection of future cash receipts and cash disbursements of the firm over various intervals of time. From it the financial manager can estimate the timing and amount of expected cash inflows and outflows over the period studied. With this information, the financial manager is better able to determine the future cash needs of the firm, plan for the financing of these needs, and exercise control over the cash and liquidity of the firm.

Cash budgets may be for almost any period of time. For near-term forecasts, monthly periods are probably the ones used most frequently because they take into account seasonal variations in cash flows. When cash flows are extremely volatile but predictable, the preparation of budgets at more frequent intervals may be necessary for determining peak cash requirements. By the same token, when cash flows are relatively stable, budgeting at quarterly or even longer intervals may be justified. Generally, the farther in the future the period for which one is trying to predict cash flows, the more uncertain the forecast. The expense of preparing monthly cash budgets is usually warranted only for predictions concerning the near future. As we shall see, the cash budget is only as useful as the accuracy of the forecasts that are relied on in its preparation.

SALES FORECAST

The key to the accuracy of most cash budgets is the sales forecast. This forecast can be based on an internal analysis, an external one, or both. With an internal approach, sales personnel are asked to project sales for the forthcoming period. The product sales managers screen these estimates and consolidate them into sales estimates for product lines. The estimates for the various product lines are then combined into an overall sales estimate for the firm. The basic problem with an internal approach is that in can be too myopic. Often, important trends in the economy and in the industry are overlooked.

For this reason, many companies use an external analysis as well. With an external approach, economic analysts make forecasts of the economy and of industry sales for several years to come. Here, regression analysis may be used to estimate the association between industry sales and the economy in general. Given these basic predictions of business conditions and industry sales, the next step is to estimate market share of individual products, the prices that are likely to prevail, and the expected reception of new products. Usually, these estimates are made in conjunction with marketing managers. However, the ultimate responsibility should lie with the economic forecasting department. With this information, an external forecast of sales can be prepared.

When the internal forecast of sales differs from the external one, as it is likely to do, a compromise must be reached. Past experience will show which of the two forecasts is more accurate. In general, the external forecast should serve as the foundation for the final sales forecast. However, it will often need to be modified by the internal forecast. For example, the firm might expect to receive several large orders from customers, and these orders might not show up in the external forecast. Basing the final sales forecast on both internal and external analyses is usually more accurate than either an internal or external forecast by itself. The final sales forecast should be based on prospective demand and should not be modified initially by internal constraints such as physical capacity. The decision to remove those constraints will depend on the forecast. The importance of accurate sales forecasts cannot be overestimated, for most other forecasts, in some measure, are based on expected sales.

CASH INFLOWS AND COLLECTION OF SALES PROCEEDS

Given the sales forecast, the next job is to determine the cash receipts from these sales. With cash sales, cash is received at the time of the sale; with credit sales, however, the receipts do not come until later. How much later will depend on the billing terms given, the type of customer, and the credit and collection policies of the firm. Suppose, for purposes of illustration, that the terms offered by Cabot Company Ltd. are net 30, meaning that payment is due within 30 days after the invoice date. Assume also that in the company's experience, 90 percent of receivables are collected, on the average, one month from the date of the sale, and that 10 percent are collected two months from the date of the sale, with no bad-debt percent losses. Moreover, on the average, 10 percent of total sales are cash sales.

If the sales forecasts are those shown in the first line of Table 7-4, we can compute a schedule of the expected sales receipts based on the above assumptions. This schedule appears in Table 7-4. For January, we see that total sales are estimated to be $250 000, of which $25 000 are cash sales. Of the $225 000 in credit sales, 90 percent or $202 500, is expected to be collected in February; and 10

TABLE 7-4 Schedule of Sales Receipts (in thousands)

	Nov.	Dec.	Jan.	Feb.	Mar.	Apr.	May	June
Total sales	$300.0	$350.0	$250.0	$200.0	$250.0	$300.0	$350.0	$380.0
Credit sales	270.0	315.0	225.0	180.0	225.0	270.0	315.0	342.0
Collections— one month		243.0	283.5	202.5	162.0	202.5	243.0	283.5
Collections— two months			27.0	31.5	22.5	18.0	22.5	27.0
Total collections			$310.5	$234.0	$184.5	$220.5	$265.5	$310.5
Cash sales			25.0	20.0	25.0	30.0	35.0	38.0
Total sales receipts			$335.5	$254.0	$209.5	$250.5	$300.5	$348.5

percent or $22 500, is expected to be collected in March. Similarly, sales in other months are broken down according to the same percentages. The firm should be alert to change its assumptions with respect to collections when there is an underlying shift in the payment habits of its customers. For example, if there is a slowdown in the economy, certain customers are likely to become slower in their trade payments. The firm must take account of this change if its cash budget is to be realistic.

From this example, it is easy to see the effect of a variation in sales on the magnitude and timing of cash receipts, all other things held constant. For most firms, there is a degree of correlation between sales and collection experience. In times of recession and sales decline, the average collection period is likely to lengthen and bad-debt losses increase. Thus, the collection experience of a firm may reinforce a decline in sales, magnifying the downward impact on total sales receipts.

CASH DISBURSEMENTS

Next comes a forecast of cash disbursements. Given the sales forecast, a production schedule may be established. Management may choose either to gear production closely to sales or to produce at a relatively constant rate over time. With the former production strategy, inventory carrying costs are generally lower, but total production costs are higher than with the latter strategy. With steady production, the opposite usually occurs. If sales fluctuate, finished goods inventories build up during certain periods and require storage. Because storage is uneven throughout the year, inventory carrying costs are generally higher than they would be if production were geared to sales. On the other hand, production is usually more efficient. The decision on which alternative is best will depend on the added cost of carrying inventory when production is geared to sales relative to the savings available if production is steady. The final production schedule embodies decisions with respect to inventory management, a topic taken up in Chapter 10.

Production outflows Once a production schedule has been established, estimates can be made of the materials that will need to be purchased, the labor that will be required, and any additional fixed assets the firm will need to acquire. As with

TABLE 7-5   Schedule of Expenses (in thousands)

	Dec.	Jan.	Feb.	Mar.	Apr.	May	June
Purchases	$100	$ 80	$100	$120	$140	$150	$150
Cash payment for purchases		100	80	100	120	140	150
Wages paid	70	80	80	90	90	95	100
Other expenses		50	50	50	50	50	50
Total cash expenses		$230	$210	$240	$260	$285	$300

receivables, there is a lag between the time a purchase is made and the time of actual cash payment. If the average billing terms given by suppliers are net 30, and the firm's policy is to pay its bills at the end of this period, there is approximately a one-month lag between a purchase and the payment. If the production program of Cabot calls for the manufacture of goods in the month preceding forecasted sales, we might have a schedule of expenses like that in Table 7-5. As we see, there is a one-month lag between the time of purchase and the payment for the purchase.

Wages are assumed to increase with the amount of production. Generally, wages are more stable over time than are purchases. When production dips slightly, workers are not usually laid off. When production picks up, labor becomes more efficient with relatively little increase in total wages. Only after a certain point is overtime work required or do new workers have to be hired to meet the increased production schedule. Included in other expenses are general, administrative, and selling expenses; property taxes; interest expenses; power, light, and heat expenses; maintenance expenses; and indirect labor and material expenses. These expenses tend to be reasonably predictable over the short run.

Other disbursements   In addition to cash expenses, we must take into account capital expenditures, dividends, income taxes, and any other cash outflows. Because capital expenditures are planned in advance, they usually are predictable for the short-term cash budget. As the forecast becomes more distant, however, prediction of these expenditures becomes less certain. Dividend payments for most companies are stable and are paid on specific dates. Estimation of income taxes must be based on projected profits for the period under review. Other cash outlays might be the repurchase of shares or payment of long-term debt. These outlays are combined with total cash expenses to obtain the schedule of total cash disbursements shown in Table 7-6.

TABLE 7-6   Schedule of Cash Disbursements (in thousands)

	Jan.	Feb.	Mar.	Apr.	May	June
Total cash expenses	$230	$210	$240	$260	$285	$300
Capital expenditures		150	50			
Dividend payments			20			20
Income taxes	30			30		
Total cash disbursements	$260	$360	$310	$290	$285	$320

TABLE 7-7   Net Cash Flow and Cash Balance (in thousands)

	Jan.	Feb.	Mar.	Apr.	May	June
Total cash receipts	$335.5	$294.0*	$209.5	$250.5	$300.5	$348.5
Total cash disbursements	260.0	360.0	310.0	290.0	285.0	320.0
Net cash flow	$ 75.5	$ (66.0)	$(100.5)	$ (39.5)	$ 15.5	$ 28.5
Beginning cash without financing	100.0	175.5	109.5	9.0	(30.5)	(15.0)
Ending cash without financing	175.5	109.5	9.0	(30.5)	(15.0)	13.5
Monthly financing (repayment)	—	—	66.0	39.5	(15.5)	(28.5)
Beginning cash with financing	100.0	175.5	109.5	75.0	75.0	75.0
Ending cash with financing	175.5	109.5	75.0	75.0	75.0	75.0
Cumulative financing**	—	—	66.0	105.5	90.0	61.5

*Includes receipts of $254 000 and cash sale of assets of $40 000

**This is the sum of the monthly financing (repayment).

NET CASH FLOW AND CASH BALANCE

Once we are satisfied that we have taken into account all foreseeable cash inflows and outflows, we combine the cash receipts and cash disbursements schedules to obtain the net cash inflow or outflow for each month. The net cash flow may then be added to beginning cash in January which is assumed to be $100 000, and the projected cash position computed month by month for the period under review. This final schedule or *cash budget* is shown in Table 7-7.

The cash budget shown indicates that the firm is expected to have a cash deficit in April and May. This deficit is caused by a decline in collections through March, capital expenditures totaling $200 000 in February and March, and a cash dividend of $20 000 in March. With the increase in collections in May and June, the cash balance without financing rises to $13 500 in June. The cash budget indicates that peak cash requirements occur in April. If the firm has a policy of maintaining a minimum cash balance of $75 000 and of borrowing from its bank to maintain this minimum, it will need to borrow an additional $66 000 in March. Additional borrowings will peak at $105 500 in April, after which they will decline to $61 500 in June, if all goes according to prediction. The effects of borrowing are shown at the bottom of Table 7-7.

Alternative means of meeting the cash deficit are available. The firm may be able to delay its capital expenditures or its payments for purchases. Indeed, one of the principal purposes of a cash budget is to determine the timing and magnitude of prospective financing needs so that the most appropriate method of financing can be arranged. A decision to obtain long-term financing should be based on long-range funds requirements and on considerations apart from a cash forecast. In addition to helping the financial manager plan for short-term financing, the cash budget is valuable in managing the firm's cash position. On the basis of a cash budget, the financial manager can plan to invest excess funds in marketable securities. The result is an efficient transfer of funds from cash to marketable securities and back.

Range of Cash-Flow Estimates

Often, there is a tendency to place considerable faith in the cash budget simply because it is expressed in figures. It is important to stress again that a cash budget represents merely an *estimate* of future cash flows. Depending on the care devoted to preparing the budget and the volatility of cash flows resulting from the nature of the business, actual cash flows will deviate more or less widely from those that were expected. In the face of uncertainty, we must provide information from the range of possible outcomes. Analyzing cash flows under only one set of assumptions, as is the case with conventional budgeting, results in a faulty perspective of the future.

DEVIATIONS FROM EXPECTED CASH FLOWS

To predict deviations from the expected cash flows, it is desirable to work out additional cash budgets. For example, we might want to base one cash forecast on the assumption of a maximum probable decline in business, and another on the assumption of the maximum probable increase in business. By bringing possible events into the open for discussion, management is better able to plan for contingencies. Not only will such discussion sharpen its perspective on the probability of occurrence of a particular event, but it will give management a better understanding of the magnitude of its impact on the firm's cash flows.[3] Following the preparation of a cash budget based on expected cash flows, it is often a simple matter to trace a change in one or a series of figures in order to take into account a

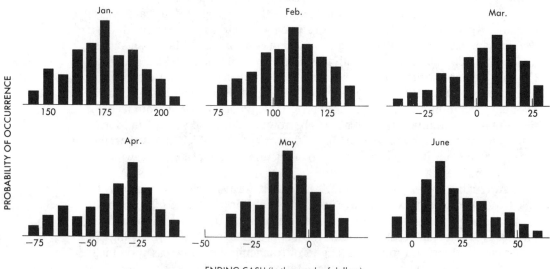

FIGURE 7-2   Distributions of ending cash

[3]See Gordon Donaldson, "Strategy for Financial Emergencies," *Harvard Business Review*, 47 (November-December 1969), 69.

large number of possibilities. Examples of a change in assumptions include a decline in sales or an increase in the average collection period. With each set of assumptions and resulting cash budget, a probability of occurrence should be included.

The final product might be a series of distributions of end of the month cash without financing. An example of frequency distributions of end of period cash for the months of January to June is shown in Fig. 7-2. Bar graphs are used. The most likely values of end of period cash are depicted by the highest bar; these conform with the values shown in Table 7-7. We note that while several of the distributions are reasonably symmetrical, others are skewed. In particular, the distributions for March and April are skewed to the left, meaning that the need for cash during these months might be considerably greater than that depicted in Table 7-7. The type of information shown in Fig. 7-2 better enables management to plan for contingencies than does information giving only single-point estimates of monthly cash flows.[4]

USE OF PROBABILISTIC INFORMATION

The expected cash position plus the distribution of possible outcomes give us a considerable amount of information. We can see the additional funds required or the funds released under various possible outcomes. This information enables us to determine more accurately the minimum cash balance, maturity structure of debt, and borrowing power necessary to give the firm a margin of safety.

We can also analyze the ability of the firm to adjust to deviations from the expected outcomes. For example, if sales should fall off, how flexible are our expenses? What can be cut? By how much? How quickly? How much effort should be devoted to the collection of receivables? In the case of an unexpected increase in business, what additional purchases will be required, and when? Can labor be expanded? Can the present plant handle the additional demand? How much in funds will be needed to finance the buildup? Answers to these questions provide valuable insight into the efficiency and flexibility of the firm under a variety of conditions.[5]

From the standpoint of internal planning, it is far better to allow for a range of possible outcomes than to rely solely on the expected outcome. This allowance is particularly important for firms whose business is relatively unstable in character. If the plans of the firm are based only on expected cash flows, the firm is likely to be caught flat-footed in the case of a significant deviation from the expected outcome, and have difficulty making an adjustment. An unforeseen deficit in cash may be difficult to finance on short notice. Therefore, it is extremely important for the

---

[4]For an additional discussion of probabilistic cash flow information, see James L. Pappas and George P. Huber, "Probabilistic Short-Term Financial Planning," *Financial Management*, 2 (Autumn 1973), 36-44.

[5]Donaldson, in "Strategy for Financial Emergencies," 71-79, develops a framework for evaluating the resources available to meet adverse financial contingencies. These resources include surplus cash, unused lines of credit, negotiated bank loans, long-term debt, new equity, the reduction of planned outflows, and the liquidation of certain assets. Once these resources have been determined together with the time necessary to put them to use, a strategy of response can be formulated. This strategy lays out the sequence in which resources will be brought into play to deal with an unanticipated event.

firm to be honest with itself and attempt to minimize the costs associated with deviations from expected outcomes by taking the steps necessary to assure accuracy and by preparing additional cash budgets so as to take into account the range of possible outcomes. When significant deviations from expected outcomes occur, the cash budget should be revised in keeping with new information.

Forecasting Financial Statements

In addition to projecting the cash flow of a firm over time, it often is useful to prepare a projected, or *pro forma*, balance sheet and income statement for selected future dates. A cash budget gives us information only as to the prospective future cash positions of the firm, whereas *pro forma* statements embody forecasts of all assets and liabilities as well as of income-statement items. Much of the information that goes into the prepartion of the cash budget can be used to derive a *pro forma* statement. In practice, the *pro forma* income statement usually precedes the cash budget. To assist in the preparation of *pro forma* financial statements, let us assume that Cabot had the following balance sheet as at December 31:

Assets (in thousands)		Liabilities (in thousands)	
Cash	$ 100	Bank borrowings	$ 50
Receivables	342	Accounts payable	200
Inventory	350	Accrued wages and expenses	250
		Accrued income taxes	70
Current assets	$ 792	Current liabilities	$ 570
Net fixed assets	800	Net worth	1 022
Total assets	$1 592	Total liabilities and net worth	$1 592

PRO FORMA INCOME STATEMENT

The *pro forma* income statement is a projection of income for a period of time in the future. As with our other projections, the sales forecast is the key input. Given this forecast, production schedules can be formulated and estimates made of production costs for the product or products. The analyst may wish to evaluate each component of the cost of goods sold. A detailed analysis of purchases, production wages, and overhead costs is likely to produce the most accurate forecasts. Often, however, costs of goods sold are estimated on the basis of past ratios of costs of goods sold to sales.

Selling and administrative expenses are estimated next. Because both of these expenses are usually budgeted in advance, estimates of them are fairly accurate. Typically, these expenses are not overly sensitive to changes in sales in the very short run, particularly to reductions in sales. Next, we estimate other income and expenses as well as interest expenses to obtain net income before taxes. Income taxes are then computed based on the applicable tax rate and deducted, to arrive at estimated net income after taxes. All of these estimates are then combined into an income statement.

TABLE 7-8 Cabot Company Ltd.—*Pro Forma* Income Statement for the Six Month Period Ending June 30 (in thousands)

Sales Table 7-4		$1 730
Cost of goods sold:		
Raw materials		
Opening stock (Dec. 31 balance sheet)	$ 350	
Add: purchases (Table 7-5)	740	
	1 090	
Less: closing stock (management estimate)	400	690
Wages (Table 7-5)		505
Depreciation (based on schedules for various assets)		110
Total		$1 305
Gross profit		425
Selling and administrative expenses (Table 7-5)		300
Profit before taxes		125
Taxes (48%)		60
Net profit		65
Common dividends (Table 7-6)		40
Earnings retained		$ 25

The *pro forma* income statement for Cabot for the six months ending June 30 is shown in Table 7-8. Details for sales, purchases of raw materials, wages and selling and administrative expenses are taken from the cash budgets as identified in Table 7-8. Opening stock for the period comes from the December 31 balance sheet and closing stock is an estimate made by the production manager. Depreciation is calculated using the capital cost allowance rates allowed for the various classes of assets. Taxes payable are calculated using the firm's tax rate of 48 percent. The projected net profit of $65 000 will be used for dividends ($40 000) and reinvestment ($25 000).

The *pro forma* income statement need not be based on a cash budget. Instead, we can make direct estimates of expenses using the *percentage-of-sales* method. In Chapter 6, we prepared a common sized income statement where expense items are expressed as a percent of sales. Now if we expect these historical relationships to continue in the near future, we can use those percentages to estimate expenses and prepare a *pro forma* income statement.

PRO FORMA BALANCE SHEET

Given the cash budget and the *pro forma* income statement we are ready to prepare a *pro forma* balance sheet as at June 30. We will forecast the asset base needed to support projected sales and then identify sources of financing.

Forecasting Assets   Receivables at June 30 can be estimated by adding to the receivable balance at December 31 the total projected credit sales from January through June, less total projected credit collections for the period. On the basis of the information in the cash budget, receivables at June 30 would be

Opening receivables (Table 7-9)	$ 342 000
Add: credit sales (Table 7-4)	1 557 000
Less: collection (Table 7-4)	(1 525 500)
Equals: closing receivables	$ 373 500

If a cash budget is not available, the receivable balance may be estimated on the basis of a turnover ratio. This ratio, which depicts the relationship between credit sales and receivables, should be based upon past experience. To obtain the estimated level of receivables, projected sales simply are divided by the turnover ratio. If the sales forecast and turnover ratio are realistic, the method will produce a reasonable approximation of the receivable balance.

The estimated investment in inventories at June 30 may be based upon the production schedule, which, in turn, is based upon the sales forecast. This schedule should show expected purchases, the expected use of inventory in production, and the expected level of finished goods. On the basis of this information, together with the beginning inventory level, a *pro forma* estimate of inventory can be made. Rather than use the production schedule, estimates of future inventory can be based upon a turnover ratio of cost of goods sold to inventory. This ratio is applied in the same manner as that for receivables. Suppose that on the basis of a turnover ratio, we estimate inventory to be $400 000 on June 30, a figure that represents a moderate increase over the inventory level of December 31, in keeping with the buildup in sales.

Future net fixed assets are estimated by adding planned expenditures to existing net fixed assets and subtracting from this sum depreciation for the period, plus any sale of fixed assets at book value. If fixed assets will be sold at their depreciated values and depreciation is expected to be $110 000, the net fixed assets as at June 30 are

Opening net fixed assets (Table 7-9)	$ 800 000
Add: capital expenditures (Table 7-6)	200 000
Less: sales of fixed assets (Table 7-7)	(40 000)
Less: depreciation	(110 000)
Equals: closing balance	$ 850 000

Forecasting liabilities and net worth Turning now to the liabilities, accounts payable are estimated by adding total projected purchases for January through June, less total projected cash payments for purchases for the period, to the December 31 balance. Our estimate of accounts payable, therefore, is

Opening payables (Table 7-9)	$ 200 000
Add: credit purchases (Table 7-5)	740 000
Less: payments (Table 7-5)	(690 000)
Equals: closing payables	$ 250 000

The calculation of accrued wages and expenses is based upon the production schedule and the historical relationship between these accruals and production. We assume the estimate of accrued wages and expenses to be $220 000. Accrued income taxes are estimated by adding to the current balance taxes on forecasted income for the 6-months' period, less the actual payment of taxes. If income taxes for the period are forecast at $60 000, as shown in the *pro forma* income statement, and the firm is scheduled to make $60 000 in actual payments, estimated accrued income taxes at June 30 would be $70 000.

Net worth at June 30 would be the net worth at December 31 plus profits after taxes for the period, less the amount of cash dividends paid. If profits after taxes are estimated at $65 000 in the *pro-forma* income statement, net worth at June 30 would be $1 022 000 plus $65 000 minus dividends of $40 000, or $1 047 000. Two items remain: cash and bank loans. We see from the cash budget that estimated cash at June 30 would be $13 500 without additional financing. If the firm has the policy of maintaining a minimum cash balance of $75 000 and borrowing from its bank to maintain this balance, cash at June 30 would be $75 000, and bank borrowings would increase by $61 500 to $111 500. In general, cash and notes payable serve as balancing factors in the preparation of *pro forma* balance sheets, whereby assets and liabilities plus net worth are brought into balance.

Once we have estimated all the components of the *pro forma* balance sheet, they are combined into a balance sheet format. The *pro forma* balance sheet at June 30 is shown in Table 7-9.

PRO FORMA SOURCE AND USE OF FUNDS STATEMENT

Given the *pro forma* income statement and balance sheet, we can prepare a *pro forma* source and use of funds statement for the six month period ended June 30. Following the procedures outlined earlier in this chapter, we prepare the statement shown in Table 7-10. We see that the firm is expecting to get about 54 percent of its funds from internal sources, one-third from increases in current

TABLE 7-9   Cabot Company Ltd.—Balance Sheets at Selected Dates (in thousands)

	Actual as at Dec. 31	Pro Forma as at June 30
Cash	$ 100	$ 75.0
Receivables	342	373.5
Inventory	350	400.0
Current assets	792	848.5
Net fixed assets	800	850.0
	$1 592	$1 698.5
Bank borrowings	$ 50	$ 111.5
Accounts payable	200	250.0
Accrued wages and expenses	250	220.0
Accrued income taxes	70	70.0
Current liabilities	570	651.5
Net worth	1 022	1 047.0
	$1 592	$1 698.5

liabilities and the balance from the sale of fixed assets. On the other hand, the funds will be used mainly for increases in assets—fixed assets, 61 percent and current assets, 25 percent of net funds.

As before, the cash-budget method is but one way to prepare a *pro forma* statement; one can also make direct estimates of all of the items on the balance sheet by projecting financial ratios into the future and then making estimates on the basis of these ratios. Receivables, inventories, accounts payable, and accrued wages and expenses frequently are based upon historical relationships to sales and production when a cash budget is not available. For example, if the average collection period is 45 days, turnover would be eight times a year. If receivables were $500 000 but the firm were predicting a $2 million increase in sales for the coming year, it would take approximately $2 million/8 = $250 000 in additional receivables to support the added sales. Thus the level of receivables one year hence might be forecast at $750 000.

Pro forma statements allow us to study the composition of expected future balance sheets and income statements. Financial ratios may be computed for analysis of the statements; these ratios and the raw figures may be compared with those for present and past balance sheets. Using this information, the financial manager can analyze the direction of change in the financial condition and performance of the firm over the past, the present, and the future. If the firm is

TABLE 7-10   Cabot Company Ltd.—*Pro Forma* Sources and Uses of Funds Statement for the Six Months Ending June 30 (in thousands)

Sources of Funds			
Funds from operation			
Net profit	$ 65		
Depreciation	110	$175.0	54%
Sale of fixed assets		40.0	12%
Increase in current liabilities			
Bank borrowing	$ 61.5		
Accounts payable	50.0	111.5	34%
Total sources		$326.5	100%

Uses of Funds			
Increase in current assets			
Receivables	$ 31.5		
Inventory	50.0	$ 81.5	25%
Increase in fixed assets		200.0	61%
Decrease in current liabilities			
Accrued wages and expenses		30.0	10%
Payments to shareholders			
Dividends		40.0	12%
		$351.5	108%
Decrease in cash		(25.0)	(8%)
Total Uses		$326.5	100%

accustomed to making accurate estimates, the preparation of a cash budget, *pro forma* statements, or both literally forces it to plan ahead and to coordinate policy in the various areas of operation. Continual revision of these forecasts keeps the firm alert to changing conditions in its environment and in its internal operations. Again, it is useful to prepare more than one set of *pro forma* statements in order to take into account the range of possible outcomes.

Summary

Continuing our examination of the analytical tools of the financial manager, we looked at source and use of funds statements, the cash budget, and *pro forma* statements. The source and use of funds statement gives the financial analyst considerable insight into the uses of funds and how these uses are financed over a specific period of time. Funds-flow analysis is valuable in analyzing the commitment of funds to assets and in planning the firm's intermediate- and long-term financing. The flow of funds studied, however, represents net rather than gross transactions between two points in time.

A cash budget is a forecast of a firm's future cash receipts and cash disbursements. This forecast is particularly useful to the financial manager in determining the probable cash balances of the firm over the near future and in planning for the financing of prospective cash needs. In addition to analyzing expected cash flows, the financial manager should take into account possible deviations from the expected outcome. An analysis of the range of possible outcomes enables management to better assess the efficiency and flexibility of the firm and to determine the appropriate margin of safety.

Finally, we considered the preparation of *pro forma* income statements and balance sheets. These statements offer financial managers insight into the prospective future financial condition and performance of their firms, giving them yet another tool for financial planning and control.

Questions

1. Contrast the source and use of funds statements with a cash budget as planning tools.
2. In constructing a cash budget, which variable is most important in order to arrive at accurate projections? Explain.
3. Discuss the benefits that can be derived by the firm from cash budgeting.
4. Explain why a decrease in cash constitutes a source of funds while an increase in cash is a use of funds in the source and use statement.
5. Explain why selling inventory to credit customers is considered as a source of funds when in fact no funds were generated.
6. Why do most audited financial reports to the shareholders include a source and use of funds statement in addition to the balance sheet and income statement?
7. Is depreciation a source of funds? Under what conditions might the "source" dry up?
8. Why do bankers closely analyze the source and use of funds statement in considering credit applications?

9. Which of the following are sources of funds and which are uses of funds?
- (a) Sale of land
- (b) Quarterly dividend payment
- (c) Lease payment
- (d) Decrease in raw-materials inventory
- (e) Increase in depreciation charges
- (f) Sale of government bonds

10. On what items should the financial manager concentrate to improve the accuracy of the cash budget? Explain your reasoning.

11. Is the cash budget a better measure of liquidity than traditional measures such as the current ratio and acid test ratio?

12. Why is the sales forecast so important in preparing the cash budget?

13. What is the principal purpose of *pro forma* statements? Being a projection of the future, how do they differ from the cash budget?

Problems with Solutions

1. The balance sheets for Parker Poultry Ltd. for the years ending Dec. 31, 19X1 and 19X2 are shown in columns (1) and (2) below. Prepare a source and use of funds statement.

Parker Poultry Ltd.
Changes in Selected Balance Sheet Accounts

	(1) Dec. 31/19X1	(2) Dec. 31/19X2	(3) Changes (2)−(1)	
Current Assets				
Cash on hand & in bank	$ 2 700	$ 1 900	$− 800	(source)
Accounts receivable	0	5 500	+ 5 500	(use)
Inventory	10 000	12 000	+ 2 000	(use)
Prepaid expenses	0	1 300	+ 1 300	(use)
Total current assets	$12 700	$20 700		
Fixed Assets				
Land (cost)	$10 000	$10 000	0	
Building (cost)	30 000	30 000	0	
Less: accumulated depreciation	0	900	N/A	
Equals: net book value	$30 000	$29 100	N/A	
Equipment (cost)	$25 000	$30 000	+ 5 000	(use)
Less: accumulated depreciation	0	3 000	N/A	
Equals: net book value	$25 000	$27 000	N/A	
Motor vehicles (cost)	0	$12 000	+12 000	(use)
Less: accumulated depreciation	0	2 400	N/A	
Equals: net book value	0	$ 9 600	N/A	
Furniture & fixtures (cost)	$ 5 000	$ 5 000	0	
Less: accumulated depreciation	0	1 000	N/A	
Equals: net book value	$ 5 000	$ 4 000	N/A	
Total net book value	$70 000	$79 700		
Total Assets	$82 700	$100 400		

Current Debts				
Accounts payable	$ 7 700	$7 880	+ 180	(source)
Bank loan	5 000	8 000	+ 3 000	(source)
Taxes payable	0	4 008	+ 4 008	(source)
Accrued expenses	0	1 500	+ 1 500	(source)
Total current debts	$12 700	$21 388		
Long Term Debts				
Mortgage	$30 000	$28 000	– 2 000	(use)
Term loan	10 000	15 000	+ 5 000	(source)
Total long term debts	$40 000	$43 000		
Shareholders' Equity				
Common shares	$30 000	$30 000	0	
Retained earnings	0	6 012	N/A	
Total equity	$30 000	$36 012		
Total Debts and Equity	$82 700	$100 400		

(a) Verify the changes in each balance sheet item as shown in column (3). The designation N/A (i.e. not applicable) refers to those items which will be picked up from the income statement or items which are irrelevant.

(b) Review the income statement shown below and identify net profit, depreciation and dividends, if any.

Parker Poultry Ltd.
Profit and Loss Statement

			For the year ending Dec. 31, 19X2
Sales			$114 000
Cost of goods sold			
Cost of poultry		38 000	
Processing expenses		10 000	
Wages		24 980	
Depreciation:			
Building	900		
Equipment	3 000	3 900	76 880
Gross margin			$37 120
Other expenses			
Selling & general admin.		20 600	
Depreciation:			
Motor vehicle		2 400	
Furniture & fixtures		1 000	
Interest		2 500	
Miscellaneous		600	27 100
Earnings before taxes			10 020
Taxes (40%)			4 008
Earnings after taxes			$ 6 012

(c) Using the above information, prepare the source and use of funds statement as follows:

Parker Poultry Ltd.—Sources and Use of Cash Statement for the Year Ended Dec. 31, 19X2

			%
Sources of funds			
Funds from operation			
Earnings after tax	$6 012		
Depreciation	7 300	$13 312	48%
Increases in Debts			
Accounts payable	180		
Bank loan	3 000		
Taxes payable	4 008		
Accrued expenses	1 500		
Term loan	5 000	13 688	49
		27 000	
Liquidation of assets			
Cash		800	3
Total sources		$27 800	100%
Uses of funds			
Increases in assets			
Accounts receivable	$5 500		
Inventory	2 000		
Prepaid expenses	1 300		
Equipment	5 000		
Motor vehicles	12 000	25 800	93
Decreases in debt			
Mortgage		2 000	7
Total uses		$27 800	100%

2. Use the information in problem 1 above and prepare a source and use of working capital statement.
   (a) Review problem 1, part (c) and identify items which relate to current assets and current liabilities. These items are usually not included in a sources and uses of working capital statement.
   (b) Prepare the sources and uses of working capital statement as follows:

Parker Poultry Ltd.—Sources and Uses of Working Capital for the Year Ended Dec. 31, 19X2

		$	%
Sources of working capital			
Funds from operation			
Earnings after tax	$6 012		
Depreciation	7 300	$13 312	73
Increases in long term debt			
Term loan		5 000	27
Total sources		18 312	100%
Uses of working capital			

Increases in fixed assets			
Equipment	$ 5 000		
Motor vehicles	12 000	$17 000	93
Decrease in long term debt			
Mortgage		2 000	11
		19 000	104%
Decrease in working capital		(688)	(4)
Total uses		$18 312	100%

(c) Working capital decreased by $688 over the year. (Check to see if this is correct by following the procedures outlined in the text).

Problems

1. Galow Fish Canning Company Ltd. reports the following changes from the previous year end. Categorize these items as either a source of funds or a use of funds.

Item		Item	
Cash	−$100	Accounts payable	$300
Accounts receivable	700	Accruals	− 100
Inventory	− 300	Long term debt	− 200
Gross fixed assets	900	Net profit	600
Depreciation	1 000	Dividends	400

2. Serap-Jones Company Ltd. had the following financial statements for 1983 and 1984. Prepare a source and use of funds statement and evaluate your findings.

		1983	1984	
Assets				
S Cash		$ 53 000	$ 31 000	− 22,000
S Marketable securities		87 000	0	− 87,000
U Accounts receivable		346 000	528 000	+182,000
U Inventories		432 000	683 000	+251,000
Current assets		918 000	1 242 000	
U Net fixed assets		1 113 000	1 398 000	+285,000
Total		$2 031 000	$2 640 000	
Liabilities and equity				
S Accounts payable		$ 413 000	$ 627 000	+214,000
S Accruals		226 000	314 000	+ 88,000
S Bank borrowings		100 000	235 000	+135,000
Current liabilities		739 000	1 176 000	
S Common stock		100 000	100 000	N/A.
S Retained earnings		1 192 000	1 364 000	+172,000
		$2 031 000	$2 640 000	

Note: Depreciation was $189 000 for 1984 and no dividends were paid.

(Hint: Since no income statement is given, prepare a statement of retained earnings to find net profits for 1984).

3.

Kohn Company Ltd. Comparative Balance Sheets at Dec. 31 (in millions)

Assets	19X1	19X2	Liabilities and net worth	19X1	19X2
Cash	$ 5	$ 3	Notes payable	$ 20	$ 0
Accounts receivable	15	22	Accounts payable	5	8
Inventories	12	15	Accrued wages	2	2
Fixed assets, net	50	55	Accrued taxes	3	5
Other assets	8	5	Long term debt	0	15
			Common stock	20	26
			Retained earnings	40	44
Total assets	$ 90	$100	Total liabilities and net worth	$ 90	$100

Kohn Company Ltd. Statement of Income and Retained Earnings, Year Ended December 31, 19X2 (in millions)

Net sales		$50
Expenses		
Cost of goods sold	$25	
Selling, general, and administrative expenses	5	
Depreciation	5	
Interest	1	36
Net income before taxes		$14
Less: taxes		7
Net income		$ 7
Add: retained earnings at 12/31/X1		40
Subtotal		$47
Less: dividends		3
Retained earnings at 12/31/X2		$44

(a) Prepare a source and use of funds statement on a cash basis for 19X2 for the Kohn Company Ltd.

(b) Prepare a source and use of working capital statement for 19X2 for the Kohn Company Ltd.

4. Rodriguez Malting Company Ltd. has received a large order and anticipates the need to increase its borrowings. It must forecast its cash requirements for January, February, and March. Usually, the company collects 20 percent of its sales in the month of sale, 70 percent the next month, and 10 percent in the second month after the sale. All sales are credit sales. Purchases of raw materials to produce malt are made in the month prior to the sale and amount to 60 percent of sales in the subsequent month. However, payments for these purchases are made a month after the purchase. Labor costs, including overtime, are expected to be

$150 000 in January, $200 000 in February, and $160 000 in March. Selling, administrative, tax, and other cash expenses are expected to be $100 000 per month for January, through March. Actual sales in November and December and projected sales for January through April (in thousands) are as follows:

November	$ 500
December	600
January	600
February	1 000
March	650
April	750

On the basis of this information,
  (a) Prepare a cash budget for the months of January, February, and March.
  (b) Determine the amount of borrowings necessary to maintain a cash balance of $50 000 at all times. Cash on hand on January 1 is $50 000 and the outstanding bank loan is $400 000.
5. Prepare a cash budget for the Ace Manufacturing Company Ltd., indicating receipts and disbursements for May, June, and July. The firm wishes to maintain, at all times, a minimum cash balance of $20 000. Determine whether or not borrowing will be necessary during the period and if it is, when and for how much. As of April 30, the firm had a balance of $20 000 in cash.

Actual sales		Forecasted sales	
January	$50 000	May	$ 70 000
February	50 000	June	80 000
March	60 000	July	100 000
April	60 000	August	100 000

Accounts receivable: 50 percent of total sales are for cash. The remaining 50 percent will be collected equally during the following two months (the firm incurs a negligible bad-debt loss).

Cost of goods manufactured: 70 percent of sales. 90 percent of this cost is paid during the first month after incurrence; the remaining 10 percent is paid the following month.

Selling and administrative expenses: $10 000 per month plus 10 percent of sales. All of these expenses are paid during the month of incurrence.

Interest payments: A semiannual interest payment on $150 000 of bonds outstanding (12 percent coupon) is paid during July. An annual $50 000 sinking-fund payment is also made at that time.

Dividends: A $10 000 dividend payment will be declared and paid in July.

Capital expenditures: $40 000 will be invested in plant and equipment in June.

Taxes: Income tax payments of $1 000 will be made in July.

6. Downeast Nautical Company Ltd. expects sales of $2.4 million next year and the same amount the following year. Sales are spread evenly throughout the year. On the basis of the following information, prepare a pro forma balance sheet and income statement for year end:

Cash: Minimum of 4 percent of annual sales.

Accounts receivable: 60-day average collection period based on annual sales.

Inventories: Turnover of eight times a year.

Net fixed assets: $500 000 now. Capital expenditures equal to depreciation.

Accounts payable: One month's purchases.

Accruals: 3 percent of sales.

Bank borrowings: $50 000 now. Can borrow up to $250 000.

Long-term debt: $300 000 now, payable $75 000 at year end.

Common stock: $100 000. No additions planned.

Retained earnings: $500 000 now.

Net profit margin: 8 percent of sales.

Dividends: None.

Cost of goods sold: 60 percent of sales.

Purchases: 50 percent of cost of goods sold.

Income taxes: 50 percent of before-tax profits.

7. Given the information that follows, prepare a cash budget for the Central City Department Store for the first 6 months of 19X2.
   (a) All prices and costs remain constant.
   (b) Sales are 75 percent for credit and 25 percent for cash.
   (c) With respect to credit sales, 60 percent are collected in the month after the sale, 30 percent in the second month, and 10 percent in the third. Bad-debt losses are insignificant.
   (d) Sales, actual and estimated, are

October 19X1	$300 000	March 19X2	$200 000
November 19X1	350 000	April 19X2	300 000
December 19X1	400 000	May 19X2	250 000
January 19X2	150 000	June 19X2	200 000
February 19X2	200 000	July 19X2	300 000

   (e) Payments for purchase of merchandise are 80 percent of the following month's anticipated sales.
   (f) Wages and salaries are

January	$30 000	March	$50 000	May	$40 000
February	40 000	April	50 000	June	35 000

   (g) Rent is $2 000 a month.
   (h) Interest of $7 500 is due on the last day of each calendar quarter.
   (i) A tax prepayment of $50 000 for 19X2 income is due in April.
   (j) A capital investment of $30 000 is planned in June, to be paid for then.
   (k) The company has a cash balance of $100 000 at December 31, 19X1, which is the minimum desired level for cash. Funds can be borrowed in multiples of $5 000. (Ignore interest on such borrowings.)

8. Use the cash budget worked out in problem 7 and the following additional information to prepare a *pro forma* income statement for the first half of 19X2 for the Central City Department Store. (Note that the store maintains a safety stock of inventory.)

(a) Inventory at 31/12/X1 was $200 000.

(b) Depreciation is taken on a straight-line basis on $250 000 of assets with an average remaining life of 10 years and no salvage value.

(c) The tax rate is 50 percent.

9. Given the following information and that contained in problems 7 and 8, construct a *pro forma* balance sheet as of June 30, 19X2, for the Central City Department Store. (Assume that accounts payable stay the same as at December 31, 19X1.)

Central City Department Store Balance Sheet at December 31, 19X1

Assets		Liabilities and equity	
Cash	$100 000	Accounts payable	$130 000
Accounts receivable	427 500	Bonds	500 000
Inventory	200 000		
Fixed assets, net	250 000	Common stock and retained earnings	347 500
	$977 500		$977 500

Selected References

CHAMBERS, JOHN C., SATINDER K. MULLICK, and DONALD D. SMITH, "How to Choose the Right Forecasting Technique," *Harvard Business Review*, 49 (July-August 1971), 45-74.

CLARK, RICHARD S., "Statement of Changes: In Need of a Change?" *C A Magazine* (Feb. 1983), 26-33.

DONALDSON, GORDON, "Strategy for Financial Emergencies," *Harvard Business Review*, 47 (November-December 1969), 67-79.

HELFER, ERICH A., *Techniques of Financial Analysis*, 5th ed. Homewood, Ill.: Irwin, 1981, Chapters 1 and 3.

HINES, DAN R., "An Input-Output Statement for Managerial Analysis of Changes in Financial Position," *Cost and Management* (Nov.-Dec. 1980), 33-38.

HUNT, PEARSON, "Funds Position: Keystone in Financial Planning," *Harvard Business Review*, 53 (May-June), 106-15.

JAEDICKE, ROBERT K., and ROBERT T. SPROUSE, *Accounting Flows: Income, Funds, and Cash*, Englewood Cliffs, N.J.: Prentice-Hall 1965, Chapters 5 and 6.

JUDELSON, DAVID N., "Financial Controls that Work," *Financial Executive*, 45 (January, 1977), 22-27.

PAN, JUDY, DONALD R. NICHOLS, and O. MAURICE JOY, "Sales Forecasting Practices of Large U.S. Industrial Firms," *Financial Management*, 6 (Fall 1977), 72-77.

PAPPAS, JAMES L., and GEORGE P. HUBER, "Probabilistic Short-Term Financial Planning," *Financial Management*, 2 (Autumn 1973), 36-44.

PARKER, GEROGE G. C., and EDILBERTO L. SEGURA, "How to Get a Better Forecast," *Harvard Business Review*, 49 (March-April 1971), 99-109.

SMITH, KEITH V., *Guide to Working Capital Management*, New York: McGraw-Hill, 1979, Chapter 2.

IV

WORKING
CAPITAL
MANAGEMENT

8

Current Asset and Liability Structure Decisions

Introduction

Current assets, by accounting definition, are assets normally converted into cash within one year. Working capital management usually is considered to involve the administration of these assets—namely, cash and marketable securities, receivables, and inventories—and the administration of current liabilities. Administration of *fixed assets* (assets normally not converted into cash within the year), on the other hand, is usually considered to fall within the realm of capital budgeting, which we take up in Part V. By and large, investment in current assets is more divisible than investment in fixed assets, a fact that has implications for flexibility in financing. Differences in divisibility as well as in durability of economic life are the essential features that distinguish current from fixed assets.

Determining the appropriate levels of current assets and current liabilities, which determine the level of working capital, involves fundamental decisions on the firm's liquidity and the maturity composition of its debt. In turn, these decisions are influenced by a tradeoff between profitability and risk. In a broad sense, the appropriate decision variable to examine on the asset side of the balance sheet is the maturity composition, or liquidity, of the firm's assets—that is, the turnover of these assets into cash. Decisions that affect liquidity of the firm include the management of cash and marketable securities, credit policy and procedures, inventory management and control, and the administration of fixed assets. For purposes of illustration, we hold constant the last three factors; the efficiency in managing them is taken up elsewhere in the book.[1] We assume also that the cash and marketable securities held by the firm (hereafter called liquid assets) yield a return lower than the return on investment in other assets.

---

[1]See Chapter 10 and Part V.

202

For current assets, then, the lower the proportion of liquid assets to total assets, the greater the firm's return on total investment. Profitability with respect to the level of current liabilities relates to differences in costs between various methods of financing and to the use of financing during periods when it is not needed. To the extent that the explicit costs of short term financing are less than those of intermediate and long term financing, the greater the proportion of short term debt to total debt, the higher the profitability of the firm.

Although short-term rates sometimes exceed long term rates, generally they are less. Even when they are higher, the situation is likely to be only temporary. Over an extended period of time we would expect to pay more in interest cost with long-term debt than we would with short term borrowings which are continually rolled over at maturity. Moreover, the use of short term debt as opposed to longer-term debt is likely to result in higher profits because debt will be paid off during periods when it is not needed.

The profitability assumptions above suggest a low proportion of current assets to total assets and a high proportion of current liabilities to total liabilities. This strategy, of course, will result in a low level of working capital or, conceivably, even negative working capital. Offsetting the profitability of this strategy is the risk to the firm. For our purposes, risk is the probability of technical insolvency. In a legal sense, insolvency occurs whenever the assets of a firm are less than its liabilities—negative net worth. Technical insolvency, on the other hand, occurs whenever a firm is unable to meet its cash obligations.[2]

In this chapter we study the extent to which possible adverse deviations from expected net cash flows (cash inflows less cash outflows) are protected by the liquid assets of the firm. The risk involved with various levels of current assets and current liabilities must be evaluated in relation to the profitability associated with those levels. The discussion that follows concerns the financing of current assets and the level of those assets that should be maintained.

The Maturity Structure of Financing

The way in which the assets of a company are financed involves a tradeoff between risk and profitability. For purposes of analysis, we assume that the company has an established policy of payment for purchases, labor, taxes, and other expenses. Thus, the amounts of accounts payable and accruals included in current liabilities are not active decision variables.[3] These liabilities finance a portion of the current assets of the firm and tend to fluctuate with the production schedule and, in the case of

---

[2]James E. Walter, "Determination of Technical Solvency," *Journal of Business*, 30 (January 1957), 30-43.

[3]Delaying the payment of accounts payable can be a decision variable for financing purposes. However, there are limits to the extent to which a firm can "stretch" its payables. For simplicity, we assume in the above analysis that the firm has a definite policy for paying bills, such as taking advantage of all cash discounts and paying all other bills at the end of the credit period. See Chapter 11 for a discussion of trade credit as a means of financing.

taxes, with profits. As the underlying investment in current assets grows, accounts payable and accruals also tend to grow, in part financing the buildup in assets. Our concern is with how assets not supported by accounts payable and accruals are financed.

HEDGING APPROACH

If the firm adopts a hedging approach to financing, each asset would be offset with a financing instrument of the same approximate maturity. Short term or seasonal variations in current assets would be financed with short term debt; the permanent component of current assets would be financed with long term debt or equity. The situation is illustrated in Fig. 8-1. If total funds requirements behave in the manner shown, only the short term debt fluctuations shown at the top of the figure would be financed with short term debt. To finance short-term requirements with long-term debt would necessitate the payment of interest for the use of funds during times when they were not needed. This occurrence can be illustrated by drawing a straight line across the seasonal humps in Fig. 8-1 to represent the total amount of long term debt and equity. It is apparent that financing would be employed in periods of seasonal lull when it was not needed. With a hedging approach to financing, the borrowing and payment schedule for short term financing would be arranged to correspond to the expected swings in current assets, less payables and accruals. Fixed assets and the permanent component of current assets would be financed with long term debt, equity, and the permanent component of current liabilities.

A hedging approach to financing suggests that apart from current installments on long term debt, a firm would show no current borrowings at the seasonal troughs in Fig. 8-1. Short term borrowings would be paid off with surplus cash. As the firm moved into a period of seasonal funds needs, it would borrow on a short

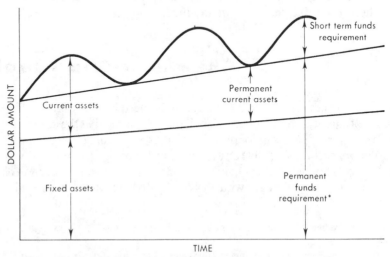

*Financed by long term debt, equity, and the permanent component of current liabilities (accounts payable and accruals).

FIGURE 8-1 Funds requirement—hedging financing policy

term basis, again paying the borrowings off as surplus cash was generated. In this way, financing would be employed only when it was needed. Permanent funds requirements would be financed with long term debt and equity. In a growth situation, permanent financing would be increased in keeping with increases in permanent funds requirements.

SHORT VERSUS LONG TERM FINANCING

Although an exact synchronization of the schedule of expected future net cash flows and the payment schedule of debt is appropriate under conditions of certainty, it usually is not appropriate under uncertainty. Net cash flows will deviate from expected flows in keeping with the business risk of the firm. As a result, the schedule of maturities of the debt contracts is very significant in a risk-profitability tradeoff. The question is, What margin of safety should be built into the maturity schedule in order to allow for adverse fluctuations in cash flows? This depends on the tradeoff between risk and profitability.

The relative risk involved   In general, the shorter the maturity schedule of a firm's debt obligations, the greater the risk that it will be unable to meet principal and interest payments. On the other hand, the longer the maturity schedule, the less risky the financing of the firm, all other things the same.

A company may borrow on a short term basis in order to build a new plant. The cash flows from the plant are not sufficient in the short run to pay off the loan. As a result, the company bears the risk that the lender may not renew the loan at maturity. This risk could be reduced by financing the plant on a long term basis, the expected cash flows being sufficient to retire the debt in an orderly manner. Thus, committing funds to a long term asset and borrowing short carries the risk that the firm may not be able to renew its borrowings. If the company should fall on hard times, creditors might regard renewal as too risky and demand immediate payment. In turn, this would cause the firm either to retrench or to go into bankruptcy.

In addition to this sort of risk, there also is the uncertainty associated with interest costs. When the firm finances with long term debt, it knows precisely its interest costs over the time period it needs the funds. If it finances with short term debt, it is uncertain of interest costs upon refinancing. In a sense, then, the uncertainty of interest costs represents risk to the borrower. We know that short term interest rates fluctuate far more than long term interest rates. During the past decade, the interest rate on short term commercial paper issued by corporations ranged from approximately 5 percent to 20 percent. A firm forced to refinance its short term debt in a period of rising interest rates may pay an overall interest cost on short term debt that is higher than it would have been on long term debt. Therefore, the absence of knowledge of future short term interest costs may represent risk to a company.

The tradeoff with costs   Differences in risk between short and long term financing must be balanced against differences in interest costs. The longer the maturity schedule of a firm's debt, the more costly the financing is likely to be. For one thing, the explicit cost of long term financing usually is more than that of short term

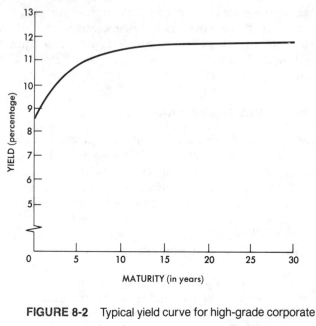

FIGURE 8-2 Typical yield curve for high-grade corporate bonds

financing. Fig. 8-2 illustrates the typical relationship which prevailed from 1970 to the present between interest rates and maturity for high-grade corporate bonds. The line is known as a *yield curve*, and it tells us the yield associated with a given maturity. As shown, the yield curve is upward sloping, which suggests that long term borrowings are more costly than short term borrowings. In addition to the higher expected interests costs of long term borrowings, the firm may pay interest on debt over periods of time when the funds are not needed. Put another way, short term financing gives the firm flexibility. If there is a probability that the firm's need for funds will decrease, the use of short term debt permits debt to be paid off in keeping with the diminished need for funds. Thus, there is an expected cost inducement to finance funds requirements on a short term basis.

Consequently, we have a tradeoff between risk and profitability. We have seen that in general short term debt has greater risk than long term debt, but also less cost. The margin of safety provided by the firm can be thought of as the lag between the firm's expected net cash flow and the contractual payments on its debt. This margin of safety will depend upon the risk preferences of management. In turn, its decision on the maturity composition of the firm's debt will determine the portion of current assets financed by current liabilities and the portion financed on a long term basis.

To allow for a margin of safety, management might decide upon the proportions of short term and long-term financing shown in Fig. 8-3. Here, we see, the firm finances a portion of its expected seasonal funds requirements, less payables and accruals, on a long term basis. If the expected net cash flows do occur, it will pay interest on debt during seasonal troughs when the funds are not needed. In contrast, if an aggressive financing policy were adopted, the situation might look

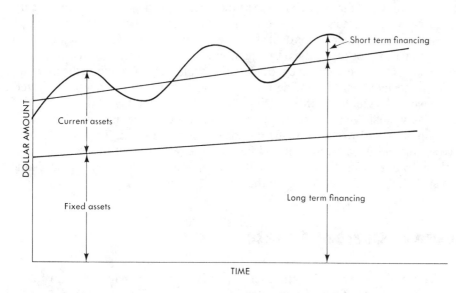

FIGURE 8-3 Funds requirement—conservative financing policy

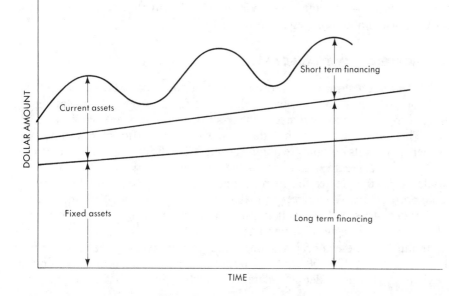

FIGURE 8-4 Funds requirement—aggressive financing policy

like that shown in Fig. 8-4. Here we see that there is a "negative" margin of safety. The firm has financed part of its permanent current assets with short-term debt. As a result, it must refinance this debt at maturity, and this involves an element of risk. The greater the portion of the permanent funds requirements financed with short-term debt, the more aggressive the financing is said to be. Therefore, the margin of safety associated with financing policy can be either positive, negative, or zero. Zero would be the case with a hedging policy, illustrated in Fig. 8-1.

As we shall see in the subsequent section, however, the firm also can create a margin of safety by increasing the proportion of liquid assets. Thus, the firm can reduce the risk of cash insolvency either by increasing the maturity schedule of its debt or by decreasing the relative "maturity" of its assets. At the end of the chapter we explore the interdependence of these two facets.

The Amount of Current Assets

In determining the appropriate level of current assets, management must again consider the tradeoff between profitability and risk. To illustrate this tradeoff, we hold constant the amount of the firm's fixed assets and vary the amount of current assets. Moreover, we assume that the management of receivables and inventories is efficient and consistent throughout the range of output under consideration. In other words, at every level of output, the investment in receivables and inventories is predetermined.[4] As a result, we are concerned only with the cash and marketable securities portion of the current assets of the firm.[5]

RISK-PROFITABILITY TRADEOFF

Under these assumptions there exists a risk-return tradeoff with respect to the relative proportion of current assets held by the firm. In general, the greater the ratio of current assets to total assets, the less risky the company's working capital policy. This makes sense in that the firm will have sufficient cash and cash equivalents to pay its bills the greater the cushion. On the other hand, the lower the ratio, the more aggressive—and risky—the company's working capital policy. At any sales level, the greater the firm's proportion of current assets, the lower its relative profitability. What happens is that the firm has money tied up in idle or near idle current assets. As a result, its profitability is not as high as it would be if the funds were invested in assets providing a higher return.

To illustrate these concepts, suppose that with its existing fixed assets a firm can produce up to 100 000 units of output a year. Production is continuous throughout the period under consideration, in which there is a particular level of

---

[4]The efficiency of management of receivables and inventory is examined in Chapter 10. The quality of these assets, as determined by the efficiency of their management, has a significant bearing upon the liquidity of the firm.

[5]The allocation of funds between cash and marketable securities, near cash, is taken up in Chapter 9.

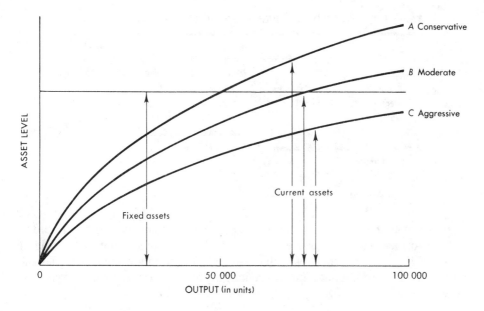

FIGURE 8-5 Relation of current to fixed assets

output. For each level of output, the firm can have a number of different levels of current assets. We assume initially three current-asset alternatives. The relationship between output and current-asset level for these alternatives is illustrated in Fig. 8-5. We see from the figure that the greater the output, the greater the need for investment in current assets. However, the relationship is not linear; current assets increase at a decreasing rate with output. This relationship is based upon the notion that it takes a greater proportional investment in current assets when only a few units of output are produced than it does later on when the firm can use its current assets more efficiently. Fixed assets are assumed not to vary with output.

Of the three alternatives, alternative A is the most conservative level of current assets, for the ratio of current assets to fixed assets is greatest at every level of output. The greater the proportion of current to fixed assets, the greater the liquidity of the firm and the lower the risk of technical insolvency, all other things held constant. Alternative C is the most aggressive policy, because the ratio of current assets to fixed assets is lowest at all levels of output. The probability of technical insolvency is greatest under alternative C if net cash flows are less than expected.

Suppose that for the forthcoming year a firm expects sales of $2 million on 80 000 units of output and expects to realize a profit margin before interest and taxes of 10 percent, or $200 000 in total profits. We assume that this figure will not vary with the levels of current assets considered. Fixed assets are $500 000 for the period under review, and management is considering current asset positions of $400 000, $500 000, or $600 000. Given this information, we are able to make the profitability calculations shown in Table 8-1. As evidenced in this table, the greater the proportion of current assets to fixed assets, the lower the rate of return.

TABLE 8-1 Profitability Under Alternative Current-Asset Positions

	A	B	C
Sales	$2 000 000	$2 000 000	$2 000 000
Earnings before interest and taxes	200 000	200 000	200 000
Current assets	600 000	500 000	400 000
Fixed assets	500 000	500 000	500 000
Total assets	1 100 000	1 000 000	900 000
Asset turnover (sales/total assets)	1.82 : 1	2 : 1	2.22 : 1
Rate of return (earnings/total assets)	18.2%	20%	22.2%

Alternative A, the most conservative plan, gives the firm the greatest liquidity cushion to meet unexpected needs for funds. It also provides the lowest rate of return of the three alternatives. Alternative C, on the other hand, provides the highest rate of return but has the lowest liquidity and, correspondingly, the greatest risk.

SOME QUALIFICATIONS

This is a very simple example of the tradeoff between risk and profitability. Our assumptions were such that changes in the level of current assets were comprised entirely of changes in liquid assets—cash and marketable securities. We should recognize that the generalizations possible become far more complicated when it comes to changes in accounts receivable and inventory. Although receivables do not provide the buffer against running out of cash that cash and marketable securities do, they provide more of a buffer than do inventories or fixed assets. By the same token, the profit foregone by holding receivables generally is less than that for holding cash or marketable securities, but greater than that for holding inventories and fixed assets. Though we may have some idea of the relative ordering of receivables and inventories with respect to risk and profits foregone, the differences are extremely difficult to quantify. In subsequent chapters we deal with the optimal level of each of these assets, taking into consideration both profitability and risk. For now, we continue to restrict our definition of liquid assets to cash and marketable securities.

Combining Liability-Structure and Current-Asset Decisions

In the preceding sections we examined two broad facets of working capital management: how to finance current assets and what proportion of liquid assets to maintain. The two facets are interdependent. All other things held constant, a firm with a high proportion of liquid assets is better able to finance its current assets on a short term basis than is a firm with a low proportion of liquid assets. On the other hand, a firm that finances its current assets entirely with equity will have less need for liquidity than it would if it financed these assets entirely with short term borrowings. Because of their interdependence, these two facets of working-capital management must be considered jointly.

UNCERTAINTY AND THE MARGIN OF SAFETY

If the firm knows its future cash flows with certainty, it will be able to arrange its maturity schedule of debt to correspond exactly with its schedule of future net cash flows. As a result, profits will be maximized, for there will be no need to hold low-yielding liquid assets nor to have more long-term financing than is absolutely necessary. When cash flows are subject to uncertainty, however, the situation is changed. As discussed in Chapter 7, cash forecasts can be prepared for a range of possible outcomes, with a probability attached to each. This information enables management to assess the possibility of technical insolvency and to plan accordingly for a margin of safety. The greater the dispersion of the probability distribution of possible net cash flows, the greater the margin of safety that management will wish to provide.

We assume initially that the firm cannot borrow on short notice to meet unexpected cash drains. As a result, it can provide a margin of safety only by (1) increasing the proportion of liquid assets, and (2) lengthening the maturity schedule of financing. Both of these actions affect profitability. In the first choice, funds are committed to low-yielding assets; in the second, the firm may pay interest on borrowings over periods of time when the funds are not needed. In addition, long-term debt has a higher expected interest cost than does short-term debt.

RISK AND PROFITABILITY

A decision on the appropriate margin of safety will be governed by considerations of risk and profitability and by the utility preferences of management with respect to bearing risk. To the extent that the cost of running out of cash is measurable, the optimal margin of safety can be determined by comparing the expected costs of running out of cash with the profits foregone when a particular solution is used to avoid that possibility. The expected cost of a cash stockout is the cost associated with a particular stockout times its probability of occurrence. Suppose that associated with a particular solution there is a 10 percent probability for a cash stockout of $50 000 and a 5 percent probability that the stockout will be $100 000. If the costs of these stockouts are $10 000 and $25 000, respectively, the expected costs will be 0.10($10 000) = $1 000 and 0.05($25 000) = $1 250, respectively. The total expected cost of cash stockout for that solution is $2 250.

The optimal solution could be determined by comparing the reduction in the expected cost of cash stockout accompanying a particular solution with the opportunity cost of implementing that solution. The optimal solution is at the point where the marginal opportunity cost equals the marginal decrease in the expected cost of cash stockout. The difficulty with this approach, however, is in estimating the cost of a cash stockout. Costs such as deterioration in a firm's credit standing and the inability to pay certain obligations are intangible and defy precise quantification.

Because of this difficulty, it may be easier for management to consider subjectively the costs associated with various cash stockouts and then simply specify a tolerable level of risk. Suppose we find that there is a 5 percent probability that the cash balance of the firm will be −$300 000 or less during the next several periods. If management is willing to tolerate a 5 percent probability of running out of cash, the firm should increase its liquid assets by $300 000. If it does so, there will be only a 5 percent probability that possible deviations from expected cash flows will result in the firm's running out of cash. The firm may be able to achieve the same results by lengthening its maturity schedule of financing. By refinancing existing debt that matures within 2 years into intermediate-term debt maturing in 5 to 7 years, the firm may be able to reduce the probability of technical insolvency to 5 percent. Likewise, various combinations of liquidity increase and debt lengthening may achieve this result.

Each solution (increasing liquidity, lengthening the maturity structure, or a combination of the two), will cost the firm something in profit-making ability. For a given risk tolerance, management may determine which solution is least costly and then implement that solution. On the other hand, management might determine the least costly solution for various levels of risk. Then management could formulate risk tolerances on the basis of the cost involved in providing a margin of safety. Presumably these tolerances would be in keeping with an objective of maximizing shareholder wealth. The approach, however, has been to provide an information framework specifying risk and profitability that management can use to make informed and rational decisions.

If the firm can borrow in times of emergency, the above analysis needs to be modified. The greater the ability of the firm to borrow, the less it needs to provide for a margin of safety by the means discussed previously. Certain companies can arrange for lines of credit or revolving credits that enable them to borrow on short notice.[6] When a company has access to such credit, it must compare the cost of these arrangements (compensating balances, interest costs, and use of debt capacity) with the cost of other solutions. There are, of course, limits on how much a firm may borrow on short notice. Consequently, it must provide for some margin of safety on the basis of the considerations discussed above.

Summary

Working capital management involves deciding upon the amount and composition of current assets and how to finance these assets. These decisions involve tradeoffs between risk and profitability. The greater the relative proportion of liquid assets, the less the risk of running out of cash; all other things being equal. Profitability, unfortunately, also will be less. The longer the composite maturity

---

[6]For a discussion of these methods, see Chapter 12.

schedule of securities used to finance the firm, the less the risk of cash insolvency, all other things being equal. Again, the profits of the firm are likely to be less. Resolution of the tradeoff between risk and profitability with respect to these decisions depends upon the risk preferences of management.

In this chapter we have been concerned with working capital management in a broad sense. We assumed the efficient management of the various components of current assets. The efficiency of credit and collection procedures and inventory control have a significant bearing upon the liquidity of the firm. Moreover, we did not differentiate between cash and marketable securities "near cash" or consider the optimal split between these two assets. In the three subsequent chapters we analyze specifically the management of cash and marketable securities, the management of receivables, and the management of inventories. Still later in this part, we consider methods of short- and intermediate-term financing.

Questions

1. Evaluate the following statement: "Returns on current assets are insignificant; therefore, a business firm should minimize its investment in these assets."

2. The amount of current assets that a firm maintains will be determined by the tradeoff between risk and profitability.
   (a) Is there a unique combination of risk and profitability for each level of current assets?
   (b) Discuss the factors that affect the risk associated with holding current assets.

3. Utilities hold 10 percent of total assets in current assets; retail trade industries hold 60 percent of total assets in current assets. Explain how industry characteristics account for this difference.

4. Some firms finance their permanent working capital with short-term liabilities (commercial paper and short-term notes). Explain the impact of this decision on the profitability and risk parameters of these firms.

5. Suppose a firm finances its seasonal (temporary) current assets with long-term funds. What is the impact of this decision on the profitability and risk parameters of this firm?

6. Risk associated with the amount of current assets is assumed to decrease with increased levels of current assets. Is this assumption correct for all levels of current assets? Explain.

7. Can you compare the net working capital position with the cash budget to measure the ability of a firm to meet maturing obligations?

8. At times, long-term interest rates are lower than short-term rates, yet the discussion in the chapter suggests that long-term financing is more expensive. If long-term rates are lower, should not the firm finance itself entirely with long-term debt?

9. How does shortening the maturity composition of outstanding debt increase the firm's risk? Why does increasing the liquidity of the firm's assets reduce that risk?

10. Why do firms invest in any current assets at all if the returns on those assets are less than the returns from fixed assets?

11. What are the costs of maintaining too large a net working capital position? Too small a net working capital position?

12. What are the main disadvantages of the use of the net working capital position as an indication of a firm's financial solvency?

Problems with Solutions

1. A Company is expanding very rapidly and is encountering some difficulty financing large increases in receivables and inventory. As treasurer of the company you are considering different ways of solving the financial problems. One proposal would have the company stretch the payment of accounts payable to 60 days and thereby generate enough funds to finance current assets. Stretching beyond 60 days is considered to be too risky. Expected purchases for the year are shown below:

Jan	$100 000	July	$240 000
Feb	100 000	Aug	300 000
March	100 000	Sept	150 000
April	150 000	Oct	100 000
May	150 000	Nov	75 000
June	200 000	Dec	75 000
	$800 000		$940 000

Half the company's suppliers offer terms 2/10, n/30, the other half require payment in 30 days. If the payables are stretched, special discounts amounting to 0.5 percent of purchases will also be lost. The company could also borrow to finance inventory and receivables but at a rate of 10 percent. Accounts payable on Dec. 31 of the current year are $55 000. Which course of action should the company take?

Accounts payable taking advantage of discounts and paying other accounts within 30 days (assuming a 360-day year)

End of	Balance*	End of	Balance
Jan	$ 66 667	July	$160 000
Feb	66 667	Aug	200 000
Mar	66 667	Sept	100 000
Apr	100 000	Oct	66 667
May	100 000	Nov	50 000
June	133 333	Dec	50 000

$$*0.5 \text{ Purchases} \times \frac{10}{30} + 0.5 \text{ Purchases} = 0.5 \text{ Purchases} \left(1\frac{1}{3}\right) = 0.667 \text{ Purchases}$$

Accounts payable stretched to 60 days

End of	Balance	End of	Balance
Jan	$155 000**	July	$440 000
Feb	200 000	Aug	540 000
Mar	200 000	Sept	450 000
Apr	250 000	Oct	250 000
May	300 000	Nov	175 000
June	350 000	Dec	150 000

**Assuming Dec. 31st accounts are paid in February.

Cost of stretching
   Lost cash discounts
      Total purchases × ½ × 0.02 =
         $1 740 000 × ½ × 0.02 = $17 400
   Lost special discount
         $1 740 000 × 0.005 = $ 8 700
                              $26 100

Interest savings
   Increased accounts payable or decreased borrowing:
   $3 460 000 − $1 160 001 = $2 299 999*
   Approx. Cost = $2 299 999 ÷ 12 × 0.10 = $19 167
*Total accounts payable stretched to 60 days minus Total accounts payable, taking advantage of discounts.

Stretching payment to 60 days would cost $6 993 ($26 100 − $19 167). Therefore the company should continue to take advantage of discounts.

2. The following information was extracted from the financial statements of three firms operating in the same industry.

December 31, 19X7

	Fixed assets	Current assets	Total assets	Net profit
Firm A	$70 000	$30 000	$100 000	$12 000
Firm B	75 000	25 000	100 000	12 500
Firm C	85 000	15 000	100 000	13 500

Assess the risk-return relationships among the three firms considering that, on average, firms in the industry invest about 25 percent of funds in current assets.
(a) Prepare the following common-size data:

	Firm A	Firm B	Firm C
Current assets	30%	25%	15%
Fixed assets	70%	75%	85%
	100%	100%	100%

(b) Compute the earning power of each firm.

Firm A (12 000/$100 000) × 100 = 12%
Firm B (12 500/$100 000) × 100 = 12.5%
Firm C (13 500/$100 000) × 100 = 13.5%

(c) Firm C has the highest earning power (or return on investment) but it has the lowest safety margin in terms of liquid assets—profits are high consistent with the liquidity risk. Firm A is the opposite—lowest profit but highest liquidity position. Firm B reflects the industry average.

3. The following information was taken from the balance sheets of three firms operating in the same industry.

	Assets		Type of financing	
	Total	Current	Short-term	Long-term
Firm D	$125 000	$22 000	$11 000	$114 000
Firm E	90 000	15 900	17 700	72 300
Firm F	170 000	30 000	13 000	157 000

Assess the strategy used to finance working capital needs for each firm considering that on average, the current ratio for the industry is 2.0.

(a) Compute the current ratio of each firm.
Firm D $22 000/$11 000 = 2.0
Firm E $15 900/$17 700 = 0.9
Firm F $30 000/$13 000 = 2.3

(b) Firm E has an aggressive (or risky) financing strategy. Current assets (and some fixed assets) are financed exclusively by current debt. Other factors remaining constant, interest costs may be less than those for Firm F which has a rather conservative financing strategy. This firm finances more than 50 percent of its current assets through long term sources (i.e. bonds and equity). Firm D reflects the average industry practice where 50 percent of current assets are financed by short term debt.

Problems

1. Anderson Corporation Ltd. has a sales level of $280 000 with a 10 percent net profit margin before interest and taxes. To generate this sales volume, the firm maintains a fixed-asset investment of $100 000. The firm currently maintains $50 000 in current assets.
   (a) Determine the asset turnover for the firm and compute the rate of return on assets.
   (b) Compute the rate of return on assets at different levels of current assets starting with $10 000 and increasing in $15 000 increments to $100 000. Note that total assets will change with each level of current assets.
   (c) What implicit assumption is being made about sales in part (b)? Appraise the significance of this assumption along with the policy to choose the level of current assets that will maximize the return on investments as computed in (b).

2. Pressler Cardboard Company Ltd. estimates the following quarterly net cash flows for the company as a whole over the next 2 years (in millions of dollars):

	19X1				19X2		
1	2	3	4	1	2	3	4
1.2	2.1	(2.7)	(1.9)	1.7	1.6	(3.6)	(1.0)

The company started in 19X1 with $1.5 million in liquid assets.

(a) What is the cumulative liquid asset balance at quarter-end, in the absence of financing?

(b) How much temporary and how much permanent financing should Pressler take on if it wishes to maintain an expected liquid asset balance of at least $1.5 million throughout the 2-year time span?

3. The Malkiel Corporation Ltd. has made the 3-year projection of its asset investment given in the following table. It has found that payables and accruals tend to equal one-third of current assets. It currently has $50 million in equity and the remainder of its capitalization in long-term debt. The earnings retained amount to $1 million/quarter.

(a) Graph the time path of total and fixed assets.

Date	Fixed assets	Current assets
3/31/X1 (now)	$50 (in millions)	$21 (in millions)
6/30/X1	51	30
9/30/X1	52	25
12/31/X1	53	21
3/31/X2	54	22
6/30/X2	55	31
9/30/X2	56	26
12/31/X2	57	22
3/31/X3	58	23
6/30/X3	59	32
9/30/X3	60	27
12/31/X3	61	23

(b) Devise a financing plan, assuming your objective is to use a hedging approach.

(c) If short-term rates average 10 percent and long-term rates average 12 percent, how much would the firm save if its entire current assets were financed by short-term debt?

4. Barnstop Aviation Company Ltd. was founded three years ago. It sells fuel and certain parts to private plane users at Western Airport, a small municipal airport in the central part of British Columbia. The company has been successful in filling an economic need and has experienced good profitability. Up to the present time, however, it has been unable to obtain term financing. As a result, it has had to finance itself by "stretching" its accounts payable and recently, by borrowing from a local finance company. At the end of June, Barnstop had the following debt and net worth:

Accounts payable	$60 000
Short term debt	40 000
Net worth	60 000
	$160 000

Willie Brown, president of Barnstop, estimates that the effective cost of stretching payables is 30 percent per annum, comprised of cash discounts foregone and, in certain cases, payment of higher prices than would otherwise prevail. Only $30 000 of the total payables is stretched; that is, the company has $30 000 in normal payables at the end of June, which are not subject to the 30 percent cost. The rate of interest on the finance company loan is 24 percent. It appears that both sources of financing will be available in the future at the same effective rates of interest.

The company has a seasonal element to its business, with peak requirements in June. In June just passed, it required $100 000 in payables and debt. By the end of December its requirements will decline by 30 percent. Mr. Brown estimates that the company's requirements for payables and debt will be the following next June under three possible states of the economy:

State	Boom	Normal	Recession
Requirements	$160 000	$120 000	$90 000

For December of next year, funds requirements will decline by 30 percent from the requirements shown above for the three possible states of the economy.

Recently the company has been exploring the use of a term loan. Monument Northern Life Insurance Company Ltd. has offered a 5-year term loan at 18 percent interest. The amount is $80 000, and the insurance company will not lend more nor less.

Mr. Brown wishes to evaluate the interest costs of the term loan in relation to the present method of financing at four times: June 30 and December 31 of this year, and June 30 and December 31 of next year. For ease of calculation, we assume that the amounts are outstanding 6 months, as increases and decreases in total financing requirements are steady. Moreover, 30 percent of the total payables and debt requirements are normal payables, for which there is no effective interest cost. The company would then borrow up to $40 000 from the finance company at 24 percent, with anything over that amount obtained from stretching accounts payable at an effective rate of 30 percent.

Which financing alternative has the lower six-month interest costs for each of the four dates and under each of the three possible states of the economy? Why?

Selected References

BIGGS, K. A. "Corporate Financing and Liquidity," *Cost and Management* (Sept.-Oct. 1977), 20-24.

BUDIN, MORRIS, and ROBERT J. VAN HANDEL, "A Rule-of-Thumb Theory of Cash Holdings by Firm," *Journal of Financial and Quantitative Analysis*, 10 (March 1975), 85-108.

EMERY, GARY W., and KENNETH O. COGGER, "The Measurement of Liquidity," Working Paper, Washington University in St. Louis, 1980.

LAMBRIX, R. J., and S. S. SINGHVI, "Managing the Working Capital Cycle," *Financial Executive*, 47 (June 1979), 32-41.

MEHTA, DILEEP R., *Working Capital Management*, Englewood Cliffs, N.J.: Prentice-Hall, 1974.

MORRIS, JAMES R., "On Corporate Debt Maturity Strategies," *Journal of Finance*, 31 (March 1976), 29-37.

PETTY, J. WILLIAM, and DAVID F. SCOTT, "The Analysis of Corporate Liquidity," *Journal of Economics and Business*, 32 (Spring/Summer 1980), 206-18.

SILVERS, J. B., "Liquidity, Risk and Duration Patterns of Corporate Financing," *Financial Management*, 5 (Autumn 1976), 54-64.

SMITH, KEITH V., *Guide to Working Capital Management*, New York: McGraw-Hill, 1979.

VAN HORNE, JAMES C., "A Risk-Return Analysis of a Firm's Working Capital Position," *Engineering Economist*, 14 (Winter 1969), 71-89.

WALKER, ERNEST W., "Towards a Theory of Working Capital," *Engineering Economist*, 9 (January-February 1964), 21-35.

WALTER, JAMES E., "Determination of Technical Solvency," *Journal of Business*, 30 (January 1957), 30-43.

Cash and Marketable Securities

We have been occupied with the overall level of liquid and current assets of the firm. By examining the tradeoff between profitability and risk, we were able to determine in a general way the proper amount of liquid assets the firm should carry. (*Liquid assets* were defined as cash and marketable securities.) Once the overall level of liquid assets is determined, other questions arise. How much will be carried in cash? How much will be carried in marketable securities? We are going to find out how to answer these questions. We shall also find out how to improve the efficiency of cash management and how to invest excess funds in marketable securities.

The Function of Cash Management

There are three motives for holding cash: the transactions motive, the precautionary motive, and the speculative motive.[1] The transactions motive is the need for cash to meet payments arising in the ordinary course of business—for things such as purchases, labor, taxes, and dividends. The precautionary motive for holding cash has to do with maintaining a cushion or buffer to meet unexpected contingencies. The more predictable the cash flows of the business, the fewer precautionary balances needed. Ready borrowing power to meet emergency cash drains also reduces the need for this type of balance. It is important to point out that not all of the firm's transactions and precautionary balances need to be held in cash; indeed, a portion may be held in marketable securities—near-money assets.

---

[1]John Maynard Keynes, *The General Theory of Employment, Interest, and Money* (New York: Harcourt Brace Jovanovich, 1936), 170-74.

219

The speculative motive relates to holding cash in order to take advantage of expected changes in security prices. When we expect interest rates to rise and security prices to fall, this motive would suggest that the firm should hold cash until the rise in interest rates ceases. When interest rates are expected to fall, cash may be invested in securities; the firm will benefit by any subsequent fall in interest rates and rise in security prices. For the most part, companies do not hold cash for the purpose of taking advantage of expected changes in interest rates. Consequently, we concentrate only upon the transactions and precautionary motives of the firm, with these balances held both in cash and in marketable securities.

Cash management involves managing the monies of the firm in order to attain maximum cash availability and maximum interest income on any idle funds. At one end, the function starts when a customer writes a check to pay the firm on its accounts receivable. The function ends when a supplier, employee, or the government realizes collected funds from the firm on an account payable or accrual. All activities between these two points fall within the realm of cash management. The firm's efforts to make customers pay their bills at a certain time fall within accounts receivable management. On the other hand, the firm's decision about when to pay its bills involves accounts payable and accrual management.

The treasurer's office of a company usually manages cash. A cash budget, instrumental in the process (see Chapter 7), tells us how much cash we are likely to have, when, and for how long. Thus, it serves as a foundation for cash planning and control. In addition to the cash budget, the firm needs systematic information on cash as well as some kind of control system. Usually the information is computer based as opposed to manually based. In either case, it is necessary to obtain frequent reports—preferably daily or even more frequently—on cash balances in each bank account, on the cash disbursed, on the average daily balances, and on the marketable-security position of the firm as well as a detailed report on changes in this position. Also, it is useful to have information on major anticipated cash receipts and cash disbursements. All of this information is essential if a firm is to manage its cash in an efficient manner.

Accelerating Collections

In this section, we analyze various collection and disbursement methods by which a firm can improve its cash management efficiency. These methods constitute two sides of the same coin; they exercise a joint impact on the overall efficiency of cash management. The general policy is to collect accounts receivable as soon as possible while paying accounts payable as late as is consistent with maintaining the firm's credit standing with suppliers. We consider first the acceleration of collections, or reducing the delay between the time a customer pays his bill and the time the cheque is collected and becomes usable funds for the firm. A number of methods have been employed in recent years to speed up this collection process and maximize available cash. These methods are designed to do one or all of the following: (1) speed the mailing time of payments from customers to the firm; (2) reduce the time during which payments received by the firm remain uncollected funds; and (3) speed the movement of funds to disbursement banks.

The second item represents float and in this regard there are two considerations. The first is the time it takes a company to process cheques internally. This interval extends from the moment a cheque is received to the moment it is deposited with a bank for credit to the company's account. The second aspect of float involves the time it takes to clear the cheque through the banking system. Float is important to the financial manager because usually a company cannot make withdrawals on a deposit until the cheques in that deposit are collected. Because a firm needs usable funds, the financial manager wants to reduce float as much as possible. Within the banking system, the need for float has steadily declined on a relative basis as chartered banks adopt more sophisticated cheque clearing methods. We now examine various ways to speed up the collection process so the firm can have more usable funds.

CONCENTRATION BANKING

Concentration banking is a means of accelerating the flow of funds of a firm by establishing strategic collection centers. Instead of a single collection center located at the company headquarters, multiple collection centers are established. The purpose is to shorten the period between the time customers mail in their payments and the time when the company has the use of the funds. Customers in a particular geographic area are instructed to remit their payments to a collection center in that area. Location of the collection centers usually is based upon the geographic areas served and the volume of billings in an area. Regional collection enters may be established in large provinces such as Ontario, Quebec, and British Columbia. On the other hand, a regional office may serve all the Atlantic Provinces or the Western Provinces (Manitoba, Saskatchewan, and Alberta). Most national firms with regional collection centers can cut mailing time by one to two days and cheque clearing by another day. Once the payments are received and cleared at the divisional level, the funds have to be transferred to the head office bank.[2] The costs of these transfers tend to partially offset the benefits of time reductions in mailing and cheque clearance.

Under concentration banking, the firm's divisions can be viewed as billings and collection centers. The advantage of such a decentralized system relative to a centralized billings and collection center is twofold:

1. The time required for mailing is reduced. Because the collection center bills customers in its area, these customers usually receive their bills earlier than they would if the bills were mailed from the head office. In turn, when customers pay their bills, the mailing time to the nearest collection center is shorter than is the time required for the typical remittance to go to the head office.
2. The time required to collect cheques is reduced because remittances deposited in the collection center's local bank account are usually presented and cleared in that general area.

Suppose that under the decentralized system the firm is able to accelerate overall collections by two days and that average daily remittances by customers are

---

[2]The Canadian system of branch banking is discussed in E. P. Neufeld, *The Financial System of Canada* (Toronto: Macmillan of Canada, 1972), Chapter 4.

$2.0 million. By saving two days in the collection process, approximately $4.0 million in funds are released for investment elsewhere. With the recent high interest rates, it is not difficult to see the opportunity cost of tying up funds. However, profits from the investment of the released funds must be compared with any additional cost of a decentralized system. Finally, the funds released by faster collection are on a one-time basis only.

LOCK-BOX SYSTEM

The collection procedures outlined in our discussion on concentration banking are popular in Canada. However, there may be some cases where a lock-box system is used. With concentration banking, remittances are received by a firm's division or collection center and deposited in the bank. The purpose of a lock-box arrangement is to eliminate the time between the receipt of remittances by the company and their deposit in the bank. A lock-box arrangement is usually made on a regional basis, with the company choosing branch offices of banks according to its billing patterns. Before determining the regions to be used, a feasibility study is made of the availability of cheques that would be deposited under different plans. If a company divided the country on a provincial basis, it might pick the provincial capital as the lock-box center for the province.

The company rents a local post office box and authorizes its bank in each of these cities to pick up remittances in the box. Customers are billed with instructions to mail their remittance to the lock-box. The bank picks up the mail several times a day and deposits the cheques in the company's account. The cheques are microfilmed for record purposes and cleared for collection. The company receives a deposit slip and a list of payments, together with any material in the envelope. This procedure frees the company from handling and depositing the cheques.

The main advantage of a lock-box system is that cheques are deposited at banks sooner and become collected balances sooner than if they were processed by the company prior to deposit. In other words, the lag between the time cheques are received by the company and the time they actually are deposited at the bank is eliminated. The principal disadvantage of a lock-box arrangement is the cost. The average cost per cheque collected can be high; therefore lock-box arrangements are usually not profitable if the average remittance is small.

The appropriate rule for deciding whether or not to use a lock-box system or, for that matter, concentration banking, is simply to compare the added cost of the more efficient system with the marginal income that can be generated from the released funds. If costs are less than income, the system is profitable; if not, the system is not a profitable undertaking. The degree of profitability depends primarily on the geographical dispersion of customers, the size of a typical remittance, and the earnings rate on the released funds.

OTHER PROCEDURES

Under concentration banking, there are some additional procedures which may be used to accelerate funds at a rate faster than would otherwise be the case. We turn to a summary discussion of these procedures.

Pre-authorized cheque payment Firms such as life insurance, mortgage, and finance companies receive fixed monthly or other periodic payments from their customers. These companies save mailing time by requesting customers to authorize automatic deductions of their payments from their bank accounts. Customers are requested to sign a form authorizing the bank to pay $X at certain time periods. The firm presents these authorizations to the customers' banks. The banks deduct $X as authorized and forward the proceeds to the firm.

Processing large cheques Frequently, firms give special attention to the handling of large remittances so that they may be deposited in a bank as quickly as possible. This special handling may involve personal pickup of these cheques or the use of airmail or special delivery. When a small number of remittances account for a large proportion of total deposits, it may be very worthwhile to initiate controls to accelerate the deposit and collection of these large cheques. Instead of processing all cheques for collection by the clearing-house system, chartered banks offer special services where high dollar volume cheques are presented directly to the drawee bank. The benefit is accelerated collection of these cheques, and it is passed on to the bank customer who can then have funds more quickly.

Surplus bank accounts Some companies maintain too many bank accounts, thereby creating unnecessary idle funds. A company that has an account in every city where it has either a sales office or a production facility might be able to reduce cash balances considerably if it were to eliminate some of these accounts. The banking activities of a sales office can often be handled from a larger bank account with little loss in service or availability of funds. Even though small accounts may create a degree of goodwill with bankers, they make little sense in the overall management of the firm. By closing such unnecessary accounts, a firm may be able to release funds that it then can put to profitable use.

Control of Disbursements

In addition to accelerating collections, effective control of disbursements can result in a faster turnover of cash. Whereas the underlying objective of collections is maximum acceleration, the objective in disbursements is to slow payments down as much as possible. The combination of fast collections and slow disbursements will result in maximum availability of funds. A company dealing with several banks or having multiple bank accounts with the same bank needs to be able to shift funds quickly to a central account from which disbursements are made, to prevent excessive balances from building up temporarily in those other accounts. Operating procedures for disbursements should be well-established.

PAYING ON DUE DATES

If cash discounts are taken on accounts payable, procedures should be geared toward eliminating or minimizing the loss of discounts due to clerical inefficiencies. The timing of payments is important. For maximum use of cash, payments should be made on the due dates, not before and not after. Creditors (or suppliers) usually insist on receiving payments on specified due dates; cheques received after due dates are regarded as late payments. For example, if a due date is December 31, the cheque should be dated December 31, and be mailed ahead of time so the creditor receives it on December 31. If the cheque is prepared and mailed on December 31, it is likely to reach the creditor after the due date. The creditor then has the option of assessing a pre-established penalty for late payment. As we discuss in Chapter 10, such a penalty imposes a rather high interest cost on the debtor firm. Where the firm's policy is to pay funds needed for deposit in the bank on those dates. Assuming that creditors use efficient collections procedures, cheques will be cleared shortly after deposit on due dates. Thus, there is usually little scope for the debtor firm to "play the float" in instances where payments are subject to due dates.

MAXIMIZING THE FLOAT

Another way of maximizing cash availability is "playing the float." In this case, float is the difference between the total dollar amount of payments drawn on a bank account and the amount shown on the bank's books. It is possible, of course, for a company to have a negative balance on its books and a positive bank balance, because payments outstanding have not been collected from the account on which they are drawn. If the size of float can be estimated accurately, bank balances can be reduced and the funds invested to earn a positive return.

Use of drafts   A company can delay disbursements through use of sight or time drafts.[3] Unlike an ordinary cheque, the draft is not payable on demand. When it is presented to the issuer's bank for collection, the bank must present it to the issuer for acceptance. The funds are then deposited by the issuing firm to cover payment of the draft. The advantage of the draft arrangement is that it delays the time the firm actually has to have funds on deposit to cover the draft. Consequently, it allows the firm to maintain smaller deposits at its banks. Possible disadvantages of a draft system are that certain suppliers may prefer cheques, and that banks do not like to process drafts because they generally require manual attention. Banks usually impose a higher service charge to process drafts than they do to process ordinary cheques.

Payroll and dividend disbursements   Many companies maintain a separate account for payroll disbursements. In order to minimize the balance in this account, one must predict when the payroll cheques issued will be presented for payment. If payday falls on a Friday, for example, not all the cheques will be cashed on that day. Consequently, the firm need not have funds on deposit to cover its

---

[3]A draft is a written order by one person (the debtor firm) addressed to another person (the bank) to pay a specific sum of money to a named person (the creditor firm) or to the bearer, on a fixed date in the future or on demand. A demand draft (a cheque) is payable upon presentation. A sight draft is payable three days after the debtor firm "accepts" the draft; the bank has to present the draft for acceptance. A time draft is payable at some specified date in the future. An example of a time draft is presented as Fig. 11-2.

entire payroll.[4] Even on Monday, some cheques will not be presented because of delays in their deposit. Based on its experience, the firm should be able to construct a distribution graph of when, on the average, cheques are presented for collection. An example is shown in Fig. 9-1. With this information, the firm can estimate the approximate value of the funds it must have on deposit to cover payroll cheques.

Many firms establish a similar separate account for dividends. Here, too, a graph can be used to predict when dividend cheques will be presented for payment so as to minimize the cash balance in the account.

By maximizing disbursement float, the firm can reduce the amount of cash it holds and employ these funds in more profitable ways. However, a debtor's gain is a creditor's loss. Maximizing disbursement float means that suppliers and other creditors will not have collectible funds as early as would otherwise be the case. To the extent that such payment habits are looked on with disfavor, creditor relations may be hurt. If so, this factor must be taken into account in planning disbursements.

ELECTRONIC TRANSFERS AND BANKING

In recent years, we have witnessed substantial changes in the way bills are paid. This progress has come about because of changes in financial institution regulation and advances in computer information systems and electronic communications. Regulatory changes have focused on permitting greater competition among financial institutions. Chartered banks have offered a variety of savings accounts and time deposits to individuals, businesses, and governments. On the other hand, non-bank deposit institutions have been allowed to develop accounts which have most of the attributes of chequing accounts. For both types of institutions, the purpose of savings deposits has been extended to allow their partial

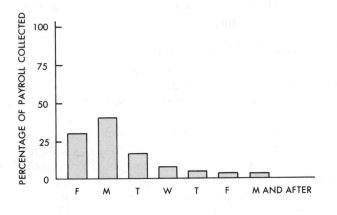

FIGURE 9-1 Percentage of payroll collected

[4]See James McN. Stancill, *The Management of Working Capital* (Scranton: Intext Educational Publishers, 1971), 19-22.

use as a payment mechanism. Pre-authorized transfers between chequing and savings accounts have permitted customers to make more efficient use of their chequing accounts and to draw interest on idle funds.

The second aspect of the changing environment is the increased sophistication in computer applications to cash management and in electronic funds transfers. There are plastic cards with magnetic coding which can be used to obtain cash, to transfer funds from one account to another, to pay bills, to borrow, and to do other things. These transactions can take place at financial institutions, at an unmanned electronic payments machine which is open 24 hours a day, and in the near future, at certain retail stores, where purchases will be paid for with such a card, and funds will be transferred electronically from the customer to the store. The advantage to the retailer is obvious; he will be assured that payment for the purchase is good and it is immediate. With such a system, a customer's cheque is scanned electronically and verified by computer. Because the bank guarantees the cheque it verifies, the retailer will not be exposed to bad cheque losses. Electronic banking is also used to deposit payrolls automatically to employee accounts, to make dividend and other payments, and to transfer funds nationally and internationally. The result is faster and more efficient financial services, which will reduce further "playing the float."

Because electronic banking is capital intensive the cost per transaction is reduced as volume increases. This has been particularly true in recent years, and a good deal of the savings are passed on to users of financial services. The customer benefits because competition among financial institutions and large retailers which provide financial services is intense. For the firm, electronic banking means less time in the collection of receivables, more efficient control of cash, and perhaps, a reduction in servicing costs.

The use of electronic banking techniques can result in higher savings for the company. Adoption of these techniques depends in part on the level of interest rates in financial markets. The higher the interest rate, the higher the opportunity cost of holding cash and the more attractive electronic banking techniques become, all other things being the same. However, the use of a new cash management technique usually involves significant startup costs. As a result, once a new method is in place, there is a tendency to keep it even if interest rates should decline somewhat thereafter. Therefore, the shifting to new cash techniques is not linearly related to interest rates prevailing in financial markets, but rather is a rachet type of function.

As mentioned earlier, optimizing cash availability involves accelerating collections as much as possible and delaying payments as long as is realistically possible. Because delaying payments may damage the firm's credit standing, the resulting cost to the firm must be taken into account. In the future, we can expect to see further improvements in electronic money payment transactions. As we move toward a "chequeless society," the length of time funds remain uncollected will become shorter. In a chequeless society where transfers are made through computers, payments will be immediate. There will be no uncollected funds, for one party's account will be debited the instant another's is credited. While the firm's deposits will be collected faster, so too will the cheques it writes. Whether it gains or loses will depend on the typical float on cheques deposited relative to the float for cheques written.

Cash Balances to Maintain

Most business firms establish a target level for maintenance of cash balances. They do not want to carry excess cash because interest can be earned by investing these funds in marketable securities. The greater the interest rate on investment, of course, the greater the opportunity cost of maintaining idle balances. The optimal level of cash should be influenced primarily by the transactions balances required when cash management is efficient, the opportunity cost of holding cash, and the cost of cash stockouts. The influence of transactions balances is determined in keeping with considerations discussed earlier in the chapter. Also, we suggested that the higher the interest rate, the greater the opportunity cost of holding cash and the greater the corresponding desire to reduce the firm's holding, all other things being the same. Furthermore, the effects of cash stockouts were discussed in Chapter 8. A number of cash management models have been developed for determining an optimal split between cash and marketable securities. These models embody the demand for cash, the interest rate on marketable securities, and the cost of transfers between marketable securities and cash. In the appendix to this chapter, two of the more widely used models are presented.

FEES AND TRANSACTIONS BALANCES

Banks provide various services to business firms and must be paid for these services. They have a schedule of costs on a per-item basis for such transactions as transfers, cheque and draft processing, credit references and so on. A business account is analyzed over some representative period and the cost of maintaining that account is determined. That is, all transactions in the account are multiplied by the appropriate per-item cost and total cost is derived. The business firm has at least two options for reimbursing the bank for its service costs: pay the fees as determined by the bank, or leave a deposit balance sufficient for the bank to reinvest, earn interest, and thereby offset the service costs.

Where a firm decides both to pay the bank charges and maintain transaction balances, the bank is over-compensated. The bank will earn interest on the transaction balances adjusted for reserve requirements—this is the amount of over-compensation. To avoid any over-compensation, transaction balances should be zero. However, firms do not consider this strategy prudent financial management. If the firm agrees to leave a deposit balance, that balance has to be large enough to provide the bank with sufficient interest income to offset the service costs of the firm's account. Usually, the bank will determine the minimum average deposit balance necessary to cover these costs. This amount is generally the average daily deposit balance over some stipulated time period, usually one month. The problem with this approach is that the bank's deposit balance may be greater than the transaction balances required for efficient cash management. If a firm feels that $100 000 is adequate as a transaction balance but the bank requires a deposit balance of $150 000, the extra $50 000 is essentially "frozen" so far as the firm is concerned. Because banks differ in the earnings rate they use as well as in their costs and method of account analysis, the determination of the minimum average deposit balance varies. The firm, therefore, may be wise to shop around to find a bank that requires a deposit balance more in line with its required transaction balance.

LOAN AGREEMENTS AND COMPENSATING BALANCES

The term *compensating balance* may appear in a loan agreement with the bank. As a provision of granting a loan, the bank may require the firm to leave between 10 percent and 15 percent of the proceeds in its account. This balance is interest-free. The Bank Act requires that the borrowing firm must agree to any compensating balance requirement. Also, the bank is under statutory obligation to disclose the full cost of the loan; full cost by definition includes interest or discounts and other charges pertaining to the loan. Compensating balances add to the effective cost of loans. For example, assume that a loan contract of $1 million requires a 15 percent compensating balance and the interest rate is 10 percent. The borrower can use only $850 000 with the balance of $150 000 remaining in a non-interest-bearing demand deposit account. If the loan is for one year, the effective interest rate is about 11.8 percent. The firm pays $100 000 (10 percent of $1 million) for the use of $850 000. The quality of the corporate borrower, past and existing banking relationships, the degree of competition for the firm's account, and money market conditions are some of the factors considered important in the loan negotiating process. In the final analysis, if a borrower refuses to agree to a compensating balance, he or she may have to look elsewhere for the required loan.

Coincidentally, the compensating balance may be equal to the minimum average deposit balance necessary to service the firm's account. However, bankers will still argue that balances compensating a lending accommodation should be "free" in the sense that they are not needed to compensate the bank for deposit activity in the firm's demand-deposit account. In fact, however, many banks overlook this differentiation of compensation when it comes to evaluating whether the requirement is being met. In other words, if a firm needed to maintain a balance of $150 000 simply to compensate for the deposit and withdrawal activity in its account, it also might be able to obtain a $1 million line of credit without increasing its balances. To the extent that a compensating balance requirement does not require the borrower to maintain balances above those that it would maintain ordinarily, such a requirement does not raise the effective cost of borrowing. However, if balances above the ordinary must be maintained, the effective cost of borrowing is raised. If the firm in the preceding example maintains an ordinary cash balance of $100 000, the effective cost of the loan will be 11.1 percent. The additional $50 000 required as minimum compensating balance increases the effective cost by about 0.7 percent.

There is some indication that the importance of the notion of compensating balances for loans has somewhat decreased. Banks are becoming more profit- as opposed to deposit-oriented and accordingly, are "fine-tuning" their profitability analyses of customer relationships. This movement has led a number of banks to prohibit the use of balances to support both account activity and lending arrangements. With the rapid and significant fluctuations in the cost of funds to banks in recent years, some banks are making loans without compensating balance requirements. The interest rate charged is higher and more in line with the bank's incremental cost of obtaining funds. The movement toward more sophisticated profitability analysis is likely to reduce further, though certainly not eliminate, the imposition of compensating balance requirements in connection with lending arrangements.

Where a compensating balance is agreed upon there is usually a provision for a *deterrent fee* in case the cash balance falls below that required. For example, if the required compensating balance is $100 000 and for a given month the average cash balance in the firm's bank account is only $80 000, there is a breach of the compensating balance agreement. Under the deterrent fee provision, the bank will regard the $20 000 difference as equivalent to a loan and will charge interest on the amount. This interest charge is the deterrent fee. If, for example, the annual interest rate is 12 percent, then the interest for the month is $200. The deterrent fee is levied to restrain a firm from violating the compensating balance agreement.

Investment of Excess Cash

In general, excess cash above some target level needed for transactions balance purposes is invested in money market instruments and certain short-term deposit-type investments. In this section, we explore the types of marketable securities available to a company as near-money investments, allowing for varying yields and for fluctuations in market price. The yield available on a security depends on its maturity, its default risk, its marketability, and perhaps its tax situation if it is selling at a price less than its face value. All these influences were explored in Chapter 3, when we reviewed the role of interest rates in financial markets. Our concern now is with various money market instruments which, by definition, are highly marketable and subject to little default risk. In addition, the usual definition restricts the maturity of a money market instrument to less than a year. Also, we review certain deposit-type investments which are offered by various domestic financial institutions. Here again maturity and default risk are crucial considerations for the financial manager. Finally, we briefly review the Eurocurrency market as a medium for the investment of excess cash. After we have discussed the various instruments available for investment, we will conclude with some observations on the overall management of the marketable security portfolio.

MONEY MARKET SECURITIES

Treasury bills Government of Canada Treasury bills constitute the largest segment of the marketable securities in the money markets. Treasury bills with maturities of 90 and 182 days are auctioned each Thursday by the Treasury. In addition, one-year bills are sold occasionally. Treasury bills carry no coupon rate but are sold on a discount basis. The return to the investor is the difference between the bid price and the face value received at maturity. These short term obligations are usually issued in large denominations, and the active bidders at the auction are the large institutional investors such as banks, insurance companies, trust and loan companies, and large nontaxable concerns. Treasury bills are extremely popular with companies as short term investments, in part because of the large number outstanding. The market is very active, and the transaction costs involved in the sale of Treasury bills in the secondary market are small. Furthermore, companies can invest in these securities subject to *repurchase agreements*. Such agreements are made with an investment dealer who contracts to repurchase the securities on a predetermined future date and price. Thus, repurchase agreements give the investor a great deal of flexibility with respect to maturity.

Bankers' acceptances   Bankers' acceptances are drafts that are accepted by commercial banks, and they are issued in the financing of foreign and domestic trade. A seller of goods will draw a commercial draft guaranteed by a chartered bank to finance inventories of finished commodities in transit to buyers. The creditworthiness of bankers' acceptances is judged relative to the bank accepting the draft, not the drawer. On acceptance by the bank, the drafts are usually bought by investment dealers and are traded in the money market. Maturities on bankers' acceptances range from 30 to 90 days, and issues have denominations of at least $100 000. The rates on bankers' acceptances tend to be slightly higher than rates on Treasury bills of like maturity but both are sold on a discount basis.

Commercial paper   Commercial paper is a short term, unsecured promissory note issued by large and well-established companies. Non-financial firms issuing commercial paper include Bell Canada, DuPont of Canada, and Steinberg's. Among the financial firms using the instrument, the larger sales finance and consumer loan companies predominate. These securities are issued mainly through investment dealers; a small proportion is placed directly with investors. Rates on commercial paper are somewhat higher than rates on Treasury bills of the same maturity and about the same as the rates available on bankers' acceptances. Paper sold directly to investors, however, generally commands a lower yield than paper sold through investment dealers. Commercial paper may be interest-bearing or sold on a discount basis. Maturities generally range from 30 to 365 days, but paper with 39-, 60-, and 90-day maturities is the most popular. Some paper may be cashed on a 24-hour notice. Commercial paper is sold only in large denominations, usually at least $100 000.

DEPOSIT-TYPE INVESTMENTS

Deposit receipts   Commercial banks issue short-term obligations (bearer deposits, certificates of deposit, and bearer deposit term notes) of varying maturities. Bearer deposits have maturities between 30 days and one year. These securities trade in the money market and can be cashed by the holder subject to an interest penalty. Yields on deposit receipts are competitive with those offered by commercial paper. Certificates of deposit, or CDs, have maturities of one to six years. These longer-term obligations are generally nonredeemable, registered, transferable, and interest-bearing securities. Bearer deposit term notes have maturities of less than seven years and are issued in multiples of over $100 00. Certificates of deposit and bearer deposit term notes are not attractive investments for companies with short-term excess cash.

Trust companies issue obligations of the nature discussed above. Trust company deposit receipts and guaranteed investment certificates are the most common.

Bank-swapped deposits   Canadian companies can take advantage of international short term interest rate differentials by investing in bank-swapped deposits. The investor can make a foreign currency bank deposit by converting available Canadian dollars. At the same time, the investor executes a futures contract to sell the foreign currency for Canadian dollars at the maturity date of the deposit. This second contract is a "swap" or "hedge" to protect the investor from the foreign exchange risk. Banks quote yields on bank-swapped deposits and such quotations take into account yields on the foreign currency deposit and the foreign exchange rate. Usually, the deposits are of a short term nature and normally are only attractive if the yield on the foreign currency bank deposit is greater than that on a domestic currency bank deposit. However, dealings in international money markets are subject to the foreign exchange risks. If the Canadian dollar appreciates in value relative to the foreign currency, the investor will receive fewer Canadian dollars on reconversion. If this happens, the attractiveness of the foreign currency deposit rate will be offset by the foreign exchange relationships. The "hedge" or "swap" contract eliminates the foreign exchange risk for the investor.

EUROCURRENCY MARKET

The Eurocurrency market is best defined by illustration. Dollars (U.S.) which are deposited in foreign banks or in foreign branches of U.S. banks are usually termed Eurodollars (U.S.). Eurodollars (Canadian) will be Canadian dollars deposited in foreign banks or in foreign branches of Canadian banks. We can use the same line of reasoning in talking of Euroyen, Euromark, Europound and Eurofranc. The term Eurocurrency is used in a general way to refer to those few national currencies which are deposited abroad and which are loaned through the auspices of the Eurocurrency market. Traditionally, the center of activity has been in Europe, hence the name Eurocurrency. Also, the Eurodollar (U.S.) is the main currency but its dominant role is decreasing given the emergence of the yen, D-mark and pound. The Canadian dollar plays a rather insignificant role in the Eurocurrency market.

There exists a substantial and very active market for the deposit and lending of Eurocurrencies—particularly the stronger currencies. The market is a wholesale one in which the amounts involved are substantial; most transactions exceed $100 000. Moreover, the market is free from government regulation because it is truly international in scope. For a given currency, the deposit rate in the Eurocurrency market is generally higher than that prevailing in the domestic market. That is, if a Canadian firm has excess Canadian dollars, it will find the Eurocurrency market relatively attractive only if the foreign deposit rate for Canadian dollars is higher than that offered in Canada, other factors being constant. Similarly, a Canadian firm with excess funds in U.S. dollars will seek a deposit in the Eurocurrency market if the deposit rate for U.S. dollars in that market is relatively higher than that offered in the U.S.A.

Also, the rates quoted on deposits vary according to the maturity of the deposit. One-day (overnight) deposits will usually have a lower rate than that on call money deposits—a deposit where one can get one's money back on demand. Time deposits will have higher rates than one-day and call money deposits; the rates on time deposits will vary with the term of the deposits. In general, most deposits have a maturity of less than a year and can be sold in the market prior to maturity if so desired. Thus, for large companies with ready contact with international money centers, the Eurodollar deposit can be an important short-term investment.

Deposits in the Eurocurrency market are loaned to high quality borrowers as sources of short-term financing. The rates quoted on loans depend on maturity and default risk. For a given maturity, the lending rate always exceeds the deposit rate; the bank makes its profit on the spread. The benchmark rates in the market are the three- and six-month London interbank rate (LIBOR) which are used by participating banks for interbank loans. All other borrowers are quoted rates higher than this rate, such as LIBOR + ½%, LIBOR + ¼%, and so on.

PREFERRED STOCK

Some companies carry preferred stocks in their marketable security portfolios. As we shall see in Chapter 22, the market price of this instrument fluctuates more than that of the short-term instruments discussed above. This fluctuation occurs because the maturity of a preferred stock is perpetual, and changes in interest rates have a pronounced impact on its market price. Default risk is greater because a preferred-stock dividend can be omitted by a company when its financial condition deteriorates. For these reasons, we usually do not think of preferred stock as being a marketable security for a corporation.

The corporate investor does gain a considerable tax advantage, in that 100 percent of preferred-stock dividends are exempt from taxation for qualified investors as we discussed in Chapter 2. Some financial managers are willing to bear the added risk in order to secure this yield, much higher than can be achieved with short-term marketable securities. Moreover, many companies actively trade in and out of preferred stocks, so that the holding period for any given stock is short. By selling a stock that has just paid its dividend, then investing in one that is about to pay a dividend, it is possible to receive a large number of preferred-stock dividends during a year for a particular level of investment.[5] The transactions costs that must be borne by the investor in such a strategy could be more than offset by the tax advantage. In final analysis, however, the substantially greater risk to the corporate investor and its liquidity needs must be balanced against the increased after-tax yield.

PORTFOLIO MANAGEMENT

The decision to invest excess cash in marketable securities involves not only the amount to invest but also the type of security in which to invest. To some extent, the two decisions are interdependent. Both should be based upon an evaluation of expected net cash flows and the certainty of these cash flows. If future

---

[5]For an analysis of this strategy in relation to the risk involved, see Michael D. Joehnk, Oswald D. Bowlin, and J. William Petty, "Preferred Dividend Rolls: A Viable Strategy for Corporate Money Managers?" *Financial Management*, 9 (Summer 1980), 78-87.

cash-flow patterns are known with reasonable certainty and the yield curve is upward sloping in the sense of longer-term securities yielding more than shorter-term ones, a company may wish to arrange its portfolio so that securities will mature approximately when the funds will be needed. Such a cash-flow pattern gives the firm a great deal of flexibility in maximizing the average return on the entire portfolio, for it is unlikely that significant amounts of securities will have to be sold unexpectedly.

To illustrate, suppose that the liquidity position of a firm, net of transactions cash needs, were expected to fluctuate in the manner shown by the dotted line in Fig. 9-2. While the figure shows only four months, we assume that the dotted line is not expected to decline below $900 000 over the next 12 months. Based on these projections, an appropriate investment strategy might be that shown by the horizontal bars in the figure. The bottom portion is represented by a 360-day investment in a certificate of deposit, followed by a Canada bond with about ten months to final maturity. Next the firm has invested in 90-day Treasury bills and these are expected to be renewed, or rolled over, at maturity. The other investments shown in the figure are designed to match the fluctuating pattern of cash flows shown. Finally, the remaining areas under the dotted line are assumed to be filled as much as possible with Treasury bills subject to repurchase agreements. With "repos", maturities of only one or a few days can be tailored to the availability of funds for investment. Overall then, the firm is able to match the maturities of its investments in marketable securities with its expected cash flow patterns. In this way, it is able to maximize its return on investment insofar as maturity decisions alone will allow.

The key, of course, is the degree of certainty in the cash flow projections. With a high degree of certainty, the maturity of a marketable security becomes its most important characteristic.[6] As illustrated in Fig. 9-2, maturities can be arranged so as to tightly fit the availability of funds and, hence, interest income can be maximized. However, if future cash flows are fairly uncertain, the most important characteristics of a security become its marketability and risk with respect to fluctuations in market value. Treasury bills and short-term repos are perhaps best suited for the emergency liquidity needs of the firm. Higher yields can be achieved by investing in longer-term, less-marketable securities with greater default risk. Although the firm should always be concerned with marketability, some possibility of loss of principal is tolerable provided the expected return is high enough. In addition to risk and marketability, transaction costs are a factor with uncertain cash flows. If securities must be sold unexpectedly, transaction costs will be incurred and their incurrence will result in a lower net return. Thus, the firm faces the familiar tradeoff between risk and profitability.

The larger the security portfolio, the more chance there is for specialization and economies of operation. A large enough security portfolio may justify a staff whose sole responsibility is managing the portfolio. Such a staff can undertake research, plan diversification, keep abreast of market conditions, and continually

---

[6]This statement assumes that all the securities considered are of reasonably high quality from the standpoint of default risk. Otherwise they would not fall within the usual definition of a marketable security.

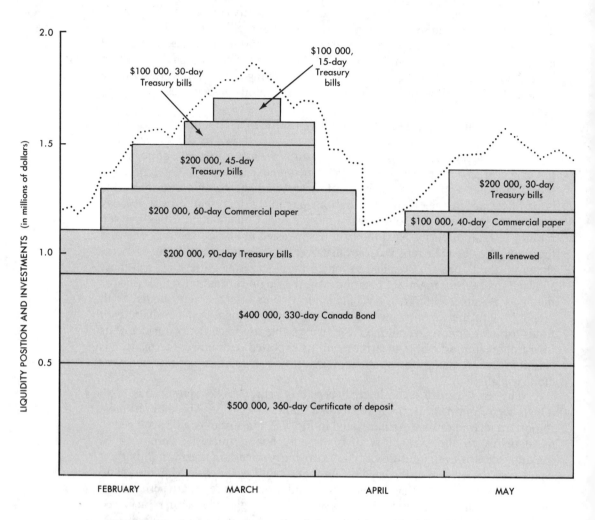

FIGURE 9-2 Investment strategy in relation to projected liquidity position

analyze and improve the firm's position. When investment is made a specialized function of the firm, the diversity of securities considered for investment is likely to be wide. Moreover, continual effort can be devoted to achieving the highest yield possible in keeping with the cash needs of the firm. Trading techniques in such a firm tend to be very sophisticated. For companies with smaller security positions, however, there may be no economic justification for a staff. Indeed, a single individual may handle investments on a part-time basis. For this type of company, the diversity of securities in the portfolio will probably be limited.

Summary

In the management of cash, companies should attempt to accelerate collections and handle disbursements so that a maximum of cash is available. Collections can be accelerated by means of concentration banking, a lock-box system, and certain other procedures. Disbursements should be handled so as to give maximum transfer flexibility and the optimum timing of payments. This applies to payments for purchases as well as to payroll disbursements. The development of electronic funds transfers and electronic banking has greatly improved the efficiency of cash management by reducing float.

The appropriate maintenance level of cash will be the higher of that required for transactions purposes or the deposit balance requirements of commercial banks to service the firm's accounts. Usually the latter dominates the former; the requirement itself depends on the activity in the firm's accounts. The level of transactions balances desirable depends in part upon the opportunity cost of holding cash as typified by the interest rate on marketable securities. In the appendix to this chapter, models are examined which allow us to take this as well as other factors into account in determining an optimal level of cash.

There are a number of money market instruments in which the firm can invest excess funds. Specific securities considered included treasury securities and repurchase agreements, bankers' acceptances and commercial paper. Also, excess funds can be invested in short-term deposits, bank-swapped deposits, deposit receipts and certificates of deposits, and Eurodollar (U.S. and Canadian) deposits. In the management of the marketable security portfolio, one tries to match to some degree the maturities of investments with the likely future need for funds.

Appendix: Cash Management Models

Given the overall liquidity of the firm (its transactions and precautionary balances), it is important to determine an optimal split between cash and marketable securities. In turn, this split tells us the average levels of cash and marketable securities to maintain. The optimal level of cash depends on the firm's needs for cash, the predictability of these needs, the interest rate on marketable securities, and the cost of effecting a transfer between marketable securities and cash. A number of formal models have been developed to provide solutions to the cash management problem, two of which are presented in this appendix. The first model approaches the problem assuming a high degree of certainty about the future cash needs of the firm. The second model assumes just the opposite—that the future cash needs of the firm are highly uncertain. Let us examine these models.

INVENTORY MODEL

Under conditions of certainty, the economic order quantity formula used in inventory management may be used to find out the optimal average amount of transactions balances to maintain. This model provides a useful conceptual foundation for the cash management problem.[7] In the model, the carrying cost of holding cash—namely, the interest forgone on marketable securities—is balanced against the fixed cost of transferring marketable securities to cash or vice versa. The model is illustrated by the saw-toothed lines in Fig. 9-3.

In the figure, we assume that the firm has a steady demand for cash over some period of time, say one month. The firm obtains cash during this period by selling marketable securities. Suppose it starts out with C dollars in cash and when this amount is expended, it replenishes it by selling C dollars of marketable securities. Thus, the transfer of funds from securities to cash occurs whenever cash touches 0. If a cushion is desired or if lead times (extra periods of time) are necessary to affect a transaction, the threshold for initiating a transfer can be higher. The principle is the same regardless of whether or not a cushion is used.

The objective is to specify the value of C that minimizes total costs—that is, the sum of the fixed costs associated with transfers and the opportunity cost of earnings forgone by holding cash balances. These costs can be expressed as

$$b\left(\frac{T}{C}\right) + i\left(\frac{C}{2}\right) \qquad \text{(9A-1)}$$

where b is the fixed cost of a transaction that is assumed to be independent of the amount transferred, T is the total amount of transaction demand for cash over the

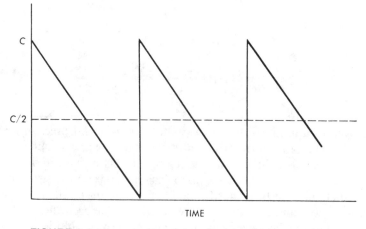

FIGURE 9-3 Inventory model applied to cash management

[7]The model was first applied to the problem of cash management by William J. Baumol, "The Transactions Demand for Cash: An Inventory Theoretic Approach," *Quarterly Journal of Economics*, 46 (November 1952) 545-56. It has been further refined and developed by a number of others.

period of time involved, and i is the interest rate on marketable securities for the period involved (the rate is assumed to be constant). T/C represents the number of transactions during the period, and when it is multiplied by the fixed cost per transaction, we obtain the total fixed cost for the period. $C/2$ represents the average cash balance, and when it is multiplied by the interest rate, we obtain the earnings forgone by virtue of holding cash. The larger the value of C, the larger the average cash balance, $C/2$, and the smaller the average investment in securities and earnings from these securities. Thus, there is a higher opportunity cost of interest income forgone. However, the larger the value of C, the fewer the transfers, T/C, which occur, and the lower the transfer costs. The object is to balance these two costs so that total costs are minimized.

The optimal level of C (C^*) is found to be

$$C^* = \sqrt{\frac{2bT}{i}} \qquad \text{(9A-2)}$$

Thus, cash will be demanded in relation to the square root of the dollar volume of transactions. This phenomenon implies that as the level of cash payments increases, the amount of transaction cash the firm needs to hold increases by a lesser percentage. In other words, economies of scale are possible. The implication is that the firm should try to consolidate individual bank accounts in order to realize economies of scale in cash management. We see from Eq. (9A-2) that C^* varies directly with order cost, b, and inversely with the interest rate on marketable securities, i. However, the relationship is nonlinear; optimal cash balance increases at a slower rate than transactions.

To illustrate the use of the economic order quantity (EOQ) formula, consider a firm with estimated cash payments of $6 million for a one-month period where these payments are expected to be steady over the period. The fixed cost per transaction is $100, and the interest rate on marketable securities is 6 percent per annum, or 0.5 percent for the one-month period. Therefore

$$C = \sqrt{\frac{2bT}{i}} = \sqrt{\frac{2(100)(6\ 000\ 000)}{0.005}} = \$489\ 898$$

Thus, the optimal transaction size is $489 898 and the average cash balance, $489 898/2 = $244 949. This means the firm should make 6 000 000/489 898 = 12 transactions of marketable securities to cash during the month.

It is useful now to consider in more detail the two costs involved. The interest rate is fairly straightforward; it simply represents the rate of interest on securities that would be sold to replenish cash. The fixed cost associated with a transaction is more difficult to measure because it consists of both explicit and implied costs. Included are the fixed component of transaction costs, the time it takes the treasurer or other official to place an order with an investment dealer, the time consumed in recording the transaction, the secretarial time needed to type the transaction and the purchase order, the time needed to record the transaction on the books, and the time needed to record the safekeeping notification. Given a number of transactions, the procedures for placing an order can be streamlined to reduce the average fixed cost per transaction. Nevertheless, these costs do exist and too often are either overlooked or underestimated.

One limitation to the use of the EOQ model is that cash payments are assumed to be steady over the period of time specified. Only if this assumption is a reasonable approximation of the situation is the model applicable. When cash payments become lumpy, it may be appropriate to reduce the period for which calculations are made so that expenditures during the period are relatively steady. The EOQ model can be applied also when receipts are continuous and there are discontinuous large payments. The decision to be made then would be the optimal purchase size of marketable securities.

Another limitation to the use of the model is that cash payments are seldom completely predictable. For modest degrees of uncertainty, one need only add a cushion so that a transfer from marketable securities to cash is triggered at some level of cash above zero. In general, the EOQ model gives the financial manager a benchmark for judging the optimal cash balance. It does not have to be used as a precise rule governing his or her behavior. The model merely suggests what would be the optimal balance under a set of assumptions. The actual balance may need to be more if the assumptions do not entirely hold.

MILLER-ORR MODEL

In those cases in which the uncertainty of cash payments is large, the EOQ model may not be applicable and other models should be used to determine optimal behavior. If cash balances fluctuate randomly, one can apply control theory to the problem. Assume that the demand for cash is stochastic (open to conjecture) and its exact timing cannot be predicted. We then can set control limits such that when cash reaches an upper limit a transfer of cash to marketable securities is undertaken, and when it hits a lower limit a transfer from marketable securities to cash is triggered. As long as the cash balance stays between these limits, no transactions take place.

How the limits are set depends in part on the fixed costs associated with a securities transaction and the opportunity cost of holding cash. As before, we assume that these costs are known and that the fixed cost of selling a marketable security is the same as that for buying it. In essence, we want to satisfy the demand for cash at the lowest possible total cost. Although there are a number of applications of control theory to the problem, we take up a relatively simple one, the Miller-Orr model. This specifies two control limits—h dollars as an upper bound and z dollars as a lower bound.[8] The model is illustrated in Fig. 9-4. When the cash balance touches the upper bound, $h-z$ dollars of marketable securities are bought, and the new balance becomes z. This is illustrated in Fig. 9-4. The minimum bound can be set at some amount higher than zero, and h and z would move up in the figure. However, we will use zero as the lower bound for purposes of illustration, recognizing that a firm can set the lower bound at some positive amount. This obviously would be necessary if there were delays in transfer.

[8]See Merton H. Miller and Daniel Orr, "A Model of the Demand for Money by Firms," *Quarterly Journal of Economics*, 80 (August 1966), 413-35.

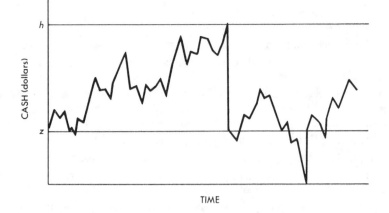

FIGURE 9-4 Miller-Orr model using control limits[9]

The solution for the optimal values of h and z depends not only on the fixed and opportunity costs but also on the degree of fluctuation in cash balances. The optimal value of z, the return-to-point for security transactions, is

$$z = \sqrt[3]{\frac{3b\sigma^2}{4i}} \qquad (9A\text{-}3)$$

where b = fixed cost associated with a security transaction
  σ^2 = variance of daily net cash flows (a measure of the dispersion of these flows)
  i = interest rate per day on marketable securities.

The optimal value of h is simply $3z$. With these control limits set, the model minimizes the total costs (fixed and opportunity) of cash management. Again, the critical assumption is that cash flows are random. The average cash balance cannot be determined exactly in advance, but it is approximately $(z + h)/3$.

We have presented two models for determining an optimal level of cash balances under the self-imposed constraint. The EOQ model assumes that the demand for cash is predictable, while the Miller-Orr model assumes it is random. For most firms, the first model is more applicable than the second owing to near-term cash flows being relatively predictable. When there is only moderate uncertainty, the EOQ model can be modified to incorporate a cushion. The second model serves primarily as a benchmark for determining cash balances under a rather extreme assumption regarding their predictability. The average cash balance will be generally much higher when this model is used than with EOQ. Thus, when cash balances of a firm are higher than those dictated by the Miller-Orr model and the demand for cash is relatively predictable, we know cash is too high.

---

[9]Source: Miller and Orr, *op. cit.*, 420.

Questions

1. Explain the concept of concentration banking.
2. Explain how the lock-box system can improve the efficiency of cash management.
3. Money market instruments are used as an investment vehicle for excess idle cash. Discuss the primary criterion for asset selection in investing temporary idle cash.
4. The assumed objective of a business firm is to maximize the wealth of shareholders, which implies that priorities should be assigned to assets on the basis of profitability. Reconcile this statement with the fact that companies keep 5 percent to 10 percent of assets in idle cash.
5. Discuss the impact of lock-box banking on corporate cash balances.
6. Explain the application of the economic order quantity model to cash balance.
7. Discuss the primary criterion for assigning priorities to assets that will serve as investment vehicles for a firm's temporary excess liquidity.
8. If the general level of interest rates is expected to fall, what maturity of securities should the firm invest in? How should this be changed if interest rates are expected to rise?
9. How can diversification reduce the risk of investment in marketable securities? What are the limits of such risk reduction?
10. Assuming that the return on real assets of a company exceeds the return on marketable securities, why should a company hold any marketable securities?
11. Under what conditions would it be possible for a company to hold no cash or marketable securities? Are these conditions realistic?

Problems with Solutions

1. The Treasurer of the Gong Company Ltd. is concerned about the lost return on daily receipts mailed by branches located in the Maritime Provinces. The daily receipts average $200 000 and time required to mail and collect the cheques is 5 days. A courier service has guaranteed collection within 3 days at an annual cost of $30 000. The company earns 12 percent on its investments. Should the offer from the courier company be accepted?

   The Gong Company would have the use of $400 000 (2 days receipts) that it did not have before. The return on this money would be $48 000 (0.12 × $400 000). Since the courier service costs only $30 000 it should be used if no other more profitable alternative is available.

2. Moosejaw Metals Ltd. sells to customers in Saskatchewan, Alberta and Manitoba. Cheques from customers take about 4 days to reach the company's offices and another day is spent in processing prior to deposit in the bank. Daily value of cheques is $25 000. The newly appointed treasurer (who recently graduated with a B. Comm. degree) feels that the system can be improved by using a lock box. In discussion with the firm's banker, the treasurer learned that the cash cycle can be reduced by two days at an annual cost of $5 000 for the lock box. The cash which is freed up can be used in either of two ways. First, the money can be used to reduce a bank loan which costs 14 percent per annum. In recent years the firm was relying on the bank for about $40 000 on a regular basis. Secondly, the money can be invested in marketable securities to earn 11 percent. What action should the treasurer take? Why?

   (a) Freed up cash is $50 000 (2 days at $25 000).
   (b) Reduce bank loan by $40 000 and save $5 600 (0.14 × $40 000) interest annually.

(c) Invest $10 000 to earn $1 100 (0.11 × $10 000) interest annually.

(d) Savings to firm: $5 600 + $1 100 − $5 000 = $ 1 700.

Problems

1. Speedway Owl Company Ltd. franchises Gas and Go stations. All payments by franchisees for gasoline and oil products are by cheque which average $420 000 a day. Presently, the overall time between the mailing of the cheque by the franchisee to Speedway Owl and the time the company has collected or available funds at its bank is 6 days.
   (a) How much money is tied up in this interval of time?
   (b) To reduce this delay, the company is considering pickups daily from the stations. In all, 3 cars would be needed and 3 additional people hired. This daily pickup would cost $93 000 on an annual basis, and it would reduce the overall delay by 2 days. Currently, the opportunity cost of funds is 9 percent, that being the interest rate on marketable securities. Should the company inaugurate the pickup plan?
   (c) Rather than mail cheques to its bank, the company could deliver them by messenger service. This procedure would reduce the overall delay by one day and cost $10 300 annually. Should the company undertake this plan?

2. The Zindler Company Ltd. currently has a centralized billing system. Payments are made by all customers to the central billing location. It requires, on the average, 4 days for customers' mailed payments to reach the central location. An additional one and one-half days are required to process payments before the deposit can be made. The firm has a daily average collection of $500 000.

   The company has recently investigated the possibility of initiating a lock-box system. It has estimated that with such a system, customers' mailed payments would reach the receipt location two and one-half days sooner. Further, the processing time could be reduced by an additional day, because each lock-box bank would pick up mailed deposits twice daily.
   (a) Determine the reduction in cash balances that can be achieved through the use of a lock-box system.
   (b) Determine the opportunity cost of the present system, assuming an 11 percent return on short-term instruments.
   (c) If the annual cost of the lock-box system were $150 000, should such a system be initiated?

3. The List Company Ltd., which can earn 7 percent on money-market instruments, currently has a lock-box arrangement with a Toronto bank for its Ontario and Quebec customers. The bank handles $3 million a day in return for a deposit balance of $2 million.
   (a) The List Company Ltd., has discovered that it could divide the region into an Ontario region (with $1 million a day in collections, which could be handled by the Toronto bank for a $1 million deposit balance) and a Quebec region (with $2 million a day in collections, which could be handled by a Montreal bank for a $2 million deposit balance). In each case, collections would be one-half day quicker than with the present arrangement. What would be the annual savings (or cost) of dividing the region?
   (b) In an effort to retain the business, the Toronto bank has offered to handle the collections strictly on a fee basis (no deposit balance). What would be the maximum fee the bank could charge and still retain List's business?

4. The Frazini Food Company Ltd. has a weekly payroll of $150 000 paid on Friday. On average, its employees cash their cheques in the following manner:

Day cheque cleared on company's account	Percent of cheques cashed
Friday	20
Monday	40
Tuesday	25
Wednesday	10
Thursday	5

As treasurer of the company, how would you arrange your payroll account? Are any problems involved?

5. Assuming an upward-sloping yield curve for marketable securities, devise a profit-maximizing maturity schedule for investment in marketable securities by Joey Brown Stereo Company Ltd., based on the following considerations. The company wishes to maintain cash balances of $100 000 at all times. There are no transaction costs for investing in, or selling, marketable securities. In the absence of any investment in marketable securities, cash balances are expected to be

Jan.	$300 000	May	$700 000	Sept.	$200 000
Feb.	500 000	June	800 000	Oct.	200 000
Mar.	600 000	July	400 000	Nov.	100 000
Apr.	500 000	Aug.	300 000	Dec.	100 000

Your schedule should indicate the amounts to be invested and the months over which the investments will be held. The maturity of the investment should correspond to the intended holding period.

Why might not such a schedule be in the best interest of the company?

Appendix Problems

6. The Schriver Company Ltd. expects to have $1 million in cash outlays for next year. The firm believes that it will face an opportunity interest rate of 5 percent and will incur a cost of $100 each time it transfers from marketable securities to cash. Cash outlays are expected to be steady over the year. Using the inventory model
   (a) Determine the optimal transfer size for the Schriver Company Ltd.
   (b) What is the total cost for the use of cash needed for transactions demand?
   (c) What will be the cash cycle for the firm (velocity)?
   (d) What will be the average cash balance for the firm?

7. Assume that the Schriver Company Ltd. (Problem 6) began the year with $1 million in cash.
   (a) How much would initially be invested in securities?
   (b) How much would be invested in securities after 231 days?

8. The Verloom Berloop Tulip Bulb Company Ltd. has experienced a stochastic demand for its product, with the result that cash balances fluctuate randomly. The standard deviation of daily

net cash flows, σ, is $1 000. The company wishes to make the transfer of funds from cash to marketable securities and vice versa as automatic as possible. It has heard that this can be done by imposing upper- and lower-bound control limits. The current interest rate on marketable securities is 6 percent. The fixed cost associated with each transfer is $100, and transfers are instantaneous.

(a) What are the optimal upper- and lower-bound control limits? (Assume a 360-day year.)

(b) What happens at these control limits?

Selected References

BATLIN, C. A., and SUSAN HINKO, "Lockbox Management and Value Maximization," *Financial Management*, 10 (Winter 1981), 39-44.

BAUMOL, WILLIAM J., "The Transactions Demand for Cash: An Inventory Theoretic Approach," *Quarterly Journal of Economics*, 46 (November 1952), 545-56.

EMERY, GARY, "Some Empirical Evidence on the Properties of Daily Cash Flow," *Financial Management*, 10 (Spring 1981), 21-28.

FROST, PETER A., "Banking Services, Minimum Cash Balances and the Firm's Demand for Money," *Journal of Finance*, 25 (December 1970), 1029-39.

GALE, BRADLEY T., and BEN BRANCH, "Cash Flow Analysis: More Important than Ever," *Harvard Business Review*, 59 (July-August 1981), 131-36.

GITMAN, LAWRENCE J., EDWARD A. MOSES, and I. THOMAS WHITE; "An Assessment of Corporate Cash Management Practices," *Financial Management*, 8 (Spring 1979), 32-41.

GITMAN, LAWRENCE J., D. KEITH FORRESTER, and JOHN R. FORRESTER, JR., "Maximizing Cash Disbursement Float," *Financial Management*, 5 (Summer 1976), 15-24.

HANKS, GEORGE F., "Finding Cash for Your Firm", *Cost and Management*, May–June 1981, 38-42.

HARTLEY, W.C.F., and YALE L. MELTZER, *Cash Management*. Englewood Cliffs, N.J.: Prentice-Hall, 1979.

JOEHNK, MICHAEL D., OSWALD D. BOWLIN, and J. WILLIAM PETTY, "Preferred Dividend Rolls: A Viable Strategy for Corporate Money Managers?," *Financial Management*, 9 (Summer 1980), 78-87.

MAIER, STEVEN F., DAVID W. ROBINSON, and JAMES H. VANDER WEIDE, "A Short-Term Disbursement Forecasting Model," *Financial Management*, 10 (Spring 1981), 9-20.

MEHTA, DILEEP R., *Working Capital Management*. Englewood Cliffs, N.J.: Prentice-Hall, 1974, Chapters 6-8.

MILLER, MERTON H., and DANIEL ORR, "The Demand for Money by Firms: Extension of Analytic Results," *Journal of Finance*, 23 (December 1968), 735-59.

_____, "A Model of the Demand for Money by Firms," *Quarterly Journal of Economics*, 80 (August 1966), 413-35.

MULLINS, DAVID W. JR., and RICHARD B. HOMONOFF, "Applications of Inventory Cash Management Models" in Stewart C. Myers, ed., *Modern Developments in Financial Management*. New York: Praeger, 1976.

NAUSS, ROBERT M., and ROBERT E. MARKLAND, "Solving Lock Box Location Problems," *Financial Management*, 8 (Spring 1979), 21-31.

SMITH, KEITH V., *Guide to Working Capital Management*, New York: McGraw-Hill, 1979, Chapters 3 and 4.

STANCILL, JAMES McN., *The Management of Working Capital*, Scranton, Pa.: Intext, 1971, Chapters 2 and 3.

STONE, BERNELL K., and NED C. HILL, "Cash Transfer Scheduling for Efficient Cash Concentration," *Financial Management*, 9 (Autumn, 1980), 35-43.

_____, "The Design of a Cash Concentration System," *Journal of Financial and Quantitative Analysis*, 16 (September 1981), 301-22.

STONE, BERNELL K. and ROBERT A. WOOD, "Daily Cash Forecasting: A Simple Method for Implementing the Distribution Approach," *Financial Management*, 6 (Fall 1977), 40-50.

VAN HORNE, JAMES C., *Financial Market Rates and Flows*. Englewood Cliffs, N.J.: Prentice-Hall, 1978.

WRIGHT, F.K., "Minimizing the Costs of Liquidity," *Australian Journal of Management*, 3 (October 1978), 203-24.

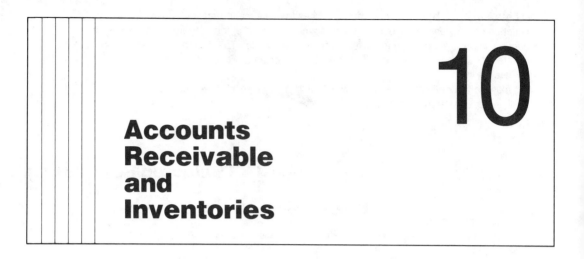

Accounts Receivable and Inventories

In Chapter 8, we saw that the investment of funds in accounts receivable involves a tradeoff between profitability and risk. The optimum investment is determined by comparing benefits to be derived from a particular level of investment with the costs of maintaining that level. This chapter will reveal the key variables involved in managing receivables efficiently, and it will show how they can be varied to obtain the optimal investment. We consider first the credit and collection policies of the firm as a whole and then discuss credit and collection procedures for the individual account. The last part of the chapter investigates techniques for efficiently managing inventories. It relates these methods to the financial manager's concern with controlling investment.

Credit and Collection Policies

Economic conditions and the firm's credit policies are the chief influences on the level of a firm's accounts receivables. Economic conditions, of course, are largely beyond the control of the financial manager. As with other current assets, however, the manager can vary the level of receivables in keeping with the tradeoff between profitability and risk. Lowering quality standards may stimulate demand which, in turn, should lead to higher profits. But there is a cost to carrying the additional receivables, as well as a greater risk of bad-debt losses. It is this tradeoff we wish to examine.

The policy variables we consider include the quality of the trade accounts accepted, the length of the credit period, the cash discount, and the collection program of the firm. Together, these elements largely determine the average collection period and the proportion of bad-debt losses. We analyze each element in turn, holding constant certain of the others, as well as all exogenous variables that affect the average collection period and the percentage of bad-debt losses. In addition, we assume that the evaluation of risk is sufficiently standardized that degrees of risk for different accounts can be compared objectively.

CREDIT STANDARDS

Credit policy can have a significant influence upon sales. If competitors extend credit liberally and we do not, our policy may have a dampening effect upon the marketing effort. Credit is one of many factors that influence the demand for a firm's product. Consequently, the degree to which credit can promote demand depends upon what other factors are being employed. In theory, the firm should lower its quality standard for accounts accepted as long as the profitability of sales generated exceeds the added costs of the receivables. What are the costs of relaxing credit standards? Some arise from an enlarged credit department, the clerical work involved in checking additional accounts, and servicing the added volume of receivables. We assume that these costs are deducted from the profitability of additional sales to give a net profitability figure for computational purposes. Another cost comes from the increased probability of bad-debt losses. We postpone consideration of this cost to a subsequent section; we assume for now that there are no bad-debt losses.

Finally, there is the opportunity cost of the additional receivables, resulting from (1) increased sales, and (2) a slower average collection period. If new customers are attracted by the relaxed credit standards, collecting from these customers is likely to be slower than collecting from existing customers. In addition, a more liberal extension of credit may cause certain existing customers to be less conscientious about paying their bills on time.

An example of the tradeoff To assess the profitability of a more liberal extension of credit, we must know the profitability of additional sales, the added demand for products arising from the relaxed credit standards, the increased slowness of the average collection period, and the required return on investment. Suppose a firm's product sells for $10 a unit, of which $7 represents variable costs before taxes, including credit department costs. The firm is operating at less than full capacity, and an increase in sales can be accommodated without any increase in fixed costs. Therefore, the contribution margin of an additional unit of sales is the selling price less variables costs involved in producing the unit, or $10 − $7 = $3.

Presently, annual credit sales are running at a level of $2.4 million, and there is no underlying trend in such sales. The firm may liberalize credit, which will result in an average collection experience of new customers of two months. Existing customers are not expected to alter their payment habits. The relaxation in credit standards is expected to produce a 25 percent increase in sales, to $3 million annually. The $600 000 increase represents 60 000 additional units if we assume that the price per unit stays the same. Finally, assume that the firm's opportunity cost of carrying the additional receivables is 20 percent before taxes.

This information reduces our evaluation to a tradeoff between the added profitability on the additional sales and the opportunity cost of the increased investment in receivables. The increased investment arises solely from new, slower-paying customers; we have assumed existing customers continue to pay in one month. With the additional sales of $600 000 and receivable turnover of six times a year (12 months divided by the average collection period of 2 months), the additional receivables are $600 000/6 = $100 000. For these additional receivables, the firm invests the variable costs tied up in them. For our example, $0.70 of every $1.00 in sales represents variable costs. Therefore, the added investment in receivables is 0.70 × $100 000 = $70 000. With these inputs, we are able to make the calculations shown in Table 10-1. Inasmuch as the profitability on additional sales, $180 000, far exceeds the required return on the additional investment in receivables, $14 000, the firm would be well advised to relax its credit standards. An optimal credit policy would involve extending trade credit more liberally until the marginal profitability on additional sales equals the required return on the additional investment in receivables necessary to generate those sales. However, as we take on poorer credit risks, we also increase the risk of the firm, as depicted by the variance of the expected cash-flow stream. This increase in risk is largely reflected in additional bad-debt losses, a subject we deal with shortly.

CREDIT TERMS

Credit period Credit terms involve both the length of credit period and the discount given. The terms "2/10, net 30" mean that a 2 percent discount is given if the bill is paid before the tenth day after the date of invoice; payment is due by the thirtieth day. The credit period, then, is 30 days. Although the customs of the industry frequently dictate the terms given, the credit period is another means by which a firm may be able to affect product demand, hoping to increase demand by extending the credit period. As before, the tradeoff is between the profitability of additional sales and the required return on the additional investment in receivables.

Let us say that the firm in our example increases its credit period from thirty to sixty days. The average collection period for existing customers goes from one month to two months. The more liberal credit period results in increased sales of $360 000, and these new customers also pay, on average, in two months. The total additional receivables are comprised of two parts. The first part represents the receivables associated with the increased sales. In our example, there are $360 000 in additional sales. With a receivable turnover of six times a year, the additional receivables associated with the new sales are $360 000/6 = $60 000. For these additional receivables, the investment by the firm is the variable costs tied up in them. For our example, we have ($7/$10)($60 000) = $42 000.

TABLE 10-1 Profitability Versus Required Return—Credit Standard Change

Profitability of additional sales	=	$3 × 60 000 units = $180 000
Additional receivables	=	(Additional sales/Receivable turnover) $600 000/6 = $100 000
Investment in additional receivables	=	(Variable costs/Sales price) (Additional receivables) (0.70)($100 000) = $70 000
Required return on additional investment	=	0.20 × $70 000 = $14 000

The second part of the total additional receivables represents the slowing in collections associated with original sales: The old receivables are collected in a slower manner resulting in a higher receivable level. With $2.4 million in original sales, the level of receivables with a turnover of 12 times a year is $2 400 000/12 = $200 000. The new level with a turnover of six times a year is $2 400 000/6 = $400 000. Thus, there are $200 000 in additional receivables associated with the original sales. For this addition, the relevant investment using marginal analysis is the full $200 000. In other words, the use of variable costs pertains only to new sales. The incremental $200 000 in receivables on original sales would have been collected earlier had it not been for the change in credit standards. Therefore, the firm must increase its investment in receivables by $200 000.

Based on these inputs, our calculations are shown in Table 10-2. The appropriate comparison is the profitability of additional sales with the opportunity cost of the additional investment in receivables. Inasmuch as the profitability on additional sales, $108 000, exceeds the required return on the investment in additional receivables, $48 400, the change in credit period from thirty to sixty days is worthwhile. The profitability of the additional sales more than offsets the added investment in receivables, the bulk of which comes from existing customers slowing their payments.

Discount given   Varying the discount involves an attempt to speed up the payment of receivables. Here we must determine whether a speedup in collections would more than offset the cost of an increase in the discount. If it would, the present discount policy should be changed. Suppose the firm has annual credit sales of $3 million and an average collection period of two months, and that the sales terms are net 45 days, with no discount given. Consequently, the average receivable balance is $500 000. By instigating terms of 2/10, net 45, the average collection period is reduced to one month, and 50 percent of the customers (in dollar volume) take advantage of the 2 percent discount. The opportunity cost of the discount to the

---

TABLE 10-2   Profitability Versus Required Return—Credit Period Change

Profitability of additional sales	=	$3 × 36 000 units = $108 000
Additional receivables associated with new sales	=	(New sales/Receivable turnover) $360 000/6 = $60 000
Additional investment in receivables associated with new sales	=	(Variable costs/Sales price)(Additional receivables) (0.70)($60 000) = $42 000
Present level of receivables	=	(Annual sales/Receivable turnover) $2.4 million/12 = $200 000
New level of receivables associated with original sales	=	$2.4 million/6 = $400 000
Additional investment in receivables associated with original sales	=	$400 000 − $200 000 = $200 000
Total additional investment in receivables	=	$42 000 + $200 000 = $242 000
Carrying cost of additional investment	=	0.20 × $242 000 = $48 400

firm is $0.02 \times 0.5 \times \$3$ million, or $30 000 annually. The turnover of receivables has improved to 12 times a year, so that average receivables are reduced from $500 000 to $250 000.

Thus, the firm realizes $250 000 from accelerated collections. The value of the funds released is their opportunity cost. If we assume a 20 percent rate of return, the opportunity saving is $50 000. In this case the opportunity saving arising from a speedup in collections is greater than the cost of the discount. The firm should adopt a 2 percent discount. If the speedup in collections had not resulted in sufficient opportunity savings to offset the cost of discount, the discount policy would not be changed. It is possible, of course, that discounts other than 2 percent may result in an even greater difference between the opportunity saving and the cost of the discount.

DEFAULT RISK

In the above examples we assumed no bad-debt losses. Our concern in this section is not only with the slowness of collection but also with the portion of the receivables defaulting. Different credit standard policies will involve both of these factors. Suppose that we are considering the present credit standard policy (sales of $2 400 000) together with two new ones and that these policies are expected to produce the following results:

	Present policy	Policy A	Policy B
Demand (sales)	$2 400 000	$3 000 000	$3 180 000
Default losses on incremental sales (percentage)	2	10	25
Average collection period on incremental sales	1 month	2 months	6 months

We assume that after six months an account is turned over to a collection agency and that, on average, 2 percent of the original sales of $2.4 million is never received by the firm, 10 percent is never received on the $600 000 in additional sales under policy A, and 25 percent on the $180 000 in additional sales under policy B is never received. Similarly, the one-month average collection period pertains to the original sales, two months to the $600 000 in additional sales under policy A, and six months to the $180 000 in additional sales under policy B.

The incremental profitability calculations associated with these two new credit standard policies are shown in Table 10-3. We would want to adopt policy A but would not want to go as far as policy B in relaxing our credit standards. The marginal benefit is positive in moving from the present policy to policy A but negative in going from policy A to policy B. It is possible, of course, that a relaxation of credit standards that fell on one side or the other of policy A would provide an even greater marginal benefit; the optimal policy is the one that provides the greatest marginal benefit.

TABLE 10-3 Profitability Versus Required Return—Bad-Debt
Losses and Collection Period Changes

	Policy A	Policy B
Additional sales	$600 000	$180 000
Profitability of additional sales (30 percent)	180 000	54 000
Additional bad-debt losses (Additional sales × bad-debt percentage)	60 000	45 000
Additional receivables (Additional sales/Receivable turnover)	100 000	90 000
Investment in additional receivables (0.7 × additional receivables)	70 000	63 000
Required return on additional investment (20 percent)	14 000	12 600
Bad-debt losses plus additional required return	74 000	57 600
Incremental profitability (2) – (7)	106 000	(3 600)

COLLECTION POLICY AND PROCEDURES

The firm determines its overall collection policy by the combination of collection procedures it undertakes. These procedures include things such as letters, phone calls, personal calls, and legal action. One of the principal policy variables is the amount expended on collection procedures. Within a range, the greater the relative amount expended, the lower the proportion of bad-debt losses and the shorter the average collection period, all other things the same.

The relationships are not linear. Initial collection expenditures are likely to cause little reduction in bad-debt losses. Additional expenditures begin to have a significant effect up to a point; then they tend to have little effect in further reducing these losses. The hypothesized relationship between expenditures and bad-debt losses is shown in Fig. 10-1. The relationship between the average collection period and the level of collection expenditure is likely to be similar to that shown in the figure.

If sales are independent of the collection effort, the appropriate level of collection expenditure again involves a tradeoff—this time between the level of expenditure on the one hand and the reduction in the cost of bad-debt losses and reduction in investment in receivables on the other. Calculations are the same as for the discount given and for default losses illustrated earlier. The reader easily can verify the tradeoff.

Because a receivable is only as good as the likelihood that it will be paid, a firm cannot afford to wait too long before initiating collection procedures. On the other hand, if it initiates procedures too soon, it may anger reasonably good customers who, for some reason, fail to make payments by the due date. Procedures, whatever they are, should be firmly established. Initially, a letter is usually sent, followed perhaps by additional letters that become ever more serious in tone. Next may come a telephone call from the credit manager and then, perhaps, one from the company's lawyer. Some companies have collection personnel who make personal calls on the account.

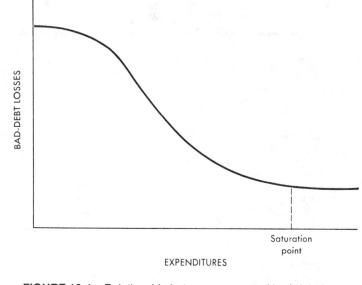

FIGURE 10-1   Relationship between amount of bad-debt losses
and collection expenditures

If all else fails, the account may be turned over to a collection agency. The agency's fees are quite substantial—frequently one-half the amount of the receivable—but such a procedure may be the only feasible alternative, particularly for a small account. Direct legal action is costly, sometimes serves no real purpose, and may only force the account into bankruptcy. When payment cannot be collected, compromise settlements may provide a higher percentage of collection.

CREDIT AND COLLECTION POLICIES—SUMMARY

We see that the credit and collection policies of a firm involve several decisions: (1) the quality of account accepted, (2) the credit period, (3) the cash discount given, and (4) the level of collection expenditures. In each case, the decision should involve a comparison of possible gains from a change in policy and the cost of the change. Optimal credit and collection policies would be those that resulted in the marginal gains equaling the marginal costs.

To maximize profits arising from credit and collection policies, the firm should vary these policies jointly until it achieves an optimal solution. That solution will determine the best combination of credit standards, credit period, cash discount policy, special terms, and level of collection expenditures. For most policy variables, profits increase at a decreasing rate up to a point and then decrease as the policy is varied from no effort to an extreme effort. Fig. 10-2 depicts this relationship with the quality of accounts rejected. When there are no credit standards, when all applicants are accepted, sales are maximized, but they are offset by large bad-debt losses as well as by the opportunity cost of carrying a very large receivable position. The latter is due to a long average collection period. As credit standards are initiated and applicants rejected, revenue from sales declines, but so do the average collection period and bad-debt losses. Because the latter two decline initially at a faster rate than do sales, profits increase. As credit standards are tightened increasingly, sales revenue declines at an increasing rate. At the same time, the average collection period and bad-debt losses decrease at a decreasing rate. Fewer and fewer bad credit risks are eliminated. Because of the combination of these influences, total profits of the firm increase at a diminishing rate with stricter credit standards up to a point, after which they decline. The optimal policy with respect to credit standards is represented by point x in the figure. In turn, this policy determines the level of accounts receivable held by the firm.

The analysis in the last several sections has purposely been rather general, to provide insight into the chief concepts of credit and collection policies. Obviously, a policy decision should be based upon a far more specific evaluation than that contained in the examples above. Estimating the increased demand and increased slowness of collections that might accompany a relaxation of credit standards is difficult. Nevertheless, management must make estimates of these relationships if it is to appraise realistically its existing policies.

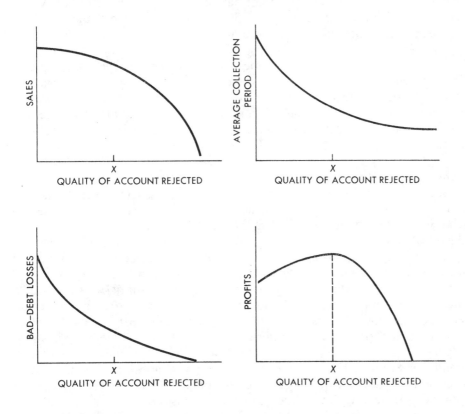

FIGURE 10-2 Relationship of sales, average collection period, bad-debt losses, and profits to the quality of account rejected

Analyzing the Credit Applicant

Having established the terms of sale to be offered, the firm must evaluate individual credit applicants and consider the possibilities of a bad debt or slow payment. The credit evaluation procedure involves three related steps: obtaining information on the applicant, analyzing this information to determine the applicant's credit-worthiness, and making the credit decision. The credit decision consists of whether to extend credit, the size of credit and the terms of credit.

SOURCES OF INFORMATION

A number of sources supply credit information; but for some accounts, especially small ones, the cost of collecting it may outweigh the potential profitability of the account. The firm extending credit may have to be satisfied with a limited amount of information on which to base a decision. In addition to cost, the firm must consider the time it takes to investigate a credit applicant. A shipment to a prospective customer cannot be delayed unnecessarily pending an elaborate credit investigation. Thus, the amount of information collected needs to be considered in relation to the time and expense required. Depending upon these considerations, the credit analyst may use one or more of the following sources of information.

Financial statement   At the time of the prospective sale, the seller may request a financial statement, one of the most desirable sources of information for credit analysis. Frequently, there is a correlation between a company's refusal to provide a statement and its weak financial position. Audited statements are preferable; and interim statements are helpful, particularly for companies having seasonal patterns of sales.

Credit ratings and reports   In addition to financial statements, credit ratings are available from various mercantile agencies. Dun & Bradstreet is perhaps the best known and most comprehensive of these agencies. It provides credit ratings to subscribers for a vast number of business firms throughout the nation. A key to its individual ratings is shown in Fig. 10-3. As we see in the figure, D&B ratings give the credit analyst an indication of the estimated size of net worth and a credit appraisal for companies of a particular size, ranging from "high" to "limited." D&B also indicates when the information available is insufficient to provide a rating for a given business. In addition to its rating service, D&B provides credit reports containing a brief history of a company and its principal officers, the nature of the business, certain financial information, and a trade check of suppliers—the length of their experience with the company and whether payments are discount, prompt, or past due. The quality of the D&B reports varies with the information available externally and the willingness of the company being checked to cooperate with the D&B reporter. In addition to Dun & Bradstreet, there are a number of credit agencies that specialize in a particular line of business or in geographic areas.

New Key to Ratings

ESTIMATED FINANCIAL STRENGTH			COMPOSITE CREDIT APPRAISAL			
			HIGH	GOOD	FAIR	LIMITED
5A	Over	$50,000,000	1	2	3	4
4A	$10,000,000 to	50,000,000	1	2	3	4
3A	1,000,000 to	10,000,000	1	2	3	4
2A	750,000 to	1,000,000	1	2	3	4
1A	500,000 to	750,000	1	2	3	4
BA	300,000 to	500,000	1	2	3	4
BB	200,000 to	300,000	1	2	3	4
CB	125,000 to	200,000	1	2	3	4
CC	75,000 to	125,000	1	2	3	4
DC	50,000 to	75,000	1	2	3	4
DD	35,000 to	50,000	1	2	3	4
EE	20,000 to	35,000	1	2	3	4
FF	10,000 to	20,000	1	2	3	4
GG	5,000 to	10,000	1	2	3	4
HH	Up to	5,000	1	2	3	4

CLASSIFICATION FOR BOTH
ESTIMATED FINANCIAL STRENGTH AND CREDIT APPRAISAL

FINANCIAL STRENGTH BRACKET	EXPLANATION
1 $125,000 and Over	When only the numeral (1 or 2) appears, it is an indication that the estimated financial strength, while not definitely classified, is presumed to be within the range of the ($) figures in the corresponding bracket and that a condition is believed to exist which warrants credit in keeping with that assumption.
2 20,000 to 125,000	

NOT CLASSIFIED OR ABSENCE OF RATING

The absence of a rating, expressed by two hyphens (--), is not to be construed as unfavorable but signifies circumstances difficult to classify within condensed rating symbols. It suggests the advisability of obtaining a report for additional information.

FIGURE 10-3 Dun & Bradstreet key to ratings

Bank checking Another source of information for the firm is a credit check through a bank. Many banks have large credit departments that undertake credit checks as a service for their customers. By calling or writing a bank in which the credit applicant has an account, a firm's bank is able to obtain information on the average cash balance carried, loan accommodations, experience, and sometimes financial information. Because banks generally are more willing to share information with other banks than with a direct inquirer, it usually is best for the firm to initiate the credit check through its own bank rather than to inquire directly.

Trade checking Credit information frequently is exchanged among companies selling to the same customer. Through various credit organizations, credit people in a particular area become a closely knit group. A company can ask other suppliers about their experiences with an account.

The company's own experience A study of the promptness of past payments, including any seasonal patterns, is very useful. Frequently, the credit department will make written assessments of the quality of the management of a company to whom credit may be extended. These assessments are very important, for they pertain to the first of the famous "three C's" of credit: *character*, *collateral*, and *capacity*. The person who made the sale to a prospective customer frequently can offer useful impressions of management and operations. Caution is necessary in interpreting this information, because a salesperson has a natural bias toward granting credit and making the sale.

CREDIT ANALYSIS

Having collected credit information, the firm must make a credit analysis of the applicant. In practice, the collection of information and its analysis are closely related. If, on the basis of initial credit information, a large account appears to be relatively risky, the credit analyst will want to obtain further information. Presumably, the expected value of the additional information will exceed the cost of acquiring it. Given the financial statements of an applicant, the credit analyst should undertake a ratio analysis, as described in Chapter 6. The analyst will be particularly interested in the applicant's liquidity and ability to pay bills on time.

In addition to analyzing financial statements, the credit analyst will consider the financial strength of the firm, the character of the company and its management, and various other matters. Then the analyst attempts to determine the ability of the applicant to service trade credit, the probability of an applicant's not paying on time and of a bad-debt loss. On the basis of this information together with information about the profit margin of the product or service being sold, a decision is reached as to whether or not to extend credit.

The amount of information collected should be determined in relation to the expected profit from an order and the cost of investigation. More sophisticated analysis should be undertaken only when there is a chance that a credit decision based upon the previous stage of investigation will be changed. If an analysis of a Dun & Bradstreet report resulted in an extremely unfavorable picture of the applicant, an investigation of the applicant's bank and its trade suppliers might have little prospect of changing the reject decision. Therefore, the added cost associated with this stage of investigation would not be worthwhile. With incremental stages of investigation each having a cost, they can be justified only if the information obtained has value in changing a prior decision.[1] Rather than perform all stages of investigation regardless of the profitability of the order, the firm should undertake investigation in stages and go to a new stage only when the expected net benefits of the additional information exceed the cost of acquiring it.

Although quantitative approaches have been developed to measure ability to service trade credit, the final decision for most companies extending trade credit rests upon the credit analyst's judgment in evaluating available information. Numerical evaluations are successful in consumer credit, where various characteristics of an individual are quantitatively rated and a credit decision is made on the basis of a total score. The plastic credit cards many of us hold are often given out

---

[1]For such an analysis, see Dileep Mehta, "The Formulation of Credit Policy Models," *Management Science*, 15 (October 1968), 30-50.

on the basis of a credit scoring system in which things such as age, occupation, duration of employment, home ownership, years of residence, telephone, and annual income are taken into account. Numerical ratings systems also are being used by companies extending trade credit.[2] With the overall growth of trade credit, a number of companies are finding it worthwhile to use numerical credit-scoring systems to screen out, clear, accept, or reject applicants. Credit analysts, then, can devote their energies to evaluating marginal applicants.

CREDIT DECISION

Once the credit analyst has marshaled the necessary evidence and has analyzed it, a decision must be reached as to the disposition of the account. In an initial sale, the first decision to be made is whether or not to ship the goods and extend credit. If repeat sales are likely, the company will probably want to establish procedures so that it does not have to evaluate the extension of credit each time an order is received. One means for streamlining the procedure is to establish a *line of credit* for an account. A line of credit is a maximum limit on the amount the firm will permit to be owing at any one time. In essence, it represents the maximum risk exposure that the firm will allow itself to undergo for an account. The establishment of a credit line streamlines the procedure for shipping goods, but the line must be reevaluated periodically in order to keep abreast of developments in the account. What is a satisfactory risk exposure today may be more or less than satisfactory a year from today. Despite comprehensive credit procedures, there will always be special cases that must be dealt with individually. Here, too, a firm can streamline the operation by defining responsibilities clearly.

Inventory Management and Control

Inventories form a link between production and sale of a product. A manufacturing company must maintain a certain amount of inventory during production, the inventory known as goods in process. Although other types of inventory—namely, in-transit, raw-materials, and finished-goods inventories—are not necessary in the strictest sense, they allow the firm to be flexible. Inventory in transit—that is, inventory between various stages of production or storage—permits efficient production scheduling and utilization of resources. Without this type of inventory, each stage of production would have to wait for the preceding stage to complete a unit. Resultant delays and idle time give the firm an incentive to maintain in-transit inventory.

---

[2]See William P. Poggess, "Screen-Test Your Credit Risks," in Keith V. Smith, ed., *Working Capital Management* (New York: West Publishing, 1974), 109-20; and Robert O. Edmister and Gary G. Schlarbaum, "Credit Policy in Lending Institutions," *Journal of Financial and Quantitative Analysis*, 9 (June 1974), 335-56. For a discussion of the updating of the underlying sample used in a credit scoring system, see Michael S. Long, "Credit Screening System Selection," *Journal of Financial and Quantitative Analysis*, 11 (June 1976), 313-28.

Raw-materials inventory gives the firm flexibility in its purchasing. Without it, the firm must exist on a hand-to-mouth basis, buying raw materials strictly in keeping with its production schedule. Finished-goods inventory allows the firm flexibility in its production scheduling and in its marketing. Production does not need to be geared directly to sales. Large inventories allow efficient servicing of customer demands. If a certain product is temporarily out of stock, present as well as future sales to the customer may be lost. Thus, there is an incentive to maintain stocks of all three types of inventory.

The advantages of increased inventories are several. The firm can effect economies of production and purchasing and can fill orders more quickly. In short, the firm is more flexible. The obvious disadvantages are the total cost of holding the inventory, including storage and handling costs, and the required return on capital tied up in the investment in inventory. Like accounts receivable, inventories should be increased as long as the resulting savings exceed the total cost of holding the added inventory. The balance finally reached depends upon the estimates of actual savings, the cost of carrying additional inventory, and the efficiency of inventory control. Obviously, this balance requires coordination of the production, marketing, and finance areas of the firm in keeping with an overall objective.

ECONOMIC ORDER QUANTITY

The economic order quantity (EOQ) is an important concept in the purchase of raw materials and in the storage of finished-goods and in-transit inventories. In our analysis, we wish to determine the optimal order quantity for a particular item of inventory, given its forecasted usage, ordering cost, and carrying cost. Ordering can mean either the purchase of the item or its production. Assume for the moment that the usage of a particular item of inventory is known with certainty. This usage is stationary or steady throughout the period of time being analyzed. In other words, if usage is 2 600 items for a 6-months' period, 100 items are used each week. Moreover, usage is assumed to be independent of the level of inventory.

We assume that ordering costs, O, are constant regardless of the size of the order. In the purchase of raw materials or other items, these costs represent the clerical costs involved in placing an order as well as certain costs of receiving and checking the goods once they arrive. For finished-goods inventories, ordering costs involve scheduling a production run. When start-up costs are large—as they are in a machined piece of metal, for example—ordering costs can be quite significant. For in-transit inventories, ordering costs are likely to involve nothing more than record keeping. The total ordering cost for a period is simply the number of orders for that period, times the cost per order.

Carrying costs per period, C, represent the cost of inventory storage, handling, and insurance, together with the required rate of return on the investment in inventory. These costs are assumed to be constant per unit of inventory, per unit of time. Thus, the total carrying cost for a period is the average number of units of inventory for the period, times the carrying cost per unit. In addition, we assume for now that inventory orders are filled without delay. Because out-of-stock items can be replaced immediately, there is no need to maintain a buffer or safety stock.

Although the assumptions made up to now may seem overly restrictive, they are necessary for an initial understanding of the conceptual framework that follows. Subsequently, we shall relax some of them.

If the usage of an inventory item is perfectly steady over a period of time and there is no safety stock, average inventory (in units) can be expressed as

$$\text{Average inventory} = \frac{Q}{2} \qquad \text{(10-1)}$$

where Q is the quantity (in units) ordered and is assumed to be constant for the period. The above problem is illustrated in Fig. 10-4. Although the quantity demanded is a step function, we assume for analytical purposes that it can be approximated by a straight line. We see that zero inventory always indicates that further inventory must be ordered.

The carrying cost of inventory is the carrying cost per unit times the average number of units of inventory, or $CQ/2$. The total number of orders for a period of time is simply the total usage (in units) of an item of inventory for that period, S, divided by Q. Consequently, total ordering costs are represented by the ordering cost per order, times the number of orders, or SO/Q. Total inventory costs, then, are the carrying costs plus ordering costs, or

$$\frac{CQ}{2} + \frac{SO}{Q} \qquad \text{(10-2)}$$

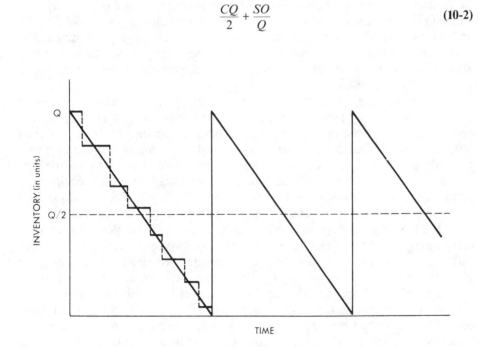

FIGURE 10-4 Order quantity example

We see from Eq. (10-2) that the higher the order quantity, Q, the higher the carrying costs but the lower the total ordering costs. The lower the order quantity, the lower the carrying costs but the higher the total ordering costs. We are concerned with the tradeoff between the economies of increased order size and the added cost of carrying additional inventory.

Optimal order quantity From Eq. (10-2) we can obtain the optimal order quantity, Q^*:

$$Q^* = \sqrt{\frac{2SO}{C}} \qquad \qquad (10\text{-}3)$$

This equation is known as the economic-lot-size formula. To illustrate its use, suppose that usage of an inventory item is 2 000 units during a 100-day period, ordering costs are \$100 an order, and carrying costs are \$10 per unit per 100 days. The most economic order quantity, then, is

$$Q^* = \sqrt{\frac{2(2\ 000)(100)}{10}} = 200 \text{ units}$$

With an order quantity of 200 units, the firm would order (2 000/200), or ten times, during the period under consideration or, in other words, every ten days. We see from Eq. (10-3) that Q^* varies directly with total usage, S, and order cost, O, and inversely with the carrying cost, C. However, the relationship is dampened by the square-root sign in both cases. As usage increases, the optimal order size and the average level of inventory increase by a lesser percentage. In other words, economies of scale are possible.

In our example, we have assumed that inventory can be ordered and received without delay. Usually, there is a time lapse between placement of a purchase order and receipt of the inventory, or in the time it takes to manufacture an item after an order is placed. This lead time must be considered. If it is constant and known with certainty, the optimal order quantity is not affected. In the above example, the firm would still order 200 units at a time and place ten orders during the specified time period, or every ten days. If the lead time for delivery were three days, the firm simply would place its order seven days after delivery of the previous order.

The EOQ function is shown in Fig. 10-5. In the figure, we plot ordering costs, carrying costs, and total costs—the sum of the first two costs. We see that whereas carrying costs vary directly with the size of the order, ordering costs vary inversely with size of the order. The total cost line declines at first as the fixed costs of ordering are spread over more units. The total cost line begins to rise when the decrease in average ordering cost is more than offset by the additional carrying costs. Point X, then, represents the economic order quantity, which minimizes the total cost of inventory. The EOQ formula taken up in this section is a very useful tool for inventory control. In purchasing raw materials or other items of inventory, it tells us the amount to order and the best timing of our orders. For finished-goods inventory, it enables us to exercise better control over the timing and size of production runs. In general, the EOQ model gives us a rule for deciding when to replenish inventories and the amount to replenish.

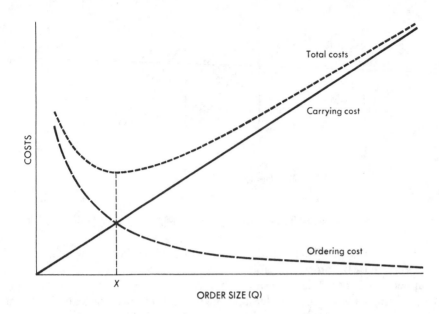

Total costs

Carrying cost

COSTS

Ordering cost

X

ORDER SIZE (Q)

FIGURE 10–5 Economic order quantity relationship

Safety Stocks and Other Considerations

In practice, the demand or usage of inventory generally is not known with certainty; usually it fluctuates during a given period of time. Typically, the demand for finished-goods inventory is subject to the greatest uncertainty. In general, the usage of raw-materials inventory and in-transit inventory, both of which depend upon the production scheduling, is more predictable. In addition to demand, the lead time required to receive delivery of inventory once an order is placed usually is subject to some variation. Owing to these fluctuations it is not feasible usually to allow expected inventory to fall to zero before a new order is anticipated, as the firm could do when usage and lead time were known with certainty. A safety stock is necessary.

ORDER POINT AND SAFETY STOCK

Before discussing safety stocks, it is necessary to consider at what point inventory will be ordered. Suppose that demand for inventory is known with certainty, but that it takes 5 days before an order is received. In our previous illustration of the economic-order-quantity formula, we found that the EOQ for our example firm was 200 units, resulting in an order being placed every 10 days. If usage is steady, the firm now would need to order 5 days before it ran out of stock, or at 100 units of stock on hand. Thus, the order point is 100 units. When the new order is received 5 days later, the firm will just have exhausted its existing stock. This example of an order point is illustrated in Fig. 10-6

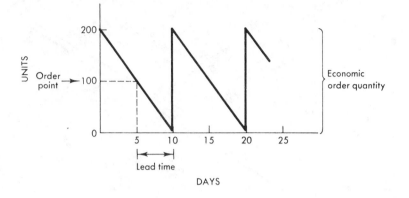

FIGURE 10-6 Order point when lead time is certain

When we allow for uncertainty in demand for inventory as well as in lead time, a safety stock becomes advisable. The concept here is illustrated in Fig. 10-7. In the upper panel of the figure we show what would happen if the firm had a safety stock of 100 units and if expected demand of 200 units every 10 days and lead time of 5 days were to occur. Note that with a safety stock of 100 units, the order point must be set at 200 units of inventory on hand as opposed to the previous 100 units. In other words, the order point determines the amount of safety stock held.

The bottom panel of the figure shows the actual experience for our hypothetical firm. In the first segment of demand, we see that actual usage is somewhat less than expected. (The slope of the line is less than the expected demand line in the upper panel.) At the order point of 200 units of inventory held, an order is placed for 200 units of additional inventory. Instead of taking the expected 5 days for the inventory to be replenished, we see that it takes only 4 days. The second segment of usage is much greater than expected and, as a result, inventory is rapidly used up. At 200 units of remaining inventory, a 200-unit order again is placed, but here it takes 6 days for the inventory to be received. As a result of both of these factors, heavy inroads are made into the safety stock.

In the third segment of demand, usage is about the same as expected; that is, the slopes of expected and actual usage lines are about the same. Because inventory was so low at the end of the previous segment of usage, an order is placed almost immediately. The lead time turns out to be 5 days. In the last segment of demand, usage is slightly greater than expected. The lead time necessary to receive the order is seven days, much longer than expected. The combination of these two factors again causes the firm to go into its safety stock. The example illustrates the importance of safety stock in absorbing random fluctuations in usage and in lead times. Without such stock, the firm would have run out of inventory on two occasions.

THE AMOUNT OF SAFETY STOCK

The proper amount of safety stock to maintain depends upon several things. The greater the uncertainty associated with forecast demand for inventory, the

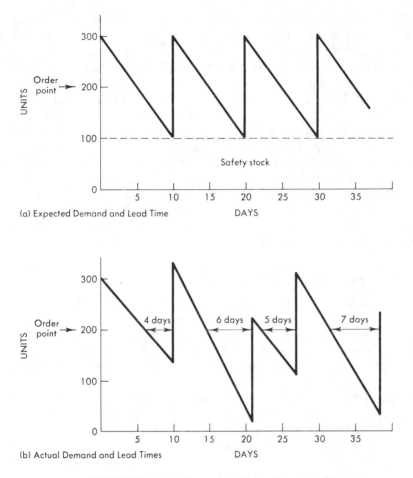

FIGURE 10-7 Safety stock when demand and lead time are uncertain

greater the safety stock the firm will wish to carry, all other things the same. Put another way, the risk of running out of stock is greater, the larger the unforeseen fluctuations in usage. Similarly, the greater the uncertainty of lead time to replenish stock, the greater the risk of running out of stock, and the more safety stock the firm will wish to maintain, all other things being equal. Another factor influencing the safety-stock decision is the cost of running out of inventory. The cost of being out of raw-materials and in-transit inventories is a delay in production. How much does it cost when production closes down temporarily? Where fixed costs are large, this cost will be quite high, as can be imagined in the case of an aluminum extrusion plant. The cost of running out of finished goods is customer dissatisfaction. Not only will the immediate sale be lost, but future sales will be endangered if customers take their business elsewhere. Although this opportunity cost is difficult to measure, it must be recognized by management and incorporated into the safety-stock decision. The greater the costs of running out of stock, of course, the more safety stock management will wish to maintain, all other things the same.

The final factor to consider is the cost of carrying additional inventory. If it were not for this cost, a firm could maintain whatever safety stock was necessary to avoid all possibility of running out of inventory. The greater the cost of carrying inventory, the most costly it is to maintain a safety stock, all other things being equal. Determination of the proper amount of safety stock involves balancing the probability and cost of a stock out against the cost of carrying enough safety stock to avoid this possibility. Ultimately, the question reduces to the probability of inventory stock out that management is willing to tolerate. In a typical situation, this probability is reduced at a decreasing rate as more safety stock is added. A firm may be able to reduce the probability of inventory stockout by 20 percent if it adds 100 units of safety stock, but only by an additional 10 percent if it adds another 100 units. There comes a point when it becomes very expensive to reduce further the probability of stockout. Management will not wish to add safety stock beyond the point at which incremental carrying costs exceed the incremental benefits to be derived from avoiding a stockout.

RELATION TO FINANCIAL MANAGEMENT

Although inventory management usually is not the direct operating responsibility of the financial manager, the investment of funds in inventory is a very important aspect of financial management. Consequently, the financial manager must be familiar with ways to control inventories effectively so that capital may be allocated efficiently. The greater the opportunity cost of funds invested in inventory, the lower the optimal level of average inventory and the lower the optimal order quantity, all other things held constant. This statement can be verified by increasing the carrying costs, C in Eq. (10-3). The EOQ model also can be used by the financial manager in planning for inventory financing.

When demand or usage of inventory is uncertain, the financial manager may try to effect policies that will reduce the average lead time required to receive inventory once an order is placed. The lower the average lead time, the lower the safety stock needed and the lower the total investment in inventory, all other things held constant. The greater the opportunity cost of funds invested in inventory, the greater the incentive to reduce this lead time. The purchasing department may try to find new vendors who promise quicker delivery, or it may pressure existing vendors to deliver faster. The production department may be able to deliver finished goods faster by producing a smaller run. In either case, there is a tradeoff between the added cost involved in reducing the lead time and the opportunity cost of funds tied up in inventory. This discussion serves to point out the value of inventory management to the financial manager.

Summary

Credit and collection policies encompass the quality of accounts accepted, the credit period extended, the cash discount given, and the level of collection expenditures. In each case, the credit decision involves a tradeoff between the additional profitability and the cost resulting from a change in any of these elements. By liberalizing the quality requirements for accounts, the firm might hope to make more on the additional sales than it spends to carry the additional receivables plus the additional bad-debt losses. To maximize profits arising from credit and collection policies, the firm should vary these policies jointly until an optimal solution is obtained. The firm's credit and collection policies, together with its credit and collection procedures, determine the magnitude and quality of its receivable position.

In evaluating a credit applicant, the credit analyst obtains financial and other information about the applicant, analyzes this information, and reaches a credit decision. If the account is new, the firm must decide whether or not to accept the order. With repeat orders, the firm must usually decide upon the maximum credit to extend. This maximum, known as a line of credit, is based upon the credit worthiness of the applicant.

The optimal level of inventories should be judged in relation to the flexibility inventories afford. If we hold constant the efficiency of inventory management, the lower the level of inventories, the less the flexibility of the firm. The higher the amount of inventories, the greater the flexibility of the firm. In evaluating the level of inventories, management must balance the benefits of economies of production, purchasing, and increased product demand against the cost of carrying the additional inventory. Of particular concern to the financial manager is the cost of funds invested in inventory.

In this chapter we examined several tools of inventory control. One is the economic order quantity (EOQ), whereby we determine the optimal size of order to place on the basis of the demand or usage of the inventory, the ordering costs, and the carrying costs. Under conditions of uncertainty, the firm must usually provide for a safety stock, owing to fluctuations in demand for inventory and in lead times. By varying the point at which orders are placed, one varies the safety stock that is held.

Questions

1. Is it always good policy to reduce the firm's bad-debt losses by "getting rid of the deadbeats"?
2. What are the probable effects on sales and profits of each of the following credit policies?
   (a) A high percentage of bad-debt loss, but normal receivable turnover and rejection rate.
   (b) A high percentage of past-due accounts and a low credit rejection rate.
   (c) A low percentage of past-due accounts, but high receivable rejection and turnover rates.
   (d) A low percentage of past-due accounts and a low rejection rate, but a high turnover rate.
3. Is an increase in the collection period necessarily bad? Explain.
4. Explain the difference between a bad-debt expense, the provision for bad debt, and a writeoff against the provision for bad debt.
5. What are the principal factors which can be varied in setting credit policy?
6. If credit standards for the quality of account accepted are changed, what things are affected?
7. Why is a saturation point reached in spending money on collections?
8. What is the purpose of establishing a line of credit for an account? What are the benefits of this arrangement?

9. The analysis of inventory policy is analogous to the analysis of credit policy. Propose a measure to analyze inventory policy which is analogous to aging of accounts receivable.

10. What are the principal implications to the financial manager of ordering costs, storage costs, and cost of capital as they relate to inventory?

11. Explain how efficient inventory management affects the liquidity and profitability of the firm.

12. The EOQ model does not provide any information about the safety stock that should be carried by a firm. Develop a conceptual model that will aid management in determining the correct amount of safety stock.

13. How can the firm reduce its investment in inventories? What costs might the firm incur from a policy of very low inventory investment?

14. Explain how a large seasonal demand complicates inventory management and production scheduling.

15. Do inventories represent an investment in the same sense as fixed assets?

16. Should the required rate of return for investment in inventories of raw materials be the same as that for finished goods?

Problems with Solutions

1. The accountant of a large wholesaler has been asked to calculate the financial implications of a change in credit policy. The accountant has collected the following information: present collection period, 30 days; variable costs, 75 percent of sales; expected increase in sales as a result of the credit policy change, 20 percent; collection period after the change, 60 days; required before tax return on investment, 20 percent. Should the credit policy be changed? Use a 360 day year.

Let $S =$ present sales

Profitability of additional sales	= increase in sales × (sales − variable cost) $= 0.25 \times 0.25 = 0.05S$
Present level of receivables	= Present sales × collection period/360 $= S \times \dfrac{30}{360} = \dfrac{1}{12}S$
New level of receivables associated with original sales	= Present sales × new collection period/360 $= S \times \dfrac{60}{360} = \dfrac{1}{6}S$
Additional investment in receivables associated with new sales	$= 0.2S \times \dfrac{60}{360} \times 0.75 = \dfrac{1}{40}S$
Total additional investment in receivables	$= \dfrac{1}{6}S - \dfrac{1}{12}S + \dfrac{1}{40}S = 0.108S$
Required return on investment	$= 0.2 \times 0.108S = 0.0216S$
Profit of $0.05S$ exceeds required return of $0.0216S$	

2. Recalculate your answer in the previous problem if the present level of sales is $6 000 000.

Profitability of additional sales

$$= 0.05S = 0.05 \times \$6\ 000\ 000$$
$$= \$300\ 000$$

Required return on investment

$$= 0.0216S$$
$$= 0.0216 \times \$6\ 000\ 000$$
$$= \$129\ 600$$

Profit of $300 000 exceeds $129 600 by $170 400

3. A few months after the change in credit policy described in problems 1 and 2 was accepted, the credit manager proposed that terms of 2/10, net 45 be offered to customers. If this were done, 60 percent of them would take advantage of the discount. The remaining customers would pay in 60 days as before. Should the proposal be accepted?

Cost of new proposal = $7 200 000 × 0.6 × 0.02 = $86 400

Present receivables = $1 200 000 (see problem 2)

New level of receivables $= \$7\ 200\ 000 \times 0.6 \times \dfrac{10}{360} = \$7\ 200\ 000 \times 0.4 \times \dfrac{60}{360}$

$$= \$120\ 000 + \$480\ 000 = \$600\ 000$$

Decrease in receivables = $1 200 000 – $600 000 = $600 000

Savings = Required rate of return × decrease in receivables
= 0.2 × $600 000 = $120 000

Savings – cost = $120 000 – $86 400 = $33 600. Accept proposal

4. Using the information presented in problems 1 and 2 assume that at a sales level of $6 000 000 bad debt losses are 1 percent of sales and that this level increases to 10 percent on incremental sales with sales of $7 200 000. If credit standards are relaxed sales will rise to $7 800 000 but bad debt losses will rise to 15% on incremental sales. No discounts are to be given at $7 800 000 the collection period will be 75 days. Which credit policy should be followed?

	Policy A	Policy B
Additonal sales	$1 200 000	$ 600 000
Profitability of additional sales (25 percent)	300 000	150 000
Additional bad debt losses (Additional sales × bad debt percentage)	120 000	90 000
Collection period	60 days	75 days
Accounts receivable (present level = $500 000)	1 200 000	1 625 000
Additional receivables	700 000	425 000
Investment in additional receivables (0.75 × additional receivables)	525 000	318 750
Required return on additional investment (20 percent)	105 000	63 750
Bad debt losses plus required return	225 000	153 750
Incremental profitability	75 000	(3 750)

5. The Falconer Company Ltd. expects to sell 4000 units over a one year period. Ordinary costs are $100 per order and carrying costs $7.50 per unit for 6 months. Calculate the most economic order quantity.

Use Eq (10-3): $Q^* = \sqrt{\dfrac{2SO}{C}}$

$$Q^* = \sqrt{\dfrac{2 \times 4\,000 \times 100}{15}} = 231$$

6. In problem 5 assume that the Falconer Company Ltd. knows with certainty that it takes 10 days before an order is received from the supplier and that a safety stock of 150 units is needed. Calculate the order point.

In problem 5 an order must be placed every 21 days

$$365 \div 4\,000 \times 231 = 21 \text{ (rounded)}$$

Since it takes 10 days to get an order, the order point becomes 110 units ($^{10}/_{21} \times 231$) plus safety stock of 150 or 260 units. Put another way, 110 units represents 10 days of stock and 150 units are needed to take care of uncertainties of demand.

7. Should the Falconer Company Ltd. in problem 5 accept an offer of a $0.05 discount per unit on a minimum order size of 300 units?

Discount savings = discount per unit × usage
$$= \$0.05 \times 4\,000 = \$200$$

Carrying cost increase = $\dfrac{(\text{new order size} - Q^*)C}{2} = \dfrac{(300 - 231)15}{2} = \$518$

Ordering cost savings = $\dfrac{SO}{Q^*} - \dfrac{SO}{\substack{\text{new} \\ \text{order} \\ \text{size}}} = \dfrac{(4\,000 \times 100)}{231} - \dfrac{(4\,000 \times 100)}{300} = \$399$

Summary: $200 + $399 − $517 = gain of $81

Problems

1. To increase sales from their present annual $24 million, MacDonald KNU Cartier Company Ltd., a wholesaler, may try more liberal credit standards. Currently, the firm has an average collection period of thirty days. It believes that with increasingly liberal credit standards, the following will result:

Credit policy	A	B	C	D
Increase in sales from previous level (in millions)	$2.8	$1.8	$1.2	$0.6
Avg. collection period for incremental sales (days)	45	60	90	144

The prices of its products average $20 per unit, and variable costs average $18 per unit. No bad-debt losses are expected. If the company has a pre-tax opportunity cost of funds of 30 percent, which credit policy should be pursued? (Assume a 360-day year.)

2. Upon reflection, MacDonald KNU Cartier Company Ltd. has estimated that the following pattern of bad-debt losses will prevail if it initiates more liberal credit terms:

Credit policy	A	B	C	D
Bad debt losses on incremental sales	3%	6%	10%	15%

Given the other assumptions in problem 1, which credit policy should be pursued?

3. Recalculate problem 2, assuming the following pattern of bad-debt losses:

Credit policy	A	B	C	D
Bad-debt losses on incremental sales	1.5%	3.0%	5.0%	7.5%

Which policy now would be best?

4. Durham-Feltz Corporation Ltd. presently gives terms of net 30 days. It has $60 million in sales and its average collection period is 45 days. To stimulate demand, the company may give terms of net 60 days. If it does instigate these terms, sales are expected to increase by 15 percent. After the change, the average collection period is expected to be 75 days, with no difference in payment habits between old and new customers. Variable costs are $0.80 for every $1.00 of sales, and the company's required rate of return on investment in receivables is 20 percent. Should the company extend its credit period? (Assume a 360-day year.)

5. The Chickee Corporation Ltd. has a 12 percent opportunity cost of funds and currently sells on terms of n/10, EOM. (This means that goods shipped before the end of the month must be paid for by the tenth of the following month.) The firm has sales of $10 million a year, which are 80 percent on credit and spread evenly over the year. The average collection period is currently 60 days. If Chickee offered terms of 2/10, net 30, 60 percent of its customers would take the discount, and the average collection period would be reduced to 40 days. Should Chickee change its terms from net/10, EOM to 2/10, net 30?

6. The Kentville Manufacturing Corporation Ltd. is considering extending trade credit to the Moose Jaw Company Ltd. Examination of the records of Moose Jaw has produced the following financial statements.

Moose Jaw Company Ltd. Balance Sheet (in millions)

	19X1	19X2	19X3
Assets:			
Current assets:			
Cash	$ 1.5	$ 1.6	$ 1.6
Receivables	1.3	1.8	2.5
Inventories (at lower of cost or market)	1.3	2.6	4.0
Other	0.4	0.5	0.4
Total current assets	$ 4.5	$ 6.5	$ 8.5

Fixed assets:			
Buildings (net)	2.0	1.9	1.8
Machinery and equipment (net)	7.0	6.5	6.0
Total fixed assets	$ 9.0	$ 8.4	$ 7.8
Other assets	1.0	0.8	0.6
Total assets	$14.5	$15.7	$16.9

Moose Jaw Company Ltd. Balance Sheet (in millions)

	19X1	19X2	19X3
Liabilities:			
Current liabilities:			
Notes payable (8½%)	$ 2.1	$ 3.1	$ 3.8
Trade payables	0.2	0.4	0.9
Other payables	0.2	0.2	0.2
Total	$ 2.5	$ 3.7	$ 4.9
Term loan (8½%)	4.0	3.0	2.0
Total	$ 6.5	$ 6.7	$ 6.9
Net worth			
Common stock	$ 5.0	$ 5.0	$ 5.0
Preferred stock (6½%)	1.0	1.0	1.0
Retained earnings	2.0	3.0	4.0
Total liabilities and net worth	$14.5	$15.7	$16.9

Moose Jaw Company Ltd. Income Statement (in millions)

	19X1	19X2	19X3
Net credit sales	$15.0	$15.8	$16.2
Cost of goods sold	11.3	12.1	13.0
Gross profit	$ 3.7	$ 3.7	$ 3.2
Operating expenses	1.1	1.2	1.2
Net profit before taxes	$ 2.6	$ 2.5	$ 2.0
Tax	1.3	1.2	1.0
Profit after taxes	$ 1.3	$ 1.3	$ 1.0
Dividends	0.3	0.3	0.0
	$ 1.0	$ 1.0	$ 1.0

The Moose Jaw Company Ltd. has a Dun & Bradstreet rating of 4A-2. Inquiries into its banking disclosed balances generally in the low millions. Five suppliers to Moose Jaw revealed that the firm takes its discounts from the three creditors offering of 2/10, net 30 terms, though it is about 15 days slow in paying the two firms offering terms of net 30. Analyze the Moose Jaw Company's application for credit.

7. Bluenose Gauge Company Ltd. makes wind and current gauges for pleasure boats. The gauges are sold throughout the Maritimes to boat dealers, and the average order size is $50. The company sells to all registered dealers without a credit analysis. Terms are net 45 days, and the average collection period is 60 days, which is regarded as satisfactory. Jane Sullivan, vice-president—finance, is now uneasy about increasing bad-debt losses on new orders. With credit ratings from local and regional credit agencies, she feels she would be able to classify new orders into one of three risk categories. Past experience shows the following:

	Order category		
	Low risk	Medium risk	High risk
Bad-debt loss (percent)	3%	7%	24%
Percent of category orders to total orders	30%	50%	20%

The cost of producing and shipping the gauges and of carrying the receivables is 78 percent of sales. The cost of obtaining credit rating information and of evaluating it is $4 per order. Surprisingly, there does not appear to be any association between the risk category and the collection period; the average for each of the three risk categories is around 60 days. Based on this information, should the company obtain credit information on new orders instead of selling to all new accounts without credit analysis?

8. Vostick Filter Company Ltd. is a distributor of air filters to retail stores. It buys its filters from several manufacturers. Filters are ordered in lot sizes of 1 000, and each order costs $40 to place. Demand from retail stores is 20 000 filters per month and the carrying cost is $0.10 a filter per month.
  (a) What is the optimal order quantity (in lot sizes)?
  (b) What would be the optimal order quantity if the carrying costs were $0.05 a filter per month?
  (c) What would be the optimal order quantity if ordering costs were $10?

9. A large bookstore is attempting to determine the optimal order quantity for a popular cookbook. The store sells 5 000 copies of this book a year at a retail price of $12.50, and the cost to the store is 20 percent less, which represents the discount from the publisher. The store figures that it costs $1 per year to carry a book in inventory and $100 to prepare an order for new books.
  (a) Determine the total costs associated with ordering 1, 2, 5, 10, and 20 times a year.
  (b) Determine the economic order quantity.
  (c) What implicit assumptions are being made about the annual sales rate?

10. A firm that sells 5 000 gidgets per month is trying to determine how many gidgets to keep in inventory. The financial manager has determined that it costs $200 to place an order. The cost of holding inventory is 4¢/month per average gidget in inventory. A 5-day lead time is required for delivery of goods ordered. (This lead time is known with certainty.)
  (a) Develop the algebraic expression for determining the total cost of holding and ordering inventory.
  (b) Plot the holding cost and the ordering cost on a graph where the abscissa represents size of order and the ordinate represents costs.
  (c) Determine the EOQ from the graph.

11. To reduce production start-up costs, Bodden Truck Company Ltd. may manufacture larger runs of the same truck. Estimated savings from the increase in efficiency are $260 000 per year. However, inventory turnover will decrease from 8 times a year to 6 times a year. Costs of goods sold are $48 million on an annual basis. If the required rate of return on investment in inventories is 15 percent, should the company instigate the new production plan?

12. Fouchee Scents Ltd. makes various scents for use in the manufacture of food products. Although the company does maintain a safety stock, it has a policy of "lean" inventories, with the result that customers sometimes must be turned away. In an analysis of the situation, the company has estimated the cost of being out of stock associated with various levels of safety stock:

	Level of safety stock (in gallons)	Annual cost of stockouts
Present safety-stock level	5 000	$26 000
New safety-stock level 1	7 500	14 000
New safety-stock level 2	10 000	7 000
New safety-stock level 3	12 500	3 000
New safety-stock level 4	15 000	1 000
New safety-stock level 5	17 500	0

Carrying costs are $0.65 per gallon per year. What is the best level of safety stock for the company?

Selected References

BARZMAN, SOL, *Everyday Credit Checking: A Practical Guide*, rev. ed. New York: National Association of Credit Management, 1980.

BEN-HORIM, MOSHE and HAIM LEVY, "Management of Accounts Receivable under Inflation", *Financial Management*, Spring 1983, 42-48.

BIERMAN, HAROLD, JR., CHARLES P. BONINI, and WARREN H. HAUSMAN, *Quantitative Analysis for Business Decisions*, 5th ed., Chapters 10-12, Homewood, Ill.: Irwin, 1977.

BROOKS, LEROY D., "Risk-Return Criteria and Optimal Inventory Stocks," *Engineering Economist*, 25 (Summer 1980), 275-99.

BROSKY, JOHN J., *The Implicit Cost of Trade Credit and Theory of Optimal Terms of Sale*. New York: Credit Research Foundation, 1969.

BUFFA, E. S., and W. H. TAUBERT, *Production-Inventory Systems: Planning and Control*, rev. ed. Homewood, Ill.: Irwin, 1972.

CARPENTER, MICHAEL D., and JACK E. MILLER, "A Reliable Framework for Monitoring Accounts Receivable," *Financial Management*, 8 (Winter, 1979), 37-40.

DEAKIN, EDWARD B., III. "Finding Optimal Order Quantity When Quantity Discounts Are Offered," *Cost and Management* (May-June 1975), 40-42.

DYL, EDWARD A., "Another Look at the Evaluation of Investment in Accounts Receivable," *Financial Management*, 6 (Winter 1977), 67-70.

GOYAL, S. K. and N. HONEYMAN, "Costing for Inventory Models," *Cost and Management* (July-August 1973), 34-37.

_____."Some Capital Investment Aspects of Stock Control," *Cost and Management* (May-June 1973), 32-35.

HALLOREN, JOHN A., and HOWARD P. LANSER, "The Credit Policy Decision in an Inflationary Environment," *Financial Management*, 10 (Winter 1981), 31-38.

HILL, NED C., and KENNETH D. RIENER, "Determining the Cash Discount in the Firm's Credit Policy," *Financial Management*, 8 (Spring 1979), 68-73.

KIM, YONG H. and JOSEPH C. ATKINS, "Evaluating Investments in Accounts Receivable: A Wealth Maximization Framework," *Journal of Finance*, 33 (May 1978), 403-12.

LEWELLEN, W. G., and R. O. EDMISTER, "A General Model for Accounts Receivable Analysis and Control," *Journal of Financial and Quantitative Analysis*, 8 (March 1973), 195-206.

LEWELLEN, W. G., and R. W. JOHNSON, "Better Way to Monitor Accounts Receivable," *Harvard Business Review*, (May-June 1972), 101-109.

LONG, MICHAEL S., "Credit Screening System Selection," *Journal of Financial and Quantitative Analysis*, 11 (June 1976), 313-28.

MAGEE, JOHN F., "Guides to Inventory Policy," I-III, *Harvard Business Review*, 34 (January-February 1956), 49-60; (March-April 1956), 103-16; and (May-June 1956), 57-70.

MARRAH, GEORGE L., "Managing Receivables," *Financial Executive*, 38 (July 1970), 40-44.

MEHTA, DILEEP, "The Formulation of Credit Policy Models," *Management Science*, 15 (October 1968), 30-50.

_____, *Working Capital Management*, Englewood Cliffs, N.J.: Prentice-Hall, 1974, Chapters 1-5.

OH, JOHN S., "Opportunity Cost in the Evaluation of Investment in Accounts Receivable," *Financial Management*, 5 (Summer 1976), 32-36.

SACHDEVA, KANWAL S., "Accounts Receivable Decisions in a Capital Budgeting Framework," *Financial Management*, 10 (Winter 1981), 45-49.

SCHIFF, MICHAEL, "Credit and Inventory Management," *Financial Executive*, 40 (November 1972), 28-33.

SMITH, KEITH V., *Guide to Working Capital Management*, New York: McGraw-Hill, 1979, Chapters 5 and 6.

SNYDER, ARTHUR, "Principles of Inventory Management," *Financial Executive*, 32 (April 1964), 16-19.

STONE, BERNELL K., "The Payments-Pattern Approach to the Forecasting and Control of Accounts Receivable," *Financial Management*, 5 (Autumn 1976), 65-82.

WESTON, J. FRED, and PHAM D. TUAN, "Comment on Analysis of Credit Policy Changes," *Financial Management*, 9 (Winter 1980), 59-63.

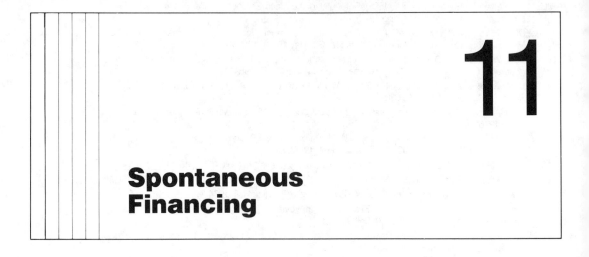

Spontaneous Financing

Short term financing can be categorized according to whether or not the source is spontaneous. Accounts payable and accruals are classified as spontaneous because their magnitude is primarily a function of a company's level of operations. As operations expand, these liabilities typically increase and finance in part the buildup in assets. While both accounts payable and accruals behave in this manner, there still remains a degree of discretion on the part of a company as to their exact magnitude. In this chapter we consider these two methods of financing and how such discretion might be used. In the next chapter we examine the other major sources of short term financing—money-market credit and short term loans, the latter being either from banks or finance companies. Unlike the sources discussed in this chapter, such financing is not spontaneous or automatic. It must be arranged on a formal basis.

Trade Credit Financing

Trade credit is a form of short-term financing common to almost all businesses. In fact, it is the largest source of short-term funds for business firms collectively. In an advanced economy, most buyers are not required to pay for goods upon delivery but are allowed a short deferment period before payment is due. During this period the seller of the goods extends credit to the buyer. Because suppliers generally are more liberal in the extension of credit than are financial institutions, small companies in particular rely on trade credit.

Of the three types of trade—open account, notes payable, and trade acceptances—by far the most common type is the open-account arrangement. The seller ships goods to the buyer and sends an invoice that specifies the goods shipped, the price, the total amount due, and the terms of the sale. Open-account credit derives its name from the fact that the buyer does not sign a formal debt instrument evidencing the amount owed the seller. The seller extends credit based upon a credit investigation of the buyer (see Chapter 10).

In some situations promissory notes are employed instead of open-account credit. The buyer signs a note that evidences a debt to the seller. The note itself calls for the payment of the obligation at some specified future date. Promissory notes have been used in business such as those dealing in furs and jewelry. This arrangement is employed when the seller wants the buyer to recognize the debt formally. A seller might request a promissory note from a buyer if the buyer's open account became past due.

A trade acceptance is another arrangement by which the indebtedness of the buyer is formally recognized. Under this arrangement, the seller draws a draft on the buyer, ordering the buyer to pay the draft at some date in the future. The seller will not release the goods until the buyer accepts the time draft.[1] Accepting the draft, the buyer designates a bank at which the draft will be paid when it comes due. At that time, the draft becomes a trade acceptance, and depending upon the credit worthiness of the buyer, it may possess some degree of marketability. If the trade acceptance is marketable, the seller of the goods can sell it at a discount and receive immediate payment for the goods. At final maturity, the holder of the acceptance presents it to the designated bank for collection.

TERMS OF SALE

Because the use of promissory notes and trade acceptances is rather limited, the subsequent discussion will be confined to open-account trade credit. The terms of sale make a great deal of difference in this type of credit. These terms, specified in the invoice, may be placed in several broad categories according to the net period within which payment is expected and according to the terms of the cash discount.

COD and CBD—no extension of credit   COD terms means *cash on delivery* of the goods. The only risk the seller undertakes is that the buyer may refuse the shipment. Under such circumstances, the seller will be stuck with the shipping costs. Occasionally a seller might ask for *cash before delivery* (CBD) to avoid all risk. Under either COD or CBD terms, the seller does not extend credit. CBD terms must be distinguished from progress payments, which are very common in certain industries. With progress payments, the buyer pays the manufacturer at various stages of production before the actual delivery of the finished product. Because large sums of money are tied up in work in progress, aircraft manufacturers request progress payments from airlines in advance of the actual delivery of aircraft.

Net period—no cash discount   When credit is extended, the seller specifies the period of time allowed for payment. The terms "net 30" indicate that the invoice or bill must be paid within 30 days. If the seller bills on a monthly basis, it might require such terms as "net 15 EOM," which means that all goods shipped before the end of the month must be paid for by the fifteenth of the following month.

---

[1]If the instrument is a sight draft, the buyer is ordered to pay the draft upon presentation. Under this arrangement, trade credit is not extended.

Net period with cash discount   In addition to extending credit, the seller may offer a cash discount if the bill is paid during the early part of the net period. The terms "2/10, net 30" indicate that the seller offers a 2 percent discount if the bill is paid within 10 days; otherwise, the buyer must pay the full amount within 30 days. Usually, a cash discount is offered as an incentive to the buyer to pay early. In Chapter 10, we discussed the optimal cash discount the seller might offer. A cash discount differs from a trade discount and from a quantity discount. A trade discount is greater for one class of customers (e.g., wholesalers) than for others (e.g., retailers). A quantity discount is offered on large shipments.

Datings   In a seasonal business, sellers frequently use datings to encourage customers to place their orders before a heavy selling period. A manufacturer of lawn mowers may give seasonal datings specifying that any shipment to a dealer in the winter or spring does not have to be paid for until summer. Earlier orders benefit the seller, who can gauge the demand more realistically and schedule production more efficiently. Also, the seller does not have to store certain finished-goods inventory. The buyer has the advantage of not having to pay for the goods until the height of the selling period. Under this arrangement, credit is extended for a longer-than-normal period of time.

TRADE CREDIT AS A MEANS OF FINANCING

We have seen that trade credit is a source of funds, because the buyer does not have to pay for goods until after they are delivered. If the firm automatically pays its bills a certain number of days after the date of invoice, trade credit becomes a built-in source of financing that varies with the production cycle. As the firm increases its production and corresponding purchases, accounts payable increase and provide part of the funds needed to finance the increase in production. As production decreases, accounts payable tend to decrease. Although the variation of accounts payable with production may not be directly proportional, because of shortages or gluts in inventory on hand, there is a strong degree of correspondence.

If a firm adheres strictly to the practice of paying its bills at a given time after invoice, trade credit is not a discretionary source of financing. It is entirely dependent upon the purchasing plans of the firm, which, in turn, are dependent upon its production cycle. In examining trade credit as a discretionary form of financing, we want to specifically consider situations in which (1) a firm does not take a cash discount but pays on the last day of the net period, and (2) a firm pays its bills beyond the net period.

PAYMENT ON THE FINAL DUE DATE

In this section we assume that the firm foregoes a cash discount but does pay its bill on the final due date of the net period. If no cash discount is offered, there is no cost for the use of credit during the net period. By the same token, if a firm takes the discount, there is no cost for the use of trade credit during the discount period. If a cash discount is offered but not taken, however, there is a definite opportunity cost. If the terms of sale are 2/10, net 30, the firm has the use of funds for an additional 20 days if it does not take the cash discount but pays on the final day of the net period. For a $100 invoice, it would have the use of $98 for 20 days. The annual interest cost is[2]

$$\frac{2}{98} \times \frac{360}{20} = 36.7 \text{ percent}$$

Thus, we see that trade credit can be a very expensive form of short-term financing when a cash discount is offered.

The cost of trade credit declines as the net period becomes longer in relation to the discount period. Had the terms in the above example been 2/10, net 60, the annual interest cost would have been

$$\frac{2}{98} \times \frac{360}{50} = 14.7 \text{ percent}$$

The relationship between the annual interest cost of trade credit and the number of days between the end of the discount period and the end of the net period is shown in Fig. 11-1. In the figure, we assume 2/10 discount terms. We see that the cost of trade credit decreases at a decreasing rate as the net period increases. The point is that if a firm does not take a cash discount, its cost of trade credit declines with the length of time it is able to postpone payment.

STRETCHING ACCOUNTS PAYABLE

In the preceding section we assumed that payment was made at the end of the due period: however, a firm may postpone payment beyond this period. We shall call this postponement "stretching" accounts payable or "leaning on the trade." The cost of stretching accounts payable is twofold: the cost of the cash discount foregone and the possible deterioration in credit rating. In Chapter 10 we discussed the rating system of credit agencies such as Dun & Bradstreet. If a firm stretches its payables excessively, so that trade payables are significantly delinquent, its credit rating will suffer. Suppliers will view the firm with apprehension and may insist upon rather strict terms of sale if, indeed, they sell at all. In assessing a company banks and other lenders do not favourably regard excessive slowness. Although it is difficult to measure, there is certainly an opportunity cost to a deterioration in a firm's credit reputation.

Notwithstanding the possibility of a deteriorating credit rating, it may be possible to postpone certain payables beyond the net period without severe consequences. Supplers are in business to sell goods, and trade credit may increase sales. A supplier may be willing to go along with stretching payables, particularly if the risk of bad-debt loss is negligible. If the funds requirement of the firm is seasonal, suppliers may not view the stretching of payables in an unfavourable light during periods of peak requirements, provided that the firm is current in the trade

---

[2]For ease of calculation, 360 rather than 365 is used as the number of days in the year.

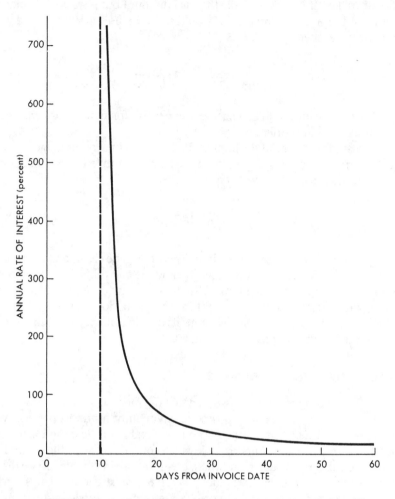

FIGURE 11–1 Annual rate of interest on accounts payable with terms of 2/10, net 30

during the rest of the year. There may be an indirect charge for this extension of credit, in the form of higher prices, a possibility that the firm should carefully consider in evaluating the cost of stretching accounts payable.

Periodic and reasonable stretching of payables is not necessarily bad per se. It should be evaluated objectively in relation to its cost and in relation to alternative sources of short-term credit. When a firm does stretch its payables, effort should be made to keep suppliers fully informed of its situation. A large number of suppliers will allow a firm to stretch payables if the firm is honest with the supplier and consistent in its payments. Sometimes a firm with seasonal funds requirements is able to obtain a dating from a supplier. When a firm obtains a dating, it does not stretch its payables; as long as it pays the bill by the final date, no deterioration in its credit rating is likely.

ADVANTAGES OF TRADE CREDIT

The firm must balance the advantages of trade credit as a discretionary source of financing against the cost of foregoing a cash discount, the opportunity cost associated with a possible deterioration in credit reputation if its stretches its payables, and the possible increase in selling price the seller imposes on the buyer. There are several advantages of trade credit as a form of short-term financing. Probably the major advantage is its ready availability. The accounts payable of most firms represent a continuous form of credit. There is no need to arrange financing formally; it is already there. If the firm is now taking cash discounts, additional credit is readily available by not paying existing accounts payable until the end of the net period. There is no need to negotiate with the supplier; the decision is entirely up to the firm. In stretching accounts payable, the firm will find it necessary, after a certain degree of postponement, to negotiate with the supplier.

In most other types of short-term financing, it is necessary to negotiate formally with the lender over the terms of the loan. The lender may impose restrictions on the firm and seek a secured position. Restrictions are possible with trade credit, but they are not nearly as likely. With other sources of short-term financing, there may be a lead time between the time the need for funds is recognized and the time the firm is able to borrow them. Trade credit is a more flexible means of financing. The firm does not have to sign a note, pledge collateral, or adhere to a strict payment schedule on the note. A suppler views an occasional delinquent payment with a far less critical eye than does a banker or other lender.

The advantages of using trade credit must be weighed against the cost. As we have seen, the cost may be very high when all factors are considered. Many firms utilize other sources of short-term financing in order to be able to take advantage of cash discounts. The savings in cost over other forms of short-term financing, however, must offset the loss of flexibility and convenience associated with trade credit. For certain firms, there are no alternative sources of short-term credit.

WHO BEARS THE COST?

We should recognize that trade credit involves a cost for the use of funds over time. In the previous sections, it was implied that there is no explicit cost to trade credit if the buyer pays the invoice during the discount period or, if no cash discount is given, during the net period. Although this supposition is valid from the standpoint of marginal analysis, it overlooks the fact that somebody must bear the cost of trade credit, for the use of funds over time is not free. The burden may fall on the supplier, the buyer, or both parties. The supplier may be able to pass the cost on to the buyer in the form of higher prices.

The supplier of a product for which demand is elastic, may be reluctant to increase prices and may end up absorbing most of the cost of trade credit. Under other circumstances the supplier is able to pass the cost on to the buyer. The buyer should determine who is bearing the cost of trade credit. A buyer who is bearing the cost may shop around for a better deal. The buyer should recognize that the cost of trade credit changes over time. In periods of rising interest rates and tight money, suppliers may raise the price of their products to take account of the rising cost of carrying receivables. This rise in price should not be confused with other rises caused by changing supply and demand conditions in the product markets.

Accrual Accounts

Perhaps even more than accounts payable, accrual accounts represent a spontaneous source of financing. The most common accrual accounts are for wages and taxes. For both accounts, the expense is incurred or accrued but not paid. Usually a date is specified when the accrual must be paid. Income taxes are paid quarterly; property taxes are paid semiannually. Wages typically are paid weekly, every other week, bimonthly, or monthly. Like accounts payable, accruals tend to expand with the scope of the operation. As sales increase, labor costs usually increase; and with them, accrued wages increase. As profits increase, accrued taxes increase in almost direct proportion.

In a sense, accruals represent costless financing. Services are rendered for wages, but employees are not paid and do not expect to be paid until the end or after the end of the pay period. The lapse is established by the company, although unions and competing employers in the labor market influence its length. Similarly, taxes are not expected to be paid until their due date. Thus, accruals represent an interest-free source of financing.

Unfortunately for the company, they do not represent discretionary financing. For taxes, the government is the creditor, and it likes to be paid on time. A company in extreme financial difficulty can postpone tax payment for a short while but there is a penalty charge. It may also postpone payment of wages—at the expense of employees and hurt morale. Employees may respond with absenteeism, reduced efficiency or seek employment elsewhere. A company must be extremely careful in postponing wages. It must fully inform employees and set a firm date for payment. Such a measure is one of last resort; nevertheless, many a company on the precipice of cash-flow disaster finds itself having to postpone wages as well as all other payments.

Accrued wages are partially discretionary in that a company can change the frequency of wage payments and thereby affect the amount of financing. If the interval of time between the last working day of a pay period and pay day stays the same, the less frequent the paydays the more the financing. Suppose a company had a weekly payroll of $400 000 with an average amount accrued of $200 000. If the company were to increase its pay period from one to two weeks, the payroll at the end of the period would be $800 000. The average amount of accrued wages now would be $400 000 ($800 000 divided by two). Therefore, the company increases its interest-free financing by $200 000.

The longer the pay period, the greater the amount of accrued wage financing. This linear relationship is illustrated in Fig. 11-2 for $1 in weekly wages. (For a specific situation, one needs to multiply the amount of accrual shown on the vertical axis by the actual weekly payroll to determine the average amount accrued.) Obviously, it should be desirable from the standpoint of a company to have as long a pay period as possible, but union pressures and competition for labor

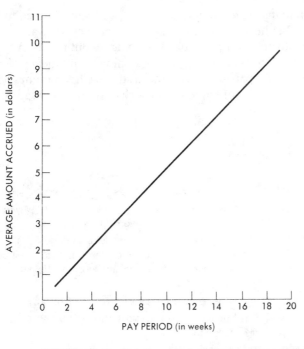

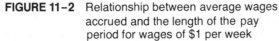

FIGURE 11-2 Relationship between average wages accrued and the length of the pay period for wages of $1 per week

from other employers limit the feasible range of options. Moreover, an increase in the pay period is usually "one-shot" in that it is not possible to repeat with a subsequent increase. In most companies, the maximum pay period is no more than one month. In summary, then, accruals are a discretionary source of financing only within a very narrow range.

Summary

Trade credit can be a significant source of short-term financing for the firm. It is a discretionary source of financing only if a firm does not have a strict policy regarding its promptness in paying bills. When a cash discount is offered but not taken, the cost of trade credit is the cash discount foregone. The longer the period between the end of the discount period and the time the bill is paid, the less the opportunity cost. "Stretching" accounts payable involves postponement of payment beyond the due period. The opportunity cost of stretching payables is the possible deterioration in the firm's credit rating. The firm must balance the costs of trade credit against its advantages and the costs of other short-term credit. The major advantage of trade credit is the flexibility it gives the firm.

Like accounts payable, accruals represent a spontaneous source of financing, albeit offering the firm even less discretion than it has with trade credit financing.

The principal accrual items are wages and taxes, and both are expected to be paid on established dates. In the interim, interest-free financing is available to the company; and for an ongoing company, this financing is continuous. A company can increase the amount of its accrued wages by lessening the frequency of paydays within a narrow range. A company in dire financial straits will sometimes postpone tax and wage payments, but the consequences of such postponement can be severe.

Questions

1. Explain why trade credit is a "spontaneous source of funds."
2. Trade credit is a very costly source of funds when discounts are lost. Explain why many firms rely on this source of funds to finance their temporary working capital.
3. Stretching payables provides "free" funds to the customers for a short period. The supplier, however, can face serious financial problems if all of its customers stretch their accounts. Discuss the nature of the problems the supplier may face and suggest different approaches to cope with stretching.
4. What may be the impact of large-scale stretching on social welfare? Explain.
5. Suppose a firm elected to tighten its trade credit policy from 2/10, net 90 to 2/10, net 30. What effect could the firm expect this change to have on its liquidity?
6. Why do small firms in particular rely heavily on trade credit as a source of funds? Why will suppliers advance credit to firms when banks will not?
7. In what ways can accruals be varied to obtain more interest-free financing?
8. Why is the Canadian government an involuntary creditor with respect to accrued taxes?
9. Why are accruals a more spontaneous source of financing than trade credit?
10. What is to prevent a company from postponing payment on its accruals?

Problems with Solutions

1. A university pays its faculty monthly. The annual faculty salaries total $6 000 000. The Faculty Association has proposed twice monthly paydays. The university invests excess cash at 13 percent and borrows when necessary at 16 percent. Currently the minimum excess cash position is $200 000 for a two month period; in every other month excess cash is more than $300 000. Calculate the cost of the proposal.

Effect of twice monthly paydays:
Monthly faculty payroll: $500 000
Excess cash is reduced by $250 000 for 10 of the 12 months but for the other 2 there is only an excess of $200 000. In these two months the university will be forced to borrow $50 000 for 15 days.

Lost interest $250 000 \times 10 \times \frac{1}{2} \times 0.13 \div 12$	$13 541.67
Lost interest $200 000 \times 2 \times \frac{1}{2} \times 0.13 \div 12$	2 166.67
Interest expense $50 000 \times 2 \times \frac{1}{2} \times 0.16 \div 12$	666.66
	$16 375.00

2. Ricketts Company Ltd. buys on credit terms 2/10, net 30 days. Included in the credit terms is a penalty clause requiring 1 1/2 percent interest per month for any balance owing at the end of the net pay period. The firm has just lost a major contract and feels that it may have to stretch its payables to 60 days for some indefinite period. Until now, the firm had always taken the discount. What will it cost the firm (on an annual basis) to stretch its payables? Is this a wise decision? Assume an invoice is for $100.

(a) By stretching payables to 60 days, the firm is essentially taking a loan of $98 ($100 less $2 discount) for a period of 50 days (60 less 10).
(b) The dollar cost (or interest) on the loan is the discount of $2 foregone plus the interest of $1.50 (1.5 percent of $100) or $3.50.
(c) The annual cost of the strategy is:

$$\frac{\$3.50}{98.00} \times \frac{360}{50} \times 100 = 25.71\%$$

The firm may be better off negotiating a bank loan for the period of expected cash shortages rather than stretch its payables.
(Note the effect of the interest penalty for non-payment after the net pay period. Without this penalty, the annual interest cost of stretching to 60 days would be:

$$\frac{\$2}{98} \times \frac{360}{50} \times 100 = 14.7\%$$

Problems

1. Determine the effective annual cost of capital for the following terms, assuming discounts are lost and a 360-day year.

(a) 1/10, n/30
(b) 2/10, n/30
(c) 3/10, n/30
(d) 10/30, n/60

(e) 3/10, n/60
(f) 2/10, n/90
(g) 3/10, n/90
(h) 5/10, n/100

2. The Dud Company Ltd. purchases raw materials on terms of 2/10, net 30. A review of the company's records by the owner, Mr. Dud, revealed that payments are usually made 15 days after purchases are received. When asked why the firm did not take advantage of its discounts, the bookkeeper, Mr. Grind, replied that it cost only 2 percent for these funds, whereas a bank loan would cost the firm 12 percent.
(a) What mistake is Grind making?
(b) What is the real cost of not taking advantage of the discount?
(c) If the firm could not borrow from the bank and were forced to resort to the use of trade credit funds, what suggestion might be made to Grind which would reduce the annual interest cost?

3. The manager of Wilstat Corporation Ltd. envisions benefits in switching from cash purchase of merchandise to credit purchase on net-60-day terms. The manager feels that the increased liquidity of purchasing $5 000/month on 60-day terms will be reflected in the liquidity ratios. The present working-capital accounts of the corporation are as follows:

Cash	$15 000	Notes payable	$10 000
Receivables	25 000	Taxes payable	6 000
Inventories	40 000	Other accruals	4 000
	$80 000		$20 000

(a) What effect would the purchase of $10 000 of merchandise on 60-day terms have on (1) the current ratio and (2) the quick ratio?

(b) Do the ratios indicate increased liquidity? Explain.

4. Determine the annual percentage interest cost for each of the following terms of sale, assuming the firm does not take the cash discount but pays on the final day of the net period (assume a 360-day year):

(a) 1/20, net 30 ($500 invoice)

(b) 2/30, net 60 ($1 000 invoice)

(c) 2/5, net 10 ($100 invoice)

(d) 3/10, net 30 ($250 invoice)

5. Does the dollar size of the invoice affect the annual interest cost of not taking discounts? Illustrate with an example.

6. Recompute problem 4, assuming a 10-day stretching of the payment date.

7. On January 1, Faville Car Company Ltd., a large car dealer, gave its employees a 10 percent pay increase in view of the substantial profits the prior year. Before the increase, the weekly payroll was $50 000. Profits were $274 000 the previous year, but only $200 000 was used in estimating quarterly tax payments. The company is in the 46 percent marginal tax bracket and intends to pay the additional taxes on April 15. What is the combined effect of these two changes on accruals?

8. The Halow Harp and Chime Company Ltd. is negotiating a new labor contract. Among other things, the union is demanding that the company pay its workers weekly as opposed to twice a month. The payroll currently is $260 000 per pay day and accrued wages average $130 000. What is the annual cost of the union's demand if the company's opportunity cost of funds is 9 percent?

Selected References

BROSKY, JOHN J., *The Implicit Cost of Trade Credit and Theory of Optimal Terms of Sale*. New York: Credit Research Foundation, 1969.

SCHWARTZ, ROBERT A., "An Economic Model of Trade Credit," *Journal of Financial and Quantitative Analysis*, 9 (September 1974), 643-58.

SMITH, KEITH V., *Guide to Working Capital Management*. New York: McGraw-Hill, 1979, Chapters 7, 8.

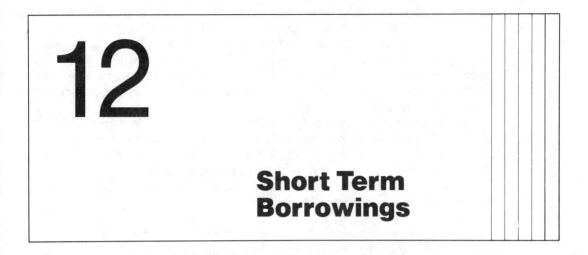

12

Short Term
Borrowings

In the previous chapter, we studied two important spontaneous sources of short-term financing—namely, trade credit and accruals. In this chapter, we examine methods of external (non-spontaneous) short term financing in the public or private market. The public market deals in various money market instruments which are sold to investors either directly by the issuer or indirectly through dealers. The private market includes short term loans which are placed privately, primarily with commercial banks and finance companies. For both money market credit and short term loans, financing must be arranged on a formal basis.

Money Market Credit

Large well-established companies sometimes borrow on a short term basis by issuing commercial paper and other money market instruments. Usually these securities are unsecured short term obligations and as such, only the most credit-worthy companies can use the money market to obtain short term financing. Two of the popular money market instruments used by non-financial companies are commercial paper and bankers' acceptances.

COMMERCIAL PAPER

Commercial paper is a short term negotiable promissory note issued by bigger firms to investors in the money market. Usually, the commercial paper of non-financial companies is unsecured. Finance company paper (that is, the commercial paper issued by sales finance and consumer loans companies), however, is usually secured by a pledge of accounts receivables. The borrowing firm may be required to deposit receivables ranging from 112 percent to 125 percent of the par value of the issue with a trustee, as a security. Generally, the issuer of commercial paper will have an unused line of credit at banks almost sufficient to redeem the issue in the event that funds expected from other sources become unavailable. Also, where applicable, a parent company will act as a guarantor of the commercial paper of its subsidiary.

Commercial paper is usually issued in multiples of not less than $100 000, and is sold on either a discount basis or an interest-bearing basis depending on the preference of the buyers. Maturities of these securities range from 1 to 365 days. Because of the unsecured and/or short term nature of these money market instruments, only the most credit-worthy companies are able to use them as a source of short term financing.

Market for commercial paper   The commercial paper market was initiated in the early 1950s by the sales and consumer loan companies.[1] In the late 1950s other borrowers (financial and non-financial) entered the market to raise short-term funds. By 1961, net issues outstanding totalled about $700 million. Since that date the commercial paper market has developed rather significantly and in 1983 net issues outstanding totalled $12.5 billion (see Table 12-1). The market is divided into two parts: the direct placement market and the dealer market.[2] The direct placement market is relatively small, accounting for about 15 percent of the new issues of commercial paper. The dealer market for commercial paper is dominated by about five of the major investment dealers of the group of money market dealers. Investment dealers purchase commercial paper from issuers and sell it to investors. The typical commission a dealer earns is 0.125 to 0.25 percent of the face value of the paper. Financial institutions, such as banks, trust companies, life insurance companies, and larger industrial and mining companies are large-scale buyers of commercial paper.[3]

The rapid growth of commercial paper in the 1960s and 1970s was closely associated with the development of the money market, the growth of the economy as a whole, and the growth of instalment financing of durable goods. In addition, this growth was attributable in part to the fact that banks curtailed credit in general and credit to finance companies in particular. Borrowers then turned to the commercial paper market as an alternative source of financing.

Non-financial companies issue commercial paper mainly to finance seasonal fluctuations in inventories and accounts receivable, and to pay accounts payable. In 1983, the outstanding commercial paper of these firms ($3.16 billion) constituted about 25 percent of the total amount of issues outstanding in the market.

---

[1]E. P. Neufeld, *The Financial System of Canada* (Toronto: Macmillan of Canada, 1972), 528-29. The Canadian money and capital markets are reviewed in Chapter 20.

[2]A discussion of the market for finance company paper is noted in J. N. Abell, "Report on the Money Market Aspects of the Failure of Atlantic Acceptance Corporation," *Report of the Royal Commission on Atlantic Acceptance*, Canada 1966, 1524-56.

[3]For a discussion of commercial paper from the standpoint of a short-term investor, see Chapter 9.

TABLE 12-1   Corporate Short Term Paper: Amounts Outstanding and Rates, 1968-83

	Amount Outstanding Dec. 31 (millions)				Average Interest Rate at Dec. 31		
	Commercial Paper						
	Sales Finance and Consumer Loan Company Paper	Other Commercial Paper		Bankers' Acceptances	Finance Company Paper 90-day	Prime Rate on Bank Loans	Bankers' Acceptance
		Financial	Non-Financial				
1968	$1 336	$ 167	$ 187	$ 116	6.54%	6.75%	6.50%
1970	1 442	313	583	395	5.58	7.50	6.10
1972	1 807	352	661	390	5.15	6.54	4.80
1974	2 961	1 529	1 437	903	10.25	11.71	9.78
1976	3 168	2 212	1 767	1 135	8.16	9.25	8.25
1978	3 880	4 318	1 472	1 664	10.78	11.50	10.23
1980	3 551	9 460	1 869	5 365	17.75	18.25	18.45
1981	3 501	7 353	2 521	6 561	15.65	17.25	14.93
1982	1 821	5 898	2 355	12 666	10.25	12.50	10.20
1983	2 372	7 374	3 161	13 859	9.85	11.00	9.57

Source: *Bank of Canada Review*

Sales finance and consumer loan companies and other financial institutions (primarily the non-banking sector) use commercial paper continuously to secure necessary funds for their operations. Note that in recent years the proportion of outstanding amounts for financial institutions other than the finance companies has increased rather dramatically (see Table 12-1). The increasing borrowing activity through commercial paper is promoting a trend towards financing on a revolving or more permanent basis.

Advantages to the borrower   The principal advantage of commercial paper to the borrower as a source of short-term financing is that it is generally cheaper than a short-term business loan from a commercial bank. Usually, the rate on prime commercial paper is 0.25 percent to 2 percent lower than the prime rate for bank loans to the highest-quality borrower. The differential tends to increase in periods of easy money and to decrease in periods of tight money. It is important to recognize that, unlike the prime rate on bank loans, commercial paper rates fluctuate considerably in keeping with money-market conditions. Table 12-1 shows the average rates for commercial paper as well as the prime rate on business loans since 1968. In assessing commercial paper as a means of financing, the firm should weight relative cost and availability in comparisons with alternative sources of funds.

Many companies consider commercial paper a desirable supplement to bank credit. Ideally, a company would borrow heavily through commercial paper when the interest-rate differential was wide and borrow more from banks when the differential narrowed. This strategy would result in the lowest average interest cost and maximum flexibility. However, commercial banks do not look favorably on credit requests only in periods of tight money. Switching from commercial paper to bank borrowing is possible, but a company must be careful not to impair relations with its bank. The commercial paper market is highly impersonal. If a firm cannot borrow from a commercial bank, it is at the mercy of the market. Therefore, it is important to maintain lines of credit at commercial banks in order to backstop adverse money-market conditions.[4]

BANKERS' ACCEPTANCES

Bankers' acceptances were introduced into the money market in 1962. Firms usually use these securities to finance inventories of finished goods in transit to buyers. Maturities on bankers' acceptances range from 30 to 180 days and the security is usually sold in multiples of not less than $100 000. Companies engaged in foreign trade find bankers' acceptances an important source of financing. To illustrate their use, suppose a Canadian company wishes to import $100 000 worth of electronic components from a company in Japan. The two companies agree that a 90-day time draft will be used in settlement of the trade. The Canadian company arranges a letter of credit with its banks whereby the bank agrees to honor drafts drawn on the company. The Japanese company ships the goods and at the same time draws a draft ordering the Canadian company to pay in 90 days. By pre-arrangement, the draft is sent by the Japanese bank to the Canadian bank and is accepted by the latter. At that time it becomes a bankers' acceptance. In essence, the bank accepts responsibility for payment, thereby substituting its credit-worthiness for that of the drawee—the Canadian company.

If the bank is large and well-known, and most banks accepting drafts are, the instrument becomes highly marketable upon acceptance. As a result, the drawer, the Japanese company, does not have to hold the draft until the final due date; it can sell the draft in the money market for less than its face value. The discount involved represents the return to the investor. At the end of 90 days, the investor presents the draft to the Canadian bank for payment and receives $100 000. At this time, the Canadian company must have funds on deposit to cover the draft.

In the example above, the Canadian company finances its import for a 90-day period. Presumably, the Japanese exporter would charge a price lower than $100 000 if he were paid upon shipment; this may be viewed as the spot price of the goods. In this sense, the Canadian company is the borrower with interest cost (comprising the difference between $100 000 and the spot cost of the goods plus a commission fee charged by the accepting bank) for its guarantee. Suppose the discount rate for outstanding acceptance is 8 percent. The Japanese company would then sell the draft for $98 000; this discount of $2000 is the interest for three months. The accepting bank generally charges $\frac{1}{2}$ of 1 percent, on an annual basis, of the face value of the draft for its guarantee. Suppose in this instance the commission fee is the annual equivalent of $\frac{1}{2}$ percent: then the dollar value of the fee for three months is $125. Total cost to the Canadian company is then $2 125 ($2 000 + $125)

---

[4]The need was well-illustrated in June 1965 when the Atlantic Acceptance Corp. defaulted on short term notes and subsequently went bankrupt. Later in June 1970 in the U.S., there was the case of the Penn Central bankruptcy.

on a "loan" of $98 000 for a term of 90 days. The effective annual interest rate is thus 8.67 percent.

The presence of an active and viable bankers' acceptance market makes possible the financing of foreign trade at interest rates approximating those on commercial paper (Table 12-1). Generally, banks take a liberal view of bankers' acceptances when they are short of Canadian dollars to loan. The instrument is also used to finance domestic trade and the procedure by which the acceptance is created is exactly the same as with a foreign trade. In recent years, bankers' acceptances have grown tremendously, increasing from $116 million in 1968 to $13.9 billion in 1983 (Table 12-1). This growth is attributed largely to the rise in Canadian foreign trade and recognition by companies of the usefulness of this form of financing.

Bank Credit—Unsecured Lending Arrangements

We now examine short-term loans, the principal sources of which are chartered banks. These loans may be secured or unsecured depending on the credit-worthiness of the borrower. In the immediate discussion we focus on the general principles applicable to short term *unsecured* bank loans; these principles also apply to short term *secured* bank loans. The secured loans of banks and non-bank financial institutions are discussed in the short-term secured lending arrangements section at the end of this chapter.

Short term bank loans are usually regarded as "self-liquidating" because the assets purchased with the proceeds generate sufficient cash flows to pay the loan in less than a year. At one time, banks confined their lending almost exclusively to this type of loan. Fortunately, banks now provide a wide variety of business loans, tailored to the specific needs of the borrower. Still, the short term self-liquidating loan is an important source of business financing. It is particularly popular in financing seasonal buildups in accounts receivable and inventories. Short term loans may be extended under a line of credit, a revolving-credit agreement, or on a transaction basis. The debt itself is evidenced formally by a promissory note signed by the borrower, showing the time and amount of payment and the interest to be paid.

LINES OF CREDIT

A line of credit is an arrangement between a bank and its customer with respect to the maximum amount of credit the bank will permit the firm to owe at any one time. Usually, credit lines are established for a one-year period and are subject to one-year renewals. Frequently, lines of credit are set for renewal after the bank receives the audited annual report and has had a chance to review the progress of the borrower. For example, if the borrower's year-end statement date is December 31, a bank may set its line to expire sometime in March. At that time, the bank and the company would meet to discuss the credit needs of the firm for the coming year in light of its past year's performance. The amount of the line is based on the bank's assessment of the credit-worthiness of the borrower and on his or her credit needs. If the borrower's credit needs change, the line of credit may be adjusted on or before the renewal date. The bank may decide to review its client's credit-rating before making any adjustment.

It is usual for banks to use a *note rollover system* with a line of credit agreement. Under the system, the bank will credit a firm's account as required with predetermined multiples of $X and will automatically reduce the firm's liability as it repays the loan but only in multiples of $X. For example, assume that a line of credit is for $1.0 million and that the loan agreement stipulates a 5.0% credit-debit note rollover. When the firm needs cash, initially an amount of $50 000 will be credited to its account. The firm will pay interest on $50 0000 whether it uses $1.00 or the full amount. It is therefore important that the firm plan its operations so as to utilize the full loan effectively. It should also avoid requesting an excessive line of credit in the first place, as a 5.0% multiple is usually the minimum acceptable to banks. However, smaller lines of credit will have higher percentage multiples so the firm should not aim too low either.

The firm will also have to watch the level of its daily deposits relative to the liability under the line of credit. The bank will not automatically reduce the loan under the line of credit unless the firm has funds in the required multiple in its deposit account. Suppose the firm in the above example has fully used the first multiple of $50 0000 and at just about the same time it has received and deposited a cheque for $30 000. The bank will not automatically offset the $30 000 against the loan of $50 000 thereby leaving a loan balance of $20 000. It will usually wait until deposits reach $50 000 when the offset will be automatically triggered. In the meantime, the firm will be paying interest on $50 000 and will receive no interest on its deposit of $30 000. To avoid this situation, the firm has to make a specific request to have the bank effect an offset equal to $30 000.

The cash budget probably gives the best insight into the borrower's short-term credit needs. For example, if maximum or peak borrowing needs over the forthcoming year are estimated at $800 000, a company might seek a line of credit of $1 million to give it a margin of safety. Whether the bank will go along with the request, of course, will depend on its evaluation of the credit-worthiness of the firm. If the bank does agree, the firm may then borrow on a short-term basis up to the full $1 million line on a demand loan basis.

Despite its many advantages to the borrower, a line of credit does not constitute a legal commitment on the part of the bank to extend credit. The borrower is usually informed of the line by means of a letter indicating that the bank is willing to extend credit up to a certain amount. This letter is not a legal obligation of the bank to extend credit. If the credit-worthiness of the borrower should deteriorate during the year, or the bank is "tight" for loanable funds, the bank may not want to extend credit and would not be required to do so. Under most circumstances, however, a bank feels bound to honor a line of credit.

REVOLVING CREDIT AGREEMENTS

A revolving credit agreement represents a legal commitment on the part of the bank to extend credit up to a maximum amount. While the commitment is in force, the bank must extend credit to the borrower any time he or she wishes to borrow, provided total borrowings do not exceed the maximum amount specified. If the revolving credit is for $1 million, and $700 0000 is already owing, the borrower can borrow an additional $300 000 at any time. Revolving credit agreements frequently extend beyond one year and usually involve a fee based on any unused portion of the revolving credit. Because lending arrangements of more than a year must be regarded as intermediate rather than short term credit, we shall examine revolving credits more extensively in Chapter 20. The purpose of introducing them at this time is to illustrate the formal nature of the arrangement in contrast to the informality of a line of credit.

TRANSACTION LOANS

Borrowing under a line of credit or under a revolving credit arrangement is not appropriate when the firm needs short term funds for only one purpose. For example, a contractor may borrow from a bank in order to complete a job. When the contractor receives payment for the job, he or she pays the loan. For this type of loan, a bank evaluates each request by the borrower as a separate transaction. In these evaluations, the cash-flow ability of the borrower to pay the loan usually is of paramount importance.

INTEREST RATES

Unlike interest rates on such impersonal money market instruments as Treasury bills, bankers' acceptances, and commercial paper, most business loans are determined through personal negotiation between the borrower and the lender(s). In some measure, banks try to vary the interest rate charged according to the credit-worthiness of the borrower; the lower the credit-worthiness, the higher the interest rate. Interest rates charged also vary in keeping with money market conditions. One measure that varies to some extent with underlying market conditions is the *prime rate*. The prime rate is the lowest rate typically charged on business loans to large, well-established, and financially sound companies. The rate itself is usually relatively uniform among banks and throughout the country. In the past, the rate has changed over time in keeping with underlying changes in market conditions. This phenomenon is evident up to the mid-1960s, as shown in Fig. 12-1. Usually, a change in the bank rate (the rate charged by the Bank of Canada on loans to chartered banks) signals a similar change in the prime rate.

In the late 1960s and early 1970s, however, banks faced new pressures that changed the traditional use of the prime rate as a means of allocating credit. Market rates of interest rose rapidly in the late 1960s to historical highs; fell over the 1971-72 period; and rose significantly thereafter especially in the early 1980s when they soared to unprecedented highs. These rates fluctuated to a much greater extent than they had in the past. Because savings deposits and other liabilities on which interest is paid have increased significantly in relation to demand deposits during the last 15 years, the increased fluctuation in market rates of interest has caused increased volatility in the cost of funds to banks. Competition among banks and non-bank institutions led to frequent changes in the interest rates offered for personal savings. Frequent changes in the cost of funds to banks led to the observed volatility in the prime rate.

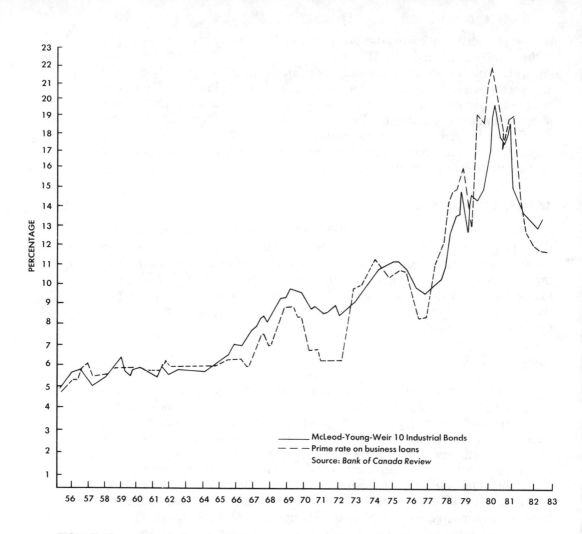

FIGURE 12-1 The relationship between the prime rate and yield on McLeod-Young-Weir 10 Industrial Bonds: Quarterly series

Differentials from prime Despite the term *prime rate* implying the price a bank charges its most credit-worthy customers, this has not been the recent practice. With banks becoming more competitive for corporate customers and facing competition from the commercial paper market, the well-established financially sound company often is able to borrow at a rate of interest below prime. The rate charged is based on the bank's marginal cost of funds, as typically reflected by the rate paid on money market certificates of deposit. An interest-rate margin is added to the cost of funds, and the sum becomes the rate charged the customer. This rate is changed daily in keeping with changes in money-market rates. Generally, the rate paid by the customer is one-quarter to one percent below the prime rate. The differential depends on competitive conditions and on the relative bargaining power of the borrower.

Other borrowers will pay either the prime rate or a rate above prime, the bank's pricing of the loan being relative to the prime rate. A bank might extend a line of credit to a company at a rate one-half percent above prime. If the prime rate is 14 percent, the borrower is charged an interest rate of 14.5 percent. If the prime rate changes to 10 percent, the borrower will pay 10.5 percent. Interest-rate differentials among the various customers of a bank supposedly should reflect only differences in credit worthiness.

Other factors, however, influence the differential. Among them are the balances maintained and other business the borrower has with a bank (such as trust business). A good customer who has maintained very attractive balances in the past may be able to obtain a more favorable interest rate than will a firm of equal credit worthiness that has carried rather meager balances.[5] Also, the cost of servicing a loan is a factor determining the differential in rate from prime. Certain collateral loans are costly to administer, and this cost must be passed on to the borrower either in the interest rate charged or in a special fee.

Thus, the interest rate charged on a short term loan will depend upon the prevailing cost of funds to banks, the existing prime rate, the credit worthiness of the borrower, the present and prospective relationship of the borrower with the bank, and sometimes upon other considerations. Because of the fixed costs involved in credit investigation and in the processing of a loan, we would expect the interest rate on small loans to be higher than the rate on large loans.

Methods of computing interest rates   There are two ways in which interest on a loan may be paid: on a collect basis and on a discount basis. When paid on a collect basis, the interest is paid at the maturity of the note; when paid on a discount basis, interest is deducted from the initial loan. To illustrate, suppose we have a $10 000 loan at 12 percent interest for one year. The effective rate of interest on a collect note is

$$\frac{\$1\ 200}{\$10\ 000} = 12.00 \text{ percent}$$

On a discount basis, the effective rate of interest is not 12 percent but

$$\frac{\$1\ 200}{\$8\ 800} = 13.64 \text{ percent}$$

When we pay on a discount basis, we have the use of only $8 800 for the year but must pay back $10 000 at the end of that time. Thus, the effective rate of interest is higher on a discount note than on a collect note. We should point out that most bank business loans are on a collect note basis.

---

[5]Transactions balances and compensating balances in loan agreements are discussed in Chapter 9.

Short Term Secured Lending Arrangements

Many firms cannot obtain credit on an unsecured basis, either because they are new and unproven or because their ability to service debt is not regarded as adequate by lenders. In order to make such a loan, lenders will require security so as to reduce their risk of loss. For non-bank financial lenders, it is common practice to extend credit only on a secured basis. Lenders have two sources of loan repayment: the cash-flow ability of the firm to service the debt; and, if that source fails for some reason, the collateral value of the security. In addition to the required security, most lenders will not make a loan unless the firm has sufficient expected cash flows to make the proper servicing of debt possible, thus reducing their risk further.

Security devices available to banks are discussed in this section. Similar statutory procedures are available to other secured lenders; such procedures vary with the location of the lender and the assets offered as security.[6] The collateral values of pledged assets are important to secured lenders.

SECURITY DEVICES UNDER THE BANK ACT

Security lending by banks is permitted under several sections of the Bank Act.[7] For example, Section 88 permits loans, secured by inventory on hand or in process, to manufacturers; to wholesalers of the products of agriculture, forests, quarries, mines, the seas, lakes, and rivers, and to farmers and fishermen, on their products, equipment, and supplies. The assets remain in the possession and control of the borrower and the bank must file a *notice of intention* (Fig. 12-2) with the provincial office of the Bank of Canada. This notice includes a statement of assets to be pledged as security and of the bank's interest in the assets (Fig. 12-3). Prior to the receipt of the loan or any portion thereof, the borrower must complete a loan application which stipulates the security device. The *notice of intention* gives public notice to other parties that the lender has a security interest in the collateral described. Before accepting collateral as security for a loan, a lender will search the public notices to see if the collateral has been pledged previously in connection with another loan. Only the lender with a valid security interest in the collateral has a prior claim on the assets and can sell the collateral in settlement of the loan.

Section 82 of the Bank Act permits loans secured by hydrocarbons. Registration requirements are controlled by provincial legislation. Warehouse receipts and bills of lading may be taken as security under Section 86 of the Bank Act.

Collateral value The excess of the market value of the security pledged over the amount of the loan determines the lender's margin of safety. If the borrower is unable to meet his or her obligation, the lender can sell the security to satisfy the claim. If the security is sold for an amount exceeding the amount of loan and

---

[6]A summary of the Acts governing secured lending can be reviewed in *Condensed Laws of Business for Credit Managers* (Toronto: the Canadian Credit Institute). Security devices are summarily discussed in *Types of Security Available to Credit Managers* (Toronto: The Canadian Credit Institute).

[7]For a discussion, see S. Sarpkaya, *The Banker and Society* (Don Mills, Ont.: Institute of Canadian Bankers, 1968), 171-76. The nature of the specific devices may change with the new Bank Act.

NOTICE OF INTENTION

FORM 710 Part 1 (9-56)

The Firm or Company must be correctly designated. In case of individuals give name in full.

TO WHOM IT MAY CONCERN:

.... (Name of Person, Firm or Company) .... (Post Office Address)

hereby gives notice that it is my/our intention to give security under the authority of Section 88 of the Bank Act, to

Dated at this

day of 19

....

....

(Only Part 1 of this form need be signed by the customer)

FIGURE 12–2 Notice of intention

interest owed, the difference is remitted to the borrower. If the security is sold for less, the lender becomes a general or unsecured creditor for the amount of the difference. Because secured lenders do not wish to become general creditors, they usually seek security with a market value sufficiently above the amount of the loan to minimize the likelihood of their not being able to sell the security in full satisfaction of the loan. However, the degree of security protection a lender seeks varies with the credit-worthiness of the borrower, the security the borrower has available, and the financial institution making the loan.

The value of the collateral to the lender varies according to several factors. Perhaps the most important is marketability. If the collateral can be sold quickly in an active market without lowering its price, the lender is likely to be willing to lend an amount higher than the collateral's stated value. On the other hand, if the collateral is a machine designed specifically for a company with no viable secondary market, the lender may choose to lend nothing at all. The life of the collateral is also important. If the life of the collateral parallels closely the life of the loan, it will be more valuable to the lender than collateral of a much longer duration. When the collateral is liquidated into cash, the proceeds may be used to pay down the loan. Therefore, a lender will usually prefer short term collateral for short term loans and long term collateral for long term loans. Still another factor is the basic riskiness associated with the collateral. The greater the fluctuation in its market value and/or the greater the uncertainty on the part of the lender concerning market value, the less desirable the collateral will be. Thus, marketability, life, and riskiness determine the attractiveness of various types of collateral to a lender and, hence, the amount of financing available to a company.

ASSIGNMENT OF ACCOUNTS RECEIVABLE

Accounts receivable are one of the most liquid assets of the firm and, consequently, they make desirable security for a loan. To illustrate the nature of the arrangement, we trace a typical assignment of an accounts receivable loan. In

AFFIDAVIT OF BONA FIDES

(To be completed when assignment to be registered in any Province except British Columbia)

CANADA

Province of..................

County of*..................

TO WIT:

I,..................
of the.................. of..................
in the Province of.................. of.................. an employee
at.................. of..................
the Assignee named in the Assignment of Book Debts hereto
annexed, make oath and say:

1. That I am an employee of .... at..................
in the Province of..................

2. That I am aware of the circumstances connected with the said Assignment of Book Debts and have a personal knowledge of the facts herein deposed in.

3. That the said Assignment of Book Debts hereto annexed was executed in good faith and for valuable consideration, and not for the †mere purpose of protecting the book debts therein mentioned against the creditors of.................., the Assignor, or for the purpose of preventing such creditors from recovering any claims which they have against the said Assignor.

SWORN before me at the..................
of.................. in the Province
of..................this..................
day of..................A.D 19..........

....
A Commissioner, etc., or a Notary Public.

AFFIDAVIT OF EXECUTION BY INDIVIDUAL OR PARTNERSHIP

(To be completed when assignment to be registered in British Columbia)

I,.................. of the.................. of
.... in the Province of.................. by
occupation .... MAKE OATH AND SAY:

1. That the paper-writing hereunto annexed is a true copy of an assignment of Book Accounts, and of every (or where the original is filed, is the assignment of Book Accounts and every) schedule or inventory thereto annexed, or therein referred to, and of every attestation of the execution thereof, as made and given and executed by *..................

2. That the assignment of Book Accounts was made and given by the said *..................
.... on the ....day
of.................. 19..........

3. That I was present and did see the said *..................
.... in the said assignment of Book Accounts mentioned, and whose name is signed thereto, sign and execute the same on the said ....day of..................,
in the year aforesaid †by its agent(s).

4. That the said *..................
.... at the time of making and giving the said Assignment of Book Accounts **resided and still resides at
††carried on business and still carries on business at ....
..................and then was and still is by occupation..................

5. That the name.................. set and subscribed as witness attesting the due execution thereof is of the proper handwriting of me, this deponent, and that I reside at .... and am by
occupation..................

SUBSCRIBED to and sworn before me
at the..................
of.................. in the
Province of..................
this..................day of..................
A.D. 19..........

....
A Commissioner, etc., or a Notary Public.

FIGURE 12–3 An example of a registration form for the assignment of accounts receivable

evaluating the loan request, the lender will analyze the quality of the firm's receivables in order to determine the amount lender the lender is willing to lend against these receivables. The greater the quality of the accounts the firm maintains, the greater the percentage the lender is willing to advance against the face value of the receivables pledged. A lender does not have to accept all the borrower's accounts receivable; usually, the lender will reject accounts that have low credit ratings or those that are unrated. Depending on the quality of the receivables accepted, a lender typically advances between 50 percent and 85 percent of their face value.

The usual Canadian practice is to take a general assignment of book debts. Under this form of security the lender has a full claim on all existing and future accounts receivable. It falls on the borrower to provide regular schedules of the accounts pledged. Also, the borrower will apply the proceeds of collections to the loan. The general assignment must be registered with provincial authorities.

Procedure   Suppose a lender has a decided to extend a loan to a firm on the basis of a 75 percent advance against the face value of accounts receivable assigned. The firm then sends in a schedule of accounts showing the name of the account, the date of billing(s), and the amounts owed. An example of the registration schedule is shown in Fig. 12-4. Having received the schedule of accounts, the lender has the borrower sign a promissory note and a general assignment. The firm then receives 75 percent of the face value of the receivables shown on the schedule of accounts.

An accounts receivable loan is a more or less continuous financing arrangement. As the firm generates new receivables that are acceptable to the lender, they are assigned, adding to the security base against which the firm is able to borrow. New receivables replace the old, and the security base and the amount of loan fluctuate accordingly. A receivable loan is a very flexible means of secured financing. As receivables build up, the firm is able to borrow additional funds to finance this buildup. Thus, it has access to "built-in" financing.

FACTORING RECEIVABLES

In the assignment of accounts receivable, the firm retains title to the receivables. When a firm *factors* its receivables, however, it actually sells them to a factor. The sale may be either with or without recourse, depending on the type of arrangement negotiated. The factor maintains a credit department and makes credit checks on accounts. Based on its credit investigation, the factor may refuse to buy certain accounts that it deems too risky. By factoring, a firm frequently relieves itself of the expense of maintaining a credit department and making collections. Any account that the factor is unwilling to buy is an unacceptable credit risk unless, of course, the firm wants to assume this risk on its own and ship the goods. If the factoring arrangement involves full recourse, the firm will want to maintain some sort of credit department in order to limit its risk exposure. On the other hand, if the receivables are sold without recourse, the factor bears both the risk of bad-debt losses and of the expenses associated with the collection of the accounts. Although it is customary in a factoring arrangement to notify the customer that his or her account has been sold and that payments on the account should be sent directly to the factor, in many instances notification is not made. The customer continues to remit payments to the firm, which, in turn, endorses them to the factor. These endorsements are frequently camouflaged to prevent the customers from learning that their accounts have been sold.

Factoring costs   For bearing risk and servicing the receivables, the factor receives a fee of around 1 percent to 3 percent of the face value of the receivables sold. This

GENERAL ASSIGNMENT UNDER SECTION 88(1) (a), (b), (c) or (e)

FOR GOOD AND VALUABLE CONSIDERATION, the undersigned hereby assigns to .... (hereinafter called "the bank") as continuing security for the payment of all loans and advances made or that may be made by the bank to the undersigned

up to and including the * .... day of ....19......, pursuant to the application for credit and

promise to give security (Form 680 of the bank) made by the undersigned to the bank and dated the † .... day

of .... 19......, and any application(s) for credit and promise(s) to give security supplemental thereto made or that may be made by the undersigned to the bank or renewals of such loans and advances or substitutions therefor and interest on such loans and advances and on any such renewals and substitutions, all property of the kind(s) hereinafter described of which the undersigned is now or may hereafter become the owner, to wit, *(describe the property assigned)*‡

and which is now or may hereafter be in the place or places hereinafter designated, to wit, *(describe the place or places where the property is located or may be located)***

and any other place or places in Canada in which any of the said property may be located.

This security is given under the provisions of section 88 of the Bank Act.

The property now owned by the undersigned and hereby assigned is free from any mortgage, lien or charge thereon, other than previous assignments, if any, to the bank, and the undersigned warrants that the property which may hereafter be acquired by the undersigned and is hereby assigned shall be free from any mortgage, lien or charge thereon, other than previous assignments, if any, to the bank.

Dated at .... the .... day of .... 19......

* Insert the EXPIRY date of the relative (original) Form 680.
† Insert the date of the relative (original) Form 680.
‡ If insufficient space insert "the property described on the reverse hereof" and set out the description on the back of this form.
** If insufficient space insert "the place or places designated on the reverse hereof" and set out the description on the back of this form.

.... (SEAL)

FIGURE 12-4 General assignment of assets form

fee will vary according to the typical size of individual accounts, the volume of receivables sold, and the quality of the accounts. We must recognize, however, that the receivables sold to the factor will not be collected from the various accounts for a period of time. If the firm wishes to receive payment for the sale of its receivables before they are actually collected, it must pay interest on the advance. Advancing payment is a lending function of the factor in addition to the functions of risk-bearing and of servicing the receivables. For this additional function, the factor requires compensation. For example, if the receivables sold total $10 000, and the factoring fee is 2 percent, the factor will credit the firm's account with $9 800. If the firm wants to draw on this account before the receivables are collected, however, it will have to pay an interest charge—say 1 percent a month—for the use of the funds. If it wishes a cash advance of the full $9 800, and the receivables are collected on the average, in one month, the interest cost will be approximately $0.01 \times \$9\ 800$, or $98.[8] Thus, the total cost of factoring is composed of a factoring fee plus an interest charge if the firm draws on its account before the receivables are collected. If the firm does not draw on its account until the receivables are collected, there is no interest charge. A third alternative is for the firm to leave its funds with the factor beyond the time when the receivables are collected and to receive interest on the account from the factor.

Flexibility   The typical factoring arrangement is continuous. As new receivables are acquired, they are sold to the factor, and the firm's account is credited. The firm then draws on this account as it needs funds. Sometimes the factor will allow the firm to overdraw its account during periods of peak needs and thereby borrow on an unsecured basis. Under other arrangements, the factor may withhold a reserve from the firm's account as a protection against losses. Factoring is done largely by banks (through factoring subsidiaries) and finance companies. Also, about 11 new factoring companies have been established in recent years to take advantage of this business opportunity. Most of these companies are members of Factors and Commercial Financing Conference of Canada Inc., an association established in 1974 to promote factoring and commercial financing in Canada. Since very little information is available publicly, we do not know the size of the operations of these companies.

In many cases, factoring is a perfectly acceptable method of financing. Its principal shortcoming is that it can be expensive. We must bear in mind, however, that the factor often relieves the firm of credit checkings, the cost of processing receivables, and collection expenses. For a small firm, the savings may be quite significant.

INVENTORY LOANS

Inventories also represent a reasonably liquid asset and are therefore suitable as security for a short-term loan. As with a receivable loan, the lender determines a percentage advance against the market value of the collateral. This percentage varies according to the quality of the inventory. Certain inventories, such as grains, are very marketable and if properly stored, resist physical deterioration over time. The margin of safety required by the lender on a loan of this sort is fairly small, and the advance may be as high as 90 percent. On the other hand, the market for a highly specialized piece of equipment may be so narrow that a lender is unwilling to make any advance against its reported market value. Thus, not every kind of inventory can be pledged as security for a loan. The best collateral is

---

[8]The actual cash advance would be $9 800 less the interest cost, or $9 702.

relatively standard and for which a ready market exists apart from the marketing organization of the borrower.

Lenders determine the percentage that they are willing to advance by considering marketability, perishability, market-price stability, and the difficulty and expense of selling the inventory to satisfy the loan. The cost of selling a certain inventory may be very high indeed. The lender does not want to be in the business of liquidating collateral, but does want to be assured that the collateral has adequate value in case the borrower defaults on the payment of principal or interest. As with most secured loans, however, the actual decision to make the loan will depend on the cash-flow ability of the borrower to service debt. There are a number of different ways a lender can obtain a secured interest in inventories, and we consider each in turn. In the case of the first group of methods (floating lien, chattel mortgage, and trust receipt), the inventory remains in the possession of the borrower. In the last two methods (terminal warehouse and field warehouse receipts), the inventory is in the possession of a third party.

Floating lien   The borrower may pledge his inventories "in general" without specifying which inventory is involved. Under this arrangement, the lender obtains a floating lien on all inventory of the borrower. This lien is very general and difficult for the lender to police. Frequently, a floating lien is requested only as additional protection and does not play a major role in determining whether or not the loan will be made. Even if the lender does regard the collateral as important, he or she is usually willing to make only a moderate advance because the lender cannot exercise tight control over the collateral. The floating lien can be made to cover both receivables and inventories, as well as the collection of receivables. This modification gives the lender a lien on a major portion of a firm's current assets. In addition, the lien can be made to encompass almost any length of time so that it includes future as well as present inventory as security.[9] The lender's right to the pledged assets materializes only when the loan is "called" for payment.

Chattel mortgage   With a chattel mortgage, inventories are specifically identified, either by serial number or by some other means. While the borrower holds title to the goods, the lender has a lien on inventory. This inventory cannot be sold without the lender's consent. Because of the rigorous identification requirements, chattel mortgages are ill-suited for inventory with rapid turnover and/or inventory that is not easily identified because of size or for other reasons. They are well-suited, however, for certain capital assets such as machine tools.

Trust receipt loans   Under a trust receipt financing arrangement, the borrower holds the inventory and proceeds from the sale of inventory in trust for the lender. This type of lending arrangement, known as floor planning, has been used extensively by automobile dealers, equipment dealers, and consumer durable goods dealers. For example, suppose an automobile manufacturer ships cars to a dealer who, in turn, finances the payment for these cars through a finance

---

[9]For further discussion, see J. Carson Quarles, "The Floating Lien," *Journal of Commercial Bank Lending*, 53 (November 1970), 51-58.

company. The finance company pays the manufacturer for the cars shipped. The dealer signs a trust receipt security agreement, which specifies what can be done with the inventory. (A copy of a typical security device used under a trust receipt arrangement is shown in Fig. 12-5). The car dealer is allowed to sell the cars but must turn the proceeds of the sale over to the lender in payment of the loan. Inventory in trust, unlike inventory under a floating lien, is specifically identified by serial number or by other means. In our example, the finance company periodically examines the cars the dealer has on hand. The serial numbers of these cars are checked against those shown in the security agreement. The purpose of the check is to see if the dealer has sold cars without remitting the proceeds of the sale to the finance company.

As the dealer buys new cars from the automobile manufacturer, a new trust receipt security agreement is signed that takes account of the new inventory. The dealer then borrows against this new collateral, which he or she holds in trust. Although there is tighter control over collateral with a trust receipt agreement than with a floating lien, there is still the risk of inventory being sold without the proceeds being turned over to the lender. Consequently, the lender must exercise judgment in deciding to lend under this arrangement. A dishonest dealer can devise numerous ways to fool the lender.

Many durable goods manufacturers finance the inventories of their distributors or dealers. Their purpose is to encourage dealers or distributors to carry reasonable stocks of goods, which then act as a sales incentive. Because manufacturers are interested in selling their products, financing terms are often more attractive than they are with an "outside" lender.

Terminal warehouse receipt loans A borrower secures a terminal warehouse receipt loan by storing inventory with a public, or terminal, warehousing company.[10] The warehousing company issues a warehouse receipt, which evidences title to specified goods that are located in the warehouse.

The warehouse receipt gives the lender a security interest in the goods, against which he or she makes a loan to the borrower. Under such an arrangement, the warehousing company can release the collateral to the borrower only when authorized to do so by the lender. Consequently, the lender is able to maintain strict control over the collateral and will release collateral only when the borrower pays a portion of the loan. For his or her own protection, the lender usually requires the borrower to take out an insurance policy with a loss-payable clause in favor of the lender.

Warehouse receipts may be either nonnegotiable or negotiable. A nonnegotiable warehouse receipt is issued in favour of a specific party—in this case, the lender—who is given title to the goods and has sole authority to release them. A negotiable warehouse receipt can be transferred by endorsement. Before goods can be released, however, the negotiable receipt must be presented to the warehousing company. A negotiable receipt is useful when title to the goods is transferred from one party to another while the goods are in storage. With a nonnegotiable receipt,

---

[10]For an excellent, discussion of warehouse receipts, see Robert W. Rogers, "Warehouse Receipts and their Use in Financing," *Bulletin of the Robert Morris Associates*, 46 (April 1964), 317-27.

WHOLESALE CONDITIONAL SALE CONTRACT

IAC LIMITED

Undersigned Seller hereby sells and undersigned Dealer hereby purchases and acknowledges to have received in good order and as ordered the following described goods:

MAKE AND DESCRIPTION	YEAR MODEL	BODY TYPE	SERIAL NUMBER	SELLING PRICE	DOWN PAYMENT	BALANCE
TOTAL						

Dealer agrees to pay to Seller, or his assigns, the balance of $ .... , remaining unpaid hereunder, on demands, with interest from the date hereof.

Title to property in and ownership of all said goods shall remain in Seller at Dealer's risk until all amounts due hereunder, or under any judgment secured, shall have been fully paid in cash and Dealer shall not have any right to impute or apportion any partial payments made against any one or more specific portions of said goods without the consent in writing of Seller. Dealer shall keep said goods unused and free from all liens and charges in his regular premises and open to inspection by Seller at any time.

If default is made in payment or in any of the other terms hereof, or if Dealer goes into bankruptcy or said goods are seized, the entire balance owing by Dealer to Seller shall immediately become due and payable and Seller may repossess all or any of said goods without legal process, or may claim the balance due. After repossession in any manner Seller may keep said goods and retain all amounts paid as liquidated damages and not as a penalty, or may sell same at public or private sale without notice to Dealer. Seller may be a purchaser at such sale. Upon such sale Seller may accept other goods as part payment, but Dealer shall be credited with only the actual proceeds when received in cash through the sale of such trade-in after deduction of all expenses, charges, and commissions in connection with the repossession, repair and sale of said goods and the repair and resale of such trade-in. Dealer shall be liable for any deficiency. If this contract is placed in the hands of a solicitor, there shall be added to the outstanding balance 15% of such balance as solicitor's fees.

To the extent not prohibited by law, the Dealer waives all of the rights, benefits and protection given by Section 19 of The Conditional Sales Act, Revised Statutes of Alberta, and agrees that the provisions of The Limitation of Civil Rights Act, Revised Statutes of Saskatchewan, as amended, shall have no application to this contract or any agreement or instrument renewing or extending or collateral to this contract, or the rights, powers or remedies of the Seller, its assignee or any other person under this contract or under any agreement or instrument renewing or extending or collateral to this contract.

Dealer takes notice that this agreement together with Seller's title to, property in and ownership of said goods and said note are to be forthwith assigned and negotiated by Seller to IAC Limited and that the said company shall be entitled to all of the rights of Seller free from all equities existing between Seller and Dealer. Dealer hereby accepts notice of such transfer and the Dealer hereby waives all benefit and advantage of any law or statute making IAC Limited, as assignee, subject to the obligations, liabilities and duties of the Seller. The Dealer further accepts notice that Seller is not an agent of said company for any purpose and that said company will accept no evidence of payment other than its official receipt. Dealer acknowledges having received a true copy of this agreement.

DATED AT .... this .... day of .... 19 ....

.... Seller

.... Dealer

(Official Title, if Company)   (Official Title, if Company)

ASSIGNMENT

FOR VALUE RECEIVED undersigned hereby sells and assigns this contract to IAC Limited, without recourse to undersigned, and also sells to said Corporation the goods therein described subject to the rights of Dealer as set out therein.

DATED the .... day of .... 19 ....

....

(Official Title, if Company)

11/70   CN-1

FIGURE 12-5 An example of a trust receipt security

the release of goods can only be authorized in writing. Most lending arrangements are based on nonnegotiable receipts.

Field warehouse receipt loans   In the case of a terminal warehouse receipt loan, the goods are located in a public warehouse. Another arrangement, known as field warehousing, permits loans to be made against inventory that is located on the borrower's premises. Under this arrangement, a field warehousing company sets off a designated storage area on the borrower's premises for the inventory pledged as collateral. The field warehousing company has sole access to the area and is supposed to maintain strict control over it. (The goods that serve as collateral are segregated from the borrower's other inventory.) The field warehousing company issues a warehouse receipt as described in the previous section, and the lender extends a loan based on the collateral value of the inventory. The field warehouse arrangement is a useful means of financing when it is not desirable, either because of the expense or because of the inconvenience, to place the inventory in a public warehouse. Field warehouse receipt lending is particularly appropriate when a borrower must make frequent use of inventory. Because of the need to pay the field warehousing company's expenses, the cost of this method of financing can be relatively high.

It is important to recognize that the warehouse receipt, as evidence of collateral, is only as good as the issuing warehousing company. When administered properly, a warehouse receipt loan affords the lender a high degree of control over the collateral. However, there have been sufficient examples of fraud to show that the warehouse receipt does not always evidence actual value. The warehousing company must exercise strict control. A grain elevator that is alleged to be full may, in fact, be empty. On close examination, it may be found that barrels reported to contain chemicals concentrate actually contain water.[11]

Composition of Short Term Financing

In this and the preceding chapter, we considered various sources of short-term financing. Because the total amount of short-term financing was assumed to have been determined according to the framework presented in Chapter 8, only determination of the best combination need be discussed in this chapter. The appropriate mix or the weighting of alternative sources will depend on considerations of cost, availability, timing, flexibility, and the degree to which the assets of the firm are encumbered. Central to any meaningful analysis of alternative sources of funds is a comparison of their costs, and inextricably bound up with the question of cost is the problem of timing. Differentials in cost between various alternatives are not necessarily constant over time. Indeed, they fluctuate in keeping with changing financial market conditions. Thus, timing bears heavily on the question of the most appropriate mix of short term financing.

Naturally, the availability of financing is important. If a firm cannot borrow by means of commercial paper or through a bank because of its low credit standing, it must turn to alternative sources. The lower the credit standing of the firm, of course, the fewer the sources of short term financing available to it. Flexibility with respect to short-term financing pertains to the ability of the firm to pay off a loan as well as to its ability to renew or increase it. With factoring and also with a bank loan, the firm can pay off the loan when it has surplus funds. As a result, interest costs are lower compared to those of commercial paper financing, where the firm must wait until the final maturity date before paying off the loan.

---

[11]For a lively discussion of the various frauds involving secured lenders, see Monroe R. Lazere, "Swinging Swindles and Creepy Frauds," *Journal of Commercial Bank Lending*, 60 (Sept. 1977), 44-52.

Flexibility relates also to how easily the firm can increase its loan on short notice. With a line of credit or revolving credit at a commercial bank, it is an easy matter to increase borrowings, assuming the maximum amount has not been reached. With other forms of short term financing, the firm is less flexible. Finally, the degree to which assets are encumbered bears on the decision. With secured loans, lenders obtain a lien on the assets of the firm. This secured position constrains the firm in future financing. Although receivables are actually sold under a factoring arrangement, the principle is the same. In this case, the firm sells one of its most liquid assets, thus reducing its credit-worthiness in the minds of creditors.

All of these factors influence the firm in deciding on the most appropriate mix of short term financing. Because cost is the key factor, differences between other factors should be compared along with differences in cost. What is the cheapest source of financing from the standpoint of explicit costs may not be the cheapest source when flexibility, timing, and the degree to which assets are encumbered are considered. Although it would be desirable to express sources of short term financing in terms of both explicit and implicit costs, the latter are hard to quantify. A more practical approach is to list available sources according to their explicit costs and then consider the other factors to see if they change the ranking as it relates to total desirability. Because the financing needs of the firm change over time, many sources of short-term financing should be explored on a continuous basis.

Summary

Commercial paper is used only by well-established, high-quality companies. The evidence of debt is a short-term promissory note that is sold in the money market. Except for some issues by finance companies, commercial paper is generally unsecured. About 85 percent of the issues of commercial paper is placed through investment dealers. The principal advantage of commercial paper is that its yield is less than the rate of interest a company would have to pay on a bank loan. Bankers' acceptance financing is another type of money market credit. Usually associated with foreign trade transactions, the acceptance is highly marketable and can be a very desirable source of short term funds.

Short-term loans can be divided into two types—unsecured loans and secured loans. Unsecured credit usually is confined to bank loans under a line of credit with a revolving-credit agreement, or on a transaction basis. Interest rates on business loans are usually influenced by the existing prime rate, the credit-worthiness of the borrower, and the profitability of the relationship for the bank.

Many firms are unable to obtain unsecured credit and are required by the lender to pledge security. In giving a secured loan, the lender looks first at the cash-flow ability of the company to service debt and, if this source of loan repayment fails, at the collateral value of the security. To provide a margin of safety, a lender will usually advance somewhat less than the market value of the collateral. The percentage advance varies according to the quality of the collateral pledged and the control the lender has over this collateral. Accounts receivable and inventory are the principal assets used to secure short term business loans. Receivables may either be pledged to secure a loan or sold to a factor. Inventory loans can be under a general lien, a trust receipt, or terminal warehouse or field warehouse receipt arrangements. Certain collateral owned outside a company may be used to secure a loan for a company.

The most appropriate mix of short term financing will depend on considerations of relative cost, availability, flexibility, timing, and the degree to which the assets of the firm are encumbered.

Questions

1. Why is the rate on commercial paper usually less than the prime rate charged by bankers and more than the Treasury bill rate?
2. Why would a firm borrow bank funds at higher rates instead of issuing commercial paper?
3. Why would a firm invest its temporary excess liquidity in Treasury bills instead of buying higher-yielding commercial paper?
4. Who is able to issue commercial paper and for what purpose?
5. What determines whether a lending arrangement is unsecured or secured?
6. As a lender, how would you determine the percentage you are willing to advance against a particular type of collateral?
7. As a financial consultant to a company, how would you go about recommending whether to use an assignment of accounts receivable or a factory arrangement?
8. Why might a company prefer an unsecured source of funds such as a line of credit or a revolving-credit agreement to some form of secured financing such as a receivable loan or chattel mortgage, even if the latter source is less expensive?
9. List assets that you would accept as collateral on a loan in your order of preference. Justify your priorities.
10. Inventory and accounts receivable are among the most liquid assets a firm owns. Does this liquidity make them the safest security available to the lender? Explain.
11. The settlements in the cases of Billie Sol Estes (the fertilizer scandal), Anthony DeAngelis (the salad oil scandal), and many other less notorious bankruptcies suggest that secured lenders are not really secure. Suggest methods of protecting the lender in short-term financing.
12. Which of the methods of short term financing considered in this chapter would be most likely to be used by the following? Explain your reasoning.
    (a) A raw-material processor such as a mining or lumber company
    (b) A retail sales concern such as an appliance retailer or high-fidelity equipment dealer
    (c) An international company
    (d) A consumer durable dealer such as an automobile sales agency
13. What reaction might a firm expect from trade creditors when it pledges its receivables to secure a bank loan?
14. As a firm's financial manager, what factors would you consider in choosing a primary bank?

Problems with Solutions

1. Calculate the annual interest rate and the annual discount rate in each of the following cases:

Loan proceeds	$ Interest	Term
a) $45 000.00	$5 000.00	1 year
b) $64 750.00	$5 250.00	6 months
c) $19 572.61	$ 427.39	60 days

Discount Rate: (Proceeds + $Interest)(Rate)(Time) = Discount
(a) $5 000 ÷ ($45 000 + $5 000) = 10%
(b) $5 250 ÷ ($64 750 + $5 250)(2) = 15%
(c) $427.39 ÷ ($19 572.61 + $427.39) $\left(\dfrac{365}{60}\right)$ = 13%

Interest Rate: Proceeds × Rate × Time = Interest
(a) $5 000.00 ÷ $45 000.00 = 11.11%
(b) $5 250.00 ÷ $64 750.00 × 2 = 16.23%
(c) $427.39 ÷ $19 572.61 × $\dfrac{365}{60}$ = 13.28%

2. Oshawa Appliance Ltd. is considering an offer from a factoring firm. The factor will buy all receivables from Oshawa Appliance for a fee of 2.5 percent of the value of the receivables. The receivables will bought without recourse and the factor will be willing to advance funds to Oshawa Appliance at a cost $\frac{1}{2}$ percent above that paid by Oshawa Appliance to its bank. If the firm factors its receivables, it will get rid of its credit department which is now costing about $70 000 per year. Average monthly credit sales are $200 000 and Oshawa Appliance Ltd. uses about $80 000 of bank credit to finance its receivables on a regular basis. The firm's banker indicated that it would be unwilling to continued this loan once the receivables were factored. Should Oshawa Appliance Ltd. factor its receivables?

Factoring cost 2.5% of $200 000 × 12	=	$60 000
Additional interest cost 0.5% of $80 000 =		400
		60 400
Less: savings in credit department		70 000
Net savings		9 600

The firm should factor its receivables.

Problems

1. The Sphinx Supply Company Ltd. needs to increase its working capital by $100 000. The following three alternatives of financing are available:

(a) Forego cash discounts, granted on basis of $^3/_{10}$, net 30.

(b) Borrow from the bank at 15 percent. This alternative would necessitate maintaining a 25 percent compensating balance.

(c) Issue commercial paper at 14 percent. The cost of placing the issue would be $1 000 each six months.

Assuming the firm would prefer the flexibility of bank financing, provided the additional cost of this flexibility was no more than 2 percent per annum, which alternative should Sphinx select?

2. Bork Corporation Ltd. wishes to borrow $100 000 for one year. It has the following alternatives available to it:

(a) An 8 percent loan on a discount basis with 20 percent compensating balances required.

(b) A 9 percent loan on a discount basis with 10 percent compensating balances required.

(c) A $10\frac{1}{2}$ percent loan on a collect basis with no compensating balance requirement.

Which alternative should Bork Corporation choose if it is concerned with the effective interest rate?

3. Commercial paper has no stipulated interest rate. It is sold on a discount basis, and the amount of the discount determines the interest cost to the issuer. On the basis of the following information, determine the percentage interest cost on an annual basis for each of the following issues (assume a 360-day year):

Issue	Face value	Price	Time to maturity
(a)	$25 000	$24 500	60 days
(b)	100 000	96 500	180 days
(c)	50 000	48 800	90 days
(d)	75 000	71 300	270 days
(e)	100 000	99 100	30 days

4. The Selby Gaming Manufacturing Company Ltd. has experienced a severe cash squeeze and needs $200 000 over the next 90 days. The company already has pledged its receivables in support of a loan. However, it does have $570 000 in unencumbered inventories. Determine the best financing alternative from the following two that are available.

(a) The Western Credit Union will lend against finished goods provided they are placed in a public warehouse under its control. As the finished goods are released for sale, the loan is reduced by the proceeds of the sale. The company currently has $300 000 in finished-goods inventory and would expect to replace finished goods that are sold out of the warehouse with new finished goods, so that it could borrow the full $200 000 for 90 days. The interest rate is 10 percent, and the company will pay warehousing costs of $3 000. Finally, it will experience a reduction in efficiency as a result of this arrangement. Management estimates that the lower efficiency will reduce before-tax profits by $5 000.

(b) The Zarlotti Finance Company Ltd. will lend the company the money under a floating lien on all of its inventories. The rate is 23 percent, but no additional expenses will be incurred.

5. The Bone Company Ltd. has been factoring its accounts receivable for the past five years. The factor charges a fee of 2 percent and will lend up to 80 percent of the volume of receivables purchased for an additional 1.5 percent per month. The firm typically has sales of $500 000 per month, 70 percent of which are on credit. By using the factor, two savings are effected:

(a) $2 000 per month that would be required to support a credit department

(b) A bad-debt expense of 1 percent on credit sales.

The firm's bank has recently offered to lend the firm up to 80 percent of the face value of the receivables shown on the schedule of accounts. The bank would charge 15 percent per annum interest plus a 2 percent processing charge per dollar of receivables lending. The firm extends terms of net 30, and all customers who pay their bills do so by the thirtieth day. Should the firm discontinue its factoring arrangement in favor of the bank's offer if the firm borrows, on the average, $100 000 per month on its receivables?

6. The Barnes Corporation Ltd. has just acquired a large account. As a result, it needs an additional $75 000 in working capital immediately. It has been determined that there are three feasible sources of funds:
   (a) Trade credit: the company buys about $50 000 of materials per month on terms of $^2/_{30}$, net 90. Discounts are taken.
   (b) Bank loan: the firm's bank will loan $100 000 at 9 percent. A 20 percent compensating balance will be required.
   (c) A factor will buy the company's receivables ($100 000 per month), which have a collection period of 60 days. The factor will advance up to 75 percent of the face value of the receivables for an annual charge of 8 percent. The factor also will charge a 2 percent fee on all receivables purchased. It has been estimated that the factor's services will save the company a credit department expense and bad-debts expense of $1 500 per month. Which alternative should Barnes select?

7. Vesco-Zultch Corporation Ltd. is a chain of appliance stores in Windsor. It needs to finance all of its inventories which average the following during the four quarters of the year:

Quarter	1	2	3	4
Inventory level (in thousands)	$1 600	$2 100	$1 500	$3 200

Vesco-Zultch presently utilizes a finance company loan secured by a floating lien. The interest rate is the prime rate plus $7\frac{1}{2}$ percent, but no additional expenses are incurred. The Boundary National Bank is bidding for the Vesco-Zultch business. It has proposed a trust receipt financing arrangement. The interest rate will be $2\frac{1}{2}$ percent above the prime rate, with servicing costs of $20 000 each quarter. Should the company switch financing arrangements?

8. The Coral Machine Tool Company Ltd. had the following balance sheet at the close of its fiscal year last month:

Cash	$ 14 000	Accounts payable	$240 000
Receivables	196 000	Bank loan	170 000
Inventories	170 000	Current liabilities	$410 000
Current assets	$380 000	Mortgage loan	240 000
Fixed assets	473 000	Common stock	50 000
		Retained earnings	153 000
	$853 000		$853 000

The company had the following income statement for the year:

Sales		$2 000 000
Cost of goods sold:		
Purchases	$960 000	
Wages	600 000	
Depreciation	60 000	1 620 000
Gross profit		$ 380 000
Expenses		310 000
Profit before taxes		$ 70 000
Taxes		30 000
Profit after taxes		$ 37 000

The company has approached the bank to increase its loan so that the company can become more current in the trade and avail itself of certain cash discounts. Suppliers are becoming very difficult. Paying higher prices and being unable to take cash discounts, Coral estimates that its costs are $40 000 more per year than they would be if its average payable were 30 days in length.

(a) How much additional financing is necessary to bring the average payable collection period to 30 days?

(b) What are some of the problems from the standpoint of the bank? Is it likely to extend the additional credit on an unsecured basis?

Selected References

ANSTIE, R. "The Historical Development of Pledge Lending in Canada," *The Canadian Banker* (Summer 1967), 81-90.

BARTLER, BRIT, JR., and RICHARD J. RENDLEMAN, JR., "Fee Based Pricing of Fixed Rate Bank Loan Commitments," *Financial Management*, 8 (Spring 1979), 13-20.

CAMPBELL, TIM S., "A Model of the Market for Lines of Credit," *Journal of Finance*, 33 (March 1978), 231-43.

CRANE, DWIGHT B., and WILLIAM L. WHITE, "Who Benefits from a Floating Prime Rate," *Harvard Business Review*, 50 (January-February 1972), 121-29.

CROSSE, HOWARE D., and GEORGE H. HEMPEL, *Management Policies for Commercial Banks*, 3rd ed. Englewood Cliffs, N.J.: Prentice-Hall, 1980.

DEL GRANDE, MICHAEL A., "Factoring: A Misunderstood Source of Financing", *C A Magazine* (June 1980), 37-40.

DENONN, LESTER E., "The Security Agreement," *Journal of Commercial Bank Lending*, 50 (February 1968), 32-40.

LAZERE, MONROE R., "Swinging Swindles and Creepy Frauds," *Journal of Commercial Bank Lending*, 60 (September 1977), 44-52.

MANSFIELD, CHARLES F., JR., "The Function of Credit Analysis in a U.S. Commercial Bank," *Journal of Commercial Bank Lending*, 61 (September 1979), 21-34.

QUARLES, J. CARSON, "The Floating Lien," *Journal of Commerical Bank Lending*, 53 (November 1970), 51-58.

QUILL, GERALD D., JOHN C. CRESCI, and BRUCE D. SHUTER, "Some Considerations about Secured Lending," *Journal of Commercial Bank Lending*, 59 (April 1977), 41-56.

SCOTT, JAMES H., JR., "Bankruptcy, Secured Debt, and Optimal Capital Structure," *Journal of Finance*, 32 (March 1977), 1-19.

SHEARER, R. A., T. F. CHANT AND D. E. BOND, *The Economics of the Canadian Financial System*, Scarborough, Ont.: Prentice-Hall of Canada Ltd., 1972.

SMITH, KEITH V., *Guide to Working Capital Management*, New York: McGraw-Hill 1979, Chapters 7 and 8.

STONE, BERNELL K., "Allocating Credit Lines, Planned Borrowing, and Tangible Services over a Company's Banking System," *Financial Management*, 4 (Summer 1975), 65-78.

V

INVESTING
IN CAPITAL
ASSETS

13

Capital
Budgeting

Capital Formation

The capital expenditure decisions of corporations have an important influence on the overall growth of the economy. A society's productive resources, such as land, machines, buildings, natural resources, and workers, are limited. These resources may all be devoted to producing goods and services for current consumption; or a part of them may go toward things that will enhance the nation's ability to produce, and hence consume, in the future. This process might involve the production of machinery, the exploration for iron ore, or the training of workers in new technology. Capital formation can be defined as any investment which increases the productive capacity of society. If resources are fully employed, the only way to make such investments is to refrain from current consumption. If resources are less than fully employed, however, it is possible to have capital formation without necessarily forgoing current consumption.

Corporate capital expenditures for new plants and equipment have ranged from 12 percent to 13½ percent of the Gross National Product in recent years. At the end of an economic downturn the percentage tends to be in the lower part of this range, and in periods of economic prosperity it tends to be in the upper part. In recent years, much of the growth in expenditures has been attributed to inflation as opposed to a growth in real outlays.

When a business firm makes a capital investment, it incurs a current cash outlay for future benefits. Usually, these benefits are expected beyond one year in the future. Examples include investment in assets such as equipment, buildings, and land, as well as the introduction of a new product, a new distribution system, or a new program for research and development. Thus, the firm's future success and profitability depends upon investment decisions made currently.

An investment proposal should be judged in relation to whether it provides a return equal to, or greater than, that required by investors.[1] To simplify our investigation of the methods of capital budgeting in this chapter, we assume the required rate of return is given and is the same for all investment projects. This assumption implies that the selection of any investment project does not alter the business-risk complexion of the firm as perceived by suppliers of capital. In Chapter 15 we investigate how to determine the required rate of return, and in Chapter 14 we allow for the fact that different investment projects have different degrees of business risk. As a result, the selection of an investment project may affect the business-risk complexion of the firm, which, in turn, may affect the rate of return required by investors. For purposes of introducing capital budgeting in this chapter, however, we hold risk constant.

Information Required

Capital budgeting involves

1. Generation of investment proposals
2. Estimate of cash flows for the proposals
3. Evaluation of cash flows
4. Selection of projects based upon an acceptance criterion
5. Continual reevaluation of investment projects after their acceptance

Starting with the first, investment proposals can emanate from a variety of sources. For purposes of analysis, projects may be classified into one of five categories:

1. New products or expansion of existing products
2. Replacement of equipment or buildings
3. Research and development
4. Exploration
5. Others

The fifth category comprises miscellaneous items such as the expenditure of funds to comply with certain health standards or the acquisition of a pollution-control device. For a new product, the proposal usually originates in the marketing department. On the other hand, a proposal to replace a piece of equipment with a more sophisticated model usually emanates from the production area of the firm. In each case, efficient administrative procedures are needed for channeling investment requests.

Most firms screen proposals at multiple levels of authority. For a proposal originating in the production area, the hierarchy of authority might run from

---

[1]The development of this chapter assumes the reader has covered Chapter 4 on the mathematics of finance.

(1) section chiefs to (2) plant managers to (3) the vice-president for operations to (4) a capital-expenditures committee under the financial manager to (5) the president to (6) the board of directors. How high a proposal must go before it is finally approved usually depends upon its size. The greater the capital outlay, the greater the number of screens usually required. Plant managers may be able to approve moderate-sized projects on their own, but only higher levels of authority approve larger ones. Because the administrative procedures for screening investment proposals vary greatly from firm to firm, it is not possible to generalize. The best procedure will depend upon the circumstances. It is clear, however, that companies are becoming increasingly sophisticated in their approach to capital budgeting.[2]

ESTIMATING CASH FLOWS

One of the most important tasks in capital budgeting is estimating future cash flows for a project. The final results we obtain are only as good as the accuracy of our estimates. Since cash, not income, is central to all decisions of the firm, we express whatever benefits we expect from a project in terms of cash flows rather than income. The firm invests cash now in the hope of receiving cash returns in a greater amount in the future. Only cash receipts can be reinvested in the firm or paid to stockholders in the form of dividends. In capital budgeting, good guys may get credit, but effective managers get cash.

For each investment proposal, we need to provide information on expected future cash flows on an after-tax basis. In addition, the information must be provided on an *incremental* basis, so that we analyze only the difference between the cash flows of the firm with and without the project. For example, if a firm contemplates a new product that is likely to compete with existing products, it is not appropriate to express cash flows in terms of the estimated sales of the new product. We must take into account probable "cannibalization" of existing products, and we must make our cash-flow estimates on the basis of incremental sales. The key is to analyze the situation with and without the new investment. Only incremental cash flows matter.

---

[2]For surveys of the administrative practices of companies with respect to capital budgeting as well as of the evaluation techniques being used, see J. William Petty, David F. Scott, Jr., and Monroe M. Bird, "The Capital Expenditure Decision-Making Process of Large Corporations," *Engineering Economist*, 20 (Spring 1975), 159-72; Lawrence D. Schall, Gary L. Sundem, and William R. Geijsbeek, Jr., "Survey and Analysis of Capital Budgeting Methods," *Journal of Finance*, 33 (March 1978), 281-87; Lawrence J. Gitman and John R. Forrester, Jr., "Forecasting and Evaluation Practices and Performance: A Survey of Capital Budgeting Techniques Used by Major U.S. Firms," *Financial Management*, 6 (Fall 1977), 66-71; J. William Petty and Oswald D. Bowlin, "The Financial Manager and Quantitative Decision Models," *Financial Management*, 4 (Winter 1976), 32-41; Meir J. Rosenblatt, "A Survey and Analysis of Capital Budgeting Decision Process in Multi-Division Firms," *Engineering Economist*, 25(Summer 1980), 259-73; and Suk H. Kim and Edward J. Farragher, "Current Capital Budgeting Practices," *Management Accounting*, 28 (June, 1981), 26-30.

See also James B. Weaver, "Organizing and Maintaining a Capital Expenditure Program," *Engineering Economist*, 20 (Fall 1974), 1-36; and E. Eugene Carter, "Designing the Capital Budgeting Process," *TIMS Studies in the Management Sciences*, 5 (1977), 25-42, for a discussion of administrative procedures. Finally, for a discussion of the importance of a post completion audit as well as of its form, see James S. Schnell and Roy S. Nicolosi, "Capital Expenditure Feedback; Project Reappraisal," *Engineering Economist*, 19 (Summer 1974), 253-61.

In this regard, sunk costs must be ignored. One is concerned with incremental costs and benefits: and the recovery of past costs is irrelevant. They are bygones and should not enter into the decision process. Also, we must be mindful that certain costs do not necessarily involve a dollar outlay. If we have allocated plant space to a project and this space can be used for something else, its opportunity cost must be included in the project's evaluation. If a presently unused building can be sold for $300 000, that amount should be treated as a cash outlay at the outset of the project. Thus, in deriving cash flows we must consider appropriate opportunity costs.

To illustrate the information needed for a capital-budgeting decision, consider the following situation. A firm is considering the introduction of a new product. To launch the product, it will need to spend $150 000 for special equipment and the initial advertising campaign. The marketing department envisions the product life to be 6 years and expects incremental sales revenue to be

Year 1	Year 2	Year 3	Year 4	Year 5	Year 6
$60 000	$120 000	$160 000	$180 000	$110 000	$50 000

Cash outflows include labor and maintenance costs, material costs, and various other expenses associated with the product. As with sales, these costs must be estimated on an incremental basis. In addition to these outflows, the firm will need to pay higher taxes if the new product generates higher profits; and this incremental outlay must be included. Suppose that on the basis of these considerations the firm estimates total incremental cash outflows to be

Year 1	Year 2	Year 3	Year 4	Year 5	Year 6
$40 000	$70 000	$100 000	$100 000	$70 000	$40 000

Because depreciation is a noncash expense, it is not included in these outflows. The expected net cash flows from the project are

	Initial cost	Year 1	Year 2	Year 3	Year 4	Year 5	Year 6
Cash inflows		$60 000	$120 000	$160 000	$180 000	$110 000	$50 000
Cash outflows	$150 000	40 000	70 000	100 000	100 000	70 000	40 000
Net cash flows	–$150 000	$20 000	$ 50 000	$ 60 000	$ 80 000	$ 40 000	$10 000

Thus, for an initial cash outflow of $150 000, the firm expects to generate net cash flows of $20 000, $50 000, $60 000, $80 000, $40 000, and $10 000 over the next six years. These cash flows represent the information needed in order to judge the attractiveness of the project. There are various methods which we can use to evaluate the feasibility of the new product using these cash flows. However, before we discuss these methods, let us look at a more complicated example involving the computation of cash flows within a marginal context.

Suppose we are considering the purchase of a turret lathe to replace an old lathe, that the purchase price of the new machine is $18 500 and that it will require an additional $1 500 to install. Thus, the total cost for the new machine is $20 000. The old machine can be sold for $2 000 making the initial net cash outflow for the investment project, $18 000 ($20 000 – $2 000).[3] Assume further that the new machine is expected to cut labor and other maintenance costs and effect other cash savings totaling $7 600 a year before taxes in each of the next five years, after which it is not expected to provide any savings. Our task is to identify the marginal cash flows of the project assuming that the new machine is acquired and that the old machine is sold on the date of acquisition of the new machine. There are three aspects of the above project which have implications for cash flows—the additional capital outlay of $18 000, the incremental capital cost allowance (CCA) which can be charged to income beginning in year 1 and continuing in future years, and the incremental cash savings of $7 600 per year for the next five years.

If we assume that the new machine is acquired at the end of year 0 or the start of year 1, the net capital outlay of $18 000 occurs at that time. Remember that this net cash outlay of $18 000 is a capital expense and is not allowed as an immediate deduction against income for tax purposes but can be written off against annual income beginning in year 1. The amount of the annual write-off (called capital cost allowances or CCA) is based on a rate specified in the Income Tax Act as discussed in Chapter 2. Now let us assume that the tax law permits the firm to depreciate the lathe at 20 percent on a double declining balance method. Then the CCA charged to income for the first five years is computed as follows:

Year	Undepreciated capital cost—end of year	Incremental CCA allowance
0	$18 000	$ —
1	16 200	1 800
2	12 960	3 240
3	10 368	2 592
4	8 294	2 074
5	6 635	1 659

Thus, the incremental CCA for the first year is $18 000 × 0.2 × 0.5 or $1 800, for the second year it is 20 percent of $16 200 ($18 000 – $1 800) or $3 240, and so on.[4] These annual incremental CCA are over and above those which would be charged to income if we had continued to use the old turret lathe. In a sense, the annual

---

[3]Chapter 2 illustrates the accounting approach followed for tax purposes for the disposal and acquisition of classes of assets to determine the cost base for depreciation purposes.

[4]For further details, see the discussion on CCA in Chapter 2.

incremental CCA serves to increase the expenses reported in the income statement. Finally, note that at the end of year 5 there is an undepreciated capital cost of $6 635 which may be charged as CCA to income in year 6 and beyond. For ease of illustration we consider this amount later.

The third aspect we consider is the before-tax cash savings of $7 600 a year for five years. These incremental savings increase the revenue of the firm over and above what it would have been if it continued to use the old machine.

Using the above information, we compute the marginal cash flows for the project as follows:

		0	1	End of year 2	3	4	5
1.	Net capital outlay	$18 000	—	—	—	—	—
2.	Increase in revenue	—	$7 600	$7 600	$7 600	$7 600	$7 600
3.	Increase in CCA	—	1 800	3 240	2 592	2 074	1 659
4.	Increase in taxable income (2-3)	—	$5 800	$4 360	$5 008	$5 526	$5 941
5.	Increase in taxes (40 percent of 4)	—	2 320	1 744	2 003	2 210	2 376
6.	Increase in earings after taxes (4-5)	—	$3 480	$2 616	$3 005	$3 316	$3 565
7.	Increase in cash flow from operations (6 + 3)	—	$5 280	$5 856	$5 597	$5 390	$5 224
8.	Cash flows for project (7-1)	−$18 000	$5 280	$5 856	$5 597	$5 390	$5 224

The increase in taxable income is the net cash savings less incremental CCA as computed earlier. Then assuming that the firm's tax rate is 40 percent, we determine incremental taxes payable each year, then derive the incremental earnings after taxes. The increase in cash flow from operations is simply the increase in earnings after taxes plus the incremental CCA. The CCA is a non-cash charge to income and has to be added back to incremental after-tax income to derive incremental cash flow from operations. The marginal cash flows of the project are simply the net cash flow of −$18 000 at the end of year 0, followed by incremental cash flows of $5 280, $5 856, $5 597, $5 390 and $5 224 in each of the next five years, respectively.

As we move to more complex examples later in this chapter, we will find it more convenient to compute the above marginal cash flows as shown in Table 13-1. The net capital outlay is derived as $20 000 less $2 000 as discussed earlier. However, the cash implications of the net cash savings and incremental CCA are treated separately. The before-tax net cash savings of $7 600 in each year are

TABLE 13-1　After-Tax Cash Flows for the Turret Lathe
Proposal for the First Five Years

End of Year			After-tax Cash Flow
0	Capital outlay		
	New lathe	−$20 000	
	Less sale price of old lathe	2 000	−$18 000
1	Cash savings [$7 600 (1 − t)]	$ 4 560	
	Tax savings on CCA [$1 800 ($t$)]	720	5 280
2	Cash savings [$7 600 (1 − t)]	$ 4 560	
	Tax savings on CCA [$3 240 ($t$)]	1 296	5 856
3	Cash savings [$7 600 (1 − t)]	$ 4 560	
	Tax savings on CCA [$2 592 ($t$)]	1 037	5 597
4	Cash savings [$7 600 (1 − t)]	$ 4 560	
	Tax savings on CCA [$2 074 ($t$)]	830	5 390
5	Cash savings [$7 600 (1 − t)]	$ 4 560	
	Tax savings on CCA [$1 659 ($t$)]	664	5 224

reduced to $4 560 after tax or $7 600 (1-$t$), where t is the tax rate. That is, other factors constant, the firm receives only $4 560 of the $7 600 after incremental taxes of $3 040. Now holding constant the effect of the net cash savings, we evaluate the net cash flow effect of incremental CCA. Remember that CCA is a non-cash expense and for our purposes is important only to the extent that it reduces taxes payable. For example, the incremental CCA of $1 800 in year 1 will reduce taxable income by $1 800 and, if operations are profitable, the taxes payable will be reduced by 40 percent of $1 800, or $720. The $720 tax savings are treated as part of the incremental cash inflow in the first year resulting from the acquisition of the new machine. The tax savings resulting from incremental CCA in each of years 2-5 are shown in Table 13-1. In each of years 1-5, the cash flow from operations is the sum of the after-tax value of $4 560 derived from the pre-tax net cash savings of $7 600 and the tax savings on incremental CCA. Note that the marginal cash flows of the project as computed above are identical to those reported in the last column of Table 13-1. It is worthwhile to remember that whenever we talk of after-tax net cash flows, procedures similar to those used in the preparation of Table 13-1 must be followed.

Efficient procedures must be set up to collect the information necessary for the capital-budgeting decision. This information must be standardized as much as possible for all investment proposals; otherwise proposals cannot be compared objectively. We recognize the difficulty in quantifying expected cash flows for certain investment proposals. The returns on all investments, other than Government of Canada securities held to maturity, are subject to varying degrees of uncertainty. In addition, projects proposed for safety or environmental reasons are difficult to quantify, often representing a constraint of what *must* be done as opposed to what *might* be done. Despite these problems, in most cases management must make some estimate of the probable outcome if it is to consider an investment proposal. These estimates can be subject to probability distributions; indeed, using probability distributions is desirable, as we shall see in Chapter 14. In this chapter, however, we work with the expected values of these estimates.

Methods for Evaluating Projects

Once we have collected the necessary information, we are able to evaluate the attractiveness of the various investment proposals under consideration. The investment decision will be either to accept or to reject the proposal. In this section, we evaluate four methods of capital budgeting:

1. Average-rate-of-return
2. Payback
3. Internal rate of return
4. Net present value

The first two are approximate methods for assessing the economic worth of a project. For simplicity, we assume throughout that the expected cash flows are realized at the end of each year.

AVERAGE RATE OF RETURN

This accounting method represents the ratio of the average annual profits after taxes to the average investment in the project. Suppose the average annual book earnings for a 5-year period are $2 000; and the average net investment in a project, assuming straight-line depreciation, is $18 000/2, or $9 000. Therefore,

$$\text{Average rate of return} = \frac{\$2\ 000}{\$9\ 000} = 22.22 \text{ percent} \qquad \textbf{(13-1)}$$

The average-rate-of-return method is sometimes based upon the original investment rather than upon the average investment. In the above example, the average rate of return would be $2 000/$18 000 = 11.11 percent under this version of the average-rate-of-return method. Once the average rate of return for a proposal has been calculated, it may be compared with a required rate of return to determine if a particular proposal should be accepted or rejected.

The principal virtue of the average-rate-of-return method is its simplicity; it makes use of readily available accounting information. The principal shortcomings of the method are that it is based upon accounting income rather than upon cash flows and that it fails to take account of the timing of cash inflows and outflows. The time value of money is ignored; benefits in the last year are valued the same as benefits in the first year.

Suppose that we have three investment proposals, each costing $9 000 and each having an economic and depreciable life of 3 years. Assume that the proposals are expected to provide the following book profits and cash flows over the next 3 years:

	Project A		Project B		Project C	
Period	Book profit	Net cash flow	Book profit	Net cash flow	Book profit	Net cash flow
1	$3 000	$6 000	$2 000	$5 000	$1 000	$4 000
2	2 000	5 000	2 000	5 000	2 000	5 000
3	1 000	4 000	2 000	5 000	3 000	6 000

Each proposal will have the same average rate of return: $2 000/ $4 500, or 44 percent; however, few, if any, firms would be equally favorable to all three projects. Most would prefer project A, which provides a larger portion of total cash benefits in the first year. For this reason, the average rate of return leaves much to be desired as a method for project selection.

PAYBACK METHOD

The payback period of an investment project gives the number of years required to recover the initial cash investment. Referring to the turret lathe proposal in Table 13-1, recovery is expected to be $16 733 ($5 280 + $5 856 + $5 597) of the net capital outlay of $18 000, by the end of year 3. The balance of $1 267 ($18 000 – $16 733) will be recovered in the first 2.8 months of year 4 assuming even monthly cash flows in that year. Thus, the payback period is approximately 3 years and 3 months.

If the payback period calculated is less than some maximum acceptable payback period, the proposal is accepted; if not, it is rejected. For example, if the required payback period is four years, the project in our example would be accepted. The major shortcoming of the payback method is that it fails to consider cash flows after the payback period; consequently, it cannot be regarded as a measure of profitability. Two proposals costing $10 000 each would have the same payback period if they both had annual net cash inflows of $5 000 in the first two years. However, one project might be expected to provide no cash flow after two years, while the other might be expected to provide a cash flow of $5 000 in each of the next three years. Thus, the payback method can be very deceptive as a yardstick of profitability. In addition to this short-coming, the method does not take account of the timing of cash flows during the payback period; it considers only the recovery period as a whole.

INTERNAL-RATE-OF-RETURN METHOD

Because of the various shortcomings in the average-rate-of-return and pay-back methods, it generally is felt that discounted cash-flow methods provide a more objective basis for evaluating and selecting investment projects. These methods take account of both the magnitude and the timing of expected cash flows in each period of a project's life. The two discounted cash-flow methods are the internal-rate-of-return and the present-value methods; the mechanics of these methods were described in Chapter 4. Recall that the internal rate of return for an investment proposal is the discount rate that equates the present value of the expected cash outflows with the present value of the expected inflows. It is represented by that rate, r, such that

$$\sum_{t=0}^{n} \left[\frac{A_t}{(1+r)^t} \right] = 0 \qquad (13\text{-}2)$$

where A_t is the cash flow for period t, whether it be a net cash outflow or inflow, and n is the last period in which a cash flow is expected. If the initial cash outlay or costs occurs at time 0, Eq. (13-2) can be expressed as

$$A_0 = \frac{A_1}{(1+r)} + \frac{A_2}{(1+r)^2} + \cdots + \frac{A_n}{1+r)^n} \qquad (13\text{-}3)$$

Thus, r is the rate that discounts the stream of future cash flows—A_1 through A_n—to equal the initial outlay at time 0—A_0. For our example in Table 13-1, the problem can be expressed as

$$18\ 000 = \frac{5\ 280}{(1+r)} + \frac{5\ 856}{(1+r)^2} + \frac{5\ 597}{(1+r)^3} + \frac{5\ 390}{1+r)^4} + \frac{5\ 224}{(1+r)^5} \qquad (13\text{-}4)$$

Solving for r either by means of a computer or by the manual method described in Chapter 4, we find the internal rate of return for the project to be 15.9 percent.[5]

When solving for r, it is important to recognize the possibility that there may be more than one internal rate of return that equates the present value of cash inflows with the present value of cash outflows. This can occur when there are net cash outflows in more than one period and the outflows are separated by one or more periods of net cash inflows. We examine the problem in Appendix A at the end of this chapter but should point out at this time that the existence of multiple internal rates of return is unusual. For the typical capital budgeting project a unique internal rate of return exists.

To arrive at the internal rate of return in this situation, we must resort to a trial-and-error process. Suppose we start with discount rates of 14 percent, 15 percent and 16 percent and calculate the present value of cash inflows. Using Appendix A, at the end of the book, we get the following results:

Discount rate	Present value of inflows
14%	$18 820
15%	$18 378
16%	$17 954

---

[5]For simplicity, we continue to ignore the tax savings on CCA in year 6 and onwards. If these tax savings are considered, the IRR will exceed 15.9 percent as we show later in this chapter.

Since the initial outlay is $18 000, we know that the internal rate of return must be between 15 percent and 16 percent. To approximate the actual return we interpolate as follows:

	Discount rate	Present value
	15%	$18 378
	16%	$17 954
Difference	1%	$ 424

$$\frac{\$378}{\$424} = 0.9 \qquad 15\% + 0.9 = 15.9\%$$

Acceptance criterion The acceptance criterion generally employed with the internal-rate-of-return method is to compare the internal rate of return with a required rate of return, known also as the cutoff, or hurdle, rate. If the internal rate of return exceeds the required rate, the project is accepted; if not, it is rejected. For example, if the required rate of return were 12 percent and this criterion is used, the investment proposal considered above would be accepted. If the required rate of return is the return investors expect the firm to earn on the project, accepting a project with an internal rate of return in excess of the required rate of return should result in an increase in the market price of the share, because the firm accepts a project with a return greater than that required to maintain the present market price per share. Much more will be said in Chapter 15 about relating the investment decision to the objective of the firm. We assume for now that the required rate of return is given.

PRESENT-VALUE METHOD

Like the internal-rate-of-return method, the present-value method is a discounted cash-flow approach to capital budgeting. With the present-value method, all cash flows are discounted to present value using the required rate of return. The net-present value (NPV) of an investment proposal is

$$NPV = -A_0 + \frac{A_1}{(1+k)} + \frac{A_2}{(1+k)^2} + \cdots + \frac{A_n}{(1+k)^n} \tag{13-5}$$

where k is the required rate of return. If the sum of these discounted cash flows is equal to or greater than 0, the proposal is accepted; if not, it is rejected. Another way to express the acceptance criterion is to say that the project will be accepted if the present value of cash inflows exceeds the present value of cash outflows. The rationale behind the acceptance criterion is the same as that behind the internal-rate-of-return method. If the required rate of return is the return investors expect the firm to earn on the investment proposal, and the firm accepts a proposal with a net-present value greater than zero, the market price of the share should rise. Again, the firm is taking on a project with a return greater than that necessary to leave the market price of the share unchanged.

If we assume a required rate of return of 12 percent after taxes, the net-present value of our example problem in Table 13-1 is

$$
\begin{aligned}
NPV &= -\$18\ 000 + \frac{5\ 280}{(1.12)} + \frac{5\ 856}{(1.12)^2} + \frac{5\ 597}{(1.12)^3} + \frac{5\ 390}{(1.12)^4} + \frac{5\ 224}{(1.12)^5} \\
&= -18\ 000 + 4\ 715 + 4\ 668 + 3\ 984 + 3\ 425 + 2\ 964 \\
&= -18\ 000 + 19\ 756 \\
&= \$1\ 756
\end{aligned}
$$

(13-6)

An easier way to solve this problem, of course, is by direct reference to Table A at the end of the book, where we find the appropriate annual discount factors, and multiply annual cash flows. Subtracting the initial outlay of $18 000, we obtain $1 756. Inasmuch as the net-present value of this proposal is greater than 0, the proposal should be accepted, using the present-value method.

With the internal-rate-of-return method, we are given the cash flows and solve for the rate of discount that equates the present value of the cash inflows with the present value of the outflows. The internal rate of return is then compared with the required rate of return to determine whether the proposal should be accepted. With the present-value method, we are given the cash flows and the required rate of return and solve for the net-present value. The acceptability of the proposal is determined by whether the net-present value is equal to, or greater than, 0.

MUTUAL EXCLUSION AND DEPENDENCY

In evaluating a group of investment proposals, it is important to determine whether the proposals are independent of each other. A proposal is said to be mutually exclusive if the acceptance of it precludes the acceptance of one or more other proposals. For example, if the firm is considering investment in one of two temperature-control systems, acceptance of one system will rule out acceptance of the other. Two mutually exclusive proposals cannot both be accepted.

A contingent or dependent proposal is one whose acceptance depends upon the acceptance of one or more other proposals. An example of a contingent proposal might be an investment in a large machine, which depends upon the construction of an addition to a plant. A combination of investment proposals containing a contingent proposal must contain the proposal(s) upon which it is dependent. When an investment proposal is not independent of all other proposals, this occurrence must be recognized and investment decisions made accordingly.

Profitability index The profitability index, or benefit-cost ratio, of a project is the present value of future net cash flows over the initial cash outlay. It can be expressed as

$$PI = \frac{\sum_{t=1}^{n} \dfrac{A_t}{(1+k)^t}}{A_0} \qquad \text{(13-7)}$$

For our example

$$PI = \frac{\$19\ 756}{\$18\ 000} = 1.10$$

As long as the profitability index is 1.00 or greater, the investment proposal is acceptable. For any given project, the net-present-value method and the profitability index give the same accept-reject signals. If we must choose between mutually exclusive projects, the net-present-value measure is preferred because it expresses in absolute terms the expected economic contribution of the project. In contrast, the profitability index expresses only the relative profitability. To illustrate, consider the following mutually exclusive projects:

	Project A	Project B
Present value of net cash flows	$20 000	$8 000
Initial cash outlay	15 000	5 000
Net present value	$ 5 000	$3 000
Profitability index	1.33	1.60

According to the net-present-value method, project A would be preferred, whereas according to the profitability indexes, project B would be preferred. Because the net present value represents the expected economic contribution of a project, we should prefer A to B. Thus, the net-present-value method is the better of the two methods when we must choose between mutually exclusive projects that involve different initial cash outlays.[6]

Comparison of Present-Value and Internal-Rate-of-Return Methods

In general, the present-value and internal-rate-of-return methods lead to the same acceptance or rejection decision. In Fig. 13-1 we illustrate graphically the two methods applied to a typical investment project. The figure shows the relationship between the net present value of a project and the discount rate employed. When the discount rate is 0, net present value is simply the total cash inflows less the total cash outflows of the project. Assuming that total inflows exceed total outflows and

---

[6]See Bernhard Schwab and Peter Lusztig, "A Comparative Analysis of the Net-Present Value and the Benefit-Cost Ratio as Measures of the Economic Desirability of Investments," *Journal of Finance*, 24 (June 1969), 507-16.

that outflows are followed by inflows, the typical project will have the highest net present value when the discount rate is 0. As the discount rate increases, the present value of future cash inflows decreases relative to the present value of cash outflows. At the intercept, the net present value of the project is 0. The discount rate at that point represents the internal rate of return that equates the present value of cash inflows with the present value of cash outflows. For discount rates greater than the internal rate of return, the net present value of the project is negative.[7]

If the required rate of return is less than the internal rate of return, we would accept the project using either method. Suppose that the required rate were 10 percent. As seen in Fig. 13-1, the net present value of the project then would be Y. Inasmuch as Y is greater than 0, we would accept the project, using the present-value method. Similarly, we would accept the project using the internal-rate-of-return method because the internal rate exceeds the required rate. For required rates greater than the internal rate of return, we would reject the project under either method. Thus, we see that the internal-rate-of-return and present-value methods give us identical answers with respect to the acceptance or rejection of an investment project.

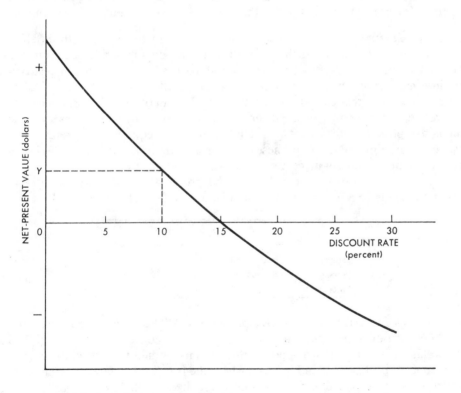

FIGURE 13-1 Relation between discount rate and net-present value

---

[7]Again, we must recognize the possibility of multiple internal rates of return. See Appendix A to this chapter.

DIFFERENCES BETWEEN METHODS

We must identify important differences between the methods. When two investments proposals are mutually exclusive, so that we can select only one, the two methods may give contradictory results. To illustrate the nature of the problem, suppose a firm had two mutually exclusive investment proposals that were expected to generate the following cash flows:

	Cash flows				
Year	0	1	2	3	4
Proposal A	−$23 616	$10 000	$10 000	$10 000	$10 000
Proposal B	− 23 616	0	5 000	10 000	32 675

Internal rates of return for proposals A and B are 25 percent and 22 percent, respectively. If the required rate of return is 10 percent, however, and we use this figure as our discount rate, the net present values of proposals A and B are $8 083 and $10 347, respectively. Thus, proposal A is preferred if we use the internal-rate-of-return method, whereas proposal B is preferred if we use the present-value method. If we can choose but one of these proposals, we obviously have a conflict.

Reinvestment rate The conflict between these two methods is due to different assumptions with respect to the reinvestment rate on funds released from the proposals. The internal-rate-of-return method implies that funds are reinvested at the internal rate of return over the remaining life of the proposal. For proposal A, the assumption is that cash flows of $10 000 at the end of years 1, 2, and 3 can be reinvested to earn a return of 25 percent, compounded annually. The present-value method implies reinvestment at a rate equivalent to the required rate of return used as the discount rate. Because of these differing assumptions, the two methods can give different rankings of investment proposals, as we have seen.

To illustrate further the nature of the problem, consider two additional mutually exclusive proposals with the following cash flows:

	Cash flows			
Time	0	1	2	3
Proposal C	−$155.22	$100.00	0	$100.00
Proposal D	− 155.22	0	0	221.00

The net present value of each of these proposals is $10.82 if we assume a required rate of return of 10 percent. However, we would be indifferent between the two proposals only if the firm had opportunities for reinvestment at a rate of 10 percent. This concept is illustrated in Fig. 13-2, where the functional relationship between net present value and the discount rate is graphed for the two proposals. The intercepts on the 0 horizontal line represent the internal rates of return of the two proposals that equate their net present values with 0. For proposal C, the internal rate of return is 14 percent; for proposal D, it is 12.5 percent. The intercepts on the vertical axis represent total cash inflows less total cash outflows for the two proposals, because the discount rate is 0. We see that proposal D ranks higher than

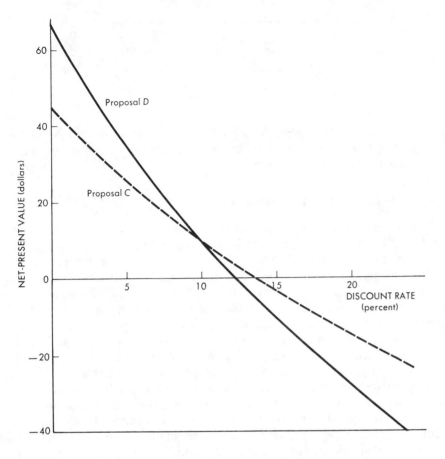

FIGURE 13-2 Relation between discount rate and net-present values, proposals C and D

proposal C if the reinvestment rate is below 10 percent and lower if it is above 10 percent. At the point of intersection, 10 percent, the proposals have identical net present values. This point represents the crossover rate. Given a reinvestment rate of 10 percent, then, the two proposals would have equal ranking. For reinvestment rates other than this percentage, we would prefer one proposal to the other. In a similar manner, other mutually exclusive investment proposals can be evaluated according to the intersections.

Scale of investment   In addition to the problem of different implicit compounding rates, a problem arises if the initial cash outlays are different for two mutually exclusive investment proposals. Because the results of the internal-rate-of-return method are expressed as a percent, the scale of investment is ignored. Without allowance for this factor, a 50 percent return on a $100 investment would always be preferred to a 25 percent return on a $500 investment. In contrast, the results of the present-value method are expressed in absolute terms. If the investment proposals above were each for one year, we would have the following, assuming a required rate of return of 10 percent:

	Cash flows			
	Year 0	Year 1	IRR	NPV (10%)
Proposal X	−$100	$150	50%	$36.36
Proposal Y	− 500	625	25	68.18

With respect to absolute returns, the second proposal is superior, despite the fact that its internal rate of return is less. The reason is that the scale of investment is greater, affording a greater net present value.

SHORTCOMINGS OF THE IRR METHOD

We have seen that the present-value method always provides correct rankings of mutually exclusive investment projects, whereas the internal-rate-of-return method sometimes does not. With the IRR method, the implied reinvestment rate will differ depending upon the cash-flow stream for each investment proposal under consideration. For proposals with a high internal rate of return, a high reinvestment rate is assumed; for proposals with a low internal rate of return, a low reinvestment rate is assumed. Only rarely will the internal rate of return calculated represent the relevant rate for reinvestment of intermediate cash flows. With the present-value method, however, the implied reinvestment rate—namely, the required rate of return—is the same for each proposal. In essence, this reinvestment rate represents the minimum return on opportunities available to the firm. Not only is it consistently applied but it is the only theoretically correct opportunity cost that can be employed if our objective is value maximization. In addition, the present-value method takes account of differences in the scale of investment, and for this reason it also is superior to the IRR method.

Many financial managers feel that, in practice, the internal rate of return is easier to visualize and to interpret than is the net-present-value. In addition, one does not have to specify a required rate of return in the calculations. To the extent that the required rate of return is but a rough estimate, the use of the internal-rate-of-return method may permit a more realistic comparison of projects. The principal shortcoming of the method is the possibility of multiple internal rates of return, a subject that we take up in Appendix A to this chapter.

Project Evaluation—Further Analysis

In our turret lathe replacement example, we omitted the tax savings on CCA charged in year 6 and onwards, the investment tax credit, the salvage value and any working capital requirements, to keep the example simple and enable analysis of the methods for evaluating expected profitability. Now we must digress to examine the effects of the above considerations on the magnitude and timing of cash flows. Recall that the net capital outlay for the replacement was $18 000 and that the new lathe was expected to result in annual cash savings of $7 600 a year over the next five years. Then taking into account the after-tax cash savings (60% of $7 600 or

$4 560) and tax savings on CCA charges to income, we computed annual after-tax net cash flows for the next five years (Table 13-1). Later in the discussion of the present value method, we computed the NPV as $1 756 in Eq. (13-6); the IRR was computed as 15.9 percent. We now turn to a refinement of that turret lathe replacement proposal taking into account several additional factors.

TAX SAVINGS ON CCA

Since 1949, only the declining-balance method of depreciating assets has been generally acceptable for tax purposes in Canada. Assets are grouped into 35 classes and assigned fixed capital cost allowance rates. For example, the turret lathe may be a Class 19 asset subject to a capital cost allowance rate of 20 percent. This rate is always applied to the book value (cost less accumulated capital cost allowance) of the asset. All assets of a given class form a pool. Additional assets purchased are added to the pool and the proceeds of assets sold are deducted. The year-end balance forms the book value for purposes of calculating the capital cost allowance, which is also deducted from the pool.

Under the double-declining balance method, the calculation of CCA can be rather tedious. In fact, if an asset is not sold at the end of its economic life, it can be depreciated to infinity for tax purposes! Fortunately, the present value of the tax savings due to CCA may be calculated using the formula[8]

$$Q = \frac{Cdt}{K+d} - \frac{1}{(1+K)^p}\left(\frac{Sdt}{K+d}\right) = \frac{dt}{K+d}\left[C - \frac{S}{(1+K)^p}\right] \qquad (13\text{-}8)$$

---

[8]This formula is a variation of one presented by Geoffrey Walsham and Daniel McDonald in "The Effect of Taxation on DCF Investment Appraisal," *Cost and Management* (July-August 1975), 20-23. Its derivation is

$$Q = \frac{Cdt}{(1+K)} + \frac{Cdt(1-d)}{(1+K)^2} + \cdots + \frac{Cdt(1-d)^{n-1}}{(1+K)^n}$$

Since this expression is a geometric progression with a first term $= \dfrac{Cdt}{(1+K)}$

$$a \text{ ratio} = \frac{1-d}{1+K}, \text{ and } n \to \infty : Q = \frac{Cdt}{K+d}$$

When the asset is sold, the pool is simply reduced by the amount received. Future depreciation charges are also reduced accordingly. The present value at the time of the sale of the asset of the reduced tax savings (Z) is calculated exactly as above and is given by

$$Z = \frac{Sdt}{K+d}$$

This value must be brought to present value (at the time of the investment). Thus, when salvage value is taken into account,

$$Q = \frac{Cdt}{K+d} - \frac{1}{(1+K)^p}\left(\frac{Sdt}{K+d}\right)$$

where Q is the present value of tax savings on CCA, C the incremental investment, d the CCA rate, t the tax rate[9], K the required rate of return, S the scrap value, and p the year of disposal.

However, as we saw in Chapter 2, since 1981 only 50 percent of the CCA is allowed in the year of acquisition. Thus Eq. (13-8) must be modified accordingly. With this adjustment it becomes [10]

$$Q^1 = \frac{Cdt}{K + d}\left[\frac{2 + K}{2(1 + K)}\right] - \frac{1}{(1 + K)^p}\left(\frac{Sdt}{K + d}\right) \tag{13-9}$$

Since tax regulations allow only 50 percent of CCA in the year of acquisition, we will use Eq. (13-9) throughout the rest of the text. However, students should keep in mind that Eq. (13-8) was used prior to 1981 and could become appropriate again should tax law permit full deduction of CCA in the first year.

Zero salvage value   If the new lathe has no salvage value at the end of year 5, the undepreciated capital cost of the asset will remain in the pool and be charged to income in year 6 and onwards. Theoretically, the lathe will be depreciated to infinity (∞) since the undepreciated capital cost will always be positive. Where an asset is depreciated to infinity, Eq. (13-9) is reduced to

$$Q = \frac{Cdt}{K + d}\left[\frac{2 + K}{2(1 + K)}\right] \tag{13-10}$$

Thus the salvage value component of Eq. (13-9) is eliminated from consideration.

To illustrate, assume a zero value for the lathe at the end of year 5, then the present value of the tax savings to infinity is

$$Q = \frac{\$18\ 000(0.2)(0.4)}{0.12 + 0.2}\left[\frac{2 + 0.12}{2(1 + 0.12)}\right] \tag{13-11}$$

$$= \$4\ 259$$

The net-present value of the proposal using the results of Eq. (13-11) is now \$2 697 as shown in Table 13-2. Earlier when we considered cash flows only to year 5, we derived an NPV = \$1 756 using Eq. (13-6). The differential of \$941 (\$2 697 − \$1 756) is the present value of the tax savings on CCA claimed in year 6

---

[9]For the use of varying tax rates in Eq. (14-7), see Jean-Marie Gagnon, "A Note on Depreciation" *Journal of Business Administration*, 7 (Spring 1976), 117-24.

[10]This formula is taken from "The Effect on Capital Budgeting Decisions of Recent Changes in the CCA calculation," *Cost and Management* (May-June 1982), 52-53 by Robert Welch. The derivation of the first term on the right hand side is

$$Q^1 = \left[\frac{C(d/2)dt}{(1 + k)}\right] + \left[\frac{C(1 - d/2)dt}{K + d}\right]\left[\frac{1}{1 + K}\right] = \frac{Cdt}{(1 + K)}\left[\frac{1}{2} + \frac{(1 - d/2)}{K + d}\right]$$

$$= \frac{Cdt}{1 + K}\left[\frac{K + d + 2 - d}{2(K + d)}\right] = \frac{Cdt}{K + d}\left[\frac{2 + K}{2(1 + K)}\right]$$

TABLE 13-2 NPV and IRR of the Turret Lathe Proposal Assuming
Non-Disposal of the Asset

End of Year		After Tax Cash Flow	P.V. Factor 12%	Present Value $
0	Capital costs			
	New lathe	-$20 000		
	Less sale price of old lathe	2 000	-$18 000	1.00	-$18 000
1-5	Cash savings [$7 600 (1 − t)]*	4 560		3.6048	16 438
1-∞	Tax savings on CCA as computed by Eq. (13-11)			4 259
	Net present value			2 697
	Internal rate of return			17.5%

*Since the amount is the same in all years, we use the annuity method as illustrated in Chapter 4.

and onwards; all other factors have been held constant. The internal rate of return is now 17.5 percent as compared to the 15.9 percent derived earlier.

Positive salvage value   Usually assets have some salvage value depending upon economic benefits perceived by potential buyers. When an asset is sold, the present value of the tax savings on CCA is determined using Eq. (13-9), and our calculations will have to include the present value of the sales proceeds. Assume, for example, that the turret lathe is sold for $6 635, which is the undepreciated capital cost at the end of year 5.[11] The present value of the tax savings on CCA is now

$$Q^1 = \frac{(0.2)(0.4)}{0.12 + 0.2} [\$18\ 000] \left[\frac{2 + 0.12}{2(1 + 0.12)} \right] - \frac{1}{1.12^5} \left[\frac{6\ 635 \times 0.2 \times 0.4}{0.12 + 0.2} \right] \quad \textbf{(13-12)}$$

$$= \$3\ 318$$

The present value of the salvage proceeds received at the end of year 5 is $3 765 ($6 635 times the 12 percent discount factor of 0.5674). The net-present value of the proposal is now computed as $5 521 as shown in Table 13-3; the internal rate of return is 22.4%.

The NPV of $1 756 in Eq. (13-6) is less than that of $5 521 in Table 13-3 by $3 765—the present value of the salvage proceeds which by assumption is the undepreciated capital cost of the lathe at the end of year 5. The present value of $3 318 in Table 13-3 for the tax savings on CCA is the annual CCA claimed over the first five years. Thus if salvage value equals the undepreciated capital cost, then the net capital cost of the asset ($18 000 − $6 635 in our example) is fully written off for

[11]For simplicity, we assume that if we had kept the existing lathe, the salvage value at the end of year 5 is zero. However, if we expect that the asset to be replaced will have a salvage value we then have to use net salvage value in Eq. (13-12). For example, if the existing lathe is expected to have a salvage value of $500 at the end of year 5, the net salvage value would be $6 135 ($6 635 − $500). Eq. (13-12) and Table 13-3 will be modified using $6 135 as the relevant salvage value.

TABLE 13-3 NPV and IRR of the Turret Lathe Proposal
Assuming Disposal at the End of Year 5

End of Year		After-Tax Cash Flow	P.V. Factor 12%	Present Value $
0	Capital costs (See Table 13-2)	–$18 000	1.00	–$18 000
1-5	Cash savings (See Table 13-2)	4 560	3.6048	16 438
5	Salvage value	6 635	0.5674	3 765
1-5	Tax savings on CCA as computed by Eq. (13-12)			3 318
	Net present value			5 521
	Internal rate of return			22.4%

tax purposes at the disposal date of the asset. Where the salvage value is less than the undepreciated capital cost, some portion of the net capital cost will be depreciated to infinity. The effect of this is a relative reduction in net-present value. For example, if the lathe is sold for $4 000 and if we re-compute Table 13-3 we obtain a net-present value of $4 400 compared to $5 521. Depending on the amount of the salvage value, the net-present value will vary between $2 697 in Table 13-2 and $5 521 in Table 13-3, other factors being constant. Now if the salvage value exceeds the undepreciated capital cost, the net-present value will exceed $5 521 in Table 13-3. For example, if the lathe is sold for $8 000 at the end of year 5 a re-computation of Table 13-3 will result in an NPV of $6 102.

INVESTMENT TAX CREDIT

As we discussed in Chapter 2, specific buildings, machinery and equipment are entitled to an investment tax credit based on the capital costs of the respective assets. This tax credit is used to reduce federal taxes payable in the year of acquisition of the asset and therefore should be regarded as a cash inflow. Assume that the lathe qualifies for a 10 percent investment tax credit and that the benefit is received at the end of year 1. Also, maintain the assumptions of Table 13-3. The investment tax credit is $2 000 (10 percent of $20 000) and its present value is $1 786 as shown in Table 13-4. For CCA purposes, the net capital outlay of $18 000 has to be reduced by the nominal amount of the investment tax credit. Thus, the present value of the tax savings on CCA is re-computed as

$$Q = \frac{(0.2)(0.4)}{0.12 + 0.20} \, [\$18\ 000 - \$2\ 000] \left[\frac{2 + 0.12}{2(1 + 0.12)} \right] - \frac{1}{1.12^5} \left[\frac{\$6\ 635 \times 0.2 \times 0.4}{0.12 + 0.2} \right] \qquad \textbf{(13-13)}$$

$$= \$2\ 844$$

Considering a salvage value of $6 635 and the investment tax credit, the net-present value is now $6 833 (Table 13-4) compared to $5 521 in Table 13-3 where the tax credit was not considered. The internal rate of return is now 26.3 percent compared with 22.4 percent when only salvage value is considered. Like salvage value, the investment tax credit enhances the profitability of a project.

WORKING CAPITAL REQUIREMENT

In addition to the investment in a fixed asset, a lathe in our example, it sometimes is necessary to carry additional cash, receivables or inventories. This investment in working capital is treated as a cash outflow at the time it occurs. For example, if $1 000 of additional inventory were required in connection with the new lathe and the investment occurred at the outset, there would be an additional cash outflow of $1 000 at time 0, bringing the total net capital outflow to $19 000. At the end of the project's life, the working capital investment presumably is recaptured. Table 13-4 is adjusted to reflect this working capital investment and the results are shown in Table 13-5. The lower net-present value ($6 400 as compared

TABLE 13-4 NPV and IRR of the Turret Lathe Proposal Assuming Salvage Value and Investment Tax Credit

End of Year		After-Tax Cash flow	P.V. Factor 12%	Present Value $
0	Capital outlay (see Table 13-3)	−$18 000	1.00	−$18 000
1	Investment tax credit	2 000	0.8929	1 786
1-5	Cash savings (see Table 13-3)	4 560	3.6048	16 438
5	Salvage value (see Table 13-3)	6 635	0.5674	3 765
1-5	Tax savings on CCA as computed by Eq. (13-13)			2 844
	Net present value			6 833
	Internal rate of return			26.3%

TABLE 13-5 NPV and IRR of the Turret Lathe Proposal Considering Salvage Value, Investment Tax Credit and Working Capital Investment

End of Year		After-Tax Cash Flow	P.V. Factor 12%	Present Value $
0	Capital outlay			
	Lathe (see Table 13-4)	−$18 000	1.00	−$18 000
	Working capital	− 1 000	1.00	− 1 000
				−$19 000
1	Investment tax credit (see Table 13-4)	2 000	0.8929	1 786
1-5	Cash savings (see Table 13-4)	4 560	3.6048	16 438
5	Salvage value (see Table 13-4)	6 635	0.5674	3 765
5	Recovery of working capital	1 000	0.5675	567
1-5	Tax savings on CCA (see Table 13-4)			2 844
	Net present value			6 400
	Internal rate of return			24.7%

to $6 833) is a result of the timing of the recovery of the working capital investment. An investment of $1 000 at time 0 results in a recovery with a present value of $567 —a differential of $433 in present value terms.

PROJECTS WITH DIFFERENT LIVES

Sometimes a company is faced with having to choose between two mutually exclusive investment projects having different economic lives. We may be comparing two machines that will perform equally well. The Monarch machine sells for $30 000, lasts 4 years, and costs $5 000 per year to keep it running smoothly. The Regal machine's price is $20 000, but it lasts only 3 years and costs $7 000 a year to keep it up. The question is which machine should we choose?

If we need the services of the machine for only 3 years, we simply would compute the present values of cash outflows for both alternatives and pick the one with the lowest present value. If we need the services of such a machine into the foreseeable future, the situation is different. One way to look at the problem is to assume that we can replicate each machine at the end of its life. We might assume that we can replace the Regal machine at the end of year 3 with an identical machine costing $20 000 which will last another three years and cost $7 000 a year to keep up. The same type of replication could be assumed for the Monarch machine. If the two machines are replicated at constant scale forever, we can compare them because both would have an infinite life. The cash outflow streams (in thousands) would be

	0	1	2	3	4	5	6	7	8	...
Monarch	−$30	−$5	−$5	−$5	−$35	−$5	−$5	−$5	−$35	
Regal	− 20	− 7	− 7	−27	− 7	7	−27	− 7	− 7	

The calculation of the present value of a long stream of cash flows is arduous. A much simpler way to reach a decision is to calculate the present values of the cash outflows only for the original lives of the machines and then convert these present values into annual annuity payments. If the required return were 12 percent, the present values of the two cash flow streams would be

Cash flows (in thousands)

	0	1	2	3	4	Present value (12%)
Monarch	−$30	−$5	−$5	−$5	−$5	−$45 187
Regal	− 20	− 7	− 7	−7		− 36 813

The next step is to divide these present values by the appropriate discount factor to determine the equivalent annual annuity amount. Turning to Table B at the back of the book, we see that the 12 percent discount factor for an even series of cash flows for three years is 2.4018 and for four years it is 3.0373. Therefore, we have the following annual annuity payments:

Monarch	$-\$45\,187/3.0373 = \$14\,877$
Regal	$-\$36\,813/2.4018 = -15\,327$

The Monarch machine, having the lower annuity payment, would be preferred. Its longer life and lower running expenses more than offset the difference in initial cost. The procedure, then, is to convert costs that are spread over varying years into annual equivalent costs and then to compare these annual costs. The method is appropriate when the life of each machine is essentially infinite, owing to replication at a constant scale. When this is not the case and replication occurs not at all or at different assumed costs, we must calculate the present value of cash outflow for the entire stream.

SOME OTHER CONSIDERATIONS

The above discussion assumes that the firm will continue to have Class 19 assets. However, if the firm decides to sell all assets in this class and has no intention of replacing them, Class 19 will be eliminated. In this situation, any net recaptured depreciation is deemed income and is fully taxable.[12] If there is a terminal loss, this loss is fully chargeable against income.[13] Where the disposition of any asset results in a capital gain, a special tax provision applies. A capital gain arises if the sale price of an asset exceeds its initial cost. Only one half of this capital gain is deemed income and is taxed at the normal tax rate.

Also, we have assumed the computation of CCA using the double-declining balance method. However, there are some instances where the net capital outlay may be written off in a relatively short time-period (say two to three years) using straight-line depreciation. In these cases, we cannot use Eq. (13-9) but have to follow the procedures embodied in Table 13-1 and extend them to include the present value calculations as illustrated in Eq. (13-6) and later in Tables 13-2 and 13-3.

---

[12]Assuming that salvage value of an asset is less than or equal to the initial capital cost, then recaptured depreciation arises if the net sales proceeds exceed the undepreciated capital cost of that asset as at the date of disposal. Recaptured depreciation is computed as net sales proceeds less the undepreciated capital cost. Net recaptured depreciation for a pool of assets is simply the aggregate of the recaptured depreciation less the aggregate of any terminal loss (footnote 13) of the assets in that pool.

[13]A terminal loss arises if the net sales proceeds from our asset (or a pool of assets) are less than the undepreciated capital cost of that asset (or the pool of assets) as at the date of disposal. The undepreciated capital cost less net sales proceeds is the amount of the terminal loss.

Capital Rationing

Capital rationing occurs any time there is a budget ceiling, or constraint, on the amount of funds that can be invested during a specific period, such as a year. Such constraints are prevalent in a number of firms, particularly in those that have a policy of financing all capital expenditures internally. Another example of capital rationing occurs when a division of a large company is allowed to make capital expenditures only up to a specified budget ceiling, over which the division usually has no control. With a capital-rationing constraint, the firm attempts to select the combination of investment proposals that will provide the greatest profitability.

Your firm may have the following investment opportunities, ranked in descending order of profitability indexes (the ratio of the present value of future net cash flows over the initial cash outlay):

Proposal	4	7	2	3	6	5	1
Profitability index	1.25	1.19	1.16	1.14	1.09	1.05	0.97
Initial outlay	$400 000	$100 000	$175 000	$125 000	$200 000	$100 000	$150 000

If the budget ceiling for initial outlays during the present period is $1 million, and the proposals are independent of each other, you would select proposals in descending order of profitability until the budget was exhausted. With capital rationing, you would accept the first five proposals, totaling $1 million in initial outlays. In other words, you do not necessarily invest in all proposals that increase the net present value of the firm; you invest in an acceptable proposal only if the budget constraint allows such an investment. You will not invest in proposal 5, even though the profitability index in excess of 1 would suggest its acceptance. The critical aspect of the capital-rationing constraint illustrated is that capital expenditures during a period are strictly limited by the budget ceiling, regardless of the number of attractive investment opportunities.

OPPORTUNITY COSTS AND OBJECTIONS TO CAPITAL RATIONING

A budget ceiling carries its cost, too, when it bars us from taking advantage of any opportunity beyond the cutoff. In our example, the opportunity foregone by the $1 million budget ceiling is proposal 5, which has a profitability index of 1.05. Although all cash flows are discounted at the required rate of return, we do not necessarily accept proposals that provide positive net present values. We see which proposals we can accept before we exhaust the budget; but even if we would not exhaust the budget, we would reject independent proposals yielding less than the required rate of return. However, we may reject projects that provide positive net present values, as was shown with proposal 5. Under capital rationing, the required rate of return is not the acceptance criterion. Should it then be used as the discount rate in present-value calculations, or should the opportunity cost be used? The implied discount rate in any budget period is the yield foregone on the most profitable investment opportunity rejected, or the required rate of return, whichever is the higher. This implied discount rate can vary significantly from period to period, depending upon variations in the total amount of investment projects from period to period and in the budget constraints.

Capital rationing usually results in an investment policy that is less than optimal. In some periods, the firm accepts projects down to its required rate of return; in others, it rejects projects that would provide returns substantially in excess of the required rate. If the firm actually can raise capital at that approximate real cost, should it not invest in all projects yielding more than the required rate of return? If it rations capital and does not invest in all projects yielding more than the required rate, is it not foregoing opportunities that would enhance the market price of its stock?

From a theoretical standpoint, a firm should accept all projects yielding more than the required rate of return.[14] By so doing, it will increase the market price per share, because it is taking on projects that will provide a return higher than that necessary to maintain the present market price per share. This proposition assumes that the firm actually can raise capital, within reasonable limits, at the required rate of return. Certainly, unlimited amounts of capital are not available at any one cost. However, most firms are involved in a more or less continual process of making decisions to undertake capital expenditures and to finance these expenditures. Given the assumptions above, the firm should accept all proposals yielding more than the required rate of return and raise capital to finance these proposals at that approximate real cost. Certainly, there are circumstances that complicate the use of this rule. In general, however, this policy should tend to maximize the market price of the stock over the long run. If the firm rations capital and rejects projects that yield more than the required rate of return, then the firm's investment policy, by definition, is less than optimal. Management could increase the value of the firm to the shareholders by accepting these projects.

Summary

Capital budgeting involves the outlay of current funds in anticipation of cash-flow benefits to be realized in the future. Capital-budgeting decisions by corporations have an important impact on capital formation and on the economic growth of a country. An important topic was the collection of cash-flow information essential for the evaluation of investment proposals. The key is to measure incremental cash flows with and without the investment proposal being analyzed. Later in the chapter the effects of accelerated depreciation, the investment tax credit, salvage value and a working capital requirement on the pattern of cash flows were examined.

Capital-budgeting methods, including the average-rate-of-return and pay-back methods, were evaluated under the assumption that the acceptance of any investment proposal does not change the total business-risk complexion of the firm. It was shown that the two discounted cash-flow methods—internal rate of

---

[14]We shall examine the rationale for this criterion in Chapter 15.

return and net-present value—were the only appropriate means by which to judge the economic contribution of an investment proposal.

The important distinction between the internal-rate-of-return method and the present-value method is the implied reinvestment rate and the scale of investment. Depending on the situation, contrary answers can be given with respect to the acceptance of mutually exclusive investment proposals. On theoretical grounds, a case can be made for the superiority of the present-value method. The problem of capital rationing was examined, and we concluded that such a policy is likely to result in investment decisions that are less than optimal.

Appendix A: Multiple Internal Rates of Return

In a well-known article, Lorie and Savage pointed out that certain streams of cash flows may have more than one internal rate of return.[15] To illustrate the problem, suppose that we had the following stream of cash flows corresponding to the "pump" proposal of Lorie and Savage:

Year	0	1	2
Cash flow	−$1 600	$10 000	−$10 000

In this example, a new, more effective pump is substituted for an existing pump. On an incremental basis, there is an initial outlay followed by net cash inflows resulting from the increased efficiency of the new pump. If the quantity of oil, for example, is fixed, the new pump will exhaust this supply more quickly than the old pump would. Beyond this point of exhaustion, the new pump alternative would result in an incremental outflow, because the old pump would still be productive.

When we solve for the internal rate of return for the above cash-flow stream, we find that it is not one rate but two: 25 percent and 400 percent. This unusual situation is illustrated in Fig. 13-3, where the discount rate is plotted along the horizontal axis and net present value along the vertical axis. At a zero rate of discount, the net present value of the project is simply the sum of all the cash flows. It is −$1 600 because total cash outflows exceed total cash inflows. As the discount rate increases, the present value of the second-year outflow diminishes with respect to the first-year inflow, and the present value of the proposal becomes positive when the discount rate exceeds 25 percent. As the discount rate increases beyond 100 percent, the present value of all future cash flows (years 1 and 2) diminishes relative to the initial outflow of −$1 600. At 400 percent, the present value of all cash flows again becomes 0.

This type of proposal differs from the usual case, shown in Fig. 13-1, in which net present value is a decreasing function of the discount rate, and in which there is

---

[15]See James H. Lorie and Leonard J. Savage, "Three Problems in Rationing Capital," *Journal of Business*, 28 (October 1955), 229-39.

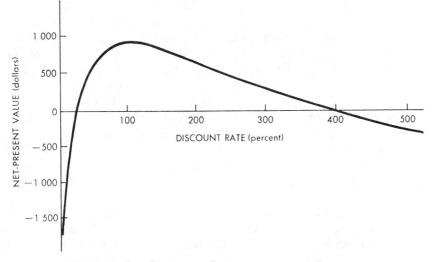

FIGURE 13-3 Dual rates of return

but one internal rate of return that equates the present value of all inflows with the present value of all outflows. An investment proposal may have any number of internal rates of return, depending upon the cash-flow pattern. Consider the following series of cash flows:

Year	0	1	2	3
Cash flow	−$1 000	$6 000	−$11 000	$6 000

In this example, discount rates of 0, 100 percent, and 200 percent result in the net present value of all cash flows equaling 0.

The number of internal rates of return is limited to the number of reversals of sign in the cash-flow stream. In the above example, we have three reversals and three internal rates of return. Although a multiple reversal in signs is a necessary condition for multiple internal rates of return, it is not sufficient for such an occurrence. The occurrence of multiple internal rates of return also depends upon the magnitude of cash flows. For the following series of cash flows, there is but one internal rate of return (32.5 percent), despite two reversals of sign:

Year	0	1	2
Cash flow	−$1 000	$1 400	−$100

When confronted with a proposal having multiple rates of return, how does one decide which is the correct rate? In our dual-rate example, is the correct rate 25 percent or 400 percent? Actually, neither rate is correct, because neither is a measure of investment worth. In essence, the firm has "borrowed" $10 000 from the project at the end of the year 1 and will pay it back at the end of year 2. The relevant question is: what is it worth to the firm to have the use of $10 000 for one year? This question, in turn, depends upon the rate of return on investment opportunities available to the firm for that period of time. If the firm could earn 20 percent on the use of these funds and realize these earnings at the end of the period, the value of this opportunity would be $2 000, to be received at the end of year 2. This amount would then be compared with the initial outlay of $1 600 to determine whether the project is worthwhile. Similarly, other proposals can be evaluated in this manner to determine whether they are worthwhile.

In general, holding risk constant a company wishes to lend at as high a rate as possible and to borrow at as low a rate as possible. In the case of a project having multiple changes in signs, both lending and borrowing are involved. The best way to tackle the problem is to separate cash flows into their lending and borrowing components and then to use the net-present value approach. In this way, the appropriate minimum required rate of return can be used on the lending side and the appropriate borrowing rate on that side.

Appendix B: Inflation and Capital Budgeting

In general, the presence of inflation in the economy distorts capital budgeting decisions. The principal reason is that depreciation charges are based on original rather than replacement costs. As income grows with inflation, an increasing portion is taxed with the result that real cash flows do not keep up with inflation. Consider an investment proposal costing $24 000, assume that no inflation is expected, the CCA rate is 30 percent double-declining and the tax rate is 50 percent. The following cash flows are expected to occur:[16]

Year	Cash savings	CCA	Taxes	Cash flow after taxes
1	$10 000	$3 600	$3 200	$6 800
2	10 000	6 120	1 940	8 060
3	10 000	4 284	2 858	7 142
4	10 000	2 999	3 501	6 499

The internal rate of return which equates the present value of cash inflows with the cost of the project is 7.4 percent.

Consider now a situation where the inflation rate is 7 percent per annum and cash savings are expected to grow at this overall rate of inflation. The after-tax cash flows become

---

[16]This example is similar to one in John A. Tatom and James E. Turley, "Inflation and Taxes: Disincentives for Capital Formation," *Review of the Federal Reserve Bank of St. Louis*, 60 (Jan. 1978), 2-8. For simplicity in presentation, we omit consideration of the tax savings on CCA in year 5 and onwards.

Year	Cash savings	CCA	Taxes	Cash flow after taxes
1	$10 700	$3 600	$3 550	$7 150
2	11 449	6 120	2 665	8 784
3	12 250	4 284	3 983	8 267
4	13 108	2 999	5 055	8 053

While these cash flows are larger than before, they must be deflated by the inflation rate if one is concerned with the real as opposed to the nominal rate of return. Therefore, the last column becomes

	Year			
	1	2	3	4
Real after-tax cash flow	$6 682	$7 672	$6 748	$6 144

As we see, the real after-tax cash flows are less than before because depreciation charges do not change with inflation; an increasing portion of the tax savings are subject to taxation. As taxes increase at a rate faster than inflation, real after-tax cash flows must decline. The internal rate of return based on real after-tax cash flows is 5.4 percent compared with 7.4 percent without inflation.

Therefore, the presence of inflation results in lower real rates of return. Consequently, there is less incentive for companies to undertake capital investments. While tax incentives for rapid write-offs in two or three years alleviate the problem somewhat, there still remains some disincentive for companies to undertake capital expenditures with the result that the typical amount invested is less than would be the case in the absence of inflation. It follows also that there will be an incentive to seek investments with faster paybacks (shorter economic lives) and that industry will become less capital intensive.[17]

THE BIAS IN CASH FLOW ESTIMATES

For the individual company, it is important in estimating cash flows to take anticipated inflation into account. Often there is a tendency to assume that price levels remain unchanged throughout the life of the project. Frequently, this assumption is imposed unknowingly; future cash flows simply are estimated on the basis of existing prices. However, a bias arises in the selection process in that the required rate of return for the project is usually based on current capital costs, which in turn embody a premium for anticipated inflation.[18]

Assume a situation where the hurdle rate for a project is its required rate of return as perceived by investors and creditors. (The ways by which it is measured

---

[17]For an analysis of these points, see Charles R. Nelson, "Inflation and Capital Budgeting," *Journal of Finance*, 31 (June 1976), 923-31.

[18]This section is based on James C. Van Horne, "A Note on Biases in Capital Budgeting Introduced by Inflation," *Journal of Finance and Quantitative Analysis*, (Jan. 1971), 653-58.

are taken up in Chapter 14). There is general agreement that security prices depend on anticipated changes in prices. In fact, over eighty years ago Irving Fisher expressed the nominal rate of interest on a financial instrument as the sum of the real rate and the rate of price change expected over the life of the instrument.[19] This observed phenomenon has come to be known as the *Fisher effect*. Implied is that the required rate of return for a project is

$$R_j = R_j^* + \rho \tag{13B-1}$$

where R_j is the required rate of return in nominal terms, R_j^* is the required rate in real terms, and ρ is the weighted average anticipated rate of inflation over the life of the project.[20]

If anticipated inflation is embodied in the acceptance criterion, it is important that it be reflected in the estimated cash flows for the project as well. The expected cash flows of a project are affected by anticipated inflation in several ways. If cash inflows ultimately arise from the sale of a product, these inflows are affected by expected future prices. As for cash outflows, inflation affects both expected future wages and material costs. Note that future inflation does not affect depreciation charges on existing assets. Once the asset is acquired, these charges are known with certainty. The effect of anticipated inflation on cash inflows and cash outflows will vary with the nature of the project. In some cases, cash inflows, through price increases, will rise faster than cash outflows; while in other cases the opposite will hold. No matter what the relationship, it is important that it be embodied in the cash-flow estimates. Otherwise, a bias of the type described before arises.

Illustration of inflation bias Assume that a project that cost $100 000 at time 0 was under consideration and was expected to provide cash-flow benefits over the next five years. The asset is subject to a 30 percent capital cost allowance rate. Scrap value at the end of year 5 is estimated to be the book value of the asset, and the firm will liquidate the pool of assets at that time. Suppose that cash flows were estimated on the basis of price levels at time 0, with no consideration to the effect of future inflation upon them, and that these estimates were

	Year				
	1	2	3	4	5
1. Expected cash inflow, I_t	$30 000	$40 000	$50 000	$50 000	$50 000
2. Expected cash outflow, O_t	10 000	10 000	10 000	10 000	10 000
3. Before tax cash savings (1-2)	20 000	30 000	40 000	40 000	40 000
4. Taxes (50% of 3)	10 000	15 000	20 000	20 000	20 000
5. After-tax cash savings (3-4)	10 000	15 000	20 000	20 000	20 000
6. CCA	15 000	25 500	17 850	12 495	8 747
7. Tax savings on CCA (50% of 6)	7 500	12 750	8 925	6 248	4 374
8. After-tax cash flow (5 + 7)	$17 500	$27 750	$28 925	$26 248	$24 374
9. Salvage value					20 408
					$44 782

[19]*Appreciation and Interest* (New York: Macmillan, 1896).

[20]Strictly speaking, $1 + R_j = (1 + R_j)(1 + \rho)$, so $R_j = R_j + \rho + R_j\rho$. Inasmuch as the cross-product term is usually small, it is conventional to drop it from consideration.

If the project's required rate of return were 13 percent, the net-present value would be −$2 331. As this figure is negative, the project would be rejected.

However, the results are biased in the sense that the discount rate embodies an element attributable to anticipated future inflation, whereas the cash-flow estimates do not. Suppose that the existing rate of inflation, as measured by changes in the price-level index, were 5 percent, and that this rate was expected to prevail over the next five years. If both cash inflows and cash outflows were expected to increase at this rate, the net-present value of the project would be

$$NPV_0 = \sum_{t=1}^{5} \frac{[I_t(1.05^t - O_t(1.05)^t][0.5] + CCA[0.5]}{(1.13)^t} + \frac{\$20\ 408}{(1.13)^5} - 100\ 000 \tag{13B-2}$$

$$= \$8\ 688$$

where I_t is the cash inflow in year t, O_t is the cash outflow in year t, and CCA is the annual depreciation in year t which is multiplied by the tax rate to give the tax-shield cash savings. Because the net-present value is positive, the project would be acceptable now, whereas before it was not. To reject it under the previous method of estimating cash flows would result in an opportunity loss to shareholders, for the project provides a return in excess of that required by investors.

The example serves to illustrate the importance of taking anticipated inflation into account explicitly when estimating future cash flows. Too often, there is a tendency not to consider its effect in these estimates. Because anticipated inflation is embodied in the required rate of return, not to take account of it in the cash-flow estimates will result in a biased appraisal of the project and, in turn, the possibility of a less than optimal allocation of capital.

Questions

1. Explain what is meant by the time value of money. Why is a bird in the hand worth two (or so) in the bush? Which capital-budgeting approaches ignore this concept? Are they optimal?

2. In evaluating the return from investments, why is depreciation included in the cash flows from a project and not deducted as are other expenses such as wages and taxes?

3. In capital budgeting for a new machine, should the following be added or subtracted from the new machine's purchase price?
   (a) The market value of the old machine is $500.
   (b) An investment in inventory of $2 000 is required.
   (c) The book value of the old machine is $1 000.
   (d) $200 is required to ship the new machine to the plant site.
   (e) A concrete foundation for the new machine will cost $250.
   (f) Training of the machine opeator will cost $300.
   (g) There is an investment tax credit on the new machine.

4. Why does the payback period bias the process of asset selection toward shortlived assets?

5. Contrast the internal rate of return with the net present value. Why might these two time-value approaches to asset selection give conflicting decision rules?

6. Why is the rate of return in future periods important in selecting a measure with which to assign priorities to projects in the current period?

7. The payback period, although it is conceptually unsound, is very popular in business as a criterion for assigning priorities to investment projects. Why is it unsound, and why is it popular?

8. Why are capital-budgeting procedures not applied to working capital decisions?

9. Discuss the adjustments in the capital-budgeting decision one should make to compensate for expected inflation.

10. Discuss the relationship between the payback period of an annuity and its internal rate of return.

11. Is the economic efficiency of a country enhanced by the use of modern capital budgeting techniques? Why?

12. What is the purpose of requiring more levels of approval, the larger the capital expenditure? Is more information also rquired in support of the request?

13. If capital rationing is not optimal, why whould any company use it?

14. The internal-rate-of-return method implies that intermediate cash flows are reinvested at the internal rate of return. Under what circumstances is this assumption likely to lead to a seriously biased measure of the economic return from the project?

15. What is the difference between a product expansion and an equipment replacement type of investment?

Problems with Solutions

1. A company is considering an investment of $24 000 in a machine that will save $12 000 in operating costs. The machine will have a salvage value of $4 000 at the end of its 4 year life. For purposes of this problem use straight-line depreciation. The tax rate is 50 percent. Calculate the payback period and the average rate of return.
Basic calculations

Year	(1) Purchase	(2) Savings	(3) Depreciation*	[(2) – (3)]0.5 = (4) Tax	(2) – (3) – (4) = (5) Net income	(6) Scrap	(3) + (5) + (6) = (7) Cash flow
0	($24 000)						($24 000)
1		$12 000	$5 000	$3 500	$3 500		8 500
2		12 000	5 000	3 500	3 500		8 500
3		12 000	5 000	3 500	3 500		8 500
4		12 000	5 000	3 500	3 500	$4 000	12 500

*($24 000 – $4 000)/4

Payback:
Required inflow = $24 000

year 1	$ 8 500
2	8 500
3	7 000
	$24 000

$$\text{Payback} = 2\frac{7\,000}{8\,500} \text{ years} = 2 \text{ years } 301 \text{ days}$$

Average rate of return = net income/average investment
= $3 500/$12 000 = 29.2%

2. A company is considering two investment proposals and has prepared the graph shown below. The investment and risk are the same in both cases.
   (a) What is the approximate internal rate of return for each proposal?
   (b) If the net present value method is used, which investment would be selected if the required rate were 6 percent? 14 percent? 17 percent?

(a) Internal rate of return
   Proposal #1   13.0%
   Proposal #2   15.5%
(b) At 6%, Proposal #1
   14%, Proposal #2
   17%, neither

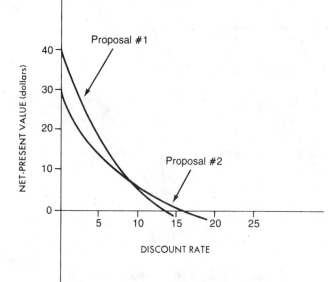

3. A company is considering the acquisition of a machine to replace an old machine that has become somewhat inefficient. The new machine costs $20 000 while the old machine, which has a book value of $4 500, can be sold for $2 500. The company's engineers estimate that the new machine will save $9 000 per year in operating costs excluding depreciation and will last 5 years after which it will have scrap value of $1 000. The scrap value of the old machine, at the end of 5 years will be $100. The company's cost of capital is 15 percent and it pays tax at a rate of 46 percent. Declining balance depreciation, at a 30 percent rate is to be charged. Calculate: (a) the internal rate of return; (b) the net present value; and (c) the profitability index. (The company has many machines of this type.)

(a) Cash flow excluding depreciation

Year	Purchase*	(2) Operating savings	(3) Incremental salvage**	(2) × 0.46 = (4) Tax 46%	(1) + (2) + (3) − (4) = (5) Cash flow
0	($17 500)				($17 500)
1		$9 000		$4 140	4 860
2		9 000		4 140	4 860
3		9 000		4 140	4 860
4		9 000		4 140	4 860
5		9 000	$900	4 140	5 760

*$20 000 − $2 500
**$1 000 − $100

Depreciation: $Q^1 = \dfrac{Cdt}{K+d} \times \dfrac{2+K}{2(1+K)} - \dfrac{1}{(1+K)P} \times \dfrac{Sdt}{K+d}$

Where C = new depreciation base − old depreciation base

C = ($20 000 + 4 500 − 2 500) − 4 500 = $17 500

Try 25%: $Q^1 = \dfrac{\$17\,500 \times 0.3 \times 0.46}{0.25 \times 0.3} \times \dfrac{2.25}{2.50} - \dfrac{1}{(1.25)^5} \times \dfrac{\$900 \times 0.3 \times 0.46}{0.25 + 0.3}$

$Q^1 = \$3\,952 - (0.32768 \times \$226) = \$3\,952 - \$74 = \$3\,878$

Present value of cash flow excluding depreciation

$4 860 × 2.3616 = $11 477
$5 760 × 0.32768 =   1 877 $13 364
        PV at 25% $17 242

Try 24%: $Q^1 = \dfrac{\$17\,500 \times 0.3 \times 0.46}{0.24 + 0.3} \times \dfrac{2.24}{2.48} - \dfrac{1}{(1.24)^5} \times \dfrac{\$900 \times 0.3 \times 0.46}{0.24 \times 0.3}$

= $4 039 − 78 = $ 3 961
  4 860 × 2.4043 $11 685
  5 760 × 0.34111   1 965   13650
  PV at 24% $17 611

$IRR = 0.24 + \dfrac{111}{369} = 24.3\%$

(b) Net present value at 15 percent

$Q = \dfrac{\$17\,500 \times 0.3 \times 0.46}{0.15 + 0.3} \times \dfrac{2.15}{2.30} - \dfrac{1}{(1.15)^5} \times \dfrac{\$900 \times 0.3 \times 0.46}{0.15 \times 0.3}$

= $5 017 − $137 = $ 4 880
  $4 860 × 2.8550
  $5 760 × 0.49718 $13 875
                         2 864   16 739
  PV at 15% $21 619

$NPV = \$21\,619 - \$17\,500 = \$4\,119$

(c) Profitability Index = $21 619/$17 500 = 1.235:1

4. Recalculate problem 3 assuming that the machine qualifies for a 10 percent investment tax credit.

Basic calculations

Year	(1) Net purchase	(2) Operating savings	(3) Incremental salvage	(4) Investment tax credit	(2) × 0.46 = (5) Tax	(1) + (2) + (3) + (4) − (5) = (6) Cash flow
0	($17 500)					($17 500)
1		$9 000		$2 000	$4 140	6 860
2		9 000			4 140	4 860
3		9 000			4 140	4 860
4		9 000			4 140	4 860
5		9 000	$900		4 140	5 760

(a) Internal rate of return method

Try 27%: $Q^1 = \dfrac{\$15\,500 \times 0.3 \times 0.46}{0.27 + 0.3} \times \dfrac{2.27}{2.54} - \dfrac{1}{(1.27)^5} \times \dfrac{\$900 \times 0.3 \times 0.46}{0.27 + 0.3}$

$$Q^1 = \$3\,354 - \$66 = \qquad\qquad \$\,3\,288$$

$\$6\,860 \times 0.78740$	\$5 402	
$\$4\,860 \times 1.4926^*$	7 254	
$\$5\,760 \times 0.30268$	1 743	14 399
PV at 27%		\$17 687

*$2.2800 - 0.7874 = 1.4926$

Try 28%: $Q^1 = \dfrac{\$15\,500 \times 0.3 \times 0.46}{0.28 + 0.3} \times \dfrac{2.27}{2.56} - \dfrac{1}{(1.28)^5} \times \dfrac{\$900 \times 0.3 \times 0.46}{0.28 + 0.3}$

$$= \$3\,285 - \$62 = \qquad\qquad \$\,3\,223$$

$\$6\,860 \times 0.78125$	\$5 359	
$\$4\,860 \times 1.45975^*$	7 094	
$\$5\,760 \times 0.29104$	1 676	14 129
PV at 28%		\$17 352

$IRR = 0.28 + \dfrac{148}{335} = 28.4\%$

*$2.2410 - 0.78125 = 1.45975$

(b) Net-present value method

$Q^1 = \dfrac{\$15\,500 \times 0.3 \times 0.46}{0.15 + 0.3} \times \dfrac{2.15}{2.30} - \dfrac{1}{(1.15)^5} \times \dfrac{\$900 \times 0.3 \times 0.46}{0.15 + 0.3}$

$$= \$4\,443 - \$137 = \qquad\qquad \$\,4\,306$$

$\$6\,860 \times 0.86957$	\$5 965	
$\$4\,860 \times 1.9854$	9 649	
$\$5\,760 \times 0.49718$	2 864	\$18 478
PV at 15%		\$22 784

$NPV = \$22\,784 - \$17\,500 = \$5\,284$

*$2.8550 - 0.8696 = 1.9854$

(c) Profitability index = $\$22\,784/\$17\,500 = 1.302{:}1$

5. A company is considering the purchase of a machine for \$50 000. It will be depreciated using the declining balance method at 30 percent and will be sold at the end of its 5 year useful life at its book value. The machine will generate annual cash savings of \$25 000 before taxes of 50 percent. Calculate the internal rate of return by: (a) using Eq. (13-9) (b) calculating depreciation directly without using the equation. (The company has many similar machines.)

(a)

Year	(1) Purchase	(2) Cash savings	(2) × 0.50 = (3) Tax	(4) Salvage	(1) + (2) + (4) − (3) = (5) Cash flow
0	(\$50 000)				(\$50 000)
1		\$25 000	\$12 500		12 500
2		25 000	12 500		12 500
3		25 000	12 500		12 500
4		25 000	12 500		12 500
5		25 000	12 500	\$10 204	22 704

Try 24%: $Q' = \dfrac{\$50\,000 \times 0.3 \times 0.5}{0.24 + 0.3} \times \dfrac{2.24}{2.26} - \dfrac{1}{(1.24)^5} \times \dfrac{\$10\,204 \times 0.3 \times 0.5}{0.24 + 0.3}$

$= \$12\,545 - \$967 =$ $\$11\,578$

$\$12\,500 \times 2.4043$ $\$30\,054$

$\$22\,704 \times 0.34111$ $\$\,7\,745$ $37\,799$

PV at 24% $\$49\,377$

Try 23%: $Q' = \dfrac{\$50\,000 \times 0.3 \times 0.5}{0.23 + 0.3} \times \dfrac{2.23}{2.46} - \dfrac{1}{(1.23)^5} \times \dfrac{\$10\,204 \times 0.3 \times 0.5}{0.23 + 0.3}$

$= \$12\,828 - \$1\,026 =$ $\$11\,802$

$\$12\,500 \times 2.4483$ $\$30\,604$

$\$22\,704 \times 0.35520$ $8\,064$ $38\,668$

PV at 23% $\$50\,470$

$IRR = 0.23 + \dfrac{470}{1093} = 23.4\%$

(b)

Year	(1) Purchase	(2) Cash savings	(3) Depreciation	(2) − (3) × 0.50 = (4) Tax	(6) Salvage	(1) + (2) − (4) + (6) = (7) Cash flow
0	($50 000)					($50 000)
1		$25 000	$ 7 500	$ 8 750		16 250
2		25 000	12 750	6 125		18 875
3		25 000	8 925	8 037		16 963
4		25 000	6 248	9 376		15 624
5		25 000	4 373	10 313	$10 204	24 891

Try 24%: $16 250 × 0.80645 = $13 105   Try 23%: $16 250 × 0.81301 = $13 211

18 875 × 0.65036 = 12 276   18 875 × 0.66088 = 12 476

16 963 × 0.52449 = 8 897   16 963 × 0.53738 = 9 116

15 624 × 0.42297 = 6 608   15 624 × 0.43690 = 6 826

24 891 × 0.34111 = 8 491   24 891 × 0.35520 = 8 841

PV at 24% $49 377   PV at 23% $50 470

$IRR = 0.23 + \dfrac{470}{1\,093} = 23.4\%$

we always show 23% 05.23

Note that the present values and the IRR are the same as those calculated in part (a). This is because the machine is sold for its book value.

6. Recalculate problem 5 assuming 8% inflation.

Year	(1) Purchase	(2) Cash savings	(3) Depreciation	(2) − (3) × 0.05 = (4) Tax	(6) Salvage	(1) + (2) − (4) + (6) = (7) Cash flow
0	($50 000)					
1		$27 000	$ 7 500	$ 9 750		$17 250
2		29 160	12 750	8 205		20 955
3		31 493	8 925	11 284		20 209
4		34 012	6 248	13 882		20 130
5		36 733	4 373	16 180	$10 204	30 757

Reduce cash flows to real dollars. Discount at 8%.

$17\ 250 \times 0.92593 = \$15\ 972$
$20\ 955 \times 0.85734 = 17\ 966$
$20\ 209 \times 0.79383 = 16\ 043$
$20\ 130 \times 0.73503 = 14\ 796$
$30\ 757 \times 0.68058 = 20\ 933$

Try 20%: $\$15\ 972 \times 0.83333 = \$13\ 310$
$\quad\quad\quad 17\ 966 \times 0.69444 = 12\ 476$
$\quad\quad\quad 16\ 043 \times 0.57870 = 9\ 284$
$\quad\quad\quad 14\ 796 \times 0.48225 = 7\ 135$
$\quad\quad\quad 20\ 933 \times 0.40188 = \underline{8\ 413}$
$\quad\quad\quad\quad$ PV at 20% $\$50\ 618$

Try 21%: $\$15\ 972 \times 0\ 82645 = \$13\ 200$
$\quad\quad\quad 17\ 966 \times 0.68301 = 12\ 271$
$\quad\quad\quad 16\ 043 \times 0.56447 = 9\ 056$
$\quad\quad\quad 14\ 796 \times 0.46651 = 6\ 902$
$\quad\quad\quad 20\ 933 \times 0.38554 = \underline{8\ 071}$
$\quad\quad\quad\quad$ PV at 21% $\$49\ 500$

$IRR = 0.20\ \dfrac{618}{1\ 118} = 20.6\%$

Problems

1. Lobears, Company Ltd. has two investment proposals which have the following characteristics:

	Project A			Project B		
Period	Cost	Profit after Taxes	Net cash flow	Cost	Profit after taxes	Net cash flow
0	$9 000	—	—	$12 000	—	—
1		$1 000	$5 000		$1 000	$5 000
2		1 000	4 000		1 000	5 000
3		1 000	3 000		4 000	8 000

For each project, compute its average rate of return, its payback period, and its net present value, using a discount rate of 15 percent.

2. In problem 1, what criticisms may be offered against the average rate of return as a capital budgeting method? What criticisms may be offered against the payback method?

3. The following are exercises on internal rates of return:
   (a) An investment of $1 000 today will return $2 000 at the end of 10 years. What is its IRR?
   (b) An investment of $1 000 will return $500 at the end of each of the next 3 years. What is its IRR?
   (c) An investment of $1 000 today will return $1 000 at the end of one year, $500 at the end of 2 years, and $100 at the end of 3 years. What is its IRR?
   (d) An investment of $1 000 will return $130 per year forever. What is its IRR?

4. Two mutually exclusive projects have projected cash flows as follows:

Period	0	1	2	3	4
A	−$2 000	$1 000	$1 000	$1 000	$1 000
B	− 2 000	0	0	0	6 000

   (a) Determine the internal rate for each project.
   (b) Determine the net present value for each project at discount rates of 0, 5, 10, 20, 30, and 35 percent.
   (c) Plot a graph of the net present value of each project at the different discount rates.
   (d) Which project would you select? Why? What assumptions are inherent in your decision?

5. The Homes Corporation Ltd. is faced with two mutually exclusive investment proposals. One would cost $100 000 and provide *net cash flows* of $30 000 per year for five years. The other would cost $50 000 and provide *net cash flows* of $16 000 for five years. Homes has a 10 percent after-tax opportunity cost of funds. Compute the net-present value and profitability index of each project. Which should be accepted?

6. Rework Problem 5, assuming a 17 percent opportunity cost of funds. How would this change your answer?

7. The L. C. Scott Company Ltd. is considering the purchase of a Class 22 machine to replace an existing machine that has a book value of $3 000 and can be sold for $1 500. The salvage value of the old machine in four years is expected to be zero, and it is depreciated at a 50 percent rate using double-declining balance. The proposed machine will perform the same function the old machine is performing; however, improvements in technology will enable the firm to reap cash benefits (before depreciation and taxes) of $7 000 *per year* in materials, labor, and overhead. The new machine has a four-year life, costs $14 000, and can be sold for an expected $2 000 at the end of the fourth year. The appropriate rate of depreciation for the new machine is 50 percent. Assuming a 40 percent tax rate and cost of capital of 16 percent, find the NPV, the IRR, and the profitability index.

8. An existing machine, which cost $4 500 when new, has a book value of $2 100; it can be operated for seven years after which it is expected to have a zero terminal value. A new machine with an expected life of seven years can be purchased to replace the existing machine for $12 500. The new machine is expected to have a salvage value of $2 000 and is expected to provide cash savings (before depreciation and taxes) of $2 300 per year. The firm acquiring the asset is located in New Brunswick and is entitled to an investment tax credit of 20 percent. The new machine qualifies for a CCA rate of 30 percent, the tax rate is 40 percent, and the cost of capital is 16 percent. The existing machine can be sold for $2 600.

(a) Compute the payback period.

(b) Compute the net-present value and profitability index.

(c) Compute the internal rate of return.

(d) Would you replace the machine?

(e) Answer (a)-(d) above assuming the old machine could not be sold and would be discarded.

9. Speedy Dating Ltd. is considering buying a small business computer costing $70 000. The presence of this machine is expected to save the wages of one full-time clerical worker and one part-time worker, an annual savings of $20 000. The computer has a useful life of seven years, will be depreciated on a 30 percent double-declining balance basis, and requires an additional $5 000 of working capital investment. Training of an operator for the computer would require an expenditure of $5 000. The company's marginal tax rate is 40 percent and the after-tax required rate of return on the project is 13 percent. Salvage value at the end of year 7 is expected to be $10 000. Should the company acquire the machine?

10. The Collingwood Ski Resort is considering a half dozen capital improvement projects. It has allocated $1 million for capital budgeting purposes. The following proposals and associated profitability indexes have been determined. The projects themselves are independent of one another.

Project	Amount	Profitability index
1. Extend ski lift 3	$500 000	1.23
2. Build a new sports shop	150 000	0.95
3. Extend ski lift 4	350 000	1.21
4. Build a new restaurant	450 000	1.18
5. Build addition to housing complex	200 000	1.21
6. Build an indoor skating rink	400 000	1.05

(a) With strict capital rationing, which of the above investments should be undertaken?

(b) Is this an optimal strategy?

11. The Ottawa River Perfect Cooker Company Ltd. is evaluating three investment situations. These are: (1) produce a new line of aluminum skillets; (2) expand its existing cooker line to include several new sizes; and (3) develop a new higher quality line of cookers. The amounts of investment required and the expected present values, if only the project in question is undertaken, are

Project	Investment required	Present value of future cash flows
1	$200 000	$290 000
2	115 000	185 000
3	270 000	400 000

If projects 1 and 2 are jointly undertaken, there will be no economies; the investment required and present values will simply be the sum of the parts. With projects 1 and 3, economies are possible in investment because one of the machines acquired can be used in both production processes. The total investment required for project 1 and 3 combined is $440 000. If projects

2 and 3 are undertaken, there are economies to be achieved in marketing and producing the products but not in investment. The expected present value of future cash flows for projects 2 and 3 is $620 000. If all three projects are undertaken simultaneously, the economies noted above will still hold. However, a $125 000 extension on the plant will be necessary, as space is not available for all three projects. Which project or projects should be chosen?

12. The City of Oshawa must replace a number of its concrete mixer trucks with new trucks. It has received several bids and has evaluated closely the performance characteristics of the various trucks. The Patterbilt truck costs $74 000 but it is "top-of-the-line" equipment. The truck has a life of eight years, assuming that the engine is rebuilt in the fifth year. Maintenance costs of $2 000 a year are expected in the first four years, followed by total maintenance and rebuilding costs of $13 000 in the fifth year. During the last three years, maintenance costs are expected to be $4 000 a year. At the end of eight years, the truck will have an estimated scrap value of $9 000.

A bid from Bulldog Trucks, Inc. Ltd. is for $59 000 a truck. However, maintenance costs for this truck will be higher. In the first year, they are expected to be $3 000 and this amount is expected to increase by $1 500 a year through the eighth year. In year 4, the engine will need to be rebuilt and this will cost the company $15 000 in addition to maintenance costs in that year. At the end of eight years, the Bulldog Truck will have an estimated scrap value of $5 000.

The last bidder, Best Tractor and Trailer Company Ltd. has agreed to sell trucks at $44 000 a piece. Maintenance costs in the first four years are expected to be $4 000 the first year and to increase by $1 000 a year. For the City of Oshawa's purposes, the truck has a life of only 4 years. At that time, it can be traded in for a new Best Truck which is expected to cost $52 000. The likely trade-in value of the old truck is $15 000. During years 5 through 8, the second truck is expected to have maintenance costs of $5 000 in year 5 and these are expected to increase by $1 000 each year. At the end of 8 years, the second truck is expected to have a resale or salvage value of $18 000.

(a) If the cost of funds is 8 percent, which bid should be accepted? (The city pays no tax).
(b) If the opportunity cost of funds were 15 percent, would your answer change?

Appendix B Problem

13. Rioka Corporation Ltd. is considering investing in a project which costs $100 000 and has a useful life of five years. The expected before-tax cash flows from the project are:

		Year		
1	2	3	4	5
$20 000	$40 000	$40 000	$30 000	$20 000

The company's tax rate is 50 percent and its cost of capital based on present conditions in the financial markets is 12 percent. The company is entitled to a 20 percent CCA rate on a double declining balance basis and the asset has a zero salvage value.

(a) Compute the net present value of the project without the consideration of inflation.
(b) If inflation of 9 percent per annum is expected over the life of the project and cash flows are adjusted upward, what is the project's present value?

Selected References

BACON, PETER W. "The Evaluation of Mutually Exclusive Investments," *Financial Management*, 6 (Summer 1977), 55-58.

BIERMAN, HAROLD JR. and SEYMOUR SMIDT, *The Capital Budgeting Decision*, 3rd ed. New York: Macmillan, 1971.

BIGER, NAHUM, "Inflation, Capital Cost Allowance and the Value of Tax Shields", *Cost and Management*, March-April 1982, 26-29.

BLUM, JAMES D. and LEROY D. BROOKS, "Capital Budgeting under Conditions of Unused Capacity," *Cost and Management* (May-June 1976), 28-32.

CARTER, E. EUGENE, "Designing the Capital Budgeting Process," *TIMS Studies in the Management Sciences*, 5 (1977), 25-42.

GAGNON, JEAN-MARIE, "A Note on Tax Depreciation," *Journal of Business Administration*, 7 (Spring 1976), 117-24.

GITMAN, LAWRENCE J. and JOHN R. FORRESTER JR. "Forecasting and Evaluation Practices and Performance: A Survey of Capital Budgeting," *Financial Management*, 6 (Fall 1977), 66-71.

GORDON, LAWRENCE A. and DAVID G. HALTRECHT, "The Relationship between the Payback Reciprocal and the IRR," *Cost and Management* (Nov.-Dec. 1976), 38-41.

HALEY, CHARLES W. and LAWRENCE D. SCHALL, "A Note on Investment Policy with Imperfect Capital Markets," *Journal of Finance*, 27 (Mar. 1972), 93-96.

HERBST, ANTHONY, "The Unique, Real Internal Rate of Return: Caveat Emptor!" *Journal of Financial and Quantitative Analysis*, 13 (June 1978), 363-70.

HONG, HAI, "Inflation and the Market Value of the Firm: Theory and Tests," *Journal of Finance*, 32 (Sept. 1977), 1031-48.

HOSKINS, C. G. and M. JAMES DUNN, "The Economic Evaluation of Capital Expenditure Proposals under Uncertainty: The Practice of Large Corporations in Canada," *Journal of Business Administration*, 6 (Fall 1974), 45-55.

HOSKINS, COLIN G. and GLEN A. MUMEY, "Payback: A Maligned Method of Asset Ranking?" *Engineering Economist*, 25 (Fall 1979), 53-65.

JONES, THOMAS W. and J. DAVID SMITH, "Improved Methods of Calculating NPV for Cash Flows Varying by a Constant Amount", *Cost and Management* (Sept.-Oct. 1981), 46-47.

KEANE, SIMON M., "The Internal Rate of Return and the Reinvestment Fallacy," *Journal of Accounting and Business Studies*, 15 (June 1979), 48-55.

KIM, SUK, H., and EDWARD J. FARRAGHER, "Current Capital Budgeting Practices," *Management Accounting*, 28 (June 1981), 26-30.

KWAN, O. YUL, "An Estimate of Asset's Uselife and Economic Depreciation Rate, by Canadian CCA Classes," *Cost and Management* (Sept.-Oct. 1978), 36-38.

LALL NIGAM, B.M., "Enhancing the ROI Credibility: Some Theoretical Underpinnings", *Cost and Management* (July-Aug. 1981), 40-43.

LORIE, JAMES H. and LEONARD J. SAVAGE, "Three Problems in Rationing Capital," *Journal of Business*, 28 (Oct. 1955), 227-39.

MAO, JAMES C. T. "A New Graphical Analysis of Fisher's Rate of Return," *Cost and Management* (Nov.-Dec. 1970), 24-27.

NELSON, CHARLES R., "Inflation and Capital Budgeting," *Journal of Finance*, 31 (June 1976), 923-31.

PETTY, J. WILLIAM, and OSWALD D. BOWLIN, "The Financial Manager and Quantitative Decision Models," *Financial Management*, 4 (Winter 1976), 32-41.

PETTY, J. WILLIAM, DAVID F. SCOTT, JR., and MONROE M. BIRD, "The Capital Expenditure Decision-Making Process of Large Corporations," *Engineering Economist*, 20 (Spring 1975), 159-72.

PUGLISI, D. J. and L. W. CHADWICK, "Capital Budgeting with Realized Terminal Values," *Cost and Management* (May-June 1977), 13-17.

QUIRIN, G. DAVID, and JOHN C. WIGINTON, *Analyzing Capital Expenditures* Homewood, Ill.: Irwin, 1981.

RAPPAPORT, ALFRED, and ROBERT A. TAGGART, JR., "Evaluation of Capital Expenditure Proposals under Inflation," *Financial Management*, 11 (Spring 1982), 5-13.

ROSENBLATT, MEIR J., "A Survey and Analysis of Capital Budgeting Decision Process in Multi-division Firms," *Engineering Economist*, 25 (Summer 1980), 259-73.

SCHALL, LAWRENCE D., GARY L. SUNDEM, and WILLIAM R. GEIJSBEEK, JR., "Survey and Analysis of Capital Budgeting Methods," *Journal of Finance*, 33 (March 1978), 281-87.

SCHNELL, JAMES S., and ROY S. NICOLOSI, "Capital Expenditure Feedback: Project Reappraisal," *Engineering Economist*, 19 (Summer 1974), 253-61.

SCHWAB, BERNHARD, and PETER LUSZTIG, "A Comparative Analysis of the Net-Present Value and the Benefit-Cost Ratios as Measures of the Economic Desirability of Investment," *Journal of Finance*, 24 (June 1969), 507-16.

TATOM, JOHN A., and JAMES E. TURLEY, "Inflation and Taxes: Disincentives for Capital Formation," *Review of the Federal Reserve Bank of St. Louis*, 60 (January 1978), 2-8.

VAN HORNE, JAMES C., "A Note on Biases in Capital Budgeting Introduced by Inflation," *Journal of Financial and Quantitative Analysis*, 6 (January 1971), 653-58.

_____, "The Variation of Project Life as a Means for Adjusting for Risk," *Engineering Economist*, 21 (Spring 1976), 151-58.

WALSHAM, GEOFF and DANIEL McDONALD, "The Effect of Taxation on DCF Investment Appraisal," *Cost and Management* (Jul.-Aug. 1975), 20-23.

WEAVER, JAMES B. "Organizing and Maintaining a Capital Expenditure Program," *Engineering Economist*, 20 (Fall 1974), 1-36.

WEINGARTNER, H. MARTIN, "Capital Rationing: *n* Authors in Search of a Plot," *Journal of Finance*, 32 (December 1977), 1403-31.

WELCH, ROBERT. "The Effect on Capital Budgeting Decisions of Recent Changes in the CCA Calculation, "*Cost and Management* (May-June 1982), 52-53.

14

Risk and Capital Budgeting

In the preceding chapter we assumed that the acceptance of any investment proposal under consideration did not change the business-risk complexion of the firm as perceived by suppliers of capital. This assumption allowed us to hold risk constant and to base our analysis of an investment project on its expected future cash flows. When we relax this assumption, we must allow for the possibility of investment projects having different degrees of risk. Because suppliers of capital to the firm (investors and creditors) tend to be risk-averse, the acceptance of a project that changes the risk complexion of the firm may cause them to change their required rates of return for investing or extending credit.

When we allow for changes in risk, then, we must take into account possible changes in the firm's value. The project that is expected to provide a high return may be so risky that it causes a significant increase in the perceived risk of the firm. In turn, this may cause a decrease in the firm's value, despite the project's considerable potential.

In this chapter we consider various ways by which management can gauge the risk of a project or a group of projects. Our ultimate objective is to come to an understanding of how risk affects value. First, we must measure project risk under a variety of circumstances, and that is the purpose of this chapter. In this regard, certain elementary probability concepts will be employed in the treatment of risk.

Given information about the expected risk of an investment proposal or proposals, together with information about the expected return, management must then evaluate this information and reach a decision. As the decision to accept or reject an investment proposal depends on the risk-adjusted return required by suppliers of capital, we defer consideration of the evaluation of risky investments until we consider required rates of return in the next chapter. In this chapter we develop the information necessary to evaluate risk investments. In Chapter 15 we examine the use of this information in reaching capital-budgeting decisions consistent with an objective of maximizing shareholder wealth. We begin this chapter with a discussion of the overall operating risk of the firm. We then move on to a general introduction to project risk, followed by the consideration of its specific measurement.

Operating Leverage and Risk

The overall business risk of a firm is related to its operating leverage. Operating leverage is simply the employment of an asset for which the firm pays a fixed cost. Expressed differently, operating leverage occurs any time a firm has fixed costs that must be met, regardless of volume. In the very long run, of course, all costs are variable. Consequently, our analysis necessarily involves the short run. We employ assets with a fixed cost in the hope that volume will produce revenues more than sufficient to cover all fixed and variable costs. One of the more dramatic examples of operating leverage is in the airline industry, where a large portion of total costs are fixed. Beyond a certain break-even load factor, each additional passenger represents essentially straight profit to the airline.

The essential thing is that fixed costs do not vary as volume changes. These costs include things such as depreciation of buildings and equipment, insurance, property taxes, part of the overall utility bills, and a portion of the cost of management. On the other hand, variable costs vary directly with the level of output. These costs include raw materials, direct labor costs, part of the overall utility bills, direct selling commissions, and certain parts of general and administrative expenses. With fixed costs, the percentage change in profits accompanying a change in volume is greater than the percentage change in volume. This phenomenon is known as operating leverage.

We should recognize that operating leverage is but one component of the overall business risk of the firm. The principal factors giving rise to business risk are variability or uncertainty of sales, and production costs. Operating leverage magnifies the impact of these factors on the variability of profits; however, operating leverage is not the source of the variability per se. Consequently, the degree of operating leverage of a firm should not be taken to represent its business risk. Because of the underlying variability of sales and costs, however, increases in operating leverage will increase the total variability of profits and, hence, magnify the company's business risk.

ANALYZING OPERATING LEVERAGE

Our firm produces a quality testing machine that sells for $50 a unit. We have annual fixed costs of $100 000, and variable costs of $25 a unit, regardless of the volume sold. We wish to study the relationship between total costs and total revenues. One way to do that is shown in the break-even chart in Fig. 14-1, which depicts the relationship between profits, fixed costs, variable costs, and volume. By profits, we mean operating profits before taxes. This definition purposely excludes interest on debt and preferred-stock dividends. These costs are not part of the total fixed costs of the firm when it comes to analyzing operating leverage. They are taken into account when we analyze financial leverage in the next part.

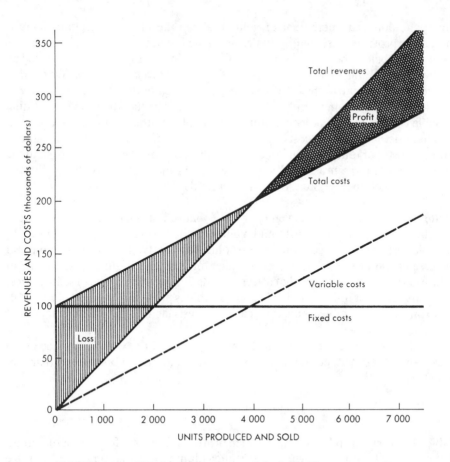

FIGURE 14-1 Break-even analysis: original conditions

The intersection of the total costs line with the total revenue line represents the break-even point. The fixed costs that must be recovered from the sales dollar after the deduction of variable costs determine the volume necessary to break even. In Fig. 14-1 this break-even point is 4 000 units of output. At the break-even point, variable costs plus fixed costs equal total revenue

$$F + V(X) = P(X) \qquad \textbf{(14-1)}$$

where F = fixed costs
V = variable costs per unit
X = volume of output (in units)
P = price per unit.
Rearranging Eq.(14-1), the break-even point is

$$X = F/(P - V)$$

$$= 100\ 000/(50 - 25) = 4\ 000$$

For each additional increment of volume above the break-even point, there is increasing profit represented by the crosshatched area in the figure. Likewise, as volume falls below the break-even point, there are increasing losses, represented by the lined area. Table 14-1 shows the profit for various levels of volume. We see that the closer the volume to the break-even point, the greater the percentage change in profit in relation to a percentage change in volume. The fact that fixed costs equal variable costs at the break-even point is attributable to the nature of the example. Because price less variable costs equals $50 – $25 = $25, this amount is the same as variable costs per unit. As total price less variable costs must equal fixed costs at the break-even point, so must total variable costs. As the example is changed in the subsequent section, this situation no longer holds.

Change in factors   A break-even chart, like that in Fig. 14-1 tells us the relationship between operating profits and volume. The greater the ratio of price to variable costs per unit, the greater the absolute sensitivity of profits to volume and the greater the degree of operating leverage for all levels of output. A change in volume is not the only factor that affects profits, however; a change in selling price, in variable cost per unit, or in fixed costs also affects profits. In the light of Fig. 14-1, we examine a favorable change in each of these factors, all other factors held constant.

An increase in price lowers the break-even point. For example, an increase in price from $50 to $65 per unit would result in the following break-even point (in units)

$$X = 100\ 000/(65 - 25) = 2\ 500$$

Table 14-2 shows the relationship between profits and volume for 5 levels of output. The original situation is shown in the second column; the situation with a $65 price is in the third column. Profits, of course, are $15 per unit greater for each level of volume.

A decrease in fixed costs also lowers the break-even point; indeed, that is the whole idea behind operating leverage. If fixed costs were lowered from $100 000 to $50 000, the break-even point would be

$$X = 50\ 000/(50 - 25) = 2\ 000$$

with this change, profits for various levels of volume are shown in the fourth column of Table 14-2.

TABLE 14-1   Relation Between Profit and Volume—Original Case

Volume (in thousand units)	0	1	2	3	4	5	6	7
Operating profit (in thousand dollars)	–$100	–$75	–$50	–$25	0	$25	$50	$75

TABLE 14-2 Relation Between Profits and Volume—
Changing Assumptions

Volume (in units)	Profits (in thousands)				
	Original case	Price ($65)	Fixed costs ($50 000)	Variable costs ($20)	All three
0	−$100	−$100	−$ 50	−$100	−$ 50
2 000	− 50	− 20	0	− 40	40
4 000	0	60	50	20	130
6 000	50	140	100	80	220
8 000	100	220	150	140	310

Finally, a decrease in variable costs again lowers the break-even point. If the change were from $25 to $20 per unit, the break-even point would be

$$X = 100\ 000/(50 - 20) = 3\ 333$$

Profits are $5 per unit greater, and the relationship of profits with volume is shown in column 5 of Table 14-2.

The last column of the table shows the relationship between profits and volume if all three of the above changes occur simultaneously. Although we have considered only a favorable change in each case, it should be clear that a decrease in price, an increase in fixed costs, and an increase in variable costs will result in a higher break-even point, the greater the percentage change in profit for a percentage change in volume.

Thus, operating leverage magnifies the overall risk of the firm. It is not the underlying cause of risk, for that depends on the variability of demand for the product plus the variability of various costs. However, increases in operating leverage increase the variability of profits that accompany the underlying fluctuations mentioned above. With this in mind, we turn now to the measurement of risk for investment projects.

The Problem of Project Risk

We define the riskiness of an investment project as the variability of its cash flows from those that are expected. The greater the variability, the riskier the project is said to be. For each project under consideration, we can make estimates of the future cash flows. Rather than estimate only the most likely cash-flow outcome for each year in the future as we did in Chapter 4, we estimate a number of possible outcomes. In this way we are able to consider the range of possible cash flows for a particular future period rather than just the most likely cash flow.

AN ILLUSTRATION

To illustrate the formulation of multiple cash-flow forecasts for a future period, suppose we had two investment proposals under consideration. Suppose further that we were interested in making forecasts for the following states of the economy: normal, deep recession, mild recession, major boom, and minor boom. After assessing the future under each of these possible states, we estimate the following cash flows for the next year:

	Annual cash flows	
State	Proposal A	Proposal B
Deep recession	$3 000	$2 000
Mild recession	3 500	3 000
Normal	4 000	4 000
Minor boom	4 500	5 000
Major boom	5 000	6 000

We see that the dispersion of possible cash flows for proposal B is greater than that for proposal A; therefore, we could say that it was riskier. In order to quantify our analysis of risk, however, we need additional information. More specifically, we need to know the likelihood of the various states of the economy occurring. Suppose our estimate of the odds for a deep recession is 10 percent, of a mild recession 20 percent, of a normal economy 40 percent, of a minor economic boom 20 percent, and of a major economic boom 10 percent. Given this information, we now are able to formulate a probability distribution of possible cash flows for proposals A and B

Proposal A		Proposal B	
Probability	Cash flow	Probability	Cash flow
0.10	$3 000	0.10	$2 000
0.20	3 500	0.20	3 000
0.40	4 000	0.40	4 000
0.20	4 500	0.20	5 000
0.10	5 000	0.10	6 000

We can graph these probability distributions, and the results are shown in Fig. 14-2. As we see, the dispersion of cash flows is greater for proposal B than it is for proposal A, despite the fact that the most likely outcome is the same for both investment proposals: $4 000. According to the discussion in Chapter 13, the firm would rank the proposals equally. The critical question is whether dispersion should be considered. If risk is associated with the probability distribution of possible cash flows, such that the greater the dispersion the greater the risk, proposal B would be the riskier investment. If management, stockholders, and creditors are averse to risk, proposal A then would be preferred to proposal B.

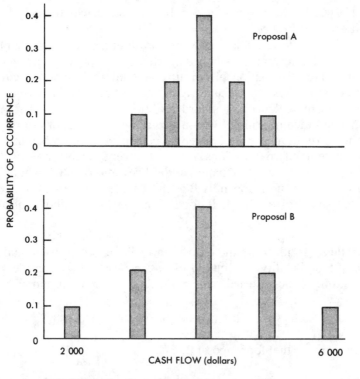

FIGURE 14-2 Comparison of two proposals

MEASUREMENT OF DISPERSION

Rather than always having to resort to graph paper, we need a measure of the dispersion of a probability distribution. The tighter the distribution, the lower this measure should be; the wider the distribution, the greater it should be. The conventional measure of dispersion is the *standard deviation*, which will be presented first mathematically and then illustrated with the previous example. The *standard deviation* can be expressed mathematically as

$$\sigma = \sqrt{\sum_{x=1}^{n} (A_x - \overline{A})^2 P_x} \qquad \text{(14-2)}$$

where A_x is the cash flow for the xth possibility, P_x is the probability of occurrence of that cash flow, and $\overline{A}$ is the expected value of cash flows, to be defined in Eq. (14-3). The greek sigma, Σ, means the sum of the bracketed amounts from possibility 1 through possibility n. In other words, n is the total number of possibilities—five in our example. the square-root sign, $\sqrt{}$, indicates that we take the square root of the calculated amount. While all of this seems rather formidable, in fact the standard deviation can be computed rather easily with the aid of a calculator. the expected value, $\overline{A}$, of a probability distribution is defined as

$$\overline{A} = \sum_{x=1}^{n} A_x P_x \qquad \text{(14-3)}$$

It is simply a weighted average of the possible cash flows, with the weights being the probabilities of occurrence.

The standard deviation is simply a measure of the tightness of a probability distribution. For a normal, bell-shaped distribution, approximately 68 percent of the total area of the distribution falls within one standard deviation on either side of the expected value. This means that there is only a 32 percent chance that the actual outcome will be more than one standard deviation from the mean. The probability that the actual outcome will fall within two standard deviations of the expected value of the distribution is approximately 95 percent, and the probability that it will fall within three standard deviations is over 99 percent. A table showing the area of a normal distribution that is so many standard deviations to the right or left of the expected value is given in Appendix B to this chapter. As we shall see later in the chapter, the standard deviation is used to assess the likelihood of an event's occurring.

An illustration   To illustrate the derivation of the expected value and standard deviation of a probability distribution of possible cash flows, consider again our previous example. The expected value of the distribution for proposal A is

$$\overline{A}_b = 0.10(2\ 000) + 0.20(3\ 000) + 0.40(4\ 000) + 0.20(5\ 000) + 0.10(6\ 000) = 4\ 000$$

which is the same as that for proposal B.

However, the standard deviation for proposal A is

$$\sigma_a = [0.10(3\ 000 - 4\ 000)^2 + 0.20(3\ 500 - 4\ 000)^2 + 0.40(4\ 000 - 4\ 000)^2$$
$$+ 0.20(4\ 500 - 4\ 000)^2 + 0.10(5\ 000 - 4\ 000)^2]^{1/2} = [300\ 000]^{1/2} = 548$$

where $[\ ]^{1/2}$ is simply the square root, the same as $\sqrt{\ }$. Note also that when we square a minus number, such as $(3\ 000 - 4\ 000)^2$, it becomes positive. The standard deviation for proposal B is

$$\sigma_b = [0.10(2\ 000 - 4\ 000)^2 + 0.20(3\ 000 - 4\ 000)^2 + 0.40(4\ 000 - 4\ 000)^2$$
$$+ 0.20(5\ 000 - 4\ 000)^2 + 0.10(6\ 000 - 4\ 000)^2]^{1/2} = [1\ 200\ 000]^{1/2} = 1\ 095$$

Thus, proposal B has a higher standard deviation, indicating a greater dispersion of possible outcomes, and so we would say it had greater risk.

Coefficient of variation   A measure of relative dispersion is the coefficient of variation, which simply is the standard deviation of a probability distribution over its expected value. For proposal A, the coefficient of variation is

$$CV_a = 548/4\ 000 = 0.14$$

while that for proposal B is

$$CV_b = 1\ 095/4\ 000 = 0.27$$

Because the coefficient of variation for proposal B exceeds that for proposal A, we would say that it had a greater degree of risk. One might question the use of the coefficient of variation when in our example it was obvious that proposal B had greater risk owing to its larger standard deviation. In our example, however, the expected values of the probability distributions of possible cash flows for the two proposals were the same. What if they were different? Here we need a measure of relative dispersion, and the coefficient of variation is such a measure. Frequent reference to the expected value, standard deviation, and coefficient of variation will be made in the remainder of this chapter.[1]

Risk for the Individual Project

If investors and creditors are risk-averse—and all available evidence suggests that they are, it behooves management to incorporate the risk of an investment proposal into its analysis of the proposal's worth. Otherwise, capital-budgeting decisions are unlikely to be in accord with an objective of maximizing share price. Having established the need for taking risk into account, we proceed to measure it for individual investment proposals. But remember that the riskiness of a stream of cash flows for a project can, and usually does, change with the length of time in the future. In other words, the probability distributions are not necessarily the same from one period to the next.

This notion is illustrated in Fig. 14-3 for a hypothetical investment project. The distributions are like those shown in Fig. 14-2 except that they are continuous instead of being discrete bars. This means that a cash-flow outcome is assigned to each possible state of the economy, and a continuous line is drawn. As before, the tighter and more peaked the distribution, the less the risk. The expected value of each of the distributions is depicted by the horizontal dashed line. We see that both the expected value of cash flow and the dispersion of the probability distribution change over time. We must come to grips with this factor so that we can quantify the risk of a prospective investment proposal.

USE OF A PROBABILITY TREE

One way of approaching the problem is with a probability tree. Here we specify the likely future cash flows of a project as they relate to the outcomes in previous periods. If a project turns out to be good in the first period, it may well turn out to be good in subsequent periods. While there frequently is a link between what happens in one period and what happens in the next, this is not always the

---

[1]We assume that risk can be judged solely in relation to the expected value and standard deviation of a probability distribution. Implied is that the shape of the distribution is unimportant. This holds when the distribution is relatively symmetric or "bell-shaped." However, if it is significantly skewed to the right or left, management may wish to take account of this fact as well. Although it is possible to incorporate a skewness measure into our analysis of risk, it is difficult mathematically to do so. For simplicity, we shall deal with only the expected value and standard deviation of a normal probability distrbution.

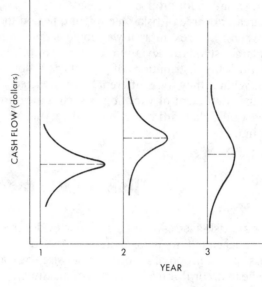

FIGURE 14-3 Illustration of changing risk over time

case. If cash flows are believed to be independent from period to period, we simply specify a probability distribution of cash-flow outcomes for each period. If there is a link, we should take this dependence into account.

With a probability tree we attempt to unfold future events as they might occur. Fig. 14-4 shows a probability tree for a three-period case. Here we see that if the outcome in period 1 is the upper branch, it results in a different set of possible outcomes in period 2 than if the lower branch occurred in period 1. The same thing applies to going from period 2 to period 3. Therefore, at time 0 the probability tree represents our best estimate of what is likely to occur in the future, contingent upon what occurs before. For each of the branches in the figure, a cash flow as well as a probability is attached.

For the first period, the cash-flow outcome does not depend on what happened before. Therefore, the probabilities associated with the two branches are said to be *initial probabilities*. For the second and third periods, however, cash-flow outcomes depend on what happened before. Therefore, the probabilities involved in these periods are said to be *conditional probabilities*. Finally, the *joint probability* is the probability that a particular sequence of cash flows might occur. For example, one sequence is the top branches in each of the three periods. The joint probability is the product of the initial probability and the two conditional probabilities for the top branches. Rather than continue to discuss probability trees in the abstract, let us proceed to an example.

AN ILLUSTRATION FOR A PROJECT

Suppose that we were considering the investment in a project costing $240 at time 0, that was expected to generate the possible cash flows shown in Table 14-3. Given a cash flow of –$100 in period 1, the probability is 0.40 that this negative flow

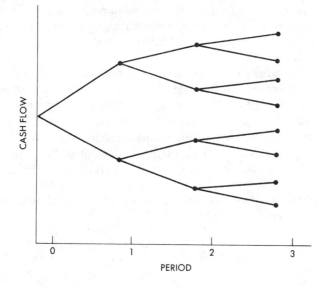

CASH FLOW

PERIOD

FIGURE 14-4 A probability tree

will become –$400 in period 2, 0.40 that it will remain at –$100, and 0.20 that it will be $200. The joint probability that a –$100 cash flow in period 1 will be followed by a –$400 cash flow in period 2 is simply the product of the initial probability and the conditional probability, or $0.25 \times 0.40 = 0.10$.

Similarly, the joint probability that a cash flow of –$100 in period 1 will be followed by a cash flow of –$100 in period 2 is $0.25 \times 0.40 = 0.10$, and the probability that a –$100 cash flow in period 1 will be followed by a $200 cash flow in period 2 is $0.25 \times 0.20 = 0.05$. If the cash flow in period 1 turns out to be $200, there is a 0.20 probability it will become –$100 in period 2; 0.60 it will remain at $200 in period 2, and 0.20 it will become $500. In the same manner as before, we can

TABLE 14-3 Illustration of a Probability Tree

Period 1		Period 2		
Initial probability P(1)	Net cash flow	Conditional probability P(2/1)	Net cash flow	Joint probability P(1,2)
0.25	–$100	0.40	–$400	0.10
		0.40	– 100	0.10
		0.20	200	0.05
0.50	200	0.20	– 100	0.10
		0.60	200	0.30
		0.20	500	0.10
0.25	500	0.20	200	0.05
		0.40	500	0.10
		0.40	800	0.10

Initial investment at time 0 = $240.

calculate the joint probabilities for this branch, and they are found to be 0.10, 0.30, and 0.10, respectively. Similarly, the joint probabilities for the last branch, where a $500 net cash flow in period 1 occurs, can be determined.

Discounting to present value   In discounting the various cash flows to their present value, one should employ the risk-free rate. This rate is used because we attempt to isolate the time value of money by discounting, and then we analyze risk separately. To include a premium for risk in the discount rate would result in double counting with respect to our evaluation. We would compensate for risk in the discounting process and then again in our analysis of the dispersion of the distribution of possible net present values. For this reason, we use the risk-free rate for discounting purposes.

For our example problem, the expected value of the probability distribution of possible net present values is

$$\overline{NPV} = -\$240 + \sum_{x=1}^{z} NPV_x P_x \tag{14-4}$$

where NPV_x is the net present value for series X of net cash flows, covering all periods, P_x is the probability of occurrence of that series, and z is the total number of cash-flow series. For our example, there are 9 possible series of net cash-flows, so $z = 9$. The first series is represented by a cash flow of $-\$100$ in period 1, followed by a $-\$400$ cash flow in period 2. The probability of occurrence of that cash flow is 0.1. If the risk-free rate used as the discount rate is 8 percent, the net present value of this series is

$$NPV_1 = -\$240 - \frac{100}{(1.08)} - \frac{400}{(1.08)^2} = -\$676$$

The second cash-flow series is represented by a cash flow of $-\$100$ in period 1, followed by a $-\$100$ cash flow in period 2. The net present value of this series is

$$NPV_2 = -\$240 - \frac{100}{(1.08)} - \frac{100}{(1.08)^2} = -\$418$$

In the same manner, the net present values for the seven other cash-flow series can be determined. When these values are multiplied by their respective probabilities of occurrence (the last column in Table 14-3) and summed, we obtain the expected value of net present value of the probability distribution of possible net present values (rounded to the nearest dollar). The calculations are shown in Table 14-4, and we see that the expected value of net present value is $116.

The standard deviation of the probability distribution of possible net present values can be determined by

$$\sigma = \sqrt{\sum_{x=1}^{z} (NPV_x - \overline{NPV})^2 P_x} \tag{14-5}$$

where the symbols are the same as for Eq. (14-4). The standard deviation for our example problem is

TABLE 14-4 Calculation of Expected Value of Net Present Value for Example Problem

(1) Cash- flow series	(2) Net present value	(3) Probability of occurrence	(4) (2) × (3)
1	-$676	0.10	-$ 68
2	- 418	0.10	- 42
3	- 161	0.05	- 8
4	- 141	0.10	- 14
5	117	0.30	35
6	374	0.10	37
7	394	0.05	20
8	652	0.10	65
9	909	0.10	91
	Weighted average		$116

$$\sigma = [0.10(- 676 - 116)^2 + 0.10(- 418 - 116)^2$$
$$+ 0.05(- 161 - 116)^2 + 0.10(- 141 - 116)^2$$
$$+ 0.30(117 - 116)^2 + 0.10(374 - 116)^2$$
$$+ 0.05(394 - 116)^2 + 0.10(652 - 116)^2$$
$$+ 0.10(909 - 116)^2]^{1/2} = [197\ 277]^{1/2} = \$444$$

Rounding to the nearest dollar, the project has an expected value of net present value of $116 and a standard deviation of $444. Although the mathematical calculation of the standard deviation is feasible for simple cases, it is not for complex situations. Here, one should resort to simulation to approximate the standard deviation. The technique is explained in Appendix A to this chapter, where the Hertz model for evaluating risky investments is considered.

USE OF INFORMATION

The expected value and the standard deviation of the probability distribution of possible net present values, whether derived by a probability tree or some other means, give us a considerable amount of information by which to evaluate the risk of the investment proposal. If the probability distribution is approximately normal, we are able to calculate the probability of the proposal's providing a net present value of less or more than a specified amount. The probability is found by determining the area under the curve to the left or to the right of a particular point of interest. To go on with our previous illustration, suppose we wish to determine the probability that the net present value will be zero or less. To determine this probability, we first calculate the difference between 0 and the expected value of net present value for the project.

In our example, this difference is – $116. We then standardize this difference by dividing it by the standard deviation of possible net present values. The formula is

$$S = \frac{X - \overline{NPV}}{\sigma}$$ (14-6)

where X is the outcome in which we are interested. $\overline{NPV}$ is the expected value of net present value, and σ is the standard deviation of the probability distribution. In our case

$$S = \frac{0 - 116}{444} = -0.26$$

This figure tells us that a net present value of 0 lies 0.26 standard deviations to the left of the expected value of the probability distribution of possible net present values.

To determine the probability that the net present value of the project will be 0 or less, we consult a normal probability distribution table found in most statistics texts or in Appendix B at the end of this chapter. We find that for the normal distribution, there is a 0.4013 probability that an observation will be less than –0.25 standard deviations from the expected value of that distribution and a 0.3821 probability that it will be less than –0.30 standard deviations from the expected value. Interpolating, we find that there is approximately a 40 percent probability that the net present value of the proposal will be zero or less. We know also that there is a 60 percent probability that the net present value of the project will be greater than zero. With a normal distribution, 0.68 of the distribution falls within one standard deviation on either side of the expected value. We know then that there is approximately a two-thirds probability that the net present value of the proposal will be between $116 – $444 = –$328 and $116 + $444 = $560. By expressing differences from the expected value in terms of standard deviations, we are able to determine the probability that the net present value for an investment proposal will be greater or less than a particular amount.[2]

The information above tells us that the dispersion of possible outcomes for the project is rather wide. There is a 40 percent probability that the net present value will be zero or less and about a one-sixth probability that it will be –$328 or worse. (The latter is simply the area of a curve that is greater than one standard deviation to the left of the expected value.)

Knowledge of these probabilities is fundamental for a realistic assessment of risk. Suppose that the firm is considering another investment proposal, call it Y. The probability distribution for this proposal is shown in Fig. 14-5, as is that for our example problem, which we call proposal X. We see that the expected value of net present value for proposal Y is $200, which is higher than that for proposal X, $116. Moreover, there is less dispersion with proposal Y than there is with proposal X. Therefore, we would say that proposal Y dominates proposal X on the basis of both risk and return. Whether proposal Y or both projects should be accepted depends on the risk tolerances of management. We address ourselves to this question in the next chapter. In this chapter we want to learn how to measure risk.

---

[2]In the examples above we have assumed normal probability distributions. Although this property is very desirable for purposes of calculation, it is not necessary for use of the above approach. Even when the distribution is not normal, we usually are able to make relatively strong probability statements by using Chebyshev's inequality.

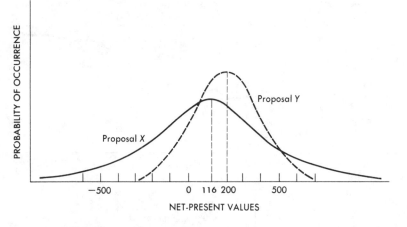

FIGURE 14-5 Probability distributions of net-present values for the two projects

Risk in a Portfolio Sense

In the last section we measured risk for a single investment proposal. When multiple investment projects are involved and we have a combined risk, the measurement procedure differs from that for a single project. The approach we take corresponds to the portfolio approach in security analysis. Portfolio theory was discussed in Chapter 5; here we apply the approach to capital-investment projects. The circumstances under which the approach is feasible are taken up in Chapter 15, where we will examine the acceptance criteria for risky investments. Our purpose here is only to show how to measure risk for combinations of risky investments, assuming that such a measure is desired.

If a firm adds a project whose future cash flows are likely to be highly correlated with those of existing assets, the total risk of the firm will increase more than if it adds a project that has a low degree of correlation with existing assets. The idea is that projects can be combined to reduce relative risk.

Fig. 14-6 shows the expected cash-flow patterns for two projects over time. Proposal A is cyclical, while proposal B is mildly countercyclical. By combining the two projects, we see that total cash-flow dispersion is reduced, and the dispersion of the return on investment is reduced even more. The combination of projects to reduce risk is known as diversification, and the principle is the same as diversification in securities. One attempts to reduce deviations in return from the expected value of return.

MEASUREMENT OF PORTFOLIO RISK

The standard deviation of the probability distribution of possible net present values is more difficult to calculate for a portfolio than for a single investment. It is

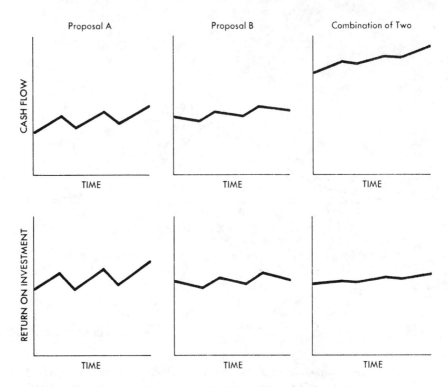

FIGURE 14-6 Effect of diversification

not the summation of the standard deviations of the individual projects making up the portfolio, but

$$\sigma = \sqrt{\sum_{j=1}^{m}\sum_{k=1}^{m}\sigma_{jk}} \qquad (14\text{-}7)$$

where j refers to project j; k to project k; m is the total number of projects in the portfolio, and σ_{jk} is the covariance between possible net present values for projects j and k. (This rather formidable expression will be illustrated shortly.)

The covariance term in Eq. (14-7) is

$$\sigma_{jk} = r_{jk}\sigma_j\sigma_k \qquad (14\text{-}8)$$

where r_{jk} is the expected correlation between possible net present values for projects j and k; σ_j is the standard deviation for project j, and σ_k is the standard deviation for project k. The standard deviations of the probability distributions of possible net present values for projects j and k are determined by the methods taken up in the previous section. When $j = k$ in Eq. (14-8), the correlation coefficient is 1.0, and $\sigma_j\sigma_k$ becomes σ_j^2 (that is, the standard deviation squared of the probability distribution of possible net present values for investment project j).

AN ILLUSTRATION

To illustrate these concepts, suppose that a firm has a single existing investment project, 1, and that it is considering investing in an additional project, 2. Assume further that the projects have the following expected values of net present value, standard deviations, and correlation coefficients:

	Expected value of net present value	Standard deviation	Correlation coefficient
Project 1	$12 000	$14 000	1.00
Project 2	8 000	6 000	1.00
Projects 1 and 2			0.40

The expected value of the net present value of the combination of projects is simply the sum of the two separate net present values.

$$NPV = \$12\ 000 + \$8\ 000 = \$20\ 000$$

The standard deviation for the combination, using Eqs. (14-7) and (14-8), is

$$\sigma = \sqrt{r_{11}\sigma_1^2 + 2r_{12}\sigma_1\sigma_2 + r_{22}\sigma_2^2}$$

$$= \sqrt{(1.00)(14\ 000)^2 + (2)(0.40)(14\ 000)(6\ 000) + (1.00)(6\ 000)^2}$$

$$= \$17\ 297$$

Thus, the expected value of net present value of the firm increases from $12 000 to $20 000 and the standard deviation of possible net present value from $14 000 to $17 297 with the acceptance of project 2. The coefficient of variation (standard deviation over expected value of net present value) is 14 000/12 000 = 1.17 without project 2 and 17 297/20 000 = 0.86 with the project. If we employ the coefficient of variation as a measure of relative business risk, we conclude that acceptance of project 2 would lower the business risk of the firm.

By accepting projects with relatively low degrees of correlation with existing projects, a firm diversifies and in so doing may be able to lower its overall business risk. We note above that the lower the degree of positive correlation, r_{12}, the lower the standard deviation of possible net present values, all other things being equal. Whether the coefficient of variation declines when an investment project is added depends also upon the expected value of net present value for the project.

CORRELATION BETWEEN PROJECTS

Estimating the correlation between possible net present values for two projects in Eq. (14-8) is the key ingredient in analyzing risk in a portfolio context. When two projects are similar to projects with which the company has had experience, it may be feasible to compute the correlation coefficients using historical data. For other investments, estimates of the correlation coefficients must be based solely upon an assessment of the future.

Management might have reason to expect only slight correlation between investment projects involving research and development for an electronic tester and a new consumer product. On the other hand, it might expect high positive correlation between investments in a milling machine and a turret lathe if both machines were used in the production of industrial lift trucks. The profit from a machine to be used in a production line will be highly, if not completely, correlated with the profit for the production line itself.

The correlation between expected net present values of various investments may be positive, negative, or 0, depending upon the nature of the association. A correlation coefficient of 1.00 indicates that the net present values of two investment proposals vary directly in exactly the same proportional manner; a correlation coefficient of –1.00 indicates that they vary inversely in exactly the same proportional manner; and a 0 correlation coefficient indicates that they are independent or unrelated. For most pairs of investments, the correlation coefficient lies between 0 and 1.00. The reason for the lack of negatively correlated investment projects is that most investments are correlated positively with the economy.

Estimates of the correlation coefficients must be as objective as possible if the total standard deviation figure obtained in Eq. (14-7) is to be realistic. It is not unreasonable to expect management to make fairly accurate estimates of these coefficients. When actual correlation differs from expected correlation, the situation can be a learning process, and estimates on other projects can be revised.

COMBINATIONS OF RISKY INVESTMENTS

We now have a procedure for determining the total expected value and the standard deviation of a probability distribution of possible net present values for a combination of investments. For our purposes, we define a *combination* as including all existing investment projects and one or more proposals under consideration. We assume, then, that the firm has existing investment projects and that these projects are expected to generate future cash flows. Thus, existing projects constitute a subset that is included in all combinations. We denote this portfolio of projects by the italic letter E.

A firm has under consideration four investment proposals, which are independent of one another; that is, they are not contingent or mutually exclusive. If these proposals are labeled 1, 2, 3, and 4, we have the following possible combinations of risky investments:

E	E,1	E,1,2	E,1,2,3	E,1,2,3,4
	E,2	E,1,3	E,1,2,4	
	E,3	E,1,4	E,1,3,4	
	E,4	E,2,3	E,2,3,4	
		E,2,4		
		E,3,4		

Thus, 16 combinations of projects are possible, with one possibility being the rejection of all of the proposals under consideration, so that the firm is left with only its existing projects, E. The expected value of net present value and standard deviation for each of these combinations can be computed in the manner described previously. The results can then be graphed.

Fig. 14-7 is a scatter diagram of the 16 possible combinations. Here the expected value of net present value is along the horizontal axis, and the standard deviation is on the vertical axis. Each dot represents a combination. Collectively, these dots constitute the total set of feasible combinations of investment opportunities available to the firm.

We see that certain dots dominate others in the sense that they represent a higher expected value of net present value and the same standard deviation, a lower standard deviation and the same expected value of net present value, or both a higher expected value and a lower standard deviation. The dominating dots are those that are farthest to the right in the figure. Four of them have been identified specifically—combinations B, H, L, and P. (The dot E represents all existing investment projects.)

Although the selection process itself is deferred until Chapter 15, we observe here that the combination ultimately chosen determines the new investment proposal or proposals that will be accepted. If combination H were selected and it consisted of E, 1, and 4, investment proposals 1 and 4 would be accepted. Those investment proposals not in the combination finally selected would be rejected. In our case, they would be proposals 2 and 3. If the combination finally selected consisted of only existing investment projects, E, all investment proposals under consideration would be rejected. The selection of any other combination implies the acceptance of one or more of the investment proposals under consideration.

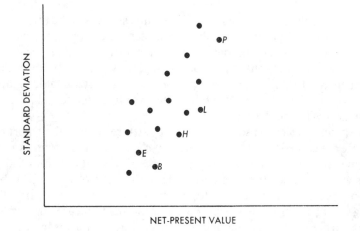

FIGURE 14-7 Opportunity set of combinations of projects

The incremental expected value of net present value and standard deviation can be determined by measuring on the horizontal and vertical axes the distance from dot E to the dot representing the combination finally selected. These distances can be thought of as the incremental contribution of expected value of net present value and standard deviation to the firm as a whole. In Chapter 15, we explore how the actual selection can be made and under what circumstances this approach is appropriate. Our purpose here has been to measure risk for combinations of risky investments in order to provide management with such information.

Summary

Operating leverage may be defined as the employment of an asset with a fixed cost in the hope that sufficient revenue will be generated to cover all fixed and variable costs. We study the operating leverage of a firm by using a break-even graph, which enables us to analyze the relationship among profits, volume, fixed costs, variable costs, and prices. By varying these factors, management may determine the sensitivity of profits and, in so doing, obtain a better understanding of the operating risk of the firm.

The risk of an investment project can be defined as the deviation in actual cash flows from those that were expected. Expressing the future in terms of probability distributions of possible cash flows, we can express risk quantitatively as the standard deviation of the distribution. The coefficient of variation is simply the standard deviation of a probability distribution over its expected value, and it serves as a relative measure of risk. Business risk is the risk associated with the operations of the firm, and it can be expressed in terms of the coefficient of variation.

One approach to the evaluation of risky investments is the direct analysis of the probability distribution of possible net present vaues of a project. Given the expected value and standard deviation of the distribution, management can determine the probability that the actual net present value will be lower than some amount such as zero. This type of information is extremely valuable in judging the risk of a project. The use of a probability tree was illustrated for taking account of changing risk over time.

Investment projects also can be judged with respect to their portfolio risk. Here we are concerned with the marginal risk of a project to the firm as a whole. By diversifying into projects not having high degrees of correlation with existing assets, a firm is able to reduce the standard deviation of its probability distribution of possible net present values relative to the expected value of the distribution. The likely degree of correlation between projects is the key to measuring portfolio risk.

Our purpose in this chapter has been to explore the means by which risk can be quantified for investment proposals and combinations of proposals. With this information, together with information about the expected profitability of the investment, we should reach much more informed, better decisions. In Chapter 15 we consider how this information can be employed in the decision process.

Appendix A: Simulation Approach to Risky Investments

In considering risky investments, we can use *simulation* to approximate the expected return and dispersion about the expected return for an investment proposal. By *simulation*, we mean testing the results of an investment decision before it actually occurs. The testing itself is based on a model coupled with probabilistic information. A simulation model proposed by Hertz considers the following factors in deriving a project's earnings stream:

Market analysis
1. Market size
2. Selling price
3. Market growth rate
4. Share of market (which results in physical sales volume)
Investment Cost Analysis
5. Investment required
6. Residual value of investment
Operating and Fixed Costs
7. Operating costs
8. Fixed costs
9. Useful life of facilities[3]

Probability distributions are assigned to each of these factors, based upon management's assessment of the probable outcomes. Thus, the possible outcomes are charted for each factor according to their probability of occurrence; examples of these probability distributions are shown in Fig. 14-8.

Once the probability distributions are determined, the next step is to determine the average rate of return that will result from a random combination of the nine factors listed above. To illustrate the simulation process, assume that the market-size factor had the following probability distribution:

Market size (in thousand units)	450	500	550	600	650	700	750
Probability	0.05	0.1	0.2	0.3	0.2	0.1	0.05

Now suppose that we have a roulette wheel with 100 numbers, on which numbers 1 to 5 represent a market size of 450 000 units, 6 to 15 represent a market size of 500 000; 16 to 35, a market size of 550 000 units, and so on through 100. As in roulette, we spin the wheel, and the ball falls in one of the 100 slots: number 26. For this trial, then, we simulate a market size of 550 000 units. Fortunately, we do not need a roulette wheel to undertake a simulation; the same type of operation can be carried out on a computer in a much more efficient manner.

Simulation trials are undertaken for each of the other eight factors. The first four factors (market analysis) give us the annual sales per year; factors 7 and 8 give

---

[3]David B. Hertz, "Risk Analysis in Capital Investment," *Harvard Business Review*, 42 (January-February 1964), 95-106.

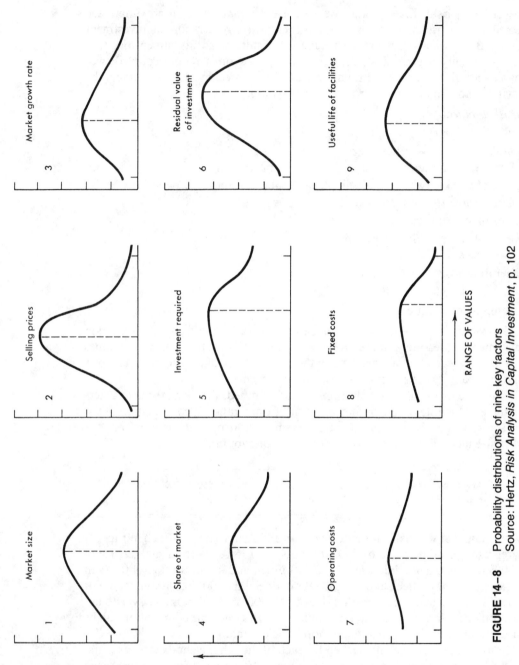

FIGURE 14-8 Probability distributions of nine key factors
Source: Hertz, *Risk Analysis in Capital Investment*, p. 102

us the operating costs and fixed costs per year. Together, these six factors enable us to calculate the annual earnings per year. When trial values for these six factors are combined with trial values for the required investment, the useful life, and the residual value of the project, we have sufficient information to calculate the return on investment for that trial run. Thus, the computer simulates trial values for each of the nine factors and then calculates the return on investment based upon the values simulated. The process is repeated a number of times: each time we obtain a combination of values for the nine factors and the return on investment for that combination. When the trial is repeated often enough, the rates of return can be plotted in a frequency distribution like that shown in Fig. 14-9.

From this frequency distribution we are able to evaluate the expected return and the dispersion about this expected return, or risk, in the same manner as before; in other words, we can determine the probability that an investment will provide a return greater or less than a certain amount. By comparing the probability distribution of rates of return for one proposal with the probability distribution of rates of return for another, management is able to evaluate the respective merits of different risky investments.

Two points should be mentioned with respect to Hertz's simulation method. Although it computes the average rate of return on investment, the method could easily be modified to calculate the internal rate of return, the net present value, or the profitability index. In addition, although Hertz allows for dependency among the nine factors, the model presented treats the factors as though they were independent. To the extent that dependency exists among factors, it must be taken into account in determining the probability distributions. For example, there is likely to be significant correlation between the market size and the selling price. These interrelationships add considerable complexity to the estimating procedure. Notwithstanding the added complexity of estimating and specifying in the model the relationships among factors, it must be done if the model is to provide realistic results. These estimates may be based upon empirical testing when such testing is feasible. Once the relationships are incorporated in the model, those factors that are correlated would then be simulated jointly. Rates of return for the simulated trials would be calculated and a frequency distribution of simulated trials formed in the same manner as before.

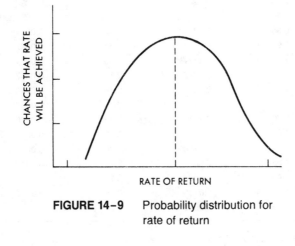

FIGURE 14-9   Probability distribution for rate of return

Appendix B: Normal Probability Distribution Table

Table 14B-1 shows the area of the normal distribution that is X standard deviations to the left or to the right of the mean. The test is "one-tail" in the sense that we are concerned with one side of the distribution or the other. If we wished to know the area of the curve, or probability, that was 1.5 standard deviations or more from the arithmetic mean on the right, it would be depicted by the colored area in Fig. 14-10. In Table 14B-1 we see that this corresponds to 6.68 percent of the total area of the normal distribution. Thus, we would say that there was a 6.68 percent probability that the actual outcome would exceed the mean by 1.5 standard deviations. In a similar manner, the table can be used to determine the probability associated with other distances from the mean.

TABLE 14B-1 Area of Normal Distribution that is X Standard Deviations to the Left or Right of the Mean

Number of standard deviations from mean (X)	Area to the left or right (one tail)	Number of standard deviations from mean (X)	Area to the left or right (one tail)
0.00	0.5000	1.55	0.0606
0.05	0.4801	1.60	0.0548
0.10	0.4602	1.65	0.0495
0.15	0.4404	1.70	0.0446
0.20	0.4207	1.75	0.0401
0.25	0.4013	1.80	0.0359
0.30	0.3821	1.85	0.0322
0.35	0.3632	1.90	0.0287
0.40	0.3446	1.95	0.0256
0.45	0.3264	2.00	0.0228
0.50	0.3085	2.05	0.0202
0.55	0.2912	2.10	0.0179
0.60	0.2743	2.15	0.0158
0.65	0.2578	2.20	0.0139
0.70	0.2420	2.25	0.0122
0.75	0.2264	2.30	0.0107
0.80	0.2119	2.35	0.0094
0.85	0.1977	2.40	0.0082
0.90	0.1841	2.45	0.0071
0.95	0.1711	2.50	0.0062
1.00	0.1577	2.55	0.0054
1.05	0.1469	2.60	0.0047
1.10	0.1357	2.65	0.0040
1.15	0.1251	2.70	0.0035
1.20	0.1151	2.75	0.0030
1.25	0.1056	2.80	0.0026
1.30	0.0968	2.85	0.0022
1.35	0.0885	2.90	0.0019
1.40	0.0808	2.95	0.0016
1.45	0.0735	3.00	0.0013
1.50	0.0668		

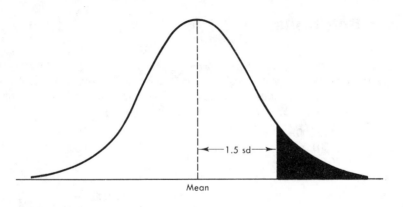

← 1.5 sd →

Mean

FIGURE 14–10 Normal distribution

Questions

1. The literature on finance assumes that the risk associated with an investment is a measurable phenomenon equivalent to the variability of returns on an investment. In your opinion, is this definition of risk adequate for asset selection by average investors? Explain.

2. Define the concept of *operating leverage*.

3. Classify the following short-run manufacturing costs as either typically fixed or typically variable. Which costs are variable at management's discretion? Are any of these costs "fixed" in the long run?

   (a) Insurance
   (b) Direct labor
   (c) Property taxes
   (d) Interest expense
   (e) Research & Development
   (f) Advertising
   (g) Raw materials
   (h) Bad-debt loss
   (i) Depletion
   (j) Depreciation
   (k) Maintenance

4. What would be the effect on the break-even point of the following?
   (a) Increased selling price
   (b) Increase in the minimum wage
   (c) Change from straight-line to accelerated depreciation
   (d) Increased sales
   (e) A 5-percent surtax on corporate profits
   (f) A liberalized credit policy

5. Discuss the importance of correlation among the expected returns of different projects.

6. Contrast uncertainly with risk as you perceive the terms. Is there a difference?

7. Risk in capital budgeting can be judged by analyzing the probability distribution of possible returns. What shape distribution would you expect to find for a safe project whose returns were absolutely certain? For a very risky project?

8. If project A has an expected value of net present value of $200 and a standard deviation of $400, is it more risky than project B whose expected value is $140 and standard deviation is $300?

9. What are the benefits of using simulation to evaluate capital-investment projects?

10. Is the standard deviation an adequate measure of risk? Can you think of a better measure?

11. Is there any business that is risk free?

Problems with Solutions

1. A company sells units of its product at $10 each. Variable cost per unit is $7.50 and total fixed cost is $100 000. Calculate (a) the break-even point in units and dollars; (b) the total revenue required to earn 10 percent of sales if taxes are paid at a 50 percent rate; and (c) the total revenue required to earn a $30 000 net income if taxes are 40 percent.

(a) $\$10(X) = \$100\ 000 + \$7.50(X)$
     $\$2.50(X) = \$100\ 000$
         $(X) = 40\ 000$ units
   Break-even sales $= 40\ 000 \times \$10 = \$400\ 000$

Proof:	Sales		$400 000
	Variable cost	$300 000	
	Fixed cost	100 000	400 000
	Net income		0

(b) $\$10(X) = \$100\ 000 + \$7.50(X) + \dfrac{NI}{1-\text{tax}}$

     $\$10(X) = \$100\ 000 + \$7.50(X) + \dfrac{(0.1)[\$10(X)]}{0.5}$

     $\$10(X) = \$100\ 000 + \$7.50(X) + \$2(X)$
    $\$0.5(X) = \$100\ 000$
         $(X) = 200\ 000$ units
    Sales $= 200\ 000 \times \$10 = \$2\ 000\ 000$

Proof:	Sales		$2 000 000
	Variable cost	$1 500 000	
	Fixed cost	100 000	1 600 000
	Profit before tax		$ 400 000
	Tax 50%		200 000
	Net income (10% of sales)		$ 200 000

(c) $\$10(X) = \$100\ 000 + \$7.50(X) + \dfrac{NI}{1-t}$

     $\$10(X) = \$100\ 000 + \$7.50(X) + \dfrac{\$30\ 000}{0.6}$

     $\$10(X) = \$100\ 000 + \$7.50(X) + \$50\ 000$
    $\$2.50(X) = \$150\ 000$
         $(X) = 60\ 000$ units
    Sales $= 60\ 000 \times \$10 = \$600\ 000$

Proof:	Sales		$600 000
	Variable cost	$450 000	
	Fixed cost	100 000	550 000
	Profit before tax		$ 50 000
	Tax 40%		20 000
	Net income		$ 30 000

2. A company has constructed a probability tree similar to the example in the text and has calculated the following expected value for net present values:

(1) Net present value	(2) Probability	(1) × (2)
−$715.98	0.10	−$71.60
− 438.61	0.10	− 43.86
− 161.24	0.05	− 8.06
− 150.15	0.10	− 15.02
127.22	0.30	38.17
404.59	0.10	40.46
415.68	0.05	20.78
693.05	0.10	69.31
970.41	0.10	97.04
	Weighted Average	$127.22

Calculate the standard deviation and the probability that the outcome would be greater than zero.

$$\sigma = \sqrt{\sum_{x=1}^{z} (NPV_x - \overline{NPV})^2 P_x} = \$480.00$$

$$S = \frac{X - \overline{NPV}}{\sigma} \qquad\qquad\qquad \textbf{(14-2)}$$

$$= \frac{0 - 127.22}{480.00} = 0.265$$

Probability that the outcome will be greater than zero is 0.3955 (see Table 14-B1) 0.25 = 0.14013, 0.30 = 0.3821 therefore 0.265 = 0.3955

3. A company is considering investing in two of four projects. The cash flows are normally distributed. Relevant data are given below:

	1	2	3	4
Expected net-present value	$4 000	$6 000	$5 000	$7 000
Standard deviations	2 000	4 000	3 000	5 000
Correlation coefficients	1.00	1.00	1.00	1.00

Combinations	Correlation coefficients
1 and 2	0.60
1 and 3	0.50
1 and 4	0.40
2 and 3	0.50
2 and 4	0.40
3 and 4	0.60

Calculate the coefficient of variation for each combination, then use your calculation to choose a combination.

Net present values:

1 and 2 $4 000 + $6 000 = $10 000
1 and 3 4 000 + 5 000 =   9 000
1 and 4 4 000 + 7 000 = 11 000
2 and 3 6 000 + 5 000 = 11 000
2 and 4 6 000 + 7 000 = 13 000
3 and 4 5 000 + 7 000 = 12 000

Standard deviations: See Eq. (14-5)

1 and 2 $= [(2\ 000)^2 + (2)(0.6)(2\ 000)(4\ 000) + (4\ 000)^2]^{1/2}$
$= [4\ 000\ 000 + 9\ 600\ 000 + 16\ 000\ 000]^{1/2} = \$5\ 441$

1 and 3 $= [(2\ 000)^2 + (2)(0.5)(2\ 000)(3\ 000) + (3\ 000)^2]^{1/2}$
$= [4\ 000\ 000 + 6\ 000\ 000 + 9\ 000\ 000]^{1/2} = \$4\ 359$

1 and 4 $= [(2\ 000)^2 + (2)(0.4)(2\ 000)(5\ 000) + (5\ 000)^2]^{1/2}$
$= [4\ 000\ 000 + 8\ 000\ 000 + 25\ 000\ 000]^{1/2} = \$6\ 083$

2 and 3 $= [(4\ 000)^2 + (2)(0.5)(4\ 000)(3\ 000) + (3\ 000)^2]^{1/2}$
$= [16\ 000\ 000 + 12\ 000\ 000 + 9\ 000\ 000]^{1/2} = \$6\ 083$

2 and 4 $= [(4\ 000)^2 + (2)(0.4)(4\ 000)(5\ 000) + (5\ 000)^2]^{1/2}$
$= [16\ 000\ 000 + 16\ 000\ 000 + 25\ 000\ 000]^{1/2} = \$7\ 550$

3 and 4 $= [(3\ 000)^2 + (2)(0.6)(3\ 000)(5\ 000) + (5\ 000)^2]^{1/2}$
$= [9\ 000\ 000 + 18\ 000\ 000 + 25\ 000\ 000]^{1/2} = \$7\ 211$

The coefficient of variation:

	σ	$\overline{NPV}$
1 and 2	$5 441 ÷	$10 000 = 0.5441
1 and 3	4 359 ÷	9 000 = 0.4843
1 and 4	6 083 ÷	11 000 = 0.5530
2 and 3	6 083 ÷	11 000 = 0.5530
2 and 4	7 550 ÷	13 000 = 0.5808
3 and 4	7 211 ÷	12 000 = 0.6009

On the basis of coefficients of variation, and assuming risks aversion, 1 and 3, would be chosen.

Problems

1. R.A. Rice Ltd., can invest in one of two mutually exclusive projects. The two proposals have the following discrete probability distributions of net cash flows for period p:

	A		B	
	Probability	*Cash flow*	*Probability*	*Cash flow*
	0.20	$2 000	0.10	$2 000
	0.30	4 000	0.40	4 000
	0.30	6 000	0.40	6 000
	0.20	8 000	0.10	8 000

(a) Without calculating a mean and a coefficient of variation, can you select the better proposal, assuming a risk-averse management?

(b) Verify your intuitive determination.

2. The Madison Company Ltd. earns monthly, after taxes, $2 400 on sales of $88 000. The average tax rate of the company is 40 percent. The company's only product sells for $20, of which $15 is variable cost.
(a) What is the monthly fixed cost of the Madison Company?
(b) What is its break-even point in units? In dollars?

3. What would be the effect of the following on the break-even point of the Madison Company Ltd. (problem 2)?
(a) An increase in price of $5 per unit (assume that volume is constant)
(b) A decrease in fixed costs of $2 000
(c) A decrease in variable costs of $1 per unit and an increase in fixed costs of $6 000

4. The D.T. Crazy Horse Hotel has a capacity to stable 50 horses. The fee for stabling a horse is $100 per month. Maintenance, depreciation, property taxes, and other fixed costs total $1 200 per moth. Variable costs per horse are $12 per month for hay and bedding and $8 per month for grain. Income is taxed at a 40 percent rate.
(a) Determine the break-even point.
(b) Compute the monthly profits after taxes if an average of 40 horses are stabled.

5. The Hume Corporation Ltd. is faced with several possible investment projects. For each, the total cash outflow required will occur in the initial period. The cash outflows, expected net present values, and standard deviations are given in the following table. All projects have been discounted at the risk-free rate, and it is assumed that the distributions of their possible net present values are normal.

Project	Cost	Net present value	Standard deviation
A	$100 000	$10 000	$20 000
B	50 000	10 000	30 000
C	200 000	25 000	10 000
D	10 000	5 000	10 000
E	500 000	75 000	75 000

(a) Ignoring size problems, are there some projects that are clearly dominated by others with respect to the coefficient of variation?
(b) May size problems be ignored?
(c) What is the probability that each of the projects will have a net present value greater than or equal to zero?

6. The probability distribution of possible net present values for project X has an expected value of $20 000 and a standard deviation of $10 000. Assuming a normal distribution, calculate the probability that the net present value will be zero or less; that it will be greater than $30 000; and that it will be less than $5 000.

7. Xonics Graphics Ltd. is evaluating a new technology for its reproduction equipment. The technology will have a 3-year life; it will cost $1 000, and its impact on cash flows is subject to risk. Management estimates that there is a 50-50 chance that the technology will either save the company $1 000 in the first year or save it nothing at all. If nothing at all, savings in the last 2 years would be zero as well. Even here there is some possibility that in the second year an additional outlay of $300 would be required to convert back to the original process, for the new technology may decrease efficiency. Management attaches a 40 percent probability to this occurrence if the new technology "bombs out" in the first year. If the technology proves itself, it is felt that second-year cash flows will be $1 800, $1 400 or $1 000, with probabilities of 0.20, 0.60, and 0.20, respectively. In the third year, cash flows are expected to be $200 greater or $200 less than the cash flow in period 2, with an equal chance of occurrence. (Again, these cash flows depend on the cash flow in period 1 being $1 000.)

(a) Set up a probability tree to depict the above cash-flow possibilities.

(b) Calculate a weighted net present value for each 3-year possibility, using a risk-free rate of 5 percent.

(c) What is the risk of the project?

8. The Windrop Company Ltd. will invest in two of three possible proposals, the cash flows of which are normally distributed. The expected net present value (discounted at the risk-free rate) and the standard deviation for each proposal are given as follows:

	1	2	3
Expected net present value	$10 000	$8 000	$6 000
Standard deviation	4 000	3 000	4 000

Assuming the following correlation coefficients for each possible combination, which combination dominates the others?

Proposals	Correlation coefficients
1	1.00
2	1.00
3	1.00
1 and 2	0.60
1 and 3	0.40
2 and 3	0.50

9. The Plaza Corporation Ltd. is confronted with various combinations of risky investments.

Combination	Net present value	Standard deviation
A	$100 000	$200 000
B	20 000	80 000
C	75 000	100 000
D	60 000	150 000
E	50 000	20 000
F	40 000	60 000
G	120 000	170 000
H	90 000	70 000
I	50 000	100 000
J	75 000	30 000

(a) Plot the above portfolios.

(b) Which combinations dominate the others?

Appendix A Problem

10. The Bertz Company Ltd. uses a simulation approach to judge investment projects. Three factors are employed: market demand, in units; price per unit minus cost per unit; and investment required at time 0. These factors are felt to be independent of one another. In analyzing a new consumer product, Bertz estimates the following probability distributions:

Annual demand		Price minus cost per unit		Investment required	
Probability	Units	Probability	Dollars	Probability	Dollars
0.05	10 000	0.10	$3.00	0.30	$1 800 000
0.10	20 000	0.20	4.50	0.40	2 000 000
0.20	30 000	0.40	6.00	0.30	2 300 000
0.30	45 000	0.20	7.00		
0.20	60 000	0.10	8.00		
0.10	75 000				
0.05	90 000				

(a) Using a random number table or some other random process, simulate 20 or more trials for these three factors and compute the return on investment for each trial. (*Note*: return = profit/investment.)

(b) Approximately what is the most likely return? How risky is the project?

Selected References

BEY, ROGER P., and J. CLAYTON SINGLETON, "Autocorrelated Cash Flows and the Selection of a Portfolio of Capital Assets," *Decision Sciences*, 8 (October 1978), 640-57.

BIERMAN, HAROLD, JR., and VITHALA R. RAO, "Investment Decisions with Sampling," *Financial Management*, 7 (Autumn 1978), 19-24.

CHESLEY, G. R. "Formal Decision Making under Uncertainty: A Structure," *Cost and Management* (Jul.-Aug. 1978), 39-42.

COZZOLINA, JOHN M., "A New Method of Risk Analysis," *Sloan Management Review*, 20 (Spring 179), 53-65.

GAHLON, JAMES M. and JAMES A. GENTRY, "On the Relationship Between Systematic Risk and the Degrees of Operating and Financial Leverage", *Financial Management*, Summer 1982, 15-23.

HAYES, ROBERTH H., "Incorporating Risk Aversion into Risk Analysis," *Engineering Economist*, 20 (Winter 1975), 99-121.

HERTZ, DAVID B., "Investment Policies That Pay Off," *Harvard Business Review*, 46 (January-February 1968), 96-108.

_____, "Risk Analysis in Capital Investment," *Harvard Business Review*, 42 (January-February 1964), 95-106.

HESPOS, RICHARD F., and PAUL A. STRASSMANN, "Stochastic Decision Trees for the Analysis of Investment Decisions," *Management Science*, 11 (August 1965), 244-59.

HILLIER, FREDERICK S., "A Basic Model for Capital Budgeting of Risky Interrelated Projects," *Engineering Economist*, 17 (Fall 1971), 1-30.

_____, "The Derivation of Probabilistic Information for the Evaluation of Risky Investments," *Management Science*, 9 (April 1963), 443-57.

KABACEK, KEITH, "Effective Risk: Management," *C A Magazine* (March 1984), 28-233.

LESSARD, DONALD R., and RICHARD S. BOWER, "Risk-Screening in Capital Budgeting," *Journal of Finance*, 28 (May 1973).

LEVY, HAIM, and MARSHALL SARNAT, *Capital Investment and Financial Decisions*. Englewood Cliffs, N.J.: Prentice-Hall, 1978.

LEWELLEN, WILBERG G., and MICHAEL S. LONG, "Simulation versus Single-Value Estimates in Capital Expenditure Analysis," *Decision Sciences* 3 (1972), 19-33.

MAGEE, J.F., "How to Use Decision Trees in Capital Investment," *Harvard Business Review*, 42 (September-October 1964), 79-96.

MOORE, BRIAN and JOHN TALBOTT, "An Application of Cost–Volume–Profit Analysis," *Cost and Management* (Mar.-Apr. 1978), 31-39.

QUIRIN, G. DAVID and JOHN C. WIGINTON, *Analyzing Capital Expenditures*. Homewood, Ill: Irwin, 1981.

ROBICHECK, ALEXANDER A., "Interpreting the Results of Risk Analysis," *Journal of Finance*, 30 (December 1975), 1384-86.

ROBICHEK, ALEXANDER A., and JAMES VAN HORNE, "Abandonment Value and Capital Budgeting," *Journal of Finance*, 22 (December 1967), 577-89; EDWARD A. DYL and HUGH W. LONG, "Comment," *Journal of Finance*, 24 (March 1969), 88-95; and ROBICHEK and VAN HORNE, "Reply," *Ibid.*, 96-97.

ROWLEY, C. STEVENSON, "Incorporating Return on Investment in Break-Even Analysis", *Cost and Management* (March-April 1981), 33-37.

SCHALL, LAWRENCE D., and GARY L. SUNDEM, "Capital Budgeting Methods and Risk: A Further Analysis," *Financial Management*, 9 (Spring 1980), 7-11.

SPAHR, RONALD W., and STANLEY A. MARTIN, "Project Pricing in Limited Diversification Portfolios," *Engineering Economist*, 26 (Spring 1981), 207-22.

VAN HORNE, JAMES C., "The Analysis of Uncertainty Resolution in Capital Budgeting for New Products," *Management Science*, 15 (April 1969), 376-86.

_____, "Capital-Budgeting Decisions Involving Combinations of Risky Investments," *Management Science*, 13 (October 1966), 84-92.

_____, "Capital Budgeting under Conditions of Uncertainty as to Project Life," *Engineering Economist*, 17 (Spring 1972), 189-99.

_____, "Variation of Project Life as a Means for Adjusting for Risk," *Engineering Economist*, 21 (Summer 1976).

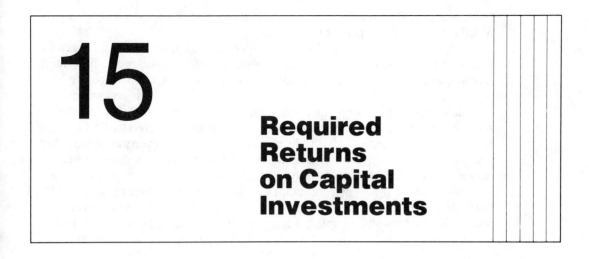

15

Required Returns on Capital Investments

The acceptance criterion for capital investments is perhaps the most difficult and controversial topic in finance. We know in theory that it should be the rate of return on a project that will leave the market price of the company's stock unchanged. The difficulty is in determining this rate in practice. Because predicting the effect of decisions on stock prices is an inexact science (some would call it an art form), estimating the appropriate required rate of return is inexact as well. Rather than skirt the issue, we address it head on and propose a general framework for measuring the required rate of return. We begin with the required rate of return for the company as a whole and then move on to consider the required rate of return for individual projects and for various subsets of an enterprise such as divisions.

Overall Cost of Capital of the Firm

For a company as a whole, there is an aggregation of assets. As a result, the use of an overall cost of capital as the acceptance criterion for investment decisions is appropriate only under certain circumstances. These circumstances are that the assets of the firm are homogeneous with respect to risk and that investment proposals under considerations are of the same character. If investment proposals vary widely with respect to risk, the required rate of return for the company as a whole is not appropriate as an acceptance criterion. The advantage of using it is its simplicity. Once it is computed, projects can be evaluated using a single rate that does not change unless underlying conditions change. This avoids the problem of computing individual required rates of return for each investment proposal. However, it is important that if the firm's overall required rate of return is used as an acceptance criterion, projects correspond in general to the above conditions.

Otherwise, one should determine an acceptance criterion for each project, a topic we take up in the latter part of this chapter.

The overall cost of capital of a firm is comprised of the costs of the various components of financing. The cost of equity capital is the most difficult to measure, and it will occupy most of our attention. We consider also the costs of debt and preferred stock. Our concern throughout will be with the marginal cost of a specific source of financing. The use of marginal costs follows from the fact that we use the cost of capital to decide whether to invest in new projects. Past costs of financing have no bearing on this decision. All costs will be expressed on an after-tax basis, to conform to the expression of investment project cash flows on an after-tax basis. Once we have examined the explicit costs of various sources of financing, we shall combine these costs to obtain an overall cost of capital to the firm. We assume in the development of this chapter that the reader has covered the foundation materials in Chapters 4 and 5 on the mathematics of finance and on valuation.

COST OF DEBT

Although debt can be both current and long-term, our concern is only with the long term. The assumption is that the firm will finance a capital project, whose benefits extend over a number of years, with long-term financing.

The explicit cost of debt can be derived by solving for the discount rate, k, that equates the net proceeds of the debt issue with the present value of interest plus principal payments, then adjusting the explicit cost obtained for the tax effect. The discount rate, k, which also is known as the yield, is solved with the following equation:

$$P_0 = \sum_{t=1}^{n} \frac{I_t + P_t}{(1 + k)^t} \tag{15-1}$$

where P_0 is the initial cash inflow to the firm, the capital Greek sigma denotes the summation for periods 1 through n, the final maturity, I_t is the interest payment in period t, and P_t is the payment of principal in period t. If principal payments occur only at final maturity, only P_n will appear. By solving for k, the rate of discount that equates the present value of cash outflows with the initial cash inflow, we obtain the before-tax cost of debt. The after-tax cost, which we denote by k_i can be approximated by

$$k_i = k(1 - t) \tag{15-2}$$

where k is the internal rate of return or yield, and t is the marginal tax rate. Because interest charges are tax deductible, the after-tax cost of debt is substantially less than the before-tax cost. If the before-tax cost, k, in Eq. (15-1) were found to be 15 percent and the tax rate were 50 percent,

$$k_i = 15.00(1 - 0.50) = 7.50 \text{ percent}$$

We note that the 7.50 percent after-tax cost in our example represents the marginal, or incremental, cost of additional debt. It does not represent the cost of debt funds already employed.

The explicit cost of debt is considerably cheaper than the cost of another source of financing having the same k but where the financial charges are not deductible for tax purposes. Implied in the calculation of an after-tax cost of debt is the fact that the firm is profitable. Otherwise, it does not gain the tax benefit associated with interest payments. The explicit cost of debt for an unprofitable firm is the before-tax cost, k.

COST OF PREFERRED SHARES

The cost of preferred stock is a function of its stated dividend. As we discuss in Chapter 22, this dividend is not a contractual obligation of the firm but is payable at the discretion of the board of directors. Consequently, unlike debt, it does not create a risk of legal bankruptcy. To holders of common shares, however, preferred stock is a security interest that takes priority over theirs. Most corporations that issue preferred stock intend to pay the stated dividend. As preferred stock has no maturity date, its cost may be represented as

$$k_p = \frac{D}{I_0} \qquad (15\text{-}3)$$

where D is the stated annual dividend and I_0 represents the net proceeds of the preferred-stock issue. If a company were able to sell a 14 percent preferred share issue ($100 par value) and realize net proceeds of $98 ½ a share, the cost of the preferred stock would be 14/98.5 = 14.21 percent. Note that this cost is not adjusted for taxes, because the preferred-stock dividend is paid after taxes. Thus, the explicit cost of preferred shares is substantially greater than that for debt.

COST OF EQUITY CAPITAL

The cost of equity capital is by far the most difficult cost to measure. In theory, it may be defined as the minimum rate of return that the company must earn on the equity-financed portion of an investment project in order to leave unchanged the market price of the shares. If the firm invests in projects having an expected return less than this required return, the market price of the share over the long run will suffer.

In the context of the dividend-capitalization model presented in Chapter 5, the cost of equity capital can be thought of as the rate of discount that equates the present value of all expected future dividends per share, as perceived by investors at the margin, with the current market price per share. Recall from Chapter 5 that

$$P_0 = \frac{D_1}{(1 + k_e)} + \frac{D_2}{(1 + k_e)^2} + \cdots + \frac{D_\infty}{(1 + k_e)^\infty}$$

$$P_0 = \sum_{t=1}^{\infty} \frac{D_t}{(1 + k_e)^t} \qquad (15\text{-}4)$$

where P_0 is the value of a share of stock at time 0; D_t is the dividend per share expected to be paid in period t; k_e is the appropriate rate of discount, and the capital Greek sigma represents the sum of discounted expected future dividends from period 1 through infinity, where infinity is depicted by the symbol ∞.

Estimating future dividends If we can successfully estimate the stream of future dividends that the market expects, it is an easy matter to solve for the rate of discount that equates this stream with the current market price of the share. Because expected future dividends are not directly observable, they must be estimated. Herein lies the major difficulty in estimating the cost of equity capital. For reasonably stable patterns of past growth, one might project this trend into the future. However, we must temper the projection to take account of current market sentiment. Insight into such sentiment can come from reviewing various analyses about the company in financial newspapers and magazines.

On the basis of the long-range plans of the company, the financial manager can make internal estimates of the expected future growth in earnings per share and in dividends per share. These estimates should take account of economic and other factors that bear on the firm's future operating performance. With access to a great deal of relevant information, the financial manager's estimates of future earnings may be the most accurate of all, but it is important that investors also expect these earnings. There is an obvious bias if the financial manager's estimate of growth used to solve for k_e differs significantly from that of the market. The important question is, What growth in dividends are investors at the margin expecting when they pay x dollars for a share of stock? Every effort should be made to get as accurate a handle as possible on this expected growth pattern. Thus, in estimating future dividends for the company, the financial manager must think as investors do.

If, for example, dividends were expected to grow at an 8 percent annual rate into the foreseeable future, the perpetual growth model presented in Chapter 5 might be used to determine the required rate of return. If the expected dividend in the first year were $2 and the present market price per share were $27, we would have

$$k = \frac{\$2}{\$27} + 0.08 = 0.154 = 15.4 \text{ percent.}$$

This rate then would be used as an estimate of the firm's required return on equity capital. If the growth in dividends is expected to taper off in the future, another growth model explained in Chapter 5 must be used.

Capital-asset pricing model approach to the cost of equity Rather than estimating the future dividend stream of the firm and then solving for the cost of equity capital, one may approach the problem directly by estimating the required rate of return on the company's equity. From our discussion of the capital-asset pricing model in Chapter 5, we know that it implies the following required rate of return for a share:

$$R_j = i + (\overline{R}_m - i)\beta_j \tag{15-5}$$

where i is the risk-free rate, $\overline{R}_m$ is the expected return for the market portfolio, and β_i is the beta coefficient for stock j.

Recall from Chapter 5 that beta is a measure of the responsiveness of the excess returns for security j (in excess of the risk-free rate) to those of the market, using some broad-based market index such as the Toronto Stock Exchange Index as a surrogate for the market portfolio. If the historical relationship between security returns and those for the market portfolio is believed to be a reasonable proxy for the future, one can use past returns to compute the beta for a share. This was illustrated in Chapter 5, where a characteristic line was fitted to the relationship between returns in excess of risk-free rate for the share and those for the market index. *Beta* is defined as the slope of this line. To free us of the need to calculate beta information directly, several services provide historical beta information on a large number of publicly traded shares. These services allow one to obtain the beta for a share with ease, thereby facilitating greatly the calculation of the cost of equity capital.

Again, if the past is thought to be a good proxy for the future, one can use Eq. (15-5) to compute the cost of equity capital for a company. To illustrate, suppose that the beta for the Silva-Chin Company Ltd. were found to be 1.20, based on monthly excess return data over the last five years. This coefficient tells us that the share's excess return goes up or down by a somewhat greater percentage than does the excess return for the market. (A beta of 1.00 means that excess returns for the stock vary proportionally with excess returns for the market portfolio.) Thus, the stock of Silva-Chin Company Ltd. has more unavoidable, or systematic, risk than does the market as a whole. But management believes that this past relationship is likely to hold in the future. Furthermore, a rate of return of about 17 percent on stocks in general is expected to prevail and a risk-free rate of 12 percent is expected.

This is all the information we need in order to compute the required rate of return on equity for Silva-Chin Company Ltd. Using Eq. (15-5), the cost of equity capital would be

$$R_j = 0.12 + (0.17 - 0.12)1.20 = 18 \text{ percent.}$$

Thus, the estimated required rate of return on equity for Silva-Chin Company Ltd. is approximately 18 percent. In essence, we are saying that this is the rate of return that investors expect the company to earn on its equity.

If measurement were exact and certain assumptions held,[1] the cost of equity capital determined by this method would be the same as that provided by a dividend capitalization model. Recall that the latter estimate is the rate of discount

---

[1] As discussed in Chapter 5, the capital-asset pricing model assumes the presence of perfect capital markets. When this assumption is relaxed to take account of real-world conditions, the residual risk of a stock may take on a degree of importance. We know that the total risk of a security is comprised of its systematic as well as its residual risk. The assumption of the capital-asset pricing model is that residual risk can be completely diversified away, leaving us with only systematic risk.   If imperfections exist in the capital markets, these may impede efficient diversification by investors. (One example of an imperfection is the presence of significant bankruptcy costs.) The greater the imperfections that are believed to exist, the greater the allowance that must be made for residual risk. As a result, it will be necessary to adjust upward the required rate of return. For amplification of this point, see James C. Van Horne, Dipchand and Hanrahan, *Financial Management and Policy*, 5th ed., Chapters 7–8.

that equates the present value of the stream of expected future dividends with the current market price of the share. By now it should be apparent that we can hope only to approximate the cost of equity capital. We believe that the methods suggested above enable such an approximation more or less accurately, depending on the situation. For a large company whose stock is actively traded on the Toronto Stock Exchange and whose systematic risk is close to that of the market as a whole, we can usually estimate more confidently than we can for a moderate-sized company whose stock is inactively traded in the over-the-counter market and whose systematic risk is very large. We must live with the inexactness involved in the measurement process and try to do as good a job as possible.

Debt cost as the base   Rather than estimate the required return in this manner, some people use the company's debt cost as a basis for estimating its equity cost. A firm's cost of debt will exceed the risk-free rate by a risk premium. The greater the risk of the firm, the greater this premium and the more interest the firm must pay in order to borrow. The relationship is illustrated in Fig. 15-1. On the horizontal axis, the firm's debt is shown to have systematic risk equal to β_i. As a result, its required return is k_i, which exceeds the risk-free rate of i.

In addition to this risk premium, the common stock of a company must provide a higher expected return than the debt of the same company. The reason is that there is more systematic risk involved. This phenomenon also is illustrated in the figure. We see that for a beta of β_s, an expected return of k_s is required and that this percentage exceeds the company's cost of debt, k_i. The historical risk premium in expected return for shares over bonds has been around 4 percent. If this seemed reasonable for a particular company, one could use the firm's cost of debt as a base and add to it a premium of around 4 percent to estimate its cost of equity capital. To illustrate, suppose Valkury Corporation Ltd.'s bonds sell in the market to yield 15 percent. Using the approach outlined above, its approximate cost of equity would be

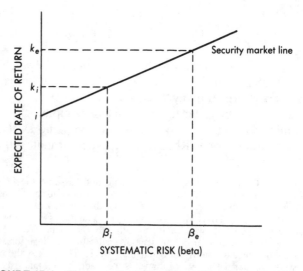

FIGURE 15-1   The security market line with debt and stock

$$k_e = k_i + \frac{\text{stock over debt}}{\text{risk premium}} = 15\% + 4\% = 19\%$$

This percentage then would be used as the cost of equity capital. The advantage of the approach is that one does not have to use beta information and make the calculation involved in Eq. (15-5). The disadvantage is that it does not allow for changing risk premiums over time; and because the 4 percent is for companies overall, the approach is not as accurate as the direct estimate of the required return on equity capital for a specific company. However, it does offer an alternative method of estimating the cost of equity capital within the overall framework of the capital-asset pricing model.

WEIGHTED-AVERAGE COST OF CAPITAL

Once we have computed costs of individual components of the capital structure,[2] we may weigh them according to some standard and calculate a weighted-average cost of capital. The firm's overall cost of capital may be expressed as

$$\text{Cost of capital} = \sum_{x=1}^{j} k_x w_x \qquad \textbf{(15-6)}$$

where k_x is the after-tax cost of the xth method of financing, w_x is the weight given to that method as a percentage of the firm's total financing, and the capital Greek sigma denotes the summation for financing methods 1 through j. To illustrate the calculations involved, suppose that a firm had the following capital structure at the latest statement date, where the amounts shown represent market values:

	Amount	Proportion
Debt	$ 30 million	30%
Preferred stock	10 million	10%
Common-stock equity	60 million	60%
	$100 million	100%

Common-stock equity includes both common-stock issues and retained earnings. In calculating proportions, it is important that we use market-value as opposed to book-value weights. Because we are trying to maximize the value of the firm to its shareholders, only market-value weights are consistent with our objective. Market

[2]While equity, debt, and preferred stock are the major types of financing, there are other types. These include leasing, convertible securities, warrants, and other options. Because determining the costs of these methods of financing involves some special and rather complex valuation issues, we treat them in individual chapters where we are able to give such issues proper attention. For our purposes in this chapter, knowing the costs of equity, debt, and preferred stock financing is sufficient for illustrating the overall cost of capital of a company. When costs are determined for other types of financing, they can be inserted in the weighting scheme to be discussed now.

values are used in the calculation of the costs of the various components of financing, so market-value weights should be used in determining the weighted average cost of capital.

To continue with our illustration, suppose that the firm computed the following after-tax costs for the component methods of financing:

	Cost
Debt	7.5%
Preferred stock	14.0
Common stock equity	18.0

Therefore, the weighted-average cost of capital for this example problem is

	(1) Proportion	(2) Cost	(3) Weighted cost (1) × (2)
Debt	30%	7.5%	2.25%
Preferred stock	10	14.0	1.40
Common-stock equity	60	18.0	10.80
			14.45%

Thus, with the assumptions of this example, 14.45 percent represents the weighted-average cost of the component methods of financing, where each component is weighted according to market-value proportions.

With the calculation of a weighted-average cost of capital, the critical question is whether the figure represents the firm's real cost of capital. The answer depends upon how accurately we have measured the individual marginal costs, upon the weighting system, and upon certain other assumptions. Assume for now that we are able to measure accurately the marginal costs of the individual sources of financing, and let us examine the importance of the weighting system.

Weighting system   The critical assumption in any weighting system is that the firm will in fact raise capital in the proportions specified. Because the firm raises capital *marginally* to make a *marginal* investment in new projects, we need to work with the marginal cost of capital to the firm as a whole. This rate depends upon the package of funds employed to finance investment projects. In other words, our concern is with new or incremental capital, not with capital raised in the past. In order for the weighted-average cost of capital to represent a marginal cost, the weights employed must be marginal; that is, the weights must correspond to the proportions of financing inputs the firm intends to employ.

If they do not, capital is raised on a marginal basis in proportions other than those used to calculate this cost. As a result, the real weighted-average cost of capital will differ from that calculated and used for capital-investment decisions. An obvious bias results. If the real cost is greater than that which is measured, certain investment projects will be accepted that will leave investors worse off than before. On the other hand, if the real cost is less than the measured cost, projects will be rejected that could increase shareholder wealth. Therefore, the 14.45 percent weighted-average cost of capital computed in our example is realistic only if the firm intends to finance in the future in the same proportions as its existing capital structure.

Raising capital is "lumpy," and strict proportions cannot be maintained. For example, a firm would have difficulty financing each project with 30 percent debt, 10 percent preferred stock, and 60 percent retained earnings. In practice, it may finance with debt in one instance and with preferred stock or retained earnings in another. Over time, most firms are able to finance in roughly a proportional manner. It is in this sense that we try to measure the marginal cost of capital for the package of financing employed.

Flotation costs   Flotation costs involved in the sale of common shares, preferred shares, or a debt instrument affect the profitability of a firm's investments. In many cases, the new issue must be priced below the market price of existing financing; in addition, there are out-of-pocket flotation costs. Owing to flotation costs, the amount of funds the firm receives is less than the price at which the issue is sold. The presence of flotation costs in financing requires an adjustment be made in the evaluation of investment proposals.

That adjustment is made by adding flotation costs of financing to the project's initial cash outlay. Suppose that an investment proposal costs $100 000 and that to finance the project the company must raise $60 000 externally. Both debt and common shares are involved, and flotation costs come to $4 000. Therefore, $4 000 should be added to $100 000, bringing the total initial outlay to $104 000. In this way, the proposal is properly "penalized" for the flotation costs associated with its financing. The expected future cash flows associated with the project are discounted at the weighted-average cost of capital. If the project were expected to provide annual cash inflows of $24 000 forever and the weighted-average cost of capital were 20 percent, the project's net present value would be

$$NPV = \frac{\$24\ 000}{0.20} - \$104\ 000 = \$16\ 000$$

This amount contrasts with a net present value of $20 000 if no adjustment is made for flotation costs.

Thus, the adjustment for flotation costs is made in the project's cash flows and not in the cost of capital.[3] To adjust the cost of capital results in an excessive "penalty" whenever the net present value of the project is positive. In our previous example, $4 000 in flotation costs represents 4 percent of the $100 000 investment, so the "adjusted" cost of capital would be 20 percent/(1 − 0.04) = 20.83 percent.

---

[3]For a defense of the procedure, see Simon E. Keane, "The Investment Discount Rate—In Defense of the Market Rate of Interest," *Accounting and Business Research*, Summer 1976, 234; and John R. Ezzell and R. Burr Porter, "Flotation Costs and the Weighted Average Cost of Capital," *Journal of Financial and Quantitative Analysis*, 11 (September 1976), 403–13.

Therefore, the net present value of the project would be

$$NPV = \frac{\$24\,000}{0.2083} - \$100\,000 = \$15\,218$$

As we see, the use of an adjusted cost of capital results in a biased, low estimate of the net present value of a project whenever this value is positive. The appropriate procedure is to adjust the project's initial cash outlay and to use the weighted-average "unadjusted" cost of capital as the discount rate.

RATIONALE FOR WEIGHTED-AVERAGE COST

The rationale behind the use of a weighted-average cost of capital is that by financing in the proportions specified and accepted projects yielding more than the weighted-average cost, the firm is able to increase the market price of its shares. This increase occurs because investment projects accepted are expected to yield more on their equity-financed portions than the cost of equity capital, k_e. Once these expectations are apparent to the marketplace, the market price of the share should rise, all other things the same, because expected future earnings per share (and dividends per share) are higher than those expected before the projects were accepted. The firm has accepted projects that are expected to provide a return greater than that required by investors at the margin, based on the risk involved.

We must return to the critical assumption that over time the firm finances in the proportions specified. If it does so, the financial risk of the company remains roughly unchanged. As we shall see in Chapter 17, the "implicit" costs of financing are embodied in the weighted-average cost of capital by virtue of the fact that a firm has to supplement nonequity financing with equity financing. It does not raise capital continually with supposedly cheaper debt funds without increasing its equity base. The firm's capital structure need not be optimal for the firm to employ the weighted-average cost of capital for capital-budgeting purposes. The important consideration is that the weights used be based upon the future financing plans of the company. If they are not, the weighted-average cost of capital calculated does not correspond to the actual cost of funds obtained; as a result, capital-budgeting decisions are likely to be suboptimal.

The use of a weighted-average cost of capital figure must be qualified also for the points raised earlier. It assumes that the investment proposals being considered do not differ in systematic, or unavoidable, risk from that of the firm and that the residual risk of the proposals does not provide any diversification benefits to the firm. Only under these circumstances is the cost-of-capital figure obtained appropriate as an acceptance criterion. These assumptions are extremely binding. They imply that the projects of a firm are completely homogeneous with respect to risk and that only projects of the same risk will be considered.

In practice, of course, the issue is one of degree. If the conditions above are approximately met, then the company's weighted-average cost of capital may be used as the acceptance criterion. If a firm produced only one product and all proposals considered were in conjunction with the marketing and production of that product, the use of the firm's overall cost of capital as the acceptance criterion probably would be appropriate. (Even here, however, there may be significant enough differences in risk among investment proposals to warrant separate consideration.) For a multiproduct firm with investment proposals of varying risk, the use of an overall required rate of return is inappropriate. Here the required rate of return for the specific proposal should be used, as determined with the methods proposed in the next section. The key, then, is the homogeneity with respect to risk of existing investment projects and investment proposals under consideration.

The CAPM: Project-Specific and Group-Specific Required Returns

When the existing investment projects of the firm and investment proposals under consideration are not homogeneous with respect to risk, the use of the firm's cost of capital as an acceptance criterion will not do. In these cases, we must formulate a specific acceptance criterion for the particular project involved. One means for doing so is with the capital-asset pricing model, and this approach is described in this section.

CAPITAL-ASSET PRICING MODEL APPROACH TO PROJECTS

Essentially, the capital-asset pricing model approach is the same as that for determining the cost of equity capital of the firm. However, instead of the expected relation between excess returns for the stock (returns in excess of the risk-free rate) and those for the market portfolio, one is concerned with the expected relation of excess returns for the project and those for the market portfolio. The required return for an equity-financed project would be

$$R_k = i + (\overline{R}_m - i)\beta_k \tag{15-7}$$

where β_k is the slope of the characteristic line that describes the relationship between excess returns for project k and those for the market portfolio. As can be seen, this equation is identical to Eq. (15-5) except for the substitution of the project return and its beta for those of the share.

Assume that the firm intends to finance a project entirely with equity. The acceptance criterion then would be to invest in the project if its expected return exceeded the required return, R_k, as determined with Eq. (15-7). Recall from Chapter 5 that the market-determined relationship between systematic risk, as described by beta, and the required rate of return is depicted by the security market line. To illustrate the acceptance criterion for projects using this concept, we turn to Fig. 15-2. All projects with internal rates of return lying on or above the line should be accepted, for they provide expected excess returns. Acceptable projects are depicted by x's. All projects lying below the line, shown by the o's, would be rejected. Note that the greater the systematic risk of a project, the greater the return that is required. If the project had no risk, only the risk-free rate would be required.

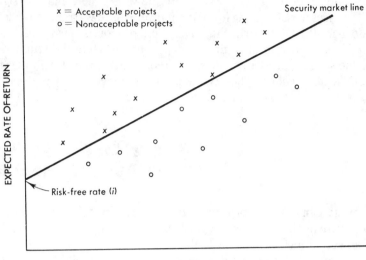

FIGURE 15-2 The security market line as applied to risky investment

For projects with more risk, however, a risk premium is demanded, and it increases with the degree of systematic risk of the project. The goal of the firm in this context is to search for investment opportunities lying above the line.

Application of the model—the use of proxy companies   The difficulty in applying this approach is in estimating the beta for a project. Recall from Chapter 5 that derivation of the characteristic line is based on changes in market value for a stock and those for the market portfolio. It is therefore necessary to estimate changes in the market value of the project over time in relation to changes in value for the market portfolio. Estimation of the former represents unfamiliar ground for most people accustomed to thinking in terms of net present values and internal rates of return.

In many cases, the project is sufficiently similar to a company whose shares are publicly held so that we can use that company's beta in deriving the required rate of return on equity for the project. For large projects, such as new products, one frequently can identify publicly traded companies that are engaged entirely, or almost entirely, in the same type of operation. The important thing is to identify a company or companies with systematic risk characteristics similar to those of the project in question.

Suppose that a steel company is considering the formation of a real estate subsidiary. As there are a number of real estate companies with publicly traded shares, one simply could determine the beta for one of those companies or a group of them and use it in Eq. (15-5) to derive the required rate of return for the project. Note that the relevant required rate of return is not that for the steel company, but that for other real estate firms. Stated differently, the market views the steel company's venture in the same way it views other firms engaged solely in real estate. By concentrating on companies in the same line as the firm desires to enter, we can find surrogates that approximate the systematic risk of the project. An exact duplication of the project's risk is unlikely, but reasonable approximations frequently are possible.

To illustrate the calculations, suppose that the average beta for a sample of real estate companies whose shares were publicly traded and whose basic businesses were similar to the venture contemplated by the steel company was 1.6. We can use this beta as a surrogate for the beta of the project. If we expect the average return on the market portfolio of stocks to be 17 percent and the risk-free rate to be 12 percent, the required return on equity for the project would be

$$R_k = 0.12 = (0.17 - 0.12)1.6 = 20 \text{ percent}$$

Therefore, 20 percent would be used as the required equity return for the project.

When there are no companies whose shares are publicly traded, so we cannot find proxies for the project, the task becomes much more difficult. Even here, however, there sometimes exists information on the market value of the project in question. For machine tools, a secondary market of sorts exists, where prices are established for used machines of various ages. Other assets have similar markets where prices can be determined. Given these prices, we can measure the market return for a particular period and then use such information to derive an estimate of beta for the project.[4] The approach is hampered however, by a number of measurement problems. Unless one is able to use a company or companies whose stock is publicly traded as a proxy for the project, the derivation of a beta for a specific project is a difficult matter. For this reason we will restrict our attention to the use of proxy company information.

THE REQUIRED RETURN WITH LEVERAGE

If the firm consistently finances projects with equity, one would use R_k as the required rate of return for the project. If some debt financing is employed, however, we need to determine a weighted-average required return. Here the weighting system is the same as that illustrated earlier for the firm's overall cost of capital. Rather than vary the proportion of debt financing project by project, a more consistent approach is to apply the same weights to all projects. Presumably these weights will correspond to the proportions with which the firm intends to finance over time. If the firm intends to finance with one part debt for every two parts equity, and the after-tax cost of debt is 7.50 percent while the required return on equity for the project is 20 percent, the overall required return for the project is

$$R_k = 0.075(1/3) + 0.200(2/3) = 15.83 \text{ percent}$$

If the project were expected to provide an internal rate of return in excess or equal to this rate, the project would be accepted. If not, it would be rejected. Thus, the acceptance criterion is specifically related to the systematic risk of the project through the cost of equity capital.

---

[4]For such an example, see Van Horne, Dipchand and Hanrahan, *Financial Management and Policy*, 5th Can. ed., Chapter 7.

GROUP-SPECIFIC REQUIRED RETURNS

Rather than determine project-specific required returns, some companies categorize projects into roughly homogeneous groups and then apply the same required return to all projects emanating from that group. One advantage is that it is not as time consuming as computing required returns for each project. Another is that it often is easier to find proxy companies for a group than it is for an individual project. By group, we mean some subunit of the company that carries on a set of activities that can be differentiated from the other activities of the firm. Usually these activities are differentiated along product or service lines as well as along management lines. Frequently the subunits are divisions or subsidiaries of the company, though a group is not restricted to this definition.

If the products or services of the group are homogeneous with respect to risk, and new proposals are of the same sort, a group-specific required return is an appropriate acceptance criterion. It represents the transfer price of capital from the company to the group. Stated differently, it is the rate of return the company expects the group to earn on its capital investments. The greater the systematic risk of the group, the greater its required return.

The computation of the required rate of return is the same as that for the specific project. For each group, proxy companies whose shares are publicly traded are identified. On the basis of these surrogates, betas are derived for each group and from these a required return on equity capital is calculated.[5] If debt is used, a weighted average required return for the group is derived in the same manner as in the previous section. Once group specific required returns are computed, capital is allocated, or transferred, throughout the firm on a risk-adjusted return basis. The approach provides a consistent framework for allocating capital among groups with greatly different risks.

The approach is illustrated in Fig. 15-3. Here, the bars represent the required returns for four groups. The weighted average cost of capital for the firm as a whole is depicted by the dashed line. Projects providing expected returns above the bars should be accepted; those below the bars rejected. Note that this criterion means that for the two "safer" groups, some accepted projects may provide expected returns below the firm's overall cost of capital but above the required return for the group. For the two "riskier" groups, rejected projects may have provided returns greater than the overall cost of capital but less than the group's required return. Indeed, capital is allocated on a risk-return basis specific to the systematic risk of the group.

Some qualifications Whether the required returns be project specific or group specific, there are certain problems in the application of the capital-asset pricing

---

[5]For an illustration of this approach, which was used by an actual company, see James C. Van Horne, "An Application of the Capital Asset Pricing Model to Divisional Required Returns," *Financial Management*, 9 (Spring 1980), 14–19. Russell J. Fuller and Halbert S. Kerr, "Estimating the Divisional Cost of Capital: An Analysis of the Pure-Play Technique," *Journal of Finance*, 36 (December 1981). 997–1009, collected proxy company betas for the various divisions of some sixty multi-division firms. The authors found that an appropriately weighted average of the betas of the proxy firms closely approximated the beta of the multi-division firm. Although an adjustment for leverage was made, the results here did not provide as good an estimate of the multi-division firm beta as the unadjusted betas.

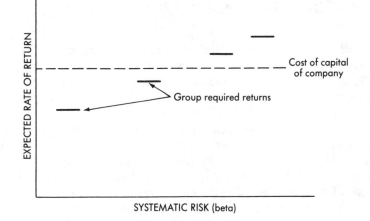

FIGURE 15-3   Group—specific required returns

model. For one thing, the amount of nonequity financing that is assigned to a project is an important consideration. For the above procedure to hold, it should approximate the same relative amount as that used by the proxy company. In other words, the proportion of nonequity financing allocated to a project should not be significantly out of line with that for the proxy company being used. Otherwise, one will not get a reasonable proxy for the systematic risk of the project. Where the proportions are not nearly the same, the proxy company's beta should be adjusted before it is used as the cost of equity capital for the project. A procedure for adjusting the beta is presented in the Appendix to this chapter. Using this procedure, one can approximate the beta for the proxy company, assuming it had the same relative proportion of nonequity financing as that contemplated for the project. The cost of equity capital for the project can then be determined in the same manner as before.

In addition to the practical problems, there is an underlying assumption in the capital-asset pricing model approach which must be questioned. As we know, this assumption is that only the systematic risk of the firm is important. However, the probability of a firm's becoming insolvent depends on its total risk, not just its systematic risk. When insolvency or bankruptcy costs are significant, investors may be served by the firm's paying attention to the impact of a project on the total risk of the firm. The total risk is comprised of both systematic and residual risk. Systematic risk means more to investors; but residual risk may be a factor,[6] and the greater its weight, the less relevant is the capital-asset pricing model approach to risky investments.

---

[6]When there are significant bankruptcy costs, these work to the detriment of stockholders as residual owners of the company. It therefore may be important for the firm to keep the probability of becoming bankrupt within reasonable bounds. To do so, it must consider the impact of the project on the firm's total risk (systematic and residual). This approach is taken up in the last section of the chapter.

Evaluation of Projects on the Basis of Their Total Risk

When for either theoretical or practical reasons it is not appropriate to compute a required rate of return for a project or group using the capital-asset pricing model, we must turn to more subjective means for evaluating risky investments. In fact, most firms approach the problem in this manner. Many, of course, deal with risky investments in informal ways. Decision makers simply try to incorporate risk into their judgment on the basis of their "feel" for the projects being evaluated. This "feel" can be improved upon by discussions with others familiar with the proposals and the risks inherent in them. Frequently, such discussions center around "what if" types of questions. In a general way, then, an allowance can be made for risk in capital-expenditure decisions. The problem with informal approaches to risk, of course, is that the information developed usually is sketchy, and the treatment of it is not consistent from project to project or over time.

We know from our discussion in Chapter 14 that expected return and risk can be quantified in a consistent manner. Given this information, the question is whether a project should be accepted or rejected. We will begin by examining how management might evaluate a single investment proposal and then move on to combinations of risky investments. These methods are firm-risk oriented in the sense that management does not consider explicitly the effect of the project on investors' portfolios. The focus is on total risk, the sum of systematic and residual risk. Management assesses the likely effect of the project on the variability of cash flows and earnings of the firm. From this assessment, it then can estimate the likely effect on share price. The critical factor from the standpoint of valuation is how accurately management is able to link share price with risk-profitability information for an investment proposal. As we shall see, the linkage tends to be subjective, which detracts from the accuracy of the approaches.

EVALUATION OF A PROPOSAL

You will recall from Chapter 14 that the information generated for an investment proposal was the probability distribution of possible net present values. We saw also that by standardizing the dispersion in terms of so many standard deviations from the expected value of the distribution, we can determine the probability that the net present value of the project will be zero or less. In the evaluation of a single proposal, it is unlikely that management would accept an investment proposal having an expected value of net present value of zero unless the probability distribution had no dispersion. In this special case the proposal, by definition, would be riskless. For risky investments, the net present values would have to exceed zero. How much they would have to exceed zero by before acceptance was warranted depends upon the amount of dispersion of the probability distribution and the utility preferences of management with respect to risk.

In order to facilitate project selection as well as to make it consistent over time, management may wish to formulate maximum risk profiles. To express the probability distributions in relative instead of absolute terms, we can convert the net present value probability distribution into a distribution of possible profitabil-

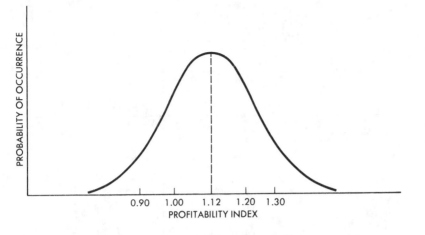

FIGURE 15–4 Probability distribution of profitability indices proposal X

ity indexes. (Recall that the profitability index is simply the present value of future net cash flows over the initial cash outlay.) Suppose we had a proposal costing $10 000 where the expected value of the probability distribution of possible net present values was $1 200. The profitability index for this expected value would be ($1 200 + $10 000)/$10 000 = 1.12. The profitability index for zero net present value is (0 + $10 000)/$10 000 = 1.00. Similarly, we can convert the entire distribution of possible profitability indexes. An example of such distribution is shown in Fig. 15-4.

If management has specified maximum risk profiles for various expected value of profitability indexes, one would simply compare the proposal shown in Fig. 15-4 with the maximum risk profile for an expected value of profitability index of 1.12. If the dispersion of the proposal is less than that for the risk profile, the proposal will be accepted. If not, it will be rejected. The maximum level of dispersion permitted, as depicted by the risk profile, will increase with the expected value of profitability index. For a profitability index of 1.02 the dispersion of the maximum risk profile will be narrower than that for a profitability index of 1.10. Some hypothetical risk profiles are shown in Fig. 15.5. We note that the greater the expected value of profitability index, the greater the dispersion that is tolerable to management. To illustrate their application, compare the probability distribution in Fig. 15-4 with that shown in the third row, first column, of Fig. 15-5. The latter is for a profitability index of 1.12. We see that the dispersion of the probability distribution for the hypothetical project (Fig. 15-4) is somewhat wider than the dispersion tolerable to management for that level of expected profitability. Therefore, the proposal would be rejected according to this method.

Some qualifications   The real problem with this approach is that the link with share price is not direct. Management is presented with information about the expected return and risk of a project; and on the basis of this information it reaches a decision. However, there is no direct link to the likely reaction of well-diversified investors. This link depends entirely upon the perceptiveness of management in judging investors' tradeoff between profitability and risk. Moreover, there is no analysis of the impact of the project on the overall risk of the firm; as we know, this

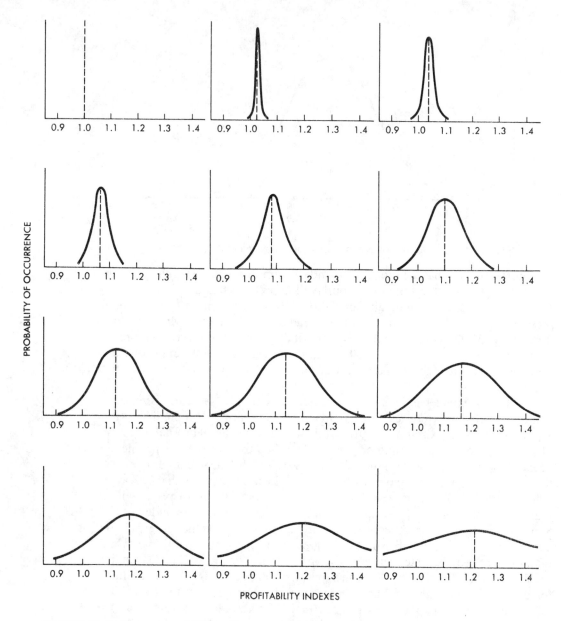

FIGURE 15-5 Management risk profiles

factor becomes important if capital markets are less than perfect. In essence, the project is evaluated in isolation of investors and of existing investment projects.

For these reasons, the approach leaves much to be desired. Still, we must recognize that in practice most investment decisions are made by management in this or some similar way. By providing management with information about the dispersion of possible outcomes, more informed decisions are possible than in the conventional capital-budgeting analysis, which considers only the expected values of cash flows.

COMBINATIONS OF RISKY INVESTMENTS

From Chapter 14 we know that the marginal risk of an individual proposal to the firm as a whole depends upon its correlation with existing projects as well as its correlation with proposals under consideration that might be accepted. The appropriate information is the standard deviation and expected value of the probability distribution of possible net present values for all feasible combinations of existing projects and investment proposals under consideration. Assume for now that management is interested only in the marginal impact of an investment proposal on the risk complexion of the firm as a whole.

The selection of the most desirable combination of investments will depend upon management's risk preferences with respect to net present value and variance, or standard deviation. Fig. 15-6 shows various combinations of risky investments available to the firm. This figure is the same as Fig. 14-7 in Chapter 14. Each dot represents a combination of proposals under consideration and existing investment projects for the firm. We see that certain dots dominate others in the sense that they represent a higher expected value of net present value and the same standard deviation, a lower standard deviation and the same expected value of net present value, or both a higher expected value and a lower standard deviation. The dots that dominate others are those that are farthest to the right. With information of this sort before it, management can eliminate most combinations of risky investments simply because they are dominated by other combinations.

In this case, management would probably consider only four combinations of risky investments—*B, H, L,* and *P.* From these it would choose the one that it felt offered the best combination of expected return and risk. If it were moderately averse to risk, it might choose combination *L.* While combination *P* provides a

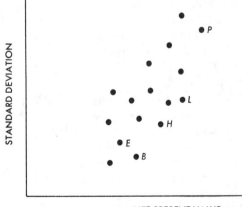

FIGURE 15-6 Opportunity set of combinations of projects

somewhat higher expected value of net present value, it also has a much higher standard deviation. Combinations B and H have lower risk, but also lower expected value of net present values. If management were fairly averse to risk, one of these two combinations might be chosen.

As discussed in Chapter 14, the final selection determines the new investment proposal or proposal that will be accepted. An exception would occur only when the combination selected was comprised of existing projects. In this situation, no investment proposals under consideration would be accepted. If the portfolio of existing projects was represented by combination E in the figure, the selection of any of the four outlying combinations would imply the acceptance of one or more new investment proposals. Investment proposals under consideration that were not in the combination finally selected would, of course, be rejected.

CONCEPTUAL IMPLICATIONS

On the basis of the information presented, management determines which investment proposals under consideration offer the best marginal contribution of expected value of net present value and standard deviation to the firm as a whole. In determining the standard deviation for a combination, management must consider the correlation between an investment proposal and existing and other proposed investments. This evaluation suggests that the total risk of the firm is what is important; investment decisions are made in light of their marginal impact on total risk.

This approach implies that from the standpoint of shareholders, management should be concerned with the firm's solvency. As discussed, such solvency depends on the total risk of the firm. Owing to less-than-perfect correlation with each other, certain projects have diversification properties. As a result, the total risk of the firm will be less than the sum of the parts. Management presumably will endeavor to accept investment proposals in a way that will keep the probability of insolvency within reasonable bounds while maximizing net present value.

As indicated before, the problem with this approach is that it ignores the fact that investors can diversify the portfolios of common stocks they hold. They are not dependent on the firm to diversify away risk. Therefore, diversification by the firm may not be a thing of value in the sense of doing something for investors that they cannot do for themselves. To the extent that investors are concerned only with the unavoidable or systematic risk of a project, the capital-asset pricing model approach illustrated earlier should be used.

It may be reasonable to use both approaches. The capital-asset pricing model approach might serve as the foundation for judging the valuation implications of an investment project. To the extent the possibility of insolvency exists and the bankruptcy costs which result are considerable, the project also would be judged in a total firm-risk context. If both approaches give clear accept or reject signals, those signals should be followed. The obvious problem occurs if one approach gives an accept signal while the other gives a reject signal. In this case, management should place more weight on one or the other signal, depending on which approach is more applicable.

If the shares of a large company are publicly held, and if the possibility of insolvency is remote, a strong case can be made for using the signal given by the capital-asset pricing model. If the stock is traded in a market with high transaction and information costs, if the possibility of insolvency is significant, and if the expression of project returns in terms of market-based returns is crude, greater reliance should be placed on the total firm-risk approach. Even here, one should recognize that a portion of the residual risk can be diversified away.

Summary

In theory, the required rate of return for an investment project should be the rate that leaves the market price of the share unchanged. If existing investment projects and investment proposals under consideration are homogeneous with respect to risk, it is appropriate to use the overall cost of capital of a company as the acceptance criterion. This can be a weighted-average cost of the various instruments with which the company intends to finance. By far the most difficult cost to measure is the cost of equity capital. Using a dividend-capitalization model, this cost is the rate of discount that equates the present value of the stream of expected future dividends with the market price of the shares. The key ingredient in the formula is the accuracy of estimates of expected future dividends. Approaching the problem directly, we can estimate the cost of equity capital with the capital-asset pricing model. The model itself was presented in Chapter 5, and its application to determining equity costs was illustrated in this chapter.

Given the measurement of marginal costs of debt, preferred stock, and equity, a weighted-average cost of capital can be computed. The weights employed should correspond to the proportions with which the firm intends to finance. Once computed, the weighted-average cost is used as a basis for accepting or rejecting investment proposals. The rationale for its use was discussed, as were certain qualifications. When investment projects, both existing and new, are widely variant with respect to risk, use of the company's overall cost of capital as an acceptance criterion is not appropriate.

In such cases, we should determine an acceptance criterion for each investment project or group of projects under consideration. One means for computing a risk-adjusted required rate of return for a proposal is with the capital-asset pricing model. One relates excess returns (in excess of the risk-free rate) for the project to excess returns for the market portfolio. Once a beta is computed, the required rate of return on equity can easily be determined. The key to this approach is to find a company whose shares are publicly traded and whose business closely corresponds to the investment proposal being contemplated. This company's stock is then used as a surrogate for the proposal in computing beta. If debt financing is employed, a weighted average required return for the project is calculated, based on the proportions the firm uses in its financing. In the same manner, a group-specific required return may be determined for a division, a subsidiary, or some other subunit of the firm. On a theoretical level, the capital-asset pricing model assumes that the only risk that is relevant is the systematic risk of the firm, an assumption that may not be appropriate in some situations.

A practical means for evaluating risky investments is to analyze the expected value and standard deviation of the probability distribution of possible returns for an investment proposal and, on the basis of this information, reach a decision. The greater the dispersion of the distribution, the greater the expected value that presumably would be required by management. The problem with this approach is that the link between the investment decision and share price is not direct. It depends on the perceptions of management with respect to likely investor reaction.

Finally, we examined the marginal impact of an investment project on the total risk of the firm. This becomes a concern if there is a possibility of insolvency. By analyzing the expected return and risk of various possible combinations of existing projects and investment proposals under consideration, management is able to select the best one, usually on the basis of dominance. The selection itself determines which proposals will be accepted and which will be rejected. With this approach, the diversification properties of a project are recognized in the computation of the standard deviation for a combination. Again, this is important if one is concerned with the impact of investment proposals accepted on the total risk of the firm as opposed to only its systematic risk.

Appendix: Adjusting the Beta for Leverage

The systematic risk of a stock is due to both the business and the financial risk of the company. In the calculation of a project's or group's cost of equity capital, the external company used as a proxy for the business risk of the project or group will sometimes have a significantly different proportion of debt than that used by the firm. As a result, it may be desirable to adjust the beta of the proxy company for this difference in relative debt. In what follows, we present a procedure for making such an adjustment under the assumptions of the capital-asset pricing model. In the end, we will qualify the results for the considerations to be taken up in Chapter 17.

With corporate income taxes, interest payments are deductible for tax purposes. Under these circumstances. Hamada, as well as others, has demonstrated that the required rate of return for a stock is[7]

$$R_j = i + \left(\frac{R_m - i}{\sigma_m^2}\right)(r_{ju,m}\sigma_{ju}\sigma_m)\left[1 + \frac{B}{S}(1 - T)\right] \qquad \text{(15A-1)}$$

where i = risk-free rate

R_m = the expected return on the market portfolio

σ_m = standard deviation of the probability distribution of possible market returns

σ_{ju} = standard deviation of the probability distribution of possible returns for security j *in the absence of leverage*

$r_{ju,m}$ = correlation coefficient between returns for security j *in the absence of leverage* and the market portfolio

---

[7]Robert S. Hamada, "Portfolio Analysis, Market Equilibrium and Corporation Finance," *Journal of Finance*, 24 (March 1969), 19–30.

B/S = the debt-to-equity ratio in market value terms

T = corporate tax rate

The important thing to note is that the covariance between returns, which is the second bracketed term in the equation, is as if the company had an all-equity capital structure.

Equation (15A-1) can be expressed in terms of the more familiar beta

$$R_j = i + (R_m - i)\beta_{ju}\left[1 + \frac{B}{S}(1 - T)\right] \tag{15A-2}$$

where β_{ju} is the beta measuring the responsiveness of the excess return for the security in the absence of leverage to the excess return for the market portfolio. Thus the overall required rate of return is comprised of the risk-free rate, i, plus a premium for business risk, $(R_m - i)\beta_{ju}$, and a premium for financial risk,

$$(R_m - i)\beta_{ju}\left[\frac{B}{S}(1 - T)\right]$$

The measured beta for the stock, β_j, embodies both risks and it is simply

$$B_j = \beta_{ju}\left[1 + \frac{B}{S}(1 - T)\right] \tag{15A-3}$$

Rearranging, the beta for the stock *in the absence of leverage* is

$$\beta_{ju} = \frac{B_j}{\left[1 + \frac{B}{S}(1 - T)\right]} \tag{15A-4}$$

Given these expressions, we are able to derive the beta *in the absence of leverage* for a particular stock. Suppose the measured beta, B_j, for security j were 1.4; the debt-to-equity ratio, B/S, were 0.6; and the tax rate were 50 percent. Therefore the beta *in the absence of leverage* would be

$$B_{ju} = \frac{1.4}{[1 + 0.6(0.5)]} = 1.08$$

If we now wished to determine the beta for a different amount of leverage, we would use Eq. (15A-3). Suppose that we were interested in using security j as a proxy for the systematic risk of our project or group. However, we employ a debt-to-equity ratio of 0.3 as opposed to the 0.6 for security j. Therefore the adjusted beta would be

$$\text{Adjusted } B_j = 1.08[1 + 0.3(0.5)] = 1.24$$

This beta contrasts with 1.08 for security j *in the absence of leverage*, and with 1.40 for security j with a debt-to-equity ratio of 0.6.

In summary, we are able to derive an adjusted beta for a security under the assumption of a different proportion of debt than what occurs. We first estimate the beta for the stock *in the absence of leverage* and then adjust this figure for the proportion of leverage we wish to employ. The final result is an approximation of the beta that would prevail if the external company were to employ the desired proportion of debt.

Note that the adjustment procedure assumes that all the tenets of the capital-asset pricing model hold. One of these is that in the absence of taxes, changes in the capital structure of a firm do not affect its valuation. With taxes, value increases in a linear manner with leverage. Chapter 16 analyzes this proposition in depth. The adjustment procedure presented provides an approximate beta when the proportion of debt is varied, but it is only an approximation.

Questions

1. Why is it important to use marginal weights in calculating a weighted-average cost of capital?
2. Under what circumstances is it appropriate to use the weighted-average cost of capital as an acceptance criterion?
3. Do the funds provided by sources such as accounts payable and accruals have a cost of capital? Explain.
4. What is the critical assumption inherent in the capital-asset pricing model as it relates to the acceptance criterion for risky investments?
5. What is the distinction between evaluating the expected value and standard deviation for an individual investment project and for a group or combination of projects?
6. If management of a company has significant holdings of stock in the company, with little in the way of "outside" wealth, how is this likely to affect its behavior with respect to risky investment decisions? Is this in the shareholders' best interests?
7. Trace the effects of the following on the cost of capital.
    (a) The Bank of Canada increases the money supply by buying bonds from the public.
    (b) The public decides to save a larger proportion of its income.
    (c) The capital-gains tax rate is lowered.
    (d) Major economic depressions are eliminated.
    (e) The corporation income tax rate is lowered.
8. Is it possible to find projects that consistently provide returns in excess of those required? What if the product markets are competitive and highly efficient?
9. Should companies in the same industry have approximately the same required rates of return on investment projects? Why or why not?
10. If you use debt funds to finance a project, why is not their cost the required return for the project? As long as the project earns more than enough to pay interest and service the principal, does it not benefit the firm?
11. If the cost of bankruptcy proceedings (fees, trustee fees, delays, inefficiencies and so on) were to rise substantially, would this occurrence have an effect on a company's required rate of return and on the way it looks at investment opportunities?
12. Should a company with multiple divisions establish separate required rates of return, or costs of capital, for each division as opposed to using the company's overall cost of capital?

Problems with Solutions

1. A company has the following capital structure:

Debt	$2 000 000
Preferred	1 000 000
Common shares	4 000 000
Retained earnings	3 000 000
	10 000 000

The amounts shown represent book values. The market values and costs of the components are as follows:

	MV	After-tax cost
Debt	$1 800 000	0.06
Preferred	700 000	0.11
Common equity	12 500 000	0.15
	$15 000 000	

Calculate the weighted-average cost of capital. Use market values.

	Proportion	Cost	Weighted cost
Debt	0.120	0.06	0.0072
Preferred	0.047	0.11	0.0052
Common	0.883	0.15	0.1250
	1.000		0.1374

Weighted-average cost of capital is 13.74 percent.

2. A company is considering an investment of $40 000 in a machine which will generate an annual cash flow of $12 000 for 5 years. Flotation costs associated with an issue of common shares which will be required to finance part of the project are $2 000. The company uses a weighted average cost of capital of 15 percent. Using the net present value method determine whether the investment should be made. If there were no flotation costs would your decision be different?

Cost of machine	$40 000
Flotation costs	2 000
Initial outlay	$42 000

PV of $12 000 per year for 5 years at 15% = $40 226
Net present value = $40 226 – $42 000 = –$1 1774
The investment should be rejected.
With no flotation costs: Net present value = $40 226 – $40 000 = $226.
The investment would be acceptable.

3. A company has the following optimal capital structure:

Debt	30%
Preferred	10%
Common equity	60%

Debt now costs the company 7 percent after tax, the cost of preferred is 10 percent and of common 16 percent. The company expects earnings of $10 000 000 and has the following investment opportunities:

Project	Cost	After tax return
1	$4 000 000	15%
2	1 500 000	16%
3	2 000 000	11%
4	2 500 000	14%

The company wishes to invest in all projects earning more than the weighted-average cost of capital and pay whatever dividends it can.

Weighted-average cost of capital

	Weights	Cost	Weighted cost
Debt	0.30	0.07	0.021
Preferred	0.10	0.10	0.010
Common	0.60	0.16	0.096
	1.00		0.127

Weighted average cost of capital = 12.7 percent. Projects 1, 2 and 4 are acceptable at a total cost of $8 000 000. The $8 000 000 of investments would be financed as follows:

	Weight	Financing	
Debt	0.3	$2 400 000	
Preferred	0.1	800 000	
Common equity	0.6	4 800 000	
		$8 000 000	
Net income			$10 000 000
Retained earnings needed to finance investment			4 800 000
Amount of dividend			$ 5 200 000

Note: Each additional dollar of earnings retained permits the company to issue more debt and preferred. For example, if the company has $15 of earnings and $10 of investment opportunities, it should raise money as follows in order to maintain its optimal capital structure:

Debt	$ 3
Preferred	1
Common equity*	6
	$10

*retained earnings

Since only $6 of earnings are needed to finance the investments, the other $9 can be paid out as dividends.

Problems

1. Lee Enterprises Ltd. is financed by two sources of funds: bonds and common stock. The cost of capital for funds provided by bonds is K_i while K_e is the cost of capital for equity funds. The capital structure consists of amount B of bonds and S of stock. Compute the weighted-average of cost of capital, K_o.

2. Assume B (problem 1) is $3 million and S is $7 million. The bonds have a 14 percent cost, and the stock is expected to pay $500 000 in dividends this year. The growth rate of dividends has been 11 percent and is expected to continue at the same rate. Find the cost of capital if the corporate tax rate on income is 40 percent.

3. On March 10, International Copy Machines Ltd. (ICOM), one of the favorites of the stock market, was priced at $300 per share. This price was based on an expected annual growth rate of at least 20 percent for quite some time in the future. In July, economic indicators turned down, and investors revised downward to 15 percent their estimate for future growth of ICOM. What should happen to the price of the stock? Assume the following:
   (a) A perpetual-growth valuation model is a reasonable representation of the way the market values ICOM.
   (b) The measured cost of equity capital to the firm is the true cost.
   (c) The firm does not change its dividend, the risk complexion of its assets, or its degree of financial leverage.
   (d) The expected dividend in the first year is $3 per share.

4. K-Far Stores Ltd. has launched an expansion program, which should result in the saturation of the Toronto marketing region in 6 years. As a result, the company is predicting a growth in earnings of 12 percent for 3 years, 6 percent for years 4 through 6, after which it expects constant earnings forever. The company expects to increase its dividends per share, how $2 in keeping with this growth pattern. Currently, the market price of the stock is $25 per share. Estimate the company's cost of equity capital.

5. The Manx Company Ltd. was recently formed to manufacture a new product. It has the following capital structure in market value terms:

13% Debentures of 2005	$ 6 000 000
12% Preferred stock	2 000 000
Common stock (320 000 shares)	8 000 000
	$16 000 000

The common stock sells for $25 a share, and the company has a marginal rate of 50 percent. A study of publicly held companies in this line of business suggests that the required return on equity is about 17 percent for a company of this sort. (The capital-asset pricing model approach was used to determine the required rate of return.) Compute the firm's present weighted-average cost of capital.

6. The Tumble Down D Ranch in Alberta would like a new mechanized barn, which will cost $600 000. The new barn is expected to provide annual cash savings of $90 000 indefinitely (for practical purposes of computation, forever). The ranch, which is incorporated and has a public market for its stock, has a weighted-average cost of capital of 14.5 percent. For this project, Howard Kelsey, the president, intends to use $200 000 in retained earnings and to finance the balance half with debt and half with a new issue of common stock.

Flotation costs on the debt issue amount to 2 percent of the total debt raised, whereas flotation costs on the new common stock issue come to 15 percent of the issue. What is the net present value of the project after allowance for flotation costs? Should the ranch invest in the new barn?

7. Cohn and Sitwell Co. Ltd., may begin to manufacture special drill bits and other equipment for oil rigs. This is currently regarded as a "hot" area, and the company has certain expertise by virtue of its having a large mechanical-engineering staff. Because of the large outlays required to get into the business, management is concerned that Cohn and Sitwell earn a proper return. Since the new venture is believed to be sufficiently different from the company's existing operations, management feels that a required rate of return other than the company's present one should be employed.

The financial manager's staff has identified several companies engaged solely in the manufacture and sale of oil-drilling equipment whose stocks are publicly traded. Over the last 5 years, the average beta for these companies has been 1.28. The staff believes that 18 percent is a reasonable estimate of the average return on stocks in general for the foreseeable future and that the risk-free rate will be around 12 percent. In financing projects, Sitwell and Cohn uses 40 percent debt and 60 percent equity. The after-tax cost of debt is 8 percent.

(a) On the basis of this information, determine a required rate of return for the project, using the capital-asset pricing-model approach.

(b) Is the figure obtained likely to be a realistic estimate of the required rate of return on the project?

8. Acosta Sugar Company Ltd. has estimated that the overall return for the Toronto Stock Exchange Index will be 15 percent for the next ten years. The company also feels that the interest rate on Treasury bills will average 10 percent over this interval. The company is thinking of expanding into a new product line: almonds. It has no experience in this line but has been able to obtain information on various companies involved in producing and processing nuts. Although no company examined produces only almonds, Acosta's management feels that the beta for such a company would be 1.10, once the almond operation was ongoing. There is some uncertainty about the beta that will actually prevail. Management has attached the following probabilities to possible outcomes:

Probability	0.2	0.3	0.2	0.2	0.1
Beta	1.00	1.10	1.20	1.30	1.40

(a) What is the required rate of return for the project using the mode beta of 1.10?
(b) What is the range of required rates of return?
(c) What is the expected value of required rate of return?

9. George and Yuji Tanaka, who are brothers, own a small motel on Vancouver Island. There are no loans against their property. Because of its location, they have been offered $500 000 for the property. If they were to sell, they feel they could obtain a return of $100 000 a year before taxes in alternative investments of comparable risk. The other option is to expand and modernize the motel and install a swimming pool. The total cost would be $300 000. Knowing the value of fee-simple land (owned land) on Vancouver Island, a savings and loan company is willing to make a long-term mortgage loan for the full cost at an interest rate of 15 percent.

(a) What should be the lowest acceptable rate of return to George and Yuji on the improvement project?

(b) What incremental annual profits before taxes must the new project earn in order to provide George and Yuji with exactly their minimum required return?

10. After a careful study of the risk preferences of its management, the Henken Aviation Company Ltd. has determined certain risk profiles for investment projects. These risk profiles depict the maximum standard deviation of profitability index that is tolerable for a particular expected value of profitability index. (The profitability index is the present value of future cash flows of a project divided by the initial cash outlay.) The risk profiles for various profitability indexes are as follows:

Expected profitability index	1.00	1.05	1.10	1.15	1.20	1.25
Maximum standard deviation	0	0.04	0.10	0.15	0.21	0.26

The company is considering two new investment proposals, which are expected to have the following characteristics:

Proposal X Cost = $2 million		Proposal Y Cost = $5 million	
Net present value	Probability of occurrence	Net present value	Probability of occurrence
−$0.5 million	0.10	−$0.4 million	0.10
0	0.20	0.1 million	0.15
0.5 million	0.40	0.5 million	0.50
1.0 million	0.20	0.9 million	0.15
1.5 million	0.10	1.4 million	0.10

Given the risk profiles of the company, should either or both of the two proposals be accepted?

11. Benzo Tube Company Ltd. wishes to evaluate three new investment proposals. It is concerned with the impact of the proposals on its total risk. Consequently, it has determined expected values and standard deviations of the probability distributions of possible net present values for the possible combinations of existing projects, E, and investment proposals under consideration:

Combination	Expected value of net present value (in thousands)	Standard deviation (in thousands)
E	$6 500	$5 250
E,1	6 800	5 000
E,2	7 600	8 000
E,3	7 200	6 500
E,1,2	7 900	7 500
E,1,3	7 500	5 600
E,2,3	8 300	8 500
E,1,2,3	8 600	9 000

Which combination do you feel is most desirable? Which proposals should be accepted? Which should be rejected?

Appendix Problem

12. Willie Sutton Bank Vault Company Ltd. has a debt-to-equity ratio (market value) of 0.75. Its present cost of debt funds is 15 percent, and it has a marginal tax rate of 40 percent. Willie Sutton Bank Vault Ltd. is eyeing the automated bank teller business, a field that involves electronics and is considerably different from its own, so the company is looking for a benchmark or proxy company. The Peerless Machine Company Ltd., whose stock is publicly traded, produces only automated teller equipment. Peerless has a debt-to-equity ratio of 0.25, a beta of 1.15, and an effective tax rate of 0.40.

(a) If Willie Sutton Bank Vault Company Ltd. wishes to enter the automated bank teller business, what systematic risk (beta) is involved if it intends to employ the same amount of leverage in the new venture as it presently employs?

(b) If the risk-free rate presently is 13 percent and the expected return on the market portfolio is 17 percent, what return should the company require for the project if it uses a capital-asset pricing model approach?

Selected References

AIVAZIAN, VAROUJ, and JEFFREY L. CALLEN, "Investment, Market Structure, and the Cost of Capital," *Journal of Finance*, 34 (March 1979), 85-92.

ALBERTS, W.W., and S.H. ARCHER, "Some Evidence on the Effect of Company Size on the Cost of Equity Capital," *Journal of Financial and Quantitative Analysis*, 8 (March 1973), 229-42.

ARDITTI, FRED D., and HAIM LEVY, "The Weighted Average Cost of Capital as a Cutoff Rate: A Critical Analysis of the Classical Textbook Weighted Average," *Financial Management*, 6 (Fall 1977), 24-34.

BERANEK, WILLIAM, "The Weighted Average Cost of Capital and Shareholder Wealth Maximization," *Journal of Financial and Quantitative Analysis*, 12 (March 1977), 17-32.

CORR, ARTHUR V. "Economic Evaluation of Capital Investment Proposals," *Cost and Management* (Jan.-Feb. 1978), 24-31.

ELLIOTT, J. WALTER, "The Cost of Capital and U.S. Investment," *Journal of Finance*, 35 (September 1980), 981-1000.

EZZELL, JOHN R., and R. BURR PORTER, "Flotation Costs and the Weighted Average Cost of Capital," *Journal of Financial and Quantitative Analysis*, 11 (September 1976), 403-13.

FAMA, EUGENE F., "Risk-Adjusted Discount Rates and Capital Budgeting under Uncertainty," *Journal of Financial Economics*, 5 (1977), 3-24.

FINDLAY, M. CHAPMAN, III, ARTHUR E. GOODING, and WALLACE Q. WEAVER, JR., "On the Relevant Risk for Determining Capital Expenditure Hurdle Rates," *Financial Management*, 5 (Winter 1976), 9-16.

FULLER, RUSSELL J., and HALBERT S. KERR, "Estimating the Divisional Cost of Capital: An Analysis of the Pure-Play Technique," *Journal of Finance*, 36 (December 1981), 997-1009.

GALLINGER, GEORGE W., and GLENN V. HENDERSON, JR., "The SML and the Cost of Capital," Research Paper, Arizona State University, 1981.

GUP, BENTON E., and SAMUEL W. NORWOOD III, "Divisional Cost of Capital: A Practical Approach," *Financial Management*, 11 (Spring 1981), 20-24.

KEANE, SIMON E., "The Investment Discount Rate—In Defence of the Market Rate of Interest," *Accounting and Business Research*, Summer 1976, 228-36.

LESSARD, DONALD R., and RICHARD S. BOWER, "An Operational Approach to Risk Screening," *Journal of Finance*, 27 (May 1973), 321-38.

MILES, JAMES A., and JOHN R. EZZELL, "The Weighted Average Cost of Capital, Perfect Capital Markets, and Project Life: A Clarification," *Journal of Financial and Quantitative Analysis*, 15 (September 1980), 719-30.

MYERS, STEWART C., and STUART M. TURNBULL, "Capital Budgeting and the Capital Asset Pricing Model: Good News and Bad News," *Journal of Finance*, 32 (May 1977), 321-32.

NANTELL, TIMOTHY J. and C. ROBERT CARLSON, "The Cost of Capital as a Weighted Average," *Journal of Finance*, 30 (December 1975), 1343-55.

REILLY, RAYMOND R., and WILLIAM E. WECKER, "On the Weighted Average Cost of Capital," *Journal of Financial and Quantitative Analysis*, 8 (January 1973), 123-26.

SCOTT, DAVID F., JR., "Determining the Cost of Common Equity Capital: The Direct Method," *Journal of Business Research*, 8 (March 1980), 89-103.

VAN HORNE, JAMES C., "An Application of the Capital Asset Pricing Model to Divisional Required Returns," *Financial Management*, 9 (Spring 1980), 14-19.

VI

CAPITAL STRUCTURE AND DIVIDEND POLICIES

16

Leveraging
the Firm

Financial leverage involves the use of funds for which the firm pays a fixed cost in the hope of increasing the return to its common shareholders. Since increases in leverage also increase the risk of the earnings stream to common shareholders, however, we face the familiar tradeoff between risk and expected return. Higher expected return leads to higher share prices, all other things being the same. Greater risk results in lower share prices, again holding all else constant. With respect to financial leverage, the goal is to strike a happy balance between risk and expected return, maximizing the market price of the firm's shares.

In this chapter we are going to explore ways a company may evaluate the impact of leverage on expected return and risk. Our purpose here is to show how we might approach the problem in practice. In the next chapter, we shall explore the conceptual underpinnings to the problem. The additional discussion in that chapter will provide a richer insight into the problem and reinforce the presentation in this chapter. Thus, the two chapters are closely related. Before proceeding further, however, let us take a moment to define financial risk.

Financial Risk

Broadly speaking, financial risk encompasses both the risk of possible insolvency and the variability in earnings available to common shareholders. As a firm increases the proportion of debt, lease financing, and preferred stock in its capital structure, fixed charges increase. As a result, the probability of cash insolvency increases. To illustrate this notion, suppose that two firms have different degrees of leverage but are identical in every other respect. Each has expected annual cash earnings of $80 000 before interest and taxes. Firm A has no debt; Firm B has

$300 000 worth of 10 percent perpetual bonds outstanding. Thus, the total annual financial charges for Firm B are $30 000, whereas Firm A has no financial charges. If cash earnings for both firms happen to be 75 percent lower than expected—namely, $20 000—Firm B will be unable to cover its financial charges with cash earnings. We see, then, that the probability of cash insolvency increases with the financial charges incurred by the firm.

The second aspect of financial risk involves the relative dispersion of income available to common shareholders. Suppose that the expected future annual operating incomes over the next 5 years for Firms A and B were subjective random variables where the expected values of the probability distributions were each $80 000 and the standard deviations $40 000. As before, assume that Firm A has no debt, while Firm B has $300 000 in 10 percent bonds. If, for simplicity, we neglect federal income taxes, the expected value of earnings available to common shareholders would be $80 000 for Firm A and $50 000 for Firm B. Because the standard deviation about the expected values is the same for both firms, the relative dispersion of expected earnings available to common shareholders is greater for Firm B than for Firm A. For Firm A the coefficient of variation, which is simply the standard deviation divided by the expected value, is

$$\text{Coefficient of variation} = \frac{\$40\ 000}{\$80\ 000} = 0.50$$

while for Firm B it is

$$\text{Coefficient of variation} = \frac{\$40\ 000}{\$50\ 000} = 0.80$$

Graphically, the relationship is shown in Fig. 16-1. We see that the degree of dispersion from the expected value of earnings available to common shareholders is the same for both firms, but the expected value of these earnings is greater for Firm A than for Firm B. As a result, the relative dispersion, as measured by the coefficient of variation, is less for Firm A.

The dispersion in earnings available to common shareholders is to be distinguished from the dispersion of operating income, known as business risk. In our example above, both firms had the same degree of business risk, as defined, because the coefficient of variation of expected future operating income was the same

$$\text{Coefficient of variation} = \frac{\$40\ 000}{\$80\ 000} = 0.50$$

Only in the degree of financial risk did the two firms differ. In summary, we regard financial risk as encompassing the volatility of earnings available to common shareholders as well as the probability of insolvency. Both aspects are related directly to the dispersion of expected operating income, or the business risk, of the firm.

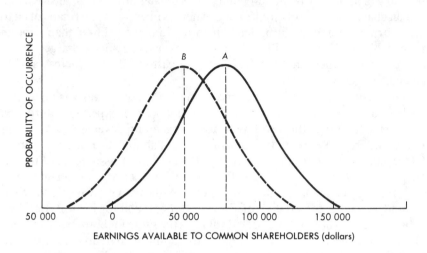

PROBABILITY OF OCCURRENCE

EARNINGS AVAILABLE TO COMMON SHAREHOLDERS (dollars)

FIGURE 16-1   Probability distribution of earnings available to common shareholders

EBIT-EPS Relationships

To analyze the appropriate degree of financial leverage for a firm, we need among other things to understand the sensitivity of earnings per share (EPS) to earnings before interest and taxes (EBIT) for various financing alternatives. EBIT does not depend on financial leverage, but rather is a result of the operations and the business risk of the firm. We must know what happens to a firm's earnings per share under various financing options as changes in EBIT occur.

CALCULATION OF EARNINGS PER SHARE

To illustrate an EBIT-EPS analysis of leverage, suppose Brandon Tire Company Ltd. with long-term capitalization of $10 million, consisting entirely of common stock, wishes to raise another $5 million for expansion through one of three possible financing plans. The company may finance with (1) all common stock, (2) all debt at 12 percent interest, or (3) all preferred stock with an 11 percent dividend. Present annual earnings before interest and taxes (EBIT) are $2 million, the income tax rate is 50 percent, and 200 000 shares of stock are now outstanding. Common stock can be sold at $50 per share under financing option 1, or 100 000 additional shares of stock.

In order to determine the EBIT break-even, or indifference, points between the various financing alternatives, we begin by calculating earnings per share for some hypothetical level of EBIT. Suppose we wished to know what earnings per share would be under the three financing plans if EBIT were $2.4 million. The calculations are shown in Table 16-1. We note that interest on debt is deducted before taxes, while preferred-stock dividends are deducted after taxes. As a result,

TABLE 16-1   Calculations of Earnings Per Share Under Three Financing Alternatives

	All common	All debt	All preferred
Earnings before interest and taxes (hypothetical)	$2 400 000	$2 400 000	$2 400 000
Interest	—	600 000	—
Earnings before taxes	2 400 000	1 800 000	2 400 000
Income taxes (50%)	1 200 000	900 000	1 200 000
Earnings after taxes	1 200 000	900 000	1 200 000
Preferred stock dividend	—	—	550 000
Earnings available to common stockholders	$1 200 000	$ 900 000	$ 650 000
Number of shares	300 000	200 000	200 000
Earnings per share	$4.00	$4.50	$3.25

earnings available to common shareholders are higher under the debt alternative than they are under the preferred stock alternative, despite the fact that the interest rate on debt is higher than the preferred stock dividend rate.

BREAK-EVEN, OR INDIFFERENCE, ANALYSIS

Given the information in Table 16-1, we are able to construct a "break-even" or indifference chart similar to the one we did for operating leverage. On the horizontal axis we plot earnings before interest and taxes (EBIT) and on the vertical axis, earnings per share (EPS). For each financing alternative, we must draw a straight line to reflect EPS for all possible levels of EBIT. To do so, we need two datum points for each alternative. The first is the EPS calculated for some hypothetical level of EBIT. For $2.4 million in EBIT, we see in Table 16-1 that earnings per share are $4.00, $4.50, and $3.25 for the common, debt, and preferred-stock financing alternatives. We simply plot these earnings per share at the $2.4 million mark in EBIT. Note that it does not matter which hypothetical level of EBIT we choose for calculating EPS. On good graph paper, one level is as good as the next.

The second datum point is simply the EBIT necessary to cover all fixed financial costs for a particular financing plan, and it is plotted on the horizontal axis. For the common-stock alternative, there are no fixed costs, so the intercept on the horizontal axis is zero. For the debt alternative, we must have EBIT of $600 000 to cover interest charges; so $600 000 becomes the horizontal axis intercept. For the preferred-stock alternative, we must divide total annual dividends by one minus the tax rate in order to obtain the EBIT necessary to cover these dividends. Thus we need $1.1 million in EBIT to cover $550 000 in preferred-stock dividends, assuming a 50 percent tax rate. Again, preferred dividends are deducted after taxes, so it takes more in before-tax earnings to cover them than it does to cover interest. Given the horizontal axis intercepts and earnings per share for some hypothetical level of EBIT, we draw a straight line through the two sets of points. The break-even or indifference chart for Brandon Tire Company Ltd. is shown in Fig. 16-2.

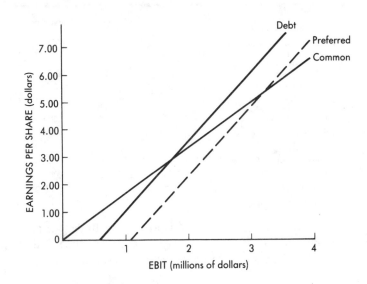

FIGURE 16-2 Indifference chart for three financing alternatives

We see from the figure that the earnings-per-share indifference point between the debt and common stock financing alternatives is $1 800 000 in EBIT. If EBIT is below that point, the common stock alternative will provide higher earnings per share; above that point the debt alternative is best. The indifference point between the preferred stock and the common stock alternative is $3 300 000 in EBIT. Above it, the preferred stock alternative is favored with respect to earnings per share; below it, the common stock alternative is best. We note that there is no indifference point between the debt and preferred-stock alternatives. The debt alternative dominates for all levels of EBIT and by a constant amount of earnings per share, namely $1.25 (or $4.50 less $3.25 from Table 16.1).

Indifference point mathematically   The indifference point between two methods of financing can be determined mathematically by

$$\frac{(\text{EBIT}^* - C_1)(1 - t)}{S_1} = \frac{(\text{EBIT}^* - C_2)(1 - t)}{S_2} \qquad \textbf{(16-1)}$$

where EBIT* = the EBIT indifference point between the two methods of financing for which we solve

C_1, C_2 = annual interest expenses or preferred stock dividends on a *before tax basis* for financing methods 1 and 2

t = corporate tax rate

S_1, S_2 = number of shares of common stock to be outstanding after financing for methods 1 and 2

Suppose we wished to determine the indifference point between the common stock and the debt-financing alternative in our example. We would have

$$\frac{(\text{EBIT*} - 0)(0.5)}{300\ 000} = \frac{(\text{EBIT*} - 600\ 000)(0.5)}{200\ 000}$$

Rearranging, we obtain

$$0.5(\text{EBIT*})(200\ 000) = 0.5(\text{EBIT*})(300\ 000)$$
$$- 0.5\ (600\ 000)(300\ 000)$$
$$50\ 000\ \text{EBIT*} = 90\ 000\ 000\ 000$$
$$\text{EBIT*} = \$1\ 800\ 000$$

The indifference point in EBIT, where earnings per share for the two methods of financing are the same, is $1.8 million. This amount can be verified graphically in Fig. 16-2. Thus, indifference points for financial leverage can be determined either graphically or mathematically.

EFFECT ON RISK

So far our concern has been only with what happens to the return to common shareholders. We have seen in our example that if EBIT is above $1.8 million, debt financing is the preferred alternative from the standpoint of earnings per share. We know from our earlier discussion, however, that the impact on expected return is only one side of the coin. The other side is the effect of leverage on risk. An EBIT-EPS chart does not permit a precise answer to this question: nevertheless, certain generalizations are possible. For one thing, the financial manager should compare the indifference point between debt and common stock financing with the most likely level of EBIT. The higher the level of EBIT, assuming it exceeds the indifference point, the stronger the case that can be made for debt financing, all other things the same.

In addition, the financial manager should assess the likelihood of EBIT's falling below the indifference point. Suppose that the EBIT in our example is $3 million. Given the business risk of the company and the resulting possible fluctuations in EBIT, the financial manager should assess the probability of EBIT's falling below $1.8 million. If the probability is negligible, the use of the debt alternative will be supported. On the other hand, if EBIT presently is only slightly above the indifference point and the probability of EBIT's falling below this point is high, the financial manager may conclude that the debt alternative is too risky.

This notion is illustrated in Fig. 16-3, where two probability distributions of possible EBIT's are superimposed on the indifference chart shown in Fig. 16-2. In Fig. 16-3, however, we focus on only the debt and common-stock alternatives. For the "safe" distribution, there is virtually no probability that EBIT will fall below the indifference point. Therefore, we might conclude that debt should be used, because the effect on shareholder return is substantial, whereas risk is negligible. For the "risky" distribution, there is a significant probability that EBIT will fall below the indifference point. In this case, the financial manager may conclude that the debt alternative is too risky.

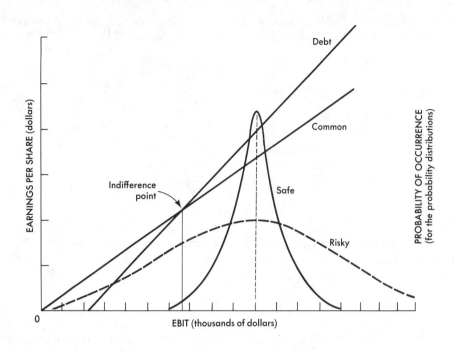

FIGURE 16-3 Indifference chart with EBIT probability distributions

In summary, the greater the level of EBIT above the indifference point and the lower the probability of downside fluctuation, the stronger the case that can be made for the use of debt financing. EBIT-EPS analysis is but one of several methods for determining the appropriate amount of debt a firm might carry. No one method of analysis is satisfactory by itself. When several methods are undertaken simultaneously, however, generalizations are possible. Let us examine the other methods for analyzing the appropriate degree of financial leverage for a firm.

Cash-Flow Ability to Service Debt

When considering the appropriate capital structure, it is necessary to analyze the cash-flow ability of the firm to service fixed charges. The greater the dollar amount of senior securities the firm issues and the shorter their maturity, the greater the fixed charges of the firm. These charges include principal and interest payments on debt, lease payments, and preferred-stock dividends. Before assuming additional fixed charges, the firm should analyze its expected future cash flows, for fixed charges must be met with cash. The inability to meet these charges, with the exception of preferred-stock dividends, may result in financial insolvency. The greater and more stable the expected future cash flows of the firm, the greater the debt capacity of the company.

COVERAGE RATIOS

Among the ways we can gain insight into the debt capacity of a firm is through the use of coverage ratios. In the computation of these ratios, one typically uses earnings before interest and taxes as a rough measure of the cash flow available to cover debt-servicing obligations. Perhaps the most widely used coverage ratio is *times interest earned*, which is simply

$$\text{Times interest earned} = \frac{\text{EBIT}}{\text{Interest on debt}} \tag{16-3}$$

Suppose that the most recent annual earnings before interest and taxes for a company were $6 million, and interest payments on all debt obligations were $1.5 million. Therefore, times interest earned would be four times. This tells us that EBIT can drop by as much as 75 percent and the firm still will be able to cover its interest payments out of earnings.

A coverage ratio of only one indicates that earnings are *just* sufficient to satisfy the interest burden. Although generalizations about what is an appropriate interest coverage ratio are difficult, one usually is concerned when the ratio gets much below 3 : 1. Circumstances differ however. In highly stable industry, a relatively low times-interest-earned ratio may be appropriate, whereas it is not appropriate in a highly cyclical industry.

Note that the times-interest-earned ratio tells us nothing about the firm's ability to meet principal payments on its debt. The inability to meet a principal payment constitutes the same legal default as failure to meet an interest payment. Therefore, it is useful to compute the coverage ratio for the full debt-service burden. This ratio is

$$\text{Debt-service coverage} = \frac{\text{EBIT}}{\text{Interest} + \dfrac{\text{Principal payments}}{1 - \text{Tax rate}}} \tag{16-4}$$

Here principal payments are adjusted upward for the tax effect. The reason is that EBIT represents earnings before taxes. Because principal payments are not deductible for tax purposes, they must be paid out of after-tax earnings. Therefore, we must adjust principal payments so that they are consistent with EBIT. If principal payments in our previous example were $1 million per annum and the tax rate were 40 percent, the debt-service coverage ratio would be

$$\text{Debt-service coverage} = \frac{\$6 \text{ million}}{\$1.5 \text{ million} + \dfrac{\$1 \text{ million}}{1 - 0.4}} = 1.89$$

A coverage ratio of 1.89 means that EBIT can fall by 47 percent before earnings coverage is insufficient to service the debt.[1] Obviously, the closer the ratio is to 1.0,

---

[1]This percent is determined by $1 - (1/1.89) = 0.47$

the worse things are, all other things the same. However, even with the coverage ratio of less than one, a company may still meet its obligations if it can renew some of its debt when it comes due.

The financial risk associated with leverage should be analyzed on the basis of the firm's ability to service total fixed charges. While lease financing is not debt per se, its impact on cash flows is exactly the same as the payment of interest and principal on a debt obligation. (See Chapter 20 for an analysis of lease financing.) Annual lease payments, therefore, should be added to the numerator and denominator of Eq. (16-4) in order to properly reflect the total cash-flow burden associated with financing.

As with the times-interest-earned ratio, exact rules of thumb are lacking for what constitutes a good or bad debt-service ratio. It varies according to the business risk of the firm. This is illustrated in Fig. 16-4, which shows the probability distributions of EBIT for two hypothetical companies. The expected value of EBIT is the same for both companies, as is the debt-service burden as described by the denominator in Eq. (16-4). Therefore, the debt-service coverage ratios also are the same, $100/$60 = 1.67. Company A, however, has much more business risk. The probability that EBIT will fall below the debt-service burden is depicted by the shaded areas in the figure. We see that this probability is much greater for Company A than it is for Company B. While a debt-service coverage ratio of 1.67 may be appropriate for Company B, it may not be appropriate for Company A. Simply put, a company with stable cash flows is able to take on relatively more fixed charges. This explains why electric utility companies have low coverage ratios when compared with manufacturing companies.

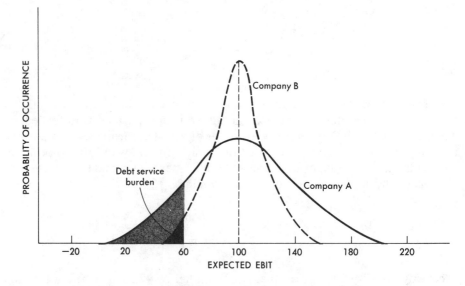

FIGURE 16-4   Possible EBIT in relation to debt service burden

As discussed in Chapter 6 on financial ratios, two comparisons should be undertaken with a coverage ratio. First, it should be compared with past and expected future ratios of the same company. Called trend analysis, the comparison determines if there has been an improvement or deterioration in coverage over time. The second comparison is with similar companies, perhaps in the same industry. The idea here is to try to isolate business risk as nearly as possible by comparing like companies. Sources of data and types of analysis possible are described in Chapter 6, so we do not dwell on them here.

Ultimately, one wants to make generalizations about the appropriate amount of debt (and leases) for a firm to have in its capital structure. It is clear that over the long run the wherewithal to service debt for the going concern is earnings. Therefore, coverage ratios are an important tool of analysis. However, they are but one tool by which a person is able to reach conclusions with respect to appropriate capital structure for the firm. Coverage ratios are subject to certain limitations and consequently, cannot be used as a sole means for determining a capital structure. For one thing, the fact that EBIT falls below the debt-service burden does not spell immediate doom for the company. Often alternative sources of funds, including renewal of the loan are available, and these sources must be considered.

PROBABILITY OF CASH INSOLVENCY

The vital question for the firm is not so much whether a coverage ratio will fall below one, but what are the chances of insolvency? The answer depends on whether all sources of payment—EBIT, cash, a new financing arrangement, or the sale of assets—are collectively deficient. A coverage ratio tells only part of the story. In order to address the broader question of cash insolvency, we must obtain information on the possible deviation of actual cash flows from those which are expected. As we discussed in Chapter 7, cash budgets can be prepared for a range of possible outcomes, with a probability attached to each. This information is extremely valuable to the financial manager in evaluating the ability of the firm to meet fixed obligations. Not only expected earnings are taken into account in determining this ability, but other factors as well: the purchase or sale of assets, the liquidity of the firm, dividends, seasonal patterns, and any other factors impacting on cash flows. Given the probabilities of particular cash-flow sequences, the financial manager is able to determine the amount of fixed charges and debt the company can undertake while still remaining within insolvency limits tolerable to management.

Management may feel that a 5 percent probability of being out of cash is the maximum it can tolerate, and that this probability corresponds to a cash budget prepared under pessimistic assumptions. In this case, debt might be undertaken up to the point where the cash balance under the pessimistic cash budget is just sufficient to cover the fixed charges associated with the debt. In other words, debt would be increased to the point at which the additional cash drain would cause the probability of cash insolvency to equal the risk tolerance specified by management. Note that the method of analysis simply provides a means for assessing the effect of increases in debt on the risk of cash insolvency. On the basis of this information, management would arrive at the most appropriate level of debt.

Donaldson has proposed a similar type of analysis.[2] He suggests that the ultimate concern of a company is whether cash balances during some future period will be involuntarily reduced below zero. Therefore, he advocated examining the cash flows of the company under the most adverse circumstances; that is, in his definition, under recession conditions. These conditions may or may not be the most adverse; however, in keeping with the spirit of his proposal, the firm should evaluate its cash flows under adverse circumstances. Donaldson defines the net cash balance during a recession (CB_r) as

$$CB_r = CB_o + NCF_r \tag{16-5}$$

where CB_o = cash balance at start of recession
NCF_r = net cash flows during recession.

Donaldson then calculates a probability distribution of expected net cash flows,[3] and analyzes the cash-flow behavior of a firm during a recession. Combining the beginning cash balances, CB_o, with the probability distribution of recession cash flows, NCF_r, he prepares a probability distribution of cash balances during the recession—CB_r.

To ascertain its debt capacity, a firm first would calculate the fixed charges associated with additional increments of debt. For each addition, the firm then would determine the probability of being out of cash. As before, management could set tolerance limits on the probability of being out of cash. Suppose the firm were considering issuing $20 million in additional debt and that the annual fixed charges were $4 million. By subtracting $4 million from the expected cash balances shown for the probability distribution of CB_r, we obtain the probability distribution of CB_r with the addition of $20 million in debt. If the probability of being out of cash with this increment of debt is negligible, Donaldson would contend that the company has unused debt capacity. Therefore, it would be possible to increase the amount of debt until the probability of being out of cash equaled the risk tolerance of management.

Donaldson extends his analysis to calculate the probability of cash inadequacy. Our discussion before was in terms of cash insolvency, which is defined as lack of cash after all nonessential expenditures have been cut. Cash inadequacy is said to occur if the firm is out of cash after making certain desired expenditures such as dividends, R & D expenditures, and capital expenditures. Thus, cash insolvency is the extreme form of cash inadequacy.

The analysis of the cash-flow ability of the firm to service fixed charges is perhaps the best way to analyze financial risk, but there is some question as to whether the external market analyzes a company in this manner. Sophisticated lenders and institutional investors certainly analyze the amount of fixed charges

---

[2]Gordon Donaldson, *Corporate Debt Capacity* (Boston: Division of Research, Harvard Business School, 1961). See also Donaldson, "Strategy for Financial Emergencies," *Harvard Business Review*, 47 (November-December 1969), 67-79.

[3]The determinants of net cash flows with which he works are sales collections, other cash receipts, payroll expenditures, raw-material expenditures, and nondiscretionary cash expenditures. By analyzing each of these determinants, he determines the range and probability of recession net cash flows.

and evaluate financial risk in keeping with the ability of the firm to service these charges, but individual investors may judge financial risk more by the book-value proportions of debt to equity. There may or may not be a reasonable correspondence between the ratio of debt to equity and the amount of fixed charges relative to the firm's cash-flow ability to service these charges. Some firms may have relatively high ratios of debt to equity but substantial cash-flow ability to service debt. Consequently, the analysis of debt-to-equity ratios alone can be deceiving and an analysis of the magnitude and stability of cash flows relative to fixed charges is extremely important in determining the appropriate capital structure for the firm.

Other Methods of Analysis

COMPARISON OF CAPITAL STRUCTURE RATIOS

Another method of analyzing the appropriate capital structure for a company is to evaluate the capital structure of other companies having similar business risk. Companies used in this comparison may be those in the same industry. If the firm is contemplating a capital structure significantly out of line with that of similar companies, it is conspicuous in the marketplace. This is not to say, however, that the firm is wrong; other companies in the industry may be too conservative with respect to the use of debt. The optimal capital structure for all companies in the industry might call for a higher proportion of debt to equity than the industry average. As a result, the firm may well be able to justify more debt than the industry average. However, if the firm is noticeably out of line in either direction, it should be able to justify its position, because investment analysts and creditors tend to evaluate companies by industry.

There are wide variations in the use of financial leverage among business firms. However, this is not true of industry classifications because firms in an industry tend to cluster together when it comes to debt ratios. Among industries there are wide differences in debt ratios. For example, the real estate industry makes extensive use of debt in financing projects, chemical and mining companies do not employ as much leverage. For selected industries, the total liabilities-to-total-equity ratios are as follows. These data are drawn from Statistics Canada Catalogue 61-207, (1980).

Industry	Debt to equity
Construction	3.22
Dairy products	1.47
Transportation	2.25
Chemical	1.21
Paper	1.04
Mining	1.03
Real estate	4.83
Publishing	1.79

The firm may profit also by talking with investment analysts, institutional investors, and investment houses to obtain their views on the appropriate amount of leverage. These analysts examine many companies and are in the business of recommending stocks. Therefore, they have an influence on the market, and their judgments with respect to how the market evaluates leverage may be very worthwhile. Similarly, a firm may wish to interview lenders to see how much debt it can undertake before the cost of borrowing is likely to rise. Finally, the management of a company may develop a "feel" for what has happened in the past to the market price of the share when they have issued debt.

The methods described above for analyzing the appropriate amount of leverage do not give an exact answer. Nevertheless, by undertaking a variety of analyses, the financial manager should be able to determine, within some range, the appropriate capital structure for the firm. By necessity, the final decision has to be somewhat subjective. However, it can be based on the best information available. In this way, the firm can obtain the capital structure most appropriate for its situation—the one that will tend to maximize the market price of the share, all other factors held constant.

Summary

Financial leverage involves the use of funds for which the firm agrees to pay a fixed charge. The greater the financial leverage of a firm, the greater the fluctuation in earnings available to common stockholders, all other things the same. Therefore, the advantage of higher expected returns to common stockholders must be balanced against the risks to them.

By using an indifference chart, we can study the relationship between earnings before interest and taxes (EBIT) and earnings per share under alternative methods of financing. The degree of sensitivity of earnings per share to EBIT depends upon the explicit cost of the method of financing, the number of shares of common stock to be issued, and the nearness to the indifference point. It is important in this analysis to evaluate the indifference point in relation to the level of EBIT as well as likely fluctuations in EBIT.

In addition, the cash-flow ability of the firm to service debt should be evaluated. The firm's debt capacity can be assessed by analyzing coverage ratios and the probability of cash insolvency under various levels of debt. Other methods of analysis include a comparison with capital-structure ratios of like companies, such as those within the same industry, and discussions with investment analysts, investment bankers, and lenders. In deciding upon an appropriate capital structure, all of these factors should be considered. In addition, certain concepts involving valuation should guide the decision. These concepts are discussed in the next chapter.

Questions

1. Define the concept of *financial leverage*.
2. Discuss the similarities and differences of financial and operating leverage.
3. Can the concept of financial leverage by analyzed quantitatively? Explain.
4. The EBIT-EPS chart suggests that the higher the debt ratio, the higher the earnings per share for any level of EBIT above the indifference point. Why do firms choose financing alternatives that do not maximize EPS?
5. Why is the percentage of debt for an electric utility higher than that for the typical manufacturing company?
6. Is the debt/equity ratio a good proxy for financial risk as represented by the cash-flow ability of a company to service debt? Why or why not?
7. How can a company determine in practice if it has too much debt? Too little debt?
8. How can coverage ratios be used to determine an appropriate amount of debt to employ? Are there any shortcomings to the use of these ratios?
9. In financial leverage, why not simply increase leverage as long as the firm is able to earn more on the employment of the funds than they cost? Would not earnings per share increase?

Problems with Solutions

1. A company expects earnings before interest and tax of $200 000 after the modernization of its plant facilities. If the company uses debt to finance the modernization it will incur interest of $60 000 per year. The expected standard deviation is $35 000. Calculate the coefficient of variation with debt and equity if the tax rate is 50 percent.

	Debt	Equity
Earnings before interest and tax	$200 000	$200 000
Interest	60 000	—
Earnings before tax	$140 000	$200 000
Tax 50%	70 000	100 000
Net income	$ 70 000	$100 000
Coefficient of variation with debt	$\dfrac{\$35\ 000}{\$70\ 000} = 0.50$	
Coefficient of variation with equity		$\dfrac{\$35\ 000}{\$100\ 000} = 0.350$

2. A company is considering an investment of $2 000 000 to add to its line of office equipment. It is the view of the directors that such a move is absolutely necessary if the company is to remain competitive. In addition to the expenditure, capital outlays of $1 500 000 are expected in each of the next five years. The company is considering two alternative methods of financing the $2 000 000: 1) an issue of 12 percent, 10-year debentures with an annual sinking fund requirement of $200 000 per year, and 2) an issue of common stock at a net price of $20 per share. The board hoped to increase the quarterly dividend to $0.25 per share. The current capital structure of the firm, which is close to the industry norm, is shown below.

Long term debt (10%)*	$3 000 000	
Common stock (par $10)	3 000 000	
Retained earnings	4 000 000	
	$10 000 000	

*$75 000 annual sinking fund requirement

Shown below is the earnings record of the company during the last five years:

	1980	1981	1982	1983	1984
Earnings before interest and tax (EBIT)	$1 000 000	$1 500 000	$400 000	$1 000 000	$200 000
Interest	330 000	322 500	315 000	307 500	300 000
Earnings before tax	$ 670 000	$1 177 500	$ 85 000	$ 692 500	$(100 000)
Tax 50%	335 000	588 750	42 500	346 750	—
	$ 335 000	$ 588 750	$ 42 500	$ 346 750	$(100 000)

Depreciation charges have averaged $1 000 000 per year; this is expected to increase to $1 100 000 per year starting in 1985. EBIT for 1985 is expected to be $1 200 000 and should increase by $200 000 per year until the end of 1989.

Using an indifference chart, assess the two financing alternatives. Also, consider the firm's ability to service debt and pay dividends.

Calculation of earnings per share at selected levels of EBIT*

	Debentures	Stock	Debentures	Stock
EBIT	$1 000 000	$1 000 000	$2 000 000	$2 000 000
Interest	532 500(1)	292 500(2)	532 500	292 500
Earnings before tax	$ 467 500	$ 707 500	$1 467 500	$1 707 500
Tax 50%	233 750	353 750	733 750	853 750
Net income	$ 233 750	$ 353 750	$ 733 750	$ 853 750
Number of shares outstanding	300 000(3)	400 000(4)	300 000	400 000
Earnings per share	$0.7792	$0.8844	$2.4458	$2.1344

(1) 0.1(3 000 000 − 75 000) + 0.12(2 000 000) = $532 500
(2) 0.1(3 000 000 − 75 000) = $292 500
(3) $3 000 000 ÷ $10 = 300 000
(4) $3 000 000 ÷ $10 + $2 000 000 ÷ $20 = 400 000

*Any two levels of EBIT are acceptable since the earnings per share is a linear function of EBIT

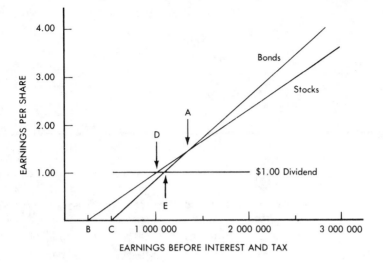

Significant points:

A   Indifference point ($1 252 500) at which earnings per share are the same under both alternatives ($1.20 per share).

B   EBIT required to cover interest charges under stock alternative, $292 500.

C   EBIT required to cover interest charges under bond alternative, $532 500.

D   EBIT required to pay interest and dividend of $1.00 under stock alternative.

$$= \$292\ 500 + \frac{\$400\ 000}{1 - 0.5)} = \$1\ 092\ 500$$

E   EBIT required to pay interest and a $1.00 dividend under bond alternative

$$= \$532\ 500 + \frac{\$300\ 000}{1 - 0.5} = \$1\ 132\ 500.$$

Other significant calculations

Overall ability to service debt:

EBIT required to cover interest and sinking fund under debt alternative

$$= \$532\ 500 + \frac{\$75\ 000 + \$200\ 000}{1 - 0.5} = \$1\ 082\ 500$$

EBIT required to cover interest and sinking fund under stock alternative

$$= \$292\ 500 + \frac{\$75\ 000}{1 - 0.5} = \$442\ 500$$

Debt service coverage under debt alternative Eq. (16.4)

$$\frac{\$1\ 200\ 000}{\$1\ 082\ 500} = 1.1085$$

Debt service coverage under stock alternative Eq. (16-4)

$$\frac{\$1\ 200\ 000}{\$442\ 500} = 2.7119$$

Future Flow of Funds—Debt Alternative Excluding Dividends

	1985	1986	1987	1988	1989
EBIT	$1 200 000	$1 400 000	$1 600 000	$1 800 000	$2 000 000
Interest	532 500	501 000	469 500	438 000	406 500
Earnings before tax	$ 667 500	$ 899 000	$1 130 500	$1 362 000	$1 593 500
Tax 50%	333 750	449 500	565 250	681 000	796 750
Net income	$ 333 750	$ 449 500	$ 565 250	$ 681 000	$ 796 750
Depreciation	1 100 000	1 100 000	1 100 000	1 100 000	1 100 000
Sources	$1 433 750	$1 549 500	$1 665 250	$1 781 000	$1 896 750
Sinking fund	$ 275 000	$ 275 000	$ 275 000	$ 275 000	$ 275 000
Investments	1 500 000	1 500 000	1 500 000	1 500 000	1 500 000
Uses	$1 775 000	$1 775 000	$1 775 000	$1 775 000	$1 775 000
Net inflow (outflow)	($ 341 250)	($ 225 500)	($ 109 750)	$ 6 000	$ 121 750

Future Flow of Funds—Stock Alternative Excluding Dividend

	1985	1986	1987	1988	1989
EBIT	$1 200 000	$1 400 000	$1 600 000	$1 800 000	$2 000 000
Interest	292 500	285 000	277 500	270 000	262 500
Earnings before tax	$ 907 000	$1 115 000	$1 322 500	$1 530 000	$1 737 500
Tax 50%	453 750	557 500	661 250	765 000	868 750
Net income	$ 453 750	$ 557 500	$ 661 250	$ 765 000	$ 868 750
Depreciation	1 100 000	1 100 000	1 100 000	1 100 000	1 100 000
Sources	$1 553 750	$1 657 500	$1 761 250	$1 865 000	$1 968 750
Sinking fund	$ 75 000	$ 75 000	$ 75 000	$ 75 000	$ 75 000
Investments	1 500 000	1 500 000	1 500 000	1 500 000	1 500 000
Uses	$1 575 000	$1 575 000	$1 575 000	$1 575 000	$1 575 000
Net inflow (outflow)	($ 21 250)	$ 82 500	$ 186 250	$ 290 000	$ 393 750

Summary Analysis:

At the highest anticipated level of EBIT ($2 000 000) the earnings per share under the debt alternative are only 14.6 percent more than under the stock alternative. The earnings per share are identical at an EBIT level of $1 252 500. Thus, given the earnings estimates and ignoring the risk considerations for the moment, the advantage, if any, of the debt alternative is small at EBIT levels expected for the next few years.

Turning to risk, earnings have fluctuated considerably over the last five years. In four of these years, interest and sinking fund payments ($1 082 500) under the debt alternative would have been in excess of EBIT.

With an excessive use of debt (see *pro forma* capital structure below) what will likely take place is an increase in the cost of capital. Assuming that 30 percent debt and 70 percent equity (the industry norm) is the optimal capital structure, what will happen to the cost of capital is shown in the familiar graph below:

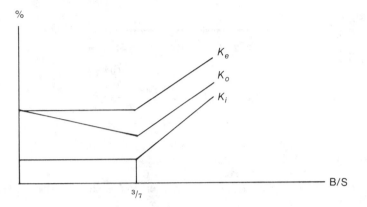

An increase in the use of debt beyond present levels will likely increase risk to such an extent that the average cost of capital will increase so as to offset the benefits of increased earnings per share under the debt alternative.

The funds flow calculations clearly show that new financing will be required in the near future even without the payment of dividends. If debt is issued this time around then the capital structure becomes:

	Amount	%
Debt	$5 000 000	41.7
Common	3 000 000	25.0
Retained earnings	4 000 000	33.3
	$12 000 000	100.0

With an industry average of only 30 percent and with the added risk described above, the debt alternative would paint the company into a corner and restrict future financing options. There can be no doubt that another issue of debt in the near future would be out of the question.

In summary, since the debt alternative does not generate a large increase in earnings per share (leverage), provides only marginal coverage (risk), and limits future financing alternatives (flexibility), the stock alternative is the more attractive.

Finally, a dividend of $1.00 per share appears unrealistic in the circumstances under either alternative. If the proposed investments are in fact necessary for the continued existence of the company, then, to conserve cash, the dividend must not be raised. Perhaps a cut in the dividend might even be in order depending on how soon the company wants to be in the market for funds once more.

Problems

1. The Lemaster Company Ltd. is a new firm that wishes to determine an appropriate capital structure. It can issue 16 percent debt or 15 percent preferred stock. The total capitalization of the company will be $5 million, and common will be sold at $20 per share. The company is expected to have a 50 percent tax rate. The possible capital structures are

Plan	Debt	Preferred	Equity
1	0%	0%	100%
2	30	0	70
3	50	0	50
4	50	20	30

   (a) Construct an EBIT-EPS chart for the four plans.
   (b) Determine the relevant indifference points.
   (c) Using Eq. (16-1), verify the indifference points on your graph for the dominant plans.
   (d) What plan is best?

2. Hi Grade Regulator Company Ltd. currently has 100 000 shares of common stock outstanding with a market price of $60 per share. It also has $2 million in 6 percent bonds. The company is considering a $3 million expansion program that it can finance with either (1) all common stock at $60 a share, (2) straight bonds at 8 percent interest, (3) preferred stock at 7 percent, (4) half common stock at $60 per share and half 8 percent bonds.
   (a) For a hypothetical EBIT level of $1 million after the expansion program, calculate the earnings per share for each of the alternative methods of financing. Assume a corporate tax rate of 50 percent.
   (b) Construct an EBIT-EPS chart. What are the indifference points between alternatives? What is your interpretation of them?

3. Hi Grade Regulator Company Ltd. (see problem 2) expects the EBIT level after the expansion program to be $1 million, with a two-thirds probability that it will be between $600 000 and $1 400 000.
   (a) Which financing alternative do you prefer? Why?
   (b) Suppose the expected EBIT level were $1.5 million and there were a two-thirds probability that it would be between $1.3 million and $1.7 million. Which financing alternative would you prefer? Why?

4. Niagara Power and Light Company Ltd. currently has the following long-term capitalization:

	Amount	Average before-tax cost
Debt	$ 80 million	9.50%
Preferred stock	10 million	8.00%
Common stock (1 million shares)	5 million	
Retained earnings	65 million	
	$160 million	

Earnings before interest and taxes (EBIT) are presently $16 million. Because Niagara services a recreational area, however, its revenues are more volatile than those of most public utilities.

The company needs to undertake a $20.million plant expansion program in order to keep up with growing demand. Management estimates the following EBIT possibilities for the near future if the expansion program is undertaken:

EBIT (in millions)	$17	$18	$19	$20	$21	$22	$23	$24
Probability of occurrence	5%	5%	10%	20%	25%	20%	10%	5%

The bonds of the company currently are rated A and the tax rate is 50 percent. To finance the expansion program, common stock could be sold at a price which would result in net proceeds to the company of $33⅓ per share. If debt financing were used, the company's bond rating would be lowered to Baa, and the interest rate would be 10½ percent on the new debt.

(a) What are present earnings per share?
(b) What are the earnings per share for the various possible levels of EBIT if common stock is used to finance the expansion program?
(c) What are earnings per share if debt is used?
(d) Which method of financing would you recommend? Is there adequate information? Does the use of debt affect the value of existing debt and equity?

5. Cornwell Real Estate Speculators Ltd., and the New Brunswick Electric Utility Company Ltd. have the following EBIT and debt-servicing burden:

	Cornwell	New Brunswick
Expected EBIT	$5 000 000	$100 000 000
Annual interest	1 600 000	45 000 000
Annual principal payments on debt	2 000 000	35 000 000

The tax rate for Cornwell is 40 percent; for New Brunswick Electric Utility, 50 percent. Compute the times-interest-earned ratio and the debt-service coverage ratio for the two companies. With which company would you feel more comfortable if you were a lender? Why?

6. Gamma Tube Company Ltd. plans to undertake a $7.5 million capital improvement program and is considering how much debt to use. It feels that it could obtain debt financing at the following interest rates (assume that this debt is perpetual):

Amounts (in millions)	First $3	Next $2	Next $1.5	Next $1
Interest cost	10%	11%	12%	13%

The company has made projections of its net cash flows (exclusive of new financing) during a period of adversity such as a recession. In a recession, it expects a net cash flow of $3 million with a standard deviation of $2 million (assume a normal distribution). Its beginning cash balance is $1 million. If the company is willing to tolerate only a 5 percent probability of running out of cash during a recession, what is the maximum proportion of the $7.5 million capital improvement program that can be financed with debt? (Use the probability concepts discussed in Chapter 14 and the table in Appendix B to that chapter.)

7. The debt ratios of four companies are shown below:

Company	Total debt/ total assets	Long term debt/ total capitalization
A	0.56	0.43
B	0.64	0.66
C	0.47	0.08
D	0.42	0.26

The companies are part of the following industries: supermarket, chemical, apparel making, and airline (not in order). Match the company with the industry.

Selected References

CRITTA, RICHARD D., "The Effect of Financial Leverage on Air Carrier Earnings: A Break-Even Analysis," *Financial Management*, 8 (Summer 1979), 53-60.

DONALDSON, GORDON, *Corporate Debt Capacity*, Boston: Division of Research, Harvard Business School, 1961.

———, "Strategy for Financial Emergencies," *Harvard Business Review*, 47 (November-December 1969), 67-79.

FERRI, MICHAEL G., and WESLEY H. JONES, "Determinants of Financial Structure: a New Methodological Approach," *Journal of Finance*, 34 (June 1979), 631-44.

HANDORF, WILLIAM C., "Flexible Debt Financing," *Financial Management*, 3 (Summer 1974), 17-23.

HELFERT, ERICH A., *Techniques of Financial Analysis*, 5th ed., Homewood, Ill.: Irwin, 1981, Chapter 2.

HONG, HAI, and ALFRED RAPPAPORT, "Debt Capacity, Optimal Capital Structure, and Capital Budgeting," *Financial Management*, 7 (Autumn 1978), 7-11.

LITZENBERGER, ROBERT H., and HOWARD B. SOSIN, "A Comparison of Capital Structure Decisions of Regulated and Non-regulated Firms," *Financial Management*, 8 (Autumn 1979), 17-21.

MARSH, PAUL, "The Choice Between Equity and Debt: An Empirical Study," *Journal of Finance*, 37 (March 1982), 121-44.

SCOTT, DAVID R., JR., and JOHN D. MARTIN, "Industry Influence on Financial Structure," *Financial Management*, (Spring 1975), 67-73.

SHALIT, SOL S., "On the Mathematics of Financial Leverage," *Financial Management*, 4 (Spring 1975), 57-66.

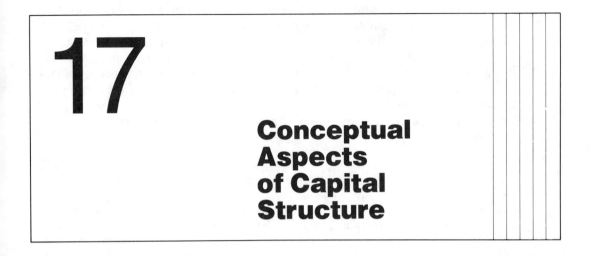

17

Conceptual Aspects of Capital Structure

We have just observed a company approaching the question of how much debt it should have in its capital structure. The incremental expected return and risk to common shareholders are very much a part of the answer. Now we explore the valuation underpinnings to the question of capital structure. As we shall see, much controversy surrounds the issue. Despite the unsettled nature of the matter, we hope that this presentation will provide the conceptual backdrop necessary to guide the financial manager in capital-structure decisions.

Throughout our discussion, we assume that the investment and dividend decisions of the firm are held constant. We wish to determine the effect of a change in financing mix on share price. The focus is different from before in that we are concerned with how security prices are determined in the overall financial markets. That is, how do suppliers of capital value a company in relation to other companies when it changes its capital structure? We shall see that financial market imperfections play a major role. For simplicity, we consider only debt-versus-equity financing, though the principles taken up apply to preferred-stock financing as well.

Introducing the Theory

The key question with which we are concerned is whether a firm can affect its total valuation (debt plus equity) and its cost of capital by changing its financing mix. Changes in the financing mix are assumed to occur by issuing debt and repurchasing shares or by issuing shares and retiring debt. In what follows, our attention is directed to what happens to the total valuation of the firm and to its cost of capital when the ratio of debt to equity, or degree of leverage, is varied.

For ease of illustration, let us assume that we are concerned with a company whose operating earnings are not expected to grow and which pays out all of its earnings to shareholders in the form of dividends. Moreover, suppose that we live in a world where, happily, there are no income taxes. Later this assumption will be relaxed to consider the issue in the real, and perhaps cruel, world of taxes. For now, the issue can be best understood if we assume no taxes and later treat taxes as a market imperfection.

In the subsequent discussion we are concerned with the three different rates of return. The first is

$$k_i = \frac{F}{B} = \frac{\text{Annual interest charges}}{\text{Market value of debt outstanding}} \qquad \text{(17-1)}$$

In this equation, k_i is the yield on the company's debt, assuming this debt to be perpetual. The second rate of return with which we are concerned is

$$k_o = \frac{E}{S} = \frac{\text{Earnings available to common shareholders}}{\text{Market value of shares outstanding}} \qquad \text{(17-2)}$$

With our assumptions of a firm whose earnings are not expected to grow and that has 100 percent dividend-payout ratio, the earnings/price ratio represents the market rate of discount that equates the present value of the stream of expected future dividends with the current market price of the stock.[1] This is not to say that it should be used as a general rule to depict the cost of equity capital. (See Chapter 15.) We use it only because of its simplicity in illustrating the theory of capital structure. The final rate we consider is

$$k_o = \frac{O}{V} = \frac{\text{Net operating earnings}}{\text{Total market value of the firm}} \qquad \text{(17-3)}$$

where $V = B + S$. Here, k_o is an overall capitalization rate for the firm. It is defined as the weighted-average cost of capital, and may also be expressed as

$$k_o = k_i\left(\frac{B}{B+S}\right) + K_e\left(\frac{S}{B+S}\right) \qquad \text{(17-4)}$$

We want to know what happens to k_i, k_e, and k_o when the degree of leverage, as denoted by the ratio B/S, increases.

The Boundaries to Valuation

It is useful to consider the two extremes to the valuation of a company when debt is employed in the capital structure. These extremes or boundaries are definitional

---

[1]In Chapter 5 we saw that the price of a security that is expected to pay a fixed payment of C forever is $P = C/k$, where k is the yield required on a perpetual investment. Rearranging, we have $k = C/P$, which is the same as Eq. (17-2) above.

only. That is, we do not attach any behavioral or economic meaning to them. They merely provide the basis for further discussion of the issue, at which time we will consider their validity. Therefore, the reader should not accept either position as necessarily true, but reserve judgment until we cover additional ground. The two extremes to the valuation of the earnings of a company are the *net income approach* and the *net operating income approach*, and we consider each in turn.[2]

NET INCOME APPROACH

This approach can best be presented with an illustration. Assume that a company has $1 000 in perpetual debt at 15 percent interest, or $150 in interest per annum. Moreover, the annual net operating earnings of the company now and in the future are $1 000; that is, no growth is expected. Net operating earnings are simply earnings before interest payments. Finally, suppose the required return on equity of the company, k_e, is 20 percent. With this information and according to the net income approach, the value of the firm is

O	Net operating earnings	$1 000
F	Interest	150
E	Earnings available to common shareholders	$ 850
k_o	Equity-capitalization rate (divide by)	0.20
S	Market value of shares	$4 250
B	Market value of debt	1 000
V	Total value of firm	$5 250

With the net income approach, earnings available to common shareholders are capitalized at a constant rate, k_e. The implied overall capitalization rate in the above example is

$$k_o = \frac{O}{V} = \frac{\$1\ 000}{\$5\ 250} = 19.05 \text{ percent}$$

Here the rate calculated is merely the result of dividing the net operating earnings of the firm by the total value of the firm which is derived. Therefore, the k_o is an implied rate of return as opposed to being given.

Assume now that the firm increases its debt from $1 000 to $3 000 and uses the proceeds of the debt issue to repurchase shares. The interest rate on debt remains unchanged at 15 percent. The value of the firm then is

[2]These approaches were originally considered by David Durand. "The Cost of Debt and Equity Funds for Business," in *The Management of Corporate Capital*, Ezra Solomon, ed. (New York: Free Press, 1959), 91-116.

O	Net operating earnings	$1 000
F	Interest	450
E	Earnings available to common shareholders	$ 550
k_o	Equity-capitalization rate (divide by)	0.20
S	Market value of shares	$2 750
B	Market value of debt	3 000
V	Total value of firm	$5 750

The implied overall capitalization rate now is

$$k_o = \frac{O}{V} = \frac{\$1\ 000}{\$5\ 750} = 17.39 \text{ percent}$$

According to the net income approach, the firm is able to increase its total valuation, V, and lower its cost of capital, k_o, as it increases the degree of leverage. As a result, the market price per share increases. To illustrate, assume in our example that the firm with $1 000 in debt has 425 shares of common stock outstanding. Thus, the market price per share is $10 a share ($4 250/425). The firm issues $2 000 in additional debt and at the same time repurchases $2 000 of stock at $10 a share, or 200 shares in total. It then has 225 shares outstanding. We saw in the example that the total market value of the firm's shares after the change in capital structure is $2 750. Therefore, the market price per share is $2 750/225 = $12.22, whereas before it was $10 a share.

Graphically, the approach is illustrated in Fig. 17-1. The degree of leverage, B/S, is plotted along the horizontal axis, while the percentage rate for k_i, k_e, and k_o is on the vertical axis. This graph can be constructed based upon the hypothetical examples we have shown. As can be seen, the critical assumptions of the net-income approach are that k_i and more particularly k_e remain unchanged as the

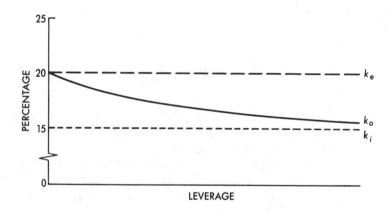

FIGURE 17-1 Capital costs: net income approach

degree of leverage increases. As the proportion of cheaper debt funds in the capital structure is increased, the weighted-average cost of capital, k_o, decreases and approaches the cost of debt, k_i. The significance of this approach is that a firm can lower its cost of capital continually and increase its total valuation by the use of debt funds.

NET OPERATING INCOME APPROACH

We turn now to the net operating income approach. The assumption here is that the overall capitalization rate of the firm, k_o, is constant for all degrees of leverage. Assume the same example as before but with k_o equal to 20 percent. In other words, we are given the overall capitalization rate as opposed to the equity-capitalization rate. For $1 000 in debt, we have

O	Net operating income	$1 000
k_o	Overall capitalization rate (divide by)	0.20
V	Total value of firm	$5 000
B	Market value of debt	1 000
S	Market value of shares	$4 000

The implied equity-capitalization rate in this case is

$$k_o = \frac{E}{S} = \frac{\$850}{\$4\,000} = 21.25 \text{ percent}$$

With this approach, net operating income is capitalized at an overall capitalization rate to obtain the total market value of the firm. The market value of the debt then is deducted from the total market value to obtain the market value of the shares.

Suppose, as before, that the firm increases the amount of debt from $1 000 to $3 000 and uses the proceeds of the debt issue to repurchase shares. The valuation of the firm then is

O	Net operating income	$1 000
k_o	Overall capitalization rate (divide by)	0.20
V	Total value of firm	$5 000
B	Market value of debt	3 000
S	Market value of shares	$2 000

The implied equity-capitalization rate is

$$K_e = \frac{E}{S} = \frac{\$550}{2\,000} = 27.50 \text{ percent}$$

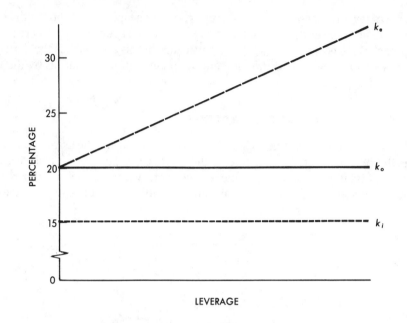

FIGURE 17-2 Capital costs: net operating income approach

We see that the equity-capitalization rate, k_e, rises with the degree of leverage. This approach implies that the total valuation of the firm is unaffected by its capital structure. Fig. 17-2 shows the approach graphically.

The critical assumption with this approach is that k_o is constant regardless of the degree of leverage. The market capitalizes the value of the firm as a whole; as a result, the breakdown between debt and equity is unimportant. An increase in the use of supposedly "cheaper" debt funds is offset exactly by the increase in the equity-capitalization rate, k_e. Thus, the weighted average of k_e and k_i remains unchanged for all degrees of leverage. As the firm increases its degree of leverage, it becomes increasingly more risky; and investors penalize the stock by raising the equity-capitalization rate (lowering the *P/E* ratio) directly in keeping with the increase in the debt-to-equity ratio. As long as k_i remains constant, k_e is a constant linear function of the debt-to-equity ratio. Because the cost of capital of the firm, k_o, cannot be altered through leverage, the net operating income approach implies that there is no one optimal capital structure.

So far, our discussion of the net operating income approach has been purely definitional; it lacks behavioral significance. Modigliani and Miller offered behavioral support for the independence of the total valuation and the cost of capital of the firm from its capital structure.[3] Before taking up the implications of their position, however, we examine the traditional approach to valuation.

---

[3]Franco Modigliani and Merton H. Miller, "The Cost of Capital, Corporation Finance and the Theory of Investment," *American Economic Review*, 48 (June 1958), 261-97.

TRADITIONAL APPROACH

The traditional approach to valuation and leverage assumes that there is an optimal capital structure and that the firm can increase the total value of the firm through the judicious use of leverage. Actually, this approach encompasses all the ground between the net income approach and the net operating income approach. The traditional approach suggests that the firm initially can lower its cost of capital and raise its total value through leverage. Although investors raise the equity-capitalization rate, the increase in k_e does not offset entirely the benefit of using "cheaper" debt funds. As more leverage occurs, investors increasingly penalize the firm's equity capitalization rate until eventually this effect more than offsets the use of "cheaper" debt funds.

In one variation of the traditional approach, shown in Fig. 17-3, k_e is assumed to rise at an increasing rate with leverage, whereas k_i is assumed to rise only after significant leverage has occurred. At first, the weighted-average cost of capital declines with leverage because the rise in k_e does not offset entirely the use of cheaper debt funds. As a result, the weighted-average cost of capital, k_o, declines with moderate use of leverage. After a point, however, the increase in k_e more than offsets the use of cheaper debt funds in the capital structure, and k_o begins to rise. The rise in k_o is supported further once k_i begins to rise. The optimal capital structure is the point at which k_o bottoms out. In the figure, this optimal capital structure is point X.

Thus, the traditional position implies that the cost of capital is not independent of the capital structure of the firm and that there is an optimal capital structure. At that optimal structure, the marginal true cost of debt is the same as the marginal true cost of equity. For degrees of leverage before that point, the marginal

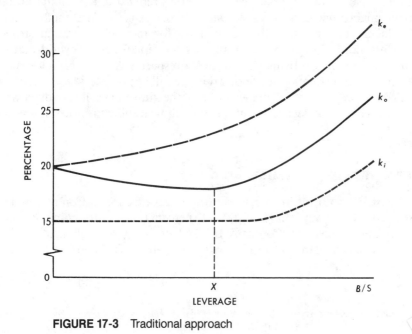

FIGURE 17-3 Traditional approach

true cost of debt exceeds that of equity. There are wide variations in the traditional approach. As we mentioned earlier, the approach falls somewhere between the extremes of the net income approach and the net operating income approach.

Total-Value Principle

Modigliani and Miller (MM) advocate that the relationship between leverage and the cost of capital is explained by the net operating income approach. They make a formidable attack on the traditional position by offering behavioral justification for having the cost of capital, k_o, remain constant throughout all degrees of leverage.

MM argue that the total risk for all security holders of a firm is not altered by changes in its capital structure. Therefore, the total value of the firm must be the same, regardless of its financing mix. Simply put, the Modigliani-Miller position is based on the idea that no matter how you divide up the capital structure of a firm among debt, equity, and other claims, there is a conservation of investment value.[4] That is, because the total investment value of a corporation depends upon its underlying profitability and risk, it is invariant with respect to relative changes in the firm's financial capitalization. Thus, the total pie does not change as it is divided into debt, equity, and other securities. The sum of the parts must equal the whole; so regardless of financing mix, the total value of the firm stays the same, according to MM.

The support for this position rests on the idea that investors are able to substitute personal for corporate leverage, thereby replicating any capital structure the firm might undertake. Because the firm is unable to do something for its shareholders (leverage) that they cannot do for themselves, capital structure changes are not a thing of value in the perfect capital market world that MM assume. Therefore, two firms alike in every respect except for capital structure must have the same total value. If not, arbitrage will be possible, and its occurrence will cause the two firms to sell in the market at the same total value. In other words, arbitrage precludes perfect substitutes from selling at different prices in the same market.

ARBITRAGE SUPPORT ILLUSTRATED

Consider two firms identical in every respect except that Company A is not levered, while Company B has $30 000 of 12 percent bonds outstanding. According to the traditional position, Company B may have a higher total value and lower average cost of capital than Company A. The valuation of the two firms is assumed to be the following:

---

[4]This idea was first espoused by John Burr Williams, *The Theory of Investment Value (Amsterdam: North-Holland Publishing Co., 1938), 72-73.*

		Company A	Company B
O	Net operating income	$10 000	$10 000
F	Interest on debt		3 600
E	Earnings available to common shareholders	$10 000	$ 6 400
k_o	Equity-capitalization rate (divide by)	0.15	0.16
S	Market value of shares	$66 667	$40 000
B	Market value of debt		30 000
V	Total value of firm	$66 667	$70 000
k_o	Implied overall capitalization rate	15%	14.3%
B/S	Debt-to-equity ratio	0	75.0%

MM maintain that this situation cannot continue, for arbitrage will drive the total values of the two firms together. Company B cannot command a higher total value simply because it has a financing mix different from Company A's. MM argue that by investing in Company A, investors in Company B are able to obtain the same dollar return with no increase in financial risk. Moreover, they are able to do so with a smaller investment outlay.[5] Because investors would be better off with the investment requiring the lesser outlay, they would sell their shares in Company B and buy shares in Company A. These arbitrage transactions would continue until Company B's shares declined in price and Company A's shares increased in price enough to make the total value of the two firms identical.

If you are a rational investor who owns 1 percent of the stock of Company B, the levered firm, worth $400 (market value), you should

1. sell the stock in Company B for $400.
2. borrow $300 at 12 percent interest. This personal debt is equal to 1 percent of the debt of Company B, your previous proportional ownership of the company.
3. buy 1 percent of the shares of Company A, the unlevered firm, for $666.67.

Prior to this series of transactions, your expected return on investment in Company B's stock was 16 percent on a $400 investment, or $64. Your expected return on investment in Company A is 15 percent on a $666.67 investment, or $100. From this return, you must deduct the interest charges on your personal borrowings, so your net dollar return is

Return on investment in Company A	$100
Less interest ($300 × 0.12)	36
Net return	$ 64

---

[5]This arbitrage proof appears in Franco Modigliani and Merton H. Miller, "Reply to Heins and Sprenkile," *American Economic Review*, 59 (September 1969), 592-95.

Your net dollar return, $64, is the same as it was for your investment in Company B; however, your cash outlay of $366.67 ($666.67 less personal borrowings of $300) is less than the $400 investment in Company B, the levered firm. Because of the lower investment, you would prefer to invest in Company A under the conditions described. In essence, you "lever" the shares of the unlevered firm by taking on personal debt.

The action of a number of investors undertaking similar arbitrage transactions will tend to drive up the price of Company A shares, and lower its k_e, drive down the price of Company B, and increase its k_e. This arbitrage process will continue until there is no further opportunity for reducing one's investment outlay and achieving the same dollar return. At this equilibrium, the total value of the two firms must be the same. As a result, their average costs of capital, k_o, must also be the same.

The important thing is the presence of rational investors in the market who are willing to substitute personal, or "homemade," leverage. The analysis can be extended further to cross risk classes and include general equilibrium in the capital markets. Here, however, we must take account of differences in business-risk premiums. On the basis of the arbitrage process illustrated, MM conclude that a firm cannot change its total value or its weighted-average cost of capital by leverage. Consequently, the financing decision does not matter from the standpoint of our objective of maximizing market price per share. One capital structure is as suitable as the next.

PRESENCE OF MARKET IMPERFECTIONS

With perfect capital markets, the arbitrage argument assures the validity of MM's thesis that the cost of capital and total valuation of a firm are independent of its capital structure. To dispute the MM position, we need to look for reasons why the arbitrage process may not work perfectly. If perfect capital markets do not exist in practice, opponents of the MM position are able to contest its behavioral support and argue that the cost of capital can decline with the appropriate use of leverage. The following are the major arguments against the MM arbitrage process.

Bankruptcy costs If there is a possibility of bankruptcy, and if administrative and other costs associated with bankruptcy are significant, the levered firm may be less attractive to investors than the unlevered one. With perfect capital markets, zero bankruptcy costs are assumed. If the firm goes bankrupt, assets presumably can be sold at their economic values with no liquidating or legal costs involved. Proceeds from the sale are distributed according to the priority of claims on assets described in Chapter 27. If capital markets are less than perfect, however, there may be administrative costs, and assets may have to be liquidated at less than their economic values. These costs and the "shortfall" in liquidating value from economic value represent a drain in the system from the standpoint of debt and equityholders.

In the event of bankruptcy, securityholders as a whole receive less than they would in the absence of bankruptcy costs. To the extent the levered firm has a greater possibility of bankruptcy than the unlevered one, it would be less attractive

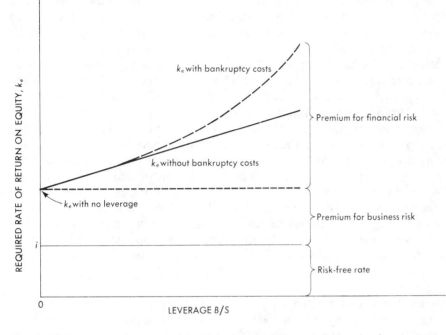

FIGURE 17-4   Required rate of return for equity capital when bankruptcy costs exist

investment, all other things the same. The possibility of bankruptcy is not a linear function of the debt/equity ratio but increases at an increasing rate beyond some threshold. As a result, the expected cost of bankruptcy increases in this manner and would be expected to have a corresponding negative effect upon the value of the firm.

Put another way, investors are likely to penalize the price of the stock as leverage increases. The nature of the penalty is illustrated in Fig. 17-4 for the case of a no-tax world. Here the required rate of return for investors, k_e, is broken down into its component parts. There is the risk-free rate, i, plus a premium for business risk. This premium is depicted on the vertical axis by the difference between the required rate of return for an all-equity capital structure and the risk-free rate. As debt is added, the required rate of return rises, and this increment represents a financial-risk premium. In the absence of bankruptcy costs, the required return would rise in a linear manner according to Modigliani-Miller, and this relationship is shown. However, with bankruptcy costs and an increasing probability of bankruptcy with leverage, the required rate of return would be expected to rise at an increasing rate beyond some point. At first there might be a negligible probability of bankruptcy, so there would be little or no penalty. As leverage increases, so does the penalty; for extreme leverage, the penalty becomes very substantial indeed.

Differences in corporate and personal leverage   The perceived risks of personal leverage and corporate leverage may differ. Despite the implication in the MM analysis that personal and corporate leverage are perfect substitutes, in the case of corporate borrowings the individual has only limited liability. If the levered company goes bankrupt, the investors' losses are limited to their investments in the shares. They are not liable for the debts of the company. If they borrow personally and default, lenders can claim assets in addition to the shares. Therefore their total risk exposure is greater with personal leverage and investment in the unlevered company than it is with a straight investment in the levered company.

In addition to greater risk, there are other reasons why investors may have a greater aversion to personal leverage than they do to corporate leverage. If investors borrow personally and pledge their shares as collateral, they are subject to possible margin calls. Many investors view this possibility with considerable alarm. Moreover, personal leverage involves a certain amount of inconvenience for investors, which they do not experience with corporate leverage. For these reasons, personal leverage may not be a perfect substitute for corporate leverage in the minds of many investors. Owing to market imperfections, the risk-adjusted cost of borrowing may be higher for the individual than for the corporation. If so, the levered company could have a somewhat greater total value than the unlevered firm for this reason alone.

Institutional restrictions   Restrictions on investment behavior may retard the arbitrage process. Many institutional investors, such as pension funds and life insurance companies, are not allowed to engage in the "homemade" leverage that was described. Regulatory bodies often restrict stock and bond investments to a list of companies meeting certain quality standards such as only a "safe" amount of leverage. If a company breaches that amount, it may be removed from the acceptable list, thereby precluding certain institutions from investing in it. This reduction in investor demand can have an adverse effect on the market value of the company's financial instruments. Moreover, if there are enough restrictions on lenders, a firm may find that credit is unavailable to it beyond a certain degree of leverage.

Transaction costs   Transaction costs tend to restrict the arbitrage process. Arbitrage will take place only up to the limits imposed by transaction costs, after which it is no longer profitable. As a result, the levered firm could have a slightly higher or slightly lower total value. The direction of the net effect of this imperfection is not predictable.

All of the factors listed above impede the effectiveness of the arbitrage process. If the arbitrage process is less than perfectly effective, a firm may be able to increase its total valuation and lower its cost of capital with an appropriate amount of leverage. As a result, the financing decision would matter, for it could affect the market value of the shares. In other words, the irrelevance-of-capital-structure argument depends on an equilibration in financial markets among security prices according to their respective risks and expected returns. If market imperfections systematically affect the arbitrage process, then capital-structure decisions would matter. To develop a complete picture, we must include the important role of taxes, to which we now turn.

The Effect of Taxes

When we allow for taxes, most would agree that the use of leverage can have a favorable impact on a company's total valuation if used judiciously. We must consider two taxes—corporate and personal—and because their effects are very different, we take them up separately. In the end, we will draw together their separate effects along with those of the market imperfections previously considered. For now, we assume that there are no market imperfections other than the presence of corporate taxes.

CORPORATE TAXES

The advantage of debt in a world of corporate taxes is that interest payments are deductible as an expense. They elude taxation at the corporate level, whereas dividends or retained earnings associated with stock are not deductible by the corporation for tax purposes. Consequently, the total amount of payments available both for debtholders and shareholders is greater if debt is employed.

To illustrate, suppose that the earnings before interest and taxes are $2 000 for companies X and Y, and they are alike in every respect except in leverage. Company Y has $5 000 in debt at 12 percent interest, whereas Company X has no debt. If the tax rate (federal and provincial) is 50 percent for each company, we have

	Company X	Company Y
Earnings before interest and taxes	$2 000	$2 000
Interest–income to debtholders	0	600
Profit before taxes	2 000	1 400
Taxes	1 000	700
Income available to shareholders	$1 000	$700
Income to debtholders plus income to shareholders	$1 000	$1 300

Thus, total income both to debtholders and shareholders is larger for levered Company Y than it is for unlevered Company X. The reason is that debtholders receive interest payments without the deduction of taxes at the corporate level, whereas income to shareholders is after corporate taxes have been paid. In essence, the government pays a subsidy to the levered company for the use of debt. Total income to all investors increases by the interest payment times the tax rate. In our example, this amounts to $600 \times 0.50 = $300. This figure represents a tax shield that the government provides the levered company. If the debt employed by a company is permanent, the present value of the tax shield using the perpetuity formula is

$$\text{Present value of tax shield} = \frac{t_c r B}{r} = t_c B \qquad (17\text{-}5)$$

where t_c is the corporate tax rate, r is the interest rate on the debt, and B is the market value of the debt. For Company Y in our example

$$\text{Present value of tax shield} = 0.50(\$5\ 000) = \$2\ 500$$

What we are saying is that the tax shield is a thing of value and that the overall value of the company will be $2 500 more if debt is employed than if the company has no debt. This increased valuation occurs because the stream of income to all investors is $300 per year greater. The present value of $300 per year discounted at 12 percent is $300/0.12 = $2 500. Implied is that the risk associated with the tax shield is that of the stream of interest payments, so the appropriate discount rate is the interest rate on the debt. Thus, the value of the firm is

$$\text{Value of firm} = \frac{\text{Value if}}{\text{unlevered}} + \frac{\text{Value of}}{\text{tax shield}} \qquad \textbf{(17-6)}$$

For our example, suppose that the equity capitalization rate for Company X, which has no debt, is 16 percent. Therefore, the value of the firm if it were unlevered would be $1 000/0.16 = $6 250. The value of the tax shield is $2 500, so the total value of the Company Y, the levered firm, is $8 750.

We see in Eqs.(17-5) and (17-6) that the greater the amount of the debt, the greater the tax shield and the greater value of the firm, all other things being the same. By the same token, the greater the leverage, the lower the cost of capital of the firm. Thus, the original MM proposition as subsequently adjusted for corporate taxes suggests that an optimal strategy is to take on a maximum amount of leverage.[6] This implies a capital structure consisting almost entirely of debt. Since this is not consistent with the behaviour of corporations, we must seek alternative explanations.

PERSONAL TAXES

The presence of taxes on personal income may reduce the corporate tax advantage associated with debt financing. With the combination of corporate taxes and personal taxes on both debt and share income, the present value of the corporate tax shield shown in Eq.(17-5) may change. The equation becomes[7]

$$\text{Present value of tax shield} = \left[1 - \frac{(1 - t_c)(1 - t_{ps})}{1 - t_{pd}}\right] B \qquad \textbf{(17-7)}$$

where t_{ps} is the personal income rate applicable to common-stock income to the

---

[6]Modigliani and Miller, "Corporate Income Taxes and the Cost of Capital: A Correction," *American Economic Review*, 64 (June 1963), 433-42.

[7]Merton H. Miller, "Debt and Taxes," *Journal of Finance*, 32 (May 1977), 266-68. See also Donald E. Farrar and Lee L. Selwyn, "Taxes, Corporate Financial Policies and Returns to Investors," *National Tax Journal*, 20 (December 1967), 444-54; and M.J. Brennan, "Taxes, Market Valuation and Corporate Financial Policy," National Tax Journal, 23 (December 1970), 417-27.

investor; t_{pd} is the personal tax rate applicable to income from the company's debt; and B is the market value of the firm's debt. We see that as long as t_{pd} is greater than t_{ps}, the tax advantage of debt is less than t_cB, which we determined to be the advantage in a world of corporate but not personal taxes.

If the income from holding a common share consists only of dividends and if dividends and interest both are taxed as ordinary income, t_{ps} would equal t_{pd}. As a result, the tax advantage in Eq.(17-7) would reduce to t_cB, which is the same as appears in Eq.(17-5) for the valuation of a levered firm with corporate income taxes but no personal income taxes. Suppose, however, that part of the income from holding a share consists of capital gains. Assuming the tax rate on capital gains is less than that on ordinary income, t_{pd} would be greater than t_{ps}. As a result, the tax advantage associated with leverage would be less than t_cB. In other words, investors overall must hold both a company's common stock and its debt instruments. If the tax on debt income is greater than that on common-stock income, increases in a company's debt ratio result in an increase in the personal income taxes that must be paid. Therefore the existence of personal income taxes, differential tax rates on ordinary income and capital gains, and share repurchase will reduce but probably not eliminate the corporate income tax advantage associated with leverage.[8]

Suppose that the corporate tax rate is 0.46, the effective personal tax rate on debt income 0.40, and the market value of DSS Corporation's perpetual debt is $1 million. If the effective tax rate on stock income is 0.40, the present value of the tax shield is

$$\text{Present value of tax shield} = \left[1 - \frac{(1 - 0.46)(1 - 0.40)}{(1 - 0.40)} \right] \$1 \text{ million}$$

$$= [0.46]\$1 \text{ million} = \$460\ 000$$

which, of course, is the straight corporate tax shield. If the effective personal tax rate on stock income is 0.20 instead of 0.40, we have

$$\text{Present value of tax shield} = \left[1 - \frac{(1 - 0.46)(1 - 0.20)}{(1 - 0.40)} \right] \$1 \text{ million}$$

$$= [0.28]\$1 \text{ million} = \$280\ 000$$

Thus, the tax advantage associated with debt is less if the effective personal tax rate on debt income exceeds that on stock income. Moreover, the greater the personal tax on debt income relative to stock income, the lower the corporate tax shield.

---

[8]Miller, "Debt and Taxes," 261-75, argues that the tax advantage of corporate debt is eliminated in market equilibrium. If this were the case, the value of the firm and its cost of capital would be independent of its capital structure even with taxes. Essentially his argument is based on corporations adjusting the supply of corporate debt to take advantage of clienteles of investors with different tax brackets. In market equilibrium, Miller claims that $(1 - t_c)(1 - t_{ps}) = (1 - t_{pd})$, so that the term in brackets in Eq. (17-7) is zero. This provocative claim has been challenged by a number of authors who argue that the tax on stock income is positive, empirical relationships between market instruments are inconsistent with the claim, and that Miller's position is deficient theoretically. Space does not permit a review of these articles, but the reader should appreciate the controversy generated by Miller's position.

The magnitude of net tax shield is an empirical question. Perhaps the only evidence that bears directly upon the issue comes from the study of changes in value when companies significantly recapitalize their capital structures. These changes occur when a company exchanges one type of security for another. Unfortunately, there have been few such studies, and the evidence from them is fragmentary.[9] Those available in the U.S. show that the net tax shield is less than the corporate tax rate, namely t_cB. These as well as certain indirect tax-effect studies imply that the net tax effect associated with debt may be in the neighborhood of 0.20.[10] That is, if there is a $1 increment in corporate debt, the net tax advantage is roughly $0.20. Again, such estimates must be taken as crude.

The tax advantage associated with leverage is reduced but not eliminated when we allow for different personal tax rates. As a result, an optimal leverage strategy would still call for the corporation to have a large proportion of debt. As this is not true for corporations overall, we must search for other factors affecting the valuation of the corporation when it alters the proportion of debt in its capital structure.

Taxes and Market Imperfections Combined

This statement brings us back to the influence of the various market imperfections considered earlier. Only if in some way they restrict the use of debt financing can the observed capital structure behavior of corporations be explained.

BANKRUPTCY COSTS AND TAXES

If one allows for bankruptcy costs, and if the probability of bankruptcy increases at an increasing rate with the degree of leverage, extreme leverage is likely to be penalized by investors. (As discussed earlier, bankruptcy costs represent a drain on the system to securityholders.) In a world of both taxes and bankruptcy costs, there would likely be an optimal capital structure even if all of the other behavioral tenets of the MM position held. The cost of capital of a firm would decline as leverage was first employed because of the net tax advantage of debt (corporate less personal). Gradually, however, the prospect of bankruptcy would become increasingly important, causing the cost of capital to decrease at a decreasing rate as leverage increased. As leverage became extreme, the bankruptcy effect might more than offset the tax effect, causing the cost of capital of the firm to rise. By definition, this would be the point at which the capital structure of the firm was optimal. The joint effect of taxes and bankruptcy is illustrated in Fig. 17-5 for a hypothetical firm.

---

[9]Ronald W. Masulis, "The Effects of Capital Structure Change on Security Prices: A Study of Exchange Offers," *Journal of Financial Economics*, 8 (June 1980), 139-78; and J.J. McConnell and R. Schlarbaum, "Evidence on the Impact of Exchange Offers on Security Prices: The Case of Income Bonds," *Journal of Business*, 54 (January 1981), 65-85.

[10]For an indirect study of the effect, see David Flath and Charles R. Knoeber, "Taxes, Failure Costs, and Optimal Industry Capital Structure," *Journal of Finance*, 35 (March 1980), 99-117.

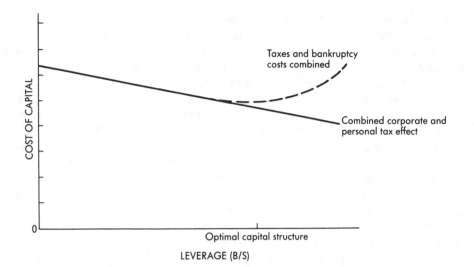

FIGURE 17-5   Cost of capital with taxes and bankruptcy costs

IMPACT OF ADDITIONAL IMPERFECTIONS

If other imperfections and behavioral factors dilute the MM position further, the point at which the cost-of-capital line turns up would be earlier than that depicted in the figure. Consider now the cost of borrowing. After some point of leverage, the interest rate charged by creditors usually rises. The greater the leverage, of course, the higher the interest rate charged. As a result, the cost of debt would turn up after a point. This phenomenon was illustrated earlier in Fig. 17-3. In turn, this factor exerts upward influence on the overall cost-of-capital line. Institutional restrictions on lenders also might cause the cost-of-line to turn up sooner than it does in Fig. 17-5. If, because of extreme leverage, a company no longer is able to sell debt securities to institutions, it must seek out unrestricted investors, and they will demand even higher interest rates. If institutional imperfections are serious enough, debt funds may not be available beyond a point of leverage, in which case there would be a discontinuity in Fig. 17-5.

Other capital-market imperfections work to hamper the arbitrage process so that "homemade" leverage is not a perfect substitute for corporate leverage. Recall that these imperfections include transaction costs, higher costs of borrowing for individuals than for corporations and imperfections in information. The greater the importance one attaches to these factors, the less effective the arbitrage process becomes, and the stronger the case can be made for an optimal capital structure.

In conclusion, there are a number of reasons for believing that an optimal capital structure exists in theory. Depending upon one's view as to the strengths of the various capital-market and behavioral imperfections, the expected optimal capital structure may occur earlier or later along the scale of possible leverage.

Summary

Much controversy has developed over whether the capital structure of a firm, as determined by its financing decision, affects its cost of capital. Traditionalists argue that the firm can lower its capital and increase market value per share by the judicious use of leverage. Modigliani and Miller, on the other hand, argue that in the absence of taxes and other market imperfections, the total value of the firm and its cost of capital are independent of capital structure. This position, which is the same as the net operating income approach, is based on the notion that there is a conservation of investment value. No matter how you divide the pie between debt and equity claims, the total pie or investment value of the firm stays the same. Therefore, leverage is said to be irrelevant. We saw that behavioral support for the MM position was based on the arbitrage process.

In a world of corporate income taxes, there is a substantial advantage to the use of debt, and we can measure the present value of the tax shield. When we allow for personal income taxes and a higher personal tax rate on debt income than on stock income, we find the tax advantage of debt to be lower. Bankruptcy costs work to the disadvantage of leverage, particularly extreme leverage. A combination of net tax effect with bankruptcy costs will result in an optimal capital structure. Other market imperfections—such as differences between corporate and "home-made" leverage and institutional restrictions on lender and stock investor behavior—impede the equilibration of security prices according to expected return and risk. As a result, leverage may affect the value of the firm because of these reasons.

In order for the financial manager to make proper capital structure decisions, these decisions must be rooted in theory. Every effort should be made to judge an alternative with respect to the imperfections described. In practice, such analysis can be accomplished with the tools taken up in the preceding chapter.

Questions

1. Contrast the net operating income approach with the Modigliani-Miller approach to the theory of the capital structure.

2. As a financial manager who believes the cost of capital to the firm can be minimized by using moderate amounts of debt, you have been asked to defend your proposal to change the debt/equity proportions of the firm to the board of directors. The majority shareholder argues that the cost of capital to the firm is the shareholders' return. Because you work for the shareholders, the majority shareholder wants your resignation unless you can defend wanting to minimize the shareholders return. Discuss your rebuttal.

3. Why might you suspect that the optimal capital structure would differ significantly from one industry to another? Would the same factors produce differing optimal capital structures within all industry groupings?

4. What factors determine the interest rate a firm must pay for debt funds? Is it reasonable to expect this rate to rise with an increasing debt/equity ratio? Why?

5. Explain why the following three firms with similar asset structures and growth rates sell at different market prices. Are any of the firms overlevered? Explain carefully.

	Firm A	Firm B	Firm C
Dividend/share	$ 4	$ 3	$ 2
Market price	18	20	15

6. If there were not imperfections in financial markets, what capital structure should the firm seek? Why are market imperfections important in finance? Which imperfections are most important?

7. Why do the effects of corporate taxes and personal taxes tend to be in opposite directions when it comes to the capital structure issue?

8. Suppose a company has a large tax-loss carryforward and then goes bankrupt. If there are no out-of-pocket costs involved in bankruptcy proceedings, is there a cost of bankruptcy?

9. There are frequent complaints that debt funds are not available for capital-formation purposes, particularly for small and medium-sized firms. Is there any truth in this assertion?

10. If the corporate tax rate were cut in half, what would be the effect on debt financing?

11. Dividends may be taxed twice. The corporation must pay taxes on its earnings and then some stockholders pay taxes on the dividends distributed depending on their marginal income tax rates. What would be the effect on corporate financing if this double taxation were eliminated by permitting companies to deduct dividend payments as an expense?

Problems with Solutions

1. A company reports net operating income of $20 000 and interest expense of $6 000. The cost of equity capital (K_e)is 14 percent and the market value of debt is $60 000. Using the net income approach, calculate the cost of debt (K_i) and the overall capitalization rate (K_o) assuming the company pays no tax.

K_i = $6 000 ÷ $60 000 = 10 percent
$20 000 − $6 000 = $14 000 = Net income
$14 000 + 0.14 = $100 000 = Market value of stock
$100 000 + $60 000 = $160 000 = Total value of the firm
K_o = $20 000 (div) $160 000 = 12.5 percent = Overall capitalization rate

2. A company reports net operating income of $20 000, interest expense of $6 000 and has an overall capitalization (K_o) of 12 percent. If K_i is 8 percent, calculate the market value of debt and K_e using the net operating income approach, assuming no tax.

$6 000 ÷ 0.08 = $75 000 = Market value of debt
$20 000 ÷ 0.12 = $166 667 = Total value of the firm
$166 667 − $75 000 = $91 667 = Market value of stock
($20 000 − $6 000) + $91 667 = 15.3% = Equity capitalization rate, K_e

3. You have been approached by an investor who is considering buying 10 percent of the shares of either Company X or Company Y, which are identical except that X has no debt and Y currently has outstanding $500 000 of 8 percent debentures. The equity capitalization rates for X and Y are 14 percent and 15 percent respectively and both companies report net operating income of $200 000. The investor knows that you agree with the Modigliani and Miller position and asks you which shares to buy.

	Company X	Company Y
Net operating income	$200 000	$200 000
Interest	—	40 000
Earnings available to common shareholders	$200 000	$160 000
Equity capitalization rate	0.14	0.15
Market value of stock	$1 428 571	$1 066 666
Market value of debt ($40 000 ÷ 0.08)	—	500 000
Total value of firm	$1 428 571	$1 566 667
Implied overall capitalization rate (K_o)	14.0% (1)	12.8% (2)
Debt to equity ratio	0	46.9%

(1) $200 000 ÷ $1 428 571 = 14%
(2) $200 000 ÷ $1 566 667 = 12.8%
Purchase of Y:
  Cost of shares 0.1 × $1 066 667 = $106 667
  Return on investment $106 667 × 0.15 = $16 000
Purchase of X:

Cost of shares 0.1 × $1 428 571	=	$142 857
Personal borrowing (see below	=	50 000
Net outlay		$ 92 857
Return on investment 0.14 × $142 857	=	$20 000
Cost of personal borrowing 0.08 × $50 000	=	4 000
Net return		$16 000

When shares of X are purchased, the investor, since X has no debt, can take on personal debt equal to 10 percent of the debt of Y without increasing his or her financial risk relative to an investment in Y. Thus, with X and Y, the investor's return would be the same ($16 000) and he or she would face the same financial risk, but investing in X would leave $13 810 ($106 667 − 92 857)free for other investments. Company X therefore is the better investment.

Problems

1. The E.W. Lambert Company Ltd., has net operating earnings of $10 million and $20 million of debt with a 7 percent interest charge. In all cases, assume no taxes.
   (a) Using the net income approach and an equity capitalization rate of $12\frac{1}{2}$ percent, compute the total value of the firm and the implied overall capitalization rate.
   (b) Next, assume that the firm issues an additional $10 million in debt and uses the proceeds to retire stock; the interest rate and equity capitalization rate remain the same. Compute the new total value of the firm and overall capitalization rate.
   (c) Using the net operating income approach and an overall capitalization rate of 11 percent, compute the total market value, the stock market value, and the implied equity-capitalization rate for the E.W. Lambert Company Ltd. prior to the sale of additional debt.
   (d) Determine the answers to part c if the company were to sell the additional $10 million in debt.

2. Abacus Calculation Company Ltd., and Zoom Calculators Ltd. are identical except for capital structures. Abacus has 50 percent debt and 50 percent equity, while Zoom has 20 percent debt and 80 percent equity. (All percentages are in market value terms.) The borrowing rate for

both companies is 13 percent, we live in a no-tax world, and capital markets are assumed to be perfect.

(a) If you own 2 percent of the stock of Abacus, what is your dollar return if the company has net operating income of $360 000 and the overall capitalization rate of the company, k_o, is 18 percent? What is the implied equity capitalization rate?

(b) What would be your dollar return if you invested the same amount of money in Zoom? (Zoom has the same net operating income as Abacus.) What percentage of the total stock of Zoom would you own? What is the implied equity capitalization rate of Zoom? Why does it differ from that of Abacus?

3. The Kelly Company Ltd. and the Green Company Ltd. are identical in every respect except that the Kelly Company is not levered, while the Green Company has $2 million in 12 percent bonds outstanding. There are no taxes, and capital markets are assumed to be perfect. The valuation of the two firms is the following:

	Kelly	Green
Net operating income	$ 600 000	$ 600 000
Interest on debt	0	240 000
Earnings to common	$ 600 000	$ 360 000
Equity capitalization rate	0.15	0.16
Market value of stock	$4 000 000	$2 250 000
Market value of debt	0	2 000 000
Total value of firm	$4 000 000	$4 250 000
Implied overall capitalization rate, k_o	15.00%	14.12%
Debt/equity ratio, B/S	0	0.89

(a) You own $22 500 worth of Green stock. Show the process and the amount by which you could reduce your outlay through the use of arbitrage.

(b) When will this arbitrage process cease?

4. The C.T. Carlisle Corporation Ltd. had a $1 million capital structure and will always maintain this book-value amount. Carlisle currently earns $250 000 per year before taxes of 50 percent, has an all-equity capital structure of 100 000 shares, and pays all earnings in dividends. The company is considering issuing debt in order to retire stock. The cost of the debt and the price of the stock at various levels of debt are given in the following table. It is assumed that the new capital structure would be reached all at once by purchasing shares at the current price. In other words, the table is a schedule at a point in time.

Amount of debt	Average pre-tax cost of debt	Price of stock
$ 0	—	$10.00
100 000	10.0%	10.00
200 000	10.0	10.50
300 000	10.5	10.75
400 000	11.0	11.00
500 000	12.0	10.50
600 000	14.0	9.50

(a) Construct a chart in terms of k_e, k_i, and k_o based upon the above data.

(b) What is the optimal capital structure?

5. Sawchuk Safflowerseed Oil Company Ltd. has $1 million in earnings before interest and taxes. Currently it is all equity financed. It may issue $3 million in perpetual debt at 15 percent interest in order to repurchase shares, thereby recapitalizing the corporation. There are no personal taxes.

(a) If the corporate tax rate is 46 percent, what is the income to all security holders if the company remains all equity financed? If it is recapitalized?

(b) What is the present value of the debt tax shield?

(c) The equity capitalization rate for the company's shares is 20 percent while it remains all equity financed. What is the value of the firm? What is the value if it is recapitalized?

6. Petroles Vintage Wine Company Ltd., is presently family owned and has no debt. The Petroles family is considering going public by selling some of their shares in the company. Investment dealers tell them the total market value of the company is $10 million if no debt is employed. In addition to selling shares, the family wishes to consider issuing debt that, for computational purposes, would be perpetual. The debt then would be used to purchase shares, so the size of the company would stay the same. Based upon various valuation studies, the present value of tax shield is estimated at 22 percent of the amount borrowed when both corporate and personal taxes are taken into account. The investment dealer has estimated the following present values for bankruptcy costs associated with various levels of debt:

Debt (in millions)	Present value of bankruptcy costs
$1	0
2	$ 50 000
3	100 000
4	200 000
5	400 000
6	700 000
7	1 100 000
8	1 600 000

Given this information, what amount of debt should the family choose?

7. Acme-Menderhall Corporation Ltd. is trying to determine an appropriate capital structure. It knows that as its leverage increases, its cost of borrowing will eventually increase as will the required rate of return on its common shares. The company has made the following estimates for various leverage ratios.

		Required rate of return on equity	
Debt/(debt + equity)	Interest rate on borrowings	Without bankruptcy costs	With bankruptcy costs
0	—	10 %	10 %
0.10	8 %	10½	10½
0.20	8	11	11¼
0.30	8½	11½	12
0.40	9	12¼	13
0.50	10	13¼	14½
0.60	11	14½	16¼
0.70	12½	16	18½
0.80	15	18	21

(a) At a tax rate of 50 percent, what is the weighted average cost of capital of the company at various leverage ratios in the absence of bankruptcy costs? What is the optimal capital structure?

(b) With bankruptcy costs, what is the optimal capital structure?

Selected References

ARDITTI, FRED D., "The Weighted Average Cost of Capital: Some Questions on its Definition, Interpretation and Use," *Journal of Finance*, 28 (September 1973), 1001-9.

_____, and JOHN M. PINKERTON, "The Valuation and Cost of Capital of the Levered Firm with Growth Opportunities," *Journal of Finance*, 33 (March 1978), 65-73.

BARNEA, AMIR, ROBERT A. HAUGEN, and LEMMA W. SENBET, "Market Imperfections, Agency Problems, and Capital Structure: A Review," *Financial Management*, 10 (Summer 1981), 7-22.

BAXTER, NEVINS D., "Leverage, Risk of Ruin, and the Cost of Capital," *Journal of Finance*, 22 (September 1967), 395-404.

CASTANIAS, RICHARD, "Bankruptcy Risk and Optimal Capital Structure", *Journal of Finance*, December 1983, 1617-1636.

CHEN, ANDREW H., and E. HAN KIM, "Theories of Corporate Debt Policy: A Synthesis," *Journal of Finance*, 34 (May 1979), 371-84.

CORDES, JOSEPH J. and STEVEN M. SHEFFRIN, "Estimating the Tax Advantage of Corporate Debt", *Journal of Finance*, March 1983, 95-105.

DEANGELO, HARRY and RONALD W. MASULIS, "Optimal Capital Structure under Corporate and Personal Taxation," *Journal of Financial Economics*, 8 (March 1980), 3-29.

DURAND, DAVID, "Costs of Debt and Equity Funds for Business: Trends and Problems of Measurement," reprinted in *The Management of Corporate Capital*, ed. Ezra Solomon, New York: Free Press, 1959, 91-116.

FAMA, EUGENE F., and MERTON H. MILLER, *The Theory of Finance*, New York: Holt, 1972, Chapter 4.

FLATH, DAVID, and CHARLES R. KNOEBER, "Taxes, Failure Costs, and Optimal Industry Capital Structure: An Empirical Test," *Journal of Finance*, 35 (March 1980), 99-117.

GLENN, DAVID W., "Super Premium Security Prices and Optimal Corporate Financing Decisions," *Journal of Finance*, 31 (May 1976).

GORDON, MYRON J., and CLARENCE C.Y. KWAN, "Debt Maturity, Default Risk, and Capital Structure," *Journal of Banking and Finance*, 3 (December 1979), 313-29.

HAMADA, ROBERT S., "The Effect of the Firm's Capital Structure on the Systematic Risk of Common Stocks," *Journal of Finance*, 27 (May 1972), 435-52.

HAUGEN, ROBERT A., and LEMMA W. SENBET, "The Irrelevance of Bankruptcy Costs to the Theory of Optimal Capital Structure," *Journal of Finance*, 33 (June 1978), 383-94.

HEINS, A. JAMES, and CASE M. SPRENKLE, "A Comment on the Modigliani-Miller Cost of Capital Thesis," *American Economic Review*, 59 (September 1969), 590-92.

HELLWIG, MARTIN F., "Bankruptcy, Limited Liability, and the Modigliani-Miller Theorem," *American Economic Review*, 71 (March 1981), 155-70.

HONG, HAI, and ALFRED RAPPAPORT, "Debt Capacity, Optimal Capital Structure, and Capital Budgeting," *Financial Management*, 7 (Autumn 1978), 7-11.

JENSEN, MICHAEL C., and WILLIAM E. MECKLING, "Theory of the Firm: Managerial Behavior, Agency Cost and Ownership Structure," *Journal of Financial Economics*, 3 (October 1976), 305-60.

LITZENBERGER, ROBERT H., and JAMES C. VAN HORNE, "Elimination of the Double Taxation of Dividends and Corporate Financial Policy," *Journal of Finance*, 33 (June 1978).

MILLER, MERTON H., "Debt and Taxes," *Journal of Finance*, 32 (May 1977), 266-68.

MODIGLIANI, FRANCO, and M. H. MILLER, "The Cost of Capital, Corporate Finance, and the Theory of Investment," *American Economic Review*, 48 (June 1958), 261-97.

_____, "The Cost of Capital Corporation Finance, and the Theory of Investment: Reply," *American Economic Review*, 51 (September 1959), 655-69; "Taxes and the Cost of Capital: A Correction," ibid., 53 (June 1963), 433-43; "Reply," *ibid.*, 55(June 1965), 524-27; "Reply to Heins and Sprenkle," *ibid.*, 59 (September 1969), 592-95.

NANTELL, TIMOTHY J., and C. ROBERT CARLSON, "The Cost of Capital as a Weighted Average," *Journal of Finance*, 30 (December 1975), 1343-55.

RENDLEMAN, RICHARD J., "The Effects of Default Risk on the Firm's Investment and Financing Decision," *Financial Management*, 7 (Spring 1978), 45-53.

SCOTT, JAMES H., JR., "Bankruptcy, Secured Debt, and Optimal Capital Structure," *Journal of Finance*, 32 (March 1977), 1-20.

SCHALL, LAWRENCE D., "Firm Financial Structure and Investment," *Journal of Financial and Quantitative Analysis*, 6 (June 1971), 925-42.

SMITH, CLIFFORD W. JR., and JEROLD B. WARNER, "On Financial Contracting: An Analysis of Bond Covenants," *Journal of Financial Economics*, 7 (June 1979), 117-61.

VAN HORNE, JAMES C., "Optimal Initiation of Bankruptcy Proceedings by Debt Holders," *Journal of Finance*, 31 (June 1976), 897-910.

18

Dividend Policy and Retained Earnings

Over the years, businesses have relied heavily on retained earnings as a source of financing. Since the dividend-payout ratio, the percentage of earnings paid to stockholders in cash, reduces the amount of earnings the firm retains, a dividend decision is a financing decision. The dividend-payout ratio is a major aspect of the dividend policy of the firm, which affects the value of the firm to the stockholder. But other aspects also affect valuation: stability of dividends, certain factors that influence the payout ratio from the standpoint of the firm, stock dividends and stock splits, the repurchase of stock, and the procedural and legal elements of dividend policy. We are going to turn to these now.

Dividend-Payout Ratio

The first questions before us are whether the payment of cash dividends can affect shareholder wealth and, if it can, what dividend-payout ratio will maximize shareholder wealth. Again, we assume that business risk is held constant. In order to evaluate the question of whether the dividend-payout ratio affects shareholder wealth, it is necessary to examine first the firm's policy solely as a financing decision involving the retention of earnings. Consider the situation in which the use of funds from earnings, and the dividend policy that results, is strictly a financing decision. As long as the firm's investment projects have returns that exceed the required return, it will use retained earnings—and the amount of senior securities the increase in equity base will support—to finance these projects. If the firm has retained earnings left over after financing all acceptable investment opportunities, these earnings will be distributed to stockholders in the form of cash dividends. If not, there will be no dividends. If the number of acceptable investment opportunities involves a total dollar amount that exceeds the amount of retained earnings plus the senior securities these retained earnings will support, the firm will finance the excess with a combination of a new equity issue and senior securities.

When we treat dividend policy strictly as a financing decision, the payment of cash dividends is a passive residual. The amount of dividend payout will fluctuate from period to period in keeping with fluctuations in the amount of acceptable investment opportunities available to the firm. If these opportunities abound, the percentage of dividend payout is likely to be zero. On the other hand, if the firm is unable to find profitable investment opportunities, dividend payout will be 100 percent. For situations between these two extremes, the payout will be a fraction between 0 and 1.

WALTER'S FORMULA

To illustrate dividend policy as a financing decision determined solely by the profitability of investment opportunities available, let us examine Walter's formula.[1] His model was one of the earlier dividend models, and certain later models correspond to this one. His formula is

$$P = \frac{D + \frac{r}{p}(E - D)}{p}$$ (18-1)

where P = market price per share of common stock
  D = dividends per share
  E = earnings per share
  r = return on investment
  p = market capitalization rate

Suppose that r = 24 percent, p = 20 percent, E = $4, and D = $2. The market price per share would be

$$P = \frac{2 + (0.24/0.20)(4-2)}{0.20} = \$22$$

The optimal dividend-payout ratio is determined by varying D until you obtain the the maximum market price per share. Under a strict interpretation of the Walter formula, the optimal dividend-payout ratio should be 0 if r is greater than p. Thus, in our example,

$$P = \frac{0 + (0.24/0.20)(4-0)}{0.20} = \$24$$

With a payout ratio of 0, market price per share is maximized. Similarly, if r is less than p, the optimal payout ratio should be 100 percent. Suppose that r = 0.16 percent, p = 0.20 percent, E = $4, and D = $2. The market price per share then would be

---

[1] James E. Walter, "Dividend Policies and Common Stock Prices," *Journal of Finance,* 11 (March 1956), 29-41

$$P = \frac{2 + (0.16/0.20)(4-2)}{0.20} = \$18$$

However, with a dividend-payout ratio of 100 percent,

$$P = \frac{4 + (0.16/0.20)(4-4)}{0.20} = \$20$$

Thus, market price per share can be maximized with a complete distribution of earnings. If $r = p$, market price per share is insensitive to the payout ratio.

The Walter formula implies that the optimal dividend payout should be determined solely by the profitability of investments. If the firm has had an abundance of profitable investment opportunities, there should be no cash dividends, for the earnings are needed to finance these opportunities. On the other hand, if the firm has no profitable investment opportunities, all earnings should be distributed to stockholders in the form of dividends. In this case, the funds are not needed for financing.

DIVIDENDS AS A PASSIVE RESIDUAL

The treatment of dividend policy as a passive residual determined solely by the availability of acceptable investment proposals implies that dividends are irrelevant; investors are indifferent between dividends and retention by the firm. If investment opportunities promise a return greater than their required return, investors would prefer to have the company retain earnings. If the return is equal to the required return, they would be indifferent between retention and dividends. Contrarily, if the return were less than the required return, they would prefer dividends. Supposedly, if the firm can earn more on projects than the required return, investors are perfectly happy to let the firm retain as much in earnings as it needs to finance the investments. With irrelevance, the required return is invariant with respect to changes in dividend payout. Are dividends more than just a means of distributing unused funds? Should dividend policy in any way be an active decision variable? To answer these questions, we must examine more thoroughly the argument that dividends are irrelevant, so that changes in the payout ratio (holding investment opportunities constant) do not affect shareholder wealth.

IRRELEVANCE OF DIVIDENDS

Modigliani and Miller's 1961 article[2] is the most comprehensive argument for the irrelevance of dividends. They assert that, given the investment decision of the firm, the dividend payout ratio is a mere detail. It does not affect the wealth of shareholders. MM argue that the value of the firm is determined solely by the earning power of the firm's assets, or its investment policy, and that the manner in which the earnings stream is split between dividends and retained earnings does not affect this value. As in the previous chapter, when we considered the capital-structure decision, MM assume perfect capital markets where there are no transac-

---

[2]Merton H. Miller and Franco Modigliani, "Dividend Policy, Growth, and the Valuation of Shares," *Journal of Business,* 34 (October 1961), 411-33.

tion costs, no flotation costs to companies issuing securities, and no taxes. Moreover, the future profits of the firm are assumed to be known with certainty. (Later this assumption is removed.)

Dividends versus terminal value   The crux of MM's position is that the effect of dividend payments on shareholder wealth is offset exactly by other means of financing. Consider first selling additional stock in lieu of retaining earnings. When the firm has made its investment decision, it must decide whether to retain earnings, or to pay dividends and sell new stock in the amount of these dividends in order to finance the investments. MM suggest that the sum of the discounted value per share after financing and dividends paid is equal to the market value per share before the payment of dividends. In other words, the stock's decline in market price because of the dilution caused by external financing offsets exactly the payment of the dividend. Thus, the stockholder is said to be indifferent between dividends and the retention of earnings.

One might ask: how does this correspond to our earlier chapters, when we said that dividends are the foundation for the valuation of common stocks? Although it is true that the market value of a share of stock is the present value of all expected future dividends, the timing of the dividends can vary. The irrelevance position simply argues that the present value of future dividends remains unchanged even though dividend policy changes their timing. It does not argue that dividends, including liquidating dividends, are never paid, only that their postponement is a matter of indifference when it comes to market price per share.

Conservation of value   Given MM's assumptions of perfect certainty as well as their other assumptions, the irrelevance of dividends follows. As with our example for corporate leverage in the previous chapter, the conservation-of-value principle assures that the sum of market value plus current dividends of two firms identical in all respects other than dividend-payout ratios will be the same.

Investors are able to replicate any dividend stream the corporation might pay. If dividends are less than desired, investors can sell portions of their stock to obtain the desired cash distribution. If dividends are more than desired, investors can use the dividends to purchase additional shares in the company. Thus, investors are able to manufacture "homemade" dividends in the same way they devise "homemade" leverage in capital-structure decisions. In order for a corporate decision to be a thing of value, the company must be able to do something for stockholders that they cannot do for themselves. Because investors can manufacture "homemade" dividends, which are perfect substitutes for corporate dividends under the above assumptions, dividend policy is irrelevant. As a result, one dividend policy is as good as the next. The firm is unable to create value simply by altering the mix of dividends and retained earnings. As in capital structure theory, there is a conservation of value so that the sum of the parts is always the same. The total size of the pie is what will be eaten, and it is unchanged in the slicing.

ARGUMENTS FOR RELEVANCE

A number of arguments have been advanced in support of the contrary position; namely, that dividends are relevant under conditions of uncertainty. In other words, investors are not indifferent to whether they receive their returns on investment in dividend income or stock-price appreciation. We shall examine these arguments under conditions of uncertainty.

Preference for dividends   Certain investors in the market may have a preference for dividends over capital gains. The payment of dividends may resolve uncertainty in their minds. It might be argued that because dividends are received on a current, on-going basis, whereas the prospect of capital gains is off in the future, investors in a dividend-paying company resolve their uncertainty earlier than do those investing in a nondividend paying company. To the extent investors prefer the early resolution of uncertainty, they may be willing to pay a higher price for the stock that offers the greater current dividend, all other things held constant. If in fact investors can manufacture "homemade" dividends, such a preference is irrational. Nonetheless, sufficient statements from investors make it difficult to dismiss the argument. Perhaps, for either psychological or inconvenience reasons, investors prefer not to manufacture "homemade" dividends but to get the "real thing" directly from the company.

Informational content of dividends   This argument implies that dividends have an impact on share price because they communicate information to investors about the firm's profitability. When a firm has a target payout ratio that is stable over time, and it changes this ratio, investors may believe that management is announcing a change in the expected future profitability of the firm. Accordingly, the price of the stock may react to this change in dividend. Dividends may offer proof of a company's ability to generate cash, whereas management's words about the bright prospects of the company and the potential for capital gains are far less clear. MM do not deny the possibility of this effect but continue to maintain that present and expected future earnings are what determine value. They assert that dividends are merely a reflection of these factors and do not in themselves determine value; therefore, the irrelevance proposition holds.[3] Thus, dividends are said to be used by investors as predictors of the firm's future performance; they convey management's expectation of the future.

Taxes on the Investor   When we allow for taxes, there are a variety of effects. The most important of these is the special tax treatment of capital gains from any source and of dividends from Canadian companies. We saw in Chapter 2 that half of capital gains over the first $1 000 are taxed at the marginal income tax rate. Also, one half of any capital losses can be offset against taxable capital gains; any remaining allowable capital loss can be charged against other income to a maximum of $1 000. Dividends from Canadian companies are first multipled by 3/2; then this grossed-up amount less a $1 000 tax-free allowance is fully taxed at the marginal tax rate. The taxpayer is then allowed a dividend tax credit equal to $22^{2/3}$ percent of the grossed-up value (or 68 percent of the amount of the gross-up). Provincial taxes are determined by applying a stated percentage to the federal tax payable. The dividend tax credit is merely a device to reduce, in some manner, the incidence of double taxation.

---

[3]Miller and Modigliani, "Dividend Policy," 429-30.

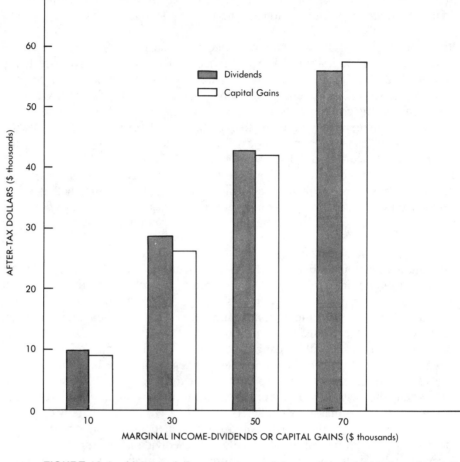

FIGURE 19-1   After-tax dollars on incremental amounts of dividends and capital gains

The individual investor's preference for dividends or capital gains would be influenced to some extent by his or her marginal tax rate. For example, assume that in 1983 a resident of Ontario earned just enough salary to cover personal and other miscellaneous allowances and thus any taxes payable would be on an incremental income derived from other sources. Now assume that he or she had the option to receive incremental income in the form of dividends or capital gains. Fig. 18-1 shows the after-tax dollars the investor would have received at varying levels of dividends and capital gains. Investors facing a marginal federal tax rate of less than 34 percent, should have a preference for dividends. The marginal income examples of $10 000, $30 000, $50 000 and $70 000 in Fig. 18-1 offer higher after tax cash flows for the dividend option. These income brackets have marginal federal tax rates of less than 34 percent (see Table 2-3). The $120 000 marginal income bracket is subject to the marginal federal tax rate of 34 percent; here both the capital gains and dividend option have about the same after tax cash flows.

However, other tax laws tend to favor current dividends over capital gains. Some corporate investors are permitted to exclude intercompany dividends in determining their tax obligations. Accordingly, these investors would prefer current dividends.

Flotation costs   The irrelevance of dividend payout is based upon the idea that in accordance with the investment policy of the firm, funds paid out of the firm must be replaced by funds acquired through external financing. The introduction of flotation costs favors the retention of earnings in the firm. For each dollar paid out in dividends, the firm nets less than a dollar after flotation costs per dollar of external financing.

Transaction costs and divisibility of securities   Transaction costs involved in the sale of securities tend to restrict the arbitrage process in the same manner as that described for debt. Stockholders who desire current income must pay brokerage fees on the sale of portions of their stocks if the dividend paid is not sufficient to satisfy their current desire for income. This fee varies inversely, per dollar of stock sold, with the size of the sale. For a small sale, the brokerage fee can be rather significant. As a result of this fee, stockholders with consumption desires in excess of current dividends will prefer the company to pay additional dividends. Perfect capital markets also assume that securities are infinitely divisible. The fact that the smallest integer is one share may result in "lumpiness" with respect to selling shares for current income. This, too, acts as a deterrent to the sale stock in lieu of dividends. On the other hand, stockholders not desiring dividends for current consumption purposes will need to reinvest their dividends. Here again, transaction costs and divisibility problems work to the disadvantage of the stockholder, although in the opposite direction. Thus, transaction costs and divisibility problems cut both ways.

Institutional restrictions   The law limits the types of common stock that certain institutional investors may buy. The prescribed list of eligible securities is determined in part by the duration over which dividends have been paid. If a company does not pay dividends or has not paid them over a sufficiently long period, certain institutional investors are not permitted to invest in the stock.

Universities, on the other hand, sometimes have restrictions on the expenditure of capital gains from their endowment. Also, a number of trusts have a prohibition against the liquidation of principal. In the case of common stocks, the beneficiary in entitled to the dividend income, but not to the proceeds from the sale of stock. As a result of this stipulation, the trustee who manages the investments may feel constrained to pay particular attention to dividend yield and seek stocks paying reasonable dividends. Though the two influences described are small in aggregate, they work in the direction of a preference for dividends as opposed to retention and capital gains.

A SUMMING UP

A company should endeavor to establish a dividend policy that will maximize shareholder wealth. Almost everyone agrees that if a company does not have sufficiently profitable investment opportunities, it should distribute any excess funds to its stockholders. The firm need not pay out the exact unused portion of earnings every period. Indeed, it may wish to stabilize the absolute amount of dividends paid from period to period. But over the longer run the total earnings retained, plus the senior securities the increasing equity base will support, will correspond to the amount of profitable investment opportunities. Dividend policy still would be a passive residual determined by the amount of investment opportunities.

For the firm to be justified in paying a dividend larger than that dictated by the amount left over after profitable investment opportunities, there must be a net preference for dividends in the market. It is very difficult to "net out" the arguments discussed above in order to arrive at the bottomline. Only institutional restrictions and some investors' preference for dividends, for tax and other reasons, argue strongly for dividends. The other arguments suggest either a neutral effect or a systematic bias favoring retention. Empirical evidence concerning the effect of dividends on the market price of a stock is far from clear. There does appear to be some positive value associated with a modest dividend as opposed to none at all. This occurrence may be due to institutional restrictions and a signaling effect. Beyond that, the picture is very cloudy, and some argue that even a modest dividend has no effect on valuation.

Despite the unsettled nature of the issue, we should point out that many companies behave as if dividends are relevant. A number of growth companies, which expand at a rate faster than their growth in earnings, pay small dividends. If these companies believed dividend policy were irrelevant, they would retain all their earnings. A number of companies pay significant dividends and go to the capital markets for additional equity capital, rather than retain a greater portion of earnings. Examples include public utilities and airlines. Whereas these actions do support the idea that dividends are relevant, they do not indicate that many companies behave as though they are. The dividend payout ratio that these firms believe is optimal is greater than that dictated by investment opportunities alone.

Managerial Considerations in Determining a Dividend Payout

So far we have discussed only the theoretical aspects of dividend policy. Yet when a company establishes a dividend policy it looks at a number of things. These considerations should be related back to the theory of dividend payout and the valuation of the firm. In what follows, we take up various factors that firms in practice can and should analyze when approaching a dividend decision.

FUNDS NEEDS OF THE FIRM

Perhaps the place to begin is with an assessment of the funds needs of the firm. In this regard, cash budgets and projected source and use of funds statements (topics taken up in Chapter 7) are of particular use. The expected operating cash flows of the firm, expected future capital expenditures, any likely buildups in receivables and inventories, scheduled reductions in debt, and any other thing that affects the cash position of the firm should be taken into account. The key is to determine the likely cash flows and cash position of the company in the absence of a change in dividend. In addition to looking at expected outcomes, we should factor in business risk, so that we may obtain a range of possible cash flow outcomes, a procedure spelled out in Chapter 7.

In keeping with our earlier discussion of the theory of dividend payout, the firm wishes to determine if anything is left over after servicing its funds needs, including profitable investment projects. In this regard, the firm should look at its situation over a reasonable number of future years, to iron out fluctuations. The likely ability of the firm to sustain a dividend should be analyzed relative to the probability distributions of possible future cash flows and cash positions. On the basis of this analysis, the firm can determine its likely future residual funds.

LIQUIDITY

The liquidity of a company is a prime consideration in many dividend decisions. Because dividends represent a cash outflow, the greater the cash position and overall liquidity of a company, the greater its ability to pay a dividend. A company that is growing and profitable may not be liquid, for its funds may go into fixed assets and permanent working capital. Because the management of such a company usually desires to maintain some liquidity cushion to give it flexibility and a protection against uncertainty, it may be reluctant to jeopardize this position in order to pay a large dividend. The liquidity of the company, of course, is determined by the firm's investment and financing decisions. The investment decision determines the rate of asset expansion and the firm's need for funds; and the financing decision determines the way in which this need will be financed.

ABILITY TO BORROW

A liquid position is not the only way to provide for flexibility and thereby protect against uncertainty. If a firm has the ability to borrow on comparatively short notice, it may be relatively flexible. This ability to borrow can be in the form of a line of credit or a revolving credit from a bank, or simply the informal willingness of a financial institution to extend credit. In addition, flexibility can come from the ability of a firm to go to the capital markets with a bond issue. The larger and more established a company, the better its access to the capital markets. The greater the ability of the firm to borrow, the greater its flexibility, and the greater its ability to pay a cash dividend. With ready access to debt funds, management should be less concerned with the effect that a cash dividend has upon its liquidity.

ASSESSMENT OF ANY VALUATION INFORMATION

To the extent there are insights into the effect of a dividend on valuation, they should be gathered. Regression analysis involving similar companies may give some indication, even though studies of this sort have statistical problems in addition to the troublesome job of trying to hold all else constant. As a result, it usually is difficult to make company-specific generalizations concerning the effect of dividends on valuation. Most companies look at the dividend payout ratios of other companies in the industry, particularly those having about the same growth. It may not matter that a company is out of line with similar companies, but it will be conspicuous and usually a company will want to justify its position. Finally, a company should judge the informational effect of a dividend. What do investors expect? Here security analysis and security reports are useful. The company should ask itself what information it is conveying with its present dividend and what it would convey with a possible change in dividend.

CONTROL

If a company pays substantial dividends, it may need to raise capital at a later time through the sale of stock in order to finance profitable investment opportunities. Under such circumstances, the controlling interest of the company may be diluted if controlling stockholders do not or cannot subscribe for additional shares. These stockholders may prefer a low dividend payout and the financing of investment needs with retained earnings. Such a dividend policy may not maximize overall shareholder wealth, but it still may be in the best interests of those in control.

Control can work two ways, however. When a company is being sought by another company or by individuals, a low dividend payout may work to the advantage of the "outsiders" seeking control. The outsiders may be able to convince stockholders that the company is not maximizing shareholder wealth and that they (the outsiders) can do a better job. Consequently, companies in danger of being acquired may establish a high dividend payout in order to please stockholders.

RESTRICTIONS IN BOND INDENTURE OR LOAN AGREEMENT

The protective covenants in a bond indenture or loan agreement often include a restriction on the payment of dividends. This restriction is employed by the lenders to preserve the company's ability to service debt. Usually, it is expressed as a maximum percentage of cumulative earnings. When such a restriction is in force, it naturally influences the firm's dividend policy. Sometimes the management of a company welcomes a dividend restriction imposed by lenders because then it does not have to justify to the stockholders the retention of earnings. It need only point out the restriction.

A FINAL OBSERVATION

In determining a dividend payout, the typical company will analyze a number of the factors described above. These factors largely dictate the boundaries within which a dividend can be paid. When a company pays a dividend in excess of its residual funds, it implies that management and the board of directors believe the payment has a favorable effect on shareholder wealth. The frustrating thing is that we have so little in the way of clear generalizations from the empirical evidence. The lack of firm footing for predicting the long-run effect of a specific dividend policy on valuation makes the dividend decision more difficult in many ways than either the investment or financing decisions. Considerations taken up in this section allow a company to determine with reasonable accuracy what would be an appropriate passive dividend strategy. An active dividend policy involves an act of faith, because it demands that a portion of the cumulative dividends ultimately be replaced with common stock financing. Such a strategy may enhance shareholder wealth, but it is undertaken in a foggy area where nobody can have much confidence in predicting the results.

Dividend Stability

In addition to the percentage of dividend payout, stability is attractive to investors. By stability, we mean maintaining its position in relation to a trend line, preferably one that is upward sloping. All other things the same, a stock may be higher in price if it pays a stable dividend over time than if it pays out a fixed percentage of earnings. Suppose Company A has a long-run dividend payout ratio of 50 percent of earnings. It pays out this percentage every year, despite the fact that its earnings are cyclical. The dividends of Company A are shown in Fig. 18-2. Company B, on the other hand, has exactly the same earnings and a long-run dividend payout ratio of 50 percent, but it maintains a relatively stable dividend over time. It changes the absolute amount of dividend only in keeping with the underlying trend of earnings. The dividends of Company B are shown in Fig. 18-3.

Over the long run, the total amount of dividends paid by these two firms is the same; however, the market price per share of Company B may be higher than that of Company A, all other things being the same. Investors may well place a positive utility on dividend stability and pay a premium for the company that offers it. To the extent that investors value dividend stability, the overall dividend policy of Company B would be better than that of Company A. This policy includes not only the percentage of dividend payout in relation to earnings but also the manner in which the actual dividends are paid. Rather than vary dividends directly with changes in earnings per share, Company B raises the dividend only when reasonably confident a higher dividend can be maintained.

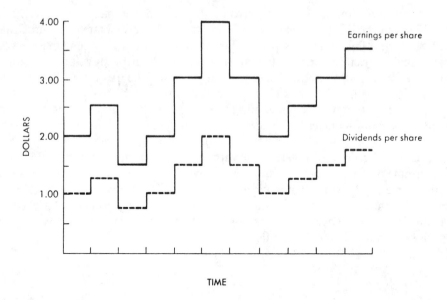

FIGURE 18-2 Hypothetical dividend policy of Company A

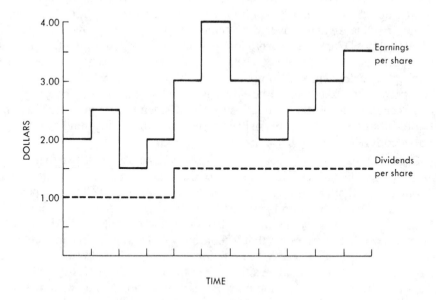

FIGURE 18-3 Hypothetical dividend policy of Company B

VALUATION OF STABILITY

Investors are willing to pay a premium for stable dividends because of the informational content of dividends, the desire of investors for current income, and certain legal considerations.

Informational content When earnings drop and a company does not cut its dividend, the market may have more confidence in the stock than it would have if the dividend were cut. The stable dividend may convey management's view that the future of the company is better than the drop in earnings suggests. Thus, management may be able to affect the expectations of investors through the informational content of dividends. Management will not be able to fool the market permanently. If there is a downward trend in earnings, a stable dividend will not convey forever an impression of a rosy future. Moreover, if a firm is in an unstable business with wide swings in earnings, a stable dividend cannot give the illusion of underlying stability.

Current income desires A second factor may favor stable dividends. Investors who desire a specific periodic income will prefer a company with stable dividends to one with unstable dividends, even though both companies may have the same pattern of earnings and long-run dividend payout. Although investors can always sell a portion of their stock for income when the dividend is not sufficient to meet their current needs, many investors have an aversion to dipping into principal. Moreover, when a company reduces its dividend, earnings usually are down and the market price of the stock depressed. Overall, income conscious investors place a positive utility on stable dividends, even though they can always sell a few shares of stock for income.

Legal considerations A stable dividend may be advantageous from the legal standpoint of permitting certain institutional investors to buy the stock. Various governmental bodies prepare legal lists of securities in which pension funds, trustees, insurance companies, and others may invest. In order to qualify, a company must have an uninterrupted pattern of dividends. A cut in the dividend may result in the removal of a company from these legal lists.

The arguments presented in support of the notion that stable dividends have a positive effect on the market price of the share are only theoretical. There is little in the way of empirical evidence to bolster this view.[4] While studies of individual stocks often suggest that stable dividends buffer the market price of the share when earnings turn down, there have been no comprehensive studies of a large sample of stocks dealing with the relationship between dividend stability and valuation. Nevertheless, most companies strive for stability in their dividend payments. Overall, companies behave in a manner consistent with the belief that stable dividends have a positive effect on value.

---

[4]Mantripragada argues that a stable dividend policy may be a preference of management rather than investors in the market. See K.G. Mantripragada "Stable Dividends and Share Prices," *Journal of Finance,* 27 (Sept. 1972), 951-52.

TARGET PAYOUT RATIOS

A number of companies appear to follow the policy of a target dividend payout ratio over the long run. Lintner contends that dividends are adjusted to changes in earnings, but only with a lag.[5] When earnings increase to a new level, a company increases dividends only when it feels it can maintain the increase in earnings. Companies are also reluctant to cut the absolute amount of their cash dividend. Both of these factors explain the lag in dividend changes behind changes in earnings. In an economic upturn, the lag relationship becomes visible when retained earnings increase in relation to dividends. In a contraction, retained earnings will decrease relative to dividends.

REGULAR AND EXTRA DIVIDENDS

One way for a company to increase its cash distribution in periods of prosperity is to declare an *extra* dividend in addition to the *regular* quarterly or semiannual dividend. By declaring an extra dividend, the company warns investors that the dividend is not an increase in the established dividend rate. The declaration of an extra dividend is suitable particularly for companies with fluctuating earnings. General Motors, for example, has declared extra dividends in good years. The use of the extra dividend enables the company to maintain a stable record of regular dividends but also to distribute to stockholders some of the rewards of prosperity. If a company pays extra dividends continuously, it defeats its purpose. The extra becomes the expected.

Stock Dividends and Stock Splits

Stock dividends and stock splits typically are used for different purposes: nevertheless, in an economic sense the two are very similar. Only from an accounting standpoint is there a significant difference.

STOCK DIVIDENDS

A stock dividend is simply the payment of additional stock to stockholders. It represents nothing more than a recapitalization of the company; a stockholder's proportional ownership remains unchanged. Chen Industries Ltd. had the following capital structure before issuing a stock dividend:

Common stock ($5 par, 400 000 shares)	$ 2 000 000
Contributed capital	1 000 000
Retained earnings	7 000 000
Net worth	$10 000 000

---

[5]See John Lintner, "Distribution of Income of Corporations," *American Economic Review, 46 (May 1956), 97-113.*

Chen pays a 5 percent stock dividend, amounting to 20 000 additional shares of stock. The fair market value of the stock is $40 a share. For each 20 shares of stock owned, the stockholder receives an additional share. The balance sheet of the company after the stock dividend would be

Common stock ($5 par, 420 000 shares)	$ 2 100 000
Contributed capital	1 700 000
Retained earnings	6 200 000
Net worth	$10 000 000

With a stock dividend, $800 000 is transferred ($40 × 20 000 shares) from retained earnings to the common-stock and contributed capital accounts. Because the par value stays the same, the increase in number of shares is reflected in a $100 000 increase in the common-stock account ($5 × 20 000 shares). The residual of $700 000 goes into the contributed capital account. The net worth of the company remains the same.

Because the number of shares of stock outstanding is increased by 5 percent, earnings per share of the company are reduced proportionately. Total net profit after taxes is $1 million. Before the stock dividend, earnings per share were $2.50 ($1 million/400 000). After the stock dividend, earnings per share would be $2.38 ($1 million/420 000). Thus, stockholders have more shares of stock but lower earnings per share. Their proportion of total earnings available to common stockholders remains unchanged.

Value to investors   If the company pays no cash dividend, what do stockholders receive with a stock dividend? In theory, nothing but an additional stock certificate. Their proportionate ownership of the company is unchanged. Presumably, the market price of the stock will drop, all other things being equal, so that the total market value of their holdings stays the same. If you had held 100 shares of stock previously, and market price per share were $40, the total value of your holdings would be $4 000. After the stock dividend, the price of the stock should drop by $40(1 − 1.00/1.05), or by $1.90. The total value of your holdings then would be $38.10 × 105, or $4 000. Under these conditions, the stock dividend does not represent a thing of value to you. You merely have an additional stock certificate evidencing ownership.

To the extent that the investor wishes to sell a few shares of stock for income, the stock dividend may make it easier to do so. Without the stock dividend, of course, stockholders also could sell a few shares of their original holdings for income. In either case, the sale of stock represents the sale of principal and is subject to the capital-gains tax. It is probable that certain investors do not look at the sale of a stock dividend as a sale of principal. To them, the stock dividend represents a windfall gain; they can sell it and still retain their original holdings. The stock dividend may have a favorable psychological effect on these stockholders.

The stock dividend can also be a thing of value to the investor if the cash dividend per share remains the same after the stock dividend. Suppose an investor owns 100 shares of a company paying a $1 dividend. The company declares a 10 percent stock dividend and, at the same time, announces that the cash dividend per share will remain unchanged. The investor then will have 110 shares; and total cash dividends will be $110 rather than $100, as before. In this case, a stock dividend increases the total cash dividends. Whether this increase in cash dividend has a positive effect upon shareholder wealth will depend upon the tradeoff between current dividends and retained earnings, which we discussed earlier. Clearly, the stock dividend in this case represents a decision by the firm to increase modestly the amount of cash dividends.

Use of the stock dividend may convey some information. Stock dividends typically are associated with growth companies. The dividend may connote to investors that management expects earnings to continue to grow and to more than offset the dilution in earnings per share because there are more shares. The underlying cause for the rise in value is the company's growth, however, not the stock dividend itself.

Possible advantages to company   Frequently, a stock dividend is employed to conserve cash. Instead of increasing the cash dividend as earnings rise, a company may desire to retain a greater portion of its earnings and declare a stock dividend. The decision then is to lower the dividend payout ratio; for as earnings rise and the dividend remains the same, the payout ratio will decline. Whether shareholder wealth is increased by this action will depend upon considerations discussed previously. The decision to retain a higher proportion of earnings, of course, could be accomplished without a stock dividend. However, the stock dividend may tend to please certain investors by virtue of its informational content as well as its psychological impact. In addition, if the cash dividend per share is kept the same, total cash dividends will increase slowly in keeping with the increase in the number of shares.

A firm may also use a stock dividend to keep the market price of the stock within a desired trading range. Some companies do not like to see the market price of their stocks above a certain amount—say $60 a share—because a high price will not appeal to small investors. Consequently, they endeavor to keep the price below a desired ceiling either by using stock dividends or, more commonly, by means of stock splits. Increasing the total number of shares outstanding may increase the total number of stockholders, resulting in greater overall popularity for the stock. The principal disadvantage of stock dividends is that they are much more costly to administer than cash dividends.

STOCK SPLITS

With a stock split, the number of shares is increased through a proportional reduction in the par value of the stock. A lumber company has the following capital structure before a two-for-one stock split:

Common stock ($5 par, 400 000 shares)	$ 2 000 000
Contributed capital	1 000 000
Retained earnings	7 000 000
Net worth	$10 000 000

After the split, the capital structure is

Common stock ($2.50 par, 800 000 shares)	$ 2 000 000
Contributed capital	1 000 000
Retained earnings	7 000 000
Net worth	$10 000 000

With a stock dividend, the par value is not reduced, whereas with a split, it is. As a result, the common-stock, contributed capital, and retained-earnings accounts remain unchanged. The net worth, of course, also stays the same; the only change is in the par value of the stock. Except in accounting treatment, the stock dividend and stock split are very similar. A stock split, however, is usually reserved for occasions when a company wishes to achieve a substantial reduction in the market price per share. The principal purpose of a split is to place the stock in a more popular trading range, thereby attracting more buyers.[6] One might expect that the increased shares would provide a better market for trading. However, in an empirical study by Thomas E. Copeland, market liquidity of a stock, as measured by the relative volume of trading and transaction costs, was found to decline following a stock split.[7]

Like the stock dividend, the stock split does not represent a thing of value to investors. They have more shares than before, but their proportional ownership of the company remains unchanged. The market price of the stock should decline proportionately, so that the total value of their holdings stays the same. Again, however, the split may have a favorable informational content. The announcement of the split may indicate to investors that management believes that earnings will continue to grow. As a result, the market price per share may increase upon the announcement or rumor of the split, and it may remain higher. The underlying cause for the increase in market price, again, is growth and not the split itself.

Very seldom will a company maintain the same cash dividends per share before and after a split, but it might increase the effective dividends to stockholders. A company may split its stock two-for-one and establish a dividend rate of $1.20 a share; whereas before, the rate was $2 a share. A stockholder owning 100 shares before the split would receive $200 in cash dividends per annum. After the split, the stockholder would own 200 shares and would receive $240 in dividends. The market price of the stock (on an after-split basis) may react favorably to the increase in cash dividends.

Reverse split Rather than increase the number of shares of stock outstanding, a company may want to reduce the number. It can accomplish this with a *reverse split*. In our example above, had there been a one-to-four reverse split instead of the two-for-one straight stock split, for each four shares held, the stockholder would receive one share in exchange. The par value per share would become $20, and

---

[6]For a survey of opinions of financial officers regarding stock splits, see H. Kent Baker and Patricia L. Gallagher, "Management's View of Stock Splits," *Financial Management,* 9 (Summer 1980), 73-77.

[7]"Liquidity Following Stock Splits," *Journal of Finance,* 34 (March 1979), 115-41.

there would be 100 000 shares outstanding rather than 400 000. Reverse stock splits are employed to increase the market price per share when the stock is considered to be selling at too low a price. Many companies have an aversion to seeing their stock fall significantly below $10 per share. If financial difficulty or some other depressant lowers the price into this range, it can be increased with a reverse split. The reverse split is regarded by many as an admission by the company that it is in financial difficulty, although that is not always the reason for the split. The stock market's reaction to it depends primarily upon the company's past and expected earnings.

Repurchase of Stock

In recent years a number of companies have repurchased a portion of their outstanding common stock. Some companies repurchase stock in order to have it available for stock options. In this way, the total number of shares is not increased with the exercise of the options. Another reason for repurchase is to have shares available for the acquisition of other companies. In certain cases, companies no longer wishing to be publicly owned "go private" by purchasing all of the stock of the outside stockholders. In still other situations, stock is repurchased with the full intention of retiring it. Under these circumstances, repurchase of stock may be treated as a part of the firm's dividend decision.

REPURCHASING AS PART OF A DIVIDEND DECISION

If a firm has excess cash and insufficient profitable investment opportunities to justify the use of these funds, it may be in the shareholders' interests to distribute the funds. The distribution can be accomplished either by the repurchase of stock or by paying the funds out in increased dividends. In the absence of personal income taxes and transaction costs, the two alternatives, theoretically, should make no difference to stockholders. With repurchase, fewer shares remain outstanding, and earnings per share rise. As a result, the market price per share should rise as well. In theory, the capital gain arising from repurchase should equal the dividend that otherwise would have been paid.

A hardware company has the following earnings and market price per share:

Net profit after taxes	$2 000 000
Number of shares outstanding	500 000
Earnings per share	$4
Market price per share, after distribution	$60
Price/earnings ratio	15

The company is considering the distribution of $1.5 million, either in cash dividends or in the repurchase of its own stock. If investors are expecting the cash dividend, the value of a share of stock before the dividend is paid will be $63; that is, $3 a share in expected dividends ($1.5 million/500 000) plus the $60 market price.

The firm chooses to repurchase its stock, however, and makes a tender offer to stockholders at $63 a share. It then will be able to repurchase $1.5 million/$63, or 23 810 shares. Earnings per share will be

$$EPS = \$2\ 000\ 000/476\ 190 = \$4.20$$

If the price/earnings ratio stays at 15, the total market price per share will be $63 ($4.20 \times 15$), the same total value as under the dividend alternative. Thus, the amount of distribution to stockholders is $3 per share, whether dividends or repurchase of stock (and subsequent capital gain) is used.

With a differential tax effect on dividends and capital gains, the repurchase of stock decision should take into account the nature of the firm's shareholders. If a firm's shareholders fall mainly in the relatively low-income bracket, they may prefer dividend payments. As discussed earlier, investors with low marginal tax rates would derive more after-tax dollars from dividend income rather than from capital gains income. The opposite is true for shareholders in the high marginal tax bracket who may prefer capital gains from the repurchase of shares. In practice, some firms have shareholders across the spectrum of marginal tax rates and it becomes difficult to identify any one dominant income group. This situation complicates the decision on whether surplus should be distributed as dividends or indirectly as capital gains through the repurchase of shares. A common problem facing management is how to determine the income levels and marginal tax positions of its shareholders. This tends to limit the use of such information in the repurchase decision and other considerations may take precedence. Also, corporate investors in common shares will prefer dividends since they are usually nontaxable. Capital gains, on the other hand, are usually taxed. For tax reasons, then, the attractiveness of stock repurchase or cash dividends as a means of distributing unused funds will depend on the type of investor (individual versus corporate) and the marginal tax rates of these investors.

It is important that the repurchase of stock be somewhat of a "one-shot" nature and not be used as a substitute for regular dividends or even for receiving extra dividends. A steady program of repurchase in lieu of paying dividends might result in investors expecting a higher level of distribution of earnings relative to what might be the case using a cash dividend policy.

STOCK REPURCHASE—INVESTMENT OR FINANCIAL DECISION?

Some regard the repurchase of stock as an investment decision instead of a dividend decision. Indeed, in a strict sense, it is. However, shares held in the treasury do not provide an expected return as other investments do. No company can exist by investing only in its own shares. The decision to repurchase should involve distribution of unused funds when the firm's investment opportunities are not sufficiently attractive to employ those funds, either now or in the foreseeable future. Therefore, the repurchase of stock cannot be treated as an investment decision as we define the term.

Repurchase may be regarded as a financing decision, however, provided its purpose is to alter the capital-structure proportions of the firm. By issuing debt and repurchasing shares, a firm can immediately change its debt-to-equity ratio toward a greater proportion of debt. In this case, repurchase of stock is a financing decision, because the alternative is not to pay out dividends. Only when there is excess cash can the repurchase of stock be treated as a dividend decision.

METHOD OF REPURCHASE

The two most common methods of repurchase are through a tender offer and through the purchase of stock in the marketplace. With a tender offer, the company makes a formal offer to stockholders to purchase so many shares, typically at a set price. This bid price is above the current market price; stockholders can elect either to sell their stock at the specified price or to continue to hold it. Typically the tender-offer period is between two and three weeks. If stockholders tender more shares than originally sought by the company, the company may elect to purchase all or part of the excess. It is under no obligation to do so. In general, the transaction costs to the firm in making a tender offer are higher than those incurred in the purchase of stock in the open market. The principal costs involve the fee paid to the investment dealer who manages the repurchase and the fees paid to soliciting dealers.

In open-market purchases, a company buys its stock as any other investor does—through an investment dealer. Usually, the brokerage fee is negotiated. Certain securities regulations restrict the manner in which a company bids for its shares. As a result, it takes an extended period of time for a company to accumulate a relatively large block of stock. For this reason, the tender offer is more suitable when the company seeks a large amount of stock.

Before the company repurchases stock, stockholders must be informed of the company's intentions. In a tender offer, these intentions are announced by the offer itself. Even here, the company must not withhold other information. It would be unethical for a mining company, for example, to withhold information of a substantial ore discovery while making a tender offer to repurchase shares.

In open-market purchases, especially, it is necessary to disclose the company's repurchase intentions. Otherwise, stockholders may sell their stock not knowing about a repurchase program that will increase earnings per share. Given full information about the amount of repurchase and the objective of the company, the stockholders can sell their stock if they so choose. Without proper disclosure, the selling stockholder may be penalized. When the amount of stock repurchased is substantial, a tender offer is particularly suitable, for it gives all stockholders equal treatment.

Since October 1, 1983, firms with shares listed on the Toronto Stock Exchange have been required to file details of stock repurchase intentions with the securities authorities. The primary objective is to have relevant information disclosed prior to the actual acquisition of shares. Also, a company is limited to buying two percent of the outstanding shares in a calendar month with a maximum of 5 percent of outstanding shares within a twelve month period. These and other rules seek to prohibit the repurchase of shares where such actions would push up the price of the shares in the marketplace. It would take several years for a firm to repurchase a large percentage of outstanding shares.

Additional Considerations

PROCEDURAL ASPECTS

When the board of directors of a corporation declares a cash dividend, it specifies a *date of record*. At the close of business that day, a list of stockholders is drawn up from the stock transfer books of the company. Stockholders on the list are entitled to the dividend, whereas stockholders who come on the books after the date of record are not entitled to the dividend. When the board of directors of Ottawa Chemical Company Ltd. met on May 8, it declared a dividend of 25 cents a share payable June 15 to stockholders of record on May 31. Jennifer Doakes owned the stock on May 31, so she is entitled to the dividend even though she might sell her stock prior to the dividend actually being paid on June 15.

A problem can develop in the sale of stock in the days immediately prior to the date of record. The buyer and the seller of the stock have several days to settle; that is, to pay for the stock or to deliver it, in the case of the seller. As a result, the company may not be notified of the stock transfer in sufficient time. For this reason, the brokerage community has a rule whereby new stockholders are entitled to dividends only if they purchase the stock five business days prior to the date of record. If the stock is purchased after that time, the stockholder is not entitled to the dividend. The date itself is known as the *ex-dividend date*. In our example, the date of record was May 31. If this were a Friday, five business days before would be May 24, and this would be the ex-dividend date. In order to receive the dividend, a new stockholder must purchase the stock on May 23 or before. If purchased on May 24 or after, the stock is said to be ex-dividend. That is, it is without the 25 cent dividend.

On the ex-dividend date, the market price of the stock should decline by approximately the amount of the dividend. Suppose the stock of Ottawa Chemical Company Ltd. in our example were selling for $20 a share on May 23. If nothing else changed, the stock should sell for approximately $19.75 on May 24 because the purchaser on that date is not entitled to the 25 cent dividend. Because other factors influence the market price of the stock, this effect is sometimes difficult to measure. Once a dividend is declared, stockholders become creditors of the company until the dividend is actually paid; the declared but unpaid dividend is a current liability of the company.

Dividend Reinvestment Plans Recently some companies have established Dividend Reinvestment Plans (DRPs) where shareholders have the option to receive cash or stock dividends. A DRP is administered by an agent (usually a trust company) on behalf of participating shareholders. Those shareholders who want stock dividends register with the agent. When a dividend is declared, the firm will pay cash to those shareholders who are not participating in the plan. Otherwise, the cash is sent to the agent who in turn buys new common shares from the firm paying the dividends. These new shares are credited to the accounts of participating shareholders in proportion to the dividends that each shareholder should have received under the cash dividend option. The dividends for a participating shareholder are automatically "reinvested" until membership is terminated (by writing to the agent) by the shareholder.

Most plans provide for the purchase of new common shares at about a 5 percent discount from market price and at zero brokerage costs. These features serve as inducements for reinvestment. So far as the firm is concerned, the reinvestment of dividends under the plan is a mechanism to raise new equity capital at relatively lower costs. By the end of 1983, about 42 firms had DRPs and most of these established their plans in 1980 and thereafter. The list includes some of Canada's largest firms—Bank of Nova Scotia, Bank of Montreal, Canadian Imperial Bank of Commerce, Canadian Pacific, Imperial Oil and Trans Alta Utilities.

LEGAL CONSIDERATIONS

Capital restriction   Directors are prohibited from the payment of dividends if these dividends impair capital. Capital is defined as the par value of the common shares. For example, if a firm had one million shares outstanding with a $2 par value, total capital would be $2 million. If the net worth of a company were $2.1 million, the company could not pay a cash dividend totaling $200 000 without impairing capital. Where a company has no par value shares, capital is the price for which the shares are issued. The purpose of the capital impairment restriction is to protect creditors of a company. For a relatively new company, these laws may afford creditors a degree of protection. However, for established companies that have been profitable in the past and have built up retained earnings, substantial losses will usually have been incurred before the restriction has an effect. By this time, the situation may be so hopeless that the restriction gives creditors little protection.

Insolvency   Directors are forbidden to pay dividends if the company is insolvent or if the dividend payment will render the company insolvent. Insolvency is defined either in a legal sense, as liabilities exceeding assets, or in a technical sense, as the firm's inability to pay its creditors as obligations become due. As the ability of the firm to pay its obligations is dependent on its liquidity rather than on its capital, the technical insolvency restriction gives creditors a good deal of protection. When cash is limited, a company is prohibited from favoring shareholders to the detriment of creditors.

Summary

The critical question in dividend policy is whether dividends have an influence upon the value of the firm, given its investment decision. If dividends are irrelevant, as Modigliani and Miller believe, the firm should retain earnings only in keeping with its investment opportunities. If there are not sufficient investment opportunities to provide expected returns in excess of those required, the unused funds should be paid out as dividends. The key issue is whether dividends are more than just a means of distributing unused funds. With perfect capital markets and an absence of taxes, stockholders can manufacture "homemade" dividends, making dividend payout irrelevant. With differential taxes on dividends and capital gains, there seemingly is a bias in favor of paying dividends particularly if shareholders have lower marginal federal tax rates.

The market imperfection of flotation costs biases things in favor of retention because retention is less expensive than the common-stock financing used to replace the dividend. Restrictions on the investment behavior of financial institutions work in the direction of a preference for dividends. Other imperfections also are part of the picture.

Unfortunately, empirical evidence on the relevance of dividends in a world with market imperfections is conflicting. In final analysis, we are not able to state whether or not the dividend payout of the firm should be more than a passive decision variable. While many companies behave as if dividend policy is relevant, the case for it is not conclusive.

When a company is faced with a dividend decision, managerial considerations include the funds needs of the firm, business risk, liquidity, ability to borrow, assessment of any valuation information, control, and restrictions in a bond indenture or loan agreement. Many people feel that the stability of dividends has a positive effect upon the market price of the stock. Stable dividends may tend to resolve uncertainty in the minds of investors, particularly when earnings per share drop. Stable dividends also may have a positive utility to investors interested in current periodic income. Many companies appear to follow the policy of a target dividend payout ratio, increasing dividends only when they feel that an increase in earnings can be sustained. The use of an extra dividend permits a cyclical company to maintain a stable record of regular dividends while paying additional dividends whenever earnings are unusually high.

A stock dividend pays additional stock to stockholders. It is used frequently to conserve cash and to reduce the cash dividend payout ratio of the firm. Theoretically, the stock dividend is not a thing of value to the stockholder unless cash dividends per share remain unchanged or are increased. A much more effective device for reducing market price per share is a stock split. With a split, the number of shares is increased by the terms of the split; for example, a three-for-one split means that the number of shares is tripled.

A company's repurchase of its own shares should be treated as a dividend decision when the firm has funds in excess of present and foreseeable future investment needs. It may distribute these funds either as dividends or by the repurchase of shares. In the absence of a tax differential between dividends and capital gains, the monetary value of the two alternatives should be about the same. However, the tax provisions governing repurchase transactions add complexity to the decision-making process. Finally, we examined various procedural aspects associated with paying dividends as well as certain legal restrictions.

Questions

1. Justify borrowing money in order to have liquidity with which to pay dividends on common stock.
2. What is the impact of a stock dividend on the wealth of stockholders? Is the answer different for a stock split?

3. The performance of some institutional investors (some pension funds, for example) is measured on the basis of income yield, recognizing capital gains or losses only if the securities are sold. Does this method of measuring performance have an impact on corporate dividend policy? Discuss the wisdom of this method of measuring performance.

4. Discuss the factors that would tend to bias dividend policy toward a high payout.

5. Discuss the factors that would tend to bias dividend policy toward a zero payout.

6. What effect would you expect on the firm's optimal dividend policy if the federal government began taxing all capital gains at the ordinary income tax rate?

7. What weakness do you see in the Walter formula as the indicator of an optimal dividend policy? Consider carefully the firm's investment opportunities and optimal capital structure before you answer.

8. As firm's financial manager, would you recommend to the board of directors that the firm adopt as policy a stable dividend payment per share or a stable payout ratio? What are the disadvantages of each? Would the firm's industry influence your decision? Why?

9. As an investor, would you prefer the firm to repurchase its stock by means of a tender offer or through open market operations? Why?

10. Why do companies with high growth rates tend to have low dividend-payout ratios, and companies with low growth rates high payout ratios?

11. Are regular stock dividends valuable to investors? Why or Why not?

12. How does an investor manufacture "homemade" dividends? What is the effect of the actions of a number of investors doing so, all other things held constant?

13. When earnings turn bad, why are boards of directors of companies reluctant to reduce the dividend?

14. Why do lenders frequently place a formal restriction in the loan agreement or the indenture on the amount of dividends that can be paid?

15. Is the dividend decision really a financing decision in disguise?

Problems with Solutions

1. Shown below is the shareholders' equity of a company as at December 31, 19X1

Common stock, No par value, 100 000 shares authorized, 90 000 issued of which 10 000 are in the treasury	800 000
Retained earnings (of which $120 000 is restricted by the purchaseof treasury stock)	1 000 000
Treasury stock	(120 000)
	$1 680 000

During 19X2 the following transactions occurred in chronological order:
(a) paid a dividend of $0.50 per share
(b) declared and distributed a 20 percent stock dividend when the market price of a share was $13
(c) split the shares three for one
(d) transferred 19X2 net income of $100 000 to retained earnings.
Prepare the shareholders' equity section of the balance sheet after each of the above transactions.

| | Transaction | | | |
	A	B	C	D
Common stock	$800 000	$1 008 000 (2)	$1 008 000 (4)	$1 008 000
Retained earnings ($120 000 restricted)	960 000 (1)	752 000 (3)	752 000	852 000 (5)
Treasury stock	(120 000)	(120 000)	(120 000)	(120 000)
	$1 640 000	$1 640 000	$1 640 000	$1 740 000

(1) Dividend = number of shares outstanding × $0.50
$$= 80\ 000 \times \$0.50 = \$40\ 000$$
Retained earnings = $1 000 000 − $40 000 = $960 000
(2) Stock dividend = number of shares outstanding × 0.20 × $13
$$= 80\ 000 \times 0.20 \times \$13 = \$208\ 000$$
Common stock = $800 000 + $208 000 = $1 008 000
(3) Retained earnings = $960 000 − stock dividend
$$= \$960\ 000 - \$208\ 000 = \$752\ 000$$
(4) Stock split does not change dollar value of common shares on the balance sheet but the number of shares outstanding is now (80 000 + 16 000)(3) = 288 000.
(5) $752 000 + net income of $100 000 = $852 000.

2. Assume that you own 8 000 shares of the company in problem 1 on December 31, 19X1 and that you neither buy nor sell shares during 19X2. Show the effect of each transaction on the book value of your investment.

	Per share (rounded)	Total
Book value Dec. 31, 19X1 ($1 680 000 ÷ 80 000)	$21.00	$168 000 (1)
Book value after (a) ($1 680 000 − 40 000) ÷ 80 000	20.50	164 000
Book value after (b) $1 640 000 ÷ (80 000 + 16 000)	17.08	164 000 (2)
Book value after (c) $1 640 000 ÷ (96 000 × 3)	5.69	164 000 (3)
Book value after (d) $1 740 000 ÷ 288 000	6.04	174 000

(1) The book value of all outstanding shares equals the total shareholders' equity, or $1 680 000 (see problem 1). Since you hold 10 percent of the shares (8 000 of 80 000) the book value of your investment equals 10 percent of $1 680 000 or $168 000.
(2) The book value per share has fallen to $17.08 but you now own 9 600 shares because of the stock dividend. (9 600 × $17.08 = $164 000)
(3) $5.69(9 600 × 3) = $164 000
Note that the book value per share is changed by each transaction but the total is affected only by dividends and earnings. The stock dividend and the split are really paper transactions and alone cannot affect wealth.

3. An investor owns 5 000 common shares of a company and expects the company to earn $10 000 after tax and pay dividends of $0.20 per share in teach of the next two years. The company has outstanding 250 000 shares of common stock that sell at a price-earnings ratio of 12:1. The investor has asked you as a financial advisor, the following questions: If the company

decided to repurchase shares rather than pay the dividends, what price must it pay for the shares in order to leave me in the same position I would be in if I received a dividend? If the shares were repurchased rateably from all shareholders how many shares would I have at the end of two years? Ignore tax considerations throughout.

Market price + dividend = repurchase price first year
Market price = ($100 000 ÷ 250 000 shares)(12) = $4.80

$4.80 + $0.20 = $5.00 = repurchase price first year.
Repurchase price first year + dividend = repurchase price second year
$5.00 + $0.20 = $5.20

Proof of calculation:
Repurchase of shares = $50 000 ÷ $5.00 = 10 000 shares
Number of shares outstanding after repurchase = 250 000 − 10 000 = 240 000
Market price start of second year = $100 000 ÷ 240 000 × 12 = $5.00
Repurchase price second year = $5.00 + $0.20 = $5.20
Number of shares repurchased = $240 000 × $0.20 ÷ $5.20) = 9 231 shares
Number of shares outstanding after repurchase = 240 000 − 9 231 = 230 769
Price of shares = $100 000 ÷ 230 769 × 12 = $5.20

Our investor held 2 percent of the total number of shares outstanding (5 000 ÷ 250 000). After the second repurchase the investor's holdings would be 0.02 × 230 769 or 4 516 shares. In the first year 200 of the investor's shares were repurchased and in the second, 185, leaving our investor with 4 615 as shown above.

Problems

1. The Peters Company Ltd.'s equity account (book value) is as follows:

The Peters Company Ltd. Equity Accounts December 31, 19X8

Common stock ($5 par, 1 000 000 shares)	$ 5 000 000
Contributed capital	5 000 000
Retained earnings	15 000 000
	$25 000 000

Currently, Peters is under pressure from stockholders to pay some dividends. Peters' cash balance is $500 000, all of which is needed for transaction purposes. The stock is trading for $7 a share.

(a) What is the legal limit that can be paid in cash dividends?
(b) Compute the equity account if the company pays a 20 percent stock dividend.
(c) Compute the equity account if the company declares a 6-for-5 stock split.
(d) Discuss the stock price movements that should occur after parts (b) and (c) above.

2. The Beta-Alpha Company Ltd. expects with some degree of certainty to generate the following net income and to have the following capital expenditures during the next five years (in thousands):

Year	1	2	3	4	5
Net income	$2 000	$1 500	$2 500	$2 300	$1 800
Capital expenditures	1 000	1 500	2 000	1 500	2 000

Presently the company has one million shares of common stock outstanding and pays dividends of $1 per share.

(a) Determine dividends per share if dividend policy is treated as a residual decision.

(b) Determine the amounts of external financing that will be necessary if the present dividend per share is maintained.

(c) Determine dividends per share and the amounts of external financing that will be necessary if a dividend payout ratio of 50 percent is maintained.

(d) Under which of the three dividend policies are aggregate dividends maximized? Under which of them is external financing minimized?

3. The Axalt Corporation Ltd. and the Baxalt Corporation Ltd. have had remarkably similar earnings patterns over the last five years. In fact, both firms have had identical earnings per share. Further, both firms are in the same industry, produce the same product, and face the same business and financial risks. In short, these firms are carbon copies of each other in every respect but one: Axalt paid out a constant percentage of its earnings (50 percent) in dividends while Baxalt has paid a constant cash dividend. The financial manager of the Axalt Corporation has been puzzled by the fact that the price of Axalt's stock has been generally lower than the price of Baxalt's stock, even though in some years Axalt's dividend was substantially larger than Baxalt's.

(a) What might account for the condition that has been puzzling the financial manager of Axalt?

(b) What might be done by both companies to increase the market price of their stock?

	Axalt			Baxalt		
Years	EPS	Div.	Mkt. price	EPS	Div.	Mkt. price
1	$1.00	0.50	$6	$1.00	0.23	$4⅞
2	0.50	0.25	4	0.50	0.23	4⅜
3	−0.25	nil	2	−0.25	0.23	4
4	0.30	0.15	3	0.30	0.23	4¼
5	0.50	0.25	3½	0.50	0.23	4½

4. The Mann Company Ltd. belongs to a risk class for which the appropriate capitalization rate is 15 percent. It currently has outstanding 100 000 shares selling at $100 each. The firm is contemplating the declaration of a $5 dividend at the end of the current fiscal year, which just began. Answer the following questions based on the Modigliani and Miller model and the assumption of no taxes.

(a) What will be the price of the stock at the end of the year if a dividend is not declared? What will it be if one is?

(b) Assuming that the firm pays the dividend, has net income of $1 million, and makes new investments of $2 million during the period, how many new shares must be issued?

(c) Is the MM model realistic with respect to valuation? What factors might mar its validity?

5. Forte Papers Corporation Ltd. and Great Northern Ltd. Paper Company, are in the same industry, both are publicly held with a large number of stockholders, and they have the following characteristics:

	Forte	Great Northern
Expected annual cash flow (in thousands)	$ 50 000	$35 000
Standard deviation of cash flows (in thousands)	30 000	25 000
Annual capital expenditures (in thousands)	42 000	40 000
Cash and marketable securities (in thousands)	5 000	7 000
Existing long-term debt (in thousands)	100 000	85 000
Unused short-term line of credit (in thousands)	25 000	10 000
Flotation costs and underpricing on common stock issues as a percent of proceeds	0.05	0.08
Present annual inflation rate	0.13	0.13

On the basis of this information, which company is likely to have the higher dividend payout ratio? Why?

6. The Canadales Copper Company Ltd. declared a 25 percent stock dividend on March 10 to stockholders of record on April 1. The market price of the stock is $50 per share. You own 160 shares of the stock.
   (a) If you sold your stock on March 20, what would be the price per share, all other things the same?
   (b) After the stock dividend is paid, how many shares of stock will you own?
   (c) At what price would you expect the stock to sell on April 2, all other things the same?
   (d) What will be the total value of your holdings before and after the stock dividend, all other things the same?

7.

The Sherill Corporation Ltd. capital structure
December 30, 19X3

Common stock ($1 par, 1 000 000 shares)	$1 000 000
Contributed capital	300 000
Retained earnings	1 700 000
Net worth	$3 000 000

The firm earned $300 000 after taxes in 19X3 and paid out 50 percent of these earnings as cash dividends. The price of the firm's stock on December 30 was $5.
   (a) If the firm declared a stock dividend of 3 percent on December 31, what would the reformulated capital structure be?
   (b) Assuming the firm paid no stock dividend, how much would earnings per share for 19X3 be? Dividends per share?
   (c) Assuming a 3 percent stock dividend, what would happen to EPS and DPS for 19X3?
   (d) What would the price of the stock be after the 3 percent stock dividend?

8. The T.N.Cox Ltd. Company is owned by several wealthy Albertans. The firm earned $3 500 000 after taxes this year. With one million shares outstanding, earnings per share were $3.50. The stock recently has traded at $72 per share, among the current stockholders. Two dollars of this value is accounted for by investor anticipation of a cash dividend. As financial manager of T.N.Cox, you have contemplated the alternative of repurchasing the company stock by means of a tender offer at $72 per share.

(a) How much stock could the firm repurchase if this alternative were selected?

(b) Ignoring taxes, which alternative should be selected?

(c) Considering taxes, which alternative should be selected?

Selected References

BAKER, H. KENT, and PATRICIA L. GALLAGHER, "Management's View of Stock Splits," *Financial Management,* 9 (Summer 1980), 73-77.

BAR-YOSEF, SASSON, and LAWRENCE D. BROWN, "A Reexamination of Stock Splits Using Moving Averages," *Journal of Finance,* 21 (December 1966), 1069-80.

BIERMAN, HAROLD, JR. and RICHARD WEST, "The Acquisition of Common Stock by the Corporate Issuer, " *Journal of Finance,* 21 (December 1966), 687-96.

BIERMAN, HAROLD, and JEROME E. HASS, "Investment Cut-off Rates and Dividend Policy", *Financial Management*, Winter 1983, 19-24.

BLACK, FISCHER, and MYRON SCHOLES, "The Effects of Dividend Yield and Dividend Policy on Common Stock Prices and Returns," Journal of Financial Economics, 1 (May 1974), 1-22.

BRITTAIN, JOHN A., *Corporate Dividend Policy.* Washington, D.C.:Brookings Institution, 1966.

CHAREST, GUY, "Split Information, Stock Reurns and Market Efficiency," *Journal of Financial Economics,* 6 (June-September 1978), 265-96.

DIELMAN, TERRY, TIMOTHY J. NANTELL, and ROGER L. WRIGHT, "Price Effects of Stock Repurchasing: A Random Coefficient Regression Approach," *Journal of Financial and Quantitative Analysis, 15 (March 1980), 175-89.*

EADES, KENNETH M., "Empirical Evidence on Dividends as a Signal of Firm Value", *Journal of Financial and Quantitative Analysis,* November 1982, 471-499.

ELTON, EDWIN J., and MARTIN J. GRUBER, "The Cost of Retained Earnings—Implications of Share Repurchase," *Industrial Management Review,* (Spring 1968), 87-104

FERRIS, KENNETH R., ARIE MELNIK, and ALFRED RAPPAPORT, "Factors Influencing the Pricing of Stock Repurchase Tenders," *Quarterly Reviews of Economics and Business,* 18 (Spring 1978), 31-39.

GOULD, LAWRENCE I., and STANLEY N. LAIKEN. "Dividends vs. Capital Gains under Share Redemptions, " *Canadian Tax Journal* (Mar.-April. 1979), 161-71

HIGGINS, ROBERT C., "The Corporate Dividend-Saving Decision," *Journal of Financial and Quantitative Analysis,* 7 (March 1972), 1527-41.

KWAN, CLARENCE C.Y., "Efficient Market Tests of the Informational Content of Announcements: Critique and Extension," *Journal of Financial and Quantitative Analysis,* 16 (June 1981), 193-206

LINTNER, JOHN, "Distribution of Income of Corporations among Dividends, Retained Earnings, and Taxes," *American Economics and Statistics*, 46 (May 1956), 97-113.

———"Dividends, Earnings, Leverage, Stock Prices and the Supply of Capital to Corporations," *Review of Economics and Statistics,* 44 (August 1962), 243-69

LITZENBERGER, ROBERT H., and KRISHNA RAMISWAMY, "Dividends, Short Selling Restrictions, Tax Induced Investor Clienteles and Market Equilibrium," *Journal of Finance,* 35 (May 1980), 469-82.

MANTRIPRAGADA, K.G. "Stable Dividends and Share Prices," *Journal of Finance,* 27 (Sept. 1972), 951-52.

MANTRIPRAGADA, K.G. and H. BISHARA. "The Dividend Policies of Canadian Corporations: An Empirical Study," Working Paper, College of Commerce, University of Saskatchewan, 1974.

MILLAR, JAMES 1., "Split or Dividend: Do the Words Really Matter?" *Accounting Review,* 52 (January 1977), 52-55.

MILLER, MERTON H., and FRANCO MODIGLIANI, "Dividend Policy, Growth, and the Valuation of Shares," *Journal of Business,* 34 (October 1961), 411-33.

MORGAN, IEUAN and JACQUES SAINT-PIERRE. "Dividend and Investment Decisions of Canadian Firms," *Canadian Journal of Economics* (Feb. 1978), 20-37.

PALMON, DAN and UZI YAARI, "Retention and Tax Avoidance: A Clarification," *Financial Management,* 10 (Spring 1981), 29-35.

PENMAN, STEPHEN H., "The Predictive Content of Earnings Forecasts and Dividends", *Journal of Finance,* September 1983, 1181-1200

PETTIT, R. RICHARDSON, "The Impact of Dividend and Earnings Announcements: A Reconciliation." *Journal of Business,* 49 (January 1976), 86-96. Watts, Ross, "Comments," *Journal of Business,* 49 (January 1976), 97-106.

PETTWAY, RICHARD H., and R. PHIL MALONE, "Automatic Dividend Reinvestment Plans for Nonfinancial Corporations," *Financial Management,* 2 (Winter 1973), 11-18.

REILLY, FRANK K., and EUGENE F. DRZYCIMSKI, "Short-Run Profits from Stock Splits," *Financial Management,* 10 (Summer 1981), 64-74.

SHILLER, ROBERT H., "Do Stock Prices Move Too Much to be Justified by Subsequent Changes in Dividends?" *American Economic Review,* 71 (June 1981), 421-36.

STEWART, SAMUEL S., JR., "Should a Corporation Repurchase its Own Stock?" *Journal of Finance,* 31 (June 1976), 911-21.

VAN HORNE, JAMES C., and JOHN G. McDONALD, "Dividend Policy and New Equity Financing," *Journal of Finance,* 26 (May 1971), 507-29.

WALTER, JAMES E., "Dividend Policies and Common Stock Prices," *Journal of Finance,* 11 (March 1958), 29-41.

WOOLRIDGE, J. RANDALL, "Dividend Changes and Security Prices", *Journal of Finance,* December 1983, 1607-1616.

_____"Stock Dividends as Signals", *Journal of Financial Research,* Spring 1983, 1-12.

WOOLRIDGE, J. RANDALL and DONALD CHAMBERS, "Reverse Splits and Shareholder Wealth", *Financial Management,* Autumn 1983, 5-15.

VII

LONGER TERM FINANCING- INSTRUMENTS AND MARKETS

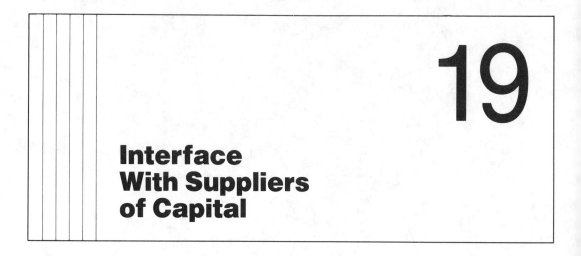

Interface With Suppliers of Capital

In Part VI, we studied how business firms arrange their long-term capitalization and how they finance internally through retained earnings. We now consider how firms raise long-term funds externally. More specifically, the purpose of this chapter is to explore the ways in which bond and preferred and common share issues are sold. We consider public issues which are usually placed through investment dealers, privileged issues to the company's own shareholders (known as rights offering), and private or direct placements by the firm with institutional investors. We also present a summary of the relative use of debt and equity securities in long-term financing. An understanding of the institutional framework presented in Chapter 3 is particularly important in the present discussion.

Public Issues Through Investment Dealers

When a company issues securities to the public, it frequently avails itself of the services of an investment dealer. The principal function of the investment dealer is to buy the securities from the company and then resell them to investors. This is known as the *underwriting function.*[1] For this service, the investment dealers receive the difference, or spread, between the price they pay for the security and the price at which the securities are resold to the public. Because most companies only

---

[1] Instead of underwriting a security issue, an investment dealer may sell the issues on a *best efforts* basis. Under this arrangement, the investment dealer agrees to sell only as many securities as possible at an established price. The investment dealer has no responsibility for securities that are unsold. In other words, the investment dealer bears no risk. Investment dealers are frequently unwilling to underwrite the security issue of a small company. For these companies, the only feasible means by which to place securities may be through a best-efforts offering.

make occasional trips to the capital market, they are not specialists in the distribution of securities. Selling securities directly to investors would be both costly and risky. Investment dealers have the knowledge, the contacts, and the sales organization needed for the efficient marketing of securities. Because they are in the business of buying securities from companies and selling them to investors, investment dealers can perform this operation at a lower cost than can the individual firm.

A security offering through an investment dealer to the investing public, known as a public offering, is usually done on a negotiated basis.[2] With a negotiated offering, the company issuing the securities selects a securities firm and works directly with that firm in determining the essential features of the issue. Together they negotiate a price for the security and determine the timing of the issue. Depending on the size of the issue, the investment dealer may invite other firms to join in sharing the risk and selling the issue; the combination is known as a syndicate. If a company has had satisfactory experience with a securities firm, it usually will use the same firm for subsequent security issues.

Functions of an Investment Dealer

UNDERWRITING FUNCTION

One of the key functions the investment dealer performs is that of bearing risk. When an investment dealer (or group of investment dealers) buys a security issue, he or she underwrites the sale of the issue by giving the company a cheque for the purchase price. At that time, the company is relieved of the risk of not being able to sell the issue to investors at the established price. If the issue does not sell well, either because of an adverse turn in the market or because it is overpriced, the underwriter, and not the company, takes the loss. Thus, the investment dealer insures, or underwrites the issue against the risk of adverse market price fluctuations during the period of distribution.

Usually, the investment dealer with whom a company discusses the offering does not handle the underwriting alone. A *banking group* may be established to finance the underwriting. Members of this group and their degree of participation are determined primarily on the basis of their ability to sell securities. The originating firm is usually the manager and has the largest participation. For the risk-bearing function of the offering, these investment dealers are compensated by an underwriting profit. We discuss this aspect of compensation later in this chapter. Also, a *selling group* may be established to assist in the sale of the new issue and just as important, to promote a wider distribution of the securities. All parties are usually signatories to one or more agreements—underwriting agreement, banking group agreement, or selling group agreement.

---

[2]Another method of issuing new securities is through competitive bidding. The issuer invites bids from investment dealers and specifies the date that sealed bids will be received. The bidder with the highest price wins the security case. Competitive bidding is not used by Canadian companies; it is used by the Federal Government for the sale of Treasury bills. In the U.S., certain utilities and railroads are required by law to use competitive bidding.

ADVISING

The investment dealer advises the firm on a wide variety of matters pertinent to the success of the offering. For a company that makes infrequent trips to the capital markets, this advice can be very valuable; the matters considered include the timing of the issue, its pricing, and the features that are necessary to assure a successful sale. Because of their expertise and experience in the market, investment dealers can recommend the best package of terms for the particular issue under consideration. Even in cases where firms make frequent trips to the capital markets, advice from investment dealers may still be valuable.

Remember that the investment dealer is not the only advisor to the company. Auditors are used to prepare the necessary financial statements and company lawyers are consulted on the legal aspects regarding the issue. Sometimes other corporate executives and even outside consultants are involved. However, the investment dealer is the "master planner" and must analyze and evaluate all available information relevant to the company's business and financial risk, particularly as these relate to the new issue.

Preparation of the prospectus   We discussed the need for the prospectus in Chapter 3. The investment dealer is instrumental in preparing this document. He or she is on continuous call from the time the preliminary prospectus is filed with the securities authorities to the time when the final prospectus is approved. The investment dealer advises the firm on queries raised by the securities authorities and assists in amendments, if needed.

Pricing the issue   The offering price is always an important consideration for both the issuing company and the investment dealer. The investment dealer would like to see a price low enough to assure a successful sale, but is also aware that if the price is too low, the issuing company will be dissatisfied. An investment dealer can ill afford dissatisfied customers, for news of such dissatisfaction spreads quickly in the financial community. Moreover, the issuing company must agree to the price recommended by the underwriter. Otherwise, of course, there can be no offering.

In the case of bonds, the issue will be priced in relation to the price of other new issues of the same grade. The underwriter and the issuing company must assess the tone of the market with respect to expectations of future interest rates. In addition to recent interest rate movements in the money and capital markets, they consider the forthcoming supply of new issues, the expected future of the economy, and expectations created by monetary and fiscal policies. A typical new issue will have to be sold at a lower price and higher yield to maturity than a seasoned or outstanding issue of the same maturity and grade. The offering price is generally set the night before issue date.

For a common stock issue, the problem of pricing is perhaps more difficult because of the greater volatility of the stock market. When a company already has shares outstanding that are held by the public, the principal factor that governs the price of any new issue is the market price of the existing shares. The new issue will need to be underpriced in order to sell, however. The degree of underpricing will depend on the volatility of the share price and the tone of the market. When it becomes known in the marketplace that a company is going to offer new shares, downward pressure is usually exerted on the market price of the outstanding shares. This pressure reflects investors' concern over dilution in earnings per share. Pressure usually develops on the day the new issue is announced, or before, if rumors of the new issue are out. This pressure contributes to the problem of underpricing the issue properly. Where a firm has shares outstanding and these are publicly traded, the price of the new shares is usually not established until the night before the offering.

If a company is issuing shares to the public for the first time, the pricing problem is much more difficult because there is no current market price to serve as a benchmark. For privately held companies that are going public, a comparison with similar companies is usually made to determine the appropriate price/earnings ratio. For this comparison, regression studies and other types of statistical analyses may be helpful. However, some companies may be so specialized that comparison with other companies is very difficult. The pricing of these issues is usually resolved by consideration of such essentials as present earnings, the growth rate, and the volatility of earnings. When a company goes public for the first time, the underwriter and company may agree on a share price well before the offering date. Because there is no secondary market for existing shares, it is not necessary to delay pricing until the last minute.

It is important to recognize that there is a tradeoff between the price per share to the public and the underwriting spread. The higher the price, the greater the risk that the investment dealer will be unable to sell the entire issue or that the distribution period will be prolonged. As a result of this greater risk, greater compensation is needed in the form of the spread between the price paid to the company and the reoffering price to the public. The important thing to the company, of course, is the net price paid to it by the underwriter.

Selling the securities   Once approval of the issue has been given, the next major function of the investment dealer is that of selling the securities to investors. As we discussed earlier, investment dealers are invited to form syndicates where their degree of participation is determined primarily by their ability to distribute securities. For this function, an investment dealer is rewarded by a selling commission of so many dollars a share. The ultimate seller can be either a member of the underwriting syndicate or a qualified outside security dealer of a selling group. The selling group is usually set up by the manager of the underwriting syndicate to facilitate wider distribution of the security issue. An outside security dealer must purchase the bond(s) or shares from a member of the underwriting syndicate, but can only obtain a dealer concession, which pays less than the full selling commission. That is, a non-syndicate seller receives a lower commission per unit of security sold than would syndicate members.

Once the preliminary prospectus has been filed with the securities commission, the underwriter will start to line up prospective buyers. The preliminary prospectus is distributed to interested investors and the underwriter ascertains which of these are likely to buy the securities. Note that the issue cannot be sold until final approval is given by the securities commission. Once the registration is approved, the offering price to the public is established, and a final prospectus is printed. At that time, security salespeople seek orders from investors. If the issue is priced fairly, it will be sold within a day or two or, perhaps, even within a few hours. Sometimes "hot" issues are sold out in advance to preorder subscribers. Once the issue is sold, the underwriting syndicate is dissolved.

STABILIZATION OF THE MARKET

During the period when the investment dealer or syndicate is attempting to sell a new issue, it is important that the market price of the new bond or share be reasonably stable, to bolster investors' confidence in the issue. If the price should drop, the investment dealer or syndicate stands to lose a great deal. To reduce this risk, the investment dealer or managing underwriter for the syndicate will often attempt to stabilize the market price during the distribution period, by placing orders to buy the security at a pegged price. For example, if the price of a bond to the public is $990, the managing underwriter may stand ready to buy any bonds offered at that price for the syndicate account. In this way, the market price will not fall below $990 during the distribution period. In a sharply falling market, the managing underwriter may not be able to peg the price without having to buy the better part of the issue—a self-defeating process, to say the least. However, for an issue that is realistically priced in a reasonably stable market, the pegging operation does tend to reduce the risk of the underwriter. Without such stabilization, the risk to the underwriters would be greater; and they would compensate for it by bidding a lower price to the company and/or increasing the underwriting spread.

UNDERWRITING COMPENSATION

To illustrate the way investment dealers are compensated, we turn to an example. Fig. 19-1 shows the cover of the prospectus for an issue of common shares of Pacific Western Airlines Corp. The issue was a negotiated one, and the underwriting syndicate consisted of Wood Gundy Ltd., Pemberton Houston Willoughby Inc., Dominion Securities Ames Ltd. and McLeod Young Weir Ltd. Wood Gundy Ltd. was the manager of the syndicate and would be regarded as the principal underwriter. All members of the syndicate financed the issue and were members of the banking group. The selling group included all members of the syndicate as well as other security dealers.

We see that the syndicate bought 10 000 000 common shares from the company, paying $10.1856 for each share priced to sell at $10.75. Thus, the underwriting spread was $0.5644 per share, or 5.25 percent of gross proceeds. This spread of $0.5644 per share would be split three ways—underwriting, banking group, and selling group commissions. The principal underwriter, and any other member of the syndicate who assists the principal underwriter, have a claim to the underwriting commission. This fee is compensation for the effort expended in negotiating with the issuing firm and in helping to prepare the details and necessary documents for the new issue. Suppose the underwriting agreement (which is signed by the principal underwriter and other members of the banking group) stipulates a 15 percent management fee. In this case, then, the underwriting commission is $0.0847 ($0.5644 × 0.15) per share. This fee structure implies that the principal underwriter has agreed to "sell" the issue to the banking group at $10.2703 ($10.1856 plus $0.0847) per share.

The gross commission now available for the banking group is $0.4797 ($0.5644 less $0.0847) per share. The amount of this commission available to the group depends on the manner in which the securities are sold to the public. Normally, there are three approaches taken in the sale of the issue. First, members

New Issue and Secondary Offering

◀ Pacific Western Airlines Corporation

$107,500,000

10,000,000 Common Shares

**(plus 500,000 Common Shares to be issued pursuant to
the Employee Share Purchase Plan)**

Of the Common Shares offered by this prospectus, 6,300,000 are being issued by the Company and 3,700,000 are being sold by the Province of Alberta (the "Selling Shareholder").

In the opinion of counsel, the Common Shares are investments which qualify for investment under those statutes referred to under "Eligibility for Investment" on page 6.

Price: $10.75 per Common Share

	Price to public	Underwriters' fees	Proceeds to the Company (1)	Proceeds to the Selling Shareholder (2)
Per Common Share	$10.75	$0.5644	$10.1856	$10.1856
Total	$107,500,000	$5,643,750	$64,169,437	$37,686,813

    (1) Before payment of estimated expenses of $267.750 payable by the Company.

    (2) Before payment of estimated expenses of $157,250 payable by the Selling Shareholder. The Company will not receive any part of the
        proceeds of the sale of Common Shares by the Selling Shareholder.

The price of the Common Shares offered hereby was determined by negotiation among the Company, the Selling Shareholder and the Underwriters.

The Toronto, Alberta and Vancouver stock exchanges have conditionally approved the listing of the Common Shares offered hereby. The listings are subject to the Company's fulfilling all the requirements of such exchanges on or before February 20, 1984, including distribution of the Common Shares to a minimum number of public shareholders.

The Common Shares carry restrictions on ownership. Reference is made to "Certain Provisions of the PWA Act" on page 20. The Province of Alberta is not bound by the provisions of the securities legislation in any jurisdiction and therefore is not liable for the remedies referred to under "Purchaser's Statutory Rights" on page 26.

We, as principals, conditionally offer these Common Shares, subject to prior sale, if, as and when issued by the Company and sold by the Selling Shareholder and accepted by us in accordance with the conditions contained in the underwriting agreement referred to under "Plan of Distribution" on page 24 and subject to approval of certain legal matters on behalf of the Company by Bennett Jones, Calgary, and on our behalf by Macleod Dixon, Calgary.

Subscriptions will be received subject to rejection or allotment in whole or in part and the right is reserved to close the subscription books at any time without notice. It is expected that definitive share certificates will be available for delivery on or about December 15, 1983.

Merrill Lynch Canada Inc.

⌂ Merrill Lynch

VICTORIA · VANCOUVER · CALGARY · EDMONTON · WINNIPEG · LONDON · KITCHENER · HAMILTON · MISSISSAUGA
TORONTO · OTTAWA · MONTREAL · QUEBEC · SAINT JOHN · HALIFAX · CHARLOTTETOWN · ST. JOHN'S · LONDON, ENGLAND

December 2, 1983

FIGURE 19-1   Prospectus of Western Airlines Corporation.
                  Note: Merrill Lynch Canada Inc. was a member of the selling
                  group.

of the syndicate have institutional customers (primarily the financial institutions) and these are placed on an *exempt list* of potential purchasers. The principal underwriter will sell to these customers on behalf of the banking group at the issue price of $10.75. Thus, the full spread of $0.4797 per share is retained. Suppose the exempt purchasers bought 2 million common shares, then the gross commission earned from sales to those buyers is $959 400. Second, the members of the syndicate have retail customers (e.g., individuals) whom they sell to at the issue price of $10.75. Assuming that 7 million shares were sold to such customers, then the gross commission from these sales would be $3 357 900 (7 million shares × $0.4797). Finally, approved non-syndicate security dealers can buy the shares from the banking group and sell them to their customers. Assume that the selling agreement stipulates that such dealers can buy from the banking group at $10.60 per share. This means a gross commission to the banking group of $0.3297 ($10.60 − $10.2703) per share on 1 000 000 shares (10 000 000 − 9 000 000 sold by the banking group) for a total of $329 700. Upon resale of the share to the public, the non-syndicate sellers receive a commission of $0.1500 ($10.75 − $10.60) per share for a total of $150 000 ($0.15 × 1 000 000 shares).

Given our assumptions in the above discussion, the distribution of the gross commission on the issue is summarized in Table 19-1. It should be noted that most of the compensation to the syndicate ($4 647 000 in Table 19-1) is derived from the sale of the securities by members of the banking group. The distribution of this commission is based on the proportion of shares sold by each member of the group. The banking group agreement stipulates the percentage of shares for which each member is responsible for the unsold shares. That is, he or she buys and holds them as inventory.

We assume that for the issue in Table 19-1, the shares are sold at the offering price of $10.75. Under this assumption, the syndicate receives the full amount of the expected compensation. However, there could be instances where an issue may have to be sold at a price below the offering price because of adverse conditions in the market following the date. Also, the issue may have been priced at too high a level relative to the prevailing market price. Whatever the reasons, sales to the public below the offering price reduce expected compensation.

TABLE 19-1   Hypothetical Illustration of the Distribution of Gross Commission

	No. of Shares	Commission per Share	Total Commission
A. Principal underwriter(s)	10 000 000	$0.0847	$ 847 000
B. Banking group			
Exempt purchasers	2 000 000	0.4797	959 400
Retail customers	7 000 000	0.4797	3 357 900
Non-syndicate dealers	1 000 000	0.3297	329 700
			4 647 000
C. Non-syndicate dealers	1 000 000	0.15	150 000
Total	10 000 000	0.5644	$5 644 000

Flotation costs The flotation costs of a new issue of securities tend to vary with the size and the type of the issue. These costs include the underwriting spread, registration expenses, and other out-of-pocket expenses. In general, the larger the issue, the lower the cost of flotation as a percentage of gross proceeds. Because certain company expenses—printing and legal fees in particular—are essentially fixed, the larger the issue, the lower their percentage cost. The underwriter also has certain "fixed" expenses. Thus, the larger the issue, the smaller the percentage of underwriting expense. Additionally and more significantly, there usually is a direct relationship between the size of an issue and the quality of the issuing company. Also, the relative cost of flotation tends to be highest for a common stock issue and lowest for a debt issue—a fact not surprising in view of the differences in underwriting risk.

For a large issue, say over $50 million, of a high quality company, the total cost of a debt issue (underwriting and other expenses) will be around 2 percent of the gross proceeds. This percentage compares with about 3 percent for a preferred stock issue and around 4 percent for a common stock issue. For a smaller issue, say $5 million, the percentages will be much higher. here percentage costs of around 4 percent, 6 percent, and 8 percent, respectively, are likely to be incurred.

Rights Offerings

Instead of selling a security issue to the public, many firms first offer the securities to existing shareholders on a privileged-subscription basis. This type of offering is known as a rights offering. Frequently, the corporate charter requires that a new issue of common shares or an issue of securities convertible into common shares be offered first to existing shareholders because of their preemptive right. Even if there is no legal obligation or provision in the corporate charter, existing shareholders are usually given the first opportunity to buy into any new issue. The use of the rights offering is popular with Canadian companies. Over the 1956–75 period about two thirds of new common stock issues were rights issues. These issues accounted for about 75 percent of new equity funds over that period.

PREEMPTIVE RIGHT

Under a preemptive right, existing common shareholders have the right to preserve their proportionate ownership in the company. If the company issues additional common shares, they must be given preferential rights to subscribe to the new shares so that they maintain their pro rata interest in the company. Suppose an individual owns 100 shares of a company which decided to increase by 10 percent the number of shares outstanding through a new common stock offering. If the shareholder has a preemptive right, then he or she must be given the first option to buy ten additional shares in order to preserve proportionate ownership in the company.

TERMS OF OFFERING

When a company sells securities by privileged subscription, each shareholder is awarded one right for each share of stock held. With a common share offering, the rights give the shareholder the option to purchase additional shares according to the terms of the offering. The terms specify the number of rights required for an additional share of stock, the subscription price per share, and the expiration date of the offering. The holder of rights has three choices: to exercise them and subscribe for additional shares; to sell them, as they are transferable; or to simply do nothing and let them expire. The latter usually occurs only if the value of a right is negligible and/or if the shareholder owns only a few shares of stock. Generally, the subscription period is relatively short (about one or two months). If a shareholder wishes to buy a share of additional stock, but does not have the necessary number of rights, he or she may purchase additional rights. For example, suppose a person owns 85 shares of stock in a company, and the number of rights required to purchase one additional share is ten. Given only 85 rights, he or she can purchase only eight full shares of stock. However, the ninth share can be bought by purchasing an additional five rights.

In a rights offering, the board of directors establishes *a date of record*. Persons holding the company's shares prior to five business days before that date receive the right to subscribe to the new issue. The share is said to sell with *rights on* prior to five business days before the date of record. After the ex-rights date (i.e., five business days before the date of record), the share is said to sell *ex-rights*; that is, the share is traded without the rights attached.

VALUE OF RIGHTS

The market value of a right is a function of the present market price of the stock, the subscription price, and the number of rights required to purchase an additional share of stock. The theoretical market value of one right after the offering is announced but while the stock is still selling rights-on is

$$R_o = \frac{P_o - S}{N + 1} \tag{19-1}$$

where R_o = market value of one right when stock is selling rights-on
P_o = market value of a share of stock selling rights-on
S = subscription price per share
N = number of rights required to purchase one share of stock.

If the market price of a stock is $100 a share, the subscription price is $90 a share, and it takes 4 rights to buy an additional share of stock, the theoretical value of a right when the stock is selling rights-on is

$$R_o = \frac{100 - 90}{4 + 1} = \$2 \tag{19-2}$$

We note that the market value of the stock with rights on contains the value of one right.

When the stock goes ex-rights, the market price theoretically declines, for investors no longer receive the right to subscribe to additional shares. The theoretical value of one share of stock when it goes ex-rights is

$$P_x = \frac{(P_o \times N) + S}{N + 1} \tag{19-3}$$

Where P_x = market price of stock when it goes ex-rights. For our example,

$$P_x = \frac{(100 \times 4) + 90}{4 + 1} = \$98$$

From this example, we see that, theoretically, the right does not represent a thing of value to the stockholder, whose stock is worth $100 before the date of record; after the date of record, it is worth $98 a share. The decline in market price is offset exactly by the value of the right. Thus, theoretically, the stockholder does not benefit from a rights offering; the right represents merely a return of capital.

The theoretical value of a right when the stock sells ex-rights is

$$R_x = \frac{P_x - S}{N} \tag{19-4}$$

where R_x = the market value of one right when the stock is selling ex-rights. If, in our example, the market price of the stock is $98 when it goes ex-rights,

$$R_x = \frac{98 - 90}{4} = \$2$$

or the same value as before.

We should be aware that the actual value of a right may differ somewhat from its theoretical value on account of transaction costs, speculation, and the irregular exercise and sale of rights over the subscription period. However, arbitrage limits the deviation of actual value from theoretical value. If the price of a right is significantly higher than its theoretical value, stockholders will sell their rights and purchase the stock in the market. Such action will exert downward pressure on the market price of the right and upward pressure on its theoretical value. The latter occurs because of the upward pressure on the market price of the stock. If the price of the right is significantly lower than its theoretical value, arbitragers will buy the rights, exercise their option to buy stock, and then sell the stock in the market. This occurrence will exert upward pressure on the market price of the right and downward pressure on its theoretical value. These arbitrage actions will continue as long as they are profitable.

SUCCESS OF THE OFFERING

One of the most important aspects of a successful rights offering is the subscription price. If the market price of the stock should fall below the subscription price, stockholders obviously will not subscribe to the stock, for they can buy it in the market at a lower price. Consequently, a company will set the subscription price at a value lower than the current market price to reduce the risk of the market price's falling below it. We know that the stock should fall in price when it goes ex-rights. Its new theoretical value is determined by Eq. (19-3); and we see that it strongly depends upon N, the number of rights required to purchase one share of stock. The greater the N, the less the theoretical price decline when the stock goes ex-rights. Thus, the risk that the market price will fall below the subscription price is inversely related to N.[3] To illustrate, suppose the following were true:

	Company A	Company B
Market value per share rights-on, P_o	$60.00	$60.00
Subscription price, S	$46.00	$46.00
Number of rights needed to purchase one share, N	1	10
Theoretical value of one share ex-rights, P_x	$53.00	$58.73

We see that Company A will have a greater decline in value per share when its stock goes ex-rights than will Company B. All other things the same, there is a greater probability, or risk, that Company A's stock will fall below the subscription price of $46 than there is that Company B's stock will fall below it.

Apart from the number of rights required to purchase one share, the risk that the market price of a stock will fall below the subscription price is a function of the volatility of the company's stock, the tone of the market, expectations of earnings, and other factors. To avoid all risk, a company can set the subscription price so far below the market price that there is virtually no possibility that the market price will fall below it. The greater the discount from the current market price, the greater the value of the right, and the greater the probability of a successful sale of stock. As long as stockholders do not allow their rights to expire, theoretically they neither gain nor lose by the offering. Therefore, it might seem feasible to set the subscription price at a substantial discount in order to assure a successful sale.

The greater the discount, however, the more shares that will have to be issued to raise a given amount of money, and the greater the dilution in earnings per share. This dilution may be of practical concern, for the investment community analyzes closely the growth trend in earnings per share. Significant underpricing of the new issue will dampen the growth trend in earnings per share. Although theoretically the stockholders should be equally well off regardless of the subscription price set, in practice the market value of their stock holdings may suffer if investors are fooled by the dilution in reported earnings per share and they lower the stock's price/earnings ratio. Obviously this would be an imperfection in the market, but imperfections on occasion can make a difference. There is no empirical evidence, however, to support the view that the amount of dilution in a rights offering matters.

---

[3]See Haim Levy and Marshall Sarnat, "Risk, Dividend Policy, and the Optimal Pricing of a Rights Offering," *Journal of Money, Credit, and Banking*, 3 (November 1971), 840-49.

If the firm wishes to maintain the same dividend per share, underpricing, which will result in more shares issued, will increase the total amount of dividends the company will need to pay and lower its coverage ratio. The disadvantages of underpricing must be balanced against the risk of the market price's falling below the subscription price. The primary consideration in setting the subscription price is to reduce the probability of this occurrence to a tolerable level. If, then, the subscription price appears to result in excessive dilution and this dilution seems to matter, the company should consider a public issue, wherein the amount of underpricing usually is less. For most rights offerings, the subscription-price discount from the current market price ranges between 15 and 30 percent.[4]

STANDBY ARRANGEMENT AND OVER-SUBSCRIPTIONS

A company can insure the complete success of a rights offering by having an investment dealer or group of investment dealers "stand by" to underwrite the unsold portion of the issue. For this standby commitment, the underwriter charges a fee that varies with the risk involved in the offering. Often the fee consists of two parts: a flat fee and an additional fee for each unsold share of stock that the underwriter has to buy. From the standpoint of the company issuing the shares, the greater the risk of an unsuccessful sale, the more desirable a standby arrangement, even if it is more costly.

Another way to increase the probability that the entire issue will be sold is through over-subscriptions. With this device, each stockholder is given not only the right to subscribe for his proportional share of the total offering, but also the right to over-subscribe for any unsold shares. Over-subscriptions are then awarded on a *pro rata* basis relative to the number of unsold shares. For example, suppose a rights offering calls for 500 000 to be sold and that stockholders subscribe for 460 000 shares. However, certain subscribing stockholders wish to purchase more shares and their over-subscriptions total 100 000 shares. As a result each stockholder over-subscribing is awarded 4/10's of a share for each share oversubscribed. This results in the entire issue being sold. While the use of the over-subscription increases the chances that the issue will be sold entirely, it does not have this assurance as does the standby agreement. It is possible that the combination of subscriptions and over-subscriptions will not successfully sell the amount of stock the company desires to sell.

PRIVILEGED ISSUE VERSUS PUBLIC ISSUE

By offering shares first to existing shareholders, the company taps investors who are familiar with the operations of the company. As a result, a successful sale is more probable. The principal sales tool is the discount from the current market price, whereas with a public issue, the major selling tool is the investment dealer organization. Because the issue is not underwritten, the flotation costs of a rights

---

[4]See Cecil R. Dipchand, "The Canadian Experience with Inherent Stock Splits of Rights Issues," *Financial Management*, 6 (Summer 1977), 34-41.

offering are lower than the costs of an offering to the public. Moreover, many shareholders feel that they should be given the first opportunity to buy new common shares. A public offering will also tend to result in a wider distribution of shares which may not be desirable to management particularly from a control viewpoint.

These advantages may be offset to some degree by the fact that a rights offering will have to be sold at a lower price than will a public issue. If a company goes to the equity market with reasonable frequency, this means that there will be somewhat more dilution with rights offerings than there will be with public issues. While this consideration is not relevant theoretically, many companies may wish to minimize dilution and thus choose the public offering. If there are information and legal and institutional imperfections which influence this choice, existing shareholder wealth may be enhanced by a firm's decision to go the public issue route. Examples of imperfections include financial reporting that masks the "true" trend in earnings per share, restraints on a company issuing stock at below its book value, and possible institutional incentives for a company to sell stock at as high a price per share as possible. These factors may have only a slight effect on shareholder wealth, but they are important in influencing management to favor a public issue.

Private Placements

Rather than sell securities to the public or to existing shareholders through a privileged subscription, a company can sell the entire issue to a single institutional investor or a small group of such investors. This type of sale is known as a *private* or *direct placement*, for the company negotiates the terms of the offering directly with the investors, eliminating the function of the underwriter. Some issues of common stock are placed privately, but the vast majority of private placements involve debt issues. Consequently, in the discussion that follows, we shall be concerned only with the direct placement of debt issues.

In the mid-1960s, private placements accounted for about 60 percent of gross debt issues of companies. However, with the rising volume of corporate bond financing in the late 1960s and in the 1970s, the composition of financing has shifted significantly toward public offerings. In recent years, public offerings have accounted for about three quarters of total corporate bond financing. The relative decline in private placements reflects in part the limited capacity of the private placement market to handle the present volume, the increasing financial strength of smaller companies which previously were not considered suitable candidates for public issues, and/or the increasing growth of the Canadian bond market.

FEATURES

One of the more frequently mentioned advantages of a private placement is the speed of the commitment. A public issue must be registered with the Securities Commission, documents prepared and printed, and extensive negotiations undertaken. All these require a certain lead time. In addition, a public issue always involves risks with respect to timing. With a private placement, the terms can be tailored to the needs of the borrower, and the financing can be consummated more quickly. Because the issue is negotiated, the exact timing in the market is not a critical problem. The fact that there is but a single investor or small group of investors is attractive if it becomes necessary to change any of the terms of the issue. It is easier to deal with a single investor or a small group of investors than with a large group of public security holders.

Another advantage of a privately placed debt issue is that the actual borrowing does not necessarily have to take place all at once. The company can enter into an arrangement whereby it can borrow up to a fixed amount over a period of time. For this non-revolving credit arrangement, the borrower will usually pay a commitment fee. This type of arrangement gives the company flexibility, allowing it to borrow only when it needs the funds. With a public issue, it is necessary to sell the entire issue at one time. Because the private placement does not have to be registered with the Securities Commission, the company avoids having to make the detailed information required by the Securities Acts available to the public.

Private placements allow medium-sized and sometimes small companies to sell a bond issue economically, whereas with a public offering the flotation costs would be prohibitive. Institutional investors are willing to invest in the bonds of these smaller companies, provided the company is credit-worthy. It is doubtful whether institutional investors would seek an issue of less than $100 000 (and many insist on a higher minimum), but we must remember that a $5 million bond issue is considered a small public offering.

COST OF ISSUE

There are two costs to consider in comparing a private placement of debt with a public offering: the initial costs and the interest cost. As the negotiations are usually direct, private placement involves no underwriting or selling expenses. Frequently, however, a company seeks the services of an investment dealer for advice in planning and negotiating the issue. Investment dealers have become increasingly involved as agents in private placements, thus offsetting to a certain degree their loss of underwriting and selling business. However, the overall initial cost of a private placement is significantly less than that of a public offering.

The second aspect of the cost of a private placement of debt is the interest cost. Here, fragmentary evidence indicates that the yield on private placements is significantly above that on public offerings. In addition to interest costs, institutional investors will sometimes request an equity "sweetener" such as warrants, to entice them to invest in the debt issue of a company. While the exact cost of this "sweetener" is difficult to measure, it certainly adds to the total cost of a private placement. Some contend that the private placement market is segmented and that the yield differential between a private placement and a public offering varies inversely with the flow of funds to life insurance companies and to other private placement lenders. Furthermore, it is suggested that with direct contact markets, such as the private placement market, nonprice factors are used to allocate credit. Owing to credit rationing and to the alleged aversion of lenders to sharp changes in rates, a lag is felt to exist between changes in public market rates and changes in private placement rates. Burton Zwick tested these notions and found little support for the segmented market effect but did find strong indication of a lag of approximately a quarter between changes in public rates and changes in private placement rates.[5]

In summary, it appears that the initial cost of a private placement of debt is less than that of a public offering; however, the interest cost and any additional compensation appear to be higher. For a long-term debt issue, the total cost is likely to be somewhat higher for a private placement than for a public offering. Moreover, the difference in cost will vary somewhat over time as interest rates, in general, change. The difference in cost between the private placement and the public markets must be balanced against the advantages of the private placement.

Net New Issues of Long Term Securities

The net new issues (gross issues less retirements) of Canadian financial and non-financial companies for the 1968-83 period are presented in Table 19-2. A major proportion of the funds is raised through the sale of bonds. Preferred stock issues accounted for less than 10 percent of long term financing prior to 1974. Thereafter, their use increased rather significantly and by 1978, accounted for 50 percent of the funds. The increasing use of preferred stocks during the 1974-78 period may be attributed, in part, to a special tax amendment[6] and the use of term preferreds. Companies took advantage of the tax amendment and designed preferred shares with a tax-deferred feature. On the other hand, term preferreds with relatively short terms to maturities were designed largely to attract funds from financial institutions. We discuss term preferreds in Chapter 22 but for our purposes here we should note that a tax amendment in 1979 was aimed at limiting the use of these securities. We do not expect preferred shares to increase in popularity; in fact, their use should decline relative to 1974-78 levels. Finally, common shares have traditionally accounted for about 10 percent to 15 percent of new funding.

The statistics in Table 19-2 show that the non-financial companies accounted for about 70 percent to 80 percent of the net issues in recent years. In general, we expect that non-financial corporate issues will continue to dominate in the capital markets.

Summary

When companies finance their long term needs externally, they may obtain funds from the capital markets or directly from a single institutional investor or a small

---

[5]"Yields on Privately Placed Corporate Bonds," *Journal of Finance*, 35 (March 1980), 23-29.

[6]An amendment in 1974 permitted firms to pay a 15 percent tax on undistributed income accumulated over the 1950-71 period. The balance designated "tax-paid undistributed surplus" and any other amounts under the category "1971 capital surplus" could be distributed tax-free. Instead of distributing these funds to existing equity holders (which was probably the intent of the Income Tax Act), some firms opted for the issuance of preferred shares using the tax-free dividends as the major selling feature.

TABLE 19-2 Net New Issues of Corporate Long-Term Securities (Financial & Non-Financial) for Selected Years ($ billions)

	Bonds		Preferred and Common Shares		
	Financial	Non-Financial	Financial	Non-Financial	Total
1968	$ 55	$ 670	$ 30	$ 328	$ 1 083
1970	212	1 287	47	305	1 851
1972	720	866	174	445	2 205
1974	584	1 216	312	468	4 785
1976	1 656	2 328	205	971	5 160
1978	1 445	3 277	1 060	5 900	11 682
1980	1 387	2 318	1 341	3 816	8 862
1982	996	3 795	471	3 885	9 147
1983	978	2 539	1 377	5 492	10 386

Source: *Bank of Canada Review*.

group of them. If the financing involves a public offering, the company will usually use the services of an investment dealer. The investment dealer's principal functions are risk bearing, or underwriting, and selling the securities. For these functions, the underwriting firm is compensated by the spread between the price it pays for the securities and the price at which it resells the securities to investors. The investment dealer provides an additional service in advising the company as to the pricing and timing of the issue and as to procedures and features involved in the issue.

A company may give its existing shareholders the first opportunity to purchase a new security issue on a privileged-subscription basis. This type of issue is known as a rights offering, because existing shareholders receive one right for each share of stock they hold. A right represents an option to buy the new security at the subscription price; and it takes a specified number of rights to purchase the security. Depending on the relationship between the current market price of the shares and the subscription price, a right will usually have a market value. Both security offerings to the general public and offerings on a privileged-subscription basis must comply with federal and provincial regulations. The enforcement agency for the government is the Securities Commission, or an equivalent body, whose authority encompasses both the sale of new securities and the trading of existing securities in the secondary market.

Rather than offer securities to existing shareholders or the public, a company may place them privately with an institutional investor. With a private placement, the company negotiates directly with the investor; there is no underwriting and no registration of the issue with the Securities Commission. The private placement has the virtue of flexibility and affords the medium-sized and even the small company the opportunity to sell its securities.

Questions

1. If competitive bidding, as opposed to negotiated offerings, were required for all security sales, would business firms benefit in higher prices for their securities?

2. How does the brokerage function of buying and selling securities differ from the underwriting function for an investment dealer?

3. The financial manager handling a stock issue must choose between going directly or going through the intermediary, the investment dealer, to the ultimate investor. Discuss the advantages and disadvantages of each alternative.

4. In issuing a new bond issue, the firm may decide to sell the bonds through a private placement or through a public issue. Evaluate these two alternatives.

5. There exists an inverse relationship between flotation costs and the size of the issue being sold. Explain the economic forces that cause this relationship.

6. For all sizes of issues, flotation costs for common stock are higher than those for preferred stock, and flotation costs for common stock are higher than those for bonds. Explain this cost structure.

7. What factors enable the investment dealer to continue to earn a profit on the underwriting and sale of securities? Are the dealer's profits in the best interests of society as a whole? Why?

8. Many major corporations, notably the commercial banks, have extensively used rights offerings in the past decade. Why do you feel these corporations have chosen to raise funds with a rights offering rather than a new equity issue, especially when a fair percentage of the rights (2 percent-5 percent) are never exercised?

9. Which of the following companies would you expect to use a private placement of long-term debt as opposed to a public offering?
   (a) An electric utility serving Ontario
   (b) A maker of electronic components with an annual volume of $13 million
   (c) A consortium of oil companies to finance an oil discovery in the Arctic
   (d) A running-shoe retreading company serving southern Alberta.

10. Should the preemptive right be required of all companies that issue common stock or securities convertible into common?

Problems with Solutions

1. The Niagara Company Ltd. has outstanding 1 000 000 shares selling on the market at $15 per share. The company is contemplating the issue of 100 000 shares at $12 per share using rights. Calculate (a) the number of rights required to purchase one share at $12; (b) the value of a right; and (c) the value of a share ex-rights.
   (a) 1 000 000 old shares ÷ 100 000 new shares = 10
   (b) Eq. (19-1)

$$\text{Price of a right} = \frac{\$15 - \$12}{10 + 1} = \$0.2727$$

   (c) Eq. (19-3)

$$\text{Price of share ex rights} = \frac{(\$15 \times 10) + \$12}{10 + 1} = \$14.7273$$

2. In problem 1, after the stock is sold ex-rights but while the rights are still traded, the price of stock goes to $20 per share. Calculate the price of a right. Given this increase would you rather have held the shares or the rights?

Eq. (19-4)

New value of a right $\dfrac{\$20 - \$12}{10} = \$0.80$

The investor would have made more holding rights

$$\text{If shares held, profit} = \frac{\$20 - \$14.7273}{\$14.7273} = 35.8\%$$

$$\text{If rights held, profit} = \frac{\$0.80 - \$0.2727}{\$0.2727} = 193.4\%$$

Problems

1. Labrador Copper Ltd. needs to raise $75 million in long-term debt funds and is negotiating with Quebec Investment Dealer Ltd. The investment dealer believes it can bring together a syndicate to underwrite and sell the issue. The bonds will have a coupon rate so that they can be priced to the public at their face value of $1 000. The price to the syndicate is expected to be $940 per bond. Quebec Investment Dealer Ltd. will be in the manager and will get 15 percent of the total spread as a management fee. The sale of the issue is expected to be distributed as follows: exempt purchasers 60 percent of the issue, retail customers of the banking group 15 percent, and non-syndicate dealers 25 percent. The bonds will be sold to non-syndicate dealers at $960.
   (a) What is the total flotation cost?
   (b) What will be the net proceeds of the issue to Labrador Copper?
   (c) How much compensation is available to each group of participants (principal underwriter, banking group, and selling group) involved in the sale of the issue?

2. The Ville Platte Artists School will issue 200 000 shares of common stock at $40 per share through a subscription issue. The 800 000 shares of stock currently outstanding have a market price of $50 per share.
   (a) Compute the number of rights required to buy a share of stock at $40.
   (b) Compute the value of a right.
   (c) Compute the value of the stock ex-rights.

3. The stock of the Mic Mac Corporation Ltd. is selling for $50 per share. The company issues rights to subscribe for one new share at $40 for each 5 shares held.
   (a) What is the theoretical value of a right if the stock is selling rights-on?
   (b) What is the theoretical value of one share of stock when it goes ex-rights?
   (c) What is the theoretical value of a right when the stock sells ex-rights at $50?

4. The stock of the Dunbar Company Ltd. is selling for $150 per share. If the company were to issue rights to subscribe for one additional share of stock at $125 a share for each 9 held, compute the following:
   (a) The theoretical value of a right when the stock is selling rights-on
   (b) The theoretical value of one share of stock when it goes ex-rights
   (c) The theoretical value of a right when the stock sells ex-rights and the actual market price goes to $143 per share.

5. Two different companies are considering rights offerings. The current market price per share is $48 in both cases. In order to allow for fluctuations in market price, Company X wants to set a subscription price of $42 while Company Y feels a subscription price of $41½ is in order. The number of rights necessary to purchase an additional share is 14 in the case of Company X and 4 in the case of Company Y.

    (a) Which company has the larger stock issue relatively? Is it the larger stock issue in absolute terms?

    (b) In which case is there less risk that the market price will fall below the subscription price?

6. The Vancouver Island Diving Company Ltd. wishes to sell a preferred-stock issue. Flotation costs are expected to be 8.5 percent of the gross proceeds. Moreover, the company feels that the stock will need to provide a yield of 9 percent to investors in order to find acceptance in the marketplace. Assuming the issue is perpetual, what is the effective cost of the preferred-stock issue to the company?

7. Obtain a prospectus on a recent security issue of a corporation. Analyze it according to

    (a) The type of security being offered. Are there any special features? If a bond, is it secured? How is it secured?

    (b) The size of the issue and the type of company involved. How sound is the company financially? How stable are its earnings? What is the growth potential? Is the size of the issue appropriate?

    (c) The flotation cost. What is the underwriter spread? Is it too high a percentage of gross proceeds? What portion of the spread is in support of underwriting? In support of selling? What is the dealer concession? Under what conditions may it be earned?

    (d) The underwriting syndicate. How many underwriters are there? What is the maximum participation? The minimum participation? Who is the manager? Are there provisions made for support of the price during the distribution period?

    (e) The pricing. Is the issue priced properly from the standpoint of the company? Of the investor? Of the underwriter? How successful was the issue?

Selected References

BACON, PETER W., "The Subscription Price in Rights Offerings," *Financial Management*, 1 (Summer 1972), 59-64.

BLOCH, ERNEST, "Pricing a Corporate Bond Issue: A Look behind the Scenes," *Essays in Money and Credit*, 72-76. New York: Federal Reserve Bank of New York, 1964.

BLOCK, STANLEY, and MARJORIE STANLEY, "The Financial Characteristics and Price Movement Patterns of Companies Approaching the Unseasoned Securities Market in the Late 1970s," *Financial Management*, 9 (Winter 1980), 30-36.

DIPCHAND, CECIL R., "The Canadian Experience with Inherent Stock Splits of Rights Issues," *Financial Management*, 6 (Summer 1977), 34-41.

_____. "Chartered Banks and the Rights Offering," *Cost and Management* (Jan.-Feb. 1977), 12-17.

EDERINGTON, LOUIS H., "Negotiated Versus Competitive Underwritings of Corporate Bonds," *Journal of Finance*, 30 (September 1975), 1129-33.

_____, "Uncertainty, Competition, and Costs in Corporate Bond Underwriting," *Journal of Financial Economics*, 2 (March 1975), 71-94.

EVANS, G. H., JR., "The Theoretical Value of a Stock Right," *Journal of Finance*, 10 (March 1955), 55-61.

HAYES, SAMUEL L., III, "The Transformation of Investment Banking," *Harvard Business Review*, 57 (January-February 1979), 153-70.

_____, "Investment Banking: Power Structure in Flux," *Harvard Business Review*, 49 (March-April 1971), 136-52.

HUNTSMAN, BLAIN, and JAMES P. HOBAN, JR., "Investment in New Enterprise: Some Empirical Observations on Risk, Return, and Market Structure," *Financial Management*, 9 (Summer 1980), 44-51.

JOHNSON, KEITH B., T. GREGORY MORTON, and M. CHAPMAN FINDLAY, III. "An Empirical Analysis of the Flotation Cost of Corporate Securities, 1971-1972," *Journal of Finance*, 30 (September 1975), 1129-33.

KEANE, SIMON M., "The Significance of the Issue Price in Rights Issues," *Journal of Business Finance*, 4, No. 3 (1972), 40-45.

LEVY, HAIM, and MARSHALL SARNAT, Risk, Dividend Policy, and the Optimal Pricing of a Rights Offering," *Journal of Money, Credit and Banking*, 3 (November 1971), 840-49.

LOGUE, DENNIS E., and ROBERT A. JARROW, "Negotiation vs. Competitive Bidding in the Sale of Securities by Public Utilities," *Financial Management*, 7 (Autumn 1978), 31-39.

LOGUE, DENNIS E., and JOHN R. LINDVALL, "The Behavior of Investment Bankers: An Econometric Investigation," *Journal of Finance*, 29 (March 1974), 203-16.

LOGUE, DENNIS E., and RICHARD J. ROGALSKI, "Does It Pay to Shop for Your Bond Underwriter? *Harvard Business Review*, 57 (July-August 1979), 111-17.

McQUILLAN, P.C., *Going Public in Canada: The Fact and the Fads*. Toronto: The Canadian Institute of Chartered Accountants, 1971.

PARKER, GEORGE G.C., and DANIEL COOPERMAN, "Competitive Bidding in the Underwriting of Public Utilities Securities," *Journal of Financial and Quantitative Analysis*, 13 (December 1978), 885-902.

PETERS, J.R. *Economics of the Canadian Corporate Bond Market*. Montreal: McGill—Queen's University Press, 1971.

SHAPIRO, ELI, and CHARLES R. WOLF, *The Role of Private Placements in Corporate Finance*, Boston: Division of Research, Graduate School of Business Administration, Harvard University, 1972.

SHAW, DAVID C., "The Cost of Going Public in Canada," *Financial Executive* (July 1969), 20-28.

SHAW, DAVID C. and T. ROSSARCHIBALD. *A Survey of Research Operations of Brokerage Firms in Canada*. Toronto: T.S.E., and London: The School of Business Administration, U.W.O., 1975.

SMITH, CLIFFORD W., JR., "Alternative Methods for Raising Capital," *Journal of Financial Economics*, 5 (November 1977), 273-307.

STROETMAN, KARLA, "The Operational Efficiency of the Canadian New Issues Market for Corporate Bonds: An Analysis of Flotation Costs," *Proceedings*, Canadian Association of Administrative Sciences, 1974.

TALLMAN, GARY D., DAVID F. RUSH and RONALD W. MELICHER, "Competitive versus Negotiated Underwriting Costs for Regulated Industries," *Financial Management*, 3 (Summer 1974), 49-55.

VAN HORNE, JAMES C., *Financial Market Rates and Flows*. Englewood Cliffs, N.J.: Prentice-Hall, 1978.

———, "Implied Fixed Costs in Long-Term Debt Issues," *Journal of Financial and Quantitative Analysis*, 8 (December 1973).

WHITE, R.W., and P.A. LUSZTIG, "The Price Effects of Rights Offerings," *Journal of Financial and Quantitative Analysis*, 15 (March 1980), 25-40.

ZWICK, BURTON, Yields on Privately Placed Corporate Bonds," *Journal of Finance*, 35 (March 1980), 23-29.

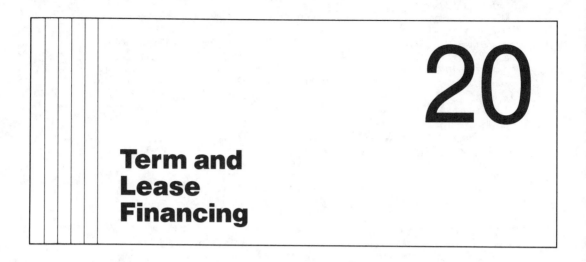

Term and Lease Financing

In Chapter 11 we discussed the use of trade credit and accruals as spontaneous sources of funds to business firms. Then in Chapter 12 we reviewed the types and sources of short term financing. These sources of funds are popularly called current liabilities, which are self-liquidating during a firm's fiscal year. Frequently, they are employed to finance seasonal and temporary funds requirements. Intermediate term financing, on the other hand, is employed to finance more permanent funds requirements, such as fixed assets and underlying buildups in receivables and inventories. The means for payment of the loan usually come from the generation of cash flows over a period of years. As a result, most of these loans are paid in regular, periodic instalments. We regard intermediate term financing as involving final maturities of one to ten years. These boundaries are arbitrary, although the one-year boundary is rather commonly accepted. In this chapter, we examine various types of intermediate term debt. We also study leasing as a means of financing certain fixed assets. Lease financing is similar to financing through debt and has become popular in recent years.

Term Loans

Commercial banks have become increasingly involved in providing intermediate-term financing to industry. There are two features of a bank term loan that distinguish it from other types of business loans. First, it has a final maturity of more than one year, and second, it most often represents credit extended under a formal loan agreement. Both ordinary term loans and revolving credits are classified under the broad heading of bank term loans. For the most part, these loans are repayable in periodic instalments; for example, quarterly, semiannually, or yearly. The payment schedule of the loan is usually geared to the borrower's cash flow ability to service the debt. Typically, this schedule calls for equal periodic instalments, but it may be irregular with respect to amounts or may simply call for repayment in a lump sum at final maturity. Sometimes the loan is amortized in equal periodic instalments except for the final payment, known as a "balloon" payment, which is larger than any of the others.

Most bank term loans are written with original maturities in the one- to six-year range. Some banks are willing to make longer-term loans, but only rarely will a bank make a term loan with a final maturity of more than 10 years. In recent years, however, banks have been making longer-term loans. Whereas a four- to six-year loan once was considered dangerous to a bank's liquidity, term loans in this maturity range are now common.

The final maturity of a term loan does not always convey the length of time the loan is likely to remain outstanding. In some cases, both the bank and the company expect the loan to be renewed successively with maturity. These loans are known as "evergreen" loans and are typically characterized by credits to companies in growth phases. Despite the expectation of "evergreen" refunding upon maturity, the bank is not legally obligated to extend the loan. As a result most requests for extensions and additional credit are analyzed afresh based on changed conditions from the time of the original loan. An "evergreen" loan may turn out to be a "deciduous" one if the financial condition and performance of the borrower deteriorate.

COSTS AND BENEFITS

Generally, the interest rate on a term loan is higher than the rate on a short-term loan to the same borrower. For example, if a firm could borrow at the prime rate on a short-term basis, it might pay 0.25 percent to 0.50 percent more on a term loan. The interest rate on a term loan can be set in one of two ways: (1) a fixed rate which is effective over the life of the loan may be established at the outset, or (2) a variable rate may be set that is adjusted in keeping with changes in the prime rate.

In addition to interest costs, the borrower is required to pay the legal expenses that the bank incurs in drawing up the loan agreement. Also, a commitment fee may be charged for the time during the commitment period when the loan is not taken down. For an ordinary term loan, these additional costs are usually rather small in relation to the total interest cost of the loan. A typical fee on the unused portion of a commitment is 0.50 percent with a range of 0.25 percent to 0.75 percent. This means that if the commitment fee were 0.50 percent on a commitment of $1 million and the company took down all of the loan three months after the commitment, the firm would owe the bank $1 million $\times$ 0.005 $\times$ 3/12 = $1 250. In addition to the commitment fee, an indirect cost to the borrower may be the need to maintain compensating balances, which we discussed in Chapter 9.

The principal advantage of an ordinary bank term loan is flexibility. The borrower deals directly with the lender, and the loan can be tailored to the borrower's needs through direct negotiation. The bank usually has had previous experience with the borrower, so it is familiar with the company's situation. Should the firm's requirements change, the terms and conditions of the loan may be revised. It is considerably more convenient to negotiate with a single lender or a reasonably small group of lenders than with a large number of public security holders such as bondholders. In addition, the borrower can deal confidentially with a bank, or, for that matter, with any private lending institution, without having to reveal certain financial information to the public.

In many instances, bank term loans are made to small businesses which do not have access to the capital markets and thus cannot readily float a public issue. Even for those firms which do have access to the capital markets, the ability to sell a public issue varies over time in keeping with the mood of the capital markets. In the 1960s, a number of these companies found a receptive market, particularly when an option involving common stock was involved. The economy was in an expansive mood and the capital markets were generally "bullish". In the 1970s some companies of moderate size but with good growth potential were unable to go to the public market with debt issues. A sluggish economy and high inflation had adverse effects on the capital markets and investors were less receptive than in the 1960s. Finally, large companies which have access to the public market may find it quicker and more convenient to seek a bank term loan than to float a public issue. A term loan can be arranged in several weeks, whereas a public issue takes a good deal longer.

REVOLVING CREDIT

As discussed in Chapter 12 a revolving credit is a formal commitment by a bank to lend a maximum amount of money to a company over a specified period of time. The actual notes evidencing debt are short-term, usually 90 days; but the company may renew them or borrow additionally, up to the specified maximum, throughout the duration of the commitment. Many revolving-credit commitments are for three years, although it is possible for a firm to obtain a shorter commitment. As with an ordinary term loan, the interest rate is usually 0.25 percent to 0.50 percent higher than the rate at which the firm could borrow on a short-term basis under a line of credit. When a bank makes a revolving-credit commitment, it is legally bound under the loan agreement to have funds available whenever the company wants to borrow.

This borrowing agreement is particularly useful at times when the firm is uncertain about its funds requirements. A revolving-credit agreement has the features of both a short-term borrowing arrangement and a term loan, for the firm can borrow a fixed amount for the entire duration of the commitment. Thus, the borrower has flexible access to funds over a period of uncertainty and can make more definite credit arrangements when the uncertainty is resolved. Revolving-credit agreements can be set up so that at the maturity of the commitment, borrowings then owing can be converted into a term loan at the option of the borrower. To illustrate, suppose a company introduces a new product and is faced with a period of uncertainty over the next several years. To provide maximum financial flexibility, the company might arrange a three-year revolving credit that is convertible into a five-year term loan at the expiry of the revolving-credit commitment. At the end of three years, the company should know its fund requirements better. If these requirements are permanent, or nearly so, the firm might wish to exercise its option and take the term loan.

INSURANCE COMPANY TERM LOANS

In addition to banks, life insurance companies lend money on a term basis. However, there are important differences in the maturity of the loan extended and in the interest rate charged. In general, life insurance companies are interested in term loans with final maturities of over ten years. Because these companies do not have the benefit of compensating balances or other business from the borrower, and because their loans usually have a longer maturity than bank term loans, typically, the rate of interest is higher. To the insurance company, the term loan represents an investment and must yield a return commensurate with the costs involved in making the loan, the risk, the maturity, and prevailing yields on alternative investments. Because an insurance company is interested in keeping its funds employed without interruption, it normally has a prepayment penalty, whereas the bank usually does not. One of the simpler formulas calls for a penalty of three to six months' interest if the loan is retired before maturity.

Insurance company term loans are generally not competitive with bank term loans. Indeed, they are complementary, for they serve different maturity range needs. Sometimes a bank and an insurance company will participate in the same loan. The bank may take the early maturities, perhaps the first five years, with the insurance company taking the remaining maturities. Including an insurance company in the credit permits a longer maturity range than the bank can provide, and the bank can offer a lower interest rate on the early maturities. Usually, there will be only one loan agreement, drawn up jointly by the bank and the insurance company. A term loan of this sort may serve both the intermediate and long term funds requirements of the firm.

Loan Agreements

When a lender makes a term loan or revolving-credit commitment, it provides the borrower with available funds for an extended period of time. Much can happen to the financial condition of the borrower during that period. In order to safeguard itself, the lender requires the borrower firm to maintain its financial condition and, in particular, its current position at a level at least as favorable as when the commitment was made. The provisions for protection contained in a loan agreement are known as protective covenants.

The loan agreement itself simply gives the lender legal authority to step in should the borrower default under any of the provisions. otherwise, the lender would be locked up into a commitment and would have to wait until maturity before being able to effect corrective measures. Under a well-written loan agreement, if the borrower should suffer losses or if there are other adverse developments, he or she will default; the lender will then be able to act. The action usually takes the form of working with the company to straighten out its problems. Seldom will a lender demand immediate payment, although it has the legal right to do so in cases of default. More typically, the condition under which the borrower defaults is waived or the loan agreement is amended. It is important to note that the lender has the authority to act, even though the lender may choose, instead, to negotiate with the borrower in order to settle the problem.

FORMULATION OF PROVISIONS

The formulation of the different restrictive provisions should be tailored to the specific loan situation. These provisions are the tools by which the lenders fashion the overall protection of their loans. No one provision is able by itself to provide the necessary safeguards, but collectively, provisions ensure the borrower's overall liquidity and ability to pay a loan. The important protective covenants of a loan agreement may be classified as follows: (1) general provisions used in most agreements, which are variable to fit the situation; (2) routine provisions used in most agreements, which are usually not variable; and (3) specific provisions that are used according to the situation. Although we focus here on a loan agreement, the protective covenants used and the philosophy underlying their use are the same as for the indenture for a bond issue which we discuss in Chapter 21.

General provisions   The *working capital requirement* is the most commonly used and most comprehensive provision in a loan agreement. Its purpose is to preserve the company's current position and ability to pay the loan. Frequently, a straight dollar amount, such as $2 million, is set as the minimum working capital the company must maintain during the duration of the commitment. When the lender feels that it is desirable for a specific company to build working capital, it may increase the minimum working-capital requirement throughout the duration of the loan. The establishment of a working capital minimum is normally based on the amounts of present working capital and projected working capital, allowing for seasonal fluctuations. The requirements should not restrict the company unduly in the ordinary generation of profit. However, should the borrower incur sharp losses or spend too much for fixed assets, purchase of stock, dividends, redemption of long-term debt, and so forth, it would probably breach the working capital requirement.

The *cash dividend* and *repurchase-of-stock restriction* is another important restriction in this category. Its purpose is to limit cash going outside the business, thus preserving the liquidity of the company. Most often, cash dividends and repurchase of stock are limited to a percentage of net profits on a cumulative basis after a certain base date, frequently the last fiscal year end prior to the date of the term-loan agreement. A less flexible method is to restrict dividends and repurchase of stock to an absolute dollar amount each year. In most cases, the prospective borrower must be willing to accept cash dividend and repurchase-of-stock restrictions. If tied to earnings, these restrictions will still allow adequate dividends as long as the company is able to generate satisfactory profits.

The *capital expenditures limitation* is third in the category of general provisions. Capital expenditures may be limited to a fixed dollar amount each year. However, it is probably more usual to limit annual capital expenditures either to depreciation or to a percentage thereof. The capital expenditures limitation is another tool used by the lender to ensure the maintenance of the borrower's current position. By limiting capital expenditures directly, the lender can be more certain that it will not have to look to liquidation of fixed assets for payment of its loan. Again, however, the provision should not be so restrictive as to prevent the adequate maintenance and improvement of facilities.

A *limitation on other indebtedness* is the last general provision. This limitation may take a number of forms, depending on the circumstances. Frequently, a loan agreement will prohibit a company from incurring any other long-term debt. This provision protects the lender, inasmuch as it prevents future lenders from obtaining a prior claim on the borrower's assets. Usually a company is permitted to borrow within reasonable limits for seasonal and other short-term purposes arising in the ordinary course of business.

Routine provisions The second category of restrictions includes routine provisions, usually variable, found in most loan agreements. Ordinarily, the loan agreement requires the borrower to furnish the lender with financial statements and to maintain adequate insurance. Additionally, the borrower is normally required not to sell a significant portion of its assets and is required to pay, when due, all taxes and other liabilities, except those contested in good faith. A provision forbidding the pledging and mortgaging of any of the borrower's assets is almost always included in a loan agreement; this important provision is known as a negative pledge clause.

Ordinarily, the company is required not to discount or sell its receivables. Moreover, the borrower is generally prohibited from entering into any leasing arrangement of property, except up to a certain dollar amount of annual rental. The purpose of this provision is to prevent the borrower from taking on a substantial lease liability, which might endanger its ability to pay the loan. A lease restriction also prevents the firm from leasing property instead of purchasing it and thereby getting around the limitations on capital expenditures and debt. Usually there is a restriction on other contingent liabilities. The provisions in this category appear as a matter of routine in most loan agreements. Although somewhat mechanical, they are important because they close many loopholes and provide a tight comprehensive loan agreement.

Special provisions Special provisions are used in specific loan agreements by lenders in order to achieve desired total protection of their loans. For instance, a loan agreement may contain a definite understanding regarding the use of the loan proceeds, so that there will be no diversion of funds to purposes other than those contemplated when the loan was negotiated. A provision for limiting loans and advances often is found in a term-loan agreement. Closely allied to this restriction is a limitation on investments, which is used to safeguard liquidity by preventing certain nonliquid investments.

If one or more executives are essential to a firm's effective operations, a lender may insist that the company carry life insurance on their lives. Proceeds of the insurance may be payable to the company or directly to the lender, to be applied to the loan. An agreement may also contain a management clause, under which certain key individuals must remain actively employed in the company during the time the loan is owing. Aggregate executive salaries and bonuses are sometimes limited in the loan agreement, to prevent excessive compensation of executives, which might reduce profits. This provision closes another loophole; it prevents large shareholders who are officers of the company from increasing their own salaries in lieu of paying higher dividends, which are limited under the agreement.

NEGOTIATION OF RESTRICTIONS

The provisions described above represent the most frequently used protective covenants in a loan agreement. From the standpoint of the lender, the aggregate impact of these provisions should be to safeguard the financial position of the borrower and his or her ability to pay the loan. Under a well-written agreement, the borrower cannot get into serious financial difficulty without defaulting under the agreement, thereby giving the lender legal authority to take action. Although the lender is instrumental in establishing the restrictions, the restrictiveness of the protective covenants is subject to negotiation between the borrower and the lender. The final result will depend on the relative bargaining power of each of the parties involved.[1]

Equipment Financing

Equipment is another asset of the firm that may be pledged to secure a loan. If the firm either has equipment that is marketable or is purchasing such equipment, it can usually obtain some sort of secured financing. Because such loans are usually for more than a year, we consider them in this chapter rather than under the short-term secured loans. As with other secured loans, the lender is concerned with the marketability of the collateral. Depending on the quality of the equipment, the lender will make a percentage advance against the equipment's market value. Frequently, the repayment schedule for the loan is set in keeping with the economic life of the equipment. In setting the repayment schedule, the lender wants to be sure that the market value of the equipment always exceeds the balance of the loan.

The excess of the expected market value of the equipment over the amount of the loan is the margin of safety, which will vary according to the specific situation. In the case of the rolling stock of a trucking company, the collateral is movable and reasonably marketable and the advance may be as high as 80 percent. Less marketable equipment, such as that with a limited use, will not command as high an advance. A certain type of lathe, for example, may have a thin market; and a lender might not be willing to advance more than 50 percent of its reported market value. Some equipment is of such a special-purpose nature that it has no value for collateral purposes. Frequently, the lender either will have its own appraiser or will hire an appraiser to estimate the approximate value of a piece of equipment if it should have to be sold. As with other collateral, the lender is interested not only in the estimated market price of the equipment but also in the cost of selling it.

SOURCES OF EQUIPMENT FINANCING

Sources of equipment financing include commercial banks, finance companies, and the sellers of equipment. Because the interest charged by a finance

---

[1]For a linear programming approach in evaluating the opportunity costs of the protective-covenant restrictions, see James Van Horne, "A Linear-Programming Approach to Evaluating Restrictions Under a Bond Indenture or Loan Agreement," *Journal of Financial and Quantitative Analysis*, 1 (June 1966), 68-83.

company on an equipment loan is usually higher than that charged by a commercial bank, a firm will turn to a finance company only if it is unable to obtain the loan from the bank. The seller of the equipment may finance the purchase either by holding the secured note itself or by selling the note to its captive finance subsidiary. The interest charge will depend on the extent to which the seller uses financing as a sales tool. If he or she uses it extensively, only a moderate interest rate may be charged, and may make up for part of the cost of carrying the notes by charging higher prices for the equipment. The borrower must consider this possibility in judging the true cost of financing. Equipment loans may be secured either by a chattel mortgage or by a conditional sales contract arrangement.

CHATTEL MORTGAGE

A chattel mortgage is a lien on property other than real property. The borrower signs a security agreement which gives the lender a lien on the equipment specified in the agreement. In order to perfect the lien, the lender files a copy of the security agreement with a registry office of the province in which the equipment is located. Given a valid lien, the lender can sell the equipment if the borrower defaults in the payment of principal or interest on the loan.

CONDITIONAL SALES CONTRACT

With a conditional sales contract arrangement, the seller of the equipment retains title to it until the purchaser has satisfied all the terms of the contract. The buyer signs a conditional sales contract security agreement under which he or she agrees to make periodic instalment payments to the seller over a specified period of time. These payments are usually monthly or quarterly. Until the terms of the contract are satisfied completely, the seller retains title to the equipment. Thus, the seller receives a down payment and a promissory note for the balance of the purchase price on the sale of the equipment. The note is secured by the contract, which gives the seller the authority to repossess the equipment if the buyer does not meet all the terms of the contract.

The seller may either hold the contract or sell it, simply by endorsing it, to a commercial bank or finance company. The bank or finance company then becomes the lender and assumes the security interest in the equipment. If the buyer should default under the terms of the contract, the bank or finance company could repossess the equipment and sell it in satisfaction of its loan. Often, the vendor will sell the contract to the bank or finance company with recourse. Under this arrangement, the lender has the additional protection of recourse to the seller in case the buyer defaults.

Lease Financing

A firm may use debt and equity financing to acquire assets; that is, the firm has title to such assets. Alternatively, the firm may lease assets for a stated period of time under specified rental terms.[2] In both instances, the firm acquires the economic use of assets for its normal business operations. However, under leasing, the title to an asset remains with the lessor and the asset is returned at the end of the lease period unless provided for otherwise. The acquisition of the economic use of assets through leasing is an important source of financing.

In recent years, reporting of the lease obligation for accounting purposes has undergone substantial change. For some companies, the accounting treatment of the lease is an important issue; and we consider the present rules later on in the chapter. However, our principal concern is with the cash flow evaluation of the lease contract. In this regard, our focus in on financial leases.

A *financial lease* is a noncancelable contractual commitment on the part of a lessee to make a series of payments to a lessor for the use of an asset. The lessee acquires most of economic values associated with outright ownership of the asset, even though the lessor retains title to it. With a financial lease, the lease period generally corresponds to the economic life of the asset. In addition, the total payments the lessee agrees to make must exceed the purchase price of the asset. The distinguishing feature between a financial and an operating lease is cancelability— an operating lease can be cancelled by giving proper notice whereas a financial lease cannot. An example of an operating lease is one for telephone service.

In lease financing, the nature of the obligations of the lessor and the lessee is specified in the lease contract. This contract sets out

1. The basic lease period during which the lease is noncancelable;
2. The timing and amounts of periodic rental payments during the basic lease period;
3. Any option to renew the lease or to purchase the asset at the end of the base period; and
4. Provision for the payment of the costs of maintenance and repairs, taxes, insurance, and other expenses. With a "net lease", the lessee pays all of these costs. Under a "maintenance lease", the lessor maintains the asset and pays the insurance.

FORMS OF LEASE FINANCING

There are three types of lease financing which we will discuss: a sale and leaseback arrangement; the direct acquisition of an asset under a lease; and leveraged leasing. Virtually all lease financing arrangements fall into one of these three categories. Our purpose in this section is to briefly describe the categories preparatory to presenting a framework for the analysis of lease financing and to discussing the basic valuation implications.

Sale and Leaseback   Under a sale and leaseback arrangement, a firm sells an asset it owns to another party, and this party leases it back to the firm. Usually, the asset is sold at approximately its market value. The firm receives the sale price in cash and the economic use of the asset during the base lease period. In return, it

---

[2]See Richard F. Vancil, "Lease or Borrow: New Method of Analysis," *Harvard Business Review*, 39 (Sept.-Oct. 1961), 22-36.

contracts to make periodic lease payments and, of course, gives up title to the asset. As a result, the lessor realizes any residual value the asset might have at the end of the lease period where before this would be realized by the firm. Lessors engaged in sale and leaseback arrangements include insurance companies, trust companies, finance companies, pension funds, and independent leasing companies.

Direct Leasing   Under direct leasing, a company acquires the use of an asset it did not own previously. For example, a firm may simply lease an asset from the manufacturer or another lessor; indeed, a number of capital goods are available today on a lease-financed basis. Common examples are computers and photo-copiers. There are a wide variety of direct leasing arrangements available to meet various needs of the firm. The major types of lessors are manufacturers, finance companies, independent leasing companies, special-purpose leasing companies, and partnerships.

Leveraged leasing   A special form of leasing has developed in conjunction with the financing of assets requiring large capital outlays. It is known as *leveraged leasing*. In contrast to the two parties involved in the forms of leasing previously described, there are three parties involved in leveraged leasing: (1) the lessee; (2) the lessor or equity participant; and (3) the lender. We examine each in turn.

From the standpoint of the lessee, there is no difference between a leveraged lease and any other type of lease. The lessee contracts to make periodic payments over the basic lease period and, in return, is entitled to the use of the asset over that period of time. The role of the lessor, however, is changed. The lessor acquires the asset in keeping with the terms of the lease arrangements. This acquisition is financed in part by an equity investment by the lessor of, say 20 percent (hence the name "equity participant"). The remaining 80 percent is provided by a long-term lender or lenders. Usually, the loan is secured by a mortgage on the asset, as well as by the assignment of the lease and lease payments. The lessor, however, is the legal borrower.

As owner of the asset, the lessor is entitled to deduct allowable depreciation charges associated with the asset as well as utilize the investment tax credit. The cash flow pattern for the lessor typically involves: (1) a cash outflow at the time the asset is acquired, which represents its equity participation; (2) a period of cash inflows represented by lease payments and tax benefits, less payments of the debt (principal and interest); and (3) a period of net cash outflows where, because of declining tax benefits, the sum of lease payments and tax benefits falls below the debt payments due. If there is any residual value at the end of the lease period, this of course represents a cash inflow to the lessor. While the leveraged lease may seem like the most difficult of the three forms of leasing we have described, it reduces to certain basic concepts. From the standpoint of the lessee, which is our concern, the leveraged lease can be analyzed in the same manner as any lease. Therefore, we will not treat it separately in the rest of this chapter.

SOURCES OF LEASE FINANCING

Chartered banks are indirectly involved in leasing services. For example, First Canadian Leasing, a division of Canadian Dominion Leasing Corporation

Ltd., accommodates leases for customers of the Bank of Montreal. Also RoyNat Ltd., a finance company, gets referrals from the Royal Bank of Canada and the National Bank of Canada. Revisions to the Bank Act permit banks to be directly involved in certain leasing transactions. Independent leasing companies, such as Canadian Dominion Leasing Corp., finance the purchase of a wide variety of equipment. In doing so, they frequently borrow from banks, securing the loan with the assignment of the lease payments. Special-purpose leasing companies confine their operations to certain types of assets; computer leasing companies, for example, mainly lease computer hardware and peripheral equipment. Wealthy individuals have formed partnerships for the purpose of purchasing equipment and leasing it to companies. Until 1976, attractive tax provisions encouraged the proliferation of lessors; thereafter tax changes operated against lessors. We review the tax position of lessors later in this chapter.

ACCOUNTING TREATMENT

Accounting for leases has changed dramatically in recent years. A number of years ago lease financing was attractive to some because the obligation did not appear on the company's financial statements. As a result, leasing was regarded as a "hidden" or "off balance sheet" method of financing. However, accounting requirements have changed and now many leases must be shown on the balance sheet as a capitalized asset with the associated liability being shown as well. For these leases, the reporting of earnings is affected. Other leases must be fully disclosed in footnotes to the financial statement. The important thing to realize is that it is no longer possible for a firm to "fool" investors and creditors by using leasing as opposed to debt financing. The full impact of the lease obligation is apparent to any supplier of capital who makes the effort to read the financial statements. (The accounting treatment of leases is taken up in the Appendix to this chapter.)

TAX TREATMENT AND CONSIDERATIONS

A lease payment is deductible as an expense for federal income tax purposes. If the asset is purchased, it must be capitalized and the annual depreciation charge deducted as an expense. If the purchase of an asset is financed by debt, the annual interest payments are also tax-deductible. If the asset qualifies for the investment tax credit, this benefit is available to the firm (see Chapter 2).

For the lease payments to be tax-deductible, the lessee must satisfy the tax authorities that the lease contract truly represents a lease and not an instalment sale. Revenue Canada may check whether the length of the lease approximates the economic life of the asset (say 75 percent of the life of the asset or more). It may also check if the lessor earns a reasonable return and if any renewal or repurchase option is based on market values prevailing at the date of expiration of the lease. In summary, the tax authorities have to be convinced that the contract does not "disguise" a purchase of the asset. For a lessor, such a contract would allow him or her to effectively "depreciate" the asset more quickly than allowed under a straight purchase.

Lease financing provides a special tax advantage. With leasing, the cost of any land is amortized in the lease payments. By deducting the lease payments as an expense for federal income tax purposes, in essence, the lessee is able to write-off the original cost of the land if it is a part of the assets acquired under a lease arrangement. On the other hand, if the land is purchased, the firm cannot depreciate it for tax purposes. When the value of land represents a significant portion of the asset acquired, lease financing can offer a tax advantage to the firm. Offsetting this tax advantage, however, is the likely residual value of land at the end of the basic lease period which otherwise would be available to the firm if it had purchased the land instead.

Evaluating Lease Financing in Relation to Debt Financing

To determine which is the best financing for the firm, it must compare the benefits of lease financing versus debt financing. Whether leasing or borrowing is better will depend on the patterns of cash outflows for each financing method and on the opportunity cost of funds. To illustrate a method of analysis, we compare lease financing with debt financing, using a hypothetical example. We assume that the firm has decided to invest in a project on the basis of considerations discussed in Part IV. In other words, the investment-worthiness of the project is evaluated separately from the specific method of financing to be employed.[3] We assume also that the firm has determined an appropriate capital structure and has decided to finance the project with a fixed-income type of instrument—either debt or lease financing.

LEASING IS AN INVESTMENT DECISION FOR A LESSOR

The lessor of a leased asset is the owner of that asset. Lease payments from the lessee are the gross revenue to the lessor. Operating expenses paid by the lessor are deducted from lease payments to derive operating income. The usual operating expenses include capital cost allowance on the leased asset, insurance, maintenance and administrative costs. The lessor will conduct an investment analysis similar to that done in Chapter 13 to determine the feasibility of leasing the asset. As a result of this analysis, the lessor determines the lease payments which are required to give an acceptable rate of return on the project. Where the lessor has to cover some or all of the cash operating expenses the lease payments will be higher than they would be if some or all of the cash operating expenses were paid by the lessee.

---

[3]For analysis in which the leasing contract is viewed as an investment rather than a financing decision, see Robert W. Johnson and Wilbur G. Lewellen, "Analysis of the Lease-Or-Buy Decision," *Journal of Finance*, 27 (Sept. 1972), 815-23. They hold that the lease is a long-term acquisition of services and that the relevant comparison is lease versus buy, not lease versus borrow. For a comparison of various methods for analyzing lease versus borrowing, see Richard S. Bower, "Issues in Lease Financing," *Financial Management*, 2 (Winter 1973), 25-34.

Leasing an asset   Suppose a firm has decided to acquire an asset costing $200 000 with an expected economic life of five years, after which the asset is expected to have a residual value of $30 000. Once the lessee has made the investment decision using the principles discussed in Chapter 13, the question becomes, Is it better to secure the asset through a lease arrangement or borrow funds to buy and own the asset? If the asset is leased, the lessor wants $51 103 in advance and four payments of $51 103 at the end of each of the next four years. Note that lease payments are usually made in advance and in an amount sufficient to provide the lessor with a desired rate of return on the project. Another way of looking at leasing is to say that the lessor is making a loan of $200 000 to the lessee and that this deal has an implicit interest cost, thus the comparison of leasing to acquisition of the asset through borrowing.

Borrowing to buy an asset   If the asset is purchased, it is assumed that the firm can finance the acquisition entirely with a 12 percent five-year unsecured term loan. This loan requires equal annual payments of $55 482 at the end of each year calculated as follows:[4]

$$\$2000\ 000 = \sum_{t=1}^{5} \frac{y}{(1.12)^t}$$

$$\$200\ 000 = 3.6048\ y$$

$$y = \frac{\$200\ 000}{3.6048}$$

$$y = \$55\ 482$$

(20-1)

LEASING VERSUS BORROWING ANALYSIS

From our previous discussion, we know that the firm will make annual lease payments of $51 103 if the asset is leased. Because these payments are an expense, they are deductible for tax purpose, but only in the year for which the payment applies. The $51 103 payment at the end of year 0 represents a prepaid expense and is not deductible for tax purposes until year 1. Similarly, each of the other four payments is not deductible until the year following the year of payment. If we assume an income tax rate of 46 percent, cash outflows after taxes each year would be those in column 3 of Table 20-1. Since we have cash outflow/inflows in different time periods, we need to find the present value of the cost of leasing. We are comparing the cost of leasing to the cost of purchasing using debt to finance the acquisition. Therefore, the appropriate discount rate is the after-tax cost of the borrowing alternative. The before-tax cost of borrowing is 12 percent and given a tax rate of 46 percent, the after-tax cost is 6.48 percent (i.e. 12 percent times 0.54).

Given the information in the paragraph above, we are able to compute the present value of cash outflows. The computations are shown in the last column of Table 20-1. We see that the present value of the total cash outflows under the leasing alternative is $128 486. This figure, then must be compared with the present value of cash outflows under the borrowing alternative.

---

[4]See Chapter 4 for the method used to calculate instalments for loan repayments.

TABLE 20-1 Schedule of Cash Outflows: Leasing Alternative

End of Year	(1) Lease Payment	(2) Tax Shield (1) × (0.46)	(3) Cash Outflow After Taxes (1) – (2)	(4) Present Value Factor (6.48%)	(5) Present Value of Cash Outflows
0	$51 103	—	$51 103	1.000	$ 51 103
1-4	51 103	$23 507	27 596	3.426	94 543
5	—	23 507	– 23 507	0.730	17 163
Present value of cost of leasing option					$128 483

If the asset is purchased, it is assumed that the firm can finance the acquisition entirely with a 12 percent five-year unsecured term loan. The loan is payable over this period in equal annual payments of $55 482 at the end of each year. These payments include both principal and interest. The proportion of interest in each payment depends on the unpaid balance of the principal amount owing during the year. For example, the principal amount owing during year 1 is $200 000; therefore, the annual interest for that year is $24 000. Table 20-2 shows the schedule of debt payments.

The procedures for the calculation of the annual cash flows for the borrowing alternative are shown in Table 20-3. The loan payment and interest charges are taken directly from Table 20-2. Assume also that the asset qualifies for a CCA rate of 30 percent and depreciation charges are determined along the principles discussed in Chapters 2 and 13. Given annual interest and depreciation, we can compute the cash outflows after taxes for the borrowing alternative; these outflows are shown in the fifth column in Table 20-3. Because both depreciation and interest are tax-deductible, they provide a tax shield equal to their sum times the tax rate. When this shield is deducted from the total payment of $55 482, we obtain the cash outflow after taxes at the end of each year. Then taking residual value into consideration we compute the present value of these outflows; and they are found to total $115 863. According to this analysis, the firm should acquire the asset through debt financing, because the present value of cash outflows with borrowing is less than that with leasing.

TABLE 20-2 Schedule of Debt Payments

End of Year	Interest Plus Principal Payments	Principal Amount Owing at End of Year	Annual Interest	Principal Repaid
0	$ —	$200 000	$ —	$ —
1	55 482	168 518	24 000	31 482
2	55 482	133 258	20 222	35 260
3	55 482	93 767	15 991	39 491
4	55 482	49 537	11 252	44 230
5	55 481	—	5 944	49 537

TABLE 20-3 Schedule of Cash Outflows: Borrowing Alternative

End of Year	(1) Loan Payment	(2) Interest	(3) Depreciation*	(4) Tax Shield [(2) + (3)] 0.46	(5) Cash Outflow After Taxes (1) − (4)	(6) Present Value Factor (6.48%)	(7) Present Value of Cash Outflows
1	$55 482	$24 000	$30 000	$24 840	$30 642	0.938	$ 28 742
2	55 482	20 222	51 000	32 762	22 720	0.881	20 016
3	55 482	15 991	35 700	23 778	31 704	0.827	26 219
4	55 482	11 252	24 990	16 671	38 810	0.777	30 155
5	55 481	5 944	17 493	10 781	44 700	0.730	32 631
							137 763
Less: present value of salvage ($30 000 at 0.730)							− 21 900
Present value of cost of borrowing option							115 863

*For simplicity we omit consideration of the tax savings on undepreciated capital cost of $10 817 which would be depreciated to infinity assuming the pool of assets is maintained.

By using declining-balance depreciation, the firm obtains a greater tax shield in the early years and a lower shield in later years. As a result, cash outflows after taxes in the early years are reduced relative to cash outflows in later years, and the present value of costs under the borrowing alternative is decreased. The pattern of after-tax cash flows under the borrowing alternative will be more attractive where a project is expected to generate greater earnings in the later years of its economic life. In the early years, declining-balance depreciation offers lower after-tax cash outflows, but the burden increases in the later years. Under the lease alternative the financial obligation is fixed for the entire period. It is easy to see that if the company expects the project to generate greater earnings in its early years, the financial risk of the borrowing alternative is significantly increased in the later years. Increasing after-tax cash outflows under the borrowing alternative will have to be met from decreasing cash inflows from operations.

Short-cuts in Calculations The above calculations can be reduced considerably by treating the loan repayment and depreciation separately. In the case of the loan repayment, if the after-tax cost of the loan and the discount rate are the same, then the present value of the cost of the loan is its principal value. For example, we assumed that the discount rate is 6.48 percent after taxes which is the same as the after-tax cost of debt. Thus, the present value of the $200 000 loan is $200 000. Then the present value of the tax savings on depreciation, using Eq. (13-8), is

$$\frac{Cdt}{k+d} \times \frac{2+k}{2(1+k)} - \frac{1}{(1+k)^5} \times \frac{5dt}{k+d}$$

$$= \frac{\$200\ 000(0.3)(0.46)}{0.0648 + 0.3} \times \frac{2.0648}{2.1296} - (0.730) \times \frac{\$30\ 000(0.3)(0.46)}{0.0648 + 0.3}$$

$$= \$65\ 064$$

where C = the net capital outlay
  d = the CCA rate
  k = the discount rate
  t = the tax rate
  s = the residual value at the end of year 5.

The calculations assume that the firm will continue to have assets in the pool and that an undepreciated capital cost of $10 817 will be depreciated to infinity.

The present value of the cash outflows of the borrowing option is thus:

Loan	$200 000
Tax savings on CCA	− 65 064
Present value of salvage	− 21 900
	$113 036

The figure $113 036 exceeds $115 863 in Table 20-3 by $2 827. This difference is the present value of the tax savings on the undepreciated capital cost claimed after year 5; Table 20-3 omitted that consideration.

Our calculations can be easily adjusted to handle such factors as differential operating costs and the investment tax credit. The principles for these adjustments were discussed and illustrated in Chapter 13 and hence will not be taken up here.

Transferring the tax benefits to a lessor   In the preceding illustration we assumed that the firm had sufficient earnings to take full advantage of all the tax benefits. Sometimes this may not be the case and a firm may for some reason, prefer leasing. Before 1976 and by using a lease, such a firm could then "transfer" some or all of the tax benefits to a lessor who may give a "kick-back" in the form of lower lease payments. The lessor, as owner, would claim the investment tax credit on eligible assets and benefit on capital cost allowances. The lessee would then negotiate lower rentals than would be paid otherwise. The lessor would agree to the above-mentioned kick-back deal only if he or she could take full advantage of the available tax benefits.

Since 1976 however, the maximum amount of capital cost allowances which a lessor of movable property can claim in any given year is net lease payments. Net lease payments are defined as gross rentals less overhead associated with lease contracts and interest on debt used to finance the acquisition of leased assets. This means that lessors are not allowed to use capital cost allowances to create a loss on leasing operations. Prior to the 1976 amendment, such a loss could be written off to non-leasing income; this is now not possible.

Summary

Term financing is generally considered to include maturities of one to ten years. There are a number of sources of intermediate-term financing. Commercial banks, insurance companies, and other institutional investors make term loans to business firms. Banks also provide financing under a revolving-credit arrangement, which is a formal commitment on the part of the bank to lend up to a certain amount of money over a specified period of time. Lenders who offer unsecured credit usually impose restrictions on the borrower. These restrictions are called protective covenants and are contained in a loan agreement. If the borrower defaults under any of the provisions of the loan agreement, the lender may initiate immediate corrective measures. On a secured basis, firms can obtain intermediate-term financing by pledging equipment that they own or are purchasing. Banks, finance companies, and sellers of the equipment are active in providing this type of secured financing.

Lease financing involves the acquisition of the economic use of an asset through a contractual commitment to make periodic lease payments to a lessor who owns the asset. Because of this contractual obligation, leasing is regarded as a method of financing similar to borrowing. Leasing can involve either the direct acquisition of an asset under a lease or a sale and leaseback arrangement, whereby the firm sells an asset it owns and leases it back from the buyer. One way to analyze lease financing in relation to debt financing is to discount to present value of the net cash outflows after taxes under each alternative, using the after-tax cost of debt as the discount rate. The preferred alternative is the one that provides the lower present value of cost.

Appendix: Accounting Treatment of Leases

The accounting treatment of leases has undergone sweeping changes in the past two decades. Where once leases were not disclosed, gradually disclosure was required in the footnotes to the financial statement. With only minimal disclosure, however, leasing was attractive to certain firms as an off balance sheet method of financing. While there was no evidence that such financing had a favorable effect on valuation, all other things being constant, many a company proceeded on the assumption that off balance sheet financing was a good thing. Then the Canadian Institute of Chartered Accountants (CICA) in December 1978 made an explicit ruling which called for the capitalization on the balance sheet of certain types of leases.[5] In essence, this statement says that if the lessee acquires essentially all of the economic benefits and risks of the leased property, then the value of the asset, along with the corresponding lease liability, must be shown on the balance sheet. The discussion in this appendix is primarily of an accounting nature and does not affect the financial analyses in the chapter.

Capital and Operating Leases

A *capital lease* transfers essentially all the benefits and risks associated with ownership of property to the lessee. More specifically, a lease is regarded as a capital lease if one or more of the following conditions are present:

[5]CICA, *Accounting Recommendations–Leases, Section 3065*, Dec. 1978.

1. If it is reasonable to expect that the lessee will obtain title to the asset at the end of the lease period. Usually, the contract will provide for an option to purchase the asset at a bargain price.
2. If the lease period is equal to or greater than 75 percent of the estimated economic life of the asset.
3. If at the beginning of the lease, the present value of the minimum lease payments equals or exceeds 90 percent of the fair value of the leased property to the lessor.

If any of these conditions is met, the lessee is said to have acquired most of the economic benefits and risks associated with the leased property and, therefore, a capital lease is involved. If a lease does not meet one of these conditions, it is classified as an *operating lease*. Essentially, operating leases give the lessee the right to use the leased property over a period of time, but they do not give the lessee all of the benefits and risks that are associated with the asset.

DETERMINING THE VALUE OF A CAPITAL LEASE

With a capital lease, the lessee must report the value of the leased property on the asset side of the balance sheet. The amount reflected is the present value of the minimum lease payments over the lease period. If executory costs, such as insurance, maintenance, and taxes are a part of the total lease payment, these are deducted and only the remainder is used for purposes of calculating the present value. The discount rate employed is the lower of (1) the lessee's incremental borrowing rate or, (2) the lessor's implicit interest rate if in fact that rate can be determined. In the latter case, it is assumed that the lessor is making a loan equal to the value of the asset to the lessee.

To illustrate these computations, suppose that Gaudet Gear Company Ltd. wishes to lease a stamping machine that calls for lease payments of $17 040 due at the beginning of each of the next eight years. (The lease payments are due in advance). The company's marginal borrowing rate is 8 percent. The cost of the machine to the lessor is $100 000 and the machine is not expected to have any residual value at the end of the lease period. The implicit interest rate of the lessor can be determined by solving the following equation for r

$$\$100\ 000 = \sum_{t=0}^{7} \frac{\$17\ 040}{(1 + r)^t} \tag{20A-1}$$

Because lease payments are made in advance, the first payment can be thought of as being due at time 0 with seven other payments due in yearly intervals. We then turn to Table B at the end of the book for the present-value discount factors for an even stream of cash flows over seven years. To the discount factor we must add 1 because the payment at time 0 is not discounted. For an interest rate of 9 percent, we see that the discount factor shown in Table B is 5.0329 to which we add 1 to obtain a discount factor of 6.0329. Dividing $100 000 by 6.0329, we obtain $16 575. As this amount is less than the lease payment, we know the implicit interest rate must be higher. For 10 percent, the discount factor is 4.8684 to which we add 1 to obtain 5.8684. Dividing $100 000 by 5.8684, we obtain $17 040, exactly the lease payment. Therefore, the lessor's implicit interest rate is 10 percent. By trial and error then, we can determine the lessor's implied interest rate provided we know the purchase price of the asset and certain other information.

As the lessor's implicit interest rate in our example is higher than the lessee's incremental borrowing rate of 8 percent, the latter would in most cases be used in determining the capitalized value of the lease. However, the lessee, in so far as is practical, must try to determine the lessor's implicit interest rate. When the implicit rate is less than the lessee's incremental borrowing rate, it must be used as the discount rate. Given the amount of the lease payments and the discount rate to employ, one can easily determine the amount that should be recorded on the balance sheet for a capital lease. For our example, the present value at time 0, after, the initial lease payment, is

$$\$17\ 040 \text{ for seven years at } 8\% = \$17\ 040 \times 5.2064$$

$$= \$88\ 717 \qquad\qquad (20A\text{-}2)$$

Considering now the initial lease payment, the capitalized value is \$105 757 (\$88 717 + \$17 040).

RECORDING THE CAPITAL LEASE ON THE BALANCE SHEET

The amount of \$105 757 should be recorded on the lessee's balance sheet as an asset. (However, if the fair value of the leased property is lower than the present value of the minimum lease payments, then the fair value would be shown.) The associated lease obligation should be shown on the liability side of the balance sheet, the present value of payments due within one year reflected as current liabilities, and the present value of payments due after one year shown as non-current liabilities. The leased property must be kept separate from assets which are owned by the firm; and related lease obligations should be kept separate from other long-term obligations. The gross amounts of leased assets and related accumulated depreciation should be disclosed by major categories of assets—land, building, and machinery, for example.

In addition to this information, more detailed information is required in footnotes, including the total future minimum lease payments, a schedule by years of future lease payments required over the next five years, the total minimum sublease rentals to be received, the existence and terms of purchase or renewal options and of escalation clauses, rentals which are contingent on some factor other than the passage of time, and any restrictions imposed in the lease agreement.

Disclosure of operating leases   As in the case of capital leases, for operating leases disclosure is required, but this can be done in footnotes. For noncancelable leases with remaining terms of over one year, the lessee must disclose total future minimum lease payments, a schedule by year for the next five years, the total sublease rentals to be received, the basis for contingent rental payments, the existence and terms of purchase and renewal options and of escalation clauses, and any lease agreement restrictions. The last two categories are included in a general description of the leasing arrangement.

Amortizing the Capital Lease and Reducing the Obligation

A capital lease must be amortized and the liability reduced over the lease period. The method of amortization is that used by the lessee to depreciate assets which are owned. In our example, if the firm normally depreciates its assets on a straight line basis (for reporting to shareholders), the leased asset will be subject to a similar treatment over the lease term or the estimated economic life of the asset. If the lease contract provides that ownership of the asset is to be passed on to the lessee or there is a bargain purchase option, the period of amortization would be the estimated economic life of the asset. Otherwise, the asset should be amortized over the lease period. Now assuming straight line depreciation and a period of amortization equal to the lease period, the asset in our illustration will be depreciated at \$13 220 (\$105 757 ÷ 8) per year. Following this procedure, the written down value of the asset at the end of year 1 will be \$92 537 (\$105 757 − \$13 220); at the end of year 2 it will be \$79 317 (\$92 537 − \$13 220) and so on.

If it is reasonable to assume that ownership of the leased asset will be passed on to the lessee at the end of the lease period, then we have to estimate the economic life of the asset, which, in general, will be equal to or greater than the lease period. This estimated economic life will then be used to determine annual depreciation and year-end amortized asset value. The principles are similar to those illustrated in the preceding paragraph.

The CICA recommendations also require that the capital lease obligation be reduced over the lease period by the "interest" method. Under this method, each lease payment is broken down into two components—the payment of principal and the payment of interest. The obligation is reduced by the amount of the principal payment. To illustrate, recall our example where the firm had the obligation to pay \$17 040 at the beginning of each year, that its incremental borrowing rate was 8 percent, and that this rate is used as the discount rate. In Table 20A-1 the calculation of interest and principal payments are shown. At the beginning of year 1, which is the beginning of the lease period, the lease payment is represented entirely by a payment of principal. After that initial period, interest payment is also shown, but the amount declines proportionally over the lease period. For balance sheet purposes, at the end of year 1 (the beginning of year 2) the capital lease obligation will be \$78 774 for long-term debt and \$17 040 for current liabilities; at the end of year 2, \$68 030 and \$17 040 respectively; and so on. These values are taken directly from Table 20A-1.

REPORTING OF EARNINGS

For income reporting purposes, both the amortization of the leased property and the annual interest embodied in the lease payment should be treated as expense. In our example, the lease expense allowable as a deduction against income at the end of each of the eight years is shown in Table 20A-2. This treatment differs from that for the operating lease where only the lease payment is deductible as an expense. Also, it differs from the way all leases were treated prior to the CICA recommendations, where again, only the lease payment was deductible.

TABLE 20A-1 Illustration of the "Interest" Method to Reduce the Lease Obligation

Beginning of Year	Principal Amount Owing at Beginning of Year	Annual Lease Payment	Annual Interest at 8%	Annual Principal Payment
1	$88 717	$17 040	0	$17 040
2	78 774	17 040	$7 097	9 943
3	68 034	17 040	6 302	10 738
4	56 437	17 040	5 443	11 597
5	43 912	17 040	4 515	12 525
6	30 385	17 040	3 512	13 527
7	15 775	17 040	2 431	14 609
8	0	17 040	1 262	15 775

TABLE 20A-2 Lease Expenses Allowable as Write-Offs Against Income

End of Year	Amortization of Asset (Straight Line)	Annual Interest (Table 20A-1)	Annual Lease Expense
1	$13 220	$7 097	$20 317
2	13 220	6 302	19 522
3	13 220	5 443	18 663
4	13 220	4 515	17 735
5	13 220	3 512	16 732
6	13 220	2 431	15 651
7	13 220	1 262	14 482
8	13 220	0	13 220

Questions

1. What reasons can you cite for the firm's use of intermediate-term debt? Why isn't long-term debt substituted in its place? Short-term debt?

2. Why do insurance companies not compete more actively with banks for short- and intermediate-term financing?

3. What is the purpose of protective covenants in a term-loan agreement?

4. How does a revolving credit agreement differ from a line of credit?

5. How should a lender go about setting the working-capital protective covenant in a loan agreement? the capital-expenditure covenant?

6. As a borrower, how would you negotiate over the working-capital and capital-expenditure restrictions a lender wished to impose?

7. What are the key financial institutions providing intermediate-term financing to business firms?

8. Chapter 1 suggests that the decision-making processes of investing funds (buying assets) and of raising funds (financing assets) are two separate and distinct functions of the financial

manager. This chapter suggests that, at least in the case of leasing, the decision-making processes cannot be separated. Discuss the problems raised by this sort of situation and prepare your analytical method for making decisions in this situation.

9. Explain the concept of sale and leaseback. Compare this arrangement with a mortgage loan on the leased asset.

10. Discuss the probable impact that a sale and leaseback arrangement will have on
   (a) Liquidity ratios
   (b) Return on investment
   (c) Return on equity
   (d) The risk-class of the corporation's stock
   (e) The price of the stock.

11. Some business people consider that the risk of obsolescence and inflexibility is being transferred from the lessee to the lessor. How is the lessor induced to accept higher risk and greater inflexibility?

12. In your opinion, would the following factors tend to favor borrowing or leasing as a financing alternative? Why?
   (a) Increased corporate tax rate
   (b) Accelerated depreciation
   (c) Rising price level
   (d) Increased residual value of the leased asset

Problems with Solutions

1. A manufacturing company purchased a building in 19X1 at a cost of $2 700 000. Of the total cost, $700 000 was deemed to be the cost of the land, and the remaining $2 000 000 the cost of the building. Immediately after the purchase, a national leasing firm offered to purchase the property for $2 700 000 and lease it back to the manufacturing company for twenty years at $300 000 per year, payable in advance. The leasing company would bear no maintenance or property tax cost and would grant no option to purchase the building. The CCA rate is 5 percent, the firm can obtain a mortgage at a cost of 15 percent, and the tax rate is 40 percent. The value of the building in 20 years is estimated to be $100 000. The land is expected to have a value of $1 000 000. Should the firm accept the sale and lease back offer?

Sale and leaseback

Year	Cash inflow (outflow) before tax	Tax savings (40%)	Cash inflow (outflow) after tax	Discount factor (9%)	PV
0	$2 700 000	–	$2 700 000	1.0	$2 700 000
0	(300 000)	–	(300 000)	1.0	(300 000)
1-19	(300 000)	120 000	(180 000)	8.9501	(1 611 018)
20	–	120 000	120 000	0.1784	21 408
	Present value of cash inflow				$ 810 390

Ownership

Depreciation tax shield:

$$\frac{\$2\ 000\ 000(0.05)(0.4)}{0.09 + 0.05} \times \frac{2.09}{2.18} - 0.1784 \times \frac{\$100\ 000(0.05)(0.4)}{0.09 + 0.05} \qquad = \$271\ 370$$

Sale of building $100 000 (0.1784)		= 17 840
Sale of land	$1 000 000	
Capital gains tax (0.4 × 150 000)	60 000	
	$940 000 (0.1784)	= 167 696
Present value of cash inflow		$456 906

Summary

Present value of sale and leaseback	$810 390
Present value of ownership	456 906
Advantage of sale and leaseback	$353 484

2. A company is considering the purchase of a new machine for $40 000. The new machine will replace an old machine which has a book value of $10 000 and which could be sold for $7 500. The new machine has an expected life of 5 years, after which it would have a salvage value of $5 000. The operating cost of the new machine is $12 500 per year.

The old machine could be overhauled at a cost of $25 000 which would be capitalized and depreciated for tax purposes. The operating cost of the old machine after overhaul is $15 000 per year. Its expected life is 5 years and it would have no scrap value at the end of that time.

The new machine could also be leased at a cost of $12 000 per year paid in advance. No operating costs would be borne by the leasing company.

The company require a return of 15 percent on investments, use a CCA rate of 30 percent paid tax at 50 percent and borrow from its bank at 12 percent.

What should the company do?

We must first decide whether the company should overhaul the old machine or acquire the new one. If the decision is to acquire the new machine, then we must decide whether to buy or lease.

Acquire new machine:

Net cost = Purchase price − proceeds from sale of old machine

$32 500 = $40 000 − $7 500

Operating cost

Annual outflow	Tax saving	After tax outflow	15% Discount factor	PV
$12 500	$6 250	$6 250	3.3522	$20 951

The depreciation tax shield on the incremental investment is

$$\frac{32\ 500(0.3)(0.5)}{0.15 + 0.3} \times \frac{2.15}{2.30} - 0.4972 \times \frac{5\ 000(0.3)(0.5)}{0.15 + 0.3} = \$9\ 299$$

Summary

Incremental capital cost	($32 500)
Operating cost	(20 951)
Present value of salvage ($5 000 × 0.4972)	2 486
Present value of tax shield	9 299
	($41 666)

Overhaul old machine
Net capital cost = $25 000
Operating cost 15 000 $(1 - t) \times 3.3522 = \$25\ 142$
Tax savings from depreciation:

$$\frac{25\ 000(0.3)(0.5)}{0.15 + 0.3} \times \frac{2.15}{2.30} = \$7\ 790$$

Summary

$$\$25\ 000 + \$25\ 142 + \$7\ 790 = (\$42\ 352)$$

Decision:
Acquire new machine since *PV* cost of new machine is less than the *PV* of overhauling the old machine.
Cost of the borrowing option

Loan	= $ 40 000
Depreciation tax shield	
	= (14 636)

$$\frac{(40\ 000)(0.3)(0.5)}{0.06 + 0.3} \times \frac{2.06}{2.12} - 0.7472 \times \frac{5\ 000(0.3)(0.5)}{0.06 + 0.3}$$

Residual value $5 000 (0.7472)	= (3 736)
Net Cost	$ 21 628

Note: The discount rate is the after-tax cost of borrowing.

Lease

Year	Payment	Tax saving	Net cash outflow (in)	Discount 6% factor	Present value
0	$12 000	–	$12 000	1.0	$12 000
1 – 4	12 000	$6 000	6 000	3.4651	20 791
5		6 000	(6 000)	0.7472	(4 483)
					$28 308

Machine should be purchased, since leasing is $6680 ($28 308 – $21 628) more costly than borrowing.

Problems

1. Zenda Fashions Corporation Ltd. wishes to borrow $600 000 on a 5-year term basis. Oysterman's National Bank is willing to make such a loan at a 14 percent rate, provided the loan is completely amortized over the 5-year period. Payments are due at the end of each of the five years. Set up an amortization schedule of equal annual loan payments that will satisfy the above. Be sure to show both the principal and interest components of each of the overall payments.

2. On January 1, Sharpe Razor Corporation Ltd. is contemplating a 4-year, $3 million term loan from the Fidelity National Bank. The loan is payable at the end of the fourth year and would involve a loan agreement that would contain a number of protective covenants. Among these restrictions are that the company must maintain working capital of $3 million at all times, that it cannot take on any more long-term debt, that its total liabilities cannot be more than 0.6 of its total assets, and that capital expenditures in any year are limited ot depreciation plus $3 million. The company's balance sheet at December 31, before the term loan, is

Current assets	$ 7 million	Current liabilities	$ 3 million
Net fixed assets	10 million	Long-term debt (due in 5 years)	5 million
		Net worth	9 million
	$17 million		$17 million

The proceeds of the term loan will be used to increase Sharpe's investment in inventories and receivables in response to introducing a new "closer-to-the-face" razor blade. The company anticipates a subsequent need to grow at a rate of 24 percent a year for current and net fixed assets. Profits after taxes of $1.5 million are expected this year, and these profits are expected to grow by $250 000 per year over the subsequent three years. The company pays no dividends and does not intend to pay any over the next four years. Depreciation in the past year was $2.5 million, and this is predicted to grow over the next four years at the same rate as the increase in net fixed assets.

Under the loan agreement, will the company be able to achieve its growth objective?

3. Given the following information, compute the annual lease payment (paid in advance) that a lessor will require:
   (a) Purchase price of $260 000, implicit interest rate of 13 percent, 5-year lease period, and no residual value
   (b) Purchase price of $138 000, implicit interest rate of 6 percent, 9-year lease period, and a near-certain residual value of $20 000
   (c) Purchase price of $773 000, implicit interest rate of 9 percent, 10-year lease period, and no residual value.

4. Bork Electronics Company Ltd. is considering leasing one of its products in addition to selling it outright to customers. The product, the Zeus Tester, sells for $18 600 and has an economic life of 8 years.
   (a) Assume 12 percent implicit interest, what annual lease payment must Bork require as lessor? (Assume lease payments are payable in advance.)
   (b) If the product has a salvage value (known with certainty) of $4 000 at the end of 8 years, what annual lease payment will be required?

5. Shaw Company Ltd. which has a 40 percent tax rate wishes to acquire a $100 000 stamping machine. The machine has a capital cost allowance rate of 20 percent. It would be possible to secure a machine through an eight-year lease for $20 000 per year, payable in advance Alternatively, it would be possible to borrow the $100 000 at 15 percent; this would require annual payments of $22 285. At the end of eight years the machine could be sold for $10 000. The firm is entitled to an investment tax credit of 10 percent of the cost of the asset at the end of the first year. Which is the superior method of financing a 40 percent tax rate?

Appendix Problem

6. Conrad Reduction Company Ltd. has just leased a press that calls for annual lease payments of $40 000 payable in advance. The lease period is 9 years, and the leased property is classified as a capital lease. The company's incremental borrowing rate is 7 percent, whereas the lessor's implied interest rate is 12 percent. The company depreciates all of its owned assets on a straight-line basis. On the basis of this information, compute
(a) The value of the leased property to be shown on the balance sheet after the initial lease payment.
(b) The annual lease expense in each year as it will appear on the accounting income statement.

Selected References

ANDERSON, PAUL F., and JOHN D. MARTIN, "Lease vs. Purchase Decisions: A Survey of Current Practice," *Financial Management*, 6 (Spring 1977), 41-47.

BOWER, RICHARD S., "Issues in Lease Financing," *Financial Management*, 2 (Winter 1973), 25-34.

———, FRANK C. HERRINGER, and J. PETER WILLIAMSON, "Lease Evaluation," *Accounting Review*, 41 (April 1966), 257-65.

BOWER, RICHARD S., and GEORGE S. OLDFIELD, JR., "Of Lessees, Lessors, and Discount Rates and Whether Pigs Have Wings," *Journal of Business Research*, 9 (March 1981), 29-38.

BREALEY, R. A., and C. M. YOUNG, "Debt, Taxes and Leasing—A Note," *Journal of Finance*, 35 (December 1980), 1245-50.

CAPETTINI, ROBERT, and HOWARD TOOLE, "Designing Leveraged Leases: A Mixed Integer Linear Programming Approach," *Financial Management*, 10 (Autumn 1981), 15-23.

CRAWFORD, PEGGY J., CHARLES P. HARPER, and JOHN J. McCONNELL, "Further Evidence on the Terms of Financial Leases," *Financial Management*, 10 (Autumn 1981), 7-14.

DUNCAN, IAN D., "The Leasing Issue–Some Important Considerations", *Cost and Management*, March-April, 1980, 21-25.

DYL, EDWARD A., and STANLEY A. MARTIN, JR., "Setting Terms for Leveraged Leasing," *Financial Management*, 6 (Winter 1977), 20-27.

FINDLAY, M. CHAPMAN, III, "A Sensitivity Analysis of IRR Leasing Models," *Engineering Economist*, 20 (Summer 1975), 231-42.

GAUMNITZ, JACK E., and ALLEN FORD, "The Lease or Sell Decision," *Financial Manager*, 7 (Winter 1978), 69-74.

GILL, RICHARD C., "Term Loan Agreements," *Journal of Commercial Bank Lending*, 62 (February 1980), 22-27.

GORDON, MYRON J., "A General Solution to the Buy or Lease Decision: A Pedagogical Note," *Journal of Finance*, 29 (March 1974).

HANRAHAN, ROBERT, J. KUSHNER and I. MASSE, "The Purchase/Lease Decision from the Viewpoint of Government", *Cost and Management*, March-April, 1984, 35-39.

IDOL, CHARLES R., "A Note on Specifying Debt Displacement and Tax Shield Borrowing Opportunities in Financial Lease Valuation Models," *Financial Management*, 9 (Summer 1980), 24-29.

JOHNSON, ROBERT W., and WILBUR G. LEWELLEN, "Analysis of the Lease-or-Buy Decision," *Journal of Finance*, 27 (September 1972), 815-23.

KIM, E. HAN, WILBUR G. LEWELLEN, and JOHN J. McCONNELL, "Sale and Leaseback Agreements and Enterprise Valuation," *Journal of Financial and Quantitative Analysis*, 13 (December, 1978), 871-84.

LAU, C.T. and M. NELSON, "A Note on Accounting for Leases", *Cost and Management*, March-April, 1981, 38-41.

LEWELLEN, WILBUR G., and DOUGLAS R. EMERY, "On the Matter of Parity Among Financial Obligations," *Journal of Finance*, 36 (March 1981), 97-111.

LEWELLEN, WILBUR G., MICHAEL S. LONG, and JOHN J. McCONNELL, "Asset Leasing in Competitive Capital Markets," *Journal of Finance*, 31 (June 1976), 787-98.

LONG, MICHAEL S., "Leasing and the Cost of Capital," *Journal of Financial and Quantitative Analysis*, 12 (November 1977), 579-86.

MIDDLETON, J. WILLIAM, "Term Lending–Practical and Profitable," *Journal of Commercial Bank Lending*, 50 (August 1968), 31-43.

MILLER, MERTON H., and CHARLES W. UPTON, "Leasing, Buying, and the Cost of Capital Services," *Journal of Finance*, 31 (June 1976), 787-98.

MOYER, R. CHARLES, "Lease Financing and the Investment Tax Credit: A Framework for Analysis," *Financial Management*, 4 (Summer 1975), 39-44.

MYERS, STEWART C., DAVID A. DILL, and ALBERTO J. BAUTISTA, "Valuation of Financial Lease Contracts," *Journal of Finance*, 31 (June 1976), 799-820.

OFFER, AHARON R., "The Evaluation of the Lease versus Purchase Alternatives," *Financial Management*, 5 (Summer 1976), 67-74.

PACKHAM, E. RICHARD, "An Analysis of the Risks of Leveraged Leasing," *Journal of Commercial Bank Lending*, 57 (March 1975), 2-29.

ROENFELDT, RODNEY L., and JEROME S. OSTERYOUNG, "Analysis of Financial Leases," *Financial Management*, 2 (Spring 1973), 74-87.

SCHALL, LAWRENCE D., "The Lease-or-Buy and Asset Acquisition Decisions," *Journal of Finance*, 29 (September 1974), 1203-14.

SMITH, CLIFFORD W., JR., and JEROLD B. WARNER, "On Financial Contracting: An Analysis of Bond Covenants," *Journal of Financial Economics*, 7 (June 1980), 117-61.

SORENSEN, IVAR W., and RAMON E. JOHNSON, "Equipment Financial Leasing Practices and Costs: An Empirical Study," *Financial Management*, 6 (Spring 1977), 33-40.

VANCIL, RICHARD F., "Lease or Borrow: New Method of Analysis," *Harvard Business Review*, 39 (September-October 1961), 122-36.

VAN HORNE, JAMES, "A Linear-Programming Approach to Evaluating Restrictions under a Bond Indenture or Loan Agreement," *Journal of Financial and Quantitative Analysis*, 1 (June 1966), 68-83.

_____, "The Cost of Leasing with Capital Market Imperfections," *Engineering Economist*, 23 (Fall 1977), 1-12.

_____, "Optimal Initiation of Bankruptcy Proceedings by Debtholders," *Journal of Finance*, 31 (June 1976), 897-910.

WIAR, ROBERT C., "Economic Implications of Multiple Rates of Return in the Leverage Lease Contest," *Journal of Finance*, 28 (December 1973), 1275-86.

ZIMMERMAN, CHARLES S., "An Approach to Writing Loan Agreement Covenants," *Journal of Commercial Bank Lending*, 58 (November 1975), 2-17.

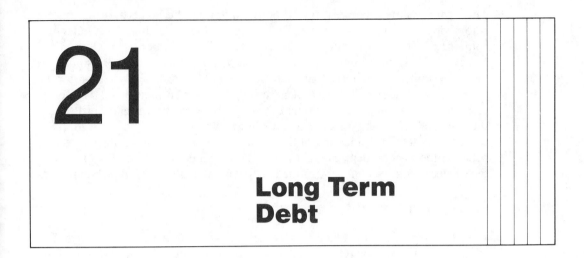

21

Long Term
Debt

In Chapters 11,12, and 20, we discussed short term and intermediate term debt instruments. In this chapter we study longer-term debt issues with original maturities of more than ten years. We first take up the features of long term debt, move on to consider various types of instruments, and then explore the nature of the call provision and the retractable and extendible options attached to some bonds. Finally, the profitability of refunding an existing bond issue will also be analyzed.

Features Of Debt

The fixed return of a long term debt instrument is denoted by the *coupon rate*. A 13 percent debenture indicates that the issuer will pay bondholders $130 per annum for every $1 000-face-value bond they hold. The *yield to maturity* on a bond is determined by solving for the rate of discount that equates the present value of principal and interest payments with the current market price of the bond. (See Chapter 4 for the mathematics of bond interest.)

A company issuing bonds to the public designates a qualified *trustee* to represent the interests of the bondholders. The obligations of a trustee are specified in the Trustee Acts of the respective provinces. The trustee's responsibilities are to authenticate the bond issue's legality at the time of issuance, to watch over the financial condition and behavior of the borrower to make sure all contractual obligations are carried out, and to initiate appropriate actions if the borrower does not meet any of these obligations. The trustee is compensated directly by the corporation, a compensation that adds to the costs of borrowing.

The legal agreement between the corporation issuing the bonds and the trustee, who represents the bondholders, is defined in the *indenture*. The indenture contains the terms of the bond issue as well as the restrictions placed upon the company. These restrictions, known as *protective covenants*, are very similar to those contained in a term-loan agreement. Because we analyzed protective covenants in Chapter 20, it is not necessary to describe them here. The terms contained in this indenture are established jointly by the borrower and trustee. If the issue is a negotiated underwriting, the underwriter also will be involved. If the corporation defaults under any of the provisions of the indenture, the trustee, on behalf of the bondholders, can take action to correct the situation. If not satisfied, the trustee then can call for the immediate payment of all outstanding bonds.

RETIREMENT

The retirement of bonds may be accomplished in a number of ways. For example, bonds may be retired by payment at final maturity, by conversion if the bonds are convertible, by calling the bonds if there is a call feature, by redeeming the bonds if there is a retractable or an extendible feature, or by periodic repayment. Periodic repayment of the debt is possible if the bond issue is either a sinking-fund issue or a serial-bond issue. (Conversion is discussed in Chapter 23, and callable, retractable, and extendible bonds are examined later in this chapter.) We turn now to a discussion of sinking-funds and serial bonds.

Sinking funds The majority of corporate bond issues carry a provision for a sinking fund which requires the corporation to make periodic sinking-fund payments to a trustee, in order to retire a specified face amount of bonds each period. Payments can be cash or bonds that the company purchases in the open market. The trustee uses cash to call bonds for redemption. Usually, bonds are called on a lottery basis by their serial numbers, which are published in *The Financial Post, The Globe and Mail*, and other papers. The corporation should purchase the bonds in the open market as long as the market price is less than the call price stated in the indenture; when the market price exceeds the call price, it should make cash payments to the trustee.

Because of the orderly retirement of debt as well as the liquidity provided by the regular purchase activity, many investors find the sinking-fund provision valuable. In general, sinking-fund bonds yield less than comparable bond issues that have no sinking-fund provision[1], partly because of the shorter duration. Many sinking funds begin not at the time of issuance of the bond, but after a period of 5 or 10 years. Also, sinking-fund payments do not necessarily retire the bond issue. There can be a "balloon" payment at final maturity.

Some corporations, in purchasing bonds for sinking-fund payment, find that *accumulators* have got there first. Accumulators are institutional or other investors who buy bonds in advance of the corporation going into the market to acquire them for sinking funds. If supply is sufficiently restricted, the corporation will be

---

[1]For empirical support of this phenomenon, see Edward A. Dyl and Michael D. Joehnk, "Sinking Funds and the Cost of Corporate Debt," *Journal of Finance*, 34 (September 1979), 887-93.

able to purchase bonds only by bidding up the price. In this way, the accumulator hopes to sell the bonds at an inflated price, knowing the corporation must purchase them in order to satisfy the sinking-fund requirement. Though perfectly legal, accumulators are not looked upon with great favor by financial managers. Only when the bonds sell at a discount from the sinking-fund call price, of course, does accumulation occur. Otherwise, the corporation will make a cash payment to the trustee, who will purchase bonds at the call price.

The amount of required sinking-fund payment may be either fixed or variable, depending upon the terms in the indenture. Under the fixed arrangement, the corporation retires a fixed face amount of bonds each period. Variable periodic sinking-fund payments are those that are not equal in amount. These payments may be tied to the earnings of the corporation, so that the greater the earnings, the greater the sinking-fund payment. This variability obviously is appealing to a company and its stockholders. In periods of poor earnings, the company is not constrained by the need to make a fixed sinking-fund payment. Bondholders, of course, would prefer fixed payments, because they assure a steady reduction of the debt. A borrower who cannot meet these payments is in clear default under the terms of the indenture. This default enables the trustee to take corrective actions. The amount of sinking-fund payment may vary also with the number of years to final maturity. For some bond issues the amount of sinking-fund payment may increase over the years; for others it may decrease. Overall, variable sinking-fund payments are employed far less often than fixed payments.

Serial bonds All sinking-fund bonds in an issue mature on the same date, although specific bonds are retired before that date. Serial bonds mature periodically until final maturity; a $20 million issue of serial bonds might have $1 million of the bonds maturing each year for 20 years. Giving investors a choice of maturity that best suits their needs, a serial bond issue appeals to a larger group of investors than does an issue in which all the bonds have the same maturity. However, serial bonds are seldom used by corporations. Their principal use is found in the government (federal, provincial and municipal) bond market.

Types Of Debt Instruments

DEBENTURES

The word *debenture* usually applies to the unsecured bonds of a corporation. Investors look to the earning power of the corporation as their security. Because these general credit bonds are not secured by specific property, in the event of liquidation the holder becomes a general creditor. Although the bonds are unsecured, debenture holders are protected by the restrictions imposed in the indenture, particularly the negative pledge clause, which precludes the corporation from pledging its assets to other creditors. This provision safeguards the investor in that the borrower's assets will not be impaired in the future. Because debenture holders must look to the general credit of the borrower to meet principal and interest payments, only well-established and credit-worthy companies are able to issue debentures.

SUBORDINATED DEBENTURES

Subordinated debentures represent debt that ranks behind debt senior to these debentures with respect to the claim on assets. In the event of liquidation, subordinated debenture holders receive settlement only if all senior creditors are paid the full amount owed them. These holders still would rank ahead of preferred and common stockholders in the event of liquidation. The existence of subordinated debentures works to the advantage of senior bondholders, because senior holders are able to assume the claims of the subordinated debenture holders. To illustrate: a corporation is liquidated for $600 000. It had $400 000 in straight debentures outstanding, $400 000 in subordinated debentures outstanding, and $400 000 in obligations owed to general creditors. One might suppose that the straight debenture holders and the general creditors would have an equal and prior claim in liquidation, that each would receive $300 000. The fact is, the straight debenture holders are entitled to the subordinate debenture holders' claims, giving them $800 000 in total claims. As a result, they are entitled to two-thirds of the liquidating value, or $400 000; whereas general creditors are entitled to only one-third or $200 000.

Because subordinated debentures are subordinate to all existing and future debt, senior creditors regard them as equity when evaluating the financial condition of the company. In fact, subordinated debt usually is employed to increase the equity base and support further borrowing. The popularity of the instrument stems in part from the fact that interest payments are deductible for tax purposes, whereas dividends on preferred stock, the closest substitute method of financing, are not.

Because of the nature of the claim, a straight subordinated debenture issue has to provide a yield significantly higher than a regular debenture issue in order to be attractive to investors. Frequently, subordinated debentures are convertible into common stock and therefore may sell at a yield that actually is less than what the company would have to pay on an ordinary debenture. From the standpoint of a creditor, the equity base of the firm is the same whether the issue remains as subordinated debentures or is converted into common stock.

MORTGAGE BONDS

A mortgage bond issue is secured by a lien on specific assets of the corporation—usually fixed assets. The specific property securing the bonds is described in detail in the mortgage, which is the legal document giving the bond-holder a lien on the property. As with other secured lending arrangements, the market value of the collateral should exceed the amount of the bond issue by a reasonable margin of safety. If the corporation defaults in any of the provisions of the bond indenture, the trustee, on behalf of the bondholders, has the power to foreclose. In a foreclosure, the trustee takes over the property and sells it, using the proceeds to pay the bonds. If the proceeds are less than the amount of the issue outstanding, the bondholders become general creditors for the residual amount.

A company may have more than one bond issue secured by the same property. A bond issue may be secured by a *second mortgage* on property already used to secure another bond issue under a *first mortgage*. In the event of foreclosure, the first-mortgage bondholders must be paid the full amount owed to them before there can be any distribution to the second-mortgage bondholders. For the obvious reason of lack of appeal to investors, second-mortgage bonds are seldom used. When they are, investors usually conclude that the financial state of the company is rather desperate.

INCOME BONDS

With an income bond, a company is obliged to pay interest when earnings permit. There may be a cumulative feature in the issue where unpaid interest in a particular year accumulates. If the company does generate earnings, it will have to pay the cumulative interest to the extent that earnings permit. However, the cumulative obligation is usually limited to no more than three years. As should be evident, this type of security offers the investor a rather weak promise of a fixed return. Nevertheless, the income bond debt is still senior to preferred and common stock as well as to any subordinated debt. Interest payments on income bonds are not allowable as a deduction for tax purposes. these payments are treated in the same manner as preferred and common dividends—that is, they are paid only if the firm earns a profit—and are not necessarily expenses incurred in the generation of revenue. This tax situation, among other things, makes income bonds unattractive to companies. They have been used principally in reorganizations.[2]

EQUIPMENT TRUST CERTIFICATES

Although equipment trust financing is a form of lease financing, the certificates themselves represent an intermediate-to long-term fixed-income investment. This method of financing is used by railways to finance the acquisition of rolling stock. Under this method, the railway arranges with a trustee to purchase equipment from a railway equipment manufacturer. The railway signs a contract with the manufacturer for the construction of specific equipment. When the equipment is delivered, equipment trust certificates are sold to investors. The proceeds of this sale, together with the down payment by the railway, are used to pay the manufacturer for the equipment. Title to the equipment is held by the trustee, who in turn leases the equipment to the railway. Lease payments are used by the trustee to pay a fixed return on the certificates outstanding—actually a dividend—and to retire a specified portion of the certificates at regular intervals. On the final lease payment by the railway, the last of the certificates is retired, and title to the equipment passes to the railway.

The duration of the lease varies according to the equipment involved, but 15 years is rather common. Because rolling stock is essential to the operation of a railway and has a ready market value, equipment trust certificates enjoy a very high standing as fixed-income investments. As a result, railways are able to acquire cars and locomotives on extremely favorable financing terms. In addition to railways, airlines use a form of equipment trust certificate to finance jet aircraft.

---

[2]For an extensive analysis of income bonds, see John J. McConnell and Gary G. Schlarbaum, "Returns, Risks, and Pricing of Income Bonds," *Journal of Business*, 54 (January 1981), 33-57.

Though these certificates are usually sold to institutional investors, some issues may be sold to the public.

PROJECT FINANCING

Project financing is a term that is now used to describe a variety of financing arrangements for large individual investment projects. Often a separate legal entity is formed which owns the project. Suppliers of capital then look to the earnings stream of the project for repayment of their loan or for the return of their equity investment. With the energy problems of recent years has come the need to finance large explorations of gas, oil, and coal, as well as to finance tankers, port facilities, refineries, and pipelines. Other projects include aluminum plants, fertilizer plants, and nuclear plants. These projects require huge amounts of capital which are often beyond the financial resources of a single company. Sometimes a consortium of companies is formed to finance the project. Part of the funds come from equity participations by the companies and the rest come from lenders and/or lessors.

If the loan or lease is made on a non-recourse basis, the lender or lessor pays exclusive attention to the size of the equity participation and to the economic feasibility of the project. In other words, the lender or lessor can only look to the project for payout, so the larger the equity cushion and the more confidence that can be placed in the projections, the better the project. Sometimes the project's sponsors guarantee the completion of the project, which simply assures the lender or lessor that the project will be brought to completion. After completion, however, the suppliers of capital are on their own. Repayment must come from the project's earnings, so the economic feasibility of the project continues to be of concern.[3] In still another type of arrangement, each sponsor may guarantee his share of the project's obligation. Under these circumstances, the lender or lessor places emphasis on the credit-worthiness of the sponsors as well as on the economic feasibility of the project.

For the sponsors of the project, there are several types of sharing rules. In a "take-or-pay" type of arrangement, each sponsor agrees to purchase a specific percentage of the output of the project and to pay that percentage of the operating costs of the project plus debt servicing charges. For pipelines, a frequent sharing rule is a "through put" arrangement. Here each sponsor is required to ship through the facility a certain amount, or percentage, of the product. If the total shipped is insufficient to cover the expenses of running the facility, sponsors are assessed additional amounts to cover the shortfall. The amount of assessment is proportional to their participation. The maturity of the loan or lease corresponds to the likely ability of the project to generate cash over time. While the financing need not be long-term, in most cases financing is eight or more years in duration.

It is important to recognize that the term "project financing" conveys nothing more than the financing of a large project. The methods of financing are

---

[3]For further discussion of these two kinds of arrangements see Grover R. Castle, "Project Financing—Guidelines for the Commercial Banker," *Journal of Commercial Bank Lending*, 57 (April 1975), 14-30.

no different from those we have studied. They include debt and lease financing. What is different is the size and complexity of the financing. It is tailored to the needs of the sponsors as well as to the needs of potential suppliers of capital. Tax considerations become very important in tailoring the financing to the best advantage of all parties. In addition, certain environmental restrictions must be observed and these influence the type of financing undertaken. When the project is located on foreign soil, political risks arise. These may be reduced by guarantees from the Export Development Corporation, or from some other government agency. Nonetheless, foreign projects are complicated by different laws and political risks from those which prevail for domestic projects.

As indicated earlier, project financing has become important in recent years with the need to finance very large energy-related investments. Their size necessitates financing separate from the sponsoring company's main line of business. This is particularly true when several sponsors enter into a consortium in order to spread risk. The key then is that the project stands alone in the sense that the sponsoring companies are liable for no more than their equity parcipitations. With the continuing energy needs and the large amounts of capital financing such needs require, project financing is likely to continue to grow in importance in the years to come.

Call Provision

Nearly all corporate bond issues provide for a call feature, which gives the company the option to buy back the bonds at a stated price before their maturity. The call price is usually above the par value of the bond and decreases over time. For example, a bond with 20 years to maturity might be callable at $105 ($1 050 per $1 000 face value bond) the first five years, $104 the next five years, and so on until the final four years, when it is callable at $101. Frequently, the call price in the first year is established at one year's interest above the face value of the bond. If the coupon rate is 8 percent, the initial call price may be $108($1 080 per $1 000 face value).

There are two types of call provision, depending on when they can be exercised. Some issues state that the call privilege can be exercised immediately after issuance; with other issues, the call privilege is deferred for a period. The most widely used deferred call periods are five to ten years. During this deferment period, the investor is protected from a call by the issuer. In recent years, virtually all issues of corporate bonds have involved a deferred call as opposed to an immediate call.

The call provision gives the company flexibility in its financing., If interest rates should decline significantly, it can call the bonds and refinance the issue at a lower interest cost. Thus, the company does not have to wait until the final maturity to refinance. In addition, the provision may be advantageous to the company if it finds any of the protective covenants in the bond indenture to be unduly restrictive. By calling the bonds before maturity, the company can eliminate these restrictions. Of course, if the issue is refinanced with bonds, similar restrictions may be imposed.

VALUE OF CALL PRIVILEGE

Although the call privilege is beneficial to the issuing company, it works to the detriment of investors. If interest rates fall and the bond issue is called, they can invest in other bonds only at a sacrifice in yield to maturity. Consequently, the call privilege usually does not come free to the borrower. Its cost, or value, is measured at the time of issuance by the difference in yield on the callable bond and the yield that would be necessary if the security were noncallable. This value is determined by supply-and-demand forces in the market for callable securities. When interest rates are high and expected to fall, the call feature is likely to have significant value. Investors are unwilling to invest in callable bonds unless such bonds yield more than bonds that are noncallable, all other things being the same. In other words, they must be compensated for assuming the risk that the bonds might be called. On the other hand, borrowers are sometimes willing to pay a premium in yield for the call privilege if they believe that yields will fall and that it will be advantageous to refund the bonds.

When interest rates are low and expected to rise, the call privilege may have a negligible value in that the company might pay the same yield if there were no call privilege. For the privilege to have value, interest rate expectations must be such that there is a possibility that the issue will be called. If interest rates are very low and are not expected to fall further, there is little probability that the bonds will be called. The key factor is that the borrower has to be able to refund the issue at a profit. In order to do so, interest rates have to drop significantly; for the issuer must pay the call price, which is usually at a premium above par value, as well as the flotation costs involved in refinancing. If there is no probability that the borrower can refund the issue at a profit, the call privilege is unlikely to have a value.

Refunding a Bond Issue

Refunding a bond issue before its maturity[4] is possible only if the firm has a call option as a term of the bond indenture. We assume that the decision to refund is based on profitability alone; other considerations, such as removing restrictive protective covenants, are not involved. Under this assumption the refunding is likely to occur only if interest rates have fallen relative to the levels prevailing on the date the bond was issued. The refunding decision can be regarded as a form of capital budgeting; there is an initial cash outlay followed by future interest savings. These savings are represented by the difference between the annual net cash outflow required under the old bonds and the net cash outflow required on the new, or refunding, bonds. Calculating the initial cash outlay is more complex. Consequently, it is best to use an example to illustrate the method of evaluation.

The refunding decision can be complex but we make certain simplifying assumptions in our hypothetical example. Suppose that a company currently has a

---

[4]This section draws upon Oswald D. Bowlin, "The Refunding Decision: Another Special Case in Capital Budgeting," *Journal of Finance*, 21 (March 1966), 55-68. Its development assumes the reader has covered Chapter 13.

$20 million, 16 percent debenture issue outstanding and that the issue still has 20 years to final maturity. These bonds are callable at $112. In addition, assume that interest rates are significantly lower now than at the time of the original offering. As a result, the company can now sell a $20 million issue of 20-year bonds at a coupon rate of 12 percent at par, but would have to pay an underwriting commission of $1 million. Issue costs—legal fees and other issuing expenses—are $225 000. Assume a tax rate of 45 percent and a 30-day period of overlap. The period of overlap is the lag between the time the new bonds are sold and the time the old bonds are called. This lag occurs because most companies wish to have the proceeds from the new issue on hand before they call the old issue. Otherwise, there is a certain amount of risk associated with calling the old issue and being at the mercy of the bond market in raising new funds. During the period of overlap, the company pays interest on both bond issues.

Framework for analysis   With this rather involved background information in mind, we can calculate the initial cash outflow and the future cash benefits. Remember that the underwriting commission and issue costs are allowable as a deduction for tax purposes in the year of the refunding. The net cash outflow at the time of the refunding is as follows:

Cost of calling of bonds (call price $112)	$22 400 000
Net proceeds of new bond issue ($20 000 000 − $1 000 000)	19 000 000
Difference	3 400 000
Expenses	
Interest expense on old bonds during overlap period	266 667
Issue costs of new bonds	225 000
Gross cash outlay	3 891 667
Tax savings on:	
Underwriting commission ($1 000 000 × 0.45)	(450 000)
Issue costs of new bond issue ($225 000 × 0.45)	(101 250)
Interest expense on old bonds during overlap period ($266 667 × 0.45)	(120 000)
Net cash outflow	$ 3 220 417

The annual net cash benefits may be determined by calculating the difference between the net cash outflow required on the old bonds and the net cash outflow required on the new or refunding bonds. The annual cash outflow on the old bonds is

Interest expense 16%	$3 200 000
Tax savings (45% of above)	1 440 000
Annual net cash outflow–old bonds	1 760 000
The annual net cash outflow on the new bonds is:	
Interest expense 12%	2 400 000
Tax savings (45% of above)	1 080 000
Annual net cash outflow–new bonds	1 320 000
Difference between annual net cash outflows	$ 440 000

Discounting   Thus, for an initial net cash outflow of $3 220 417, the company can achieve annual net cash benefits of $440 000 over the next 20 years. Because the net cash benefits occur in the future, they must be discounted back to present value. But what discount rate should be used? Certain authors advocate the use of the cost of capital. However, a refunding operation differs from other investment proposals. Once the new bonds are sold, the net cash benefits are known with certainty. From the standpoint of the company, the refunding operation is essentially a risk-free investment project. The only risk associated with the cash flows is that of the firm defaulting in the payment of principal or interest. Because a premium for default risk is embodied in the market rate of interest the firm pays, the appropriate discount rate is the after-tax cost of borrowing on the refunding bonds. Using this cost (6.6 percent) as our discount factor, the refunding operation would be worthwhile if the net-present value were positive.[5] For our example, the net-present value is $1 589 452 indicating that the refunding operation is worthwhile. The internal rate of return is approximately 12.3 percent, indicating again that the refunding is worthwhile, because the internal rate of return exceeds the required rate of 6.6 percent which is the after-tax cost of the refunding bonds.

OTHER CONSIDERATIONS

We must recognize, however, that just because a refunding operation is found to be worthwhile, it should not necessarily be undertaken right away. If interest rates are declining, and this decline is expected to continue, management may prefer to delay the refunding. At a later date, the refunding bonds can be sold at an even lower rate of interest, making the refunding operation even more worthwhile. The decision concerning timing must be based on expectations of future interest rates.

Finally, two points should be raised with respect to the calculations in our example. First, most firms refund an existing issue with a new bond issue of a longer maturity. In our example, we assumed that the new bond issue has the same maturity as that of the old bond issue. Our analysis needs to be modified slightly when the maturity dates are different. The usual procedure is to consider only the net cash benefits up to the maturity of the old bonds. A second assumption in our example is that neither issue involves sinking-fund bonds or serial bonds. If either issue calls for periodic reduction of the debt, we must adjust our procedure for determining future net cash benefits.

Retractable and Extendible Options

A *rectractable option* gives the bondholder an opportunity to redeem or "recall" a bond at a specified date before maturity. For example, the 7.25 percent Debentures, Series C, due February 1, 1987 and issued by the Bank of Montreal of February 1, 1973, could have been redeemed on August 1, 1979. The bondholders

---

[5]We recall from Chapter 13 that the net-present value is the present value of net cash benefits less the initial cash outflow.

were required to give notice of such intention during the period August 1, 1978-February 1, 1979. Such advance notice gives the issuer time to seek funds to retire the obligation on August 1, 1979. The retractable option will be attractive to the bondholder if interest rates have increased by the retractable option date, as alternative investment opportunities will be offering higher yields at that time. If the investor has to sell the bond at the end of thee years, in the absence of a retractable option, there will be a capital loss. Also, remember that in a period of rising interest rates the company will likely not call the bond. The retractable option enables the bondholder to "shorten" the maturity date. If the required advance notice is not received by the Trustee, the bond automatically matures on February 1, 1987, with interest payments continuing to that date.[6]

An *extendible* option is usually attached to a short-term bond (3 to 5 years maturity) giving bondholders the privilege to exchange the debt for a similar amount of long term debt. The long term bond may have the same coupon rate or a slightly higher coupon rate. For example, the 9 percent Government of Canada bond due October 1, 1980 could be exchanged for the 9.5 percent October 1, 1985 bond. Bondholders had to indicate their intentions to exchange the 9 percent October 1, 1980 for the 9.5 percent October 1, 1985 over the period January 1, 1980-June 30, 1980. If no such notice was received, the former bond matured on October 1, 1980.[7] If interest rates decline over the extendible option period and this trend is expected to continue, it may be attractive for the bondholder to exchange the short term bond for the longer-term bond. However, if interest rates are rising and this rise is expected to continue, the bondholder may wish to let the short term bond mature.

Retractable and extendible options originated in the late 1960s and are increasing in popularity. The past decade was one of rising levels of interest rates and persistently rising inflation. Investor demand for long-term debt securities was declining and new issues of long-term bonds were somewhat difficult to sell. The retractable and extendible options developed as incentives aimed at increasing investor demand for debt securities. The securities offer investors some protection against monetary losses which may result from rising interest rates. For this protection, one might expect these securities to sell at a higher price relative to securities without the retractable options.[8] That is, the yield on a bond with a retractable or an extendible option may be lower than that on a similar bond without these features. Investors will likely accept a lower yield since the retractable or extendible options provide that they will have the opportunity to protect themselves against any monetary loss should interest rates increase. Remember that investors require a call premium in the case of a callable bond. This call premium is viewed as a return for any income loss investors may incur if the bond is called by the issuer. It is therefore logical to expect that investors will agree to a lower yield for a bond with a retractable or an extendible option relative to a bond without these options.

---

[6]Most bondholders exercised the retractable option on this issue.

[7]Bondholders did not exercise the extendible option on this issue.

[8]See Cecil R. Dipchand and J. Robert Hanrahan, "Exit and Exchange Option Values on Government of Canada Retractable Bonds," *Financial Management* (Autumn 1979), 62-71.

Summary

Our concern in this chapter has been with the various features and types of long-term debt. The decision to use long-term debt in the capital structure and the amount of debt to be employed were considered in Chapters 16 and 17. The principal features of debt include the fixed return, the priority of claim on assets, the call privilege, and the method of retirement of the debt. Retractable or extendible options on bonds are new features being added to these securities, primarily for the benefit of bondholders. We saw that periodic reduction of the debt can be accomplished by issuing either sinking-fund bonds or serial bonds.

In financing with long term debt, the company must bargain with investors over the terms of the debt instrument. If the company wishes to include terms that are not beneficial to investors, it must be prepared to pay a higher yield in order to sell the instrument. For example, if debentures are subordinated, investors will demand a higher yield than if the issue involves straight debentures. Another interesting aspect of the bargaining process between the borrower and investors relates to the call privilege. If interest-rate expectations in the market are such that investors think that the issue may be called, the company will have to pay a higher yield for the privilege of being able to call it.

A method was proposed for analyzing the refunding of an existing bond issue before maturity. This method treats the refunding operation as a risk-free capital-budgeting project.

Questions

1. Contrast serial bonds and bonds requiring a sinking fund.
2. In the refunding decision, differential cash flows are discounted at the after-tax cost of debt. Explain why these cash flows are not discounted at the average cost of capital.
3. Explain why a commercial bank loan officer would be particularly concerned with subordinating debt owed to the principal stockholders or officers of a company.
4. Which of the principal features of bond issues would you seek as a borrower and avoid as a lender under the following circumstances?
   (a) A continuing period of inflation
   (b) A period of declining interest rates
   (c) Considerable short-term borrowing projected in the near future
   (d) Cash inflows exceeding cash outflows for the foreseeable future.
5. Why would a corporation ever issue bonds that were immediately callable if the interest rate were higher than that for a deferred callable bond?
6. In issuing long-term debt, which types of instruments would be most used by railroads? By public utilities? By industry firms?
7. Why would you expect very long-term bonds (30-50 years) to be *unsecured*? If the earning power of a secured bond's collateral were in doubt, would the collateral have any value to a bondholder?
8. Why do callable bonds typically have a higher yield to maturity than noncallable bonds holding all other things constant? Is the yield differential likely to be constant over time? If not, why not?

9. There are two ways in which sinking-fund payments may be used by the trustee. What are the benefits and drawbacks of each to the bondholders and the company?

Problems with Solutions

1. In January 1984 a company was considering the possibility of refunding $2 million of callable bonds issued in March 1981, that mature in 1999. The new bonds could be issued at 12 percent at $100 per bond. The company would net $97 after payment of underwriting expenses associated with the issue. The 1981 bond has a 14 percent coupon rate and is callable at 111. There would be a two month period during which the company would be paying interest on both issues. Other expenses (excluding underwriting) associated with the issue amounted to $21 000. The company could invest excess funds without risk at 9 percent. The tax rate was 50 percent. Should the issue be refunded?

Net outlay:	Before tax	After tax
Call premium (0.11 × $2 000 000)	$220 000	$220 000
Overlap period interest cost ($2 000 000 × 1/6 × 0.14)	46 667	23 334
Other expenses	21 000	10 500
Overlap interest earned ($2 000 000 × 1/6 × 0.09)	(30 000)	(15 000)
Underwriting expense	60 000	30 000
		$268 834
Savings:		
Old interest ($2 000 000 × 0.14)	280 000	140 000
New interest ($2 000 000 × 0.12)	240 000	120 000
		$ 20 000

The discount rate is the after-tax cost of borrowing or 0.12 (1 − 0.5) = 0.06.
The present value factor of 6 percent for 15 years (the remaining life of the old issue) is 9.7122.
The present value of the interest savings is $ 20 000 × 9.7122 = $194 244.
The issue should not be refunded in January 1984.

Problems

1. The Hirsch Corporation Ltd. is in bankruptcy. Mortgaged assets have been sold for $5 million and other assets have yielded $10 million. Hirsch has $10 million in mortgage bonds. $5 million in subordinated (to the mortgage bonds) debentures, $15 million owed to general creditors, and $10 million par value of common stock. How would distribution in bankruptcy be made?

2. Five years ago, Stavropoulos International Ltd. issued $50 million of 10 percent, 25-year debentures at a price of $990 per bond. The call price was originally $1 100 per bond the first year after issuance, and this price declined by $10 each subsequent year. Stavropoulos now is calling the bonds in order to refund them at a lower interest rate.

(a) Ignoring taxes, what is the bondholder's return on investment for the five years? (Assume that interest is paid once a year and that the investor owns one bond.)

(b) If the bondholder now can invest $1 000 in a 20-year bond of equivalent risk that provides 8 percent interest, what is the overall return over the 25-year holding period? How does this compare with the return on the Stavropoulos bonds had they not been called? (Assume again that interest is paid once a year. Both rates of return can be approximated using the present-value tables at the end of the book.)

3. In January 1980 Roberts Company Ltd. floated a $20 million bond issue with a 15 percent coupon rate and maturing January 2010. Currently, the issue is callable at $110. Investment dealers suggest refunding the issue with a $20 million, 12 percent bond to be issued in January 1985 with a 25-year maturity. The new issue will net the firm $19.5 million from the underwriters and there will be other issue costs of $150 000 payable by the firm. There would be a 60-day overlap between the issue of new bonds and the calling of the old bonds. Excess short-term cash can be invested in 60-day Treasury bills expected to yield 10 percent annually. The firm's tax rate is 50 percent.

(a) Compute the cash outlay required by the firm to refund the bond issue.

(b) Should the issue be refunded?

4. Five years ago, Cawsey Inc. Ltd. issued a $30 million of 10 percent, 25-year debenture at par. The terms of the issue provided bondholders the option to "redeem" the issue at the end of year 5; otherwise, the issue will mature at the end of year 25. Since the issue date of the debt interest rates have been rising and now, a 20-year debenture (of similar risk) would sell to yield 12 percent. Consequently, the appropriate notice was given to the firm to redeem the obligation at the end of year 5.

(a) Ignoring taxes, what is the bondholder's return on the Cawsey bond for the five years? (Assume that interest is paid once a year and that the investor owns one bond.)

(b) The bondholder can invest $1 000 in a 20-year bond of equivalent risk that provides 12 percent interest commencing year 6. What is the overall return over the 25-year holding period? How does this compare with the Cawsey bond had it not been redeemed? (Assume again that interest is paid once a year.)

5. Northern Manitoba Public Service Company Ltd. is considering refunding its preferred stock. The dividend rate on this stock is $6 and it has a par value of $50 a share. The call price is $52 a share, and 500 000 shares are outstanding. Georgia Petrenko, vice-president finance, feels the company can issue new preferred stock in the current market at an interest rate of 11 percent. With this rate, the new issue could be sold at par; the total par value of the issue would be $25 million. Flotation costs of $780 000 are tax deductible, but the call premium is not tax deductible; the company's marginal tax rate is 50 percent. A 90-day period of overlap is expected between the time the new preferred stock is issued and the time the old preferred stock is retired. Should the company refund its preferred stock? (Preferred stock dividends are assumed to be paid forever unless the issue is called. The problem may be set up in the same way as a bond refunding, except for the qualifications noted above.)

6. The Lemand Corporation Ltd. has $8 million of 10 percent mortgage bonds outstanding under an open-end indenture. The indenture allows additional bonds to be issued as long as all of the following conditions are met.

(a) Pretax interest coverage [(income before taxes + bond interest)/bond interest] remains greater than 4.

(b) Net depreciated value of mortgaged assets remains twice the amount of mortgage debt.

(c) Debt/equity ratio remains below 0.5.

The Lemand Corporation has net income of $2 million and a 50 percent tax rate, $40 million in equity, and $30 million in depreciated assets, covered by the mortgage. Assuming that 50 percent of the proceeds of a new issue would be added to the base of mortgaged assets and that the company has no sinking-fund payments until next year, how much more 10 percent debt could be sold?

7. Crakow Machine Company Ltd. wishes to borrow $10 million for 10 years. It can issue either a noncallable bond at 11.40 percent interest or a bond callable at the end of 5 years for 12 percent. For simplicity, we assume that the bond will be called only at the end of year 5. The interest rate that is likely to prevail 5 years hence for a 5-year straight bond can be described by the following probability distribution:

Interest rate	9%	10%	11%	12%	13%
Probability	0.1	0.2	0.4	0.2	0.1

Issuing and other costs involved in selling a bond issue five years hence will total $200 000. The call price is assumed to be par.

(a) What is the total absolute amount of interest payments for the noncallable issue over the ten years? (Do not discount.) What is the expected value of total interest payments and other costs if the company issues callable bonds? (Assume the company calls the bonds and issues new ones only if there is a savings in interest costs after issuing expenses.) On the basis of total costs, should the company issue noncallable or callable bonds?

(b) What would be the outcome if the probability distribution of interest rates 5 years hence were the following?

Interest rate	7%	9%	11%	13%	15%
Probability	0.2	0.2	0.2	0.2	0.2

Assume all other conditions stay the same.

8. Research project: Obtain copies of several bond indentures. Pay particular attention to the restrictive covenants concerning things such as dividends, working capital, additional debt, and nature of the business. Try to relate the cost of debt to the firm to the relative restrictiveness of these provisions. Does management pay extra for discretion? If it does, can these covenants truly be said to be nonquantifiable? How would you go about finding a measure of the degree of restriction so that tradeoffs with interest could be made?

Selected References

AGMON, T., A. R. OFER, and A. TAMIR, "Variable Rate Debt Instruments and Corporate Debt Policy," *Journal of Finance*, 36 (March 1981), 113-26.

ANG, JAMES S., "The Two Faces of Bond Refunding," *Journal of Finance*, 30 (June 1975), 869-74.

BOARDMAN, CALVIN M. and RICHARD M. McENALLY, "Factors Affecting Seasoned Corporate Bond Prices", *Journal of Financial and Quantitative Analysis*, June 1981, 207-226.

BOWLIN, OSWALD D., "The Refunding Decision: Another Special Case in Capital Budgeting," *Journal of Finance*, 21 (March 1966), 55-68.

CALLAHAN, JOHN R. and JOHN S. McCALLUM, "The Sinking Fund Decision: Buy Forward or Wait," *Cost and Management*, (Jan.-Feb. 1978), 36-39.

DIPCHAND, CECIL R. and J. ROBERT HANRAHAN, "Exit and Exchange Option Values on Government of Canada 'Retractable Bonds'," *Financial Management* (Autumn 1979), 62-71.

DYL, EDWARD A., and WILLIAM J. SAWAYA, "The Bond Issue Size Decision Revisited," *Financial Management*, 8 (Winter 1979), 60-67.

DYL, EDWARD A., and MICHAEL D. JOEHNK, "Sinking Funds and the Cost of Corporate Debt," *Journal of Finance*, 34 (September 1978), 19-20.

EMERY, DOUGLAS R., "Overlapping Interest in Bond Refunding: A Reconsideration," *Financial Management*, 7 (Summer 1978), 19-20.

EVERETT, EDWARD, "Subordinated Debt—Nature and Enforcement," *Business Lawyer*, 20 (July 1965), 953-87.

FINNERTY, JOHN D., "Evaluating the Economics of Refunding High-Coupon Sinking-Fund Debt", *Financial Management*, Spring 1983, 5-10.

HARRIS, ROBERT S., "The Refunding of Discounted Debt: An Adjusted Present Value Analysis," *Financial Management*, 9 (Winter, 1980), 7-12.

JEN, FRANK C., and JAMES E. WERT, "The Deferred Call Provision and Corporate Bond Yields," *Journal of Financial and Quantitative Analysis*, 3 (June 1968), 157-69.

KALOTAY, A. J., "On the Advanced Refunding of Discounted Debt," *Financial Management*, 7 (Summer 1978), 14-18.

_____; "Sinking Funds and the Realized Cost of Debt," *Financial Management*, 11 (Spring 1982), 43-54.

KALOTAY, ANDREW J., "On the Management of Sinking Funds," *Financial Management*, 10 (Summer 1981), 34-40.

KIRZNER, ERIC and GRANT RUSSELL, "The Refunding of Fixed Financial Obligations", *Cost and Management*, July-August 1982, 27-30.

LABER, GENE, "Repurchases of Bonds through Tender Offers: Implications for Shareholder Wealth," *Financial Management*, 7 (Summer 1978), 7-13.

LAWLOR, WILLIAM R. "Income Debentures and Term-Preferred Shares," *Canadian Tax Journal* (Mar.-Apr. 1978), 200-16.

LOGUE, DENNIS E., and RICHARD J. ROGALSKI, "Does It Pay to Shop for Your Bond Underwriter?" *Harvard Business Review*, 57 (July-August 1979), 111-17.

MARSHALL, WILLIAM J., and JESS B. YAWITZ, "Optimal Terms of the Call Provision on a Corporate Bond," *Journal of Financial Research*, 2 (Fall 1980), 203-11.

McCONNELL, JOHN J., and GARY G. SCHLARBAUM, "Returns, Risks, and Pricing of Income Bonds, 1956-76," *Journal of Business*, 54 (January 1981), 33-57.

McENALLY, RICHARD W., and MICHAEL L. RICE, "Hedging Possibilities in the Flotation of Debt Securities," *Financial Management*, 8 (Winter 1979), 12-18.

NEVITT, PETER K., *Project Financing*, 2nd ed. San Francisco: Advanced Management Research, 1979.

OFER, AHARON R., and ROBERT A. TAGGART, JR., "Bond Refunding: A Clarifying Analysis," *Journal of Finance*, 32 (March 1977), 21-30.

PINCHES, GEORGE E., and KENT A. MINGO, "The Role of Subordinate and Industrial Bond Ratings," *Journal of Finance*, 30 (March 1975), 201-6.

RIENER, KENNETH D., "Financial Structure Effects on Bond Refunding," *Financial Management*, 9 (Summer 1980), 18-23.

SMITH, CLIFFORD W., JR., and JEROLD B. WARNER, "On Financial Contracting; An Analysis of Bond Covenants," *Journal of Financial Economics*, 7 (June 1979), 117-61.

VAN HORNE, JAMES C., "Called Bonds: How Does the Investor Fare?" *Journal of Portfolio Management*, 6 (Summer 1980), 58-61.

_____, *Financial Market Rates and Flows*, Englewood Cliffs, N.J.: Prentice-Hall, 1978, Chapters 6 and 7.

_____, "Implied Fixed Costs in Long-Term Debt Issues," *Journal of Financial and Quantitative Analysis*, 8 (December 1973).

WEINSTEIN, MARK "The Systematic Risk of Corporate Bonds", *Journal of Financial and Quantitative Analysis*, September 1981, 257-278.

YAWITZ, JESS B., and JAMES A. ANDERSON, "The Effect of Bond Refunding on Shareholder Wealth," *Journal of Finance*, 32 (December 1977), 1738-46.

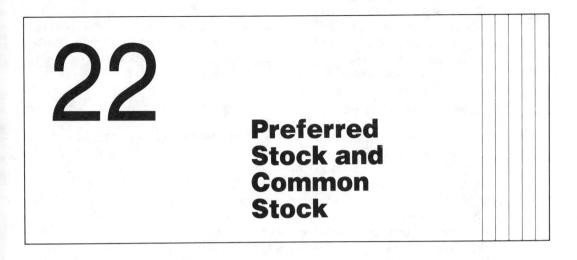

22

Preferred Stock and Common Stock

In this chapter we take up two forms of equity financing—preferred stock and common stock. Although they fall under the same general heading, their differences are far more pronounced than their similarities. From the standpoint of the ultimate owners of the corporation—namely, the common stockholders—preferred stock is a form of leverage to be evaluated much like debt. Because the theory behind the use of these securities was discussed in Chapter 18, this chapter is devoted primarily to examining their features.

Preferred Stock and its Features

Preferred stock is a hybrid form of financing, combining features of debt and common stock. In the event of liquidation, a preferred stockholder's claim on assets come after that of creditors but before that of the common stockholders. Usually, this claim is restricted to the par value of the stock. If the par value of a share of preferred stock is $100, the investor will be entitled to a maximum of $100 in settlement of the principal amount. Although preferred stock carries a stipulated dividend, the actual payment of a dividend is a discretionary rather than a fixed obligation of the company. The omission of a dividend will not result in a default of the obligation or insolvency of the company. The board of directors has full power to omit a preferred-stock dividend if it so chooses.

The maximum return to preferred stockholders usually is limited to the specified dividend, and these stockholders ordinarily do not share in the residual earnings of the company. Thus, if you own 100 shares of $10\frac{1}{2}$ percent preferred stock, $100 par value, the maximum return you can expect in any one year is

$1 050; and this return is at the discretion of the board of directors. The corporation cannot deduct this dividend on its tax return; this fact is the principal shortcoming of preferred stock as a means of financing. In view of the fact that interest payments on debt are deductible for tax purposes, the company that treats a preferred-stock dividend as a fixed obligation finds the explicit cost to be rather high.

CUMULATIVE FEATURE

Almost all preferred stocks have a cumulative feature, providing for unpaid dividends in any one year to be carried forward. Before the company can pay a dividend on its common stock, it must pay the dividends *in arrears* on its preferred stock. A board of directors may omit the preferred-stock dividend on a company's 8 percent cumulative preferred stock for 3 consecutive years. If the stock has a $100 par value, the company is $24 per share in arrears on its preferred stock. Before it can pay a dividend to its common stockholders, it must pay preferred stockholders $24 for each share of preferred stock held. It should be emphasized that just because preferred-stock dividends are in arrears, there is no guarantee that they ever will be paid. If the corporation has no intention of paying a common-stock dividend, there is no need to clear up the arrearage on the preferred. The preferred-stock dividend typically is omitted for lack of earnings, but the corporation does not have to pay a dividend if earnings are restored.

If the preferred-stock dividends are in arrears, and the company wishes to pay a common-stock dividend, it may choose not to clear up the arrearage but to make an exchange offering to preferred stockholders. Say that the dividend arrearages on an issue of $100 par value preferred stock are $56 and that the market price of the stock is $38 a share. The company might offer preferred stockholders common stock in the company valued at $90, for each share of preferred stock held. Although theoretically the preferred stockholders are asked to give up $156 ($100 par value plus $56 dividend arrearages), the exchange offering promises them $90 relative to a current preferred-stock market value of only $38 per share. In order to eliminate the preferred stock, the company must obtain the approval of a required percentage of the stock outstanding, often two-thirds. Consequently, it probably will make its exchange offering contingent upon obtaining the required acceptance.

If a preferred stock is noncumulative, dividends not paid in one year do not carry forward. As a result, a company can pay a common-stock dividend without regard to any dividends it did not pay in the past on its preferred stock. From the standpoint of an investor, a noncumulative preferred stock is little more than an income bond. In fact, there is somewhat less uncertainty with income bonds, for the conditions under which interest will be paid are specified clearly, and bondholders have a prior claim on assets. Because of the obvious disadvantage to investors, noncumulative preferred-stock issues are rare, although they may be used in reorganizations.

PARTICIPATING FEATURE

A participating feature allows preferred stockholders to participate in the residual earnings of the corporation according to some specified formula. The preferred stockholder might be entitled to share equally with common stockholders in any common-stock dividend beyond a certain amount. Suppose that a 6 percent preferred stock ($100 par value) were participating, so that the holders were entitled to share equally in any common stock dividendss in excess of $6 a share. If the common-stock dividend is $7, the preferred stockholder will receive $1 in extra dividends for each share of stock owned. The formula for participation can vary greatly. The essential feature is that preferred stockholders have a prior claim in income and an opportunity for additional return if the dividends to common stockholders exceed a certain amount. Unfortunately for the investor, practically all preferred stock issued are nonparticipating, with the maximum return limited to the specified dividend rate.

VOTING POWER

Because of their prior claim on assets and income, preferred stockholders normally are not given a voice in management unless the company is unable to pay preferred-stock dividends during a specified period. Arrearages on four quarterly dividend payments might constitute a default; under such circumstances, preferred stockholders as a class would be entitled to elect a specified number of directors. Usually, the number of directors is rather small in relation to the total; and, by the time the preferred stockholders obtain a voice in management, the company probably is in considerable financial difficulty. Consequently, the voting power that preferred stockholders are granted may be virtually meaningless.

Depending upon the agreement between the preferred stockholders and the company, they may obtain voting power under other conditions as well. The company may default under restrictions in the agreement that are similar to those found in a loan agreement or a bond debenture. One of the more frequently imposed restrictions is that dividends on common stock are prohibited if the company does not satisfy certain financial ratios. We note, however, that default under any of the provisions of the agreement between the corporation and its preferred stockholders does not result in the obligation's becoming immediately payable, as does default under a loan agreement or bond debenture. The preferred stockholders merely are given a voice in management and assurance that common-stock dividends will not be paid during the period of default. Thus, preferred stockholders do not have nearly the same legal power in default as do debtholders.

RETIREMENT OF PREFERRED STOCK

The fact that preferred stock, like common stock, has no maturity does not mean that most preferred stock issues are regarded as a means of perpetual financing, because provision for retirement of the stock invariably is made.

Call feature Almost all preferred stock issues have a stated call price, which is above the original issuance price and may decrease over time. Like the call feature on bonds, the call feature on preferred stock affords the company flexibility. Because the market price of a straight preferred stock tends to fluctuate in keeping with interest rate cycles, the value of the preferred stock call feature is determined by the same considerations as is the call feature for bonds, which we discussed in Chapter 21. Long term debt, unlike preferred stock, has a final maturity that assures the eventual retirement of the issue. Without a call feature on preferred stock, the corporation would be able to retire the issue only by the more expensive and less efficient methods of purchasing the stock in the open market, inviting tenders of the stock from preferred stockholders at a price above the market price, or offering the preferred stockholders another security in its place.

Sinking fund   Many preferred-stock issues provide for a sinking fund, which partially assures an orderly retirement of the stock. Like bond issues, a preferred-stock sinking fund is advantageous to investors because the retirement process exerts upward pressure on the market price of the remaining shares. Also, the coverage ratio on the preferred stock dividend is improved as the number of shares outstanding is reduced. Overall, sinking funds are used much less with preferred stock than with bonds.

Retractable option   Some preferred stocks may have a retractable option similar to that discussed for bond issues in Chapter 21. With this option, the preferred shareholder may cash in the security on the date specified in the issuing prospectus. Of course, such an action will be taken only if future dividend yields on comparable shares are expected to be higher than that on the retractable preferred. The exercise of the retractable option by all preferred shareholders leads to the retirement of a preferred stock.

Use in Financing

Preferred stock is not used extensively in financing; only public utilities employ it with any degree of regularity. One of the principal drawbacks to its use is that the preferred dividend is not tax-deductible. With a 46 percent tax rate, the explicit cost of preferred stock is about twice that of bonds. As an investment, however, preferred shares may be more attractive to corporate investors than bonds because the dividends received are not subject to taxation. Individual investors receive a dividends tax credit (which is discussed in Chapter 2). As a result, after-tax yields on preferred shares are usually greater that those on comparable bonds. Many preferred-stock issues sell at a lower before-tax yields than do bonds of the same company, despite their lower priority of claim.

The advantage of preferred stock financing is its flexibility as a financing arrangement. The dividend is not a legal obligation on the part of the corporation issuing the securities; if earnings turn bad and the financial condition of the company deteriorates, the dividend can be omitted. With debt financing, interest must be paid regardless of whether earnings are good or bad. To be sure, companies that are accustomed to paying dividends on their common stock certainly regard the preferred dividend as a fixed obligation. Nevertheless, under dire circumstances, a company that omits its common-stock dividend also can omit its preferred stock dividend.

Another advantage of a straight preferred stock issue is its lack of final maturity; in essence, it is a perpetual loan. In addition, the majority of preferred-stock issues do not require sinking-fund payments. Thus, a preferred-stock issue gives a company flexibility by allowing it to avoid having to make principal payments or plan for refinancing. Moreover, from the standpoint of creditors, preferred stock adds to the equity base of the company and thereby strengthens its financial condition. The additional equity base enhances the ability of the company to borrow in the future. Although the explicit cost of preferred stock is considerably higher than that of bonds, the implied benefits discussed above may offset this cost. In addition, the implicit cost of preferred stock financing, from the standpoint of the possibility of investors penalizing the price/earnings ratio of the common stock, may be somewhat less than that of debt financing.[1] To the extent that investors are apprehensive over legal bankruptcy, they would regard debt as a riskier form of leverage. Unlike creditors, preferred stockholders cannot force a company into legal bankruptcy.

Term-preferred shares Earlier in the discussion we noted that preferred shares have fixed dividends and no maturity. However, it is interesting to note that in the later part of the 1970s, the financial community developed what is known as a term-preferred share. This security is similar to the preferred share discussed earlier except that it has a stated maturity (usually short-to intermediate-term), that the dividend may be floating rather than fixed, and that the investor may have the right to call for redemption at any given time. These exceptions are generally different from the traditional concept of preferred shares. The introduction of term-preferreds may be attributed largely to the tax environment. A firm that has a significant tax-loss carry-forward to write-off may refund debt with term-preferreds. The lower interest charged to income increases before-tax income and enables the firm to write-off its tax-loss carry-forward within the stipulated five years. On the other hand, the preferred dividends received by corporate investors were not taxed before 1979. Thus, both parties—the borrowing firm and the investor—benefited. As another example, a non-taxable entity may issue term-preferreds at an attractive dividend rate to a corporate investor with a higher tax rate. The latter would have a lower effective tax rate if the dividends were tax-free, as they were before 1979.

While there are other and more complex reasons for the use of term-preferreds[2], institutions, particularly banks, invested heavily in term-preferreds, thus affecting taxation revenue. Therefore, in 1979, Revenue Canada ruled that dividends from term-preferreds with maturities less than ten years are not tax-free to financial institutions. Financial institutions receiving dividends from term-preferreds have to declare the full amount of the dividends as income and be taxed at their respective marginal tax rates. With this ruling, the use of term-preferreds has been reduced considerably. Finally, it is argued that term-preferreds are really debt instruments, and the tax ruling implicity takes this position.

---

[1]Gordon Donaldson, in "In Defense of Preferred Stock." *Harvard Business Review*, 40 (Jul.-Aug. 1962), 123-36, rigorously defends the use of preferred stock as a means of financing under certain circumstances. He argues that when a company has utilized its debt capacity it may be able to finance further with preferred stock because the preferred stock capacity of a company is distinct from its debt capacity.

[2]For further details, see William Lawlor, "Income Debentures and Term-Preferred Shares," *Canadian Tax Journal* (Mar.-Apr. 1978), 200-16.

Common Stock and Its Features

The common shareholders of a company are its residual owners; collectively, they own the company and assume the ultimate risk associated with ownership. Their liability, however, is restricted to the amount of their investment. In the event of liquidation, these shareholders have a residual claim on the assets of the company after the claims of all creditors and preferred shareholders have been settled in full. Common stock, like preferred stock, has no maturity date and shareholders can liquidate their investment by selling their shares in the secondary market.

AUTHORIZED, ISSUED, AND OUTSTANDING SHARES

The corporate charter of a company specifies the number of *authorized* shares of common stock, the maximum that the company can issue without amending its charter. Although amending the charter is not a difficult procedure, it does require the approval of existing shareholders, which takes time. For this reason, a company usually likes to have a certain number of shares that are authorized but unissued. These unissued shares allow flexibility in granting stock options, pursuing mergers, and splitting the stock. When authorized shares of common stock are sold, they become *issued* stock. *Outstanding* stock is the number of shares issued that actually are held by the public. A company incorporated in Ontario or British Columbia, for example, can buy back part of its issued stock and hold it as *Treasury* stock. A federally incorporated company may repurchase its shares and retire them.

PAR VALUE

A share of common stock can be authorized either with or without par value. The par value of a stock is merely a stated figure in the corporate charter and is of little economic significance. Only companies incorporated in New Brunswick and mining companies incorporated in Ontario, Quebec, and the Western provinces are permitted to issue stock at a price below par value. Consequently, the par values of most stocks are set at fairly low figures relative to their market values. Suppose a company sold 10 000 share of new common stock at $45 a share and the par value of the stock was $5 per share. The equity portion of the balance sheet would be

Common stock ($5 par value)	$ 50 000
Contributed capital	400 000
Shareholders' equity	$450 000

The difference between the issuing price and the par value is reflected as contributed surplus.

Under the Canada Business Corporations Act, a company can issue no-par value stock and the stock is carried on the books at its original sale price. There is no contributed capital in these instances. Since the par value is of little significance, the notion of par value securities is expected to gradually disappear.

BOOK VALUE AND LIQUIDATING VALUE

The book value of a share of stock is the net worth of a company less the par value of preferred shares outstanding, divided by the number of shares outstanding. Suppose the equity portion of the balance sheet of a company is as follows:

Preferred stock ($100 par value)	$10 000 000
Common stock ($5 par value)	5 000 000
Contributed capital	10 000 000
Retained earnings	16 000 000
Shareholders' equity	$41 000 000

The book value of a share of common stock is $31 million/1 million shares or $31 per share. Theoretically, the book value of a share of stock should correspond to the liquidating value of the company, but this situation seldom occurs. Only if the assets of a company can be liquidated for the book values shown on the financial statement will the book value per share correspond to the liquidating value per share. Even then, if liquidating costs are high, the liquidating value per share will be less than the book value per share. For most companies, the liquidating value per share is less than the book value per share because many of the assets can be liquidated only at distress prices. However, some companies carry certain assets—notably, land and mineral rights—at modest values on their books relative to the market value of the asset. For these companies, the liquidating value per share may be significantly higher than the book value.

MARKET VALUE

Market value per share is the current price at which the share is traded. For listed companies and actively traded over-the-counter shares, market-price quotations are readily available. However, the market for the shares of many companies is thin and inactive, so that market-price information is difficult to obtain. Even when obtainable, the information may reflect only the sale of a few shares of stock and not typify the market value of the firm as a whole. For companies of this sort, care must be taken in interpreting market-price information.

The market value of a share of common stock will usually differ considerably from its book value and its liquidating value. It is a function of the current and expected future dividends of the company and the perceived risk of the stock on the part of investors. Because these factors bear only a partial relationship to the book value and the liquidating value of the company, the market value per share is not tied closely to these values.

LISTING

The shares of a new company are usually traded in the over-the-counter market. In this market, one or more security dealers maintain an inventory of the shares and buy and sell them at the bid-and-ask prices they quote. As a company grows in financial stature, number of shareholders and volume of transactions, it may qualify for listing on a stock exchange. In contrast to the over-the-counter market, an exchange is a closely regulated auction market where buy-and-sell orders are matched. The listing requirements of the Toronto and Montreal Stock Exchanges are more stringent than those of the Vancouver Stock Exchange.[3]

Once a company satisfies the listing requirement of an exchange, it must decide whether or not to list. It may well want its shares to continue trading in the over-the-counter market. In fact, shares of many large companies with heavy volume are traded in the over-the-counter market. One reason often cited for listing is the increased marketability of the stock. If marketability is enhanced, shareholders will gain from the greater liquidity associated with the stock listed on an exchange. Shareholders may also gain from the greater collateral value attractiveness of a listed stock as compared with an over-the-counter one. For the company, there may be a certain amount of prestige associated with being listed on a major stock exchange. For these reasons, many feel that listing on a major exchange improves the market price of the shares.

Rights of Shareholders

RIGHT TO INCOME

Common shareholders are only entitled to share in the earnings of the company if cash dividends are paid. Shareholders prosper from the market value appreciation of their stock, but they are entirely dependent on the board of directors for the declaration of dividends that give them income from the company. Thus, the position of a common shareholder differs markedly from that of a creditor. If the company fails to pay contractual interest and principal repayments, it is liquidated. Shareholders, on the other hand, have no legal recourse against a company for not distributing profits. Only if management, the board of directors, or both, are engaged in fraud may they take their case to court and, possibly, force the company to pay dividends. With stock options, the goals of management are likely to approximate those of shareholders.

VOTING POWER

Inasmuch as the common shareholders of a company are its owners, they are entitled to elect a board of directors. In a large company, shareholders usually exercise only indirect control through the board of directors they elect. The board, in turn, selects the management; and management controls the actual operations of the company. With a proprietorship, partnership, or small company, the owners usually control the operations of the business directly. With a large company, however, there may be times when the goals of management differ from those of the

---

[3]For a discussion of listing requirements, see *The Canadian Securities Course* (Toronto: The Canadian Securities Institute, 1973), 230-40, or P. C. McQuillan, *Going Public in Canada: The Facts and the Fads* (Toronto: The Canadian Institute of Chartered Accountants, 1971).

common shareholders. The only way a shareholder can reach management is through the board of directors. Because common shareholders are often widely dispersed geographically and, therefore, disorganized, management can often exercise effective control of a large company even if it controls only a small percentage of the shares outstanding. By proposing a slate of directors that is favourable to its own interests, management is able to maintain control. Outside shareholders, however, do have the right to expect that the directors will administer the affairs of the company properly on their behalf. If the directors act in a manner that results in their personal gain, shareholders can sue to recover any amount they may be entitled to.

PROXIES

Each common shareholder is entitled to one vote for each share of stock he or she owns. Because most shareholders do not attend the annual meeting, they may vote by proxy. A proxy is simply a form by which the shareholder assigns his or her right to vote to another person. Federal and provincial Securities Acts regulate the solicitation of proxies and also require companies to disseminate information to their shareholders through proxy mailings. Prior to the annual meeting, management solicits proxies from shareholders to vote for the recommended slate of directors and for any other proposals requiring shareholder approval. If shareholders are satisfied with the company, they generally sign the proxy in favour of management, giving written authorization to management to vote their shares. If a shareholder does not vote his or her shares, the number of shares voted at the meeting and the number needed to constitute a majority are lower. Because of the proxy system and the fact that management can mail information to shareholders at the company's expense, management has a distinct advantage in the voting process. As a result, it can usually perpetuate existing practices if it so chooses.

However, outsiders can seize control of a company through a proxy contest. Obviously, outsiders would not attempt a takeover if management controlled a large percentage of shares outstanding. The outside group attempts to persuade shareholders to sign proxies giving them the authority to vote the shareholders' share. If this group is successful, the incumbent management can be replaced.

VOTING PROCEDURES

Depending on the corporate charter, the board of directors is elected either under a *majority voting system* or under a *cumulative voting system*. Under the former system, each shareholder has one vote for each share of stock owned, and must vote for each director position that is open. For example, a shareholder who owns 100 shares, will be able to cast 100 votes for each director position open. Because each person seeking a position on the board must win a majority of the total votes cast for that position, the system precludes minority interests from electing directors. If management can obtain proxies for over 50 percent of the shares voted, it can select the entire board.

Under a cumulative voting system, shareholders can accumulate votes and cast them for less than the total number of directors being elected. The total number of votes is the number of shares owned times the number of directors being elected. For example, if shareholder owns 100 shares, and 12 directors are to be elected, he or she will be entitled to cast 1 200 votes. He or she can cast these votes for whatever number of directors he or she chooses, the maximum being 1 200 votes for one director.

A cumulative voting system, in contrast to the majority system, permits minority interests to elect a certain number of directors. The minimum number of shares necessary to elect a specific number of directors is determined by:

$$\frac{\text{Total shares outstanding times specific number of directors sought}}{\text{Total number of directors to be elected plus one}} + 1 \qquad \textbf{(22-1)}$$

For example, if there are 3 million shares outstanding, the total number of directors to be elected is 14, and if a minority group wishes to elect two directors, it will need at least the following number of shares:

$$\frac{3\ 000\ 000 \times 2}{14 + 1} + 1 = 400\ 001$$

As is evident, cumulative voting gives minority interests a better opportunity to be represented on the board of directors of a company. Although the system is more democratic, there is no statutory requirement that directors be elected in this way. Even with cumulative voting, however, management can sometimes preclude minority interests from obtaining a seat on the board of directors by reducing the number of directors. For example, suppose the minority group above actually owns 400 001 shares. With 14 directors to be elected, the group can elect two directors. however, if the board is reduced to six members, the minority group can elect no directors because the minimum number of shares needed to elect a single director is

$$\frac{3\ 000\ 000 \times 1}{6 + 1} + 1 = 428\ 572$$

Another method used to thwart a minority interest from obtaining representation is to stagger the terms of the directors so that only several are elected each year. For example, if a firm had 12 directors and the term was four years, only three would be elected each year. As a result, a minority group would need considerably more shares voted in its favour to elect a director than it would if all 12 directors came up for election each year.

PREEMPTIVE RIGHT

A preemptive right (see Chapter 19) entitles common shareholders to maintain proportional ownership in the company. They are given the first opportunity to purchase, on a pro rata basis, any new shares being offered or any new securities that are convertible into common.

RIGHT TO EXAMINE BOOKS

A shareholder is legally entitled to inspect the books and records of a company. However, this access is limited, for most companies feel that the audited financial statement is sufficient to satisfy the requirement. To obtain more specific information, the shareholder may have to take the case to court in order to prove the necessity of obtaining this information. Shareholders are also entitled to a list of the shareholders of the company and their addresses. This list is vital to an insurgent group in a proxy contest. However, management may engage in delaying tactics by contending that the shareholder list will be misused. In these situations, the shareholder may have to go to court and demonstrate sufficient cause for obtaining the information. On a court order, management is required to provide the list.

Classified Common Stock

A company may have more than one class of common stock. Its common stock can be classified according to the claim on income and voting power. Class A common of a company may have no voting privilege but may be entitled to a prior claim to dividends, while the Class B common has voting rights but a lower claim to dividends. Usually, the promoters of a corporation and its management will hold the Class B common stock, whereas the Class A Common is sold to the public. Actually, the Class A shares in this example are no more than a form of preferred stock. Usually, Class A stock is given some voting power but not as much as the Class B stock per dollar of investment,

Suppose that the Class A and Class B common shareholders of a company are entitled to one vote per share, but that the Class A stock is issued at an initial price of $20 per share. If $2 million is raised in the original offering through the issuance of 80 000 shares of Class A common for $1.6 million and 200 000 shares of Class B common for $400 000, the Class B stockholders will have over twice as many votes as the Class A holders have, although their original investment is only one-quarter as large. Thus, the Class B holders have effective control of the company. Indeed,this is the purpose of classified stock.

For this control, the Class B holders must be willing to give up something in order to make Class A stock attractive to investors. Usually, they take a lower claim both to dividends and assets. An appropriate balance must be struck between voting power and the claim to dividends and assets if the company is to bargain effectively for Class A equity funds. Sometimes, the Class B common simply is given to the promoters of a corporation without any cash investment on their part.

FORD MOTOR COMPANY

Perhaps the most famous example of a company with classified common stock is the Ford Motor Company. On December 31, 1980, the issued shares of capital stock for the company were

	Shares Issued
Class B	13 935 719
Common stock	106 592 461
	120 528 180

The Class B common is owned by members of the Ford family and constitutes 40 percent of the total voting power of the company. The common is held by the general public and has 60 percent of the voting power of the company. The common stock was owned originally by the Ford Foundation but was later sold to the general public. Those who own it are entitled to one vote for each share they own. A holder of Class B common is entitled to that number of votes per share that will make the voting power of the Class B common 40 percent of the total voting power of the corporation. At December 31, 1980, this number was

$$\frac{106\ 592\ 461}{13\ 935\ 719} \times \frac{0.40}{0.60} = 5.1 \text{ votes}$$

Each shareholder of Class B stock was entitled to 5.1 votes per share at the end of 1980. Thus, members of the Ford family retain substantial voting power in the company, even though they hold far fewer shares than does the general public. All shares of common and Class B stock share equally in dividends and equally in their claim on assets in the event of liquidation.[4] The use of classified capital stock in this case affects only the voting power.

Summary

Preferred stock is a hybrid form of security having characteristics both of debt and common stock. The payment of dividends is not a legal but a discretionary obligation, although many companies regard the obligation as fixed. Preferred stockholders' claims on assets and income come after those of creditors but before those of common stockholders. The return on their investment is almost always limited to the specified dividend; very seldom do preferred stockholders participate in the residual earnings of the company. Although they may have some voting power, this power generally is restricted to situations in which the company has evolved itself into financial difficulty.

Because preferred stock has no final maturity, almost all issues have call features that give the corporation financial flexibility. Retirement of the preferred stock can be accomplished also by a sinking fund, convertibility, or an exchange offering. The principal disadvantage of preferred stock is that the dividend is not tax deductible. Implicit benefits associated with debt capacity and financial flexi-

---

[4]Annual Report, Ford Motor Company, 1980; and *Prospectus* to Ford Motor Company Stock, November 20, 1963.

bility offset in some measure the difference between explicit after-tax costs of preferred-stock and debt financing. Despite these implicit benefits, preferred stock is used only moderately as a method of financing.

The common stockholders of a corporation are its owners. As such, they are entitled to share in the residual earnings of the company if cash dividends are paid. As owners, however, they have only a residual claim on assets in the event of liquidation. Common stockholders are also entitled to a voice in management through the board of directors they elect. These directors can be elected under a majority voting system or a cumulative voting system. The cumulative system allows minority interests to obtain representation on the board of directors. Differences between authorized, issued, and outstanding shares were explained as were differences in par value, book value, liquidating value, and market value. The use of different classes of common stock allows the promoters and management of a corporation to retain voting control without having to make a large capital contribution.

Questions

1. Because the dividend payments on preferred stock are not a tax-deductible expense, the explicit cost of this form of financing is high. What are some of the offsetting advantages to the firm and to the investor that enable this type of security to be sold? Can you explain why the utilities are the principal preferred-stock issuers?

2. Why would a preferred stockholder suffer a loss on those dividend payments in arrears even if the arrearage were ultimately paid up?

3. Preferred stock is said to combine the worst features of both common stock and debt. Do you agree with the contention? From whose point of view does it make sense?

4. Why do most preferred stock issues have a cumulative feature? Would not the company be better off with a noncumulative feature?

5. If not otherwise stated, what would you assume is usual practice with respect to the following features for a preferred stock: cumulative, participation, voting power, call feature, and claim on assets?

6. What advantages to the firm are there from broad share distribution? Is the preemptive right in conflict with an objective of broad share distribution?

7. Why would a company ever wish to use classified common stock in its financing instead of straight common stock?

8. Why does most common stock have a low par value in relation to its market value?

9. Why does book value per share of common stock change over time?

10. The common stockholder is considered the residual owner of a corporation. What does this mean in terms of risk and return?

11. Why does the number of authorized shares usually exceed the number that are actually outstanding?

12. In any proxy attempt by an outside group to gain control of a company, the advantage lies with management. What are the reasons for this advantage?

13. If Parliament were to eliminate the double taxation of dividends so that a company could deduct dividend payments in the same way it does interest payments for tax purposes, what would be the effect on preferred stock and common stock financing?

Problems with Solutions

1. A Company Ltd. has outstanding 10 000 shares of $10 par value, 7 percent preferred shares and 2 000 shares of $100 par value common shares. During a 5-year period the company paid out the following amounts in dividends: 198A, nothing; 198B, $24 000; 198C, nothing; 198D, $31 000; and 198E, $35 000.

Show the total dividends paid to the preferred and to the common shares in each year assuming:

(a) The preferred is noncumulative and nonparticipating
(b) The preferred is cumulative and nonparticipating
(c) The preferred is cumulative and fully participating.

	Year	Total	Pref.	Common
(a)	A	$0	$0	$0
	B	24 000	7 000	17 000
	C	0	0	0
	D	31 000	7 000	24 000
	E	35 000	7 000	28 000
(b)	A	$0	$0	$0
	B	24 000	14 000	10 000
	C	0	0	0
	D	31 000	14 000	17 000
	E	35 000	7 000	28 000
(c)	A	$0	$0	$0
	B	24 000	14 000	10 000
	C	0	0	0
	D	31 000	15 000	16 000
	E	35 000	11 667	23 333

Problems

1. The Riting Railroad needs to raise $9.5 million for capital improvements. One possibility is a new preferred stock issue: 8 percent, $100 par value stock that would yield 9 percent to investors. Flotation costs for an issue this size amount to 5 percent of the total amount of preferred stock sold; these costs are deducted from gross proceeds in determining the net proceeds to the company. (Ignore any tax considerations.)

(a) At what price per share will the preferred stock be offered to investors? (Assume the issue never will be called.)
(b) How many shares must be issued to raise $9.5 million for Riting Railroad?

2. Lost Horizon Silver Mining Company Ltd. has 200 000 shares of $7 cumulative preferred stock outstanding, $100 par value. The preferred stock has a participating feature. If dividends on the common stock exceed $1 per share, preferred stockholders receive additional dividends per share equal to one-half of the excess. In other words, if the common stock dividend were $2, preferred stockholders would receive an additional dividend of $0.50. The company has 1 million shares of common outstanding. What would dividends per share be on the preferred stock and on the common stock if earnings available for dividends in three successive years were (a) $1 000 000; $600 000; and $3 000 000; (b) $2 000 000; $2 400 000; and $4 600 000; and (c)$1 000 000; $2 500 000; and $5 700 000. (Assume all of the available earnings are paid in dividends, but nothing more is paid.)

3. D. Sent, a disgruntled stockholder of the Zebec Corporation Ltd., desires representation on the board. The Zebec Corporation, which has 10 directors, has 1 million shares outstanding.
   (a) How many shares would Sent have to control to be assured of one directorship under a majority voting system?
   (b) Recompute part a, assuming a cumulative voting system.
   (c) Recompute parts a and b, assuming the number of directors was reduced to 5.

4. The Brampton Brass Company Ltd. has a 9-person board and has 2 million shares of common stock outstanding. It is chartered with a cumulative voting rule. Jane Irwin, a granddaughter of the founder, controls directly or indirectly 482 000 shares. As she disagrees with present management, she wants a slate of her own directors on the board.
   (a) If all directors are elected once a year, how many directors can she elect?
   (b) If director terms are staggered so that only 3 are elected each year, how many can she elect?

5. The stock of the Morlbund Corporation Ltd. is currently selling in the market for $45 per share, yet it has a liquidation value of $70 per share. The Raid Corporation Ltd. has decided to make a tender offer for the shares of Moribund. Raid feels that it must obtain at least 50 percent of the shares in order to effect the liquidation. Assuming Raid makes its tender offer on the expected relationship shown in the following table, at what price should the tender be made?

Price per share	Expected percentage of shares tendered
$55	50%
57	60
59	70
62	80
67	90
72	100

6. At last year-end, the long term capitalization of Amherst Furniture Company Ltd. consisted of the following:

Long-term bonds, 9%	$ 3 400 000
Preferred stock, 8%, $50 par value	2 000 000
Common stock, $5 par value	1 000 000
Contributed capital	500 000
Retained earnings	4 000 000
	$10 900 000

During the current year the company earned $2.5 million before interest and taxes. Its dividend payout rate with respect to profits after taxes was 40 percent, and the company's marginal tax rate is 46 percent. At the current year-end, it issues 50 000 additional shares of common stock at a price to the public of $38 per share. The underwriters' spread is $3 a share. What is the long-term capitalization of the company at the current year-end?

Selected References

BEAR, ROBERT M., and ANTHONY J. CURLEY, "Unseasoned Equity Financing," *Journal of Financial and Quantitative Analysis*, 10 (June 1975), 311-26.

BILDERSEE, JOHN S., "Some Aspects of the Performance of Non-Convertible Preferred Stocks," *Journal of Finance*, 28 (December 1973), 1187-1202.

BLOCK, STANLEY, and MARJORIE STANELY, "The Financial Characteristics and Price Movement Patterns of Companies Approaching the Unseasoned Securities Market in the Late 1970s," *Financial Management*, 9 (Winter 1980), 30-36.

DONALDSON, GORDON, "Financial Goals: Management vs. Stockholders," *Harvard Business Review*, 41 (May-June 1963), 116-29.

_____, "In Defense of Preferred Stock," *Harvard Business Review*, 40 (July-August 1962), reprinted in *Foundations for Financial Management*, ed. James Van Horne, 194-218. Homewood, Ill.; Irwin, 1966.

EIBOTT, PETER, "Trends In the Value of Individual Stockholdings," *Journal of Business*, 47 (July 1974), 339-48.

HAYES, SAMUEL L. III, "The Transformation of Investment Banking," *Harvard Business Review*, 57 (January-February 1970), 153-70.

LEVY, HAIM, "Economic Evaluation of Voting Power of Common Stock," *Journal of Finance*, March 1983, 79-93.

SOLDOFSKY, ROBERT M., "Classified Common Stock," *Business Lawyer* (April 1968), 899-902.

SORENSON, ERIC H. and CLARK A. HAWKINS, "On the Pricing of Preferred Stock," *Journal of Financial and Quantitative Analysis*, November 1981, 515-527.

VAN HORNE, JAMES C., "New Listings and Their Price Behavior," *Journal of Finance*, 25 (September 1970), 783-94.

WHITE, R. W., and P. A. LUSZTIG, "The Price Effects of Rights Offerings," *Journal of Financial and Quantitative Analysis*, 15 (March 1980), 25-40.

YOUNG, ALAN, and WAYNE MARSHALL, "Controlling Shareholder Servicing Costs," *Harvard Business Review*, 49 (January-February 1971), 71-78.

Convertible Securities and Warrants

In addition to straight debt and equity instruments, a company may finance with an option, a contract giving its holder the right to buy common stock or to exchange something for it within a specific period of time. As a result, the value of the option instrument is strongly influenced by changes in value of the stock. In this chapter, we consider two specific types of options frequently employed by business firms in their financing: the convertible security and the warrant. In the Appendix to this chapter, a more detailed discussion of option pricing theory appears.

Convertible-Security Features

A convertible security is a bond or a share of preferred stock that can be converted at the option of the holder into common shares of the same corporation. Once converted into common shares the share cannot be exchanged again for bonds or preferred stock. The ratio of exchange between the convertible security and the common share can be stated in terms of either a *conversion price* or a *conversion ratio*. Bell Canada $1.96 convertible preferred shares Series G ($25 par value), issued in April 1978, have a conversion ratio of 1.2 (six common shares for each five preferred) giving a conversion price of $20.83. We simply divide the par value of the security by the conversion ratio to obtain the conversion price, $25/1.2 = $20.83. The conversion privilege can be stated in terms of either the conversion price or the conversion ratio.

The conversion terms are not necessarily constant over time. Many convertible issues provide for increases or "step-ups" in the conversion price at periodic intervals. For example, a $1 000-face-value bond might have a conversion price of $100 a share for the first five years, $110 a share for the second five years, $120 for the third five, and so on. In this way, the bond converts into fewer shares of common stock as time goes by. Usually, the conversion price is adjusted for any stock splits or stock dividends that occur after the securities are sold. If the common stock were split two for one, the conversion price would be halved. This provision protects the convertible security holder and is known as an antidilution clause.

CONVERSION VALUE AND PREMIUM

The *conversion value* of a convertible security is the conversion ratio of the security times the market price per share of the common stock. Late in August 1983 Bell Canada common shares were selling for $27⅞, thus the conversion value at that time would be $1.2 \times \$27⅞$, or $33.45.

The convertible security provides the investor with a fixed return from a bond or preferred stock. In addition, the investor receives an option to convert the security into common stock and thereby participates in the possibility of capital gains associated with being a residual owner of the corporation. Because of this option, the company usually is able to sell the convertible security at a lower yield than it would have to pay on a straight bond or preferred stock issue. At the time of issuance, the convertible security will be priced higher than its conversion value. The differential is known as the *conversion premium*. The Bell Canada convertible preferred was sold to the public for $25. The market price of a common share (adjusted for a 3 for 1 split) at the time the convertible was issued was approximately $18. Therefore, the conversion value of each preferred share was $1.2 \times \$18 = \$21.60$, and the differential of $3.40 represented the conversion premium. Frequently, this premium is expressed as a percentage; in our example the conversion premium is $\$3.40/\$21.60 = 15.7$ percent.

Almost without exception, convertible securities provide for a *call price*. As was true with the straight bond or preferred stock, the call feature enables the corporation to call the security for redemption. Few convertible securities, however, are ever redeemed. Instead, the purpose of the call usually is to force conversion when the conversion value of the security is significantly above its call price.

OTHER FEATURES

Almost all convertible bond issues are subordinated to other creditors. That fact permits the lender to treat convertible subordinated debt or convertible preferred stock as a part of the equity base when evaluating the financial condition of the issuer. In the event of liquidation, it makes no difference to the creditor if the issue is actually converted; in either case, the lender has a prior claim. The situation is different with a convertible bond that is not subordinate. As long as the bond is not converted, its holder would be a general creditor in the event of liquidation.

Consequently, creditors tend to regard the convertible bond as debt until actual conversion takes place. For this reason, there is a strong incentive for the company to make the issue subordinated.

Investors in a company's common stock tend to recognize the potential dilution in their earnings per share position before actual conversion takes place. To illustrate the dilution effect, suppose that a company issues $20 million in 6 percent convertible debentures and that the conversion price is $20 a share. The total number of additional shares on conversion would be $20 million/$20 = 1 million. Assume further that the company has 3 million common shares outstanding and no other debt, that it expects earnings before interest and taxes two years from now to be $10 million, and that the federal income tax rate is 46 percent. Earnings per share under the two alternatives would be

	Convertible debentures outstanding	Debentures converted
Earnings before interest and taxes	$10 000 000	$10 000 000
Interest 6% debentures	1 200 000	—
Profit before taxes	8 800 000	10 000 000
Taxes	4 048 000	4 600 000
Profit after taxes	4 752 000	5 400 000
Shares outstanding	3 000 000	4 000 000
Earnings per share	$1.58	$1.35

We see that after conversion, there will be a dilution in earnings per share. It is important that the investor in common shares consider the impact of this dilution on the market price of the shares. We note also that on conversion, the company no longer has to pay interest on the debentures; this factor may have a favorable influence on earnings per share. For example, if earnings were low enough, the elimination of interest payments could result in an increase in earnings per share. However, this occurrence is the exception rather than the rule. Furthermore, any favorable impact is dampened to some extent by the fact that the company no longer enjoys the tax advantage of convertible debt.

We point out that it is now necessary for companies to report earnings per share on a fully diluted basis. In January of 1970, the Canadian Institute of Chartered Accountants required "fully diluted" earnings per share to be shown in a note to the financial statements and cross-referenced to the income statement. Full dilution means the maximum possible dilution if all convertible securities which are convertible within ten years were converted into common shares and all warrants and options to purchase common shares which are exercisable within ten years were exercised. As a result of this Institute opinion, which is binding on chartered accountants in certifying financial statements, the common stock investor is not likely to overlook the potential dilution inherent in a company's financing with convertible securities and warrants.

Use of Convertibles

Convertibles securities, in most cases, are employed as deferred common-stock financing. Technically these securities represent debt or preferred stock, but in essence they are delayed common stock. Companies that issue convertibles expect them to be converted in the future. By selling a convertible security instead of common stock, they create less dilution in earnings per share, both now and in the future. The reason is that the conversion price on a convertible security is higher than the issuing price on a new issue of common stock.

The current market price of the common stock of the mythical ABC Company Ltd. is $40 per share. If the company raises capital with an issue of common stock, it will sell the stock through underwriters and realize net proceeds of $36 per share. If the company wishes to raise $18 million, the issue will involve 500 000 shares of additional stock. On the other hand, if ABC Company Ltd. sells a convertible issue, it is able to set the conversion price above the current market price per share. If the conversion premium is 15 percent, the conversion price will be $46 per share. Assuming an $18 million issue of convertibles, the number of shares of additional stock after conversion will be

$$\frac{\$18 \text{ million}}{\$46} = 391\ 305$$

We see that potential dilution with a convertible issue is less than that with a common issue because fewer shares are being added.

As a financing strategy, management may wish to finance with convertible securities as opposed to common stock when its estimates of the firm's future are more favorable than those of the market. By so doing, it obtains less dilution for existing shareholders than it would if it financed with common stock. Once management's expectations are realized, the share will presumably rise in price. Of course, the merit of such a strategy depends upon management's estimating the future more accurately than the market does. When the share is depressed in price, however, it may be wise to avoid both common stock and convertible financing. This situation will be discussed later in the chapter when we consider the timing of a convertible issue.

Another advantage to the company in using convertible securities is that the interest rate or preferred-dividend rate typically is lower than the rate the company would have to pay on a straight bond or a straight preferred stock issue. The conversion feature makes the issue more attractive to investors. The greater the value of the conversion feature to investors, the lower the yield the company will have to pay in order to sell the issue.

FORCING OR STIMULATING CONVERSION

Companies usually issue convertible securities with the full expectation that these securities will be converted within a certain length of time. Investors can exercise their options voluntarily at any time and exchange the convertible security for common shares; however, they may prefer to hold the security, for its price will increase as the price of the common share increases. During this time, also, they receive regular interest payments or preferred stock dividends. For a security which is convertible to common stock that pays no dividend, it is to the holder's advantage never to convert voluntarily. In other words, the investor should delay conversion as long as possible. (When a company pays a common stock dividend, it may be in the interest of the convertible security holder to convert voluntarily.) On the other hand, it is in the company's interest, on behalf of existing stockholders, to force conversion as soon as possible. In this way, the cost of paying interest on the convertible debenture, or dividends on the convertible preferred stock, can be avoided.

In order to force conversion, companies issuing convertible securities usually must call the issue. If the call is to succeed, the market price of the security must be significantly higher than the call price, so that investors will convert rather than accept the lower call price. Many companies regard a 20 percent premium of conversion value over call price as a sufficient cushion for possible declines in market price and for enticing investors to convert their securities. The conversion price of a convertible debenture ($1 000 face value) might be $50 a share and the call price $1 080. For the conversion value of the bond to equal the call price, the market price of the stock must be $1 080/20, or $54 a share. If the bonds are called when the market price is $54, many investors might choose to accept the call price rather than convert. The company then would have to redeem many of the bonds for cash, in part defeating the purpose of the original financing. In order to assure almost complete conversion, it might wait to call the debentures until the conversion value of the bond was 20 percent above the call price, a value that corresponds to a common stock market price of approximately $65 a share. At this price, the investor who accepts the call price suffers a significant opportunity loss.[1] Studies show that companies tend to call their convertibles after a period of rise in their common stock price relative to the market.[2] As a result, the opportunity loss to the holder for not converting is pronounced.

Other means are available to a company for "stimulating," as opposed to "forcing," conversion. By establishing an acceleration or "step-up" in the conversion price at steady intervals in the future, there is persistent pressure on bondholders to convert, assuming the conversion value of the security is relatively high. If the conversion price is scheduled to increase from $50 to $56 at the end of next month, convertible bondholders have an incentive to convert prior to that time, all other things the same. If the holders wait, they receive fewer shares of stock. The "step-up" provision must be established at the time the convertible issue is sold; it cannot be used for purposes of stimulating conversion at a particular moment.

Another means for stimulating conversion is to increase the dividend on the common stock, thereby making the common more attractive. In certain cases, the

[1]For a discussion of ways a company can notify bondholders of the call and to assure that a very high percentage exercise their option, see Alexander B. Miller, "How to Call Your Convertibles," *Harvard Business Review*, 49 (May-June 1971), 66-70.

[2]Gordon J. Alexander and Roger D. Stover, "The Effect of Forced Conversions on Common Stock Prices," *Financial Management*, 9 (Spring 1980), 39-45.

dividend income available on the common may exceed interest income on the convertible security. Although the two stimulants discussed above enhance conversion, invariably a portion of the convertible bondholders will not convert, owing to the downside protection of the bond, the superior legal claim on assets, and other reasons. Consequently, calling the issue may be the only means for assuring that the issue will be substantially converted.

Overhanging issue If a company is unable to force or stimulate conversion because the market price of the stock has not risen sufficiently to entice the investor to convert, the issue is said to be overhanging. With an overhanging issue, the company is said to be constrained in its ability to obtain new financing. It is difficult to sell another convertible-security issue until the present one is converted. The overhanging issue creates apprehension in the market over the investment worthiness of any new issue of convertibles and may even create apprehension over the worthiness of a nonconvertible security offering.

The chance of an overhanging issue and the loss of flexibility associated with such an issue may offset, at least in part, the advantage in issuing price of the convertible security over a common stock offering. With a common stock offering, the firm obtains equity capital now. With a convertible-security issue, it is uncertain when, if ever, the security will convert and the company will obtain equity capital.

CONVERSION PREMIUMS

For most issues of convertibles, the conversion premium ranges from 10 to 20 percent. Remember that this premium is the percentage by which the issuing price of the convertible exceeds its conversion value. If a convertible bond is sold for $1 000 with a conversion price of $50, and if the market price of common at the time of issuance is $43 a share, the conversion premium will be $7/$43, or 16.3 percent. For a growth company, the conversion premium can be in the upper part of the 10 to 20 percent range, or perhaps even higher in the case of a supergrowth stock. For companies with more moderate growth, the conversion premium may be closer to 10 percent. The range itself is established mainly by market tradition, in keeping with the idea that the stock should be expected to rise in price so that it exceeds the conversion price within a reasonable period of time. The greater the growth in market price per share, the more quickly will the market price exceed the conversion price, all other things the same. Thus, the supergrowth company is able to command a higher conversion premium in the market than a company with only moderate growth potential.

The higher the conversion premium, of course, the lower the dilution. If the company sets too high a conversion price, the issue will have to be sold as essentially a fixed-income security with a yield commensurate with what the company would pay on a straight debt or preferred stock issue. Under such circumstances, the issue cannot be considered delayed equity financing; the ability of the firm to force conversion is too uncertain. For this reason, there are practical limits to how high a conversion premium can be set. For most situations, it is 20 percent or less.

Value of Convertible Securities

The value of a convertible security to an investor is twofold: its value as a bond or preferred stock and its potential value as common stock. (Because the principles of valuation of a convertible bond and a convertible preferred stock are nearly the same, our subsequent discussion will refer to convertible bonds.) Investors obtain a hedge when they purchase a convertible bond. If the market price of the stock rises, the value of the convertible is determined largely by its conversion value. If the market for the shares turns down, the investor still holds a bond whose value provides a floor below which the price of the convertible is unlikely to fall.

BOND VALUE

The value of a convertible bond is the price at which a straight bond of the same company would sell in the open market. It can be determined by solving the following equation for B:

$$B = \sum_{t=1}^{2n} \frac{I}{(1 + \frac{i}{2})^t} + \frac{F}{(1 + \frac{i}{2})^{2n}} \tag{23-1}$$

where B = straight bond value of the convertible
I = semiannual interest payments determined by the coupon rate
F = face value of the bond
n = years to final maturity
i = market yield to maturity on a straight bond of the same company.

In the equation, we assume semiannual interest payments, which are typical with corporate bonds, so the total number of payments is two times the years to maturity, n, and the semiannual interest rate on a straight bond is i divided by 2.

Amos White Company Ltd. has outstanding a 9 percent convertible debenture with a final maturity 20 years hence. If the company is to sell a straight 20-year debenture in the current market, the yield will have to be 11 percent to be attractive to investors. For a 20-year bond with a 9 percent coupon to yield 11 percent to maturity, the bond has to sell at a discount. Using the above equation and rounding, we have

$$B = \sum_{t=1}^{40} \frac{\$4.50}{(1.055)^t} + \frac{\$1\,000}{(1.055)^{40}} = \$839$$

Although it is possible to solve this equation by hand, using present-value tables, we need only consult a bond table to determine the market price. Thus the bond-value floor of Amos White Company's convertible bonds would be $839. This floor suggests that if the price of the common shares were to fall sharply so that the conversion feature had negligible value, the price of the convertible would fall only to $839. At that price, the security would sell as a straight bond in keeping with prevailing bond yields for that grade of security.

The bond-value floor of a convertible is not constant over time. It varies with (1) interest-rate movements in the capital market and (2) changes in the financial risk of the company involved. If interest rates in general rise, the bond value of a convertible will decline. If the yield to maturity on a straight bond in our example increases from 11 to 12 percent, the bond value of the convertible will drop from $839 to $774. Moreover, the company's credit rating can either improve or deteriorate over time. If it improves, and the company is able to sell a straight bond at a lower yield to maturity, the bond value of the convertible security will increase, all other things held constant. If the company's credit standing deteriorates, and the yield on a straight bond increases, the bond-value floor will decline. Unfortunately for the investor, when the market price of the stock falls because of poor earnings, the company may have financial difficulty, in which case its credit standing will suffer. As a result, the straight bond value of the convertible may decline along with the decline in its conversion value, giving investors less downside protection than they might have expected originally.[3]

PREMIUMS

Convertible securities usually sell at premiums over both their bond value and their conversion value. Recall that the conversion value of a convertible is simply the current market price per share of the company's common stock times the number of shares into which the security is convertible. The fact that the convertible bond provides the investor with a degree of downside protection, given the qualifications mentioned above, often results in its selling at a market price somewhat higher than its conversion value. In general, the more volatile the price movements of the stock, the more valuable is the downside protection afforded by the bond-value floor. For this reason as well as for additional reasons discussed later, the market price of a convertible security frequently is above its conversion value. The difference is known as the *premium-over-conversion value*.

Moreover, a convertible bond typically will sell at a *premium-over-bond value*, primarily because of the conversion feature. Unless the market price of the stock is very low relative to the conversion price, the conversion feature usually will have value, in that investors may eventually find it profitable to convert the securities. To the extent that the conversion feature does have value, the convertible will sell at a premium over its straight bond value. The higher the market price of the common relative to the conversion price, the greater this premium.

RELATION BETWEEN PREMIUMS

The tradeoff between the two premiums depicts the value of the option to investors and is illustrated in Fig. 23-1. The market price of the common is on the horizontal axis; the value of the convertible security is on the vertical. It should be

---

[3]Mathematically, the straight bond value of a convertible will rise over time, all other things held constant, if the face value of the convertible is above the straight bond value at the time of issuance. At final maturity the straight bond value will equal the face value of the convertible, assuming the company is not in default.

pointed out that the two axes are on different scales. If the conversion ratio were 20 to 1, the horizontal axis might be in units of $10, while the vertical axis would be in units of $200. The diagonal line, which starts at the origin, represents the conversion value of the bond. It is linear, as the conversion ratio is invariant with respect to the market price of the stock. The bond value line, however, is related to the market price of the common. If a company is doing badly financially, the prices of both its common stock and its bonds are likely to be low. At the extreme, if the total value of the company were zero, both the bonds and the stock would have a value of zero. As the company becomes sounder financially and the common stock increases in price, bond value increases but at a decreasing rate. After a point, the bond value line becomes flat, and further increases in common stock price are unrelated to it. At this point, the bond value floor is determined by what other high grade bonds sell for in the market. The upper curved line represents the market price of the convertible security. The distance between this line and the bond-value line is the premium over bond value, while the distance between the market-value line and the conversion-value line represents the premium over conversion value.

We see that at relatively high common stock price levels, the value of the convertible as a bond is insignificant. Consequently, its premium-over-bond value is high, whereas its premium-over-conversion value is negligible. The security sells mainly for its stock equivalent. Investors are unwilling to pay a significant premium-over-conversion value for the following reasons. First, the greater the premium of market price of the convertible over its bond value, the less valuable the bond-value protection is to the investor. Second, when the conversion value is high, the convertible may be called; if it is, the investor will want to convert rather than redeem the bond for the call price. Upon conversion, of course, the bond is worth only its conversion value.

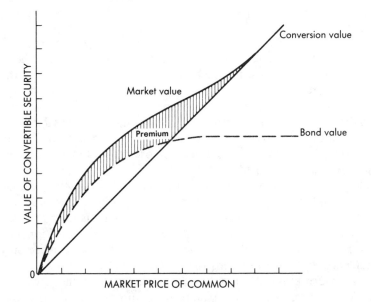

FIGURE 23-1 Relation between bond value and conversion premiums

On the other hand, when the market value of the convertible is close to its straight bond value, the conversion feature has little value. At this level, the convertible security is valued primarily as a straight bond. Under these circumstances, the market price of the convertible is likely to exceed its conversion value by a significant premium.

The principal reason for premiums in market price over both conversion value and bond value is the unusual appeal of a convertible as both a bond and a common stock. It offers the holder partial protection on the downside together with participation in upward movements in share price. Thus the distribution of possible outcomes is skewed to the right, and this characteristic finds favor with investors.

Warrants and Their Valuation

A warrant is an option to purchase a specified number of shares of common stock at a stated price. When holders exercise options, they surrender the warrants. Warrants often are employed as "sweeteners" to a public issue of bonds or debt that is privately placed. The investor obtains not only the fixed return associated with debt but also an option to purchase common shares at a stated price. If the market price of the shares should rise, this option can be valuable. As a result, the company should be able to obtain a lower interest rate than it would otherwise. For companies that are marginal credit risks, the use of warrants may spell the difference between being able and not being able to raise funds through a debt issue. In addition to being a "sweetener" to debt financing, warrants are used in the origination of a company as compensation to underwriters and venture capitalists.

FEATURES

The warrant itself contains the provisions of the option. It states the number of shares the holder can buy for each warrant held. For example, the Czar Resources Ltd. warrants provide an option to purchase one share of common stock for each warrant held. Another important provision is the price at which the warrant can be exercised. For example, Czar warrants are exercisable at $17.00 a share until April 30, 1986 when the warrants expire. The warrants of Standard Trustco Ltd. are exercisable at $15.00 a share on or prior to January 3, 1985.

Most warrants have a stated expiration date. Warrants may be either detachable or nondetachable. Detachable warrants may be sold separately from the bond. Consequently, bondholders do not have to exercise their options in order to obtain the value of the warrants. They can simply sell the warrants in the marketplace. Many detachable warrants are listed on the stock exchanges. Nondetachable warrants cannot be sold separately from the bonds; they can be detached only when the bondholders exercise their options and purchase shares.

Because a warrant is only an option to purchase shares, the warrant holders are not entitled to any cash dividends paid on the common shares, nor do they have voting power. If the common stock is split or a stock dividend is declared, the option price of the warrant is usually adjusted to take this change into account.

EXERCISE OF WARRANTS

When warrants are exercised, the common shares of the company are increased. Moreover, the debt which was issued in conjunction with the warrants remains outstanding, assuming the warrants are detachable. At the time of the issue of the warrants, the exercise price usually is set in excess of the market price of the common shares. The premium often is 15 percent or so above the share's value. If the share price is $40, this translates into an exercise price of $46.

To see how new capital can be infused with the exercise of warrants, let us take a company we shall call Westman Bodac Ltd. It has just raised $25 million in debt funds with warrants attached. The debentures carry a 12 percent coupon rate; and with each debenture ($1 000 face value) investors receive one warrant entitling them to purchase 4 shares of common stock at $30 a share. The capitalization of the company before financing, after financing, and after complete exercise of the options is as follows (in millions):

	Before financing	After financing	After exercise
Debentures		$25	$25
Common stock ($10 par value)	$10	10	11
Contributed capital			2
Retained earnings	40	40	40
Net worth	$50	$50	$53
Total capitalization	$50	$75	$78

The retained earnings of the company remain unchanged, and the debenture issue has neither matured nor been called. Exercising their options, the warrant holders purchase 100 000 shares of stock at $30 a share, or $3 million in total. Consequently, the total capitalization of the company is increased by that amount.

A company cannot force the exercise of the warrant option as it can force the exercise of the conversion option by calling a convertible security. Consequently, it is unable to control when, if ever, the warrant will be exercised and there will be an infusion of new equity capital into the corporation. Only the expiration date sets a limit on how long the warrants can remain outstanding and unexercised. As with convertibles, it is necessary for companies to report earnings per share on a fully diluted basis.

VALUATION OF WARRANTS

The theoretical value of a warrant can be determined by

$$NP_s - E \qquad (23\text{-}2)$$

where N = the number of shares that can be purchased with one warrant
P_s = the market price of one share of stock
E = the exercise price associated with the purchase of N shares.

The theoretical value of a warrant is the lowest level at which the warrant will generally sell. If, for some reason, the market price of a warrant were to go lower than its theoretical value, arbitragers would eliminate the differential by buying the warrants, exercising them, and selling the stock. A warrant is unlikely to sell below its theoretical value, and many warrants sell above that value.

Premium over theoretical value The primary reason that a warrant sells at a price higher than its theoretical value is the opportunity for leverage. To illustrate the concept of leverage, consider the Czar Resources warrants. For each warrant held, one share of common stock can be purchased, and the exercise price is $17. If the stock were selling at $20 a share, the theoretical value of the warrant would be $3. Suppose, however, that the common stock increased by 30 percent in price to $26 a share. The theoretical value of the warrant would go from $3 to $9, a gain of 200 percent.

The opportunity for increased gain is attractive to investors when the common stock is selling near its exercise price. For a particular investment, the investor can buy more warrants than common shares. If the stock moves up in price the investor will make more money on the warrants than on an equal investment in common shares. Of course, leverage works both ways; the percentage change can be almost as pronounced on the downside. However, there is a limit to how far the warrant can fall in price because it is bounded at zero. Moreover, in order for the market price to drop to zero, there would have to be no probability that the market price of the stock would exceed the exercise price during the exercise period. Usually there is some probability.

The market prices of many warrants are in excess of their theoretical values because of the potential for upside movements in the value of the warrant while, at the same time, downside movements are cushioned. In particular, this event occurs when the market price of the associated common stock is near the exercise price of the warrant.

The typical relationship between the market value of a warrant and the value of the associated common share is shown in Fig. 23-2. The theoretical value of the warrant is represented by the solid line in the figure, and the actual market value by the dashed line. When the market value of the associated share is less than the exercise price, the theoretical value of the warrant is zero. When the value of the associated common share is greater than the exercise price, the theoretical value of the warrant is positive, as depicted by the solid, diagonal line.

One might think of the theoretical value line as representing the values a warrant might take with only a moment to expiration. When there is a reasonable amount of time to expiration of the warrant, the relationship between warrant value and stock value is better depicted by the dashed line in Fig. 23-2. The greater the length of time to expiration, the more time the investor has in which to exercise the warrant and the more valuable it becomes. As a result, the further in the future the expiration date of the warrant, the higher the market-value line tends to be in relation to the theoretical-value line.

We note in the figure that when the market value of the associated common share is low in relation to the exercise price, the actual market value of a warrant

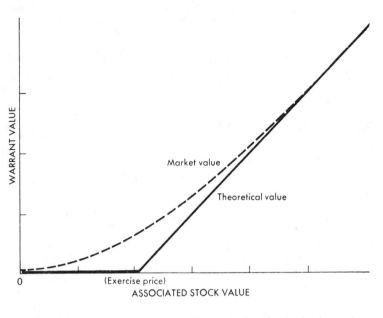

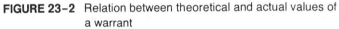

FIGURE 23-2 Relation between theoretical and actual values of a warrant

exceeds its theoretical value. As the market value of the associated stock rises, the market value of the warrant usually approaches its theoretical value. This simply suggests that a warrant has the greatest value, relative to its theoretical value, when it has the greatest potential percentagewise for upside movements and where the amount of funds invested is not all that great. The valuation of options, of which warrants are one form, is explored in more depth in the Appendix to this chapter.

The Equity Participation Record of Convertibles and Warrants

Storey and Dipchand[4] evaluated the conversion record of 99 convertible bonds and preferred stocks issued by Canadian companies over the 1956-68 period. The convertible options on the sample of securities expired at the latest, December 31, 1975 and the par value of all securities was $635.9 million. It was observed that 30 percent of the issues had a zero conversion rate (Fig. 23-3) while another 25 percent experienced conversions up to 85 percent of their respective par values. Just about 45 percent of the convertible issues had over 85 percent of par value exchanged for

---

[4]Ronald G. Storey and Cecil R. Dipchand, "Factors Related to the Conversion Record of Convertible Securities: The Canadian Experience 1946-76", *Journal of Financial Research*, 1 (Winter 1978), 71-83.

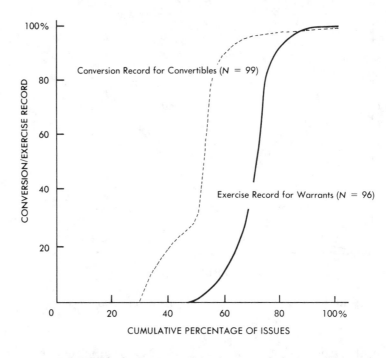

FIGURE 23-3 Equity participation record of convertibles and warrant options

Source: Ronald G. Storey and Cecil R. Dipchand, "The Conversion Record of Canadian Convertible Options," and Cecil R. Dipchand and Ronald G. Storey, "The Exercise Record of Canadian Warrant Options."

common equity. In aggregate, about 55 percent of the total par value of $635.9 million was converted into common equity. The study also showed that there was no significant difference in the distribution of conversion rates for bonds and that for preferred stocks. Further analysis revealed that conversion rates across issues were significantly related to several variables. Using a multiple discriminant analysis model, it was observed that conversion was positively influenced by the growth rate of the common stock price, the number of step-ups in the conversion ratio, and the magnitude of the common dividends relative to the income stream on the convertible security. The conversion premium at issue date was negatively related to the conversion rate. The growth in common share price and the magnitude of the conversion premium at issue date were observed to be the two most influential factors on the degree of conversion to common equity. These results are generally supportive of the theoretical framework outlined earlier in the discussion.

In a related study,[5] it was observed that 44 percent of warrant issues had a zero exercise record while 25 percent had an exercise record exceeding 85 percent (Fig. 23-3) of shares issuable under the option agreement. The remaining 31 percent of issues had exercise records exceeding zero but less than 85 percent of issuable shares. A review of Fig. 23-3 shows that most of the issues in this last group had exercise records exceeding zero but less than 20 percent of issuable shares. This study on warrants had a sample size of 96 and included options issued since January 1956 and the lastest expiry date was December 1975. The exercise record on a warrant issue is simply the number of shares purchased through exercise of the warrant option expressed as a percentage of the shares issuable if all options for each issue were exercised. A comparison of the conversion and exercise record graphs in Fig. 23-3 indicates that the conversion record is relatively higher than the exercise record of warrant issues. That is, there appears to be a higher equity participation rate for convertibles than that observed for warrant issues.

Summary

Convertible securities and warrants are two types of options under which the holder can obtain common stock. The conversion feature enables the investor to convert a debt instrument or preferred stock into common stock, whereas a warrant enables the holder to purchase a specified number of shares of common stock at a specified price. With a warrant, the exercise of the option does not result in the elimination of the bonds. Convertibles are used more than warrants in financing.

The value of the convertible in the market place is determined by its value as a straight bond or preferred stock and its conversion value as common stock. For the corporation, convertibles represent delayed common stock financing, and the timing of a convertible issue must be analyzed by the company in relation to the market for its common stock. For a given amount of financing, there will be less dilution with a convertible issue than with a common stock issue, assuming, of course, that the issue eventually converts. This advantage is offset somewhat by the risk of an "overhanging" issue, which occurs when the company is unable to force conversion. A firm encounters this difficulty when the market price of a share does not go high enough to raise the conversion value of the security significantly above the call price. An overhanging issue results in less financing flexibility for the issuer.

Normally, warrants are employed as a "sweetener" for a public or private issue of debt. The market value of a warrant usually is higher than its theoretical value when the market value of the share is close to the exercise price, because this situation gives the investor an opportunity for favorable leverage. When the market price of the share is high relative to the exercise price, warrants tend to sell at about their theoretical values.

---

[5]Cecil R. Dipchand and Ronald G. Storey, "The Exercise Record of Canadian Warrant Options," *Research Paper*, Dalhousie University, June 1977.

Appendix A: Option Pricing and the Canadian Options Market

An option is simply a contract that gives the holder the right to buy or sell the common stock of a company at some specified price. Among a variety of option contracts, the most prevalent are the *call option* and the *put option*. The call option gives the holder the right to buy a share of stock at a specified price, known as the exercise price. We might have a call option to buy one share of ABC Corporation Ltd.'s common stock at $10 through December 31, which is the expiration date. The party who provides the option is known as the *writer*. In the case of a call option, the writer must deliver stock to the optionholder when the latter exercises the option. The extendible option (Chapter 21) is another example of a call option.

As evident from our discussions in the chapter, a warrant is a form of call option, as is the convertible security, in that it gives the holder an option on the company's stock. In contrast to a call option, a put option gives the holder the right to sell a share of stock at a specified price up to the expiration date. It is the mirror image of a call option. In what follows, we will focus only on the valuation of call options.

VALUATION ON EXPIRATION DATE

Suppose that we were concerned with the value of a call option, (hereafter simply called an option) on its expiration date. The value of the option is simply

$$V_o = \text{Max}(V_s - E, O) \tag{23A-1}$$

where V_s, is the market price of one share of stock, E is the exercise price of the option, and Max means the maximum value of V_s, $- E$ or zero, whichever is greater. To illustrate the formula, suppose one share of Selby Corporation Ltd.'s stock is $25 at the expiration date and that the exercise price of an option is $15. The value of the option would be $25 - $15 = $10. Note that the value of the option is determined solely by the value of the stock less the exercise price; however, the option cannot have a negative value. When the exercise price exceeds the value of the stock, the value of the option becomes zero.

This notion is illustrated graphically in Fig. 23-2, where the theoretical value of a warrant is shown. The expiration value of the option lies along the theoretical-value line; the horizontal axis represents the price of a share of stock at the expiration date.

VALUATION PRIOR TO EXPIRATION

Consider now the value of an option with one period to expiration. For simplicity, let us assume that it can be exercised only on the expiration date. The value of stock at the expiration date is not known, but rather is subject to probabilistic beliefs. As long as there is some time to expiration, it is possible for the market value of the option to be greater than its theoretical value. The reason is that the option *may* have value in the future. This was discussed for the warrant, so further discussion is not necessary. The actual value of the option might be described by the dashed line in Fig. 23-2.

The effect of time to expiration   In general, the longer the period of time to expiration, the greater the value of the option relative to its theoretical value. This makes sense in that there is more time in which the option may have value. Moreover, the further in the future one pays the price, the lower its present value, and this too enhances the option's value. As the expiration date of an option approaches, the relationship between the option value and the stock value becomes more convex. This is illustrated in Fig. 23-A-1. Line 1 represents an option with a shorter time to expiration than that for line 2, and line 2 represents an option with a shorter time to expiration than that for line 3.

The influence of volatility   Usually the most important factor in the valuation of options is the price volalitiliy of the associated stock. More specifically, the greater the possibility of extreme outomes, the greater the value of the option to the holder, all other things the same. We may, at the beginning of a period, be considering options on two shares that have the following probability distributions of possible values at the expiration of the option:

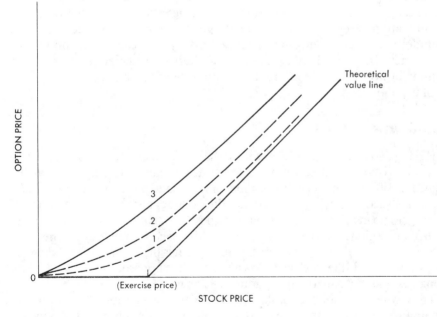

FIGURE 23A-1   Relation between price and option price for various expiration dates

Probability of occurrence	Price of Share A	Price of Share B
0.10	$30	$20
0.25	36	30
0.30	40	40
0.25	44	50
0.10	50	60

The expected stock price at the end of the period is the same for both shares: $40. For Share B, however, there is a much larger dispersion of possible outcomes. Suppose that the exercise prices of options to purchase Share A and Share B at the end of the period are also the same, say $38. Thus, the two shares have the same expected values at the end of the period, and the options have the same exercise price. The expected value of the option for Share A at the end of the period, however, is

$$\text{Option } A = 0(0.10) + 0(0.25) + (\$40 - \$38)(0.30)$$
$$+ (\$44 - \$38)(0.25) + (\$50 - \$38)(0.10) = \$3.30$$

whereas that for Share B is

$$\text{Option } B = 0(0.10) + 0(0.25) + (\$40 - \$38)(0.30)$$
$$+ (\$50 - \$38)(0.25) + (\$60 - \$38)(0.10) = \$5.80$$

Thus, the greater dispersion of possible outcomes for share B leads to a greater expected value of option price on the expiration date. The reason is that values for the option cannot be negative. As a result, the greater the dispersion, the greater the magnitude of favorable outcomes as measured by the share price minus the exercise price. Increases in the volatility of the shares therefore increase the magnitude of favorable outcomes for the option buyer and, hence, increase the value of the option.

HEDGING WITH OPTIONS

Having two related financial assets—a share and an option on that share—we can set up a risk-free hedged position. Price movements in one of the financial assets will be offset by opposite price movements in the other. A hedged position can be established by buying the share (holding it long) and by writing options. If the share goes up in price, we gain in our long position; that is, in the stock we hold. We lose in the options we have written, because the price we must pay for the share in order to deliver to the person exercising the option is higher than it was when the option was written. If the stock goes down in price, the opposite occurs. We lose on our long position, but gain on the options we have written.

Thus, when one holds a combination of shares and options written, movements upward or downward in the price of the share are offset by the opposite movements in the value of the option position written. If one does this properly, the overall position (long in stock, options written) can be made approximately risk-free. In market equilibrium, one would expect to earn only the risk-free rate on a perfectly hedged position.

BLACK-SCHOLES OPTION MODEL

In a seminal paper, Fischer Black and Myron Scholes developed a precise model for determining the equilibrium value of an option.[6] This model is based on the hedging notion discussed above. Black-Scholes assume an option that can be exercised only at maturity, no transaction costs or market imperfections, a stock that pays no dividend, a known short-term interest rate at which market participants can both borrow and lend, and finally, share price movements that follow a random pattern.

Given these assumptions, we can determine the equilibrium value of an option. Should the actual price of the option differ from that given by the model, we could establish a riskless hedged position and earn a return in excess of the short-term interest rate. As arbitragers entered the scene, the excess return would eventually be driven out and the price of the option would equal that value given by the model.

To illustrate a hedged position, suppose that the appropriate relationship between the option and the stock of XYZ Corporation Ltd. were that shown in Fig. 23A-2. Suppose further that the current market price of the stock were $20 and the price of the option $7. At $20 a share, the slope of the line in Fig. 23A-2 is one-half. A hedged position could be undertaken by buying a share of stock for $20 and writing two options at $7 each. The "net money" invested in this position would be $20 − 2($7) = $6.

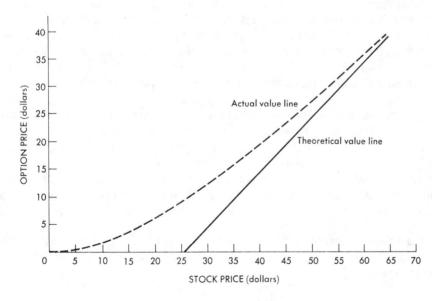

FIGURE 23A-2 Relation between the option price and the stock price for XYZ Corporation

[6]"The Pricing of Options and Corporate Liabilities," *Journal of Political Economy*, 81 (May-June 1973), 637-54.

This combination of holding one share of stock long and two options short leaves us essentially hedged with respect to risk. If the stock drops slightly in value, the value of the short position goes up by approximately an equal amount. We say *approximately* because with changes in the price of the common and with changes in time, the ideal hedge ratio changes. With a stock price increase, for example, the slope of the line in Fig. 23A-2 increases. Therefore, fewer options would need to be written. If the stock price declines, the slope decreases and more options would need to be written. If the stock price declines, the slope decreases and more options would need to be written to maintain a hedge. In addition, the line itself will shift downward as time goes on and the expiration date approaches. This was illustrated in Fig. 23A-1. The downward shift due to the passage of time causes the line to be more convex and, therefore, its slope to be affected.

Thus, one's short position in options must be continually adjusted for changes in the stock price and for changes in time if a riskless hedged position is to be maintained. The assumptions of the model make this possible; but in the real world, transaction costs make it impractical to adjust one's short position continuously. Even here, however, the risk that will appear as a result of moderate changes in share price or of the passage of time will be small. Moreover, it can be diversified away. For practical purposes, then, it is possible to maintain a hedged position that is approximately risk-free. Arbitrage will assure that the return on this position is approximately the short-term, risk-free rate.

If the price of the option got out of line with that of the share, it would be possible for a person to earn more than the short-term rate on a hedged position. In the example above, the "net money" invested in the position was $6[$20 − 2($7)]. As the total hedged position is riskless, the "net money" invested should provide a return equal only to the short-term rate. If for some reason the prices on the two instruments got out of line with each other, it would be possible to earn a return on the total position in excess of the short-term rate times the "net money" invested. In other words, excess returns would be possible on a position perfectly hedged for risk.

As a result, arbitragers would enter the picture and would borrow large sums of money, establish hedged positions, and reap the excess returns available. This action would continue until the buying or selling pressure on the prices of the stock and the option drove such prices into "equilibrium" with each other. At such time, the return on the "net money" invested in a fully hedged position would once again be the short-term rate. Thus, there are equilibrating forces that cause a riskless hedge to provide a return equal to the short-term rate.

The exact formula and implications In this context, the equilibrium value of an option that entitles the holder to buy one share of stock is shown by Black and Scholes to be

$$V_o = V_s N(d_1) - \left(\frac{E}{e^{rt}}\right) N(d_2) \qquad \text{(23A-2)}$$

where V_s = the current price of the stock
$\quad E$ = the exercise price of the option
$\quad e$ = 2.71828

r = the short-term interest rate continuously compounded

t = the length of time in years to the expiration of the option

$N(d)$ = the value of the cumulative normal density function

$$d_t = \frac{\ln(V_s/E + (r + 1/2\sigma^2)t}{\sigma\sqrt{t}}$$

$$d_2 = \frac{\ln(V_s/E) + (r - 1/2\sigma^2)t}{\sigma\sqrt{t}}$$

ln = the natural logarithm

σ = the standard deviation of the annual rate of return on the stock continuously compounded

The important implication of this formula is that the value of the option is a function of the short-term interest rate, of the time to expiration, and of the variance rate of return on the stock, but it is not a function of the expected return on the stock. The value of the option in Eq. (23A-2) increases with the increase of the duration to expiration, t, the standard deviation, σ, and the short-term interest rate, r.

The reasons for the first two relationships with option values is obvious from our earlier discussion. The last is not so obvious. Recall that a person is able to take a position in options that will provide the same dollar movements as the associated stock, but with a lower net investment. The "difference" in net money in the option relative to the stock may be invested in short-term market instruments. The greater the return on these investments, therefore, the greater the attraction of the option relative to the stock, and the greater its value. Another way to look at the matter is that the greater the interest rate, the lower the present value of exercise price that will need to be paid in the future if the option is exercised, and the greater the value of the option. Of the three factors affecting the value of the option, however, the short-term interest rate has the least impact.

In solving the formula, we know the current share price, the time to expiration, the exercise price, and the short-term interest rate. The key unknown, then, is the standard deviation. This must be estimated. The usual approach is to use the past volatility of the share's return as a proxy for the future. Black and Scholes as well as others have tested the model using standard deviations estimated from past data with some degree of success. Given the valuation equation for options, Black and Scholes derive the ratio of shares of stock to options necessary to maintain a fully hedged position. It is shown to be $N(d_1)$, which was defined earlier. Thus, the Black-Scholes model permits the quantification of the various factors that affect the value of an option. As we saw, the key factor is estimating the future volatility of the stock.

The Canadian Options Market

In Canada, call options have been traded on the Montreal Stock Exchange since September 1975 and on the Toronto Stock Exchange since 1976 while put options have been traded on both exchanges since January 1979. The trading of both call and put options is controlled by TransCanada Options Inc., a corporation jointly owned by the Toronto and Montreal Stock Exchanges and formed in April 1977 upon the merging of the Montreal Options Clearing Corporation (abbreviated MOCC and owned by the MSE) and the Canadian Clearing Corporation for Options Ltd. (abbreviated CCCO and owned by the TSE.) The resulting corporation, TransCanada Options Inc., thus acts as the sole issuing and clearing body for Exchange-traded options in Canada and functions through the facilities of both the TSE and MSE.

Prior to the creation of Exchange-traded options as noted above, option trading was carried on in the over-the-counter market but on a comparatively small scale because of the limited secondary market that was available. Once an investor purchased an over-the-counter (OTC) option, he or she either exercised the option and purchased the shares or let the option expire. The primary advantage which the introduction of Exchange-traded options brought was greater flexibility to both buyers and sellers. The buyer of the option was no longer locked in for the life of the option but could, if so desired, resell the option through the Exchange secondary market before the option contract expired.

The effective creation of a secondary market via the introduction of Exchange traded options on the TSE and the MSE was made possible by several key improvements in the options market: (1) the standardization of stock option contract and trading practices; (2) public reporting of option prices and volume in more than twenty daily newspapers across Canada; and (3) the development of TransCanada Options Inc.

The standardization of options contract and trading practices provides (1) an option contract which usually covers 100 shares of the underlying security with the option contract premium being quoted in "price per share"; (2) that all options contracts written on a particular security expire on either a January / April / July / October, a February / May / August / November, or a March / June / September / December cycle; and, (3) that all option contracts on either the MSE or TSE expire on the third Friday of the month of expiration at exactly 5:30 p.m. Toronto time. The significance of daily reporting of option prices and volume insofar as the creation of an effective secondary market is concerned is that information on the market is made public. The creation of TransCanada Options Inc., itself, provided a body which not only issues but guarantees all option contracts traded on Canadian stock exchanges. This guarantee aspect of option contract trading is crucial to the effective trading of options in Canada and as such, the corporation has developed a strict regulatory framework controlling all aspects of option trading.

Option contracts are usually written on the shares of the larger Canadian companies. The reader is encouraged to review the financial newspapers (*Financial Post, Globe and Mail, Financial Times*, etc.) for a complete listing.

A SUMMING UP

In summary, it is possible to establish a riskless hedged position by buying a stock and by writing options. The hedge ratio determines the portion of stock held long in relation to the options that are written. In efficient financial markets, the rate of return on a perfectly hedged position would be the risk-free rate. If this is the case, it is possible to determine the appropriate value of the option at the beginning of the period. If the actual value is above or below this value, arbitrage should drive the price of the option toward the correct price.

The Black-Scholes option-pricing model provides an exact formula for determining the value of an option based on the volatility of the stock, the price of the stock, the exercise price of the option, the time to expiration of the option, and the short term interest rate. The model is based on the notion that investors are able to maintain reasonably hedged positions over time and that arbitrage will drive the return on such positions to the risk-free rate. As a result, the option price will bear a precise relationship to the stock price. The Black-Scholes model provides considerable insight into the valuation of contingent claims.

Questions

1. Because the interest on convertible bonds is tax deductible, but the dividend on a convertible preferred is not, would a company be more inclined to force or stimulate conversion of a convertible preferred than it would a convertible bond?

2. This chapter has argued that convertibles are a form of delayed equity financing allowing the sale of equity at a 10 to 20 percent premium over current market price. Yet most convertibles are finally called only if the current market price is well in excess of conversion price. Would not the firm have been better off to wait and sell the common stock? Explain your position.

3. If convertible securities can be issued at a lower effective interest rate than long-term bonds, why would a company ever issue straight debt?

4. Why do warrants whose theoretical value is zero sell for positive prices?

5. Suppose you are the financial manager of a rather closely held small electronics firm. You have a favorable investment opportunity and are considering raising funds to finance it, using subordinated convertible debentures or straight bonds with warrants attached. Equity funds are not a possibility, as you feel the current stock price has been unnecessarily penalized for recent start-up expenses and the firm's high debt ratio (relative to the industry). If you expect additional large future funds requirements, which financing alternative would you adopt? Why?

6. Why might a convertible bondholder elect to convert voluntarily?

7. What reasons can you offer for the use of warrants by small, rapidly growing companies?

8. Why does the market price of an option such as a warrant usually exceed its value as common stock?

9. When a convertible security is converted into common stock, there is dilution in earnings per share. Would you expect the market price of the stock to decline as a result of this dilution?

10. If the desire of a company in selling convertible securities is delayed equity financing, would it not be wise to establish at the time the security is sold a "step-up" in conversion price every few years?

11. Why would an investor want to invest in warrants as opposed to common stock?

12. As a lender, how attractive are warrants to you as a "sweetener"? Will you give terms more favorable than you otherwise would?

Problems with Solutions

1. The common stock of a company sells at $37.50 per share. Calculate the conversion price, the conversion ratio, the initial conversion value and the number of new common shares issued assuming 100 percent conversion if the company issues $12.5 million of 10 percent convertible, $100 preferred. The initial conversion premium is 20 percent and the call price, $105.

Conversion price = $37.50 + (0.2 × $37.50) = $45.00

Conversion ratio = $100 ÷ $45 = 2.222

Initial conversion value = $37.50 × 2.222 = $83.33

Number of new common shares = $\dfrac{\$12\ 500\ 000}{100} \times 2.222 = 277\ 750$

Problems

1. The Charrier Boat Company Ltd. has current earnings of $3 a share with 500 000 shares outstanding. The company plans to issue 40 000 shares of 7 percent, $50-par-value convertible preferred stock at par. The preferred stock is convertible into two shares of common for each preferred share held. The common stock has a current market price of $21 per share.
  (a) What is the preferred stock's conversion value?
  (b) What is its conversion premium?
  (c) Assuming that total earnings stay the same, what will be the effect of the issue on earnings per share before conversion? after full conversion?
  (d) If profits after taxes increase by $1 million, what will be earnings per share before conversion? after full conversion?

2. The common stock of the Davidson Corporation Ltd. earns $2.50 per share, has a 60 percent dividend payout, and sells at a P/E ratio of 10. Davidson wishes to offer $10 million of 9 percent, 20-year convertible debentures with an initial conversion premium of 20 percent and a call price of $105. Davidson currently has 1 million common shares outstanding and has a 50 percent tax rate.
  (a) What is the conversion price?
  (b) What is the conversion ratio per $1 000 debenture?
  (c) What is the initial conversion value of each debenture?
  (d) How many new shares of common must be issued if all debentures are converted?
  (e) If Davidson can increase operating earnings (before taxes) by $1 million per year with the proceeds of the debenture issue, compute the new earnings per share and earnings retained before and after conversion.

3. Assume that the Davidson Corporation Ltd. (in problem 2) raised the $10 million through an issue of stock (total spread and expenses = 10 percent of gross proceeds of issue). How many new shares would have to be issued? If operating earnings were increased by $1 million through the use of the proceeds, compute the new earnings per share and earnings retention. Compare your answers with those obtained in 2(e) above.

4. Assume that the Davidson Corporation (in problem 2) could sell $10 million in straight debt at 12 percent as an alternative to the convertible issue. Compute the earnings per share and earnings retained after issuance of the straight debt under the assumption of a $1 million increase in operating earnings and compare your answers with those obtained in 2(e) above.

5. The Beruth Company Ltd. needs to raise $10 million by means of a debt issue. It has the following alternatives:
   (a) A 20-year, 8 percent convertible debenture issue with a $50 conversion price and $1 000 face value, or
   (b) A 20-year, 10 percent straight debt issue. Each $1 000 bond has a detachable warrant to purchase 4 shares of stock for a total of $200.
   The company has a 50 percent tax rate, and its stock is currently selling at $40 per share. Its net income before interest and taxes is a constant 20 percent of its total capitalization, which currently appears as follows:

Common stock (par $5)	$ 5 000 000
Capital surplus	10 000 000
Retained earnings	15 000 000
Total	$30 000 000

   (a) Show the capitalizations resulting from each alternative, both before and after conversion or exercise (a total of four capitalizations).
   (b) Compute earnings per share currently and under each of the four capitalizations determined in part (a).
   (c) If the price of Beruth stock went to $75, determine the theoretical value of each warrant issued under alternative (b) above.

6. Using Eq. (23-2), compute the theoretical value of each of the following warrants.

Warrant	N	P_s	E
(a)	5	$100	$400
(b)	10	10	60
(c)	2.3	4	10
(d)	3.54	$27^1/_8$	35.40

7. Stanley Zinc Company Ltd. called its 7 percent convertible subordinated debentures for redemption on March 25, 1983. The call price was $106. A holder of a $1 000 bond was entitled to convert into 34.7 shares of stock. At the time of the call announcement, the common stock of Stanley Zinc was selling at $43 per share.
   (a) What is the approximate market price at which the debentures would be selling at the time of the announcement?
   (b) By what percentage would market price per share need to drop before bondholders would rationally accept the call price?

8. Max Murphy Ltd. has warrants outstanding which allow the holder to purchase 3 shares of stock for a total $60 for each warrant that is held. Currently, the market price per share of Max Murphy common is $18. However, investors hold the following probabilistic beliefs about the stock six months hence.

Market price per share	$16	$18	$20	$22	$24
Probability	0.15	0.20	0.30	0.20	0.15

(a) What is the present theoretical value of the warrant?

(b) What is the expected value of stock price 6 months hence?

(c) What is the expected theoretical value of the warrant 6 months hence?

(d) Would you expect the present market price of the warrant to equal its theoretical value? If not, why not?

9. Suppose you have just bought a warrant which entitles you to purchase two shares of stock for $45. The market price of the stock is $26 per share, whereas the market price of the warrant is $10 in excess of its theoretical value. One year later the stock has risen in price to $50 per share. The warrant now sells for $2 more than its theoretical value.

(a) If the common stock paid $1 in dividends for the year, what is the return on investment in the common?

(b) What is the return on investment in the warrant?

(c) Why do the two rates of return differ?

10. Sadfield Manufacturing Company Ltd. plans to issue $10 million in 7½ percent convertible subordinated debentures. Currently, the stock price is $36 per share, and the company believes it could obtain a conversion premium (issuing price in excess of conversion value) of approximately 12 percent. The call price of the debenture in the first ten years is $1 060 per bond, after which it drops to $1 030 in the next ten years and to $1 000 in the last ten years. To allow for fluctuations in the market price of the stock, the company does not want to call the debentures until their conversion value is at least 15 percent in excess of the call price. Earnings per share are expected to grow at an 8 percent compound annual rate for the foreseeable future, and the company envisions no change in its price/earnings ratio.

(a) Determine the expected length of time that must elapse before the company is in a position to force conversion.

(b) Is the issuance of a convertible security a good idea for the company?

Selected References

ALEXANDER, GORDON J., and ROGER D. STOVER, "The Effect of Forced Conversion on Common Stock Prices," *Financial Management*, 9 (Spring 1980), 39-45.

_____, and DAVID B. KUHNAU, "Market Timing Strategies in Convertible Debt Financing," *Journal of Finance*, 34 (March 1979), 143-56.

BACON, PETER W., and EDWARD L. WINN, JR., "The Impact of Forced Conversion on Stock Prices," *Journal of Finance*, 24 (December 1969), 871-74.

BLACK, FISCHER, and MYRON SCHOLES, "The Pricing of Options and Corporate Liabilities," *Journal of Political Economy*, 81 (May-June 1973), 637-54:

_____, "The Valuation of Option and a Test of Market Efficiency," *Journal of Finance*, 27 (May 1972), 399-417.

BRENNAN, MICHAEL J., and EDUARDO S. SCHWARTZ, "Analyzing Convertible Bonds," *Journal of Financial and Quantitative Analysis*, 15 (November 1980), 907-29.

_____, "Convertible Bonds: Valuation and Optimal Strategies for Call and Conversion," *Journal of Finance*, 32 (December 1977), 1699-1715.

BRIGHAM, EUGENE F., "An Analysis of Convertible Debentures: Theory and Some Empirical Evidence," *Journal of Finance*, 21 (March 1966), 35-54.

FRANK, WERNER G., and CHARLES O. KRONCKE, "Classifying Conversions of Convertible Debentures over Four Years," *Financial Management*, 3 (Summer 1974), 33-42.

JENNINGS, EDWARD H., "An Estimate of Convertible Bond Premiums," *Journal of Financial and Quantitative Analysis,* 9 (January 1974), 33-56.

LEWELLEN, WILBUR G., and GEORGE A. RACETTE, "Convertible Debt Financing," *Journal of Financial and Quantitative Analysis*, 7 (December 1973), 777-92.

McDANIEL, WILLIAM R., "Convertible Bonds in Perfect and Imperfect Markets", *Journal of Financial Research*, Spring 1983, 51-65.

MERTON, ROBERT C., "On the Pricing of Corporate Debt," *Journal of Finance*, 29 (May 1974), 449-70.

MILLER, ALEXANDER B., "How to Call Your Convertible," *Harvard Business Review*, 49 (May-June 1971), 66-70.

NOREEN, ERIC, and MARK WOLFSON, "Equilibrium Warrant Pricing Models and Accounting for Executive Stock Options," *Journal of Accounting Research*, forthcoming.

PIPER, THOMAS R., and JASPER H. ARNOLD, III, "Warrants and Convertible Debt as Financing Vehicles in the Private Placement Market," *Explorations in Economic Research of the National Bureau of Economic Research* 4 (Spring 1977), 277-302.

RUBINSTEIN, MARK, and JOHN C. COX, *Option Markets*. Englewood Cliffs, N.J.: Prentice-Hall, 1982.

RUSH, DAVID F., and RONALD W. MELICHER, "An Empirical Examination of Factors Which Influence Warrant Prices," *Journal of Finance*, 29 (December 1974), 1449-66.

SHARPE, WILLIAM F., *Investments*, 2d ed. Englewood Cliffs, N.J.: Prentice-Hall, 1981, Chapter 16.

SMITH, CLIFFORD W., JR., "Option Pricing: A Review," *Journal of Financial Economics* 3 (January-March 1976), 3-51.

STONE, BERNELL K., "Warrant Financing," *Journal of Financial and Quantitative Analysis*, 11 (March 1976), 143-54.

STOREY, RONALD G. and CECIL R. DIPCHAND. "Factors Related to the Conversion Record of Convertible Securities: The Canadian Experience 1946-75," *Journal of Financial Research*, 1 (Winter 1978), 71-83.

VAN HORNE, JAMES C., "Warrant Valuation in Relation to Volatility and Opportunity Costs," *Industrial Management Review*, 10 (Spring 1969), 19-32.

VIII

SPECIAL AREAS
OF FINANCIAL
MANAGEMENT

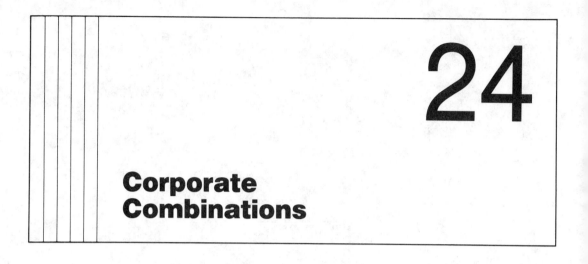

Corporate Combinations

Growth is essential to the success and vitality of virtually all companies. Without it, a company has difficulty in generating a dedication of purpose and in attracting first-rate managers. Growth can be either internal or external. Up to now, we have considered only the former category, where a firm acquires specific assets and finances them by retention of earnings and/or external financing. External growth, on the other hand, involves the acquisition of or combination with another company. In principle, growth by acquiring another company is little different from growth by acquiring a specific asset. Each requires an initial outlay, which is expected to be followed by future benefits. The objective of either type of acquisition is to maximize the value of the firm to existing shareholders.

Types of Corporate Combinations

There are three principal methods whereby corporate combinations are effected: by a statutory amalgamation or merger; by a consolidation resulting from a purchase of assets; and by a parent-subsidiary relationship resulting from a purchase of voting common shares.[1] The selection of a specific approach depends on legal, tax, and other associated factors. We discuss some of these later in the chapter. First we give a brief summary of the above-mentioned approaches to combinations.

---

[1] John R. E. Parker and George C. Baxter, *Corporate Combinations and Intercorporate Investments* (Toronto: Canadian Institute of Chartered Accountants, 1980), Chapter 1.

STATUTORY AMALGAMATIONS

A statutory amalgamation or merger involves a combination of two or more companies whereby the amalgamating corporations are continued as one corporate entity. The surviving company, by law, possesses the assets, rights, and privileges and is subject to the liabilities and contracts of each of the amalgamating companies. A statutory amalgamation is subject to certain provisions of the Canada Business Corporations Act or the various provincial Companies Acts. In general, these acts stipulate: (1) basic provisions to be included in the amalgamation agreement; (2) shareholders' approval of the agreement, depending on the province, usually two-thirds to three-quarters majority vote; and (3) recourse or remedies for dissenting shareholders. An amalgamation is done by law, and when all statutory requirements are met, an official certificate of amalgamation is issued.

PURCHASE OF ASSETS

The purchase-of-assets method results in a *consolidation* where a company buys all or substantially all of the assets of another company. The vendor or selling company receives cash or shares from the acquiring company and is responsible for its liabilities. This company may be liquidated after it has paid its creditors and has distributed any remaining funds to its shareholders. Or the vendor company may continue as a holding company or as an active entity in some other line of business. Various company statutes require that the shareholders of the vendor company approve the sale of the assets usually by a two-thirds majority vote. Also, dissenting shareholders have the right to require the company to pay a fair value for their shares. So far as the acquiring firm is concerned, the corporate charter may require final approval by shareholders; otherwise, the decision rests entirely with management.

PURCHASE OF COMMON SHARES

Where a company purchases the common shares of another corporate entity sufficient to give it a controlling interest, we may have a parent-subsidiary relationship. Both companies continue to exist as separate legal entities with each responsible for the management of its assets and for its outstanding obligations under the respective corporate administration. The authority to plan for corporate combinations usually rests with management as provided for in the corporate charter. However, these provisions tend to require that management present combination proposals for final approval by shareholders.

Combination through purchase of common shares is used widely in Canada. (The procedures will be discussed later in the chapter.) Also, while it is important to understand the distinction, the words *merger, amalgamation, consolidation*, and even *acquisition* tend to be used interchangeably to describe corporate combinations. Unless stated otherwise, we follow this loose interpretation in the rest of the chapter.

In the 1950-76 period, there were an estimated 6 122 corporate combinations in Canada.[2] The figure increased from an estimated 45 mergers in 1950 to 332 in 1976; the annual average over the 1960-76 period was 294. The peak period for mergers was 1967-69; in 1969 alone there were 504 mergers. In the early 1980s, the annual average was in excess of 400 mergers. Intense merger activity tends to coincide with buoyant markets, high corporate profits, and periods of economic prosperity. Merger activity also tends to be greatest in the construction, material supplies, food processing, merchandising, and general manufacturing industries. Furthermore, some 80 percent of the corporate combinations were by firms incorporated in Canada acquiring another company incorporated in Canada. The number of Canadian firms acquiring companies incorporated in foreign countries is relatively small.

Corporate combinations may lead to undue concentration of economic power which may reduce competition and adversely affect the national economy. Ironically, this issue has been a serious concern in Canada[3], but the fact remains that combinations operate in a relatively unconstrained legal environment.[4] Under the Combines Investigation Act, mergers which are likely to reduce competition significantly may be disallowed. However, this act is considered more as a deterrent to price fixing in restraint of trade than as anti-merger legislation. Since 1974, the acquisition activities of foreign firms in Canada have been subject to the scrutiny and approval of the Foreign Investment Review Agency (FIRA) which administers the Foreign Investment Review Act. In recent years, FIRA has approved 80 percent to 90 percent of applications by foreign firms for investment in Canada. The Agency does not appear to be unduly restrictive in allowing the entry of foreign investments and interests.

Reasons for Combination

The reasons for a corporate combination are usually many and complex; moreover, they are not mutually exclusive. In this section, we consider various reasons for corporate combinations individually, but the reader should realize that they operate collectively.

---

[2]Samuel A. Martin, Stanley N. Laiken and Douglas F. Haslam, *Business Combinations in the '60s: A Canadian Profile*, (Toronto: The Canadian Institute of Chartered Accountants, and London: The School of Business Administration, University of Western Ontario, 1970), 16; and J. Fred Weston, Eugene F. Brigham and Paul Halpern, *Essentials of Canadian Managerial Finance* (Toronto: Holt, Rinehart and Winston of Canada, 1979), 601.

[3]*Report of the Royal Commission on Corporate Concentration* (Ottawa: Supply and Services Canada, 1979), 166.

[4]For discussion, see C. W. Borgsdorf, "The Virtually Unconstrained Legal Environment for Mergers in Canada," *Journal of American and Foreign Antitrust and Trade Regulation*, Vol. XVIII, No. 4 (Winter 1973).

OPERATING ECONOMIES AND ECONOMIES OF SCALE

Operating economies can often be achieved through a combination of companies. Duplications of facilities can be eliminated, and marketing, accounting, purchasing, and other operations can be consolidated. For example, the need for two sales forces can sometimes be eliminated. The principal objective in a railway merger is to realize economies of operation through elimination of duplicate facilities and runs. With an industrial company merger, a firm with a product that complements an existing product line can fill out that line and, if all goes well, increase the total overall demand for the products of the acquiring company. The realization of operating economies is known as *synergism* and the fused company is of greater value than the sum of the parts—that is, 2 + 2 = 5.

In addition to operating economies, economies of scale may be possible with a merger of two companies. Economies of scale occur when average cost declines with increases in volume. We usually think of economies of scale in relation to production, but it is also possible to achieve economies of scale in marketing, purchasing, distribution, accounting, and even finance. The idea is simply to concentrate a greater volume of activity into a given facility, into a given number of people, into a given distribution system, and so on. In other words, increases in volume permit a more efficient utilization of resources. As in anything else, however, there are limits. Beyond a point, increases in volume may cause more problems than they remedy and a company may actually become less efficient. Economists speak of an "envelope curve", with economies of scale possible up to some optimal point after which dis-economies occur.

Operating economies can best be realized with a *horizontal merger*, in which two companies in the same line of business are combined. The economies achieved by this means result primarily from eliminating duplicate facilities and offering a broader product line in the hope of increasing total demand. A *vertical merger*, whereby a company either expands forward toward the ultimate consumer or backward toward the source of raw material, may also bring about economies. This type of merger gives a company more control over its distribution and purchasing. In the formation of Algoma Steel Corporation in 1934, one of the purposes was a complete vertical integration of steel from extraction of ore to the final sale of the product. There are few operating economies in a *conglomerate merger*, where two companies in unrelated lines of business combine.[5]

MANAGEMENT ACQUISITION

Closely related to operating economies is the acquisition of management. If a firm finds that it is unable to hire top-quality management and that it has no one

---

[5]For an example, see Dennis M. Mueller, "A Theory of Conglomerate Mergers," *Quarterly Journal of Economics*, 83 (Nov. 1969), 652-53. The *Report of the Royal Commission on Corporate Concentration* noted that in 1974, 68 percent of combinations were horizontal, 9 percent vertical, and 23 percent conglomerate. In the last three decades the percentage of horizontal mergers was relatively constant, that for vertical mergers decreased significantly in recent years, and conglomerates increased.

coming up through the ranks, it may seek a combination with another company having aggressive and competent management. The choice may be between gradual stagnation with an existing organization or combination with another company in order to obtain aggressive management and prospects for growth. To foster the long-run growth of shareholder wealth, the latter may be the only feasible alternative.

GROWTH

A company may not be able to grow at a sufficiently fast or balanced rate by internal expansion and may find that its only way of achieving a desired growth rate is by acquiring other companies. The cost of growth by acquisition may well be cheaper than the real cost of internal growth; the numerous costs and risks involved in developing and embarking on a new product line may be avoided through acquisition of a going concern. In addition, it is usually quicker to acquire new products and facilities through mergers than through internal development. An important aspect of external growth may be the acquisition of the research capabilities of another firm. Because research and development tend to be oriented towards specific goals, the acquiring company may be unable to develop such capabilities on its own. Closely related to research and development is the possession of basic patents. A company having certain patent rights may be extremely valuable for this reason alone.

Although these features may contribute to higher future earnings and growth of the acquiring company, the critical factor is the price paid for the acquisition. If the company to be acquired is reasonably priced in the market (that is, it is not undervalued or overvalued), its acquisition is unlikely to increase share price *unless* there is synergism. Increased growth in *total* earnings is not the important thing—it is increased growth in earnings *per share*, all other things being the same. Unfortunately, in certain cases growth in sales, assets, and total earnings appears to have supplanted maximization of shareholder wealth as the primary goal of the firm.

FINANCING

Rapidly growing companies can run into difficulty in financing their growth. Rather than curtail their expansion, they may seek to combine with a company having the liquidity and stability necessary for financing the contemplated growth. The "cash-rich" company can benefit by being able to utilize its liquidity in a growth situation. The growing company benefits because it does not have to give up exciting opportunities in order to provide for a period of "digestion."

TAXATION

The avoidance of corporate income taxes is a factor in some mergers. A company with a tax loss carry-forward may want to acquire one or more profitable companies in order to be able to utilize its carry-forward. Otherwise, the carry-forward may expire at the end of five years for lack of sufficient profits to utilize it completely. For this reason, a company may be willing to pay a fairly substantial price to acquire a profitable company. The tax department does not look favorably on mergers motivated solely by the tax loss carry-forward advantage. The privilege is extended only under certain conditions. For example, if the acquiring firm merges with a profitable firm in the same line of business, the tax loss carry-forward may be allowed.

DIVERSIFICATION

Diversification is the motive in some mergers. By acquiring a firm in a different line of business, a company may be able to reduce cyclical instability in earnings. Although it is virtually impossible to find two companies with negative correlation in earnings, it is possible to find situations in which there is only moderate correlation. Related to the argument for diversification is the notion of spreading risk. To the extent that investors in a company's stock dislike high risk and are concerned only with the total risk of the firm, a reduction in earnings instability would have a favorable impact on share price.

This argument assumes that investors evaluate risk solely in relation to the total risk of the firm. We know from Chapters 5 and 15, however, that investors can diversify risk on their own. If they evaluate risk in an overall market context, they will diversify at least as effectively on their own as the firm can do for them. Particularly when the stock of the company being acquired is publicly traded, there is no reason to believe that investors cannot diversify their portfolios efficiently. Diversification as a reason for merging is not of value to shareholders. Consequently, it would not lead to an increase in share price. For the most part, it is the prospect for synergism that is valuable when it comes to a merger.

PERSONAL REASONS

Personal reasons may dictate the desirability of a merger. For example, in a closely held company, the individuals who have controlling interest may want their company to be acquired by another company that has an established market for its shares. For estate planning purposes, it may be desirable for these individuals to hold shares of stock that are readily marketable and for which market-price quotations are available. The owners of a tightly held company may have too much of their wealth tied up in the company. By merging with a publicly held company, they obtain a marked improvement in their liquidity, enabling them to sell some of their shares and diversify their investments.

Combination as an Investment Decision

From the standpoint of the acquiring company, the acquisition of shares or assets of the selling company can be treated as another aspect of capital budgeting. In principle, the prospective acquisition should be evaluated in much the same manner as any capital-budgeting project. There is an initial outlay and expected future benefits. Whether the outlay be cash or stock, the firm should attempt to allocate capital optimally in order to increase shareholder wealth over the long run. The only difference is that, with acquisitions, the initial cost may not be established; indeed, it usually is subject to bargaining. If it can be assumed that the acquiring company intends to maintain its existing capital structure over the long run, it is appropriate to evaluate the prospective acquisition without reference to the way it is financed.

In evaluating the prospective acquisition, the buying company should estimate the future cash income after taxes that the acquisition is expected to add, net of any new investment. The estimates should include consideration of any synergistic effects, for their interest is in the marginal impact of the acquisition. Moreover, the cash flow estimates should be made before allowing for any financial charges. The idea is to divorce the prospective acquisition's financial structure from its overall worth as an investment. The concern is with operating cash flows that arise from operating the acquired company and not with prospective net income after financial charges. On the basis of these considerations, suppose the following incremental cash flows are expected from a prospective acquisition:

	Average for years (in thousands)				
	1-5	6-10	11-15	16-20	21-25
Annual cash income after taxes from acquisition	$2 000	$1 800	$1 400	$800	$200
New investment	$ 600	$ 300	—	—	—
Cash flow after taxes	$1 400	$1 500	$1 400	$800	$200

If the acquisition is not expected to increase or decrease the business-risk complexion of the firm as perceived by suppliers of capital, the appropriate discount rate would be the cost of capital. Assuming this rate to be 15 percent after taxes, the present value of the expected net cash flows shown above will be $8 724 000, less any liabilities assumed. This figure suggests that the company can pay a maximum price of $8 724 000 for the acquisition and still be acting in the best interests of the company's shareholders. The actual price paid will be subject to negotiation. However, the present value of the prospective acquisition should represent an upper boundary for the acquiring company. Any price up to this amount should result in a worthwhile investment for the company. As a result, the market price per share of the firm's stock should increase over the long run. If the price paid is in excess of the acquisition's present value, this suggests that capital is less than optimally allocated.

ESTIMATING CASH FLOWS

In an acquisition, there are the usual problems with respect to estimating future cash flows. However, the process may be somewhat easier than for a capital-budgeting proposal because the company being acquired is a going concern. The acquiring company buys more than assets; it buys experience, an organization, and proven performance. The estimates of sales and costs are based on past results;

consequently, they are likely to be more accurate than the estimates for a new investment proposal. Less uncertainty involved in the estimates means less dispersion of expected outcomes and lower risk, all other things remaining constant. However, an additional problem is introduced when the acquisition is to be integrated into the acquiring company. Under these circumstances, the acquisition cannot be evaluated as a separate operation; the synergistic effects must be considered. Estimates of these effects are difficult, particularly if the organization that results from the acquisition is complex.

The Accounting Treatment

While the after-tax cash flows are important in the investment decision, the management of an acquiring firm should also be interested in the accounting treatment for corporate combinations. The concern over accounting treatment is related to the impact that such treatment may have on reported earnings per share subsequent to the combination.

From an accounting standpoint, a combination of two companies is treated either as a *purchase* or as a *pooling-of- interests*. Under the purchase method, the acquiring company reports the assets acquired and the liabilities assumed at the cost to the acquiring company. The purchase price paid for the acquisition has to be allocated to the net assets acquired. These assets will be revalued in light of market conditions and be reported in the balance sheet of the acquiring company as at the acquisition date. Fair market values are determined in the negotiation process and are an integral part of the combination agreement. Otherwise, an appraisal will have to be undertaken to determine fair market values as at the acquisition date. Where the purchase price exceeds the aggregate of the fair values of the net assets acquired, the difference is deemed *goodwill*. With respect to income from operations, the acquiring company includes the results of operations of the acquired company from the date of acquisition only.

Under the pooling of interests method, the balance sheets of the combining companies are, with some exceptions, simply added together on a line-by-line basis. No accounting recognition is given either to goodwill or to any excess of fair values over the book value of the assets of the pooled company. This arises because the pooling of interests method does not recognize that the current market value of the shares issued affects the combination and hence no revaluation of assets is undertaken. Also the reported income after combination is the aggregate of the income for the combining companies for the entire fiscal year in which the combination takes place. Financial statements for previous years are restated on the above-mentioned bases. Reported earnings will be higher with the pooling of interest accounting treatment than they will be with the purchase treatment. Consequently, acquiring firms desirous of showing "instantaneous profits" may follow the pooling of interest approach, if this option is available.

Let us briefly illustrate these accounting methods focusing first on the purchase method. The balance sheets for the acquiring and acquired companies just prior to the date of consolidation are shown in Table 24-1. The acquiring company (Company A) desires to purchase all the shares of the acquired company

(Company B) and agrees to issue 9 000 shares valued at $90 000 to the shareholders of the acquired company. Assets of Company B are revalued to an aggregate of $80 000 (Table 24-1). Net assets are therefore $55 000 ($80 000 less liabilities of $25 000). Goodwill is then $35 000 ($90 000 less $55 000). The consolidated balance sheet as at the date of acquisition for the acquiring company is then determined as shown in Table 24-1. Other factors being constant, the total consolidated assets of $940 000 is obtained regardless of the type of consideration employed.

Now assume that the pooling of interests method is used and all other assumptions in the purchase of shares illustration remain. The consolidated statement for the combined company will then be as follows:

Cash	$110 000	Current liabilities	105 000
Receivables	170 000	Long-term debt	320 000
Inventories	90 000	Common stock	390 000
	370 000	Retained earnings	85 000
Fixed assets (net)	530 000		
Total	900 000	Total	$900 000

TABLE 24-1   The Purchase Method

Balance Sheets for the Acquiring and Acquired Companies just prior to date of acquisition, Revaluations of Assets and Liabilities and Consolidated Balance Sheet for Acquiring Company as at Date of Acquisition.

	Company A— Acquring Company	Company B— Acquired Company		Consolidated
	Balance Sheet	Balance Sheet	Revaluations of (2), Goodwill and Equity Adjustments	Balance Sheet (1) + (3)
	(1)	(2)	(3)	(4)
Cash	$100 000	$10 000	$ 10 000	$110 000
Receivables	150 000	20 000	20 000	170 000
Inventories	75 000	15 000	15 000	90 000
	325 000	45 000	45 000	370 000
Fixed assets (net)	500 000	30 000	35 000	535 000
Goodwill	—	—	35 000	35 000
Total	825 000	75 000	115 000	940 000
Current liabilities	100 000	5 000	5 000	105 000
Long-term debt	300 000	20 000	20 000	320 000
Shareholders' equity				
Common stock	300 000	30 000	90 000	390 000
Retained earnings	125 000	20 000	—	125 000
Total	825 000	75 000	115 000	940 000

Despite the fact that the same net price of $90 000 is paid, there are differences in the consolidated statements prepared under the two accounting approaches. One significant difference is the resulting understatement of net assets under the pooling-of-interests method. In our example the understatement is $40 000 or 80 percent of the amount of shareholders' equity in the acquired company.

The Canadian Institute of Chartered Accountants recommends the use of the purchase method to account for combinations in the books of the acquiring company. However, in cases where it is not possible to classify the parties in a combination as the acquiring and the acquired companies, the pooling of interest method is permissible. For example, in a consolidation, a new company may be established to purchase the assets of two companies of relatively equal size. The combination is of mutual interest to both managements and neither played an unusually dominant role in the negotiations and more importantly, there is continuity of management and shareholders' interest. Under these conditions it is difficult to identify which is the acquiring company, hence the pooling of interests method may be used.

Merger Terms and Their Impact

In this section we review some of the more important terms in a corporate combination agreement. Terms governing the amount of the purchase consideration and timing of payment are usually of paramount importance to all parties. When two companies are combined, a ratio for the exchange of common shares has to be determined. This ratio of exchange affects earnings per share and the market prices of the shares of the two companies involved. Since the objective in any merger is to maximize the long-run wealth of existing shareholders, we evaluate the impact on earnings and market prices in some detail.

To simplify the discussion, we assume that the combination is effected through the purchase of common shares. The acquiring firm (Company A) buys 100 percent of the shares of the acquired firm (Company B). To finance the deal, Company A issues its shares to the shareholders of Company B; thus, there is a parent-subsidiary relationship. Under tax laws, the parent and subsidiary are taxed independently of each other—each corporate entity prepares financial statements and is taxed accordingly. However, for shareholder reporting purposes, generally accepted accounting principles require that consolidated statements be prepared in accordance with the purchase method of accounting. Some rather complex issues arise here in the preparation of these statements.

The write-off of the excess of fair values for the fixed assets over book values is, under the assumption of parent-subsidiary relationship, not allowed as a deduction for tax purposes. For example, the fair value for Company B's fixed assets in Table 24-1 is $35 000 while book value is $30 000—the excess of $5 000 is not allowable as a depreciation for tax purposes. Also, the amortization of goodwill of $35 000 is not tax-deductible. Accounting principles require the acquiring firm to (a) consolidate and depreciate the excess fixed assets of $5 000 on a straight-line basis over the remaining economic life of the assets, and (b) amortize goodwill over a maximum of 40 years on a straight-line basis. These "extraordinary adjustments" are usually called *permanent differences*.

Alternatively, with the purchase of assets and the statutory amalgamation, the acquiring or surviving company will be allowed to depreciate the excess of fair values over book values for allowable assets and to amortize some portion of goodwill for tax purposes.[6]

EARNINGS IMPACT

In evaluating the desirability of an acquisition, it is important to consider the effect that the merger has on the consolidated earnings per share. In the two firms whose balance sheets as at the date of acquisition are shown in Table 24-1, additional financial data at the time the acquisition is being considered are as follows:

	Acquiring Company A	Acquired Company B
Present earnings	$150 000	$20 000
Shares outstanding	200 000	30 000
Earnings per share	$ 0.75	$0.67
Price of share	$10.00	$3.00
Price/earnings ratio	13.22	4.48

Assume that Company B has agreed to an offer of $3 per share to be paid in the shares of the acquiring firm. The exchange ratio then is $3/$10, or about 0.3 shares of the stock of Company A for each share of Company B. In total, 9 000 shares of the acquiring company will be issued for 100 percent control of Company B. Assuming that the earnings of the component companies remain the same after the acquisition, earnings per share on a consolidated basis will be as follows:

	Consolidated statement
Earnings before adjustments	$170 000
Less permanent differences*	
Depreciation ($5 000/20 years)	(250)
Amortization of goodwill $35 000/35 years)	(1 000)
Earnings after adjustments	$168 750
Shares outstanding	209 000
Earnings per share	$0.81

*It is assumed that the remaining economic life of fixed assets is 20 years and that goodwill is amortized over 35 years.

---

[6]For further discussion, see Parker and Baxter, *op. cit.*, Chapter 2.

At the assumed exchange ratio, there is an increase in the earnings per share for Company A. However, there is a reduction in earnings per share for the former shareholders of the acquired company. For each share they previously held, they now hold 0.3 shares of Company A. Thus, earnings per share on each share held before the merger is (0.3) ($0.81) = $0.243, compared with $0.30 earned previously.

Assume, however, that the price agreed on for the shares of the acquired company is $10 per share. The ratio of exchange, then, would be $10/$10, or one share of Company A for each share of Company B. Assuming that revaluations remain as shown in Table 24-1, then goodwill is now $245 000 ($300 000 market value of shares less net fair value of assets of $55 000). In total, 30 000 shares would be issued, and earnings per share after the merger would be as follows:

	Consolidated statement
Earnings before adjustment	$170 000
Less permanent differences	
Depreciation ($5 000/20 years)	(250)
Amortization of goodwill ($245 000/35 years)	(7 000)
Earnings after adjustment	$162 750
Shares outstanding	230 000
Earnings per share	$0.71

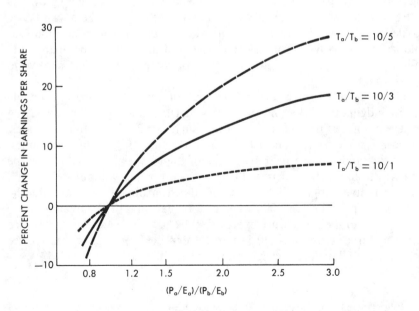

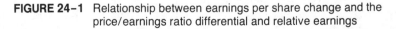

FIGURE 24-1 Relationship between earnings per share change and the price/earnings ratio differential and relative earnings

In this case, there is initial dilution in Company A's earnings per share on account of the acquisition of Company B. Dilution in earnings per share will occur any time the price/earnings ratio paid for a company exceeds the price/earnings ratio of the acquiring company. In our example, the price/earnings ratio in the first case was $3/$0.67 = 4.5, and in the second case, it was $10/$0.67 or 15. Because the original price/earnings ratio of Company A was 13.2 there would be an increase in earnings per share in the first case and a decrease in the second. Note that Company B's former shareholders get better earnings per share—$0.71 compared to $0.67 before.

Thus, both initial increases and decreases in earnings per share are possible. The *amount* of increase or decrease is a function of (1) the differential in the price/earnings ratio and (2) the relative size of the two firms as measured by total earnings.[7] The higher the price/earnings ratio of the acquiring company in relation to that of the company being acquired, and the larger the earnings of the acquired company in relation to those of the acquiring company, the greater increase in earnings per share of the acquiring company. These relationships are illustrated in Fig. 24-1 for three different earnings relationships. The a subscript for total earnings, T_a, and price/earnings ratio, P_a/E_a, denotes the acquiring company while the b subscript for T_b and P_b/E_b denotes the company being acquired.

Future earnings impact   If the decision to acquire another company is based solely on the initial impact on earnings per share, a company would never acquire another if there were an initial dilution in earnings per share. However, this type of analysis does not take into account the possibility of a future growth in earnings resulting from the merger. If the earnings of Company B are expected to grow at a faster rate than those of Company A, a high ratio of exchange for the stock may be justified, despite the fact that there is an initial dilution in earnings per share for shareholders of Company A. The superior growth of the acquired company may eventually result in higher earnings per share for these shareholders relative to earnings without the merger.

Another drawback to using the initial impact on earnings per share as the sole criterion for judging the value of a merger is that the earnings of the surviving company are not necessarily an additive affair, such that 2 + 2 = 4. In many cases, there are *synergistic* effects, such that 2 + 2 = 5. Because of operating economies, increases in demand, and so forth, earnings of the surviving company may be greater than the sum of the earnings of the two companies without the merger.

In our example, suppose that total consolidated earnings three years after the merger are expected to be $250 000 whereas total earnings of Company A three years hence without the merger are expected to be $190 000. Assuming the price paid for the acquired company is $10 a share, the expected earnings per share three years hence, with and without the merger, will be as follows:

---

[7]See Walter J. Mead, "Instantaneous Merger Profit as a Conglomerate Merger Motive," *Western Economics Journal*, 7 (Dec. 1969), 295-306.

	With merger	Without merger
Expected earnings before adjustments	$250 000	$190 000
Less permanent differences		
Depreciation ($5 000/20 years)	(250)	–
Amortization of goodwill ($245 000/35 years)	(7 000)	–
Expected earnings after adjustments	$242 750	$190 000
Shares outstanding	230 000	200 000
Expected earnings per share	$1.06	$0.95

We see, then, that despite initial dilution, the acquisition of Company B produces a favorable effect on future earnings per share above the expected growth in earnings per share for Company A without the merger. We can graph expected earnings per share (as in Fig. 24-1) with and without the acquisition under the assumption of synergism. In fact, when an acquisition is being considered, graphs should be prepared under differing earnings assumptions for the combination, for preparing such multiple graphs gives management greater information on which to base negotiations.

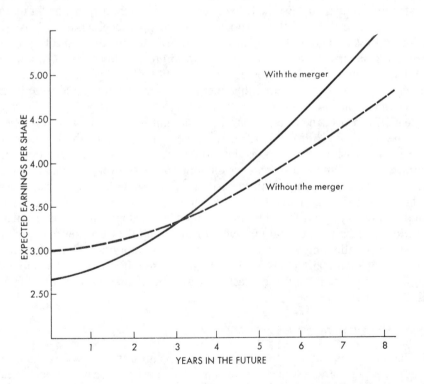

FIGURE 24–2 Expected earnings per share with and without the merger

Fig. 24-2 shows how long it will take for the dilution in earnings per share to be eliminated, and for an accretion to take place. In this example, it is three years; earnings per share drop initially, but this relative dilution is eliminated by the start of the fourth year. The greater the duration of the dilution, the less desirable the acquisition is said to be from the standpoint of the acquiring company. Some companies set a ceiling on the number of years dilution will be tolerated, and this ceiling serves as a constant in establishing the exchange ratio to be paid in the acquisition.

CASH-FLOW VERSUS EARNINGS-PER-SHARE

The analysis of an acquisition on a cash-flow basis differs from that on an earnings-per-share basis. In analyzing earnings-per-share, the question is whether earnings-per-share will improve now or in the future. In the cash-flow approach, the question is whether the expected net cash flows have a present value in excess of the acquisition cost. This approach was illustrated earlier in this chapter.

In general, the cash-flow approach looks at the valuation of an acquisition over the long run whereas the earnings-per-share approach focuses on the short run. For example, if a prospective acquisition does not result in a positive increment in earnings-per-share within a few years, it is usually ruled out if one relies only on the earnings-per-share approach. In contrast, the cash-flow approach looks at incremental cash flows likely to be generated from the acquisition for many years in the future. Thus, the earnings-per-share approach tends to bias the selection process in favor of companies with immediate growth prospects but not necessarily in favor of companies with long-term growth prospects. It should be noted that neither approach embodies a consideration of changes in business risk, which can be incorporated into either method of analysis using the techniques discussed in Chapter 14.

Aside from risk, the question is which method—cash-flow or earnings-per-share—should be used? Probably the best answer is that both methods should be employed. The cash-flow method is the more comprehensive with respect to the economic worth of an acquisition over the long run. However, if management is concerned with short-term growth in earnings-per-share and believes that this is what the market values, then a strong case can be made for the earnings-per-share method. In practice, it is difficult to imagine management ignoring the effect of an acquisition on earnings per share no matter how sound the cash-flow approach is conceptually. By the same token, an earnings-per-share approach by itself may be too short-sighted and fail to look at solid long-term growth prospects. Therefore, a strong case can be made for using a cash-flow method of analysis *in addition* to an earnings-per-share one.

MARKET VALUE IMPACT

The major emphasis in the bargaining process is on the ratio of exchange of market prices per share as well as on earnings. The market price of a publicly held stock is the focal point in the judgment of investors as to the "intrinsic" value of that company. Accordingly, it reflects the earnings potential of the company, dividends, business risk, capital structure, asset values, and other factors that bear on valuation. The ratio of exchange of market price is simply

$$\frac{\text{Market price per share of acquiring company} \times \text{Number of shares offered}}{\text{Market price per share of acquired company}}$$

For example, if the market price of Company A is $10 per share and that of Company B is $3, and Company A offers 0.3 shares of its stock for each share of Company B, the ratio of exchange would be:

$$\frac{10 \times 0.3}{3} = 1.00$$

In other words, the shares of the two companies would be exchanged on a one-to-one market price basis. If the market price of the surviving company is relatively stable at $10 a share, each set of shareholders is about as well off as before with respect to market value. However, there is little enticement to the company being acquired to accept a one-to-one market-value ratio of exchange. Consequently, the acquiring company usually must offer a price higher than the current market price per share of the company it wishes to acquire.

Even when the acquiring company offers a price higher than the current market price of the company being acquired, its own shareholders may still be better off with respect to market price per share. The reason is that there may be a difference in the price/ earnings ratios of the two companies. Suppose that Company Y is a moderate-sized company whose shares are traded in the over-the-counter market. Because, among other reasons, its shares are not particularly marketable, its price/earnings ratio is 10, which is relatively low. Company X, on the other hand, has a price/earnings ratio of 18. Assume the following financial information:

	Company X	Company Y
Present earnings	$20 000 000	$6 000 000
Shares	6 000 000	2 000 000
Earnings per share	$3.33	$3.00
Market price per share	$60.00	$30.00
Price/earnings ratio	18	10

Assume an offer of 0.667 shares of Company X for each share of Company Y, or $40 a share in value. The market-price exchange ratio for Company Y is

$$\frac{60 \times 0.667}{30} = 1.33$$

Shareholders of Company Y are being offered shares with a market value of $40 for each share of stock they own. Obviously, they benefit from the acquisition with respect to market price, because their stock was formerly worth $30 a share. However, the shareholders of Company X also stand to benefit, if the price/earnings ratio of the surviving company stays at 18. The market price per share of the surviving company after the acquisition, all other things held constant, would be:

	Consolidated statement
Total earnings after adjustments	$26 000 000
Number of shares	7 333 333
Earnings per share	$ 3.55
Price/earnings ratio	18
Market price per share	$63.90

The behavior of the P/E ratio   The reason for this apparent bit of magic whereby shareholders of both companies benefit is the difference in price/earnings ratios. Thus, companies with high price/earnings ratios would apparently be able to acquire companies with lower price/earnings ratios and obtain an immediate increase in earnings per share, despite the fact that they pay a premium on the market value exchange ratio. The key factor, however, is what happens to the price/earnings ratio after the merger. If it stays the same, the market price of the share will increase and an acquiring company would be able to show a steady growth in earnings per share if it acquired a sufficient number of companies over time in this manner.[8] It is important to recognize that this increase is not the result of operating economies or underlying growth but is due to the "bootstrap" increase in earnings per share through acquisitions. To the extent that the marketplace values this illusory growth, a company presumably could increase shareholder wealth through acquisitions alone.

However, in reasonably efficient capital markets it seems unlikely that the market will hold constant the price/earnings ratio of a company that cannot demonstrate growth potential in ways other than by acquiring companies with lower price/earnings ratios. The acquiring company must be able to manage the companies it acquired and show some degree of synergism if the benefit of acquisitions is to be lasting. If the market is relatively free from imperfections and if synergism is not anticipated, we would expect the price/earnings ratio of the surviving firm to approach a weighted average of the two previous price/earnings ratios. Under these circumstances, the acquisition of companies with lower price/earnings ratios would not enhance shareholder wealth. If synergism were expected, however, shareholder wealth could be increased through the acquisition.

EMPIRICAL EVIDENCE

In the numerous empirical studies of how mergers affect the valuation of the merged companies, differences in samples, sample periods, and research methods have rendered much of the evidence ambiguous.[9] From the more recent studies, certain generalizations seem possible. In almost all cases, the selling company's stockholders received a premium over the market price of their stock before negotiations took place. Otherwise, there would be little reason to consider a

---

[8]For further illustration of this process, see Mead, "Instantaneous Merger Profit," 298-99.

[9]For a comprehensive review of the empirical literature on mergers, see Dennis C. Mueller, "The Effects of Conglomerate Mergers," *Journal of Banking and Finance*, 1 (December 1977), 315-47. See also Pieter T. Elgers and John J. Clark, "Merger Types and Shareholder Returns: Additional Evidence," *Financial Management*, 9 (Summer 1980), 66-72.

merger, unless it were a financial bailout. The size of the premium ranged from 15 percent to 50 percent in different studies. The premium itself began to be reflected in market price increases once information of merger negotiations became available. The typical time here was 7 to 10 months in advance of the actual merger.[10] Paying a premium for an acquisition was consistent with expected synergy or more efficient management of the resources of the acquired company. Indeed, many acquired companies were characterized by relatively low returns prior to merging.

For the buying company, the evidence is less clear. Several studies show that share price relative to similar risk stocks increased moderately for several years up to roughly the time of the merger, after which there was no noticeable effect.[11] Estimates of the improvement in share price are in the neighborhood of 5 to 10 percent; however, it cannot be said that the merger caused the increase in share price. The fact that share price performs well relative to the market may be a reason for a company to expand through acquisition.

The general nature of the share price effects found in various empirical studies is illustrated in Fig. 24-3. In summary, the empirical evidence gives indication that the selling company's stockholders reap significant gains from a merger. Although there appears to be a pre-merger share price improvement for buying companies in the aggregate, the effect is far less than that for selling companies, and it begins earlier. Since the share price increase may be the cause of the merger, rather than the result, it is not clear that, on average, buying companies gain from mergers. They do not lose, however, a result implying expected synergism that offsets the premium paid for the acquired company.

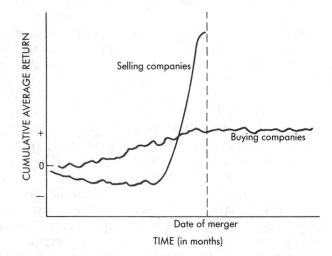

FIGURE 24-3 Typical average relative stock returns before and after merging

---

[10]See Gershon Mendelker, "Risk and Return: The Case of Merging Firms," *Journal of Financial Economics*, 1 (December 1974), 303-35.

[11]Mendelker, "Risk and Return: The Case of Merging Firms;" James C. Ellert, "Mergers, Antitrust Law Enforcement and Stockholder Returns," *Journal of Finance*, 31 (May 1976), 715-32; and Elgers and Clark, "Merger Types and Shareholder Returns: Additional Evidence."

Procedural Aspects of Combinations

We noted earlier that the purchase-of-common-shares approach is the most popular method of combinations in Canada. In this section we focus primarily on certain procedural aspects of this approach—negotiations between managements, the holding company relationships, methods of purchasing the common shares, and contingency payments. Discussion of negotiations is generally common to all three types of corporate combinations. Those on holding companies and methods of share purchase apply exclusively to the purchase-of-common-shares method. We then review the use of contingency payments in settling the claims of some acquired companies. Under this procedure, the purchase consideration is deferred until some future date depending on stipulated performance levels.

NEGOTIATIONS BETWEEN MANAGEMENTS

A merger or consolidation often begins with negotiations between the managements of the two companies. Usually, the boards of directors of the companies are kept up to date on the negotiations. The acquiring Company evaluates many facets of a target company as shown in Fig. 24-4. When initial agreement is reached as to terms, the respective boards must ratify these terms. On ratification, the agreement is submitted to the common shareholders of both companies for approval. Depending on the corporate charter, an established majority—usually three quarters—of the total shares is required. After approval by the common shareholders, the merger or consolidation can take place once the necessary papers are filed in accordance with the provisions of the respective Companies Acts.

The financial information generated on cash flows, earnings per share and market prices only assists management in negotiating more effectively; it does not establish the final terms. Management of the buying company must convince its counterpart in the selling company that a merger is in the latter's best interests. One must be mindful of the fact that if the prospective acquisition is attractive to the buying company, it is probably attractive to others as well. Consequently, the selling company may have its pick of offers. Naturally, it will want to select the best.

But what constitutes the best offer? Obviously, the market price exchange ratio is important, because it establishes the market price per share offered for the company. Apart from the exchange ratio, management of the potential acquisition often has to be convinced that a marriage of the two companies is in their best interests. Very much a part of the total picture is the role this management will play in the surviving company. To come to grips with this and related issues prior to negotiations, management of the acquiring company must thoroughly understand the operations of the potential acquisition. Then it must lay out a strategy with respect to the non-financial aspects of the prospective merger. These aspects include not only the role and compensation of management in the surviving company but also such things as the continuation and promotion of existing products, the opportunity to go into new markets, and the provision of financial resources to ensure future growth. Non-financial considerations can loom quite large in the minds of the selling company's management, often spelling the difference between its going along with the merger and turning it down.

General Information

- ☐ Exact corporate name
- ☐ Address
- ☐ Date and state of incorporation
- ☐ States in which the company is qualified to do business
- ☐ Location of minute books, by-laws, and certificate of incorporation
- ☐ History
- ☐ Description of products
- ☐ Fiscal year
- ☐ Capitalization
- ☐ Rights of each class of stock and other securities
- ☐ Stockholders' agreements and terms thereof
- ☐ Names of stockholders and holdings
- ☐ Bank depositaries and average bank balances
- ☐ Bank references
- ☐ Credit rating
- ☐ Location of company records
- ☐ Accountants: Name, address, and reputation
- ☐ Attorneys: Name and address

Personnel

- ☐ Directors and their affiliations
- ☐ Officers: For each — position, duties, age, health, salary, service, experience, personal plans for the future, other interests (including time devoted thereto), and stockholdings
- ☐ Organization chart
- ☐ Employee contracts: Terms, expiration date(s)
- ☐ Number of employees in production, sales, administration, etc.
- ☐ Union contracts: Terms, expiration dates
- ☐ Strike record, labor morale, handling of labor relations
- ☐ Labor market
- ☐ Pension, profit sharing, insurance, stock bonus, deferred compensation, and severance plans
- ☐ Comparison with industry as to number of employees, hours per week, and wage rates for the past five years and for the past twelve months

Operations

- ☐ Description, including significant changes in the past few years
  1. Capacity and per cent of utilization
  2. Production controls (scheduling and inventories)
  3. Shipping and receiving controls
  4. Accounting controls
- ☐ Principal suppliers and terms
- ☐ Distribution methods and terms (also, brokers or agents and compensation arrangements)
- ☐ Branch offices and their operations
- ☐ Subsidiaries, their operations and inter-company dealings
- ☐ Government contracts and subcontracts
- ☐ Seasonal factors
- ☐ Public and stockholder relations

Sales

- ☐ Description of market
- ☐ Number of customers and names of principal customers
- ☐ Gross and net sales for the past five years and for the past twelve months
  1. Penetration of market by product
  2. Possibilities of increase through existing lines and by diversification
- ☐ Sales comparison with the industry for the past five years and for the past twelve months
- ☐ Sales backlog, accounts receivable activity, customer continuity
- ☐ Sales correspondence
- ☐ Sales policies and method of compensation of sales personnel
- ☐ Pricing policies and fluctuations in the past five years
- ☐ Principal competitors
- ☐ Relative size in the industry
- ☐ Comparative advantages and disadvantages
- ☐ Anything significant in lines produced in the past few years
- ☐ Any nonrelated activities
- ☐ Missing product lines
- ☐ Advertising and other sales promotion programs: Cost and effectiveness in the past five years
- ☐ Research program: Cost, history, scope, potential, results, work by outsiders
- ☐ New developments
- ☐ Industry trends
- ☐ Current and future prospects

Earnings and Dividends

- ☐ Earnings record and budget for the past five years and the last twelve months, break-even point, gross profit margins and reasons for variations, nonrecurring income and expenses, changes in overabsorbed and underabsorbed burden
- ☐ Earnings comparison with the industry for the past five years
- ☐ Dividend and earnings record for the past five years in total and per share
- ☐ Potential economies
- ☐ Current and future prospects
- ☐ Analysis of selling and general and administrative expenses
- ☐ Contribution of company's effort to profit

Plant Facilities

- ☐ Location
- ☐ Shipping facilities
- ☐ Real estate taxes
- ☐ Land
  1. Acreage
  2. Cost
  3. Assessed value
  4. Fair market value

PMM & Co./Management Focus/May–June 1980. Copyright Peat, Marwick, Mitchell & Co. Reprinted by permission.

FIGURE 24-4 Acquisition evaluation checklist

□ Buildings
  1. Description, including pictures, if available
  2. Age and condition
  3. Area
  4. Depreciation: Reserves, methods, rates, policies
  5. Assessed value
  6. Fair market value (recent appraisals)
  7. Fire insurance
□ Title to realty and title policy
□ Machinery and equipment
  1. Description
  2. Age, condition, efficiency, insurance coverage
  3. Depreciation: Reserves, methods, rates, policies
  4. Total acquisitions during the past five years
  5. Analysis of most recent additions
□ Future plant, machinery, and equipment requirements
□ Capitalization versus repair policies
□ Capital expenditures and repairs for the past five years
□ Percentage relationship of production costs and comparison with the industry
□ Efficiency of operations
□ Subcontracting done by others
□ Certificates of necessity
□ Facility contracts or leases
□ Surplus or idle buildings or equipment

Assets
□ Relationship of cash to current liabilities
□ Age and number of accounts receivable (latest accounts receivable aging)
□ Provision for bad debts
□ Inventories for the past five years
  1. Relationship of inventories to current assets
  2. Location
  3. Finished goods by product
  4. Work in process by product
  5. Raw materials by product
  6. Pricing methods
  7. Accounting procedures and practices
  8. Provision for obsolete or slow-moving stock (latest inventory aging)
□ Analysis of notes receivable
□ Analysis of investments
□ Subsidiaries
  1. Treatment on parent company's balance sheet
  2. Analysis (per check list) of significant items
□ Analysis of other assets
□ Patents held

Liabilities
□ Renegotiable business
□ Renegotiation status
□ Current federal and state tax status and tax payments for the past three years
□ Commitments for new buildings, machinery, inventories
□ Long-term loans outstanding and terms
□ Debentures outstanding and terms

□ Dividend and interest arrearages
□ Leases: Locations, areas, terms
□ Insurance coverage, fidelity bonds, and amounts
□ Pensions, etc.
□ Contingent liabilities: Warranties; patent, etc., infringements; loss contracts; compensation for services
□ Litigation record and present status

Financial Data
□ Annual statements and audit reports for the past five years
□ Tax returns for the past five years
□ Surplus statements
□ Disposition of funds statements
□ Reports to Securities and Exchange Commission
□ Explanation of how consolidations, if any, were effected and separate statement for each company involved
□ Chart of accounts
□ Book, net quick, liquidating, and market values for the past five years
□ Working capital for the past five years and normal requirements based on trade practices, credit terms to customers, consignments, finished inventory, and raw inventory
□ Net working capital ratios for the past five years
□ Net quick position for the past five years
□ Annual depreciation compared with capital additions for the past five years
□ Inventory turnover for the past five years
□ Cash, inventory, and working capital requirements for the past two years
□ Interest charges for the past five years
□ Exchange, if any, on which the company's stock is traded
□ Recent stock sales and prices paid

Comparison with Comparable Companies
The following ratios for the subject company should be compared with those of comparable companies for the past five years and, if data are available, by quarters for the current year:
□ Price to earnings
□ Price to book value
□ Sales to accounts receivable
□ Sales to inventories
□ Sales to fixed assets
□ Earnings to book value

Terms of Acquisition
□ Reasons for sale
□ Price to be paid
□ Terms of payment
□ Financing
□ Brokerage fees
□ Tax considerations

Projected Financial Data
□ Pro forma balance sheet
□ Earnings forecast

FIGURE 24-4   (cont.)

To the extent that synergism is possible, the buyer can be relatively generous in the exchange ratio offered, as well as in non-financial terms. Final terms depend on the bargaining strengths of the two parties, the financial relationships described, and expectations regarding the future earnings performance of the surviving company. In the case of the buyer, negotiations should be framed in terms of what the seller will gain from the merger. Unless there is a reasonable gain, few companies will wish to sell. In contrast, the seller should think in terms of how much the merger is worth to the buyer. Just because a merger will benefit the seller it does not mean that the terms offered are the best that can be obtained by the seller.

HOLDING COMPANY RELATIONSHIPS

Instead of actually acquiring another company, a firm may purchase a portion of its stock and act as a holding company. A *holding company* is defined as one that owns sufficient voting stock to have a controlling interest in one or more companies. Where the acquiring company owns more than 50 percent of the voting shares of an acquired company, the former has undisputed majority control. Such a situation is usually regarded as a *parent-subsidiary relationship*. Under accounting rules, the parent (or acquiring company) prepares consolidated statements for the purpose of reporting to shareholders. However, we should note that a holding company does not necessarily have to own more than 50 percent of the shares of another company to gain control. For a widely held company, ownership of 20 percent or as little as 10 percent of the shares outstanding may constitute effective working control.

Management of the acquiring company has to decide if it requires 100 percent ownership, majority voting powers, or a share ownership sufficient to gain control. Each combination proposal will have to be evaluated on its own and the decision on share ownership determined. Suffice it to say that an acquiring company may have varying degrees of share ownership across different acquired companies.

Advantages One of the advantages of a holding company is that it allows a company to acquire control of another with a much smaller investment than would be necessary with 100 percent ownership. Moreover, by acquiring only a portion of the shares, the holding company usually does not have to pay as high a price per share as it would if it sought to purchase all the shares. It may purchase the shares gradually without undue upward pressure on the market price of the shares. Another advantage is that formal approval from shareholders of the acquiring company is not required. It is an informal arrangement. A further advantage of a holding company is the possibility that operating economies can be achieved through centralized management. The magnitude of economies possible here, however, is limited. Moreover, the acquiring company is not taxed for dividends received from the acquired company.

Disadvantages By pyramiding a series of holding companies, it is possible to obtain considerable leverage with respect to earnings and assets controlled. For example, suppose holding Company A owns 20 percent of holding companies B, C, and D, which, in turn, own 20 percent controlling interest in nine operating companies. Thus, for every dollar of capital in each of the operating companies— $9 in all —Company A can gain control with an investment of $0.36(0.20 × 0.20 × $9), or 4 percent of the total capital of the operating companies. As long as the operating companies are profitable and able to pay dividends to the holding companies, all may go well. However, in the U.S. in the 1920s, there was excessive pyramiding of holding companies, particularly public utilities. In the 1930s the leverage of these companies magnified the losses, and a number of the pyramids crumbled. Because of the many abuses of holding companies, the Public Utility Holding Company Act of 1935 was passed to restrict the operation of holding companies in the public utility field in the U.S. In Canada, "full disclosure" and "insider trading" provisions in the Securities Acts provide for the monitoring of the acquisition activities of holding companies.

ACQUISITION OF COMMON SHARES

There are essentially two ways to acquire the common shares of the acquired company—purchase in the open market and purchase through a tender offer. The choice of method depends on several factors, some of which are highlighted in the following discussion.

Purchase in the Open Market   Where the shares of an acquired company are closely held, the usual approach is by direct negotiations with the management and major shareholders of that company. However, where the shares of the acquired company are widely distributed and are listed on the stock exchanges, the approach may be different. The acquiring company will engage a securities firm to assist in the purchase of the shares in the open market. However, there are certain regulatory and trading considerations in this type of open market purchase which may limit its use.

The philosophy of securities regulation is "full and timely disclosure of material facts" and a decision to acquire control of a company is a material fact. The acquiring company has to disclose its acquisitions plans to the securities authorities and to the company it wishes to acquire. To gain control, an acquiring company may have to buy a significant block of common shares. It is unlikely that this can be achieved in a short time without putting upward pressures on the market price of the shares. When the market price of a share behaves rather abnormally, the securities authorities have the right to cease trading and seek an explanation for such abnormal behavior. An acquiring company may not wish the market price of shares of a company it wants to acquire to go up and even more importantly, to be a target for investigation by securities authorities.

Despite the above factors, an acquiring company may still use the open market to buy shares under certain circumstances. The company, through its investment broker, may be able to identify the few major shareholders and deal with them directly. Also, the company may be content to acquire shares on a piecemeal basis over an extended period until the desired proportion is obtained. Under this strategy, the company will eventually be classified as an "insider" and will be required to report such activity under the insider-trading rules.

Tender offers   The acquiring company can make its appeal directly to the shareholders of the company it wishes to acquire, through a tender offer. A *tender offer* is an offer to purchase shares of stock of another company at a fixed price per share from any shareholder who "tenders" his shares. The tender price is usually set significantly above the present market price in order to provide an incentive to shareholders to tender their shares. Use of the tender offer allows the acquiring company to bypass the management of the company it wishes to acquire and, therefore, serves as a threat in any negotiations with that management. If management holds out for too high a price or otherwise balks at the offer of the acquiring company, that company can always make a tender offer.

The tender offer can also be used when there are no negotiations but when one company simply wants to acquire another. In a "surprise" tender offer, the acquiring company is usually very careful not to reveal its intentions prior to the actual offer. The primary selling tool is the premium that is offered over the existing market price of the share. As a rule of thumb, many suggest a premium of 20 percent, which is adjusted up or down depending on the circumstances. In addition, brokers are often given very attractive commissions for shares tendered through them. The tender offer itself is usually communicated through financial newspapers. Direct mailings are made to the shareholders of the company being bid for if the bidder is able to obtain a shareholders' list. Although a company is legally obligated to provide such a list, it can usually delay delivery long enough to frustrate the bidder.

From the standpoint of the company being bid for, a number of defensive tactics are available. First, management may try to persuade its shareholders that the offer is not in their best interests. Usually, the argument is that the bid is too low in relation to the true, long-run value of the firm. However, in the face of an attractive premium, the long run may be too distant. Some companies raise the cash dividend or declare a stock split in hopes of gaining shareholder support. Legal actions are often undertaken, more to delay and frustrate the bidder than with the expectation of winning. To the extent that the two firms are competitors, provisions in the Combines Investigation Act may prove a powerful deterrent to the bidder. As a last resort, management of the company being bid for may seek a merger with a "friendly" company. A cartoonist's view of some of the strategies involved in tender offers is shown in Fig. 24-5.

The rising trend in tender offers has prompted the securities authorities to institute more stringent reporting regulations. We use the securities regulation in Ontario to highlight briefly some of the reporting requirements. A take-over bid is deemed to occur if the acquiring firm is seeking to own at least 20 percent of the shares of the acquired firm. This 20 percent is an aggregate of what is already held by the acquiring firm and that which will result from the tender offer if it is successful. The acquiring firm must notify the Ontario Securities Commission (OSC) of its intention to bid for the shares of another company. All shareholders are to be notified and treated equally. For example, shares will be pro-rated if an oversubscription results and the same price is paid to all shareholders. Management of the acquired firm is required to advise the shareholders either to accept or reject the bid. Other rules govern the period over which the offer is in effect, the manner in which the shares are tendered, and the privilege of shareholders to withdraw their shares without further obligation.[12]

---

[12]For an extended discussion of these and other issues involving tender-offer takeovers, see "Corporate Takeovers—The Unfriendly Tender Offer and the Minority Stockholder Freezeout," Special Issue of *The Business Lawyer*, 32 (May 1977).

A bidder takes pains to keep his intentions secret until the last minute.
"Claude; Courtesy of *Fortune Magazine*."

Management often seeks to foil a bidder by quickly arranging a merger with another company.
"Claude; Courtesy of *Fortune Magazine*."

Determined management opposition can usually fend off an unwanted take-over bid.
"Claude; Courtesy of *Fortune Magazine*."

FIGURE 24–5 Tender offers

Dissenting stockholders   Although a combination generally depends only upon the approval of a required majority of the total number of shares outstanding, minority stockholders can contest the price paid for their stock. If a dissenting stockholder and the company fail to agree on a just settlement, the stockholder can take the case to court and demand an appraisal of his shares and a settlement in cash. After a "fair market price" has been established by the court, the dissenting stockholder receives payment in cash for his or her shares. A large number of dissenting stockholders can cause considerable trouble. If the transaction is in stock, their demands for cash payments may put a severe financial strain on the combination. Thus, most combinations depend not only upon obtaining approval of a required majority of stockholders but also upon minimizing the number of dissenting stockholders by making the offer attractive to all. Dissenting stockholders may be able to block the combination if they suspect that fraud is involved, even though the required majority of stockholders has approved it.

CONTINGENT PAYMENTS

In order to provide a performance incentive to the management of the acquired company, the buyer sometimes uses a contingent payment plan based on subsequent performance. A down payment is made at the time of the merger, and the contingent payment is based on the seller meeting or exceeding certain standards. Several conditions are necessary before a contingent payment plan is feasible. For one thing, the selling company needs to be operated after the merger as a separate division or subsidiary, with major decisions affecting the profitability left in the hands of the management of the acquired company. Otherwise, management's influence on profitability is diluted. Other conditions that increase the feasibility of a contingent payment plan are the selling company's being closely held, relatively new, and having relatively low earnings.

The down payment and performance standards must be firmly established by both parties. A number of variations are possible. The most common is to specify some level of future earnings, either year by year or an average. Contingent payments then are made on the basis of how much actual earnings exceed the earnings standards. Sometimes this excess is adjusted downward for the use of the parent company's capital. Other types of standards include a moving standard and a cumulative one. When the acquisition is for cash, the contingent payment is simply excess earnings over the standard times some agreed percentage. When the acquisition is by shares, the number of shares given in a contingent payment varies according to the price of the parent company's shares at the time of the payment.

As should be apparent, the use of contingent payouts is applicable only under certain circumstances. The ground rules must be firmly established. It is no good from the standpoint of the buyer if the selling company "jacks up" earnings during the contingency period by postponing capital expenditures and research and development or "adjusts" accounting earnings. These actions work to the detriment of earnings in later years. If ground rules are equitable and firm, however, the incentive payment plan may be quite effective. The buyers benefit in that only proven performance is rewarded. If things turn bad, they are out of pocket only in the down payment. The seller also may benefit because the total price paid if post-merger earnings are good may be higher than the price paid if the total payment was made at the time of the merger.

Summary

A company may grow internally, or it may grow externally through acquisitions. The objective of the firm in either case is to maximize existing shareholder wealth.

There are a number of reasons for merging, all of which relate to expected return and risk. Among the more important are economies, acquisition of management, growth potential, financing, taxation, diversification, and personal reasons.

Expansion can be regarded as involving capital-budgeting decisions. The criterion for acceptance is essentially the same: capital should be allocated to increase shareholder wealth. There are three methods used to effect a corporate combination: statutory amalgamation or merger; purchase of assets resulting in a consolidation; and purchase of common shares resulting in a parent-subsidiary relationship. Under the first two methods, the operations of the companies are usually combined and continued by the acquiring company. With the purchase-of-shares method both the acquiring and acquired companies continue as separate corporate entities.

Whenever there is an exchange of stock between two companies, certain financial relationships become important. Many companies focus on the impact on earnings per share. When the price/earnings ratio of the company being acquired is lower than the price/earnings ratio of the acquiring company, there is an initial improvement in earnings per share of the latter company; a dilution occurs when the price/earnings ratio is higher. Instead of looking only at the effect of acquisition on initial earnings per share, it is desirable also to look at its effect on expected future earnings per share. In efficient financial markets and in the absence of synergism, the price/earnings ratio of the surviving company is expected to be a weighted average of the price/earnings ratios of the two pre-merger companies. For the most part, wealth cannot be created simply by merging with companies with low price/earnings ratios.

Once sufficient financial information is generated, management of the acquiring company usually negotiates directly with management of the target company. Under the purchase-of-common-shares method, the acquiring company can avoid this procedure by buying the common shares directly in the open market or by going directly to the shareholders of the target company with a tender offer. From the accounting viewpoint, the purchase method is the recommended approach for consolidated statements for acquiring companies. In some cases where the distinction between acquiring and acquired companies is difficult, the pooling of interests method may be used.

Questions

1. Explain the concept of synergism.
2. Illustrate and explain how the ratio of P/E multiples for two stocks affects the growth rate of reported earnings.

3. Why is the book value of a firm important in determining the exchange ratio of stock in a merger?

4. Some argue that the method of payment in a merger (stock-for-stock transaction at one end of the spectrum and cash-for-stock at the other, with various combinations of bonds, convertibles, etc., for stock in between the two extremes) is the principal factor in determining the price of the acquired firm. Explain this position.

5. Explain the concept of instantaneous merger profit. What assumptions are made about economies of scale in explaining the concept?

6. It has been noted that the number of mergers tends to vary directly with the level of relative business activity. Why would this be?

7. Can a merger with a large, stable company serve as an effective way to raise capital for a growth-oriented smaller company?

8. Company X and Company Y both have considerable variability in their earnings, but they are in unrelated industries. Could a merger of the two companies reduce the risk for stockholders of both companies? Could investors lower the risk on their own?

9. Many a corporate merger is made with the motive of increasing growth. What does this mean? Can you increase growth without increasing the overall risk of the surviving company?

10. Why is it that so many acquisition opportunities look good before the merger but later prove to be "dogs"?

11. Is an acquisition-minded company consistently able to find bargains? If so, why is it that other companies do not discover these bargains?

12. When evaluating a potential acquisition's future, why penalize the prospect by deducting the capital expenditures that will need to be made? Are not future earnings what really matter?

13. No merger is going to be attractive to all the acquired company's stockholders. Why should a company be concerned with dissenting stockholders as long as the majority favor the merger?

Problems with Solutions

1. X Company and Y Company plan to combine, with X to be the resultant parent. No earnings growth is expected from the combination. The following information is available:

	X Company	Y Company
Shares outstanding	900 000	600 000
Earnings	$1 350 000	$600 000
Price/earnings ratio	40 : 1	10 : 1

Required:

(a) Suppose the negotiated exchange ratio is $\frac{1}{6}$: 1 and that the price/earnings ratio for the combined firm is 25 : 1. What are the gains or losses accruing to the shareholders of each combining company?

(b) At what price/earnings ratio will there be no change in total shareholders wealth?

	X Company	Y Company
(a) Pre-combination wealth $(900\,000 \times \frac{\$1\,350\,000}{900\,000} \times 40)$	$54 000 000	
$(600\,000 \times \frac{\$600\,000}{600\,000} \times 10)$		$6 000 000
Post-combination wealth $(900\,000 \times \frac{\$1\,950\,000}{1\,000\,000} \times 25)$	43 875 000	
$(100\,000 \times \frac{\$1\,950\,000}{1\,000\,000} \times 25)$		4 875 000
Losses to shareholders	$10 125 000	$1 125 000

(b) At the weighted average price/earnings ratio
   Calculation:

Company	Earnings	Value (see above)
X	$1 350 000	$54 000 000
Y	600 000	6 000 000
	$1 950 000	$60 000 000

$60 000 000 ÷ $1 950 000 = 30.769 : 1

2. On Jan. 1, 19X1 P Company purchased an 80 percent interest in S Company for $280 000. On this date, S Company had capital stock of $50 000 and retained earnings of $100 000.

   An examination of S Company's assets and liabilities revealed that book values were equal to fair values for all except inventory which had a book value of $80 000 and a fair value of $90 000 and plant and equipment (net) which had a book value of $60 000 and a fair value of $140 000. The inventory should be sold in 19X1 and the plant and equipment had an expected remaining life of 5 years. Goodwill should be amortized over 40 years.

   P Company's income from its own operations was $40 000 in 19X1 and $50 000 in 19X2. S Company's income was $30 000 in 19X1 and $25 000 in 19X2. S Company did not pay dividends in either year.

   P Company had 50 000 common shares outstanding during both years.

Required:

   Calculate consolidated net income and earnings per share for 19X1 and 19X2.

Consolidated net income = P Company's income from its own operations + 0.8 × S Company's net income − permanent differences

19X1 = $40 000 + 0.8 ($30 000) − $23 000* = $41 000
19X2 = $50 000 + 0.8 ($25 000) − $15 000* = $55 000

Earnings per share

19X1 = $41 000 ÷ 50 000 = $0.82
19X2 = $55 000 ÷ 50 000 = $1.10

Cost of investment	$280 000
Book value (0.8 × $150 000)	−120 000
Excess	$160 000

*Permanent differences

	19X1	19X2
Inventory 0.8($90 000 − $80 000)	$ 8 000	—
Plant and equipment 0.8($140 000 − $60 000) ÷ 5	12 800	$12 800
Goodwill [$160 000 − 0.8 ($90 000 − $80 000) − 0.8 ($140 000 − $60 000)] ÷ 40	2 200	2 200
	$23 000	$15 000

Problems

1. The following data are pertinent for Companies A and B:

	Company A	Company B
Present earnings (in millions)	$20	$ 4
Shares (in millions)	10	1
Price/earnings ratio	18	10

(a) If the two companies were to merge and the exchange ratio were one share of Company A for each share of Company B, what would be the initial impact on earnings per share of the two companies? What is the market-value exchange ratio? Is a merger likely to take place? Ignore permanent differences.

(b) If the exchange ratio were two shares of Company A for each share of Company B, what would happen with respect to the above?

(c) If the exchange ratio were 1.5 shares of Company A for each share of Company B, what would happen?

(d) What exchange ratio would you suggest?

2.

	Expected earnings	Number of shares	Market Price per share	Tax rate
Hargrave Company Ltd.	$5 000 000	1 000 000	$100	50%
Hooper Company Ltd.	3 000 000	500 000	60	50%

Hargrave Company Ltd. wishes to acquire Hooper Company Ltd. If the merger were effected through an exchange of stock, Hargrave would be willing to pay a 25 percent premium for the Hooper shares. If payment were to be in cash, the terms would have to be as favorable to the Hooper shareholders: to obtain the cash, Hargrave would have to sell its own stock in the market.

(a) Compute the exchange ratio and the combined expected earnings per share if an exchange of stock were accomplished. Ignore permanent differences.

(b) If we assume that all Hooper shareholders have a 40 percent marginal tax rate, and paid an average of $14 for their shares, what cash price would have to be offered to make the cash offer as attractive as the terms in (a) above?

3. Assume the exchange of Hargrave shares for Hooper shares as outlined in problem 2 (a) above. Ignore permanent differences.

(a) What is the ratio of exchange?

(b) Compare the earnings per Hooper share before and after the merger. Compare the before and after earnings per Hargrave share. On this basis alone, which group fared better? Why?

(c) Why do you imagine that old Hargrave Company commanded a higher P/E than the Hooper Company? What should be the change in P/E ratio resulting from the merger?

(d) If the Hargrave Company is in a high-technology growth industry and Hooper makes cement, would you revise your answers?

(e) In determining the appropriate P/E ratio for Hargrave, should the increase in earnings resulting from this merger be added as a growth factor?

4. Three years and 20 mergers later, Hargrave (see problems 2 and 3), under pressure to report earnings growth, is looking at a proposed merger.

	Expected earnings	Number of shares	Market price
Hargrave	$35 000 000	3 500 000	$200
Fontenot	3 000 000	500 000	90

Assume the merger is consummated under the same terms as in Problem 2 and ignore permanent differences.

(a) Compute the exchange ratio and the combined expected earnings per share if an exchange of shares were accomplished.

(b) What do you think will happen to the P/E ratio?

5. Copper Tube Company Ltd. has present annual earnings of $10 million with 4 million shares of common stock outstanding and a market price per share of $30. In the absence of any mergers, Copper Tube's annual earnings are expected to grow at a compound rate of 5 percent per annum. Brass Fitting Company Ltd., which Copper Tube is considering acquiring, has present annual earnings of $2 million, 1 million shares of common outstanding, and a market price per share of $32. Its annual earnings are expected to grow at a compound annual rate of 10 percent. Copper Tube is considering offering 1.2 shares of its stock for each share of Brass Fitting Company. Permanent differences are $500 000 annually.

(a) What is the immediate effect of the proposed merger on the surviving company's earnings per share?

(b) Would you want to acquire Brass Fitting Company? If it is not attractive now, when will it be attractive from the standpoint of earnings per share?

6. The Resin Corporation Ltd. which has a 16 percent after-tax cost of capital, is considering the acquisition of the Smythe Company Ltd., which has about the same degree of systematic risk. If the merger were effected, the incremental cash flows would be as follows:

	Average for years (in millions)			
	1-5	6-10	11-15	16-20
Annual cash income attributable to Smythe	$10	$15	$20	$15
Required new investment	2	5	10	10
Net after-tax cash flow	$ 8	$10	$10	$ 5

What is the maximum price that Resin should pay for Smythe?

7. Cougar Pipe and Brass Company Ltd. is considering the cash acquisition of Red Wilson Rod Inc. Ltd. for $750 000. The acquisition is expected to result in incremental cash flows of $100 000 in the first year, and this amount is expected to grow at a 6 percent compound rate. In the absence of the acquisition, Cougar expects net cash flows (after capital expenditures) of $600 000 this year, and these are expected to grow at a 6 percent compound rate forever. Presently, suppliers of capital require a 14 percent overall rate of return for Cougar Pipe and Brass Company. However, Red Wilson Rod is much more risky, and the acquisition of it will raise the company's overall required return to 15 percent.

   (a) Should Cougar Pipe and Brass Company acquire Red Wilson Rod Inc.?

   (b) Would your answer be the same if the overall required rate of return stayed the same?

   (c) Would your answer be the same if the acquisition increased the surviving company's growth rate to 8 percent forever?

8. Let it be assumed that a holding company can always be set up with 50 percent debt at 12 percent and 20 percent preferred stock at 10 percent. Further assume that all companies pay a tax rate of 50 percent, that the 100 percent intercorporate dividend exclusion applies in all cases, and that ownership of 40 percent of the stock of another company constitutes control. The shares of the Target Company can be obtained at their book value.

Target Company

Total assets	$25 000 000	Debt (12%)	$15 000 000
		Common	10 000 000
			$25 000 000

   (a) A group of investors has set up Holding Company A to acquire control of the Target Company. If the group holds all the equity of Holding Company A, how much money must it put up? Target has operating earnings equal to 20 percent of total assets and pays all earnings in dividends, what return on investment will the group earn?

   (b) Suppose the group sets up Holding Company B to acquire control of Holding Company A. If the group holds all the equity of B, how much money must it put up? If A pays all earnings in dividends, what return on investment will the group earn? How many dollars of operating assets does the group control per dollar of its own investment?

   (c) How would your answers change if Target had operating earnings equal to 15 percent of total assets?

9. Biggo Stores, Inc. Ltd. (BSI) has acquired the Nail It, Glue It and Screw It Hardware Company Ltd. (NGS) for $4 million in stock and the assumption of $2 million in NGS liabilities. The balance sheets of the two companies before the merger were

	BSI	NGS
Tangible and total assets	$10.0 million	$5.0 million
Liabilities	4.0	2.0
Net worth	6.0	3.0

Determine the balance sheet of the combined company after the merger under the purchase and pooling of interests methods of accounting.

Selected References

ALBERTS, WILLIAM W., and JOEL E. SEGALL, eds., *The Corporate Merger*, Chicago: University of Chicago Press, 1966.

APPLEYARD, A. R. and G. K. YARROW, "The Relationship Between Take-over Activity and Share Valuation," *Journal of Finance*, 30 (December 1975), 1239-50.

AUSTIN, DOUGLAS V., "The Financial Management of Tender Offer Takeovers," *Financial Management*, 3 (Spring 1974), 37-43.

BORGSDORF, C. W. "The Virtually Unconstrained Legal Environment for Mergers in Canada," *Journal of American and Foreign Antitrust and Trade Regulation*, Vol. XVIII, No. 4 (Winter 1973).

BRAULT, REJEAN "A Simple Approach to Complex Consolidations," *CA Magazine* (April 1979), 52-54.

"Corporate Takeovers—The Unfriendly Tender Offer and the Minority Stockholder Freezeout," Special Issue of *The Business Lawyer*, 32 (May 1977).

DODD, PETER, and RICHARD RUBACK, "Tender Offers and Stockholder Returns," *Journal of Financial Economics*, 5 (November 1977), 351-73.

ELGERS, PIETER T., and JOHN J. CLARK, "Merger Types and Shareholder Returns: Additional Evidence," *Financial Management*, 9 (Summer 1980), 66-72.

ELLERT, JAMES C., "Mergers, Antitrust Law Enforcement and Stockholder Returns," *Journal of Finance*, 31 (May 1976), 715-32.

GAHLON, JAMES M., and ROGER D. STOVER, "Diversification, Financial Leverage, and Conglomerate Systematic Risk," *Journal of Financial and Quantitative Analysis*, 14 (December 1979), 999-1014.

HALPERN, PAUL, "Corporate Acquisitions: A Theory of Special Cases? A Review of Recent Studies Applied to Acquisitions," *Journal of Finance*, May 1983, 297-317.

HAUGEN, ROBERT A., and TERENCE C. LANGETIEG, "An Empirical Test for Synergism in Merger," *Journal of Finance*, 30 (September 1975), 1003-14.

HIGGINS, ROBERT C., and LAWRENCE D. SCHALL, "Corporate Bankruptcy and Conglomerate Merger," *Journal of Finance*, 30 (March 1975), 93-114.

HOFFMEISTER, J. RONALD, and EDWARD A. DYL, "Predicting Outcomes of Cash Tender Offers," *Financial Management*, 10 (Winter 1981), 50-58.

HONG, H., G. MANDELKER, and R. S. KAPLAN, "Pooling vs. Purchase: The Effects of Accounting for Mergers on Stock Prices," *Accounting Review*, 53 (January 1978), 31-47.

KEOWN, ARTHUR J., and JOHN M. PINKERTON, "Merger Announcements and Insider Trading Activity: An Empirical Investigation," *Journal of Finance*, 36 (September 1981), 855-70.

KUMMER, DONALD R., and J. RONALD HOFFMEISTER, "Valuation Consequences of Cash Tender Offers," *Journal of Finance*, 33 (May 1978), 505-16.

LAIKEN, STANLEY N., "Financial Performance of Merging Firms in a Virtually Unconstrained Legal Environment," *Journal of American and Foreign Antitrust and Trade Regulation*, Vol. XVII, No. 4 (Winter 1973).

LANGETIEG, TERENCE C., ROBERT A. HAUGEN and DEAN W. WICHERN, "Merger and Stockholder Wealth," *Journal of Financial and Quantitative Analysis*, 15 (September 1980), 689-717.

LARSON, KERMIT D., and NICHOLAS J. GONEDES, "Business Combinations: An Exchange-Ratio Determination Model," *Accounting Review*, 44 (October 1969), 720-28.

LEWELLEN, WILBUR G. and MICHAEL G. FERRI, "Strategies for the Merger Game: Management and the Market," *Financial Management*, Winter 1983, 25-35.

MARTIN, SAMUEL A., STANLEY N. LAIKEN, and DOUGLAS F. HASLAM, *Business Combinations in the 60s: A Canadian Profile*. Toronto: The Canadian Institute of Chartered Accountants, and London: The School of Business Administration, University of Western Ontario, 1970.

MEAD, WALTER J., "Instantaneous Merger Profit as a Conglomerate Merger Motive," *Western Economic Review*, 7 (December 1969), 295-306.

MELICHER, RONALD W., and THOMAS R. HARTER, "Stock Price Movements of Firms Engaging in Large Acquisitions," *Journal of Financial and Quantitative Analysis*, 7 (March 1972), 1469-75.

———, and DAVID F. RUSH, "Evidence on the Acquisition-Related Performance of Conglomerate Firms," *Journal of Finance*, 29 (March 1974), 141-50.

MENDELKER, GERSHON, "Risk and Return: The Case of Merging Firms," *Journal of Financial Economics*, 1 (December 1974), 303-35.

MORIN, DESMOND B. and WARREN CHIPPINDALE, *Acquisition and Mergers in Canada*. Toronto: Methuen Publications, 1970.

MUELLER, DENNIS C., "The Effects of Conglomerate Mergers," *Journal of Banking and Finance*, 1 (December 1977), 315-47.

NEILSEN, JAMES F., and RONALD W. MELICHER, "A Financial Analysis of Acquisition and Merger Premiums," *Journal of Financial and Quantitative Analysis*, 8 (March 1973), 139-48.

SALTER, MALCOLM S., and WOLF A. WEINHOLD, "Diversification via Acquisition: Creating Value," *Harvard Business Review*, (July-August 1978), 166-76.

SCOTT, JAMES H., JR., "On the Theory of Conglomerate Mergers," *Journal of Finance*, 32 (September 1977), 1235-50.

SHICK, RICHARD A., and FRANK C. JEN, "Merger Benefits to Shareholders of Acquiring Firms," *Financial Management*, 3 (Winter 1974), 45-53.

SMALTER, DONALD J., and RODERIC C. LANCEY, "P/E Analysis in Acquisition Strategy," *Harvard Business Review*, 44 (November-December 1966), 85-95.

SMILEY, ROBERT, "Tender Offers, Transactions Costs and the Firm," *Review of Economics and Statistics*, 58 (February 1976), 22-32.

WANSLEY, JAMES W., WILLIAM R. LANE and HO C. YANG, "Abnormal Returns to Acquired Firms by Type of Acquisition and Method of Payment," *Financial Management*, Autumn 1983, 16-22.

International Financial Management

In recent years, international trade has grown in importance to the point where it now constitutes a major portion of the total activity of many business firms. In the wake of this growth has come the development of the multinational enterprise. By definition, a multinational business is one with investment and sales in two or more countries. For many companies, foreign sales represent only a small portion of total revenues, and we would not regard these companies as multinational in any real sense. However, companies like Alcan and International Nickel derive a significant portion of their profits from international operations and are truly multinational in scope.

How does financial management in a multinational enterprise differ from that in a domestic business firm? In principle, the concepts of efficient allocation of funds among assets and the raising of funds on as favorable terms as possible are the same for both types of companies. However, the environment in which these decisions are made is different. In this chapter we review Canada's foreign trade and direct foreign investment and consider the institutional factors that make investing and financing for a multinational company somewhat different from that for a domestic company. We examine such things as the tax environment, political risks, foreign exchange risk, investment constraints imposed by all governments, financing instruments, and certain specialized documents used in foreign trade. Our examination is not an in-depth study but rather a presentation of those factors which influence the basic decisions of the firm operating in an international setting.

Investing Abroad

The decision to invest capital in a project abroad should be based upon considerations of expected return and risk, the same as any investment proposal. Quantifying these parameters is complicated by disparities in currency exchange rates, differences in taxes, differences in accounting practices, and differences in factors affecting risk; but once expected return and risk are quantified, the evaluation of the project itself is the same whether it be domestic or foreign in origin.[1] Consequently, we shall concentrate on the various factors that make foreign investment unique rather than on the evaluation process itself. That process was taken up earlier in the book and has not changed.

REASONS FOR FOREIGN INVESTMENT

Risk considerations   International diversification is often more effective than domestic diversification in reducing a company's risk in relation to expected return. You will recall from our discussion of portfolio risk in Chapter 14 that the key element was the correlation among projects in the asset portfolio. By combining projects with low degrees of correlation with each other, a firm is able to reduce risk in relation to expected return. Since domestic investment projects tend to be correlated with each other, most being highly dependent on the state of the economy, foreign investments have an advantage. The economic cycles of different countries do not tend to be completely synchronized, so it is possible to reduce risk relative to expected return by investing across countries.

If a company in the machine tool business invested in another plant domestically, the return would likely be highly correlated with the return from existing assets. Consequently, there would be little reduction in relative risk. If it invested in a plant to market machine tools in a country whose economy was not highly correlated with the domestic economy, the project's return would not likely be so highly correlated with the return from existing assets. Consequently, it may be possible to reduce risk relative to expected return by investing in the same industry internationally. The idea is simply that returns on investment projects tend to be less correlated among countries than they are in any one particular country.

Whether foreign diversification by a company benefits its stockholders depends on whether or not capital markets between countries are segmented. If they are not, there is little reason to believe that foreign diversification by a company will increase its value. This notion is the same as that for diversification of assets involving domestic projects, which was discussed earlier. If capital markets are perfect, investors can effectively replicate any asset diversification by the firm. Therefore, such diversification adds nothing at the margin to shareholder wealth. If currency restrictions, investment barriers, legal restrictions, lack of information, and other capital-market imperfections of this sort exist, capital markets between countries may be segmented. Under these circumstances, foreign diversification may enhance shareholder wealth. In general, studies of common stock investments across countries have supported the diversification potential of international investments, though there is disagreement on the degree of capital-market segmentation.

---

[1]For a survey of capital budgeting techniques employed by multinational companies, see David J. Oblak and Roy J. Helm, Jr., "Survey and Analysis of Capital Budgeting Methods used by Multinationals," *Financial Management*, 9 (Winter 1980), 37-41. The authors found that a large number of the companies surveyed used discounted cash flow methods and adjusted for risk.

The concept of diversification is applicable also to the acquisition of foreign companies. To the extent again that market imperfections result in segmentation among international capital markets, the diversification properties associated with a foreign acquisition may be of value. We know from Chapters 15 and 24 that domestic acquisitions are a thing of value only if the acquiring company can do something for its investors that they cannot do for themselves. In the case of a company with a publicly traded stock, there was little reason to believe that stockholders could not achieve the same diversification on their own by investing directly in the company involved. Making foreign acquisitions, however, the acquiring company may be able to do something for investors that they cannot do for themselves if specific international capital markets are segmented. As a result, the risk-reduction properties associated with the foreign acquisition may be a thing of value.

Return considerations   The other reason for investing abroad is the expectation of a higher return for a given level of risk. Within a firm's particular expertise, there may be gaps in markets abroad where excess returns can be earned. Domestically, competitive pressures may be such that only a normal rate of return can be earned. Although expansion into foreign markets is the reason for most investment abroad, there are other reasons. Some firms invest in order to produce more efficiently. In another country, where labor or other costs are less, a company may seek foreign production facilities simply to operate at a lower cost. The electronics industry has moved toward foreign production facilities for saving. Finally, some companies invest abroad to secure necessary raw materials. Oil companies and mining companies in particular invest abroad for this reason. All of these pursuits—markets, production facilities, and raw materials—are in keeping with an objective of securing a higher rate of return than is possible through domestic operations alone.

As we observed earlier, among the factors that make investment abroad different from investment at home are tax differences and political and foreign exchange risk. Before taking up each in turn, we should point out that there is more risk to a foreign investment than simply the political and foreign exchange risks. Frequently, the predominant risk is business risk in the country itself. We discussed methods for analyzing this risk in Chapters 14 and 15.

TAXATION

Owing to different tax laws and different treatments of foreign investment around the world, the taxation of a multinational firm is extremely complex. We will discuss some of the more important aspects of the problem, beginning with a look at the way the Canadian government taxes a company with foreign operations and then moving on to consider taxation by foreign countries.

Taxation by the Canadian government   If a Canadian company receives dividends from a Canadian subsidiary, these dividends are tax-free to the recipient. However, if business is carried on through a foreign subsidiary, the tax situation is different. The dividends from the foreign subsidiary are fully taxable. Foreign business income is calculated as dividends received plus the taxes deducted by the foreign tax authority. This foreign income is added to Canadian income and is taxed at the full Canadian tax rate. Foreign taxes paid are allowable as a credit against the Canadian federal taxes on the foreign income. The credit is limited to the actual amount of foreign taxes paid. Foreign taxes not absorbed as a foreign tax credit can be carried forward for up to five years to be claimed in the future. Foreign tax credit arrangements enable the taxpayer to avoid double taxation.

For example, suppose a Canadian company earned a before tax foreign income of $10 000 and it paid foreign taxes of $3000, and a domestic income of $5 000. The company is assessed federal taxes of $4 000 in Canada on a total income of $15 000 (that is, $10 000 foreign income plus $5 000 domestic income). Canadian taxes applicable to foreign income are ($10 000/$15 000) of $4 000 or $2 666. The company claims a foreign tax credit of only $2 666; the balance of $334 of foreign taxes is carried forward.

Taxation by foreign governments Most countries tax income of foreign companies doing business in that country. The regulations governing type of tax imposed vary. However, most of the larger industrial countries impose taxes on corporate income at rates that correspond roughly to the corporate rate in Canada. Some of these countries differentiate distributed income to shareholders from undistributed income, imposing a lower tax on distributed income. Less developed countries frequently have lower taxes and provide certain other tax incentives in order to encourage foreign investment. One method of taxation that has become very important in Europe is the value-added tax. In essence, the value-added tax is a sales tax wherein each stage of production is taxed on the value added. Suppose an aluminum fabricator buys aluminum sheets for $1 000 and cuts, shapes and otherwise works them into doors which are sold for $1 800. The value added is $800 and the fabricator would be taxed on this amount. If the fabricator sold its doors to a wholesaler who, in turn, sold them to retailers for $2 000, the value added would be $200 and the wholesaler would be taxed accordingly. In the future, the value-added tax system is likely to become increasingly important all over the world.

The taxation policies of foreign governments are not only varied but also highly complex. For example, the definition of what constitutes taxable income differs from country to country; so does tax rate. Certain nations, such as Luxembourg, Panama, and the Bahamas, have low tax rates on corporate profits in order to encourage foreign investment, whereas the tax rates in most advanced industrial countries are high. The picture is complicated further by the numerous tax treaties that Canada has with other nations. While the ability to use a low tax country as a "tax haven" is limited by the Canadian government, enough latitude remains so that companies still devise complicated legal structures in order to take advantage of such "havens."

POLITICAL RISKS

The political risk facing a multinational company range from mild interference to complete confiscation of all assets. Interference includes such things as laws that specify a minimum percentage of nationals that must be employed in various positions, required investment in environmental and social projects, and restrictions on the convertibility of currencies. The ultimate political risk is expropriation; the subsidiary of Alcan Aluminum Ltd. in Guyana suffered this fate in 1971. There are a number of degrees of risk between mild interference and outright expropriation. Such practices as higher taxes, higher utility charges, and the requirement to pay higher wages than are paid by a comparable domestic company are examples. Any of them can cause the foreign operation of the Canadian company to be placed at a competitive disadvantage.

Because political risk has an important influence on the overall risk of an investment project, it must be assessed realistically. Essentially, the job is one of forecasting the political climate. How stable is the government involved? What are the prevailing political winds? What is likely to be a new government's view of foreign investment? How efficient is the government in processing requests? How much inflation and economic stability is there? How strong and equitable are the courts? Answers to these questions should give considerable insight into the political risk involved in an investment. Some companies have categorized countries according to their political risk and will usually refuse to permit any investment in a country classified in the undesirable category, no matter how high its expected return.

Once a company decides to invest, it should take steps to protect itself. By cooperating with the host country in hiring nationals, making the "right" types of investment, and by being cooperative in other ways, political risk can be reduced. A joint venture with a company in the host country can improve the public image of the operation. Although every effort should be made to protect an investment once it is made, when sudden political changes occur there is often nothing that can be done. The time to look hardest at political risk is before the investment is made.

In the case of investments in certain less developed countries, it is possible to insure projects through the Export Development Corporation (EDC). The EDC is government-owned and insures against inconvertibility into dollars as well as against loss due to expropriation. It also insures against normal business losses. Where uncertainty is great, obtaining this insurance makes a good deal of sense to the investing company.

Currency Exposure Management

FOREIGN EXCHANGE RISK

An exchange rate represents the number of units of the currency of one country that can be exchanged for another. Currencies of major countries are traded in an active market where rates are determined by the forces of supply and demand.

Foreign exchange risk is the risk that the currency of a country in which a Canadian firm does business will be devalued relative to the dollar, that the market price of the currency will decline relative to the dollar (in the absence of an official devaluation), and/or that its convertibility will be restricted. (If the dollar declines in value relative to the currency in question, this works to the advantage of the company.) When a currency is devalued relative to the dollar, the Canadian company suffers a loss on the currency and on the assets payable in the currency it holds. For example, assume the British pound is worth $2. If XYZ Multinational Company Ltd. held currency and receivables amounting to 500 000 pounds and the pound were devalued by 10 percent, XYZ would suffer a loss in dollar terms of $100 000. Thus, a significant devaluation can be very costly to the multinational company. In addition to price fluctuations, there is the risk that a county may block its currency so that it cannot be converted into other currencies.

Accounting for gains and losses The accounting principles for the translation of assets and liabilities recorded in foreign currencies are complex. In recent years proposed changes have been controversial and have been subject to much debate. Suffice it to say that changes in exchange rates affect the balance sheet and income statement of a foreign subsidiary and consolidated statements of the parent, often quite dramatically. This arises because generally accepted accounting principles in Canada require that exchange gains and losses (realized and unrealized) be reflected in the financial statements.

To illustrate, suppose that Richmond Precision Instruments Ltd. has a subsidiary in West Germany with current assets (cash and receivables only)[2] of 500 000 DM and current liabilities of 200 000 DM. If the exchange rate were 2.0 DM to the dollar, the implied dollar value of the current assets would be $250 000 and the current liabilities, $100 000. This suggests that if the current position of the subsidiary were to be liquidated, current assets would produce 500 000 DM from which would be subtracted 200 000 DM in settlement of the current liabilities, leaving 300 000 DM. This net current asset position could then be converted to $150 000. However, if the dollar were to depreciate in terms of the deutschemark to 1.8 DM to the dollar, the dollar value of current assets would increase from $250 000 to $277 778. However, it also would cost more dollars to pay off the current liabilities, $111 111 instead of $100 000. Because the subsidiary's current assets exceed its current liabilities, the dollar value of the net current asset position increases from $150 000 to $166 667. For accounting purposes, $16 1667 (166 667 less $150 000) will be deemed income.

Thus, when the dollar falls in relation to a foreign currency, current assets increase in dollar value as do current liabilities. If the subsidiary is a net monetary creditor, the dollar value of its net current asset position increases as shown above. On the other hand, if it is a net monetary debtor, the dollar value of its net current asset position (deficit) deteriorates; an exchange loss is incurred. Conversely, when the dollar rises relative to a foreign currency, the current assets and current liabilities of a foreign subsidiary decline in dollar value. If the subsidiary is a net monetary creditor, the dollar value of its net current asset position declines, while if it is a net monetary debtor, its net current asset position increases in dollar value.

---

[2]All assets have prescribed rules for their conversion to Canadian dollars for financial reporting purposes. We select monetary assets and liabilities which are to be converted at the exchange rate prevailing on the day of translation (or the date of the balance sheet).

Because of reporting requirements, multinational companies are very sensitive to exchange rate fluctuations. As the net current asset position is what determines the magnitude and direction of risk exposure, the financial manager must devote considerable and rather continual attention to variations in the net current asset positions of foreign subsidiaries. Many a Board of Directors meeting has been devoted to agonizing over the large accounting loss that must be reported due to adverse foreign exchange fluctuations coupled with a net current asset position exposure. As translation gains and losses can result in rather sharp swings in reported earnings per share, a good deal of attention is devoted to the matter by the financial manager of a multinational company.

EXPOSURE MORE BROADLY DEFINED

The exchange-risk exposure of a company is not confined to changes in the value of monetary assets. It encompasses all factors that give rise to the foreign operation's cash flows. When a devaluation or sharp drop in currency value occurs, it may affect future sales, costs, and remittances. This effect often influences total value to a greater extent than does the immediate effect on the operation's monetary position. The long-run effects of a currency value change on cash flows and value are difficult to quantify and certainly important, but beyond the scope of this book. We shall concentrate on the way a change in currency value affects the monetary assets and liabilities of a company.

If a company believed that the currency of a country is going to drop sharply in value, it makes sense to reduce monetary assets in that currency to as low a figure as possible and to borrow extensively in that currency. As we have discussed, the drop in the value of a currency works to the advantage of a net debtor and to the disadvantage of a net creditor. In order to protect itself against adverse exchange-rate fluctuations, a multinational company can hedge its monetary position. By hedging, we mean offsetting monetary assets—such as cash, marketable securities, and receivables—with monetary liabilities, such as payables and loans, of the same amount. If a change in currency value occurs, monetary assets and liabilities will be equally affected and the company will suffer neither a gain nor a loss. Its net monetary position (assets less liabilities) is zero before and after the change in currency value.

If a company knew a currency were going to fall in value, it would want to do a number of things. First of all, it should reduce its cash to a minimum by purchasing inventories or other real assets. Moreover, the company should try to avoid extended trade credit. As quick a turnover as possible of receivables into cash is desirable. In contrast, it should try to obtain extended terms on its accounts payable. It may also want to borrow in the local currency to replace advances made by the Canadian parent. The last step will depend on relative interest rates. If the currency were going to appreciate in value, opposite steps should be undertaken. Without knowledge of the future direction of currency value movements, aggressive policies in either direction are inappropriate. Under most circumstances we are unable to predict the future, so the best policy may be one of balancing monetary assets against monetary liabilities in order to neutralize the effect of exchange-rate fluctuations.

FORWARD MARKET

In addition to the above, a company can protect itself against exchange-rate fluctuations by use of the forward, or futures, market. In this market, one buys a futures contract for the exchange on one currency for another at a specific future date and at a specific exchange ratio. A futures contract is assurance of being able to obtain conversion into the desired currency at a specific exchange ratio.

To illustrate, suppose Balog Equipment Ltd. sold machinery to a British customer through its U.K. branch for 100 000 pounds sterling with terms of 90 days. On payment, Balog intends to convert the pounds to dollars. Suppose the spot rate and 90-day futures rate on British pounds were as follows:

Spot rate	$2.35
90-day futures	2.32

The spot rate is simply the current market-determined exchange rate for pounds. If Balog wishes to avoid foreign exchange risk, it should sell £100 000 forward 90 days. When it delivers the £100 000, 90 days hence, it will receive $232 000. If the spot rate stays at $2.35, of course, Balog would have been better off not to have sold pounds forward. (It could have sold the £100 000 in the spot market for $235 000.) However, if the pound were devalued or it otherwise declined by 1.27 percent or more during the 90 days, Balog would profit from the use of the forward market. Thus, the forward exchange market allows a company to insure against devaluation and market-determined declines in value. In the case illustrated above, there is a cost if the spot rate remains at $2.35. This cost is 0.03 per pound (future spot rate minus forward rate), and on an annual basis it can be expressed as

$$\left(\frac{0.03}{\$2.35}\right)\left(\frac{365}{90}\right) = 5.18\%$$

Put another way, Balog paid $3 000 to insure its ability to convert pounds to dollars. In doing so, it protected itself against declines in the value of the pound which might have further eroded the $235 000 sale of machinery.

Quotations on selected foreign exchange as of January 19, 1984 are shown in Table 25-1. The spot and future rates shown in the second column indicate the conversion rates into dollars. Future rates are shown for the British pound, the U.S. dollar, and the German deutschemark. For example, the mark was worth $0.4464 on Jan. 19, 1984, in the spot market; in other words, 2.2401 DM ($1.00/0.4464) were required to buy $1.00. However, the 90-day future rate was $0.4508 and this is higher than the spot rate of $0.4464. The market was anticipating a strengthening of the deutschemark relative to the Canadian dollar. A similar expectation was held for the U.S. dollar and the British pound where the future rates quoted exceeded the spot rates.

The financial manager has to be knowledgeable in the operations of the foreign exchange market. He or she has to monitor current and expected trends in the exchange rates for currencies of interest to the firm. Through the use of the forward market, transactions can be undertaken to blunt the effect of foreign exchange fluctuations.

TABLE 25-1 Foreign Exchange Rates—January 19, 1984

	Currency	Canadian Dollar to Buy One Unit	Units Required to Buy One Canadian Dollar
Austria	Schilling	0.0635	15.7480
Brazil	Guzeiro	0.0012	833.3333
Britain	Pound	1.7671	0.5659
30-day future		1.7682	0.5655
90-day future		1.7695	0.5651
180-day future		1.7714	0.5645
365-day future		1.7740	0.5637
France	Franc	0.1459	6.8540
Italy	Lira	0.00073	1369.8630
Japan	Yen	0.00534	187.2659
Lebanon	Pound	0.2493	4.0112
Luxembourg	Franc	0.0219	45.6621
Mexico	Peso	0.00755	132.4503
Netherlands	Guilder	0.3968	2.5202
Pakistan	Rupee	0.0913	10.9529
Saudi Arabia	Riyal	0.3552	2.8153
South Africa	Rand	1.0035	0.9965
Sweden	Krona	0.1528	6.5445
United States	Dollar	1.2466	0.8022
30-day future		1.2469	0.8020
90-day future		1.2469	0.8020
180-day future		1.2470	0.8019
Venezuela	Bolivar	0.1018	9.8232
West Germany	Mark	0.4464	2.2401
30-day future		0.4480	2.2321
90-day future		0.4508	2.2183

Source: *The Globe and Mail*, January 20, 1984.

In summary, the forward exchange market permits a multinational company to protect itself against foreign exchange risk. This risk embodies both devaluation, where a sharp decline in currency value occurs, and downside fluctuations in the spot rate. For this protection, there is a cost which is determined by the relationship between the forward rate and the future spot rate. Whether or not one wishes to use the forward market depends on one's views of the future and one's attitude to risk. The greater the possibility of devaluation and the greater the concern over risk, the greater the case that can be made for the use of the forward market. If others feel the same way, however, the "cost" of this insurance will rise.

INFLATION, INTEREST RATES, AND EXCHANGE RATES

If product and financial markets are efficient internationally, we would expect certain consistent relationships to hold. From Chapter 3, where we discussed inflation and interest rates, we know the Fisher effect implies that the nominal rate of interest is comprised of the real rate plus the rate of inflation expected to prevail over the life of the instrument. If the real rate of interest were 3 percent and inflation of 10 percent were expected, the current nominal rate of interest would be 13 percent. When inflation expectations change so does the nominal rate of interest. Thus, the Fisher effect suggests that the expected inflation for a country has a powerful effect on interest rates in that country.

Interest-rate parity theorem.   The interest-rate parity theorem states that there is an orderly relationship between forward and spot currency exchange rates and nominal interest rates for two countries. Expressing the relationship between the Canadian dollar ($) and the British pound (£) both now and 90 days in the future, the theorem suggests that

$$\frac{F_£}{S_£} = \frac{1 + r_£}{1 + r_\$}$$ (25-1)

where $F_£$ = Current 90-day forward exchange rate in pounds per dollar
   $S_£$ = Current spot exchange rate in pounds per dollar
   $r_£$ = Nominal interest rate on risk-free 90-day British securities, expressed in terms of the 90-day return
   $r_\$$ = Nominal interest rate on risk-free 90-day Canadian securities, expressed in terms of the 90-day return

If the nominal interest rate in Britain were 16 percent and the nominal Canadian rate 12 percent, these annualized rates translate into 90-day rates of 4 percent and 3 percent, respectively. If the current spot rate were 0.50 pounds per dollar, we would have

$$\frac{F_£}{0.50} = \frac{1.04}{1.03}$$

Solving for the implied forward rate

$$1.03F_£ = 0.52$$

$$F_£ = 0.50485$$

   Thus, the implied forward rate is 0.50485 British pounds per Canadian dollar. The British pound forward rate is at a discount from the spot rate of 0.50 pounds to the dollar. That is, a pound is worth less in terms of dollars in the forward market, 1/0.50485 = $1.98079, than it is in the spot market, 1/0.50 = $2.00. The discount is equal to (0.50485 − 0.50)/0.50 = 0.0097. With interest-rate parity, the discount must equal the relative difference in interest rates and, indeed, this is the case for (1.04/1.03) 1.03 = 0.0097. If the interest rate in Britain were less than that in Canada, the implied forward rate in our example would be less than the spot rate. In this case, the British pound forward rate would be at a premium above the spot rate. For example, if the Canadian interest rate (annualized) were 16 percent and the British rate 12 percent, the implied 90-day forward rate for British pounds would be

$$\frac{F_£}{0.50} = \frac{1.03}{1.04}$$

Solving for $F_£$, we have

$$1.04F_£ = 0.515$$

$$F_£ = 0.49519$$

Therefore, the forward rate is at a premium in the sense that it is worth more in terms of dollars than in the spot market.

If interest-rate parity did not occur, presumably arbitragers would be alert to the opportunity for profit. Their actions to exploit profit opportunities would continue until interest-rate parity was established. Does this mean that interest-rate parity prevails between all sets of currencies at all times? For European and other currencies where there is largely an absence of imperfections, interest-rate parity generally holds within the limits of transaction costs. Where government restrictions on exchange and tax imperfections occur, interest-rate parity is not expected. With reasonable adherence to interest-rate parity, one is able to determine the cost in dollars of a foreign sale or purchase where a future receipt or payment is involved.

In summary, the forward exchange market permits a multinational company to protect itself against foreign exchange risk. This risk embodies both devaluation, where a sharp decline in value occurs, and downside fluctuations in the spot rate. For this protection there is a cost, determined by the relationship between the forward rate and the future spot rate. Whether or not one wishes to use the forward market depends upon one's view of the future and one's risk aversion. The greater the possibility of currency value changes and the greater the risk aversion, the greater the case that can be made for use of the forward market. If others feel the same way, unfortunately, the cost of this insurance will rise.

FOREIGN CURRENCY SWAP

Yet another means for hedging against foreign exchange risk is a swap arrangement, an agreement between two parties to exchange one currency for another at a specific future date and at a specified exchange ratio. In effect, the swap is a simultaneous spot and forward transaction, with the forward transaction reversing the original swap transaction. A Canadian parent company might wish to transfer funds temporarily abroad to a foreign subsidiary with the understanding that the funds would be returned in 120 days. In order to protect itself against exchange risk, it might enter into a swap arrangement with a private trader or commercial bank. This arrangement assures the company that it will be able to get dollars back 120 days hence. The cost of the arrangement is the difference in exchange ratios at the time of the initial swap and at reversion 120 days later.

Swap arrangements also are made available by foreign governments and central banks in an effort to encourage international trade and investment. When economic conditions are volatile and the currency markets unsettled because of the possibility of devaluation, the government is often the only party able to effectively underwrite exchange risk. In recent years, central banks have been actively using currency swaps as a means for stabilizing their own currencies. These swaps, of course, do not involve companies, but are made directly between central banks. As shown above, however, the currency swap affords protection to the firm against devaluation and is particularly important in transactions with countries whose currency is soft and where viable forward exchange markets are lacking.

Adjustment of intra-company accounts   Finally, a company with multiple foreign operations can protect itself against foreign exchange risks by adjusting transfer of funds commitments between countries. To illustrate, suppose that it was generally believed that the German mark would be revaluated upward in the near future while the French franc would hold steady. Suppose further that a company had foreign subsidiaries in both countries and that the French subsidiary purchased approximately $100 000 of goods each month from the German subsidiary. Normal billing calls for payment three months after delivery of the goods. Instead of this arrangement, the French subsidiary might be instructed to pay for the goods on delivery, in view of the likely revaluation upward of the German mark. The result of this move would be to save the parent company a good deal of money on a consolidated basis should the revaluation occur.

In addition to these arrangements, the multinational company also can adjust intercompany dividends and royalty payments. Sometimes the currency in which a sale is billed is varied in keeping with anticipated foreign exchange movements. In all of these cases as well as others, intercompany payments are arranged so that they fit into the company's overall management of its currency exposure.

Multinational Financing

The second major facet of financial management is the raising of funds on as favorable terms as possible. In the case of a multinational company, this involves raising funds to finance a foreign affiliate. These funds can come from either internal or external sources. The former comprises equity investment and loans from the Canadian parent, retained earnings, and depreciation and depletion allowances. Collectively, the largest sources are retained earnings and depreciation and depletion allowances. Recently, internal sources of funds have accounted for somewhat over 70 percent of the total financing of Canadian-owned foreign affiliates. Of the internal sources, approximately three quarters consists of retained earnings and depreciation and depletion allowances.

EXTERNAL FINANCING

Although the major sources of funds for a foreign affiliate are internal, external sources are important as well. External financing is particularly important in cases involving less permanent funds requirements. There is a wide variety of sources of external financing available to the foreign affiliate. These range from commercial bank loans within the host country to loans from international lending agencies. In this section, we consider the more important sources of external financing.

Commercial bank loans and trade bills   One of the major sources of financing abroad is commercial banks. These banks perform essentially the same financing function as domestic banks—a topic discussed in Chapter 12. One subtle difference is that banking practices in Europe allow for longer-term loans than are available in Canada. Accompanying the growth in multinational companies has been a corresponding growth in international banking by Canadian banks. The number of branches of Canadian banks abroad has increased rapidly, and now there is no important city in the free world that does not have a branch or office or a Canadian bank. Thus, Canadian banks are able to provide, directly or indirectly, banking arrangements for foreign affiliates in almost any country. For reasons of contact and familiarizaiton with local practices and customs, however, the affiliate may wish to do business with a local bank as opposed to a Canadian bank.

In addition to commercial bank loans, the discounting of trade bills is a common method of short-term financing. Although this method of financing is not used extensively in Canada, it is used extensively in Europe to finance both domestic and international trade. More will be said about the instruments involved later in the chapter.

Eurocurrency and Eurobond financing   Eurocurrency is defined as a unit of currency deposit held in a bank (usually in Europe) outside the country issuing the specific currency. For example, a Eurodollar is a U.S. dollar deposit held in a bank outside the United States. While there are other popular Eurocurrencies (German mark, yen, British pound, French franc and so on), the Eurodollar is dominant. Since the late 1950s, an active market has developed for these deposits. Foreign banks and foreign branches of domestic banks, mostly in Europe, bid actively for Eurocurrency deposits, paying interest rates that fluctuate in keeping with supply and demand conditions. These deposits are in large denominations, frequently $100 000 or more. The banks use the Eurocurrency deposits they receive to make loans to prime borrowers. These loans are made at a rate higher than the deposit rate; the differential varies according to the relative risk of the borrower. All loans are unsecured. Essentially, the borrowing and lending of Eurocurrencies is a wholesale operation, with far fewer costs than are usually associated with banking. The market itself is free from government restrictions and is truly international in scope.

The Eurocurrency market serves as an important source of short term financing for the working capital requirements of the multinational company.

Many Canadian firms arrange for lines of credit and revolving credits from Eurocurrency banks. For the latter arrangement, the firm pays a commitment fee the same as it does for a domestic revolving credit. The interest rate on loans is based on the Eurocurrency deposit rate and bears only an indirect relationship to the prime rate. Typically, the rates on loans are quoted in terms of the London interbank offering rate, commonly called the LIBOR; the greater the risk, the greater the spread above the LIBOR.[3] One should realize that the LIBOR is usually much more volatile than the prime rate of the banks owing to the sensitive nature of supply and demand conditions for Eurocurrency deposits. Consequently, it is more difficult to project the cost of a Eurocurrency loan than that of a domestic loan.

In the late 1960s the Eurobond market developed into an important source of long-term funds for the multinational company. A Eurobond is simply a bond which is denominated in another currency from that of the country in which the borrower is located. The market for Eurobonds is truly international with investment dealer syndicates composed of bankers from a number of countries and with securities placed all over the world. As with the Eurocurrency market, there is an absence of government regulation. Of the total volume, over half of the funds raised are in U.S. dollars. Canadian parent companies issue these bonds to supplement their direct investments in their foreign affiliates. Not only do foreign affiliates of Canadian companies borrow in this market but foreign companies do as well. Both straight bond issues and convertible issues have been sold.

Development banks and agencies   Many countries have development banks or agencies that make or guarantee intermediate and long term loans. The purpose of these loans is to support economic development within the country. If the investment project or international transaction qualifies, financing through a development bank may be a viable financing alternative. The bank or agency itself can be either a government agency or privately run. In order to obtain a better understanding of their operation, we will discuss briefly the Export Development Corporation programs.

The Export Development Corporation was established as a federal agency to assist in the promotion of exports through export credit insurance, guarantees of loans extended by financial institutions, long-term financing, and insurance on investments abroad. The EDC credit insurance policy protects an exporter against commercial and political risks. The EDC insures 90 percent of export sales and the foreign buyer, 10 percent. The EDC can also insure, subject to the approval of the Governor General in Council, Canadian investments abroad against non-commercial risk of loss due to expropriation, war or revolution, and the resultant impossibility of repatriating capital and revenue. The EDC can guarantee loans granted by banks or other financial institutions to foreign purchasers of Canadian goods and services. In addition, the EDC can finance projects for which commercial credit is

---

[3]LIBOR is the rate at which participating banks loan funds to each other. Corporate borrowers pay LIBOR plus a premium for their loans; the size of the premium depends on perceived default risk.

not available. These projects normally require large amounts of capital expenditures. The Canadian suppliers of capital goods are guaranteed payments through loans to the foreign buyers.

The development banks of individual countries are too numerous to list. To mention only a few of the larger ones, there is the *Export-Import Bank* in the U.S., the *Industrial Reorganization Corporation* in Britain, the *National Financiera, S.A.* in Mexico, the *Credit National* in France, the *Kreditanstalt fur Wiederaufbau* in West Germany, and the *Instituto Mobiliare Italiano* in Italy. An example of a privately owned development bank is *Adela*, which was formed in 1964. It makes private investments in Latin American firms, usually in participation with other investors.

Financing International Trade

Foreign trade differs from domestic trade with respect to the instruments and documents employed. Most domestic sales involve an open-account credit where the customer is billed and has so many days to pay. In international trade, the seller is seldom able to obtain as accurate or as thorough credit information on the potential buyer as with a domestic sale. Communication is more cumbersome and transportation of the goods slower and less certain. Moreover, the channels for legal settlement in cases of default are complicated and more costly to pursue than when a domestic customer defaults. For these reasons, a set of procedures has evolved for international trade which differ from those for domestic trade. There are three key documents: an order to pay, or a draft; a bill of lading, which covers the physical movement of the goods; and a letter of credit, which guarantees the creditworthiness of the buyer.

THE TRADE DRAFT

The international draft, sometimes called a bill of exchange, is simply a written statement by the exporter ordering the importer to pay a specific amount of money at a specific time. Though the word "order" may seem harsh, it is the customary way of doing business internationally. The draft may be either a *sight* draft or a *time* draft. A sight draft is payable on presentation to the party to whom the draft is addressed. This party is known as the *drawee*. If the drawee, or importer, does not pay the amount specified on presentation of the draft, he or she defaults and redress is achieved through the letter of credit arrangement to be discussed later. A time draft is payable so many days after presentation to the drawee.[4] For

---

[4]The draft itself can be either "clean" or "documentary." A clean draft is one where documents of title are not attached, while with a documentary draft they are attached and delivered to the importer at the time the draft is presented. Clean drafts are usually used for situations in which there is no trade as such, and the drawer is simply collecting a bill. Most drafts are documentary.

example, a 90-day time draft indicates that the draft is payable 90 days after sight. An example of a time draft is shown in Fig. 25–1.

Several features of the draft should be noted. First, it is an unconditional order in writing signed by the drawer, the exporter. It specifies an exact amount of money that the drawee, the importer, must pay. Finally, it specifies an exact interval after sight at which time this amount must be paid. On presentation of the time draft to the drawee, it is accepted. The *acceptance* can be by either the drawee or a bank. If the drawee accepts the draft, he or she acknowledges in writing on the back of the draft the obligation to pay the amount specified 90 days hence. The draft is then known as a trade acceptance. If a bank accepts the draft, it is known as a bankers' acceptance. The bank accepts responsibility for payment and thereby substitutes its credit-worthiness for that of the drawee.

If the bank is large and well-known—and most banks accepting drafts are— the instrument becomes highly marketable on acceptance. As a result, the drawer, or exporter, does not have to hold the draft until the due date; but can sell it in the market. In fact, an active market exists for bankers' acceptances of well-known banks. To illustrate the arrangement, assume that we have a 90-day draft for $10 000, that it is accepted by a well-known bank, and that 90-day interest rates in the bankers' acceptance market are 12 percent. The drawer then could sell the draft to an investor for $9 700, $10 000−[$10 000 × 0.12(90/360)]. At the end of 90 days, the investor would present the acceptance to the accepting bank for payment and would receive $10 000. Thus, the existence of a strong secondary market for bankers' acceptances has facilitated international trade by providing liquidity to the exporter.

$ 10000.00	*January 16, 1984*
– – – –Ninety– – – – Days after sight	
Pay to the order of *OURSELVES*	
*Ten thousand and no/100 – – – – – – – – – – – – – –*Dollars	
To	
Dorts Import	
Hamburg, West Germany	*J. Kelly Company, Ltd., Exporters*
	Halifax, Nova Scotia
	By

FIGURE 25–1   Example of a Trade Draft

BILLS OF LADING

A bill of lading is a shipping document used to cover the transportation of goods from the exporter to the importer. It has several functions. First, it serves as a receipt for the transportation company to the exporter that specified goods have been received. Second, it serves as a contract between the transportation company and the exporter to ship the goods and deliver them to a specific party at a specific point of destination. Finally, the bill of lading can serve as a document of title. It gives the holder title to the goods. The importer, for example, cannot take title until receipt of the bill of lading from the transportation company or its agent. This bill will not be released until the importer satisfies all the conditions of the draft.[5]

The bill of lading accompanies the draft, and the procedures by which the two are handled are well-established. Banks and other institutions able to handle these documents efficiently exist in virtually every country. Moreover, the procedures by which the goods are transferred internationally are well-grounded in international law. These procedures allow an exporter in one country to sell goods to an unknown importer in another and not release possession of the goods until paid, in the case of a sight draft, or until the obligation is acknowledged, in the case of a time draft.

COMMERCIAL LETTERS OF CREDIT

A commercial letter of credit is issued by a bank on behalf of the importer. In the document, the bank agrees to honor a draft drawn on the importer provided a bill of lading and other details are in order. In essence, the bank substitutes its credit for that of the importer. Obviously, the local bank will not issue a letter of credit unless it feels the importer is credit-worthy and will pay the draft. The letter of credit arrangement reduces almost entirely the risk to the exporter of selling goods to an unknown importer in another country. An example of a letter of credit form is shown in Fig. 25-2.

Illustration of a confirmed letter The letter of credit arrangement is strengthened further if a bank in the exporter's country *confirms* the letter of credit. To illustrate, suppose a Canadian exporter wishes to ship goods to a Brazilian importer located in Rio de Janeiro. The importer's bank in Rio regards the importer as a sound credit risk and is willing to issue a letter of credit guaranteeing payment for the goods when they are received. Thus, the Rio bank substitutes its credit for that of the importer. The contract is now between the Rio bank and the beneficiary of the letter of credit, the Canadian exporter. However, the exporter may wish to work through a Canadian bank, because of little knowledge of the Rio bank. The exporter asks his or her bank to confirm the Rio bank's letter of credit. If the bank is satisfied with the credit-worthiness of the Rio bank, it will agree to do so. When it

---

[5]The bill of lading can be negotiable, if specified at the time it is made out; and it can also be used as collateral for a loan.

Form 940A Rev. (July 67) — 38861
Printed in Canada

APPLICATION FOR COMMERCIAL CREDIT
(See Reverse Side for Instructions)

No. ....

To the Manager,

.................................19.......

....

(1 & 2) Please issue for $\frac{our}{my}$ account an IRREVOCABLE Commercial Credit by $\frac{mail}{cable}$ in favour of ....

....
(Complete name and full address of beneficiary)

(3) Available with ....
(To be completed by Credit-issuing office)

(4) by drafts at .... to the aggregate sum of ....
(Number of days after date or sight)   (Amount in figures and words and kind of currency)

....

(5) to be drawn upon ....
(To be completed by Credit-issuing office)

(6) DOCUMENTS REQUIRED ARE: (Please indicate by "X")

☐ Commercial Invoice in duplicate   ☐ Customs Invoice in quadruplicate, certified according to Canadian Customs Regulations

☐ Insurance Policy or Certificate covering marine and war risk ....

☐ Other documents: ....

....

☐ Full set of clean ....Bills of
(State if "on Board—Ocean" "Received for Shipment" or "Railroad")

Lading made out to the order of Bank of Montreal, Claused Notify ....
(As a general rule—the Applicant)

(7) Description and country of origin of goods ....

....

(8) To be shipped to .... via .... from ....

(9) Method of conveyance ....
(Viz. Steamer, Railroad, Air Shipment, Parcel Post, Etc.)

(10) Terms of Purchase ....
(C.I.F. or F.O.B., etc.—name point also)

(11) Partial shipments are ☐ permitted ☐ not permitted
(please indicate by X)

(12) Freight charges are to be paid by ....

(13) Insurance including War Risk to be covered by ....

(14) This Credit is to expire in .... on ....

(15) Special Instructions if any ....

....

(16) DISPOSAL OF ORIGINAL CREDIT INSTRUMENT (Credits opened by mail only) (Please indicate by "X")
☐ Direct to beneficiary ☐ to Correspondents for delivery ☐ to Branch for forwarding by applicant ☐ Return to applicant

It is fully understood that no liability shall attach to the Bank of Montreal or to its Correspondents for any loss or damage in consequence of any delay or mistake in transmitting this message, or for any cause beyond its control. The undersigned hereby undertake to complete and forward to you, upon request, your usual contract form covering this credit.

I/We further understand that this credit is subject to the "Uniform Customs & Practice for Documentary Credits (1962 Revision), International Chamber of Commerce, Brochure No. 222" and documents presented and conforming to these provisions will be acceptable excepting as the terms of the Credit may specifically detail otherwise.

....
Applicant.

....
Address.

FIGURE 25-2 Example of a Letter of Credit form

does, it obligates itself to honor drafts drawn in keeping with the letter of credit arrangement.

Thus, when the exporter ships the goods, he or she draws a draft in accordance with the terms of the letter of credit arrangement. The exporter presents the draft to the Canadian bank, and the bank pays the amount designated, assuming all the conditions of shipment are met. As a result of this arrangement, the exporter has the money with no worries as to payment. The Canadian bank then forwards the draft and other documents to the Rio bank. On affirming that the goods have been shipped in a proper manner, the Rio bank honors the draft and pays the Canadian bank. In turn, it goes to the Brazilian importer and collects from him or her once the goods have arrived in Rio and are delivered.

Facilitation of trade   From the description, it is easy to see why the letter of credit facilitates international trade. Instead of extending credit directly to an importer, the exporter relies on one or more banks; and their credit-worthiness is substituted for that of the importer. The letter itself can be either *irrevocable* or *revocable*. Drafts drawn under an irrevocable letter must be honored by the issuing bank. This obligation can be neither canceled nor modified without the consent of all parties. On the other hand, a revocable letter of credit can be canceled or amended by the issuing bank. This type of letter specifies an arrangement for payment but is no guarantee that the draft will be paid. Most letters of credit are irrevocable, and the process described above assumes an irrevocable letter.

The three documents described—the draft, the bill of lading, and the letter of credit—are required in most international transactions. Established procedures exist for doing business on this basis. Together, they afford the exporter protection in selling goods to unknown importers in other countries. They also give the importer assurance that the goods will be shipped and delivered in a proper manner. The financial manager should be acquainted with the mechanics of these transactions if the firm is engaged in exporting or importing.

Summary

A multinational firm is one that does business in two or more countries, and these firms have grown in importance in recent years. As with domestic operations, the financial manager is concerned with the allocation of capital to investment projects and the raising of funds. Foreign investments should be judged on the basis of expected returns and risk, the same as a domestic project. Foreign projects often afford risk-reduction properties that are not available in domestic projects. The possible advantages to companies investing abroad are new markets, the acquisition of less costly production facilities, and the securing of raw materials at lower cost.

A number of factors make foreign investment different from domestic investment. For one thing, taxation is different. Political and foreign exchange risk exist. With respect to the former, forecasting of the political climate and the effect of this climate on expected returns is essential at the time an investment is being considered. Foreign exchange risk is the risk that a foreign currency will be devalued relative to the dollar and/or that convertibility will be restricted. A company can protect itself against the risk by balancing foreign monetary assets and liabilities, by using the forward exchange market, by engaging in a foreign currency swap arrangement, or by adjusting intra-company account arrangements. Both political and foreign exchange risks must be integrated with business risk in judging the overall risk of a foreign investment. A final factor sometimes influencing foreign investment decisions is that of foreign government restrictions on direct investment from abroad.

Raising funds abroad is the second major function of the financial manager. Although internal financing—comprising equity investments and loans from the parent, retained earnings, and depreciation and depletion allowances—is the most important source of funds, external financing is important as well. The major sources of external funds are commercial banks, Eurocurrency loans, Eurobonds and development banks. Financing international trade differs from domestic trade in the procedures employed. The differences in procedures are attributable to the lower quality of credit information, poorer communications, slow transportation, and different legal processes. There are three principal documents involved in international trade. The draft is an order by the exporter to the importer to pay a specified amount of money either on presentation of the draft or a certain number of days after presentation. A bill of lading is a shipping document that can serve as a receipt, a shipping contract, and as title to the goods involved. The final document, a letter of credit, is an agreement by a bank to honor a draft drawn on the importer. It greatly reduces the risk to the exporter and may be confirmed by another bank. These three documents greatly facilitate international trade.

Questions

1. If capital and product markets are perfect, does it make any difference in which country a company invests?

2. Why would a company want to enter a joint venture when it loses partial control over its foreign operations?

3. Explain the function performed by the Eurodollar market.

4. What are the functions of a bill of lading?

5. Many countries require that nationals control more than 50 percent of the voting stock in any venture. Is this wise? Explain.

6. In the early 1970s the Chilean government took over most of the American-owned businesses in Chile. Explain the impact of such action on the short-run and long-run productivity of the assets that were taken over. Project the impact of these actions on future development of the underdeveloped countries.

7. What are monetary assets? Monetary liabilities? With respect to a foreign subsidiary, what if they are mismatched?

8. What is meant by interest-rate parity? Does it work?

9. Identify factors that will prevent the correction of a trade deficit by currency realignment (devaluation or revaluation).

10. In a letter of credit arrangement, who is the borrower? Who is the lender?

11. What is the credit worthiness of a bankers' acceptance? How does it differ from that of the trade draft? What determines the face value of the acceptance?

12. Do income taxes paid by a foreign branch work to the detriment of the Canadian parent company?

Problems with Solutions

1. An investor wishing to make a 90-day, $100 000 term deposit has asked you for advice. The investor is considering a deposit with a U.S. Bank at a rate of 15 percent rather than a Canadian dollar deposit at 14 percent. The Canadian dollar is currently trading at U.S. $0.84. Calculate the return on a Canadian deposit and on a U.S. deposit assuming that the exchange rate does not change and that transaction costs are zero. Use a 360 day year. How much does the U.S. dollar have to fall to offset the higher interest?

Canadian deposit:

$$\$100\,000 \times 0.14 \times \frac{90}{360} = \$3\,500$$

Terminal value $100 000 + $3 500 = $103 500 Canadian

U.S. deposit:

Convert $100 000 Canadian into $84 000 U.S.

$$\$84\,000 \times 0.15 \times \frac{90}{360} = \$3\,150$$

At the end of 90 days convert US $ back to Canadian $.

$84 000 ÷ 0.84 = $100 000, $3 150 ÷ 0.84 = $3 750

Terminal value $100 000 + $3 750 = $103 750 Canadian

Calculation of amount by which the US dollar must fall (or Canadian dollar must rise) to offset higher interest. Let X = new value Canadian $.

$$\frac{\$84000 + \$3\,150}{X} = \$103\,500$$

$$\$87\,150 = 103\,105X$$

$$X = \$0.842029$$

The US dollar has fallen from $1.19048 Can ($1.00 ÷ $0.84) to $1.18761 Can ($1.00 ÷ $0.842029) or 0.2402% = ($1.19048 − $1.18761) ÷ $1.19048

2. (a) What precaution could the investor in problem 1 take to remove the currency risk?

(b) If all investors are absolutely certain that the Canadian dollar will trade at U.S. $0.84 in 90 days and that interest rates will remain the same, what will happen to the extra profit calculated in the first part of problem 1?

(i) Since the investor must sell the US dollars in 90 days he or she could simply sell 90-day US dollar futures when making the initial deposit. If the US dollar goes up the investor makes money on the deposit conversion but loses on the forward contract. If the US dollar goes down the opposite happens.

For example, assume that the 90-day rate is the same as the spot rate, i.e. $0.84 US ($1.1905 Canadian) and that the spot rate in 90 days is $0.82 US or $1.2195 Canadian. The investor buys US $87 150 at $1.2195 Canadian to cover the future contract: the cost of this purchase is $106 280 Canadian. The sale of these U.S. dollars has been contracted for at $1.1905 Canadian, or $103 750. The loss ($2 530) exactly offsets the gain on the deposit transaction where the investor bought at $1.1905 Canadian and sold at $1.2195 Canadian.

(ii) If the spot rate is known with certainty to be $0.84 in 90 days and the interest rates remain the same, then the difference between the spot rate and the 90-day rate will exactly offset the $250 gain ($103 750 – $103 500) calculated in problem 1. The 90-day rate will be $0.842029 which is also calculated in problem 1.

Problems

1. Table 25-1 shows foreign exchange rates. On the basis of this information, compute to the nearest second decimal the number of
   (a) British pounds that can be acquired for $100
   (b) Dollars that 50 Dutch guilders will buy
   (c) Swedish krona that can be acquired for $40
   (d) Dollars that 200 French francs can buy
   (e) Italian lira that can be acquired for $10 (to the nearest lira.)
   (f) Dollars that 1 000 Mexican pesos will buy

2. The Labrador Imports Company purchased 100 000 marks' worth of machines from a firm in Dortmund, West Germany. The value of the dollar in terms of the mark has been decreasing. The firm in Dortmund offers 2/10, net 90 terms. The spot rate for the mark is $0.42, while the 90-day future rate is $0.43.
   (a) Compute the dollar cost of paying the account within the 10 days.
   (b) Compute the dollar cost of buying a future contract to liquidate the account in 90 days.
   (c) The differential between part (a) and part (b) is the result of the time value of money (the discount for prepayment) and protection from currency value fluctuation. Determine the magnitude of each of these components.

3. In 1977 the Vermont Maple Industries Company from the U.S.A. obtained a $100 000 loan in Canadian dollars from the Bank of Quebec to finance an exploratory maple sugar farm in Quebec. At the time of the loan the exchange rate was 1.00 U.S. dollars required to buy one Canadian dollar. Four years later, when the loan was paid, the exchange rate had dropped to 0.83 U.S. dollars to the Canadian dollar. What gain or loss did the company sustain by virtue of the change in currency value?

4. Financiera de Nuevo León in Mexico offers to pay 12 percent on one-year certificates of deposit. The Mexican government taxes interest income at the source through a withholding system much like the Canadian system of withholding on personal income. The Mexican tax rate is 21 percent. A Canadian who is in the 40 percent tax bracket in Canada invests $50 000 in the Financiera (Savings and Loan).
   (a) Determine the taxes paid to the Mexican government.
   (b) Determine the taxes paid to the Canadian government on the income from Mexico.
   (c) Qualitatively, assess the risks being borne by the Canadian investor.

5. Canadian manufacturer is going to increase its inventories in Europe financed either by a Eurodollar loan with 18 months maturity at an annual rate of 12 percent payable at maturity or by French francs at an annual rate of 15 percent. If the French francs are chosen, the position will be hedged with an 18-month future contract at $0.16 per franc. The current exchange rate is $0.17 per franc. Choose the better financing alternative.

6. Presently, the U.S. dollar is worth 220 Japanese yen in the spot market. The interest rate in Japan on 90-day government securities is 8 percent; it is 12 percent in the United States. If the

interest rate parity theorem holds, what is the implied 90-day forward exchange rate in yen per dollar? What would be implied if the U.S. interest rate were 10 percent?

7. Cordova Leather Company Ltd. of New Brunswick is in a 42 percent tax bracket. It has sales branches in Algeria and in Spain, each of which generate earnings of $200 000 before taxes. If the effective income tax rate is 52 percent in Algeria and 35 percent in Spain, what total Canadian and foreign taxes will Cordova pay on the above earnings?

8. The government of Zwill presently encourages investment in the country. Comstock International Mining Corporation Ltd. a Canadian company, is planning to open a new copper mine in Zwill. The front-end investment is expected to be $25 million, after which cash flows are expected to be more than sufficient to cover further capital needs. Preliminary exploration findings suggest that the project is likely to be a very profitable, providing an expected internal rate of return of 34 percent, based on business considerations alone.

The government of Zwill, like that of many countries, is unstable. The management of Comstock, trying to assess this instability and its consequences, forecasts a 10 percent probability that the government will be overthrown and a new government will expropriate the property, with no compensation. The full $25 million would be lost, and the internal rate of return would be −100 percent. There also is a 15 percent probability that the government will be overthrown but that the new government will make a partial payment for the properties; this would result in an internal rate of return of −40 percent. Finally, there is a 15 percent probability that the present government will stay in power, but that it will change its policy on repatriation of profits. More specifically, it will allow the corporation to repatriate its original investment, $25 million, but all other cash flows generated by the project would have to be reinvested in the host country forever. These probabilities still leave a 60 percent chance that a 34 percent internal rate of return will be achieved.

Given these political risks, approximate the likely return to Comstock. Should the mining venture be undertaken?

Selected References

ADLER, MICHAEL, and BERNARD DUMAS, "The Exposure of Long-Term Foreign Currency Bonds." *Journal of Financial and Quantitative Analysis*, 15 (November 1980), 973-94.

AGGARWAL, R., "International Differences in Capital Structure Norms: An Empirical Study of Large European Companies," *Management International Review*, 21, Nov. 1 (1981), 75-88.

AKHTAR, M.A. and A.K.M.A. ROB, "The Canadian Experience with Flexible Exchange Rates," *Atlantic Economic Journal*, 4 (Spring 1976), 19-30.

ANDERSON, GERALD L. "International Project Financing," *Financial Executive*, 45 (May 1977), 40-45.

BEAVER, WILLIAM H., and MARK A. WOLFSON, "Foreign Currency Translation and Accounting for Changing Prices in Perfect and Complete Markets," Research Paper, Stanford Business School, 1981.

CALDERON-ROSSELL, JORGE R., "Covering Foreign Exchange Risks of Single Transactions," *Financial Management*, 8 (Autumn 1979), 78-85.

COHN, RICHARD A., and DONALD R. LESSARD, "The Effect of Inflation on Stock Prices: International Evidence," *Journal of Finance*, 36 (May 1981), 277-90.

CORNELL, BRADFORD, "Inflation, Relative Price Changes, and Exchange Risk," *Financial Management*. 9 (Autumn 1980), 30-34.

———, "The Denomination of Foreign Trade Contracts Once Again," *Journal of Financial and Quantitative Analysis*, 15 (November 1980), 933-44.

———, "Spot Rates, Forward Rates and Exchange Market Efficiency," *Journal of Financial Economics*, 5 (August 1977), 55-65.

DAVIS, STEVEN I., "How Risky is International Lending?" *Harvard Business Review*, 55 (January-February 1977), 135-43.

DUFEY, GUNTER and S.L. SRINIVASULU, "The Case for Corporate Management of Foreign Exchange Risk," *Financial Management*, Winter 1983, 54-62.

EDEN, LORRAINE A.B. "Vertically Integrated Multinationals: A Microeconomic Analysis," *Canadian Journal of Economics* (Aug. 1978), 534-46.

EAKER, MARK R., "Denomination Decision for Multinational Transactions," *Financial Management*, 9 (Autumn 1980), 23-29.

EITEMAN, DAVID K., and ARTHUR I. STONEHILL, *Multinational Business Finance*. 2nd ed. Reading. Mass.: Addison-Wesley, 1979.

ERRUNZA, VIHANG R., and LEMMA W. SENBET, "The Effects of International Operations on the Market Value of the Firm: Theory and Evidence," *Journal of Finance*, 36 (May 1981), 401-18.

FEIGER, GEORGE and BERTRAND JACQUILLAT, "Currency Option Bonds, Puts and Calls on Spot Exchange and the Hedging of Contingent Foreign Earnings," *Journal of Finance*, 34 (December 1979), 1129-39.

_____, *International Finance*. Boston: Allyn and Bacon, 1982.

FINNERTY, JOSEPH E., THOMAS SCHNEEWEIS, and SHANTARAM P. HEGDE, "Interest Rates in the Eurobond Market," *Journal of Financial and Quantitative Analysis*, 15 (September 1980), 743-55.

GARMAN, MARK B., AND STEVEN W. KOHLHAGEN, "Inflation and Foreign Exchange Rates under Production and Monetary Uncertainty," *Journal of Financial and Quantitative Analysis*, 15 (November 1980), 949-68.

GIDDY, IAN H., "An Integrated Theory of Exchange Rate Equilibrium," *Journal of Financial and Quantitative Analysis*, 11 (December 1976), 883-92.

GITMAN, LAWRENCE J., "A Multinational Firm Investment Model," *Journal of Economics and Business*, 26 (Fall 1973), 41-48.

HAGEMANN, HELMUT, "Anticipate Your Long-Term Foreign Exchange Risks," *Harvard Business Review*, 55 (March-April 1977), 81-88.

HENNING, CHARLES N., WILLIAM PIGOTT, and ROBERT HANEY SCOTT, *International Financial Management*, New York: McGraw-Hill, 1978.

HUGHES, JOHN S., DENNIS E. LOGUE, and JAMES SWEENEY, "Corporate International Diversification and Market Assigned Measures of Risk and Diversification," *Journal of Financial and Quantitative Analysis*, 10 (November 1975), 627-37.

LESSARD, DONALD, "International Portfolio Diversification: A Multivariate Analysis for a Group of Latin American Countries," *Journal of Finance*, 28 (June 1973), 619-34.

_____, ed. *International Financial Management, Theory and Application*. New York: Warren, Gorham & Lamont, 1979.

LEVY, HAIM, and MARSHALL SARNAT, "International Diversification of Investment Portfolios," *American Economic Review*, 60 (September 1970), 668-75.

LIETAER, BERNARD A., *Financial Management of Foreign Exchange: An Operational Technique to Reduce Risk*. Cambridge, Mass.: M.I.T. Press, 1971.

LOGUE, DENNIS E., and GEORGE S. OLDFIELD, "Managing Foreign Assets when Foreign Exchange Markets Are Efficient," *Financial Management*, 6 (Summer 1977), 16-22.

OBLAK, DAVID J., and ROY J. HELM, JR., "Survey and Analysis of Capital Budgeting Methods used by Multinationals," *Financial Management*, 9 (Winter 1980), 37-41.

PETTY, J. WILLIAM, II, and ERNEST W. WALKER, "Optimal Transfer Pricing for the Multinational Firm," *Financial Management*, 1 (Winter 1972), 74-87.

PIPPENGER, JOHN. "Interest Arbitrage between Canada and the United States: A New Perspective," *Canadian Journal of Economics* (May 1978), 183-93.

PURVIS, D.D. "Exchange Rates and Economic Policy in Theory and Practice," *Canadian Public Policy* (Spring 1977), 205-18.

ROBERTSON, J. R. "The Use of Tax Evasion and Tax Avoidance by Multinational Companies: A Canadian View," *Canadian Tax Journal* (Sept.-Oct. 1977), 513-27.

RODRIQUEZ, RITA M., "Corporate Exchange Risk Management, Theme and Aberrations," *Journal of Finance*, 36 (May 1981), 427-38.

_____, and E. EUGENE CARTER, *International Financial Management*, 2nd ed., Englewood Cliffs, N.J.: Prentice-Hall, 1979.

SHAPIRO, ALAN C., "Exchange Rate Changes, Inflation, and the Valuation of the Multinational Corporation," *Journal of Finance*, 30 (May 1975), 485-502.

_____, "Optimal Inventory and Credit-Granting Strategies under Inflation and Devaluation," *Journal of Financial and Quantitative Analysis*, 8 (January 1973), 37-46.

_____, and DAVID P. RUTENBERG, "Managing Exchange Risks in a Floating World," *Financial Management*, 5 (Summer 1976), 48-58.

SOLNIK, BRUNO H., *European Capital Markets*. Boston: Lexington Books, 1973.

TECK, ALAN, "Control your Exposure to Foreign Exchange," *Harvard Business Review*, 52 (January-February 1974), 66-75.

VERNON, RAYMOND, et al., *Manager in the International Economy*, 4th ed. Englewood Cliffs, N.J.: Prentice-Hall, 1981.

WELLS, LOUIS T., JR., "The Multinational Business Enterprise: What Kind of International Organization?" *International Organization*, 25 (September 1971), 447-64.

WESTON, J. FRED, *Guide to International Financial Management*. New York: McGraw-Hill, 1977.

26

The Smaller Company and Financial Management

Our discussions on short , intermediate , and long term financing in Chapter 12 and Chapters 19-23 were focused exclusively on well-established private financial institutions as suppliers of funds. We discussed the procedures used by firms to acquire both debt and equity financing within the financial market structure shown in Fig. 3-1. These discussions almost invariably described the practices of large and well-established Canadian companies. We now consider sources of funds available to the smaller business firms in the country. A review of these sources of small business financing is important for a number of reasons. There are significant numbers of small businesses in Canada, and the access these smaller firms have to funds is limited. Small firms often do not have the credit rating necessary to qualify for the amounts of funds they may need to expand and grow. Lack of adequate funds for small businesses affects the growth of the economy in the regions where these firms predominate, but it also affects the growth of the entire economy.

Characteristics of the Small Firm

What is a small business? Unfortunately, there is no single answer to this question. The definition will depend on the context in which the characteristics of the firm are discussed. For example, for tax purposes a small business is a private company which is Canadian-controlled and which has accumulated taxable income (minus $^4/_3$ of taxable dividends) of less than $1 000 000 as discussed in Chapter 2. A stock market analyst may regard a firm whose shares are not listed on the stock exchange as a small business, while under the provisions of the Small Business Loans Act, a small business is a firm whose gross revenue does not exceed $1 500 000 during the year in which the loan request is made. These are but a few of the definitions available.

THE GROWTH-ORIENTED SMALLER FIRM

A new venture in a growth segment of the economy is a different genre from the more traditional small business that will always remain small. A high technology company may start out small but grow into a larger company, particularly in the electronics, computer, and information systems industries.

For the smaller growth firm, the challenge is to manage growth in an efficient manner. Fast growth brings with it the need to hire large numbers of new employees –often to double the number each year or to grow even more rapidly. With the inevitable turnover of employees, this means an even larger number of new employees who must be assimilated into the organization, and new management must be developed. Frequently, entrepreneurs who start a business are technically oriented and not necessarily good managers of increasing numbers of people. Many a growth firm flounders because its top people, who have been able to do things themselves when the firm was small, cannot manage other people.

The growth-oriented smaller business faces a number of strategic decisions in marketing, new products, production, and a host of other areas. Financing is an ever-present problem. For most smaller, growth-oriented, high technology companies, growth in assets outpaces growth in retained earnings. Though these companies typically pay no dividends, the percentage of buildup in receivables, inventories, and fixed assets usually is much greater than the percentage of buildup in retained earnings. Sometimes the problem is alleviated by leasing buildings and equipment and by being labor intensive, instead of capital intensive, in the production process. Even at that, receivables and inventories continue to grow.

Whenever growth in assets outstrips growth in retained earnings, debt increasingly must fill the gap. Debt may take the form of bank loans or increasing reliance on trade payables. Because the firm is small, even though growing, a straight bond issue to the public is out of the question. Consequently, the firm is restricted in its sources of debt funds. With the unbalanced growth mentioned above, debt ratios increase, and these ratios ultimately are questioned by lenders. Eventually it becomes necessary either to raise equity capital or to curtail growth. Equity capital often comes from venture capitalists, a topic considered later in the chapter.

Thus, the small, high technology company faces a number of problems: personnel, marketing, production, and financing. Resolution of the financing problem is instrumental in solving many of the former. Building a company on a proportionally smaller and smaller equity base is precarious. Often the problem is masked by growing profits; but, as long as assets are growing more rapidly, debt ratios deteriorate. The problem often is compounded by using short term financing–bank loans and payables–to finance long term funds requirements; that is, permanent buildups in receivables, inventories, and fixed assets. Eventually a day of reckoning must come. It is far better to face the issue of balanced financial growth earlier, rather than later.

The risks of starting and nurturing a growth-oriented, high technology company are many. Usually there is little margin for error. The equity base simply does not provide an adequate cushion. If things go wrong, the small company frequently is unable to weather the storm. Although one remedy might be to curtail growth, few entrepreneurs have the temperament to do so. Usually it is forced upon them by outside suppliers of capital, often too late. Thus, there is a higher mortality of small firms than of large ones.

THE TRADITIONAL SMALLER FIRM

The traditional smaller company tends to be outside a high technology industry. It may be a retail store, a franchise outlet, a service company, or a small manufacturing company. Even though the company may be quite successful, it probably always will remain small. This forecast does not denigrate the traditional small business, for such firms are essential to the economy. It simply recognizes the fact that high growth is not an appropriate objective. Usually the traditional small firm is heavily dependent upon one or two individuals who own it and who are involved in all areas of the enterprise. Indeed, specialization for them is not possible. They are on the firing line all the time, making most of their decisions without elaborate analysis. Their management style is loose and personal; control is informal. They take in stride their day-to-day operations but cannot extricate themselves from these operations for enough time to engage in strategic planning.

Financial management of the small, traditional firm is a good deal different from that of the large firm and even from that of the small, but growth-oriented, high technology firm. For one thing, the small firm cannot sell common stock. All equity capital must come from the owners and from earnings retained in the business. The lack of ability to engage in equity financing seriously limits any expansion plans that management might have. The chief sources of financing are trade payables and bank loans. Often trade credit serves as a cushion to offset unfavorable cash swings. When the small firm is in a temporary cash bind, it leans on the trade by slowing its payments. If it is desperate, it may use accrual financing as well. It may postpone wages and payments for sales and income taxes. Of course there frequently are costs to such actions, as discussed in Chapter 9. Moreover, such reliance may mask the fact that the funds requirements of the firm are permanent instead of temporary and should be financed by some other means. Bank loans usually must be secured, usually by receivables and inventories. Often the owners are required to guarantee the loan, to put all their personal wealth at stake and compound their risk.

Any intermediate or long term debt also must be secured. Equipment may be purchased on a conditions sales contract or through a secured loan, or its often leased. If the firm owns its building, it may use a mortgage loan, but the small business usually enters into short term debt.

Table 26-1 illustrates some financial differences between a small and a large firm. It compares the average balance sheet percentages and financial ratios for two sizes of a machine tool company. These data are compiled by Robert Morris Associates. The smaller firm has a greater need to hold cash than the large one, owing to economies of scale in liquidity management. Also, it has far lower inventories, which may be due to differences in the nature of the business. The inventory turnover ratio is more than double that for larger firms, which may support the idea of differences in the nature of the business. With respect to financing, the smaller business uses much more debt and less equity than does the larger business. This relationship may reflect the difficulties of raising equity capital. Also, profitability on sales is less, though the return on assets is about the

TABLE 26-1 Comparison of Balance Sheet Percentages and Financial Ratios for Small and Larger Manufacturers of Machine Tools and Metal Working Equipment

	Asset size	
	Under $250 000	$10 million to $50 million
Cash	11.6%	4.8%
Receivables	32.3	25.5
Inventories	15.8	37.3
Other current assets	1.8	1.2
Net fixed assets	30.9	24.1
Other noncurrent assets	7.6	7.1
Total Assets	100.0	100.0
Notes payable	16.0	10.4
Accounts payable	16.1	11.5
Accruals	7.0	6.7
Other current liabilities	1.2	3.4
Long-term debt	26.5	15.7
Net worth	33.2	52.3
Total Liabilities and Net Worth	100.0	100.0
Current ratio	1.8	2.4
Quick ratio	1.3	1.0
Average collection period	53	59
Inventory turnover	6.5	3.0
Debt/Net worth	1.9	0.9
Before-tax profit margin	7.0%	10.6%
Return on assets (before taxes)	16.1%	15.6%

same, owing to the higher turnover of assets. The other numbers speak for themselves. Thus, the most noticeable differences between the two size categories is the much heavier reliance of the smaller firm on debt financing and the lower level of inventory and higher turnover.

The typical small business is greatly involved, perhaps overly involved, in managing working capital. Because many small businesses are thinly capitalized, management worries a lot about liquidity. Planning cash flows is critical. Receivables must be watched closely, and late payers hounded. In order not to tie up funds unnecessarily, inventories must be managed efficiently. When either receivables or inventories are mismanaged, financial problems typically arise. As mentioned before, current liability management also is important. Many small businesses must delay payments to suppliers and sometimes even to employees in order to weather what is hoped to be only a temporary downturn. Some small businesses are franchises, such as fast food outlets and muffler shops, and they usually lease their buildings. Their managements' principal concern are sales, inventory management, expense control, and planning ahead to pay bills.

In summary, the small business has somewhat different characteristics from those of the large business. Typically, it must rely on internal financing. A great deal of attention should, and indeed must, be paid to working capital management.

Continual effort must be devoted simply to remaining solvent. Decision making is concentrated in one or at most only a few individuals. Management is spread thinly over all facets of the enterprise, so long-range planning receives little attention. The principles taken up in previous chapters apply to the small business as they do to any business, but the relative emphasis is different.

Special Financing Opportunities

In this chapter we review the role of governments and venture capitalists as suppliers of funds for small businesses. Remember that small businesses obtain funds from banks, life insurance companies, trust companies, and other institutional sources; this was discussed in Chapters 12 and 20. Trade credit, term loans, equipment financing, and lease financing are normally available to qualified small businesses. However, these short and intermediate term financing arrangements are likely to cost the small business more. Moreover, many of the sources of long-term financing discussed in Chapters 11-23 are not usually available to most small businesses. To a large extent, such financing has to be provided by equity or loans from the owners of the firms, or by long term capital suppliers who are willing to assume the risk.

Federal Government Financial Assistance Programs

Federal government incentives provided to industry are many and varied, and we do not intend to review all programs.[1] We will briefly examine the Federal Business Development Bank, the Regional Development Incentives programs supervised by the Department of Regional Industrial Expansion, and the Small Business Loans Act.

FEDERAL BUSINESS DEVELOPMENT BANK

The Federal Business Development Bank (FBDB) was established by the FBDB Act in 1975 as the successor to the Industrial Development Bank (IDB). The latter was established by the IDB Act in 1944 as a subsidiary of the Bank of Canada. The FBDB took over the operations of IDB as well as certain consultant and advisory services of other government agencies. Responsibility for the FBDB lies with the Department of Industry, Trade and Commerce, Ottawa, and the bank has about 100 branches throughout Canada. The name and center of responsibility were changed because the institution is expanding its scope of activities to include management counselling services and management training. The Bank makes term loans to new and existing businesses in Canada, particularly those of smaller

---

[1]For information on the various programs, the reader should contact the local offices of the Department of Industry, Trade and Commerce and the Federal Business Development Bank. Most of this information is also available at the offices of the provincial development corporations.

TABLE: 26-2 FBDB Loan Approvals During the Fiscal Year ending March 31

	1977	1978	1979	1981	1982
Number of loans					
$25 000 or less	4 327	4 605	5 562	3 553	1 403
over $25 000 to $50 000	2 812	3 085	3 498	1 936	1 074
over $50 000 to $100 000	1 475	1 362	1 880	1 452	1 065
over $100 000 to $500 000	662	812	1 240	960	984
Total up to $500 000	9 276	9 864	12 180	7 901	4 526
over $500 000	35	44	91	67	104
Total	9 311	9 908	12 271	7 968	4 630
Dollar value (in millions)					
$25 000 or less	$ 62.0	$ 64.2	$ 77.2	$ 49.7	$ 21.0
over $25 000 to $50 000	103.4	122.1	136.1	73.3	41.2
over $50 000 to $100 000	109.9	102.7	138.4	107.1	78.8
over $100 000 to $500 000	119.2	148.0	235.6	192.0	213.6
Total up to $500 000	397.5	437.0	587.3	422.1	354.6
over $500 000	26.6	42.3	81.3	62.0	121.3
Total	$424.1	$479.3	$668.6	$484.1	$475.9
Average dollar value (in thousands)	46	48	54	60	103

Source: Federal Business Development Bank, *Annual Report*

TABLE 26-3 FBDB Loan Approvals by Province During the Fiscal Year ending March 31

	1977	1978	1979	1981	1982
	(in millions)				
Newfoundland	$ 7.9	$ 15.3	$ 28.7	$ 13.7	$ 11.7
Prince Edward Island	2.2	2.6	3.6	1.7	1.5
Nova Scotia	11.4	17.7	20.4	12.0	9.5
New Brunswick	10.9	20.9	27.9	12.3	14.5
Quebec	100.7	102.7	131.2	113.2	164.9
Ontario	104.6	118.2	183.2	145.1	76.0
Manitoba	8.5	12.7	17.8	13.7	9.2
Saskatchewan	15.5	15.3	17.4	12.3	9.8
Alberta	52.5	50.0	69.4	53.3	48.4
British Columbia	104.2	119.8	161.9	98.6	122.4
Yukon	3.9	1.9	4.2	3.7	2.1
Northwest Territories	1.8	2.2	2.9	4.2	5.8
Total	$424.1	$479.3	$668.6	$484.1	$475.9

Source: Federal Business Development Bank, *Annual Report*

size. This fact is evident from the data shown in Table 26-2. The majority of loans are under $500 000. Historically, most of the loans approved by the FBDB have been for businesses located in Ontario, British Columbia, Quebec, and Alberta. (See Table 26-3.) Also, the bank makes equity investments primarily in high-technology enterprises. By March 31, 1982 FBDB had equity investments of $26.7 million.

General requirements for obtaining a loan   Before the FBDB will consider a loan, a small business firm has to satisfy five general requirements:

1. The firm must be located in and doing business in Canada. The FBDB lends money for almost any type of business. However, firms in manufacturing, wholesaling, retailing, construction, and service industries (such as restaurants, hotels, and motels) are significant users of FBDB funds. Most loans are granted for capital expansion or replacement. Loans are also given for the establishment of new businesses or to finance purchases of existing businesses.

2. The required financing must be unobtainable from other sources on reasonable terms and conditions. The FBDB is viewed as a "lender of last resort" and not as a competitor to commercial lenders. Usually an applicant is required to provide evidence (a letter of refusal) verifying that the required financing is not obtainable elsewhere. Other sources of funds would include the usual financial institutions, new bond and stock issues, and assistance offered under such legislation as the Small Business Loans Act, the Fisheries Improvement Loans Act, the Farm Improvement Loans Act, and the Farm Credit Act.

3. Financing by the FBDB must be supplemented by a reasonable amount of funds provided by the borrower or other lenders.

4. Expected earnings must be sufficient to meet the needs of the business including the repayment of obligations to the FBDB and all other creditors. Analysis of the applicant's strength follows the procedures discussed in Chapters 6-10.

5. FBDB loans are secured by the fixed assets of the borrower. Realty mortgage, chattel mortgage, or a mortgage bond are the basic security devices used in securing the loan. The FBDB may also enter into a conditional sales agreement and in the case of transportation firms, may purchase equipment trust certificates. Frequently, owners are required to offered personal guarantees and parent companies may guarantee loans to subsidiaries. Borrowers are also required to maintain adqeuate insurance on secured assets and sometimes on the lives of key management personnel.

Types of financing   The FBDB is primarily involved in the granting of term loans. The term of the loan and the repayment of principal and interest are tailored to the needs of the borrower. However, most loans are scheduled for repayment within ten years. Interest rates are based on the general level of interest rates in Canada. Normally, the interest rates on FBDB loans approximate those charged by chartered banks on new loans. It is the policy of the FBDB to set interest rates on smaller loans somewhat lower than those on larger loans. The Bank takes the position that large borrowers are most likely to obtain such funds from sources other than the FBDB.

In addition to the term loans, the FBDB may provide financing by purchasing common shares of the borrowing company. The Bank normally restricts such investments to a minor portion of the common shares. Also, any equity financing would usually be combined with a secured term loan. Equity positions taken by the FBDB have been rare in the 1960s and early 1970s but the Bank is now involved in this type of investment.

Other services   The FBDB has a Management and Counselling Service that seeks to promote good management practices in small and medium-sized companies. A series of information bulletins is currently in circulation. these bulletins cover selected topics in the area of financial planning and control. The FBDB also sponsors management seminars in smaller centers across Canada. The costs of these seminars to participating firms are rather small.

INDUSTRIAL AND REGIONAL DEVELOPMENT PROGRAM (IRDP)

The Department of Regional Industrial Expansion (DRIE) was established in 1983 to administer the Industrial and Regional Development Act of 1983. DRIE replaced the well known Department of Regional Economic Expansion (DREE) which administered the Regional Incentives Act of 1969. The objectives of the IRDP are to stimulate economic activity, industrial expansion, and new employment across Canada. The IRDP recognizes that regional disparities exist across the country and DRIE's role is to co-ordinate the efforts of several government departments (federal, provincial and municipal) to achieve the above objectives. Federal assistance to firms under the IRDP will depend on the economic conditions in their areas of location.

DRIE follows certain procedures to assess the economic hardship of each of Canada's census districts. This assessment considers such factors as level of unemployment, per capital income, and the fiscal capacity of the province in which the district is located. The districts are then classified in four Tier Groups based on population statistics and the degree of economic hardship. Tier IV includes districts where up to 5 percent of the provincial population reside and where the economic hardship is relatively severe. Tier III includes districts with 5 percent to 20 percent of the provincial population; Tier II, 20 percent to 50 percent; and Tier I, the remaining 50 percent. Other factors remaining constant, it is expected that the level of federal assistance will be greatest for firms locating in Tier IV districts and least in Tier I districts.

Type and Level of Assistance   Federal assistance is offered to new establishments and to existing firms for modernization/expansion, research and product development, and identification of new markets. Grants ranging from 35 percent to 75 percent of approved costs may be obtained depending on the type of project and the Tier Group. Also, some projects may qualify for loan guarantees by the federal government.

SMALL BUSINESS LOANS

The Small Business Loan Act permits charted banks (and other interested financial institutions) to extend loans to small businesses. These loans are guaranteed by the federal government. Loans may be made to small business firms engaged in manufacturing, trade, transportation, construction, communications, service industries, and those in the wholesale and retail trade. For the purposes of the Act, a small business is defined as one whose gross revenue does not exceed $1.5 million during the year in which the loan request is made. Loans are to be used for the purchase, installation, renovation, or modernization of equipment. In addition, loans may be granted for the purchase, construction, renovation, or modernization of business premises excluding land. Normally, the terms of the loan are determined in consultation with the lender. However, certain additional factors taken into account in the negotiations are

1. The federal government guarantees a maximum of $75 000 per firm.
2. The loan can cover a maximum of 80 percent of funds required for movable equipment and 90 percent for premises.
3. The maturity of the loan should not exceed ten years and instalments must be paid at least annually. The lender can require payments to be made more frequently. The duration of the loan will vary with the type of asset acquired.
4. The interest rate on loans is established at one percentage point above the prime rate. Thus, it is usually lower than those for regular small business loans.
5. Loans are secured by a first charge on assets acquired.

Loans by chartered banks granted under the Act increased from $64 million in 1970 to $1 142 million in 1983. However, these loans amounted to less than 2 percent of the total business loans granted by banks. (See Table 26-4)

OTHER PROGRAMS

Federal assistance may be geared towards aiding specific industries. For example, the Farm Improvement Loans Act enables farmers to obtain loans for the purchase of machines, for breeding stock, and for general improvements. These loans are granted by chartered banks and are guaranteed by the federal government. The amount of these loans for the 1970-83 period is shown in Table 26-4. A similar situation exists for fishermen under the Fisheries Improvement Loans Act.

Instead of concentrating on an industry, the federal government may focus on a single region. For example, the Cape Breton Development Corporation (DEVCO) was established to provide financial assistance to industrial firms locating or expanding in the Cape Breton area of Nova Scotia. Financial assistance can be in the form of a grant and/or a loan. In the case of larger projects, DEVCO cooperates with commercial lenders to provide the necessary funds.

Finally, the Department of Industry, Trade and Commerce has support programs to subsidize studies in research and productivity, project feasibility, export development, and management efficiency and improvement. Traditionally, most of the allocated funds have gone to business firms in Quebec and Ontario.

TABLE 26-4　Selected Loans of Chartered Banks
(in millions)

	Business Loans		Loans to Farmers	
	Total	Under Small Business Loans Act	Total	Farm Improvement Loans
1970	$ 8 900	$ 64	$1 214	$303
1972	13 461	82	1 569	373
1974	20 568	117	2 295	457
1976	28 218	211	3 399	456
1978	34 441	319	4 893	468
1980	55 385	661	7 472	521
1982	68 568	896	7 337	500
1983	68 351	1 142	7 475	528

Source: *Bank of Canada Review*

Financial Assistance Programs Provincial Government

Provincial governments have established public corporations or agencies similar to those of the federal government. These provincial bodies are often responsible for the promotion of all economic development. Such provincial efforts supplement federal financial assistance generally in the form of incentives or term loans.

Venture Capital

Venture capital may be viewed as debt or equity capital made available to small businesses prior to their going public. Alternatively, we may define venture capital as money invested in business enterprises which do not have access to such conventional sources as the stock and bond markets and banks and other financial institutions. The funds may be provided at the start of the business or for expansion of operations. Venture capital is high-risk capital. Such investments are exposed to a greater-than-normal risk of losses, and consequently, such commercial lenders as banks, life insurance companies, and trust companies will not usually directly finance a significant portion of their total investments. Most of the government financial assistance discussed earlier can be regarded as venture capital. The incentives (grants and low interest-bearing loans) are "sweeteners" offered to businesses to undertake business and financial risk in designated regions. Guaranteed loans, on the other hand, are "sweeteners" offered to commercial lenders to extend credit to firms which may not otherwise qualify for funds. The government therefore shares in the business and financial risk of these ventures. The return the government seeks from its venture capital investment is viable business enterprises promoting the economic prosperity of designated regions. A quantitative expression of such a return is not possible.

Aside from the government, a group of private venture capital suppliers is gradually emerging within the Canadian financial system. Unlike the government, these ventures capitalists are looking for stated minimum rates of return on their investments. They do not give incentives. In fact, the opposite is true. Very little is known of the amount of venture capital available in Canada, so we will limit our discussion to the type of investments venture capitalists look for and the incentives required. [2]

TYPES OF INVESTMENT

Some venture capitalists tend to specialize in certain phases of the development of a company. For example, the venture capitalist may supply funds for the start-up phase, but once the business is in commercial operation, the investment is liquidated. Other venture capitalists may be involved only after the start-up phase. In general, most prefer to invest in a business after it has been in operation for several years.

Usually, the amount invested in any one firm ranges from $50 000 to $1 million. The type of financing varies, with convertible debentures and convertible preferred stocks being perhaps the most popular. The preference for convertible securities or securities with options to purchase common shares is adopted for a number of reasons. Debt or preferred shares offer a fixed return to the venture capitalist during the holding period of the investment, while conversion to common shares becomes attractive if the company is likely to go public. The capital gains potential in such instances adds to the attractiveness of the investment. In fact, some venture capitalists may not invest in a business if it is likely that the company will not satisfy the listing requirements of a stock exchange. Debt affords the venture capitalist the opportunity to attach covenants which limit the powers of management. These covenants are similar to those discussed in Chapter 12.

REQUIRED RETURN

Venture capital is a high-risk capital, and venture capitalists expect higher-than-normal returns. Required returns of venture capitalists range from 15 percent per annum to as much as 60 percent. The higher expected rates for return are normally based on the assumption that the company will go public. A venture capitalist will usually benefit from capital gains should the firm go public.

OPERATING CONTROL

Control of the borrowing company by the venture capitalist may range from minimal supervision to absolute control. At a minimum, the venture capitalist relies on the protective covenants in the debt agreement and periodic financial statements to monitor his or her investment. In addition, the venture capitalist

---

[2]Venture capital companies are described in more detail, and most are listed in "Sources of Venture Capital," by R.C. McQuillan and H. Taylor, published by the Federal Department of Industry, Trade and Commerce, See also *The Sources of Funds Index*, ed. by M. J. Kostuch, published by the Services Division of SB Corporation Ltd., Toronto. This index is available only to subscribers.

usually has a representative on the Board of Directors. At the other extreme, the venture capitalist may take over operating control, though most venture capitalists would not consider it desirable. Normally, as investors, venture capitalists do not want to participate directly in the management of companies in which they have financial interest. Their primary concern is with the safety of their investments and they will usually only get involved with the management of day-to-day operations if they feel their investments are endangered.[2]

Summary

Small businesses are an important element in the Canadian economy. Like the larger companies, small business firms obtain funds from such sources as trade credit, loans, and lease financing from the conventional lenders (banks, life insurance companies, trust companies, and other private financial institutions). Equity capital is supplied primarily by the owners of the small businesses. For a number of reasons, many of the small business firms may not have access to funds on the same terms and conditions as the larger companies do. That is, their ability to raise needed funds may be restricted. We reviewed two main sources of funds available to small businesses–government and venture capitalists.

Federal and provincial governments provide incentives and term loans to encourage viable business enterprises. Firms may also obtain loans which are guaranteed by the government. Lenders are therefore given additional protection if the firm defaults. Incentives may be "free" capital or capital obtained at relatively low interest rates. Interest rates on loans are considered low relative to those charged by conventional lenders, given the quality of the borrowers. The underlying philosophy in government financing is the promotion of economic prosperity in designated regions.

A second source of funds is the venture capital market. Venture capital is high-risk capital on which higher-than-normal returns are demanded by the lenders. Venture capitalists normally provided debt and equity funds to small companies prior to their going public. These lenders have a strong preference for convertible securities. Such securities offer a fixed annual income and the possibility of capital gains should the value of the firm increase. The venture capital market is relatively small but current trends indicate that this market is likely to grow significantly in the future.

Questions

1. How would you define a small business? In terms of sales? Assets? Profits? Employees? Other?
2. What effect do small businesses have on the economy? Are they essential?
3. Identify some of the problems associated with a new enterprise in a high technology, fast growing area.

4. What are some of the repercussions of receivables, inventories, and fixed assets growing at a faster rate than do retained earnings? What are the remedies?

5. Are there dangers to using short-term debt for financing a small but growing company?

6. Identify the characteristics of the traditional smaller business.

7. In the traditional smaller business, with what aspects of finance is management primarily concerned?

8. What do venture capitalists hope to gain from an investment in a new enterprise? How liquid is the investment?

9. Can any small, new business look to venture capital as a source of financing?

10. Why do various departments of the government try to assist small businesses?

11. If you decide to start a retail store or take on a new franchise, how will you finance it?

Selected References

BATLER, EMANUEL, "The Growth and Development of Venture Capital," *Cost and Management*, (Jan.-Feb. 1973), 17-20.

BRIGHAM, EUGENE F., and KEITH V. SMITH, "The Cost of Capital to the Small Firm," *Engineering Economist*, 13 (Fall 1967), 1-26.

DIPCHAND, CECIL R., "Venture Capital for "Grass-Roots" Small Business–A Comparison of Provincial Legislation," *Cost and Management*, January-February, 1981, 2-9.

FELLS, GEORGE A., "Venture Capital in the Closely Held Business," *Cost and Management*, (Jul-Aug. 1970), 16-22.

_____, "Venture Capital–Can a Canadian Entrepreneur Find It There?" *Cost and Management*, (Jan.-Feb. 1975), 29-32.

GEORGE, ROY E., *The Life and Times of Industrial Estates Limited*, Halifax: Institute of Public Affairs, Dalhousie University, 1974.

GILMORE, F.F., "Formulation Strategy in Smaller Companies," *Harvard Business Review*, 49 (May 1971), 71-81.

HUNTSMAN, BLAINE, and JAMES P. HOBAN, Jr., "Investment in New Enterprise: Some Empirical Observations on Risk, Return, and Market Structure," *Financial Management*, 9 (Summer 1980), 44-51.

KNIGHT, RUSSELL M., "The Supply of Venture Capital in Canada," *Working Paper Series No. 57*, School of Business Administration, University of Western Ontario, London, October, 1971.

_____, "The Use of Incentive Contracts in Venture Capital Investments," *Journal of Business Administration*, 4 (Spring 1973), 31-42.

MACONOCHIE, MICHAEL, "New Rules in the Venture Capital Game," *Canadian Business*, (Sept 1977), 50-58.

MARTIN, JOHN D. and J. WILLIAM PETTY, "An Analysis of the Performance of Publicly Traded Venture Capital Companies," *Journal of Financial and Quantitative Analysis*, September 1983, 40-409.

MAY, J. DOUGLAS, "Investment Incentives and Industrial Strategy," *Canadian Public Policy*, (Winter, 1979), 70-79.

PLAYFAIR, JOHN L., "New Solutions to the Venture Capital Problem," *CA Magazine*, (Sept. 1976), 26-31.

POYNTON, DAVID C., "A Review of Ontario's Small Business Development Corporations Act, 1979," *Canadian Tax Journal* (Sept.-Oct. 1979), 534-51.

PUDDINGTON, JOHN C., "Venture Capital: Risk Financing for Growing Companies," *CA Magazine* (Sept. 1983), 30-35.

ROSSITER, BRUCE G., and GENE I. MILLER, "Financing the New Enterprise," in J. FRED WESTON and MAURICE B. GOUDZWAARD, eds., *The Treasurer's Handbook*, Homewood, Ill.: Dow Jones-Irwin, 1976, 861-900.

WALKER, ERNEST W., and WILLIAM J. PETTY II, "Financial Differences between Large and Small Firms," *Financial Management*, 7 (Winter 1978), 61-74.

WHEELRIGHT, STEVEN C., "Strategic Planning in the Small Business," *Business Horizons*, 14 (August 1971), 51-58.

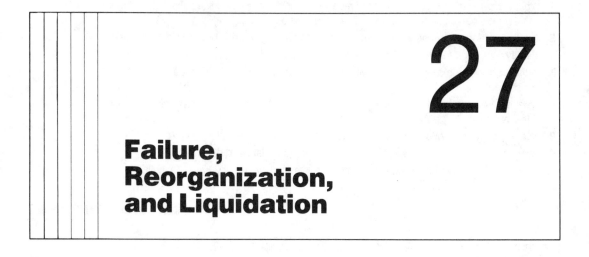

Failure,
Reorganization,
and Liquidation

In our analysis throughout this book, we have consistently viewed the firm as a going concern; nevertheless, we must not lose sight of the fact that some do fail. Recognition of possible failure is important from the standpoint of both internal management and a creditor with amounts owing from a company in financial distress. Both management and creditors should be familiar with their respective rights and remedies when financial difficulties arise. In this chapter we present a rather general description of the voluntary (or informal) and statutory proceedings which are usually undertaken when a company fails. We emphasize the fact that the exposition is general and we advise readers to seek legal and other related professional advice when faced with the complexities of actual corporate failure.

Failure

The word "failure" is vague because there are varying degrees of failure and varying procedures available to handle a failing company. Generally, a company is regarded as *insolvent* if it is unable to meet its obligations as they become due. The firm's assets may exceed its liabilities but the firm simply does not have cash to pay its current debts. Thus, there is general lack of (short-term) liquidity and the non-payment of maturing obligations results in default. The financial difficulty may be only temporary and subject to remedies which may save the firm from liquidation. At the other extreme, the firm's total liabilities may exceed a fair valuation of its total assets; that is, the net worth is negative. Here the financial difficulty is severe and the best remedy possible is liquidation. Management or creditors can, under the Bankruptcy Act, take steps to have the firm declared a *bankrupt* and effect liquidation proceedings.

Financial failure includes the entire range of possibilities from temporary financial distress which can be remedied to situations which are so chronic that the only advisable approach is to liquidate the firm. The specific procedures used to deal with failing situations will depend on the degree of financial difficulty. We discuss some of these procedures later in this chapter when we consider the remedies available to a company in financial distress: from remedies that are voluntary on the part of creditors and the company, to legal action that can be taken in connection with a failing company.

CAUSES OF FAILURE

Although the causes of financial difficulty are numerous (some are listed in Table 27-1), many failures are attributable either directly or indirectly to management. Usually, non-financial problems lead to losses which, in turn, lead to financial strain and eventual failure. Very seldom is one bad decision the cause of the difficulty; usually the cause is a series of errors, and the difficulty evolves gradually. Because with most companies the signs of potential distress are evident prior to actual failure, a creditor may be able to take corrective action before failure finally occurs. If the cause of the difficulty is financial mismanagement and the company is profitable, the situation can almost invariably be salvaged. However, when the underlying clause is principally external, and there is no way for management to curtail losses, the inevitable result is liquidation.

Despite difficulties caused by past mistakes, many companies can be preserved as going concerns and can make an economic contribution to society. Sometimes the rehabilitation is severe, in keeping with the degree of financial difficulty. Nevertheless, these measures may be necessary if the firm is to obtain a new lease on life.

TABLE 27-1 Causes of Failure as Reported by Dun & Bradstreet— Selected Years

	1968	1970	1972	1974	1977	1980
Neglect	1.0%	1.2%	1.4%	1.5%	2.2%	0.3%
Fraud	0.5	0.7	0.6	0.3	0.3	0.1
Business operating factors						
Inadequate sales	61.5	54.9	58.9	65.5	36.6	41.3
Heavy operating expenses	10.2	10.0	18.8	23.2	46.3	46.9
Receivables difficulties	9.5	7.8	2.2	2.4	3.3	0.9
Inventory difficulties	3.7	5.9	3.5	2.1	5.2	1.9
Excessive fixed assets	3.1	2.8	2.9	0.8	2.3	1.2
Poor location	1.4	1.4	1.6	1.1	1.0	0.3
Competitive weakness	10.8	15.2	10.1	3.3	4.2	5.6
Other	1.2	1.0	0.4	0.3	0.1	1.6
Disaster	0.8	0.8	1.0	0.8	0.9	0.1
Reason unknown	0.6	0.2	0.1	0.4	0.8	0.1

Source: Dun and Bradstreet, *The Canadian Failure Record*. The percentages do not total 100.0%. Some firms were subject to combinations of causes and such firms are counted more than once.

RECORD OF CORPORATE FAILURES

An index of corporate failures since 1900 is presented in Fig. 27-1. The data are reported as the number of failing firms per 10 000 businesses listed by Dun & Bradstreet. The post-World War II failure rate has been increasing, but the increase has generally been lower than that observed in the decades prior to 1940, when the failure rate averaged 1 percent per decade of the total number of businesses. The decennial average increased from 0.5 percent in 1950 to 0.9 percent in the 1970s. The trend is definitely upwards and the failure rate is currently approaching the pre-1940 experience.

We would expect the failure rate to vary with the overall performance of the economy. That is, in periods of economic boom, fewer firms should fail, while more firms should fail during periods of economic slowdown. Also, the failure rate will be higher for smaller firms than for larger firms, because larger firms tend to have more financial strength than smaller firms to withstand temporary adverse economic conditions.

Voluntary Settlements

The discussion in the rest of this chapter focuses on the different ways of dealing with corporate failures. First, we review those remedies which are voluntary: management and creditors agree on specific proposals without resort to legal action. Then we review management's right to submit a proposal for an arrangement under the Bankruptcy Act in an attempt to save the firm from liquidation.

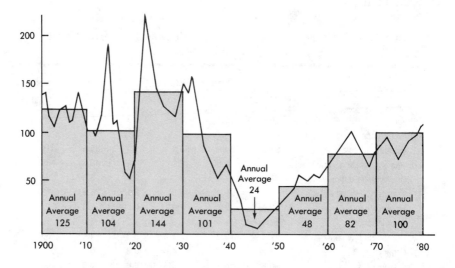

FIGURE 27-1 Number of failing firms per annum and annual average per decade per 10 000 listed concerns

Source: Dun & Bradstreet. The failure rate is based on firms listed with D & B.

Finally, we discuss liquidation under the Bankruptcy Act—such a procedure can be effected either by management or creditors. Let us now turn to the voluntary settlements or remedies.

EXTENSIONS AND COMPOSITIONS

An *extension* involves nothing more than creditors extending the maturity of their obligations. If a basically sound company is temporarily insolvent, creditors may prefer to work the problem out with the company. By not forcing the issue with legal proceedings, creditors avoid considerable legal expense and the possible shrinkage of value in liquidation. Moreover, they maintain their full claim against the company involved; they do not agree to a partial settlement. The ability of a creditor to realize the full value of his or her claim depends, of course, on the company improving its operations and its liquidity. In an extension situation, existing creditors are often unwilling to grant further credit on new sales and insist on current purchases being paid for in cash. Obviously, no one creditor is going to extend his or her obligation unless others do likewise. Consequently, a creditors' committee is usually formed by the major creditors to negotiate with the company and to formulate a plan satisfactory to all concerned.

If an extension is worked out, the creditors can institute controls over company operations to ensure proper management and to increase the probability of speedy recovery. In addition, they may elect to take security if marketable assets are available. The ultimate threat on the part of creditors is to initiate bankruptcy proceedings against the company and to force it into liquidation. By making an extension, however, they show an inclination to cooperate with the company.

A *composition* involves a pro rata settlement of creditors' claims in cash, or in cash and promissory notes. The creditors must agree to accept a partial settlement in discharge of their entire claim. For example, a debtor may propose a settlement of $0.60 on the dollar. If creditors feel that the settlement is more than they could obtain in liquidation after legal expenses, they will probably accept. Even if it is somewhat less, they may still accept, because no company likes to be responsible for forcing another into bankruptcy. The settlement is a "friendly" one in the sense that legal proceedings are avoided. As in an extension, however, the settlement must be agreed to by all the creditors.

Sometimes a voluntary settlement may be a combination of an extension and a composition. In other than cash settlements as at the date of the agreement, the promissory notes may be paid on an instalment basis over some future period.

Overall, voluntary settlements can be advantageous to the creditors as well as to the debtors, for they avoid legal expenses and complications. The settlements are "informal" and, as a result, tend to be more efficiently administered than legal settlements. Too often the latter are both cumbersome and lengthy.

LIQUIDATION BY VOLUNTARY AGREEMENT

In certain circumstances, creditors may feel that the company should not be preserved, because further financial deterioration seems inevitable. When liquidation is the only realistic solution, it can be accomplished either through a private settlement or through bankruptcy proceedings. An orderly private liquidation is likely to be more efficient and likely to result in a significantly higher settlement. With a liquidation in bankruptcy, much time is expended in court scheduling and other legal formalities, not to mention the legal and other expenses involved. The opportunity costs of delays as well as the direct expenses usually are much less with a private liquidation.

A private liquidation can be effected through an assignment in which the debtor assigns its assets to an administrator.[1] In turn, the administrator liquidates the assets and distributes the proceeds to creditors on a pro rata basis. The liquidation itself can be on a piecemeal basis, asset by asset over time, or through a public auction where assets are sold all at once. The assignment of assets by the debtor does not release the debtor from his or her obligations. For all practical purposes, however, creditors have little prospect of obtaining further settlement from a company once all of its assets are liquidated. Because voluntary liquidation requires the approval of all creditors, it is usually restricted to companies with a limited number of creditors and to situations where the securities outstanding are not publicly held.

Proposals for an Arrangement under the Bankruptcy Act

The management of a failing company may believe that if the firm is properly reorganized, it may operate successfully in the future. However, there is some uncertainty as to whether creditors will voluntarily agree to an extension or composition as discussed earlier. In some cases creditors may have already petitioned the court to declare the firm bankrupt. Under these circumstances, the debtor company may, under the provisions of the Bankruptcy Act, submit a proposal for an arrangement (popularly termed a *commercial arrangement*). The proposal may be for an extension, composition, or both, and will contain details for the reorganization of the firm, if necessary. Management of the failing firm will seek the approval of shareholders for the proposal and once this is obtained, the proposal is lodged with a trustee,[2] who then files the proposal with an Official Receiver[3] and at the same time sets a date for a meeting with creditors. Acceptance of the proposal is binding if a majority of the creditors holding three quarters of the amount of claims present or represented at the meeting votes in favor of the proposal. After acceptance by creditors the proposal must be ratified by the court.

---

[1] The administrator is usually a trustee. See fn. 2.

[2] The Bankruptcy Act requires that the property of each bankrupt estate be administered by a trustee licensed by the Minister of Justice. A candidate has to demonstrate thorough knowledge of bankruptcy law, have substantial business experience, and have sound financial and other resources to undertake the required duties.

[3] The Official Receiver is appointed by the Governor-in-Council for each bankruptcy division (province) and is an officer of the court. The Official Receiver has a number of important duties including the acceptance of a debtor's assignment, the appointment of a trustee for an estate, the conduct the first meeting of creditors, and the examination of the affairs of the debtor.

The trustee plays a key role in the proceedings relating to proposals for an arrangement. We noted earlier that the trustee files the proposal with the Official Receiver and sets the date for the first meeting of creditors. Prior to that meeting, the trustee has to appraise and investigate the affairs and assets of the debtor company with a view to ascertaining the causes of the firm's financial difficulties. Also, the trustee has to be satisfied that the financial situation of the debtor company is as represented in the proposal. The trustee's report is made available to the creditors at the meeting and is also submitted to the court as supporting evidence for ratification of the proposal.

Creditors are likely to approve a proposal if they feel that the debtor firm can be rehabilitated and that the benefits to them will be higher than those obtainable through bankruptcy proceedings. Thus, the prospects of the firm's successful operations in the future and the specific terms of the extension or composition proposal are of paramount importance. In some composition proposals, the settlement may be for cash payable after the court ratifies the proposal. Otherwise creditors' claims are settled over some defined future time period. In this situation, creditors have to be satisfied that a reorganization of the company will be in their best interest.

REORGANIZATION

It may be in the best interests of all concerned to reorganize a company rather than to liquidate it. A reorganization is an effort to keep a company alive by changing its capital structure. The rehabilitation involves the reduction of fixed charges by substituting equity and limited-income securities for fixed-income securities. In essence, a reorganization is similar to a composition in that claims are scaled down. The decision to go with a reorganization as opposed to liquidation must be based on the likely future profitability of the company. If there is little prospect for profitable operations in the foreseeable future, creditors will want to liquidate the company and take whatever losses they must at the time. Only if the present value of the company as a going concern exceeds its liquidating value will a reorganization be worthwhile from the standpoint of creditors. The plan for reorganization has to be approved at the meeting(s) of the creditors and management of the debtor company. Any plan formulated as a result of such meetings must be ratified by the court. Several factors are considered by the court before ratification is given.

Fair, equitable, and feasible standards If the court feels that the plan is fair, equitable, and feasible, it will ratify the plan. The fair and equitable standard means that all parties are treated according to their priority of claim. Junior security holders cannot receive a new security of the same value as senior security holders. The superior rights of senior security holders must be recognized in the reorganization. Feasibility has to do with the plan being workable with respect to earning power relative to the financial structure of the reorganized company. A company cannot have too great an amount of fixed financial charges in relation to this expected earning power.

REORGANIZATION PLAN

The difficult aspect of a reorganization is the recasting of the company's capital structure to reduce the amount of fixed charges. In formulating a reorganization plan, three steps are generally followed: (1) determination of the total valuation of the reorganized company; (2) formulation of a new capital structure; and (3) assignment of valuation to the old securities in exchange for the new securities.

Determining a total valuation   The first step—determining the total valuation of the reorganized company—is perhaps the most difficult and the most important. The technique favored is a capitalization of prospective earnings. For example, if future annual earnings of the reorganized company are expected to be $2 million, and the overall capitalization rate of similar companies averages 10 percent a total valuation of $20 million would be set for the company. The valuation figure is subject to considerable variation owing to the difficulty of estimating prospective earnings and determining an appropriate capitalization rate. Thus, the valuation figure is nothing more than a best estimate of potential value. Although the capitalization of prospective earnings is the generally accepted approach to valuing a company in reorganization, the valuation may be adjusted upward if the assets have substantial liquidating value. The common shareholders of the company, of course, would like to see as high a valuation figure as possible. If the valuation figure proposed is below the liquidating value of the company, common shareholders will argue for liquidation rather than reorganization.

Formulating a capital structure   Once a valuation figure has been determined, the next step is to formulate a new capital structure for the company to reduce fixed charges so that there will be an adequate coverage margin. To reduce these charges, the total debt of the firm is scaled down by being partly shifted to income bonds, preferred stock, and common stock. In addition to being scaled down, the terms of the debt may be changed. The maturity of the debt can be extended to reduce the amount of annual sinking-fund obligation. The creditors and debtor are very mindful of the need to achieve a proper balance between debt and equity in relation to the prospective earnings of the company. If it appears that the reorganized company will need new financing in the future, a more conservative ratio of debt to equity is in order to provide for future financial flexibility.

Valuation of old securities   Once a new capital structure is established, the last step involves the valuation of the old securities and their exchange for new securities. Under an *absolute priority rule*, all senior claims on assets must be settled in full before a junior claim can be settled. For example, in the exchange process, a bondholder must receive the par value of his or her bond in another security before there can be any distribution to preferred shareholders. The total valuation figure arrived at in step 1 sets an upper limit on the amount of securities that can be issued. Suppose the company undergoing reorganization has the following existing capital structure:

Debentures	$ 9 million
Subordinate debentures	3 million
Preferred stock	6 million
Common stock equity (at book value)	10 million
	$28 million

If the total valuation of the reorganized company is to be $20 million, the parties might establish the following capital structure in step 2:

Debentures	$ 3 million
Income bonds	6 million
Preferred stock	3 million
Common stock	8 million
	$20 million

Having established the "appropriate" capital structure for the reorganized company, the parties then must allocate the new securities. In this regard, they may propose that the debenture holders exchange their $9 million in debentures for $3 million in new debentures and $6 million in income bonds; that the subordinated debenture holders exchange their $3 million in securities for preferred stock; and that preferred shareholders exchange their securities for $6 million of common stock in the reorganized company. The common shareholders would then be entitled to $2 million in stock in the reorganized company, or 25 percent of the total common stock of the reorganized company. Before, these shareholders held 100 percent of the stock. It is easy to see why common shareholders would like to see as high a valuation figure as possible. To encourage high valuation, they may attempt to discount the troubles of the company as temporary and argue that the earning potential of the company is favorable.

Thus, each claim is settled in full before a junior claim is settled. The example above represents a relatively "mild" reorganization. In a "harsh" reorganization, debt instruments may be exchanged entirely for common stock in the reorganized company and the old common stock eliminated completely. Had the total valuation figure in the example been $12 million, the parties might have proposed a new capital structure consisting of $3 million in preferred stock and $9 million in common stock. Only the straight and subordinated debenture holders would receive a settlement in this case. The preferred and the common shareholders of the old company would receive nothing.

The examples serve to show that the common shareholders of a company undergoing reorganization suffer under the absolute priority rule where claims are settled in order of their legal priority. Their only recourse is to question whether the reorganization plan is fair and equitable to all security holders. Also, note that the absolute priority rule does not imply that fixed-income security holders must receive securities of the same grade. They can and usually do receive in part a security of a grade inferior to the one they held. However, their superior rights, relative to shareholders, must be recognized. Moreover, the securities they receive must be reasonably sound in the sense that their actual values in the market approximate the face values assigned in the reorganization. It would be unfair, for example, to assign a new bond with a face value of $1 000 if, because of a low interest rate and considerable default risk, it sells for only $500 in the capital markets. In this case, a greater amount of the new securities would need to be assigned in the reorganization.

Liquidation under the Bankruptcy Act

If there is no hope that a failing company can be saved, liquidation is the only feasible alternative. The creditors and debtor company may agree to a voluntary liquidation as discused earlier, or liquidation may be carried out under the provisions of the Bankruptcy Act.

DECLARATION OF BANKRUPTCY

A firm may be subject to liquidation proceedings under the Bankruptcy Act in several ways. A creditor or group of creditors with claims of at least $1 000 may petition the court to declare the debtor company as bankrupt. Any creditor's petition must allege that the debtor company had violated, within six months preceding the date of the petition, one or more of the prescribed the acts of bankruptcy. These can be summarized as follows:

1. The debtor has made an assignment of assets to a trustee for the creditors.
2. The debtor undertakes a fraudulent conveyance, gift delivery, or transfer of property or any part of such assets.
3. The debtor transfers or creates any charge on property or any part of such assets, such actions being deemed as fraudulent preference under the Bankruptcy Act.
4. The debtor is not available, the intent being to defeat or delay creditors.
5. The debtor permits any execution or other process issued against him or her to remain unsatisfied beyond the time limits specified in the Act.
6. The debtor presents in writing, at a meeting of the creditors, an admission of insolvency; insolvency can also be evaluated from any financial statements presented at such a meeting.
7. The debtor attempts to defraud creditors by assigning, secretly disposing, or secretly removing any property.
8. The debtor gives notice to creditors that he or she has suspended or is about to suspend a payment of debts.
9. The debtor defaults in any proposal under the Bankruptcy Act.
10. The debtor fails to meet maturing obligations.

If a violation of one or more of these acts is proven, the court will declare the firm a bankrupt. This is usually termed an *involuntary bankruptcy* since the debtor company did not initiate the proceedings.

Alternatively, the debtor company itself may assign all assets to a trustee for administration on behalf of creditors. In a sense, the firm is applying for bankrupt status and the trustee's job is to file the application with the Official Receiver. Once the Official Receiver accepts the submission from the trustee, the debtor firm is declared bankrupt. This is a case of *voluntary bankruptcy* since the proceedings are initiated by the debtor company.

Finally, if a proposal for an arrangement is rejected by the creditors or by the court, the debtor company is deemed to be bankrupt. There are also instances where the proposal accepted by creditors and ratified by the court is subsequently annulled by the court and the debtor company is declared a bankrupt as of the date of the filing of the proposal almost immediately after it is approved. The court may view the default with disfavor and upon petition by the creditors, will declare the firm bankrupt.

THE TRUSTEE FUNCTION

When creditors initiate bankruptcy proceedings against the debtor company, the court may appoint an *interim receiver* at their request. The interim receiver, usually a trustee, takes control of the business and supervises the receipts and disbursements of the firm. The interim receiver administers the affairs of the debtor company until the proceedings are settled in court. If the proceedings prove successful, the firm is declared bankrupt and the court issues a *Receiving Order* authorizing liquidation. The court then appoints a trustee (usually the interim receiver) to administer the estate of the bankrupt. In the case of voluntary bankruptcy, the trustee is appointed when the documents are filed with the Official Receiver and there is no receiving order.

First meeting of creditors   The initial functions of the trustee are essentially to take over the operation of the debtor company temporarily, and to call a first meeting of creditors. This first meeting is usually called within five days of the appointment of the trustee and held within fifteen days from the date that the notice is sent to creditors. At the first meeting the claims of creditors are proven, the financial affairs of the bankrupt are presented by the trustee, the creditors accept (or reject) the trustee appointed by the court or the Official Receiver, a board of inspectors is appointed, and creditors given general instructions to the trustee on matters relating to the administration of the estate. The board of inspectors has a membership not exceeding five persons and its primary function is to monitor the actions of the trustee and to offer advice and make decisions on behalf of creditors. In a sense, the board of inspectors represents the creditors throughout the bankruptcy proceedings subsequent to the date of the first meeting.

Liquidation of estate   After the preliminary procedures of the first meetings of creditors are completed, the real task begins. The trustee has to liquidate the assets of the estate and distribute the proceeds as provided for under the Bankruptcy Act. In general, the liquidation proceeds are distributed, in order of priority, to secured creditors, preferred creditors, ordinary unsecured creditors and equity shareholders.

Usually *secured creditors* take possession of assets on which they have a lien and liquidate them to satisfy their claims. Where liquidation proceeds are less than the secured claims, the secured creditors become ordinary unsecured creditors for the remaining balance. Sometimes the trustee may sell secured assets on behalf of secured creditors but the net proceeds go directly to these creditors. Generally, the trustee has little to do with secured creditors.

After any claims of secured creditors are satisfied, a distribution is then made to preferred creditors. The Bankruptcy Act lists ten groups of preferred claims and these, in order of priority of payment, are as follows:

1. Costs for funeral and other associated expenses in the case of a deceased bankrupt.
2. Costs of the administration of the estate comprising the expenses and fees of the trustee and other expenditures.
3. A special tax paid to the Superintendent of Bankruptcy to help to defray court costs—2 percent of the first $1 000 000 of liquidation proceeds, 1 percent of the next $1 000 000 and $\frac{1}{10}$ percent thereafter.
4. Wages, salaries, and compensation for employees of a bankrupt firm up to a maximum of $500 per person.
5. Outstanding municipal taxes for two years preceding the year of bankruptcy.
6. Rent in arrears for three months and for three months from date of bankruptcy, if so provided in the lease.
7. Claims for any judgment lodged against the bankrupt prior to date of bankruptcy.
8. Claims of the Crown for payments due for workmen's compensation, unemployment insurance, and income taxes.
9. Claims resulting from injuries to employees of the bankrupt where such claims are not covered by the Workmen's Compensation Act.
10. Other claims of the Crown.

After settling the above claims and if the liquidation proceeds are not fully exhausted, then a distribution is made to the ordinary unsecured creditors. Any such distribution is done on a pro rata basis depending on the amount of proven claims by each unsecured creditor relative to total proven claims. Very often the unsecured creditor receives less than 100 percent of proven claims. If the claims of unsecured creditors are settled in full and there are funds remaining, then a distribution is made to equity shareholders. The claims of preferred shareholders are settled in full before any distribution is made to common shareholders.

To show an example of priority claims, we look at the balance sheet of Bar K Products Company Ltd., shown in Table 27-2, at the time of bankruptcy. The claims of creditors are shown on the right-hand side. Suppose that in liquidating the assets of the company the trustee in bankruptcy realizes $1 500 000 on the current assets and $2 500 000 on the sale of fixed assets, only $800 000 is realized on the mortgaged assets, and this amount is paid directly to the secured creditors. From the balance of $3 200 000 of the liquidation proceedings, the claims of preferred creditors will be paid. Suppose that these claims are $568 000 for the costs of administration of the estate, $32 000 for the tax paid to the Superintendent of

TABLE 27-2 Balance Sheet of Bar K Products at Time of Bankruptcy

Current assets	$2 600 000	Accounts payable	$ 900 000
		Accrued wages	1 000 000
		Bank loan	1 100 000
		Current liabilities	$3 000 000
		First mortgage bonds	1 000 000
		Long-term debentures	600 000
Net fixed assets	5 200 000	Preferred stock	1 000 000
		Common stock	3 600 000
		Retained earnings	(1 400 000)
	$7 800 000		$7 800 000

Bankruptcy, and $500 000 for wages of 1000 employees. After these are settled, what remains available to unsecured creditors is computed as follows:

Proceedings from sale of all assets	$4 000 000
Less: paid to mortgage holders	800 000
cost of administration	568 000
tax levy	32 000
wages due employees	500 000
Amount available for unsecured creditors	$2 100 000

General creditor claims include accounts payable of $900 000, a bank loan of $1 100 000, the $200 000 in unsatisfied claim of the first mortgage bondholders ($1 million claim less $800 000 proceeds from the sale of the property securing the bonds), and long-term debentures of $600 000. These claims total $2 800 000. Thus, the claims of unsecured creditors of Bar K Products Company Ltd. exceed the amount available to them. As a result, general creditor claims are settled on a pro rata basis of $2 100 000/$2 800 000 = 75 percent. The specific settlements are as follows:

	General creditor claims	Amount of settlement
Accounts payable	$ 900 000	$ 675 000
Bank loan	1 100 000	825 000
First mortgage	200 000	150 000
Long-term debentures	600 000	450 000
	$2 800 000	$2 100 000

Obviously, nothing remains for preferred shareholders or common shareholders in this particular case. If the amount available for general creditors exceeds total claims, the residual is applied first to preferred shareholders and, if anything remains, to common shareholders.

Final discharge   When the liquidation of the company and the distribution of the proceeds are completed, the trustee files a final report to the Superintendent of Bankruptcy. A company which has paid all its creditors in full then applies for a discharge from bankruptcy—otherwise, a discharge is unavailable. Most corporate bankrupts fail to pay 100 percent of the claims of creditors and thus remain bankrupts until they "die." A company dies when it fails to renew its annual registration as required under the Companies Act.

THE COST OF BANKRUPTCY

The term *cost of bankruptcy* may be defined to include a number of direct and indirect costs associated with a bankruptcy proceeding. At the simplest level it may be defined as the direct costs incurred in the administration of the affairs of a bankrupt. These administrative costs include trustee fees and other expenses incurred in the liquidation of the assets of the bankrupt and the distribution of the liquidation proceeds. This simple definition however, fails to account for the capital loss suffered by both creditors and equity holders when liquidation proceeds (less administrative costs) are less than total investment. Another omitted component of the cost of bankruptcy is the costs incurred by creditors who have to take actions to establish and protect their claims. Finally, there is the broader consideration of socioeconomic costs to society; these also are neglected in our simple definition. Bankruptcy reflects inefficient allocation of funds within the financial market system. Such inefficient allocation tends to have depressing effects on capital formation, employment, the operations of associated firms and industries and, in general, the socioeconomic welfare of society. The socioeconomic costs are difficult (perhaps impossible) to measure.

Dipchand and George[4] reviewed the administrative costs of bankruptcy for 48 businesses in Nova Scotia over the 1965-75 period. Administrative costs averaged 40.6 percent of liquidation proceeds; trustee fees, 24.0 percent; and other expenses, 16.6 percent. The distribution to preferred creditors averaged 23.2 percent of liquidation proceeds. Finally, ordinary unsecured creditors received, on average, 36.2 percent of liquidation proceeds. When this distribution was related to the total established claims of these creditors, it was observed that unsecured creditors, on average, recovered only $14.88 for every $100.00 of credit extended to bankrupt companies. About 64 percent of the cases had a recovery factor of less than $14.88 (or 14.88 percent); in about 33 percent of the cases the unsecured creditors received nothing.

The results reported above apply to relatively small firms. They indicate that unsecured creditors tend to lose significantly in the event bankruptcy proceedings are initiated. Similar trends are expected for large bankruptcies.

---

[4]Cecil R. Dipchand and Roy E. George, "The Cost of Bankruptcy," *CA Magazine* (July 1977), 28-30.

PROPOSED CHANGES IN THE BANKRUPTCY ACT
(BILL S-14)

The present Act, enacted in 1949, is based on the Bankruptcy Act of 1919 which in turn, was based on the Bankruptcy Act of England, enacted in 1883. Since 1949 there have been numerous amendments to the Act; the latest were made in 1966. There are also several other statutes dealing with bankruptcy. In the late 1960s the federal government felt that there was a need to update the Act and consolidate the respective statutes. A committee was appointed to review bankruptcy legislation and to make recommendations for amendments. In 1970 the committee recommended about 113 amendments to the existing Act. Some of these have been passed by parliament and are now law. At present, Parliament is debating some rather sweeping changes to the Bankruptcy Act.[5]

Administrative structure Proposed changes to the administrative structure are aimed at improving the efficiency of the system and at inducing unsecured creditors to play a more active role in the administration of bankrupt estates. The extended powers of the Superintendent of Bankruptcy will enable the Superintendent to play a greater role in licensing (and revoking licenses) of trustees, and in the detection and investigation of commercial arrangements and bankruptcies. The Official Receiver will be renamed "Bankruptcy Administrator," whose job it will be to undertake the administration of an estate if no private sector trustee will do so. Trustees will be subject to stricter conflict-of-interest rules and more stringent bonding requirements. Finally, the proposed changes will reduce the number of preferred claims in the hope that unsecured creditors will have a chance of receiving a higher percentage of their claims.

Commercial arrangements Proposed changes to the Act are also aimed at giving the debtor firm more time to prepare a carefully considered and workable proposal for an arrangement. The debtor firm has to file a *notice of intention* with the Bankruptcy Administrator stating that it intends to file a proposal with a view to preventing bankruptcy. The proposal for arrangement may be submitted by a trustee (receiver or liquidator) or any creditor on behalf of a debtor who is bankrupt. Once this notice is filed, all legal proceedings against the debtor by all creditors (including secured creditors) are automatically stopped for a period of ten days, or longer if approved by the court. Under current regulations, secured creditors are not obligated to cease any legal proceeding against the debtor firm. (The proposed arrangement must be filed within the stipulated item or the notice is deemed withdrawn and normal bankruptcy proceedings may continue.) With the proposed changes, the debtor firm has more time and is subject to less pressure from creditors in the preparation of the proposal.

Other important changes The following proposed changes may be considered important so far as a corporate bankruptcy is concerned.

1. The preferred claims of the Crown will be reduced in order to increase returns to ordinary unsecured debtors.

---

[5]For details, see Consumer and Corporate Affairs, Canada, *Background Papers for the Bankruptcy and Insolvency Bill (1979)*.

2. Wage earners will continue to have priority over insecured creditors for up to $2 000 in unpaid wages per employee plus an additional $500 of amounts an employer is liable to pay as pension, health, and other related contributions.

3. Directors of a company may be personally liable for unpaid wages and contributions discussed above. Such personal liability may arise if it is proven that directors acted contrary to the interest of the company or did business with the purpose of defrauding creditors.

Summary

Business failure encompasses a wide range of financial difficulty; it occurs whenever a company is unable to meet its current obligations. The remedies applied to a failing company vary in severity with the degree of financial difficulty. Voluntary settlements are informal and must be agreed on by all creditors and by the company itself. The difficulty with a voluntary settlement is in obtaining the agreement of all parties concerned. Included in voluntary settlements are extensions, compositions, reorganizations, and private liquidations.

Legal settlements are effected, for the most part, under the Bankruptcy Act. Statutory extensions or compositions are granted under the provisions of the Act. In reorganization, the capital structure of the company is changed so as to reduce the total annual amount of fixed charges. The reorganization plan has to be fair, equitable, and feasible, and once it is approved by shareholders and creditors, it has to be ratified by the court. If the company cannot be rehabilitated, it will be declared bankrupt and be liquidated by a trustee in bankruptcy. Creditors receive liquidating dividends according to the priority of their claims.

An extended discussion of bankruptcy and reorganization would concern mostly legal matters. If the company should become involved in financial distress, a counsel or trustee experienced in bankruptcy proceedings should be engaged.

Questions

1. Contrast a technically insolvent situation with an insolvency-in-bankruptcy situation.

2. Why are taxes and administrative costs involved in the bankruptcy paid prior to any creditor's claim?

3. It is argued that a small number of bankruptcies is a healthy sign of economic development. Explain.

4. As a creditor to a financially troubled concern, would you prefer liquidation or financial reorganization? Why? Would you always prefer liquidation if the market value of the firm was less than the liquidation value?

5. Can you explain why utilities, railroads, and banks are seldom liquidated? Are the risks in these industries less than those in other industrial corporations?

6. Before a firm can be reorganized, a valuation must be placed on it. How should this valuation be arrived at? What conceptual problems would you encounter in the process?

7. Contrast an extension and composition with a reorganization of a firm in distress.

8. Contrast absolute and relative priority bases for settling claims.

9. When liquidation of a company is in litigation, do creditors whose claims originated before the trouble began have priority over recent employees and the federal government's claim for income taxes?

Problems with Solutions

1. A Company has gone into bankruptcy leaving the following assets:

	Book value	Liquidation value
Accounts receivable	200 000	150 000
Inventory	300 000	80 000
Plant building	1 000 000	450 000
Office building	600 000	500 000
Other assets	300 000	250 000
	$2 400 000	$1 430 000

The Company had the following liabilities:

Bank loan (Section 88)	$250 000
Mortgage on plant building	500 000
Mortage on office building	300 000
Trustee and legal fees	20 000
Wages	1 000
Municipal taxes	2 000
Accounts payable	550 000

Determine the distribution of proceeds.

	Claim	Value of security	Distribution
A Secured claims			
Section 88 bank loan	$250 000	$230 000*	$230 000
Mortgage on plant	500 000	450 000	450 000
Mortgage on office	300 000	500 000	300 000
	$1 050 000	$1 180 000	$980 000

*Accounts receivable + inventory

B Preferred claims	
Trustee and legal fees	$20 000
Wages	1 000
Municipal taxes	2 000
	$23 000

C Unsecured claims

Total funds available		$1 430 000
Paid to secured claims	$980 000	
Paid to preferred claims	23 000	1 003 000
Funds available for unsecured claim		$ 427 000

	Balance	Amount paid**
Accounts payable	$550 000	$378 791
Balance owing bank ($250 000–$230 000)	20 000	13 774
Balance owing mortgage on plant ($500 000–$450 000)	50 000	34 435
	$620 000	$427 000

**Amount paid = 68.871% ($427 000 ÷ $620 000) of balance

Summary:	
Liability:	
Bank loan	$ 243 774
Mortgage on plant	484 435
Mortgage on office	300 000
Trustee and legal fees	20 000
Wages	1 000
Municipal taxes	2 000
Accounts payable	378 791
	$1 430 000

Problems

1.

Fall Corporation Ltd. balance sheet

Cash	$ 1 000 0000	Note payable	$ 1 000 000
Accounts receivable	2 000 000	Accounts payable	4 000 000
Inventories	5 000 000	Accrued wages	3 000 000
Prepaid expenses	1 000 000	Accrued taxes	1 000 000
Total current assets	$ 9 000 000	Total current liabilities	$ 9 000 000
Fixed assets, net	8 000 000	Long-term debt	12 000 000
Goodwill	5 000 000	Equity	1 000 000
Total assets	$22 000 000		$22 000 000

(a) Do you feel that it is likely that the Fall Corporation either is now or will soon be technically insolvent? Why? What steps could management take to correct this situation?

(b) Answer part (*a*) with respect to the bankruptcy concept of insolvency.

(c) Compare and contrast these two concepts of insolvency.

(d) Is it possible that attempts to alleviate one form of insolvency could aggravate the other? How?

(e) Is the balance sheet the best tool for determining technical or fundamental insolvency? Can you suggest better ones?

2. Merry Land, an amusement park in Niagara, has experienced increased difficulty in paying its bills. Although the park has been marginally profitable over the years, the current outlook is not encouraging, as profits during the last two years have been negative. The park is located on reasonably valuable real estate and has an overall liquidating value of $5 million. After much discussion with creditors, management has agreed to a voluntary liquidation. A trustee, who is appointed by the various parties to liquidate the properties, will charge $200 000 for services given. The Merry Land Company owes $300 000 in back property taxes. It has a $2 million mortgage on certain amusement park equipment that can be sold for only $1 million. Creditor claims are as follows:

Party	Book value claim
General creditors	$1 750 000
Mortgage bonds	2 000 000
Long-term subordinated debt	1 000 000
Common stock	5 000 000

What amount is each party likely to receive in liquidation?

3. The Vent Corporation Ltd. has been liquidated under bankruptcy proceedings. The book and liquidation values are as follows:

	Book	Liquidation
Cash	$ 700 000	$ 700 000
Accounts receivable	2 000 000	1 600 000
Inventory	3 500 000	2 000 000
Office building	5 000 000	3 000 000
Plant	8 000 000	5 000 000
Equipment	7 000 000	3 000 000
Total	$26 200 000	$15 300 000

The liability and equity accounts at the time of liquidation were as follows:

Accounts payable	$ 2 000 000
Accrued federal taxes	500 000
Accrued local taxes	200 000
Notes payable	1 000 000
Accrued wages	500 000
Total current liabilities	$ 4 200 000
Mortgage on office building	$ 3 000 000
First mortgage on plant	3 000 000
Second mortgage on plant	2 000 000
Subordinated debentures	5 000 000
Total long term debt	$13 000 000
Preferred stock	$ 5 000 000
Common stock	7 000 000
Retained earnings	(3 000 000)
Total	$ 9 000 000
Total	$26 200 000

Expenses of liquidation (lawyers' fees, trustee fees, etc.) came to 20 percent of the proceeds. The debentures are subordinated only to the two first mortgage bonds. All of the accrued wages are less than $500 per employee. Determine the appropriate distribution of the proceeds of liquidation.

4. The Greenwood Corporation Ltd. is insolvent. The trustee has estimated that the company can earn $1.5 million before interest and taxes (50 percent) in the future. In the new capitalization, the trustee feels that debentures should bear a coupon on 10 percent and have coverage of five times, income bonds (12 percent) should have overall coverage of two times, preferred stock (10 percent) should have after-tax coverage of three times, and common stock should be issued on a price-earnings ratio basis of twelve times. Determine the capital structure that conforms to the trustee's criteria.

5. Assume that the Greenwood Corporation (see problem 4) originally had the following capital structure:

	Book value	Market value
Senior debentures	$ 6 000 000	$ 5 500 000
Subordinated debentures	7 500 000	6 000 000
Junior subordinated debentures	2 500 000	1 000 000
Preferred stock (par $100)	2 500 000	500 000
Common stock (1 000 000 shares)	−4 500 000	1 000 000
	$14 000 000	$14 000 000

Determine which of the new securities each class of holders of securities would get under an absolute priority rule.

6. Jalna Plantation Company Ltd. has run into financial difficulty and is facing possible reorganization. It currently has the following capital structure (in thousands):

	Book value
Long term bonds	$ 40 000
General unsecured debt	30 000
Preferred stock	10 000
Common stock	20 000
	$100 000

Unfortunately, the trustee estimates that Jalna has a value of only $75 million as a going concern, not the $100 million shown on the books. The trustee has recommended the following capital structure for the reorganized company (in thousands):

Long term bonds	$10 000
Unsecured debt	20 000
Preferred stock	5 000
Common stock	40 000
	$75 000

If this plan is accepted by the claimholders and confirmed by the bankruptcy court, what will be the distribution of the new securities to the holders of old claims?

7. *Research Project*

Compile data on recent bankruptcy cases involving fairly large companies. Learn as much as you can about "stockholder protective committees"; discover how many of these committees there are for each bankruptcy case you study. Finally, compare the amount of money going for legal fees, court costs, etc., as opposed to the amount the creditors finally receive. Do you begin to feel that there might be "self-interest" as well as "friendly" motives behind the creditors' acceptance of a settlement? Whom do stockholder protective committees really protect? Can you find any parallels between bankruptcy law and probate law?

Selected References

AHARONY, JOSEPH, CHARLES P. JONES and ITZHAK SWARY, "An Analysis of Risk and Return Characteristics of Corporate Bankruptcy Using Capital Market Data," *Journal of Finance*, 35 (September 1980), 1001-16.

ALTMAN, EDWARD I., *Corporate Bankruptcy in America*, Lexington, Mass.: Heath Lexington Books, 1971.

_____, "Financial Ratios, Discriminant Analysis and the Prediction of Corporate Bankruptcy," *Journal of Finance*, 23 (September 1968), 589-609.

_____, "Bankruptcy and Reorganization," in Edward I. Altman, ed., *Financial Handbook*, 5th ed. New York: Wiley, 1982.

————, and MENACHEM BRENNER, "Information Effects and Stock Market Response to Signs of Firm Deterioration," *Journal of Financial and Quantitative Analysis*, 16 (March 1981), 35-52.

ALTMAN, EDWARD I., ROBERT G. HALDEMAN, and P. NARAYANAN, "Zeta Analysis: A New Model to Identify Bankruptcy Risk of Corporations," *Journal of Banking and Finance*, 1 (June 1977).

ALTMAN, EDWARD I., and ARNOLD W. SAMENTZ, eds., *Financial Crises*. New York: Wiley, 1977.

BACKER, MORTON, and MARTIN L. GOSMAN, "The Use of Financial Ratios in Credit Downgrade Decisions," *Financial Management*, 9 (Spring 1980), 53-56.

BALDWIN, CARLISS Y. and SCOTT P. MASON, "The Resolution of Claims in Financial Distress: The Case of Massey Ferguson," *Journal of Finance*, May 1983, 505-516.

CHEN, KUNG H., and THOMAS A. SHIMERDA, "An Empirical Analysis of Useful Financial Ratios," *Financial Management*, 10 (Spring 1981) 51-60.

COLLINS, ROBERT A., "An Empirical Comparison of Bankruptcy Prediction Models," *Financial Management*, 9 (Summer 1980), 52-57.

DIPCHAND, CECIL R. and ROY E. GEORGE, "The Cost of Bankruptcy," *CA Magazine* (July 1977), 28-30.

DONALDSON, GORDON, "Strategy for Financial Emergencies," *Harvard Business Review*, 47 (Nov.-Dec. 1969), 67-79.

GORDON, MYRON J. "Towards a Theory of Financial Distress," *Journal of Finance*, 26 (May 1971), 347-56.

HONSBERGER, JOHN D. "Corporate Failure Can Be Predicted," *CA Magazine* (June 1979), 30-32.

MCKINLAY, RONALD A. "Some Reasons for Business Failures in Canada," *Cost and Management* (May-June 1979), 17-21.

MOYER, R. CHARLES, "Forecasting Financial Failure: A Re-Examination," *Financial Management*, 6 (Spring 1977), 11-17.

VAN HORNE, JAMES C., "Optimal Initiation of Bankruptcy Proceedings by Debt Holders," *Journal of Finance*, 31 (June 1976), 897-910.

WALTER, JAMES E., "Determination of Technical Insolvency," *Journal of Business*, 30 (January 1957), 30-43.

Appendix A: Present-Value Tables

TABLE A-1   Present Value of One Dollar Due at the End of N Years

N	1%	2%	3%	4%	5%	6%	7%	8%	9%	10%	N
01	0.99010	0.98039	0.97007	0.96154	0.95238	0.94340	0.93458	0.92593	0.91743	0.90909	01
02	.98030	.96117	.94260	.92456	.90703	.89000	.87344	.85734	.84168	.82645	02
03	.97059	.94232	.91514	.88900	.86384	.83962	.81630	.79383	.77218	.75131	03
04	.96098	.92385	.88849	.85480	.82270	.79209	.76290	.73503	.70843	.68301	04
05	.95147	.90573	.86261	.82193	.78353	.74726	.71299	.68058	.64993	.62092	05
06	.94204	.88797	.83748	.79031	.74622	.70496	.66634	.60317	.59627	.56447	06
07	.93272	.87056	.81309	.75992	.71068	.66506	.62275	.58349	.54703	.51316	07
08	.92348	.85349	.78941	.73069	.67684	.62741	.58201	.54027	.50187	.46651	08
09	.91434	.83675	.76642	.70259	.64461	.59190	.54393	.50025	.46043	.42410	09
10	.90529	.82035	.74409	.67556	.61391	.55839	.50835	.46319	.42241	.38554	10
11	.89632	.80426	.72242	.64958	.58468	.52679	.47509	.42888	.38753	.35049	11
12	.88745	.78849	.70138	.62460	.55684	.49697	.44401	.39711	.35553	.31863	12
13	.87866	.77303	.68095	.60057	.53032	.46884	.41496	.36770	.32618	.28966	13
14	.86996	.75787	.66112	.57747	.50507	.44230	.38782	.34046	.29925	.26333	14
15	.86135	.74301	.64186	.55526	.48102	.41726	.36245	.31524	.27454	.23939	15
16	.85282	.72845	.62317	.53391	.45811	.39365	.33873	.29189	.25187	.21763	16
17	.84438	.71416	.60502	.51337	.43630	.37136	.31657	.27027	.23107	.19784	17
18	.83602	.70016	.58739	.49363	.41552	.35034	.29586	.25025	.21199	.17986	18
19	.82774	.68643	.57029	.47464	.39573	.33051	.27651	.23171	.19449	.16351	19
20	.81954	.67297	.55367	.45639	.37689	.31180	.25842	.21455	.17843	.14864	20
21	.81143	.65978	.53755	.43883	.35894	.29415	.24151	.19866	.16370	.13513	21
22	.80340	.64684	.52189	.42195	.34185	.27750	.22571	.18394	.15018	.12285	22
23	.79544	.63416	.50669	.40573	.32557	.26180	.21095	.17031	.13778	.11168	23
24	.78757	.62172	.49193	.39012	.31007	.24698	.19715	.15770	.12640	.10153	24
25	.77977	.60953	.47760	.37512	.29530	.23300	.18425	.14602	.11597	.09230	25

N	11%	12%	13%	14%	15%	16%	17%	18%	19%	20%	N
01	0.90090	0.89286	0.88496	0.87719	0.86957	0.86207	0.85470	0.84746	0.84034	0.83333	01
02	.81162	.79719	.78315	.76947	.75614	.74316	.73051	.71818	.70616	.69444	02
03	.73119	.71178	.69305	.67497	.65752	.64066	.62437	.60863	.59342	.57870	03
04	.65873	.63552	.61332	.59208	.57175	.55229	.53365	.51579	.49867	.48225	04
05	.59345	.56743	.54276	.51918	.49718	.47611	.45611	.43711	.41905	.40188	05
06	.53464	.50663	.48032	.45559	.43233	.41044	.38984	.37043	.35214	.33490	06
07	.48166	.45235	.42506	.39964	.37594	.35383	.33320	.31392	.29592	.27908	07
08	.43393	.40388	.37616	.35056	.32690	.30503	.28478	.26604	.24867	.23257	08
09	.39092	.36061	.33288	.30751	.28426	.26295	.24340	.22546	.20897	.19381	09
10	.35218	.32197	.29459	.26974	.24718	.22668	.20804	.19106	.17560	.16151	10
11	.31728	.28748	.26070	.23662	.21494	.19542	.17781	.16192	.14756	.13459	11
12	.28584	.25667	.23071	.20756	.18691	.16846	.15197	.13722	.12400	.11216	12
13	.25751	.22917	.20416	.18207	.16253	.14523	.12989	.11629	.10420	.09346	13
14	.23199	.20462	.18068	.15971	.14133	.12520	.11102	.09855	.08757	.07789	14
15	.20900	.18270	.15989	.14010	.12289	.10793	.09489	.08352	.07359	.06491	15
16	.18829	.16312	.14150	.12289	.10686	.09304	.08110	.07078	.06184	.05409	16
17	.16963	.14564	.12522	.10780	.09293	.08021	.06932	.05998	.05196	.04507	17
18	.15282	.13004	.11081	.09456	.08080	.06914	.05925	.05083	.04367	.03756	18
19	.13768	.11611	.09806	.08295	.07026	.05961	.05064	.04308	.03669	.03130	19
20	.12403	.10367	.08678	.07276	.06110	.05139	.04328	.03651	.03084	.02608	20
21	.11174	.09256	.07680	.06383	.05313	.04430	.03699	.03094	.02591	.02174	21
22	.10067	.08264	.06796	.05599	.04620	.03819	.03162	.02622	.02178	.01811	22
23	.09069	.07379	.06014	.04911	.04017	.03292	.02702	.02222	.01830	.01509	23
24	.08170	.06588	.05322	.04308	.03493	.02838	.02310	.01883	.01538	.01258	24
25	.07361	.05882	.04710	.03779	.03038	.02447	.01974	.01596	.01292	.01048	25

TABLE A-1   Present Value of One Dollar Due at the End of N Years

N	21%	22%	23%	24%	25%	26%	27%	28%	29%	30%	N
01	0.82645	0.81967	0.81301	0.80645	0.80000	0.79365	0.78740	0.78125	0.77519	0.76923	01
02	.68301	.67186	.66098	.65036	.64000	.62988	.62000	.61035	.60093	.59172	02
03	.56447	.55071	.53738	.52449	.51200	.49991	.48819	.47684	.46583	.45517	03
04	.46651	.45140	.43690	.42297	.40906	.39675	.38440	.37253	.36111	.35013	04
05	.38554	.37000	.35520	.34111	.32768	.31488	.30268	.29104	.27993	.26933	05
06	.31863	.30328	.28878	.27509	.26214	.24991	.23833	.22737	.21700	.20718	06
07	.26333	.24859	.23478	.22184	.20972	.19834	.18766	.17764	.16822	.15937	07
08	.21763	.20376	.19088	.17891	.16777	.15741	.14776	.13878	.13040	.12259	08
09	.17986	.16702	.15519	.14428	.13422	.12493	.11635	.10842	.10109	.09430	09
10	.14864	.13690	.12617	.11635	.10737	.09915	.09161	.08470	.07836	.07254	10
11	.12285	.11221	.10258	.09383	.08590	.07869	.07214	.06617	.06075	.05580	11
12	.10153	.09198	.08339	.07567	.06872	.06245	.05680	.05170	.04709	.04292	12
13	.08391	.07539	.06780	.06103	.05498	.04957	.04472	.04039	.03650	.03302	13
14	.06934	.06180	.05512	.04921	.04398	.03934	.03522	.03155	.02830	.02540	14
15	.05731	.05065	.04481	.03969	.03518	.03122	.02773	.02465	.02194	.01954	15
16	.04736	.04152	.03643	.03201	.02815	.02478	.02183	.01926	.01700	.01503	16
17	.03914	.03403	.02962	.02581	.02252	.01967	.01719	.01505	.01318	.01156	17
18	.03235	.02789	.02408	.02082	.01801	.01561	.01354	.01175	.01022	.00889	18
19	.02673	.02286	.01958	.01679	.01441	.01239	.01066	.00918	.00792	.00684	19
20	.02209	.01874	.01592	.01354	.01153	.00983	.00839	.00717	.00614	.00526	20
21	.01826	.01536	.01294	.01092	.00922	.00780	.00661	.00561	.00476	.00405	21
22	.01509	.01259	.01052	.00880	.00738	.00619	.00520	.00438	.00369	.00311	22
23	.01247	.01032	.00855	.00710	.00590	.00491	.00410	.00342	.00286	.00239	23
24	.01031	.00846	.00695	.00573	.00472	.00390	.00323	.00267	.00222	.00184	24
25	.00852	.00693	.00565	.00462	.00378	.00310	.00254	.00209	.00172	.00142	25

TABLE A-1 Present Value of One Dollar Due at the End of N Years

N	31%	32%	33%	34%	35%	36%	37%	38%	39%	40%	N
01	0.76336	0.75758	0.75188	0.74627	0.74074	0.73529	0.72993	0.72464	0.71942	0.71429	01
02	.58272	.57392	.56532	.55692	.54870	.45066	.53279	.52510	.51757	.51020	02
03	.44482	.43479	.42505	.41561	.40644	.39754	.38890	.38051	.37235	.36443	03
04	.33956	.32939	.31959	.31016	.30107	.29231	.28387	.27573	.26788	.26031	04
05	.25920	.24953	.24029	.23146	.22301	.21493	.20720	.19980	.19272	.18593	05
06	.19787	.18904	.18067	.17273	.16520	.15804	.15124	.14479	.13865	.13281	06
07	.15104	.14321	.13584	.12890	.12237	.11621	.11040	.10492	.09975	.09486	07
08	.11530	.10849	.10214	.09620	.09064	.08545	.08058	.07603	.07176	.06776	08
09	.08802	.08219	.07680	.07179	.06714	.06283	.05882	.05509	.05163	.04840	09
10	.06719	.06227	.05774	.05357	.04973	.04620	.04293	.03992	.03714	.03457	10
11	.05129	.04717	.04341	.03998	.03684	.03397	.03134	.02893	.02672	.02469	11
12	.03915	.03574	.03264	.02934	.02729	.02498	.02287	.02096	.01922	.01764	12
13	.02989	.02707	.02454	.02227	.02021	.01837	.01670	.01519	.01383	.01260	13
14	.02281	.02051	.01845	.01662	.01497	.01350	.01219	.01101	.00995	.00900	14
15	.01742	.01554	.01387	.01240	.01109	.00993	.00890	.00798	.00716	.00643	15
16	.01329	.01177	.01043	.00925	.00822	.00730	.00649	.00578	.00515	.00459	16
17	.01015	.00892	.00784	.00691	.00609	.00537	.00474	.00419	.00370	.00328	17
18	.00775	.00676	.00590	.00515	.00451	.00395	.00346	.00304	.00267	.00234	18
19	.00591	.00512	.00443	.00385	.00334	.00290	.00253	.00220	.00192	.00167	19
20	.00451	.00388	.00333	.00287	.00247	.00213	.00184	.00159	.00138	.00120	20
21	.00345	.00294	.00251	.00214	.00183	.00157	.00135	.00115	.00099	.00085	21
22	.00263	.00223	.00188	.00160	.00136	.00115	.00098	.00084	.00071	.00061	22
23	.00201	.00169	.00142	.00119	.00101	.00085	.00072	.00061	.00051	.00044	23
24	.00153	.00128	.00107	.00089	.00074	.00062	.00052	.00044	.00037	.00031	24
25	.00117	.00097	.00080	.00066	.00055	.00046	.00038	.00032	.00027	.00022	25

TABLE A-2 Present Value of One Dollar Per Year. N Years at r%

Year	1%	2%	3%	4%	5%	6%	7%	8%	9%	10%	Year
1	0.9901	0.9804	0.9709	0.9615	0.9524	0.9434	0.9346	0.9259	0.9174	0.9091	1
2	1.9704	1.9416	1.9135	1.8861	1.8594	1.8334	1.8080	1.7833	1.7591	1.7355	2
3	2.9410	2.8839	2.8286	2.7751	2.7232	2.6730	2.6243	2.5771	2.5313	2.4868	3
4	3.9020	3.8077	3.7171	3.6299	3.5459	3.4651	3.3872	3.3121	3.2397	3.1699	4
5	4.8535	4.7134	4.5797	4.4518	4.3295	4.2123	4.1002	3.9927	3.8896	3.7908	5
6	5.7955	5.6014	5.4172	5.2421	5.0757	4.9173	4.7665	4.6229	4.4859	4.3553	6
7	6.7282	6.4720	6.2302	6.0020	5.7863	5.5824	5.3893	5.2064	5.0329	4.8684	7
8	7.6517	7.3254	7.0196	6.7327	6.4632	6.2098	5.9713	5.7466	5.5348	5.3349	8
9	8.5661	8.1622	7.7861	7.4353	7.1078	6.8017	6.5152	6.2469	5.9852	5.7590	9
10	9.4714	8.9825	8.5302	8.1109	7.7217	7.3601	7.0236	6.7101	6.4176	6.1446	10
11	10.3677	9.7868	9.2526	8.7604	8.3064	7.8868	7.4987	7.1389	6.8052	6.4951	11
12	11.2552	10.5753	9.9539	9.3850	8.8632	8.3838	7.9427	7.5361	7.1607	6.8137	12
13	12.1338	11.3483	10.6349	9.9856	9.3935	8.8527	8.3576	7.9038	7.4869	7.1034	13
14	13.0038	12.1062	11.2960	10.5631	9.8986	9.2950	8.7454	8.2442	7.7861	7.3667	14
15	13.8651	12.8492	11.9379	11.1183	10.3796	9.7122	9.1079	8.5595	8.0607	7.6061	15
16	14.7180	13.5777	12.5610	11.6522	10.8377	10.1059	9.4466	8.8514	8.3125	7.8237	16
17	15.5624	14.2918	13.1660	12.1656	11.2740	10.4772	9.7632	9.1216	8.5436	8.0215	17
18	16.3984	14.9920	13.7534	12.6592	11.6895	10.8276	10.0591	9.3719	8.7556	8.2014	18
19	17.2261	15.6784	14.3237	13.1339	12.0853	11.1581	10.3356	9.6036	8.9501	8.3649	19
20	18.0457	16.3514	14.8774	13.5903	12.4622	11.4699	10.5940	9.8181	9.1285	8.5136	20
21	18.8571	17.0111	15.4149	14.0291	12.8211	11.7640	10.8355	10.0168	9.2922	8.6487	21
22	19.6605	17.6580	15.9368	14.4511	13.1630	12.0416	11.0612	10.2007	9.4424	8.7715	22
23	20.4559	18.2921	16.4435	14.8568	13.4885	12.3033	11.2722	10.3710	9.5802	8.8832	23
24	21.2435	18.9139	16.9355	15.2469	13.7986	12.5503	11.4693	10.5287	9.7066	8.9847	24
25	22.0233	19.5234	17.4131	15.6220	14.0939	12.7833	11.6536	10.6748	9.8226	9.0770	25

TABLE A-2   Present Value of One Dollar Per Year. *N* Years at *r*%

Year	11%	12%	13%	14%	15%	16%	17%	18%	19%	20%	Year
1	0.9009	0.8929	0.8850	0.8772	0.8696	0.8621	0.8547	0.8475	0.8403	0.8333	1
2	1.7125	1.6901	1.6681	1.6467	1.6257	1.6052	1.5852	1.5656	1.5465	1.5278	2
3	2.4437	2.4018	2.3612	2.3216	2.2832	2.2459	2.2096	2.1743	2.1399	2.1065	3
4	3.1024	3.0373	2.9745	2.9137	2.8550	2.7982	2.7432	2.6901	2.6386	2.5887	4
5	3.6959	3.6048	3.5172	3.4331	3.3522	3.2743	3.1993	3.1272	3.0576	2.9906	5
6	4.2305	4.1114	3.9976	3.8887	3.7845	3.6847	3.5892	3.4976	3.4098	3.3255	6
7	4.7122	4.5638	4.4226	4.2883	4.1604	4.0386	3.9224	3.8115	3.7057	3.6046	7
8	5.1461	4.9676	4.7988	4.6389	4.4873	4.3436	4.2072	4.0776	3.9544	3.8372	8
9	5.5370	5.3282	5.1317	4.9464	4.7716	4.6065	4.4506	4.3030	4.1633	4.0310	9
10	5.8892	5.6502	5.4262	5.2161	5.0188	4.8332	4.6586	4.4941	4.3389	4.1925	10
11	6.2065	5.9377	5.6869	5.4527	5.2337	5.0286	4.8364	4.6560	4.4865	4.3271	11
12	6.4924	6.1944	5.9176	5.6603	5.4206	5.1971	4.9884	4.7932	4.6105	4.4392	12
13	6.7499	6.4235	6.1218	5.8424	5.5831	5.3423	5.1183	4.9095	4.7147	4.5327	13
14	6.9819	6.6282	6.3025	6.0021	5.7245	5.4675	5.2293	5.0081	4.8023	4.6106	14
15	7.1909	6.8109	6.4624	6.1422	5.8474	5.5755	5.3242	5.0916	4.8759	4.6755	15
16	7.3792	6.9740	6.6039	6.2651	5.9542	5.6685	5.4053	5.1624	4.9377	4.7296	16
17	7.5488	7.1196	6.7291	6.3729	6.0472	5.7487	5.4746	5.2223	4.9897	4.7746	17
18	7.7016	7.2497	6.8399	6.4674	6.1280	5.8178	5.5339	5.2732	5.0333	4.8122	18
19	7.8393	7.3658	6.9380	6.5504	6.1982	5.8775	5.5845	5.3162	5.0700	4.8435	19
20	7.9633	7.4694	7.0248	6.6231	6.2593	5.9288	5.6278	5.3527	5.1009	4.8696	20
21	8.0751	7.5620	7.1016	6.6870	6.3125	5.9731	5.6648	5.3837	5.1268	4.8913	21
22	8.1757	7.6446	7.1695	6.7429	6.3587	6.0113	5.6964	5.4099	5.1486	4.9094	22
23	8.2664	7.7184	7.2297	6.7921	6.3988	6.0442	5.7234	5.4321	5.1668	4.9245	23
24	8.3481	7.7843	7.2829	6.8351	6.4338	6.0726	5.7465	5.4509	5.1822	4.9371	24
25	8.4217	7.8431	7.3300	6.8729	6.4641	6.0971	5.7662	5.4669	5.1951	4.9476	25

TABLE A-2   Present Value of One Dollar Per Year. *N* Years at *r*%

Year	21%	22%	23%	24%	25%	26%	27%	28%	29%	30%	Year
1	0.8264	0.8197	0.8130	0.8065	0.8000	0.7937	0.7874	0.7813	0.7752	0.7692	1
2	1.5095	1.4915	1.4740	1.4568	1.4400	1.4235	1.4074	1.3916	1.3761	1.3609	2
3	2.0739	2.0422	2.0114	1.9813	1.9520	1.9234	1.8956	1.8684	1.8420	1.8161	3
4	2.5404	2.4936	2.4483	2.4043	2.3616	2.3202	2.2800	2.2410	2.2031	2.1662	4
5	2.9260	2.8636	2.8035	2.7454	2.6893	2.6351	2.5827	2.5320	2.4830	2.4356	5
6	3.2446	3.1669	3.0923	3.0205	2.9514	2.8850	2.8210	2.7594	2.7000	2.6427	6
7	3.5079	3.4155	3.3270	3.2423	3.1611	3.0833	3.0087	2.9370	2.8682	2.8021	7
8	3.7256	3.6193	3.5179	3.4212	3.3289	3.2407	3.1564	3.0758	2.9986	2.9247	8
9	3.9054	3.7863	3.6731	3.5655	3.4631	3.3657	3.2728	3.1842	3.0997	3.0190	9
10	4.0541	3.9232	3.7993	3.6819	3.5705	3.4648	3.3644	3.2689	3.1781	3.0915	10
11	4.1769	4.0354	3.9018	3.7757	3.6564	3.5435	3.4365	3.3351	3.2388	3.1473	11
12	4.2785	4.1274	3.9852	3.8514	3.7251	3.6060	3.4933	3.3868	3.2859	3.1903	12
13	4.3624	4.2028	4.0530	3.9124	3.7801	3.6555	3.5381	3.4272	3.3224	3.2233	13
14	4.4317	4.2646	4.1082	3.9616	3.8241	3.6949	3.5733	3.4587	3.3507	3.2487	14
15	4.4890	4.3152	4.1530	4.0013	3.8593	3.7261	3.6010	3.4834	3.3726	3.2682	15
16	4.5364	4.3567	4.1894	4.0333	3.8874	3.7509	3.6228	3.5026	3.3896	3.2832	16
17	4.5755	4.3908	4.2190	4.0591	3.9099	3.7705	3.6400	3.5177	3.4028	3.2948	17
18	4.6079	4.4187	4.2431	4.0799	3.9279	3.7861	3.6536	3.5294	3.4130	3.3037	18
19	4.6346	4.4415	4.2627	4.0967	3.9424	3.7985	3.6642	3.5386	3.4210	3.3105	19
20	4.6567	4.4603	4.2786	4.1103	3.9539	3.8083	3.6726	3.5458	3.4271	3.3158	20
21	4.6750	4.4756	4.2916	4.1212	3.9631	3.8161	3.6792	3.5514	3.4319	3.3198	21
22	4.6900	4.4882	4.3021	4.1300	3.9705	3.8223	3.6844	3.5558	3.4356	3.3230	22
23	4.7025	4.4985	4.3106	4.1371	3.9764	3.8273	3.6885	3.5592	3.4384	3.3254	23
24	4.7128	4.5070	4.3176	4.1428	3.9811	3.8312	3.6918	3.5619	3.4406	3.3272	24
25	4.7213	4.5139	4.3232	4.1474	3.9849	3.8342	3.6943	3.5640	3.4423	3.3286	25

TABLE A-2   Present Value of One Dollar Per Year. *N* Years at *r*%

Year	31%	32%	33%	34%	35%	36%	37%	38%	39%	40%	Year
1	0.7634	0.7576	0.7519	0.7463	0.7407	0.7353	0.7299	0.7246	0.7194	0.7143	1
2	1.3461	1.3315	1.3172	1.3032	1.2894	1.2760	1.2627	1.2497	1.2370	1.2245	2
3	1.7909	1.7663	1.7423	1.7188	1.6959	1.6735	1.6516	1.6302	1.6093	1.5889	3
4	2.1305	2.0957	2.0618	2.0290	1.9969	1.9658	1.9355	1.9060	1.8772	1.8492	4
5	2.3897	2.3452	2.3021	2.2604	2.2200	2.1807	2.1427	2.1058	2.0699	2.0352	5
6	2.5875	2.5342	2.4828	2.4331	2.3852	2.3388	2.2939	2.2506	2.2086	2.1680	6
7	2.7386	2.6775	2.6187	2.5620	2.5075	2.4550	2.4043	2.3555	2.3083	2.2628	7
8	2.8539	2.7860	2.7208	2.6582	2.5982	2.5404	2.4849	2.4315	2.3801	2.3306	8
9	2.9419	2.8681	2.7976	2.7300	2.6653	2.6033	2.5437	2.4866	2.4317	2.3790	9
10	3.0091	2.9304	2.8553	2.7836	2.7150	2.6495	2.5867	2.5265	2.4689	2.4136	10
11	3.0604	2.9776	2.8987	2.8236	2.7519	2.6834	2.6180	2.5555	2.4956	2.4383	11
12	3.0995	3.0133	2.9314	2.8534	2.7792	2.7084	2.6409	2.5764	2.5148	2.4559	12
13	3.1294	3.0404	2.9559	2.8757	2.7994	2.7268	2.6576	2.5916	2.5286	2.4685	13
14	3.1522	3.0609	2.9744	2.8923	2.8144	2.7403	2.6698	2.6026	2.5386	2.4775	14
15	3.1696	3.0764	2.9883	2.9047	2.8255	2.7502	2.6787	2.6106	2.5457	2.4839	15
16	3.1829	3.0882	2.9987	2.9140	2.8337	2.7575	2.6852	2.6164	2.5509	2.4885	16
17	3.1931	3.9071	3.0065	2.9209	2.8398	2.7629	2.6899	2.6206	2.5546	2.4918	17
18	3.2008	3.1039	3.0124	2.9260	2.8443	2.7668	2.6934	2.6236	2.5573	2.4941	18
19	3.2067	3.1090	3.0169	2.9299	2.8476	2.7697	2.6959	2.6258	2.5592	2.4958	19
20	3.2112	3.1129	3.0202	2.9327	2.8501	2.7718	2.6977	2.6274	2.5606	2.4970	20
21	3.2147	3.1158	3.0227	2.9349	2.8519	2.7734	2.6991	2.6285	2.5616	2.4979	21
22	3.2173	3.1180	3.0246	2.9365	2.8533	2.7746	2.7000	2.6294	2.5623	2.4985	22
23	3.2193	3.1197	3.0260	2.9377	2.8543	2.7754	2.7008	2.6300	2.5628	2.4989	23
24	3.2209	3.1210	3.0271	2.9386	2.8550	2.7760	2.7013	2.6304	2.5632	2.4992	24
25	3.2220	3.1220	3.0279	2.9392	2.8556	2.7765	2.7017	2.6307	2.5634	2.4994	25

Index

by voluntary agreement,
677-678
Liquidity:
of inventories, 140-141
of receivables, 136-139
Liquidity ratios:
acid-test, 136
current, 135-136
Loans:
agreements, 517-520
amortizing, 85-86
bank, 514-516
field warehouse receipt,
300-301
insurance company, 517
inventory, 297-298
receivable, 293-295
self-liquidating, 287
term, 514-520
terminal warehouse receipt,
299-300
transaction, 289
trust receipt, 298-299
Lock-box system, 222-223
London Interbank Offering Rate
(LIBOR), 649
Long term debt to total
capitalization ratio,
defined, 142
Lorie, James H., 336
Losses:
net capital, 25-26, 28, 29
non capital, 25
terminal, 23, 333 (*table*) 23

M

Majority voting system, 565-566
Management:
acquisition of, through merger,
605-606
goals of, vs. shareholders, 9
Margin of safety:
and risk and profitability,
211-212
uncertainty and, 211
Marginal cost of capital, 386
weighing system for, 392-393
Market stabilization, 498
Market value of firm,
approximation of, 8
Market value of common stock,
563
effect of merger on, 616-618
Marketability, defined, 46

Marketable securities:
bankers' acceptances, 230
and cash, 219-239
commercial paper, 230
Eurodollars, 231
investment in, 229-234
negotiable certificates of
deposit, 230
portfolio management,
232-234
preferred stock, 232
repurchase agreements, 230
treasury, 229-230
Markowitz, Harry M., 6
Maturity:
of debt, 203-208 (*fig.*) 206, 207
of ordinary term loans,
515-516
yields and, 44-45 (*fig.*) 45
Maximum risk profiles, 400-403
(*figs.*) 401, 402
Memorandum of association, 18
Mergers:
earnings impact of, 612-616
market-value impact of,
616-619
pooling of interests and, 609,
610-611
purchase, 609, 610-611
statutory, 603
Miller, Merton H., 5-6, 444,
446-449, 451-455, 465-467
Miller—Orr model for
determining cash balance,
238-239
Modigliani, Franco, 5-6, 444,
446-449, 451-455, 465-467
Modigliani—Miller position on
firm value, 5-6, 444,
446-449, 451-455, 465-467
and arbitrage, 446-448
arguments against, 466-467
and corporate income taxes,
451-452
and market imperfections,
448-450, (*fig.*) 449
Monetary policy, effect on
interest rate expectations,
51-53
Money market instruments,
examples, 59-60
Money markets: *see* Financial
markets
Montreal Options Clearing
Corporation, 594

Montreal Stock Exchange, 58,
593, 594
Moody's Investors Service, 45
Mortgage bonds, 544-545
Mortgages:
chattel, 298
first and second, 544
Mutual exclusion, 321
Mutual funds, 57

N

National Financiera, S.A.
(Mexico), 650
Negotiated offering in securities
issue, 495
Net cash flow and cash balance,
182-183, (*table*) 183
Net creditor, defined, 48
Net debtor defined, 48
Net income approach to firm
valuation, 441-443, (*fig.*)
442
Net operating income approach
to firm valuation, 443-444,
(*fig.*) 444
Net period—no cash discount,
273
Net period with discount, 274
Net present value method,
320-321
Net profit margin, defined, 144
Normal probability distribution,
376-377
Note rollover system, 288
Notice of intention:
under Bank Act, 292, (*fig.*) 293
under Bankruptcy Act, 687

O

Official receiver, in bankruptcy,
683, 687
Ontario Corporations Tax Act,
20
Ontario Securities Act, 61
Ontario Securities Commission,
61, 625
Operating leverage:
analyzing, 354-357
defined, 372
and risk, 354-357
Opportunity costs and capital
rationing, 334-335
Options, 588-594
Black-Scholes model for,
591-593
call, 588

Trade, international, *see also*
  Foreign investments,
  650-655
Transactions costs in securities
  sales, 469
Transaction loans, 289
Transactions balances, 227-228
Transactions motives for holding
  cash, 219-220
Trans Canada Options Inc.,
  593-594
Treasury bills, 229-230
  yield behavior, 50-51 (*fig.*) 50
Treasury stock, 562
Trustees, 541
  in bankruptcy, 678, 679,
    683-686
  for bond issues, 541
  role in reorganization, 678
Trustees Act, 541
Trust receipt loans, 298-299
Turnover ratio, defined,
  application of, 145

U

U.C.C.: *see* Capital cost
  allowances
Underwriting, 494-495
  compensation, 498-501 (*table*)
    509
  making a market, 498

standby arrangement in rights
  offering, 505
Unsystematic risk, 111-112

V

Valuation:
  bond, 98-101
  common stock, 103-108
  dividend stability, 473-475
  earnings,
    net-income approach,
      441-442
    net-operating-income
      approach, 443-444
    traditional approach, 445
  fixed-income securities, 98-103
  foundations for, 95-118
  warrants and, 582-587
Venture capital, 670-672
  operating control, 671-672
  required return, 671
  types of investments, 671
Vertical merger, 605
Voluntary settlements of failures,
  676-678
Voting power:
  of common shareholders,
    564-565
  of preferred shareholders, 559

W

Walter, James E., 464
Walter's formula
  (dividend-payout ratio),
    464-465
Warehouse receipts, 292
warrants, 582-585
  exercise of, 583
  features of, 582
  valuation of, 583-585
Wealth maximization vs. profit
  maximization, 8-9
Williams, John Burr, 5
Working capital:
  funds as, 176-177
  management, 202-303
Working capital requirement,
  331-332

Y

Yield curve, defined, 206
Yield to maturity 541
  defined, 98
Yields:
  behavior and corporate
    securities, 50-51
  and default risk, 45-46
  and inflation, 48-49
  marketability, 46
  maturity, 44-45
  taxability, 47-48